MICROSOFT, ANTITRUST AND THE NEW ECONOMY: SELECTED ESSAYS

The Milken Institute Series On Financial Innovation And Economic Growth

Series Editors

James R. Barth
Auburn University
Senior Fellow at the Milken Institute
Glenn Yago
Director of Capital Studies at the
Milken Institute
Other books in the series:

Barth, James R., Brumbaugh Jr., R. Dan and Yago, Glenn:
Restructuring Regulation and Financial Institutions

MICROSOFT, ANTITRUST AND THE NEW ECONOMY: SELECTED ESSAYS

edited by

David S. Evans
National Economic Research Associates, U.S.A.

KLUWER ACADEMIC PUBLISHERS
Boston / Dordrecht / London

Distributors for North, Central and South America:
Kluwer Academic Publishers
101 Philip Drive
Assinippi Park
Norwell, Massachusetts 02061 USA
Telephone (781) 871-6600
Fax (781) 681-9045
E-Mail <kluwer@wkap.com>

Distributors for all other countries:
Kluwer Academic Publishers Group
Distribution Centre
Post Office Box 322
3300 AH Dordrecht, THE NETHERLANDS
Telephone 31 78 6392 392
Fax 31 78 6546 474
E-Mail <services@wkap.nl>

Electronic Services <http://www.wkap.nl>

Library of Congress Cataloging-in-Publication Data

A C.I.P. Catalogue record for this book is available
from the Library of Congress.

Printed on acid-free paper
Printed in the United States of America

"The Microsoft Corporation supported some of the research included in this book."

The Milken Institute has chosen the material published in this book series for its quality and seriousness of purpose. But the opinions expressed in the books do not necessarily reflect the views of the Institute or its staff.

Contents

About the Authors .... **vii**

Introduction **1**
by David S. Evans

Section 1

***U.S. v. Microsoft Corp.*: The Economics** **23**

An Analysis of the Government's Economic Case in *U.S. v. Microsoft Corp.* 23
by David S. Evans, Albert L. Nichols, and Richard Schmalensee

Why Does Microsoft Charge So Little for Windows? 93
by Bernard Reddy, David S. Evans, and Albert L. Nichols

U.S. v. Microsoft Corp.: Remedy or Malady? 127
by Kenneth G. Elzinga, David S. Evans, and Albert L. Nichols

DOS Kapital: Has Antitrust Action Against Microsoft Created Value in the Computer Industry? 193
by George Bittlingmayer and Thomas W. Hazlett

The Price of Unanimity: The D.C. Circuit's Incoherent Opinion in *U.S. v. Microsoft Corp.* 221
by John E. Lopatka and William H. Page

Judicial Misconduct and the Microsoft Case 239
by Leonard Orland

Section 2

Antitrust Policy and the New Economy 253

Antitrust and the New Economy 253
by David S. Evans

The Rise and Fall of Leaders in
Personal Computer Software 265
by David S. Evans, Albert L. Nichols, and Bernard Reddy

The Failure of Structural Remedies in Sherman Act
Monopolization Cases 287
by Robert W. Crandall

Economic Perspectives on Software Design:
PC Operating Systems and Platforms 361
by Steven J. Davis, Jack MacCrisken, and Kevin M. Murphy

Preserving Competition: Economic Analysis,
Legal Standards, and Microsoft 421
by Ronald A. Cass and Keith N. Hylton

The Returns to Investments in Innovative Activities:
An Overview and an Analysis of the Software Industry 463
by Josh Lerner

About the Authors

George Bittlingmayer is the Wagnon Distinguished Professor of Finance at the University of Kansas School of Business, whose research interests include stock market volatility and antitrust. He is an associate editor of the *Journal of Corporate Finance.*

Ronald A. Cass is dean and Melville Madison Bigelow Professor of Law at the Boston University School of Law. From 1988 to June 1990, he served as a member of the United States International Trade Commission and, in 1989-90, as the Commission's vice chairman.

Robert W. Crandall is a senior fellow at the Brookings Institution who specializes in regulatory policy. He is the co-author of *Who Pays for Universal Service?* (Brookings Press).

Steven J. Davis is the William H. Abbott Professor of International Business and Economics at the University of Chicago Graduate School of Business. His research interests include the business cycle and the economics of software.

Kenneth G. Elzinga is a professor of economics at the University of Virginia. He has written extensively about antitrust and industrial organization.

David S. Evans is a senior vice president at National Economic Research Associates in Cambridge, Massachusetts, and a consultant to Microsoft and Visa. Among other works, he is the co-author of *Paying with Plastic: The Digital Revolution in Buying and Borrowing* (MIT Press).

Thomas W. Hazlett is a resident scholar at the American Economic Enterprise Institute specializing in regulation. He served as the chief economist for the Federal Communications Commission in 1991-92. He is co-author of *Public Policy Towards Cable Television: The Economics of Rate Controls* (MIT Press).

Keith N. Hylton is a professor of law at the Boston University School of Law. He specializes in the field of law and economics.

Josh Lerner is a professor of business administration at the Harvard Business School and a faculty research fellow at the National Bureau of

Economic Research. Much of his research on technology and innovation is collected in his book, *The Venture Capital Cycle* (MIT Press).

John E. Lopatka is the Alumni Professor of Law at the University of South Carolina School of Law. He served as Assistant Director for Planning in the Federal Trade Commission's Bureau of Competition.

Jack MacCrisken is a technology consultant at Chicago Partners who has served as a consultant to Microsoft. His published research includes work on data compression.

Kevin M. Murphy is the George Pratt Shultz Professor of Economics and Industrial Relations at the University of Chicago Graduate School of Business and a faculty research associate at the National Bureau of Economic Research. He is a winner of the American Economic Association's John Bates Clark medal for the most promising economist under age 40.

Albert L. Nichols is a vice president at National Economic Research Associates in Cambridge, Massachusetts, and a consultant to Microsoft. His fields of expertise include the economics of the environment and antitrust policy.

Leonard Orland is professor of law at the University of Connecticut School of Law and a member of the Federal Courts Study Committee.

William H. Page, formerly a trial attorney with the Antitrust Division of the Department of Justice, is the Marshall M. Criser Eminent Scholar at the University of Florida's Levin College of Law. He is currently revising and supplementing the Kintner treatise on Federal Antitrust Law.

Bernard Reddy is a vice president at National Economic Research Associates in Cambridge, Massachusetts, and a consultant to Microsoft. His fields of expertise include electric power regulation and the economics of information technology.

Richard Schmalensee is dean and professor of economics at the MIT Sloan School of Management, and the expert economic witness for Microsoft in the antitrust trial. He served as a member of the President's Council of Economic Advisors in the first Bush administration.

Introduction

by David S. Evans

No antitrust case in recent history has attracted as much public attention as *U.S. v. Microsoft Corp.* Nor has any antitrust case in memory raised as many complex, substantive issues of law, economics, and public policy. This volume constitutes an early effort to analyze some of the central issues and to put the case in the context of the ongoing debate over the role of government in managing markets – especially in technologically driven New Economy industries.

All of these essays, it should be noted, are written by critics of the government's efforts to regulate Microsoft. Indeed, many are by individuals who were closely involved in the company's legal defense and served as consultants to Microsoft. But their work should be judged on the merits rather than their provenance. For all represent serious scholarship by researchers committed to advancing the debate over government regulatory policies.

Part I opens with an analytic summary of the trial and its conclusions (Evans, Nichols, Schmalensee). The second essay (Reddy, Evans, Nichols) estimates what the profit-maximizing price of the Windows operating system would be if it were indeed a monopoly, and offers an explanation for why Microsoft charges so much less for a product with so dominant a share of the apparent market. The third (Elzinga, Evans, Nichols) addresses remedy – most notably, the logical gap between Microsoft's legal liability as identified by the trial judge and his proposed division of Microsoft into one company selling operating system software and another selling applications software. The fourth (Bittlingmayer, Hazlett) looks at the response of the stock market to the early legal skirmishing over Windows – and looks in vain – for confirmation that regulating Microsoft would increase efficiency. The fifth (Lopatka, Page) assays the high price the D.C. Circuit Court of Appeals paid in terms of clarity and consistency in order to generate a unanimous decision. The sixth (Orland) dissects the appeals court's logic in tossing out the judge without tossing out his opinion.

Part II examines some broader questions that divide policymakers struggling to reconcile traditional antitrust with rapidly changing economic circumstances. The first essay (Evans) asks whether the antitrust laws are adequate to the task of protecting consumers in an era of "winner-take-all" market outcomes and Schumpeterian-style competition. The second (Evans, Nichols, Reddy) challenges the conventional wisdom that the advantages of incumbency give software producers substantial protection against competition. The third (Crandall) looks at major efforts to restructure industries by means of antitrust enforcement in the past and finds little evidence that they have served the interests of consumers. The fourth (Davis, MacCrisken, Murphy) analyzes the reasons that producers of operating systems largely compete by adding features to successive versions of the software. The fifth (Cass, Hylton) uses the Microsoft case to illustrate the pitfalls in using intent as a proxy for market outcomes in weighing the benefits of government intervention. The last (Lerner) explores the dangers in using exceptionally high rates of return for individual firms after the fact as evidence of anticompetitive behavior in high-risk industries.

None of the essays, however, bring the Microsoft case up to date in light of the complex appeals court ruling that tossed out many of the trial judge's findings of liability, modified others, and directed the new judge to devise "a specific remedy" for the "drastically altered"[1] liability findings. Hence this brief summary of what stuck and what did not as the case marched through the judicial system between May 1998, when the government filed the case, and November 2001, when Microsoft, the Justice Department, and half the state plaintiffs proposed a settlement.

The government made four broad allegations: market foreclosure and tying under Section 1 of the Sherman Act, and attempted monopolization and monopoly maintenance under Section 2 of the Sherman Act. The district court judge, Thomas Penfield Jackson, rejected the Section 1 foreclosure claim as well as several of the charges included under the Section 2 monopoly maintenance claims. The government did not appeal any of the claims that it lost in the district court. The state plaintiffs also claimed that Microsoft engaged in monopoly leveraging in violation of Section 2 of the Sherman Act. Judge Jackson granted Microsoft's motion to dismiss that claim prior to the start of the trial.

The appeals court then concluded that most of the violations found by the lower court did not "withstand appellate scrutiny." It reversed the Section 2 attempted monopolization claim, affirmed a portion of the Section 2 monop-

Table 1. **Status of Key Issues**

Government's Antitrust Allegations	District Court	Appeals Court
SHERMAN ACT SECTION 1 CLAIMS		
Microsoft excluded Netscape from the market	No	Not addressed since government did not appeal.
Microsoft's inclusion of Internet Explorer in Windows was a per se illegal tie	Yes	Vacated and remanded with guidance to evaluate the rule of reason (DOJ abandoned proceedings).
SHERMAN ACT SECTION 2 CLAIMS		
Microsoft took anticompetitive actions to maintain a monopoly in PC operating systems	Yes on some actions; no on others	Affirmed some findings that Microsoft engaged in anticompetitive actions; vacated others; government did not appeal decisions on actions the district court did not find anticompetitive, and therefore appeals court did not address those actions.
Microsoft took anticompetitive actions to obtain a monopoly in Web browsers	Yes	Reversed.
REMEDIES		
Microsoft should be broken into separate operating system and applications companies	Yes	Vacated and remanded, with guidance suggesting that this type of remedy is not appropriate (DOJ abandoned breakup efforts).
Microsoft should have severe restrictions imposed on its conduct	Yes	Vacated and remanded, with guidance suggesting that conduct restrictions should be tailored to deal with the specific actions found anticompetitive by the appeals court.

Sources: Plaintiffs' Joint Proposed Conclusions of Law, *U.S. v. Microsoft Corp.*, December 6, 1999, http://www.usdoj.gov/atr/cases/f3900/3932.pdf; Judge Thomas Penfield Jackson, Conclusions of Law, *U.S v. Microsoft Corp.*, April 3, 2000, http://www.usdoj.gov/atr/cases/f4400/4469.pdf; United States Court of Appeals for the District of Columbia, Opinion, *U.S v. Microsoft Corp.*, June 28, 2001, http://ecfp.cadc.uscourts.gov/MS-Docs/1720/0.pdf.

oly maintenance claim, and vacated and remanded the Section 1 tying claims.[2] The appeals court vacated the remedies ordered by the district court in their entirety and remanded them for the district court "to determine the propriety of a specific remedy for the limited ground of liability which we have upheld."[3] Finally, the appeals court removed Judge Jackson from future proceedings, finding that he had violated a number of "ethical precepts."[4]

In September 2001, the government announced that it would not pursue the tying claims on remand. In November 2001, Microsoft settled the case with the Department of Justice and nine of the state plaintiffs. As of this writing, the remaining plaintiffs will pursue their desired remedies before a new judge.

MARKET DEFINITION AND MONOPOLY POWER

The district court and the appeals court agreed with the government that

Microsoft had monopoly power in the market for operating systems for Intel-compatible computers. This finding is significant because some of the actions alleged by the government were unlawful only if Microsoft had monopoly power in the market for operating systems – a firm must have a monopoly before it can be accused of trying to *maintain* a monopoly.

The antitrust laws have long acknowledged that there is nothing inherently wrong with a firm's having monopoly power, and of course many firms do. The government did not claim that Microsoft had acted unlawfully in achieving its leading market position. Indeed, in an earlier case, the government agreed that Microsoft had achieved its success through superior foresight, skill, and luck.[5]

The government also claimed that Microsoft was attempting to *obtain* monopoly power in the market for Web browsers. The district court did not, however, find that there was a relevant market for Web browsers in which monopoly power could be exercised. The appeals court precluded the government from revisiting this issue in a new trial. As discussed below, this conclusion was fatal to the government's claim that Microsoft had attempted to monopolize the Web browser market, and posed a substantial hurdle for the government's tying case on remand as well.

SHERMAN SECTION 1 ALLEGATIONS

Section 1 of the Sherman Act declares unlawful "every contract, combination in the form of a trust or otherwise, or conspiracy, in restraint of trade or commerce…"[6] The courts have interpreted this as prohibiting practices such as price-fixing, exclusive dealing, resale price maintenance, and tying.[7] The government claimed that Microsoft had violated Section 1 by entering into exclusive contracts with various parties as well as tying Internet Explorer (IE) to Windows – that is, attempting to extend its monopoly by linking the sale of a competitive product to a monopoly product.

Exclusive Contracts

The government asserted that Microsoft had prevented the distribution of Netscape's competing Web browser. The district court concluded that this claim required that the government show that Netscape was substantially foreclosed from getting its Web browser to consumers. The district court rejected the government's claim because:

> ... in 1998 alone, for example, Netscape was able to distribute 160 million copies of Navigator, contributing to an increase in its installed base from 15 million in 1996 to 33 million in December 1998. As such, the evidence does not support a finding that these agreements completely excluded Netscape from any constituent portion of the worldwide browser market, the relevant line of commerce.[8]

The government did not seek to reverse this finding on appeal.

Tying

The government claimed that Microsoft violated the antitrust laws against tying as defined by the Supreme Court in the *Jefferson Parish* (1984) decision. According to the Supreme Court, a tie is illegal on its face if (a) there are two distinct products; (b) the defendant requires customers to take the tied product as a condition of obtaining the tying product; (c) the arrangement affects a significant volume of commerce; and (d) the defendant has market power in the tying product.[9] The district court found that Microsoft's combination of its Web browser and its PC operating system met these four conditions and was therefore illegal.

Under the *Jefferson Parish* test, there is no inquiry into whether the tie ultimately benefits or harms consumers. A key issue at trial was whether the appropriate test was the one set forth in *Jefferson Parish* or a very different one set forth by the majority of a three-judge panel of the appeals court in a related case concerning whether Microsoft violated an earlier consent decree. The appeals court, with all seven available members reviewing the district court's decision, rejected both tests. It concluded that software like Windows, which is used as a platform to support other software, should be subject to a rule-of-reason test that weighs the pro-competitive and anticompetitive effects of combining features. In particular, it found "...that integration of new functionality into platform software is a common practice and that wooden application of per se rules in this litigation may cast a cloud over platform innovation in the market for PCs, network computers and information appliances."[10]

The appeals court's ruling allowed the government to retry its tying claim under the rule of reason: The government would have to show that the harm to competition in the Web browser market outweighs the benefits of integrating a browser into the operating system. But the ruling presented the government with substantial hurdles on both sides of the equation. It precluded the government from presenting any theory of harm that depends on a precise definition of the market for Web browsers or on claims that such a market is protected by barriers to entry. It is unclear how, under these restrictions, the government could prevail on a rule-of-reason argument.[11] Moreover, the government would be obliged to focus on harm to competition in the Web browser market; it could not consider the harm to competition in the operating system market that was at the heart of the Section 2 allegations discussed below. On the other side of the equation, the appeals court has noted that the integration of features in the operating system provides consumer benefits. "For example," the court noted, "the bundling of a browser with OSs enables an independent software vendor to count on the presence of the browser's APIs, if any, on consumers' machines and thus to omit them from its own package."[12] It also noted:

> Bundling can also capitalize on certain economies of scope. A possible example is the "shared" library files that perform OS and browser functions with the very same lines of code and thus may save drive space from the clutter of redundant routines and memory when consumers use both the OS and browser simultaneously.[13]

The government decided not to retry its tying claim on remand.

SHERMAN SECTION 2 ALLEGATIONS

Section 2 of the Sherman Act condemns "every person who shall monopolize, or attempt to monopolize, or combine or conspire with any other person or persons, to monopolize any part of the trade or commerce among the several States, or with foreign nations..."[14] The courts have defined "monopolization" as having two elements: "(1) the possession of monopoly power in the relevant market and (2) the willful acquisition or maintenance of that power as distinguished from growth or development as a consequence of a superior product, business acumen, or historical accident."[15] Although the government did not claim that Microsoft obtained its monopoly in operating systems unlawfully, it did charge that Microsoft attempted to maintain its monopoly in operating systems for Intel-compatible computers and to obtain a monopoly in Web browsers.

Monopoly Leveraging

The complaint filed by the state plaintiffs alleged that Microsoft had violated Section 2 by "leveraging" its operating system monopoly.[16] Monopoly leveraging refers to the use of market power in one market to gain a competitive advantage in another market – even if that competitive advantage does not involve an attempt to monopolize.[17] Microsoft filed a motion to dismiss this claim before the start of the trial. Judge Jackson granted that motion. He found that the "Third and Ninth Circuits and many commentators have rejected the [monopoly leveraging] theory outright, as contrary to both economic theory and the Sherman Act's plain language."[18]

Attempted Monopolization of Web Browsers

The government charged that Microsoft first attempted to persuade Netscape not to distribute Web browsers for Intel-compatible computers. When Netscape refused, the government claimed, Microsoft engaged in the exclusionary and predatory behavior described above. The district court agreed. But the appeals court reversed the trial judge's decision because he did not find that there was a Web browser market capable of being monopolized and the government had not presented sufficient evidence on this issue at trial:

> To establish a dangerous probability of success, plaintiffs must as a threshold matter show that the browser market can be monopolized, i.e., that a hypothetical monopolist in that market could enjoy market power. This, in turn, requires plaintiffs (1) to define the relevant market and (2) to demonstrate that substantial barriers to entry protect that market. Because plaintiffs have not carried their burden on either prong, we reverse without remand.[19]

As a result, the appeals court did not address whether Microsoft's meeting with Netscape violated the antitrust laws. The district court's finding concerning that meeting therefore does not provide a basis for liability and will not be considered by the new judge in formulating remedies.

Maintenance of the PC Operating System Monopoly

The monopoly maintenance portion of the government's case is the most difficult to summarize. It is based on allegations concerning numerous acts, which the government claimed were individually anticompetitive but also collectively constituted an anticompetitive course of conduct.[20] Moreover, the district judge was not always clear or consistent on which of these claims he believed violated Section 2 of the Sherman Act.

Table 2 presents a summary of the various monopoly maintenance claims and their disposition to date. The appeals court did not explicitly address more than half a dozen of the actions that the district court found to be anticompetitive. Those findings are not a basis for liability, have no significance to the

Table 2. **The Government's Monopoly Maintenance Allegations and Their Disposition by the District Court and the Appeals Court**

Act	District Court	Appeals Court
FUNDAMENTAL		
Large investment in Internet Explorer (IE)	N?	N
Making IE free for consumers	N?	N
ORIGINAL EQUIPMENT (COMPUTER) MANUFACTURERS		
Limits on promoting browsers or otherwise modifying the initial boot sequence	Y	Y
Prohibition of autoloading shells	Y	N
Prohibition of the deletion of the IE icon	Y	Y
Use of discounts, etc. to reward or punish computer manufacturers	Y	NL
CODE INTEGRATION		
Commingling of code specific to Web browsing with software code that performs other operating system functions	Y	Y
No inclusion of IE in add/remove utility	Y	Y
Override default browser choice in limited circumstances	Y	N
INTERNET ACCESS PROVIDERS		
Inducements (including free desktop space) to set IE as the default browser	N?	NL
Making IE free for Internet access providers	Y	N
Paying Internet access providers to distribute IE	Y	N
Developing and distributing at no charge a tool (the "IEAK") enabling Internet access providers to customize IE	Y	N
Quantitative restrictions on the promotion and distribution of competing Web browsers by Internet access providers	Y	Y
INTERNET CONTENT PROVIDERS, INDEPENDENT SOFTWARE VENDORS, AND APPLE		
Internet content provider agreements re Channel Bar	Y	N
First-wave requirements for software vendors to use IE	Y	Y
Use of Office to get Apple to feature IE	Y	Y
JAVA		
Developing a Java Virtual Machine incompatible with Sun's	Y	N
First-wave requirements for software vendors to use Microsoft's Java Virtual Machine	Y	Y
Failure to warn in Java development tools	Y	Y
Pressure on Intel to stop Java Virtual Machine development	Y	Y
NON-BROWSER/OTHER		
June 1995 proposed "market division" with Netscape	Y	NL
Withholding technical information from Netscape	Y	NL
Pressuring Intel not to develop NSP, platform-level software	Y	NL
Pressuring Apple re QuickTime media software on Windows	Y	NL
Pressuring RealNetworks re streaming media software on Windows	Y	NL
Pressuring IBM re promotion of OS/2 & SmartSuite	Y	NL
General course of conduct	Y	N

Note: "Y" means anticompetitive; "N" means not, "N?" means there was some ambiguity in the district court's language although the government did not press the issue; "NL" means no liability because the issue was not addressed, and is thus not a basis for liability.

Sources: Plaintiffs' Joint Proposed Conclusions of Law, *U.S. v. Microsoft Corp.*, December 6, 1999, http://www.usdoj.gov/atr/cases/f3900/3932.pdf; Judge Thomas Penfield Jackson, Conclusions of Law, *U.S. v. Microsoft Corp.*, April 3, 2000, http://www.usdoj.gov/atr/cases/f4400/4469.pdf; United States Court of Appeals for the District of Columbia, Opinion, *U.S. v. Microsoft Corp.*, June 28, 2001, http://ecfp.cadc.uscourts.gov/MS-Docs/1720/0.pdf.

monopoly maintenance ruling, and are not relevant to the question of appropriate remedies.

Here, I analyze some of the highlights, organized according to categories of violations alleged by the government. All of these violations depend on the district court's finding, which the appeals court accepted, that competing Web-browsing software presented a unique threat to Microsoft's monopoly in operating systems. The appeals court premised its analysis on the district court's finding that Web-browsing software had the potential to develop into an alternative to Windows that could have supplanted its core value, as a broad-based platform for building and running applications.

Suppression of Netscape Distribution

The government charged that Microsoft engaged in a series of actions that cut Netscape off from key channels of distribution and otherwise made it difficult for Netscape to get its Web browser into the hands of end users. The district court found that Microsoft's agreements with Internet access providers (IAPs), Independent software vendors (ISVs), and Internet content providers (ICPs) were, indeed, exclusionary. The district court also found that Microsoft made it difficult for computer makers (often referred to as original equipment manufacturers, or OEMs) to distribute computers with Netscape Navigator.

The appeals court reversed several of these findings. For example, it found insufficient evidence of anticompetitive effects of Microsoft's agreements with ICPs, and it ruled that Microsoft had legitimate reasons to prohibit OEMs from installing auto-loading shells on their PCs that would obscure the Windows desktop. But it affirmed others. Most significantly, it affirmed that, to maintain its operating system monopoly, Microsoft had imposed restrictions that made it less likely that Netscape Navigator would be distributed through the two most important channels: OEMs and IAPs.

Tying/Bundling

The government claimed that by tying IE to Windows, Microsoft made it harder for consumers to choose Netscape Navigator.[21] The district court agreed. The appeals court reversed some of the lower court's findings and accepted others.

It found that Microsoft's inclusion of IE with Windows at no separate charge – really the essence of the tying claim – was lawful. It further found that Microsoft could not be held liable for designing various aspects of

Windows, such as the Help system and Windows Explorer, to use built-in Web-browsing software. In that sense, it found that Microsoft's integration of browsing features into the operating system was not an antitrust violation.

But the appeals court did accept the lower court's findings that (a) commingling of code specific to Web browsing with code that supplies operating system functions, (b) failing to include IE in the Add/Remove Programs utility in Windows, and (c) prohibiting OEMs from deleting certain items from the desktop and Start menu did make it harder for consumers to choose Netscape Navigator. In effect, the appeals court accepted the lower court's finding that Microsoft had taken actions that made it difficult for OEMs and end users to hide access to the IE integrated with Windows.

Predatory Pricing and Investment

The government distinguished predatory behavior from legal behavior by considering whether the defendant made business decisions that would have been the most profitable if the defendant were not anticipating monopoly profits from destroying a rival.[22] It claimed that, in several cases, Microsoft had given up profits for the purpose of maintaining its monopoly in the operating system. These cases included: (a) investing $100 million a year in the development of IE; (b) giving away IE to Internet access providers and end users; (c) reducing the royalties paid for Windows by OEMs that agreed to promote IE; (d) giving AOL valuable space on the Windows desktop in return for its agreement to distribute IE exclusively; (e) giving other firms valuable consideration in return for their either agreeing to distribute IE or agreeing not to distribute Netscape Navigator; and (f) giving Internet access providers a valuable set of software tools (IEAK) for installing and maintaining IE on their Web servers.

The district court agreed with the government's novel definition of predation. However, it did not seem to agree that investing in the development of IE was by itself illegal:

> Even absent the strategic imperative to maximize its browser usage share at Netscape's expense, Microsoft might still have set the price of an Internet Explorer consumer license at zero. It might also have spent something approaching the $100 million it has devoted each year to developing Internet Explorer and some part of the $30 million it has spent annually marketing it.[23]

Nor did the district court seem to find that Microsoft's agreement to allow AOL to use IE technology for its subscription software was predatory, although it condemned the aspects of that agreement that restricted the promotion and distribution of other browsers.[24]

But the district court did conclude that Microsoft had engaged in predation by (a) developing the IEAK software; (b) giving the IEAK away; (c) not charging Internet access providers for IE; and (d) paying Internet access providers a bounty for securing additional IE users. The appeals court rejected these findings:

> The rare case of price predation aside, the antitrust laws do not condemn even a monopolist for offering its product at an attractive price, and we therefore have no warrant to condemn Microsoft for offering either IE or the IEAK free of charge or even at a negative price. Likewise, as we said above, a monopolist does not violate the Sherman Act simply by developing an attractive product. Therefore, Microsoft's development of the IEAK does not violate the Sherman Act.[25]

Other Anticompetitive Acts

The district court agreed with the government that Microsoft demanded that Netscape withdraw from platform competition – and then withheld crucial information about Windows 95 following Netscape's rejection of Microsoft's alleged proposal to divide the Web browser market. But the appeals court did not hold Microsoft liable for these actions.

The government identified additional actions by Microsoft that were said to undermine other threats to Microsoft's operating system monopoly.

• The district court found that Microsoft put Sun Microsystems' Java programming language at a competitive disadvantage. The appeals court agreed with some of the lower court's findings in this area but rejected others.

• The district court also found that Microsoft took actions to discourage Intel from distributing native signal processing (NSP) software and from developing other software that could serve as a platform for applications. The appeals court did not address NSP but did find liability for threatening Intel regarding its work on a version of Java that met Sun's requirements.

• The district court found that Microsoft had tried to prevent the distribution of Apple's QuickTime software for Windows, but the appeals court did not explicitly address that finding.

Similarly, the district court found that Microsoft had attempted to induce RealNetworks to halt development of its streaming audio software, but the appeals court was silent on the issue.

Course of Conduct

The government claimed that Microsoft should be held liable for engaging in a course of anticompetitive conduct, regardless of whether any of Microsoft's individual actions were anticompetitive. The district court agreed, but the appeals court vacated the finding:

> The "course of conduct" section of the District Court's opinion contains, with one exception, only broad, summarizing conclusions. See, e.g., Conclusions of Law, at 44 ("Microsoft placed an oppressive thumb on the scale of competitive fortune"). The only specific acts to which the court refers are Microsoft's expenditures in promoting its browser, see id. ("Microsoft has expended wealth and foresworn opportunities to realize more."), which we have explained are not in themselves unlawful. Because the District Court identifies no other specific acts as a basis for "course of conduct" liability, we reverse its conclusion that Microsoft's course of conduct separately violates § 2 of the Sherman Act.[26]

REMEDIES

The government asked the district court to break Microsoft into two companies, one that would hold the assets related to its operating system products and another that would hold the assets related to its office productivity and other applications products. The government also asked the district court to impose a series of restrictions on the conduct of both companies (principally the operating system company) for a period of time. The restrictions included some forced sharing of intellectual property with other firms and limitations on the integration of certain features into Windows.

Microsoft opposed the remedies and sought to have a hearing at which it could present evidence concerning the government's proposed remedies and potential alternatives. The district court judge decided not to hold any evidentiary hearings. Instead, he adopted the government's proposed remedies with minimal changes. The appeals court reversed:

> [W]e vacate the District Court's remedies decree for three reasons. First, the District Court failed to hold an evidentiary hearing despite the presence of remedies-specific factual disputes. Second, the court did not provide adequate reasons for its decreed remedies. Finally, we have drastically altered the scope of Microsoft's liability, and it is for the District Court in the first instance to determine the propriety of a specific remedy for the limited ground of liability which we have upheld.[27]

In addition to reversing the district court's decisions, the appeals court provided some guidance for the fashioning of appropriate remedies. In particular, it noted that:

> If the court on remand is unconvinced of the causal connection between Microsoft's exclusionary conduct and the company's position in the OS market, it may well conclude that divestiture is not an appropriate remedy. While we do not undertake to dictate to the District Court the precise form that relief should take on remand, we note again that it should be tailored to fit the wrong creating the occasion for the remedy.[28]

DISQUALIFICATION OF THE DISTRICT COURT JUDGE

The appeals court held that the district judge's secret meetings with reporters while the trial was under way violated several "ethical precepts" set forth in the Code of Conduct for United States Judges, as well as Section 455(a) of the Judicial Code, a federal statute. His violations were "deliberate, repeated, egregious, and flagrant." The appeals court disqualified the trial judge retroactive to the remedy stage of the case and removed him from the case going forward.

Microsoft had asked the appeals court to disqualify the trial judge retroactive to the start of trial, while the government had argued that the judge's behavior did not warrant his disqualification at all. Microsoft unsuccessfully petitioned the Supreme Court on this issue, arguing that the disqualification should be retroactive to the date of the judge's first disqualifying act.[29]

THE SETTLEMENT BETWEEN MICROSOFT, THE JUSTICE DEPARTMENT, AND SEVERAL STATES

Most of the claims brought by the government against Microsoft did not survive review by the district court and then by the appeals court. The states' monopoly leveraging claim was dismissed before the trial. Two of the four major claims that went to trial were ultimately discarded – the district court rejected the exclusive contract claim under Section 1 of the Sherman Act, and the appeals court rejected the attempted monopolization of the browser market claim under Section 2 of the Sherman Act. A third claim – tying under Section 1 – was vacated and remanded under conditions that made it unlikely that the government could prevail.

The fourth claim – monopoly maintenance under Section 2 of the Sherman Act – was affirmed in part and reversed in part. Many of the specific allegations against Microsoft were made only under the monopoly maintenance claim. Some of these were rejected by the district court, and the appeals court rejected many more.

After the appeals court rendered its decision, the government decided not to ask the district court to reconsider the Section 1 tying claim under the rule of reason and announced that it would not seek a breakup of Microsoft.[30] In September, Judge Jackson's replacement – Judge Colleen Kollar-Kotelly – ordered the parties to engage in an intense effort to settle the case. After their failure to do so on their own, she appointed a mediator, Professor Eric Green of Boston University Law School, to assist them in the process. The Justice Department and Microsoft informed Judge Kollar-Kotelly that they had reached a settlement agreement on November 2, 2001. On November 6, nine states indicated that they would join in that settlement, and at the time of my writing, the remaining 10 plaintiffs[31] had indicated they intended to continue the litigation.

The proposed consent decree limits Microsoft's ability to counter rivals' middleware and other competing products. Some portions of the agreement prevent Microsoft from taking particular business actions, such as entering into exclusive distribution contracts, offering selective price cuts to individual computer manufacturers, or restricting computer manufacturers from modifying the appearance of the Windows desktop in prescribed ways. Other portions require Microsoft to disclose information about its operating system products that could help competitors design their own products.

The proposed consent decree defines a "Microsoft Middleware Product" as "the functionality provided by Internet Explorer, Microsoft's Java Virtual Machine, Windows Media Player, Windows Messenger, Outlook Express and their successors," plus certain types of functionality if Microsoft trademarks it and adds it to its client operating systems in the future. Most of the products included in this definition do not match either what most people in the computer industry think of as "middleware" or the way the term was used at trial. For example, media playing and instant-messaging software are not considered middleware by industry specialists.[32]

Table 3 summarizes the terms of the proposed consent decree. For each clause in the decree, the table notes whether the clause is a specific remedy for a violation found by the appeals court,[33] for a claim that was raised at trial but not found to be a basis for liability by the appeals court, or for an issue that was not addressed at trial. Table 4 adds a column to Table 2 that relates the

Table 3. **Terms of Proposed Consent Decree**

Item	Brief Description	Relevance
III.A.1	No retaliation against OEMs for distributing, etc., software that competes with Microsoft's operating systems or middleware.	Trial
III.A.2	No retaliation against OEMs for shipping PCs with a second operating system in addition to Windows.	None
III.B	Uniform pricing, terms, and conditions for top 20 OEMs, but volume discounts are permitted, and marketing allowances can be different for top 10 than for next 10.	Trial
III.C.1	OEMs permitted to put icons, etc., for products that compete with Microsoft's wherever such items might generally be displayed.	Liability
III.C.2	OEMs permitted to use icons of any size and shape that do not interfere with the user interface.	Liability
III.C.3	OEMs permitted to launch non-Microsoft middleware in a boot sequence if any Microsoft middleware product would otherwise launch.	Liability
III.C.4	OEMs permitted to provide dual-boot options, letting user choose between Windows and another OS.	None
III.C.5	At initial boot, OEMs permitted to offer their own lists of Internet access providers.	Liability
III.D	Microsoft must document APIs used by Microsoft middleware to interoperate with the rest of Windows, for use by ISVs, IHVs, IAPs, ICPs, and OEMs, "for the sole purpose of interoperating with a Windows operating system product."	None
III.E	Microsoft must document communications protocols used by Windows client computers to interoperate "with a Microsoft server operating system product."	None
III.F.1	No retaliation against any ISV or IHV for developing, distributing, etc., software that competes with Microsoft's operating systems or middleware or runs on software that competes with Microsoft's operating systems or middleware.	Liability
III.F.2	No agreements with ISVs conditioned on their agreeing not to develop, distribute, etc., software that competes with Microsoft's operating systems or middleware or runs on software that competes with Microsoft's operating systems or middleware.	Liability
III.G.1	No agreements with any IAP, ICP, ISV, IHV, or OEM that conditions consideration on exclusivity or near-exclusivity for Microsoft operating systems or middleware. Microsoft can enter agreements based on fixed percentages for such Microsoft products, provided "that it is commercially practicable" for competing products to obtain "equal or greater distribution."	Liability
III.G.2	No agreements with IAPs or ICPs to grant placement on the desktop, etc., conditioned on restrictions on distribution, etc. of "software that competes with Microsoft middleware."	Liability
III.H.1	Provide Add/Remove type of mechanism for end users and OEMs "to enable or remove access to each Microsoft middleware product or Non-Microsoft middleware product."	Liability
III.H.2	Provide mechanism that (in essence) extends the "default browser" concept to all Microsoft middleware products, permitting end users, OEMs, and competing middleware to make non-Microsoft middleware products the default.	None
III.H.3	Place limitations on a feature new to Windows XP, which identifies desktop icons not used within a recent time period and sweeps them (with the user's permission) into	

	a special desktop folder for unused icons. The major limitation is that this "desktop cleanup wizard" cannot be invoked automatically for at least 14 days after first boot.	Liability/ None
III.I	Microsoft must license intellectual property, when relevant, to permit ISVs, IHVs, IAPs, ICPs, and OEMs to exercise rights (e.g., III.D and III.E), under "reasonable and non-discriminatory" terms, with right to prohibit sublicensing.	None
III.J.1	Under some circumstances, Microsoft need not provide API and communications protocol information if doing so would compromise particular installations of anti-piracy, encryption, etc. systems.	None
III.J.2	Microsoft may condition the license of APIs and communications protocols related to anti-piracy, encryption, etc., to entities that do not violate intellectual property rights, have a business need for the information, meet objective standards for business viability, etc.	None

Note: "Liability" means the provision addresses a liability finding affirmed by the appeals court, but may go beyond the specific liability findings. "Trial" means related to charges raised at trial that did not survive the judicial process. "None" means unrelated to charges raised at trial. Restrictions on the new "desktop cleanup wizard" in Windows XP is designed to ensure that Microsoft cannot remove icons that an OEM put on the desktop before consumers have a chance to use them. The feature was not a trial issue, but the right of OEMs to put icons on the desktop was.

Sources: Plaintiffs' Joint Proposed Conclusions of Law, *U.S. v. Microsoft Corp.*, December 6, 1999, http://www.usdoj.gov/atr/cases/f3900/3932.pdf; Judge Thomas Penfield Jackson, Conclusions of Law, *U.S. v. Microsoft Corp.*, April 3, 2000, http://www.usdoj.gov/atr/cases/f4400/4469.pdf; United States Court of Appeals for the District of Columbia, Opinion, *U.S. v. Microsoft Corp.*, June 28, 2001, http://ecfp.cadc.uscourts.gov/MS-Docs/1720/0.pdf. Revised Proposed Final Judgment, *U.S. v. Microsoft Corp.*, November 6, 2001, http://www.usdoj.gov/atr/cases/f9400/9495.htm.

Table 4. **Monopoly Maintenance Allegations and Disposition**

Act	District Court	Appeals Court	Judgment
FUNDAMENTAL			
Large investment in IE	N?	N	
Making IE free for consumers	N?	N	
ORIGINAL EQUIPMENT (COMPUTER) MANUFACTURERS			
Limits on promoting browsers or otherwise modifying the initial boot sequence	Y	Y	III.C
Prohibition of autoloading shells	Y	N	
Prohibition of the deletion of the IE icon	Y	Y	III.H
Use of discounts, etc. to reward or punish computer manufacturers	Y	NL	III.A,B
CODE INTEGRATION			
Commingling of code specific to Web browsing with software code that performs other operating system functions	Y	Y	III.H
No inclusion of IE in add/remove utility	Y	Y	III.H
Override default browser choice in limited circumstances	Y	N	
INTERNET ACCESS PROVIDERS			
Inducements (including free desktop space) to set IE as the default browser	N?	NL	
Making IE free for Internet access providers	Y	N	
Paying Internet access providers to distribute IE	Y	N	
Developing and distributing at no charge a tool (the "IEAK") enabling Internet access providers to customize IE	Y	N	
Quantitative restrictions on the promotion and distribution of competing Web browsers by Internet access providers	Y	Y	III.G
INTERNET CONTENT PROVIDERS, INDEPENDENT SOFTWARE VENDORS, AND APPLE			
Internet content provider agreements re Channel Bar	Y	N	III.G

First-wave requirements for software vendors to use IE	Y	Y	III.F,G
Use of Office to get Apple to feature IE	Y	Y	III.G
JAVA			
Developing a Java Virtual Machine incompatible with Sun's	Y	N	(moot)
First-wave requirements for software vendors to use Microsoft's Java Virtual Machine	Y	Y	III.F,G
Failure to warn in Java development tools	Y	Y	(moot)
Pressure on Intel to stop Java Virtual Machine development	Y	Y	III.F
NON-BROWSER/OTHER			
June 1995 proposed "market division" with Netscape	Y	NL	III.G
Withholding technical information from Netscape	Y	NL	(note)
Pressuring Intel not to develop NSP, platform-level software	Y	NL	III.F
Pressuring Apple re QuickTime media software on Windows	Y	NL	III.F
Pressuring RealNetworks re streaming media software on Windows	Y	NL	III.F
Pressuring IBM re promotion of OS/2 & SmartSuite	Y	NL	III.A (OS/2)
General course of conduct	Y	N	

Note: "Y" means anticompetitive; "N" means not, "N?" means there was some ambiguity in the district court's language, although the government did not press the issue; "NL" means no liability because the issue was not addressed, and is thus not a basis for liability. "Withholding technical information from Netscape" involved an API to dial (for example) an Internet access provider, which was not published until about the time that Windows 95 shipped; the proposed judgment involves making available what have been internal APIs. Some Java-related items are moot as a result of events in the Sun–Microsoft lawsuit involving Java.

Sources: Plaintiffs' Joint Proposed Conclusions of Law, *U.S. v. Microsoft Corp.*, December 6, 1999, http://www.usdoj.gov/atr/cases/f3900/3932.pdf; Judge Thomas Penfield Jackson, Conclusions of Law, *U.S. v. Microsoft Corp.*, April 3, 2000, http://www.usdoj.gov/atr/cases/f4400/4469.pdf; United States Court of Appeals for the District of Columbia, Opinion, *U.S. v. Microsoft Corp.*, June 28, 2001, http://ecfp.cadc.uscourts.gov/MS-Docs/1720/0.pdf. Revised Proposed Final Judgment, *U.S. v. Microsoft Corp.*, November 6, 2001, http://www.usdoj.gov/atr/cases/f9400/9495.htm.

terms of the proposed consent decree to the Section 2 allegations, some of which became the basis (and the only basis) for the appeals court liability findings.

These two tables show that the consent decree addresses all of the areas in which the appeals court found violations, prevents Microsoft from engaging in many actions that were not the basis of the liability findings by the appeals court, and imposes requirements on Microsoft in some areas that were not addressed in the trial. Moreover, the unusual definition of middleware further expands the reach of the consent decree beyond the specific issues that were the subject of the trial.

The consent decree thus goes well beyond providing "specific remedy for the limited ground of liability."[34] Several examples are noteworthy. The decree prevents Microsoft from offering price cuts or various incentives to individual computer manufacturers. At trial Microsoft was accused of cutting good deals with computer manufacturers that cooperated in not carrying competitive products and raising prices to those that did. But this was not a basis for any finding of liability by the appeals court.

The proposed consent decree requires Microsoft to reveal communication protocols between the operating systems used by individuals at home or at the office (so-called "client" operating systems) and the operating systems used for performing tasks on computer networks ("server" operating systems). The interoperability of client and server operating systems was not an issue at trial. Nor was there any allegation that directly concerned server operating systems.

Consider yet another example. The proposed consent decree requires Microsoft to disclose information concerning Windows APIs that are used by Microsoft middleware products. This requirement goes beyond the appeals court decision in two ways. First, the appeals court did not find Microsoft liable for failing to provide API information to Netscape, Sun, or any other competitor. Second, the requirement covers middleware products, irrespective of whether they might evolve into competing platforms.

The proposed consent decree falls short of the conduct remedies imposed by Judge Jackson and, of course, does not provide for the breakup he ordered. For example, the district court remedy required Microsoft to enable third parties to examine the Windows source code.[35] The proposed consent decree does not have this provision, although it does establish a three-person technical committee that would have access to the Windows source code.[36] Nor does the proposed consent decree include a requirement that Microsoft write Windows in a way that allows computer manufacturers to remove whatever parts of it they want – and to earn discounts from Microsoft based on how much of Windows they remove!

After the appeals court decision, the government indicated that it would ask for the same conduct remedies that Judge Jackson had imposed. However, that position was not tenable. In remanding the remedies to the new district court judge, the appeals court concluded, "Finally, we have drastically altered the scope of Microsoft's liability, and it is for the district court in the first instance to determine the propriety of a specific remedy for the limited ground of liability which we have upheld."[37]

It is unknowable whether Microsoft could have settled the case for less or whether the Justice Department could have settled the case for more – that is the nature of settlement negotiations. However, the review above may provide some help in understanding that the proposed consent decree is not surprising, given the constraints Microsoft and the Justice Department were under.

Microsoft had to accept restrictions that addressed the specific violations found by the appeals court. There is some case law that suggests that the district court could impose remedies that go beyond enjoining the specific conduct that violates the Sherman Act. By the same token, since the appeals court specifically indicated that it remanded the remedies in light of its drastically altered liability findings, the Justice Department had to cede conduct remedies that it had obtained from Judge Jackson.[38] As of this writing, several states have decided not to accept the proposed consent decree. Under the schedule adopted by the new judge, these remaining plaintiffs are supposed to present their proposed remedies by early December 2001.

[1] United States Court of Appeals for the District of Columbia, Opinion, *U.S. v. Microsoft Corp.*, June 28, 2001, http://ecfp.cadc.uscourts.gov/MS-Docs/1720/0.pdf (hereafter, Appeals Court Decision), p. 102.

[2] "In a case such as the one before us where sweeping equitable relief is employed to remedy multiple violations, and some – indeed most – of the findings of remediable violations do not withstand appellate scrutiny, it is necessary to vacate the remedy decree…" Appeals Court Decision, p. 102.

[3] Appeals Court Decision, p. 106.

[4] Appeals Court Decision, p. 106.

[5] Memorandum of the United States of America in Support of Motion to Enter Final Judgment and in Opposition to the Positions of I.D.E. Corporation and Amici, *U.S. v. Microsoft Corp.*, Civil Action No. 94-1564 (SS), January 18, 1995, http://www.usdoj.gov/atr/cases/f0000/0044.htm, p. 22; Declaration of Kenneth J. Arrow, *U.S. v. Microsoft Corp.*, Civil Action No. 94-1564 (SS), January 17, 1995, p. 11.

[6] 15 U.S.C. Section 1.

[7] See *U.S. v. Socony Vacuum Oil Co.*, 310 U.S. 150 (1940); *Tampa Electric Co. v. Nashville Coal Co.*, 365 U.S. 320 (1961); *Dr. Miles Medical Co. v. John D. Park & Sons Co.*, 220 U.S. 373 (1911); *Jefferson Parish Hospital District No. 2 v. Hyde*, 466 U.S. 2 (1984).

[8] Judge Thomas Penfield Jackson, Conclusions of Law, *U.S. v. Microsoft Corp.*, April 3, 2000, http://www.usdoj.gov/atr/cases/f4400/4469.htm, p. 38.

[9] *Jefferson Parish Hospital District No. 2 v. Hyde*, 466 U.S. 2 (1984).

[10] Appeals Court Decision, p. 86.

[11] For opposing views on the government's chances for success in pursuing the tying claim on remand, compare Lawrence Lessig, "Will Microsoft Admit It Has Lost?" *The New Republic Online*, July 12, 2001, http://www.tnr.com/072301/lessig072301.html, to Herbert Hovenkamp, quoted in Edmund Sanders and Joseph Menn, "Officials May Drop Microsoft Tying Issue," *The Los Angeles Times* (*latimes.com*), July 20, 2001, http://www.latimes.com/business/la-000059155jul20.story.

[12] Appeals Court Decision, p. 83. An "API" is an application programming interface, which exposes functionality for a program to take advantage of.

[13] Appeals Court Decision, p. 73 (internal citation omitted).

[14] 15 U.S.C. Section 2.

[15] *United States v. Grinnell Corp.*, 384 U.S. 563 (1966).

[16] Plaintiff States' First Amended Complaint, *U.S. v. Microsoft Corp.*, July 17, 1998, http://www.naag.org/features/microsoft/amendco.cfm, Paragraphs 91-92.

[17] *Berkey Photo v. Eastman Kodak Co.*, 603, F.2d 263, 276 (1979).

[18] Memorandum and Order, *U.S. v. Microsoft Corp.*, September 14, 1998, p. 51.

[19] Appeals Court Decision, p. 63.

[20] A useful starting point is found in the Conclusions of Law the government proposed to the district court after that court issued its Findings of Fact. The government identified 14 specific anticompetitive acts. Government' Joint Proposed Conclusions of Law, *U.S. v. Microsoft Corp.*, http://www.usdoj.gov/atr/cases/f3900/3932.pdf, pp. 22-23.

[21] Although the factual background is similar, the tying claim here differs from the one discussed above because it is addressed under Section 2 of the Sherman Act and because it is based on the argument that the tying was used to maintain a monopoly in operating systems; the Section 1 claim is based on the argument that the tying was used to extend that monopoly to browsers.

[22] Direct Testimony of Franklin M. Fisher, *U.S. v. Microsoft Corp.*, January 5, 1999, Paragraphs 48-49; Rebuttal Testimony of Franklin M. Fisher, *U.S. v. Microsoft Corp.*, June 1, 1999, a.m. Session, pp. 38-39.

[23] Judge Thomas Penfield Jackson, Findings of Fact, *U.S. v. Microsoft Corp.*, November 5, 1999, http://www.usdoj.gov/atr/cases/f3800/msjudge.pdf, Paragraph 140. There is other language in the decision that could be interpreted to suggest that the district court did not find this illegal: Compare Paragraph 140 to Paragraph 137. While the Findings of Fact are ambiguous, the district court appears to condemn these investments as predatory, but seems to stop short of finding them violations of the antitrust laws. On appeal, the government chose not to challenge Microsoft's investment in developing IE. See Transcript of Oral Arguments before the Court of Appeals for the District of Columbia, *U.S. v. Microsoft Corp.*, February 26, 2001, http://www.microsoft.com/presspass/trial/transcripts/feb01/02-26.asp.

[24] The district court recognized that AOL was going to pick a single browser, and that AOL wanted to be promoted by Microsoft in return for making IE its default browser. Judge Thomas Penfield Jackson, Findings of Fact, *U.S. v. Microsoft Corp.*, November 5, 1999, http://www.usdoj.gov/atr/cases/f3800/msjudge.pdf, Paragraphs 274, 275, 279, 283, 293. The court explicitly acknowledged that some form of exclusivity could be pro-competitive: "A desire to limit free-riding on the firm's investment in consumer-oriented features, such as the Referral Server and the Online Services Folder, can, in some circumstances, qualify as a procompetitive business motivation; but that motivation does not explain the full extent of the restrictions that Microsoft imposed upon IAPs." Judge Thomas Penfield Jackson, Conclusions of Law, *U.S. v. Microsoft Corp.*, April 3, 2000, http://www.usdoj.gov/atr/cases/f4400/4469.htm, p. 15. From the court's subsequent discussion of the "full extent of the restrictions," it seems that the court objected only to the aspects of the deal that placed restrictions on the promotion and distribution of Navigator. *Ibid.*, pp. 15-16.

[25] Appeals Court Decision, p. 42.

[26] Appeals Court Decision, p. 59.

[27] Appeals Court Decision, p. 106.

[28] Appeals Court Decision, pp. 105-106.

[29] Microsoft Corp., Petition for a Writ of Certiorari, included as the Annex to Microsoft Corp., Appellant's Motion for Stay of the Mandate Pending Petition for Writ of Certiorari, August 7, 2001, http://ecfp.cadc.uscourts.gov/MS-Docs/1744/0.pdf. The Supreme Court

denied certiorari in *U.S. v. Microsoft Corp.* on October 9, 2001. See http://a257.g.akamaitech.net/7/257/2422/09oct20011045/www.supremecourtus.gov/orders/courtorders/100901pzor.pdf.

[30] "Plaintiffs have advised Microsoft that they do not intend to pursue further proceedings on remand regarding the Section 1 tying claim and do not intend to pursue on remand the restructuring of Microsoft into separate operating system and applications companies that had previously been ordered by the district court." Joint Status Report in *U.S. v. Microsoft Corp.*, September 20, 2001, p. 2.

[31] One state, New Mexico, settled in July after the appeals court decision, http://www.ago.state.nm.us/PIO/Archived_Press_Releases/2001/MicrosoftCase.htm.

[32] "Middleware" generally refers to software that runs on top of operating systems and provides a set of APIs that other applications can use. Java is a good example: It provides a platform so that applications can run on different operating systems and hardware. At least some business strategists at Netscape hoped to make Navigator middleware in this sense, although they never got very far – Navigator has never had many APIs that other programs can use. To the extent that middleware succeeds, it makes Windows less valuable, because developers write applications to run on the middleware, not on Windows. The other products listed lack at least one of the key characteristics that made Java and Navigator plausible threats to Windows. Media Player and Windows Messenger both expose some APIs, and hence are middleware in that sense. But no one expects competing products (such as RealPlayer or AOL Instant Messenger) to evolve into serious platforms that could threaten Windows. And Outlook Express is simply an e-mail program for client computers – a type of application that is not middleware by any stretch of the imagination. Thus, the unusual definition of middleware in the consent decree appears designed to reduce Microsoft's ability to compete in a much wider range of product segments than those for which its actions were found anticompetitive at trial.

[33] Note that in many cases the remedy may go beyond the specific liability finding to which we have attached it.

[34] Appeals Court Decision, p. 106.

[35] Final Judgment in *U.S. v. Microsoft*, June 7, 2000, http://www.dcd.uscourts.gov/ms-final2.pdf, p. 8.

[36] Microsoft and the Justice Department each appoint one member, and those two members appoint a third, subject to court approval.

[37] Appeals Court Decision, p. 106.

[38] "Other officials said the consent decree was the product of a more narrow reading by the Bush administration than by Microsoft's critics as the parties considered last June's decision by the United States Court of Appeals here." Stephen Labaton and Steve Lohr, "Judge to Hear From 9 States on Microsoft," *The New York Times*, November 7, 2001, http://www.nytimes.com/2001/11/07/technology/07SOFT.html.

Section 1: *U.S. v. Microsoft Corp.*: The Economics

Essay 1

An Analysis of the Government's Economic Case in *U.S. v. Microsoft Corp.*

by David S. Evans, Albert L. Nichols, and Richard Schmalensee*

Interested observers, even those well acquainted with the legal and economic underpinnings of antitrust policy, no doubt had a hard time following the arguments in the Microsoft trial by reading about them in the media. And for good reasons.

For one thing, the government's case turned on novel interpretations of the law. For another, the government altered its case through the course of the proceedings, in part in response to inconsistencies of logic and fact revealed by cross-examination of its expert witnesses.

This paper, written by economists working for Microsoft's defense team, explores the economic underpinnings of the government's case. And each pillar of the government's case is found to be fragile.

The case conflated the market for PC operating systems with the market for software platforms, where Microsoft was challenged on a variety of fronts. In charging that Microsoft was a predator, the government ignored the legitimate reasons why the company would invest heavily in browsing features and add them to Windows free. And nowhere did the government feel compelled to forge durable links between its legal case and the modern economic rationale for antitrust enforcement: the protection of consumer interests.

The very origins of the legal case are troubling. For it seemed to be about punishing winners in the market and leveling the playing field – a reversion to an older notion of antitrust as a means of balancing equities among competitors rather than as a means of furthering the efficiency of markets. —*D.S.E.*

U.S. v. Microsoft Corp. was mainly about what was known as the "browser war."[1] Netscape Navigator was introduced in the fall of 1994,[2] and it quickly became one of the most widely used software applications ever offered. Navigator's popularity peaked in early 1996, when it accounted for more than 80 percent of browser use outside of proprietary online services.[3] But it continued to retain a majority of users well into 1998. Microsoft introduced Internet Explorer (IE) as part of the first release of Windows 95 in August 1995. Little used at first, IE's share rose rapidly after the introduction of IE 3 in August 1996 and after America Online (AOL) began using IE components in its proprietary subscriber software that November. By June 2000, when the trial concluded, Microsoft's share of browser use (including AOL's subscriber software) was just under 70 percent, while Netscape's share was about 30 percent.[4]

Microsoft fought the browser battle as part of a broader struggle to remain the leading provider of software platforms. A software platform contains modules of code that are accessed through application programming interfaces (APIs). APIs provide a wide variety of features and services to software developers. Applications software developers use these APIs to economize on writing code for computer users who have the corresponding software platform installed on their computers. Today, most personal computers use Microsoft Windows[5] as their software platform, and many software developers have written applications that utilize some of the more than 5,000 APIs in Windows.[6] Microsoft included browsing features in Windows to encourage software developers to write Web-enabled applications for Windows, with the goal of increasing the demand for Windows by computer users.

Microsoft concluded that Netscape Navigator could become a competing software platform if it added enough APIs that software developers wanted.[7] The company also concluded that, if Navigator maintained its overwhelming popularity as a browser, Netscape could be in a position to dictate evolving Internet standards, and in the process deter applications developers from using Windows' Web-related features.[8]

Microsoft competed aggressively to win the browser battle and the platform war. It invested about $100 million annually to develop improved versions of IE.[9] It also invested in distributing IE technologies. For example, it gave AOL its IE technologies to use in AOL's subscriber software. It also gave AOL a place in the Windows Online Services folder so Windows users could click on an icon to sign up for the AOL service.[10] Microsoft never sought to make money from IE directly. The payback from developing and distributing IE, as from its investments in other Windows features, came from increasing the value of Windows to make it more likely that Windows would remain the leading software platform.

The government claimed Microsoft's efforts to win the browser battle violated Sections 1 and 2 of the Sherman Act.[11] This article argues that the economic analysis presented in support of that accusation was internally inconsistent, was based on unsound economic theory, and conflicted with the facts. The government refused to acknowledge that the relevant antitrust product market was software platforms – even though its case was mainly about Microsoft's efforts to remain the purveyor of the leading platform in the face of threats from Netscape, Sun, and others. That conceptual error forced the government to depend on a series of economic arguments whose logic hinged on software platforms' *not* being a relevant market.

In its economic analysis of alleged predation, the government would not acknowledge that Microsoft had reasons to invest in the development and distribution of IE for the purpose of competing to sell software platforms. In its economic analysis of tying, the government refused to accept that Web-browsing capabilities logically belong in software platforms, even though all platform vendors, including IBM and Apple, also have included browsers. Other analytic and factual errors compounded these fundamental mistakes.

This article also argues that the district court's Findings of Fact did not support its conclusions that Microsoft had violated Sections 1 and 2 of the Sherman Act.[12] The district court did not accept the government's claims that almost everything Microsoft did to win the browser war violated the Sherman Act. Instead, it found that Microsoft's principal anticompetitive actions entailed not allowing computer vendors to remove IE from Windows and preventing AOL and some Internet service providers from providing Navigator to all subscribers who asked for it.[13] Yet there was no evidence in the record that the actions the district court found unlawful had a material effect on Netscape's share of browser use, or significantly harmed consumers. The district court also found that Microsoft had engaged in tying only because it had failed to provide a version of Windows that prevented end users from using IE.[14] Yet no evidence was offered that there was significant demand for a browser-disabled software platform, and no other vendor promoted a browser-disabled version of its platform.

The second section provides some background on the case. We show that the government's case was based on the propositions that Microsoft had no legitimate "business reason" to fight to win the browser war since it did not expect to earn revenue from IE.

The third section examines the government's market analysis. We show that the government refused to acknowledge that the relevant product market consisted of software platforms, even though, according to the government's witnesses, that is the arena in which Microsoft was battling Navigator and Sun's Java platform.

The fourth section analyzes the government's monopoly maintenance case, the centerpiece of the district court's findings and the government's case on appeal. We show that the government's predation analysis relies on both an indefensibly narrow conception of how Microsoft earns a legitimate return on investments in its platform and an analytic approach incapable of distinguishing predation from vigorous competition.

The fifth section examines the government's Section 1 tying and exclusive dealing allegations. The government charged that Microsoft designed Windows and contracted with distribution channels so that Netscape could not compete effectively. We do not dispute the theory of this part of the government's case; these are potentially troublesome charges. However, we show that the inclusion of IE in Windows and Microsoft's contracts did not, in fact, prevent consumers from obtaining and using Navigator.

The sixth section summarizes the district court's findings. We show that these findings – taken as true and as interpreted by the government in its appeals brief – failed to establish a causal link between (a) the actions found to be anticompetitive; (b) substantial effects in the market; and (c) impacts on consumer welfare.

This article focuses on the trial record rather than the district court's Findings of Fact and Conclusions of Law for three reasons.[15] First, the district court rejected many of the implications of the government's case, even though it accepted much of the government's logic. Since our focus is on the economic foundations of the government's case, we must go directly to the source. Second, the district court's findings are sometimes contradictory. For instance, at one point the district court finds that Microsoft's inclusion of IE at no charge was predation but at another finds it to have been competition on the merits.[16] While the district court appears to condemn many of Microsoft's actions, it stops short of finding them violations of the antitrust laws. Third, the district court's findings lack citations to the trial record, making it impossible to verify the findings.[17] Events subsequent to the trial have also raised other issues concerning the objectivity and reliability of the district court's findings.[18]

BACKGROUND

The government claimed that Microsoft had tied IE and Windows together and entered into exclusive distribution contracts that foreclosed Netscape from the market in violation of Section 1 of the Sherman Act, and that it had engaged in anticompetitive actions (including tying and foreclosing distribution) to maintain a monopoly in operating systems and to obtain a monopoly in browsers in violation of Section 2 of the Sherman Act.[19] To expedite the trial, the district court limited each side to 12 summary witnesses who filed written testimony and were cross-examined between October 1998 and February 1999.[20] Three rebuttal witnesses from each side testified in June 1999. Both sides then submitted proposed Findings of Fact to the district court. The district court issued its Findings of Fact (FOF) in November 1999.[21] After a failed mediation effort, the district court issued its Conclusions of Law (COL) in April 2000.[22] The government then submitted its proposed remedies, with supporting declarations from three economists who had not participated in earlier phases of the trial.[23] It proposed dividing Microsoft into separate operating system and applications companies, and imposing stringent conduct restrictions and disclosure requirements dealing with a variety of software products in addition to Windows. The district court held three hours of non-evidentiary hearings, after which it issued a Final Order imposing the government's proposed remedies largely unchanged.[24] We focus on the liability case.

Software Products and Technology at Issue

The Microsoft case involved consideration of three different functions that computer software provides.[25] A *software platform* provides software services that applications developers can use rather than writing the code for those services themselves. Examples include the code that stores a file on the hard disk or instructs a modem to dial a telephone number. It is common to refer to the modules of code that provide these services, as well as the specifications that provide access to these modules, as "APIs."[26] Many platforms are part of an *operating system*, which controls the computer hardware. For example, an operating system sends instructions to the microprocessor to perform calculations and to move information to the hard disks and other storage devices. A *Web browser*, in its most narrow incarnation, is software that enables users to navigate the World Wide Web and to display files in the HTML format that has become the standard on the Web.

Relationships

There is a close relationship among software platforms, operating systems, and Web browsers. All operating systems provide APIs for communication with the hardware and therefore provide some platform services. Many commercial operating systems, such as the Apple Mac OS and Windows, have added APIs that provide a more extensive platform that eliminates the need for applications developers to write their own code or to license third-party software to provide many functions. The fact that most operating system vendors promote their products as platforms for applications developers suggests that this is efficient and responsive to consumer demand. With the emergence of the Web as a popular resource, essentially all platform vendors added "free" browsing capabilities to their products. Apple developed CyberDog for the Mac OS, IBM developed Web Explorer for OS/2, and Sun developed HotJava for Solaris.[27] In the open-source movement, the popular KDE graphical user interface for the Linux operating system uses an integrated browser to view files stored on the computer's own drives as well as files retrieved from the Web.[28]

A browser is a natural addition to an operating system because it allows the user to obtain information from the Web in the same way operating systems historically have obtained information from an increasing array of sources and storage media. A browser is also a natural extension to a platform because it enables software developers to access APIs that display HTML files and provide other application features that can be used in conjunction with the Web.

Economics of Software Platform Products

The software platform is an example of a product sold in a "two-sided market" characterized by "network externalities."[29] A product serves a two-sided market if the product is valuable only when both sides of the market use it. The simplest example is a heterosexual singles bar: It is valuable only when it attracts both men and women. A two-sided market has externalities when the value obtained by customers on each side of the market is higher the more customers there are on the other side of the market.[30] Men and women value a singles bar more when there are more members of the opposite sex in it.

Software platforms are valued by end users if they are popular with applications developers and thus run attractive applications. They are popular with applications developers if they economize on programming efforts and if they are popular with end users. As with a singles bar, the externalities appear on both sides and are interdependent. A consumer values a software platform more if the platform has more applications he wants. A software developer values a platform more if the platform has more consumers who are potential customers for her applications and it has APIs that make it possible to write powerful applications quickly. To attract developers to this two-sided market, platform vendors undertake wide-ranging efforts beyond providing desirable APIs.[31]

The economics of software platforms generate economies of scale on both the demand side and the supply side. Platforms that have more end users and run more applications are more valuable products. Platforms also have economies of scale in production, because there are substantial fixed costs in writing software and marginal costs close to zero in copying and distributing it. As a result, competition tends to lead to the emergence of a dominant platform product. But the dominant platform product remains vulnerable to displacement by alternative products that are substantially better from the standpoint of end users and applications developers.

Network externalities and scale economies preclude me-too competition against established leaders. Rather, competition comes from major innovations that can displace the incumbent. As a practical matter, the dominant platform is vulnerable because of rapid technological improvements in microprocessor speeds, storage capacity, and, with the emergence of the Internet, bandwidth. We return to this dynamic competition in the next section.

Alternative Platform Models

Middleware and *Web application servers* offer two alternative ways of servicing this two-sided market. Middleware is software that provides APIs to applications software – thus serving as a platform – while obtaining hardware services through the operating system. Middleware could be written to run on a variety of different operating systems and hardware while providing the same APIs to applications – just as many applications provide similar user interfaces on Windows and Macintosh platforms.[32] Thus, applications written for such middleware would, with its aid, run on that same set of operating systems without modification.[33]

An alternative model involves having the platform software and the applications reside primarily on a Web server. The user employs browsing software to access applications through the Web (or via a company intranet employing Internet protocols), with the interface determined by open Web standards, like those governing HTML files. Thus a user running, say, the Macintosh operating system on a desktop computer can use a Web browser to link to and operate a tax-preparation program running on a Linux-based Web server.

The Microsoft case was mainly about the threat posed to Microsoft's Windows software platform by two potential middleware products – Netscape's Navigator and Sun's Java. Navigator was designed to run on many operating systems. It could have become middleware if it had included enough useful APIs to attract software developers to use it for their applications.[34] A browser is potentially well suited as a Web-centric platform if it makes the functions it performs for end users also available to applications developers through APIs. Navigator could also have become middleware by distributing certain Java technologies that provided an additional set of APIs.

Figure 1 illustrates the three platform models. The platform model on the left is based on the marriage between a specific operating system and type of hardware. The one in the center is based on middleware that sits on top of many different operating system – hardware combinations. The one on the right is based on applications that run off a central server computer and communicate through standard Web protocols to browsers running on "client" computers with many different operating system – hardware combinations.

Figure 1. **Three Alternative Software Platforms: Operating Systems, Middleware, and the Web**

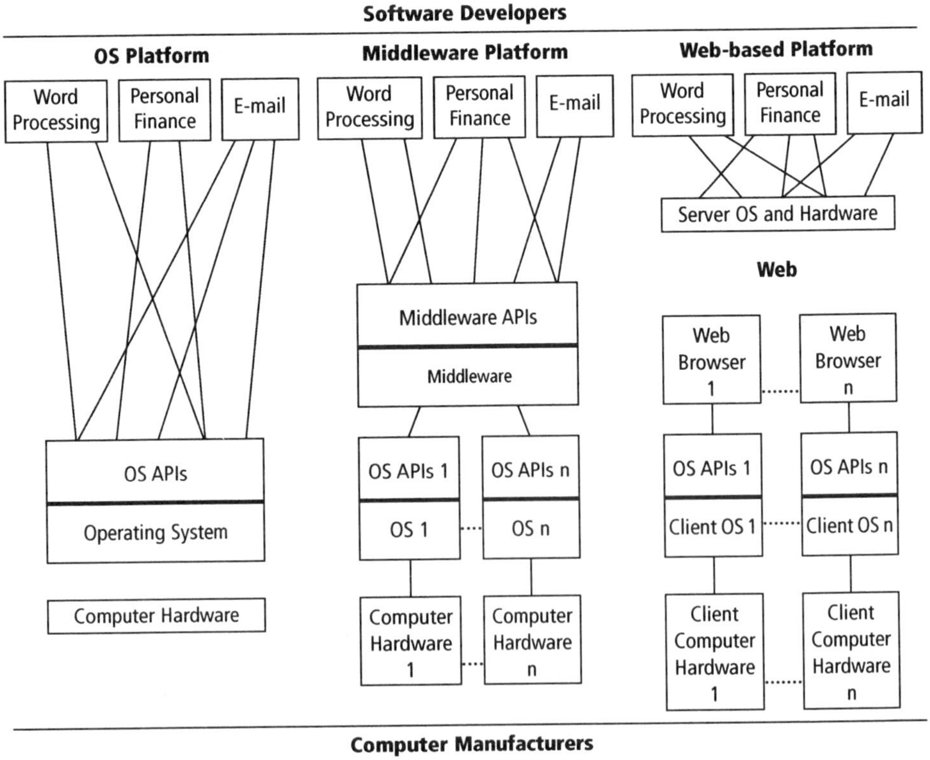

The Browser Battle and the Platform War

Microsoft saw Netscape as a threat to its highly successful Windows software platform. It fought the browser battle to win the war to be the leading Web-centric platform.

Netscape's Threat to Microsoft

In 1994, Microsoft began to develop its own browser for inclusion in Windows 95, but when that effort proved too slow, it licensed code from a third party, while continuing its internal efforts to develop its own.[35] Microsoft had strong incentives to invest in the development and distribution of browsing features and functions in Windows. First, the expansion of Windows' capacity as an operating system would make it more attractive to end users. In 1994-95, IBM's OS/2 was mounting a significant challenge to Windows, and IBM had announced in the fall of 1994 that it would include a "free" Web browser in OS/2 in early 1995. It used this as a selling point, with full-page ads that stressed its Internet capabilities: "The new 32-bit, multitasking, multimedia, Internet-accessed, crash-protected, Windows-friendly, totally cool way to run your computer."[36] All else being equal, the more attractive a platform is to end users, the more attractive it is to applications developers. In addition, by making browsing functions available to software developers through APIs, Microsoft could increase the supply of applications for Windows and thereby increase its value to computer users.

In October 1994, Netscape, a company that had been founded a few months before, released a free beta version of its new Navigator Web browser. Navigator 1, which was released in final form in December, was an instant hit – "the most widely used software application of all time."[37] Netscape distributed most copies at no cost. With the release of Windows 95 in August 1995, Microsoft's browser, IE 1, was preinstalled on every new computer shipped with the new operating system. However, despite the great success of Windows 95 and the release of an improved IE 2 in December 1995, most Web users continued to choose Navigator. One industry source estimated that at the end of 1995, 20 times more copies of Navigator were in use than copies of IE.[38]

Microsoft competed fiercely to reduce Netscape's overwhelming lead. At least two economic concerns motivated Microsoft. First, one of Netscape's founders, Marc Andreessen, boasted that Navigator would include enough APIs to make it attractive to software developers. Navigator's potential as a platform was augmented by the fact that it was the first browser to include a run-time environment for Sun's Java, which included many more APIs. If Navigator/Java included enough useful APIs, and developers wrote popular applications to those APIs rather than to Microsoft's, Windows could, in Andreessen's famous words, become a "mundane collection of not entirely debugged device drivers."[39]

As it turns out, Netscape did not invest in developing significant APIs for its browser software, and it never broke Navigator into functional components that could be used by developers of third-party applications.[40] (Beginning with IE 3, Internet Explorer was "componentized" in this fashion.) Indeed, Netscape's CEO, Jim Barksdale, denied that he or Netscape as a whole had ever shared Andreessen's expansive platform vision.[41] Moreover, Java has thus far proved inadequate as a platform for developing major PC applications.[42]

Microsoft had a second concern. If Navigator continued to be the overwhelming favorite of Web-browser users, Netscape would be able to set *de facto* standards for the Web, determining the path of the Web's future development. These Netscape-driven standards would put Microsoft at a disadvantage both by making it more difficult for it to offer useful Web-related APIs to developers and by making it more difficult for it to compete with Netscape in the market for Web servers (the software on which Web content resides and on which Web-based applications run). Although Netscape emphasized its reliance on "open" standards, in fact it was implicitly extending those standards in proprietary ways in 1995 and 1996. Tens of thousands of Web sites carried the "Best Viewed with Netscape Navigator" logo. Indeed, until IE caught up, Navigator was the only browser that could view Web content relying on Netscape's newest features. Even in late 1996, *PC Magazine* wrote:

> Not surprisingly, Netscape Communications Corp., the maker of Navigator – the leader with 80 to 90 percent market share for browsers – wants to continue to set the pace for the emerging interactive Web. Its HTML extensions, notably those for presenting tables and frames, have become standards for Web designers. Netscape's Navigator plug-in architecture is the de facto standard for adding multimedia pizzazz to a Web site, and its support for Sun Microsystems' Java is the most popular way of embedding interactive elements into Web pages.[43]

As the government correctly observed, Microsoft sought to prevent Netscape from continuing to dominate the evolution of the Web.[44]

Competition Between Microsoft and Netscape

Over the next few years, Microsoft and Netscape competed in three major ways. First, they engaged in innovation competition. Each raced to release versions that would include new or improved features. At first Microsoft played catch-up, adding support for "frames" and animated graphics. Later Microsoft added its own new features, such as dynamic HTML. Microsoft spent about $100 million a year between 1995 and the time of trial to improve IE.[45]

Table 1 shows quality comparisons between IE and Netscape over this time period, based on third-party reviews drawn from 13 major computer magazines.[46] For the first two versions, Navigator was the unanimous choice of the reviewers. With the release of IE 3 in August 1996, Internet Explorer achieved rough parity; with the release of IE 4 in October 1997, Microsoft passed Netscape: three-quarters of the reviews ranked IE as superior, and none labeled Navigator as better. Internet Explorer continued to lead with IE 5, which bested Navigator 4.5 by similar margins.[47]

Table 1. **Reviews of Navigator and IE in Major Computer Publications**

	CHOICES AMONG BROWSERS			
MAGAZINES' CHOICES	**VERSIONS 1/2**	**VERSION 3**	**VERSION 4**	**VERSION 4.5/5**
Navigator	100%	50%	0%	0%
Tie/Mixed	0%	25%	27%	25%
IE	0%	25%	73%	75%
Number of magazines with reviews	13	12	11	8

Source: Schmalensee Direct, *supra* note 3, App. F

IE 3 also offered advantages to developers over Navigator. IE 3 had components that provided services to other parts of Windows and also exposed numerous APIs useful to third-party developers. IE 4 made even more services available.[48] By contrast, Navigator provided software developers minimal access to its features. For example, when a user asked Intuit's Quicken personal financial software to access information on the Web using Navigator, Navigator launched in a separate window, retrieved the information from the Web, and then reactivated Quicken. In contrast, Quicken was able to use IE 3's components to obtain information from the Web without ever leaving the Quicken environment.[49]

Microsoft and Netscape also engaged in price competition. Microsoft gave its browser away to all users: It included the browser in the operating system, made upgrades available free, and (starting with IE 3) developed and distributed free versions of IE for Apple's Macintosh and for major versions of the Unix operating system (used on high-level workstations in corporations and universities). Netscape followed a "free but not free" strategy.[50] Some users (e.g., students and professors) were entitled to free licenses. Other individuals could use trial or beta versions free but were supposed to pay $39 to $79 for final versions (depending on the period and the model). Although Netscape let anyone download copies and made little attempt to collect license fees from individuals, many in fact paid.[51] Netscape also charged license fees to businesses and to Internet service providers (ISPs), as well as to others who wanted to distribute Navigator to their customers. As IE's quality improved, Netscape found customers increasingly resistant to its charges, and it eliminated all license fees in early 1998.[52]

Last, Microsoft and Netscape competed in making their browsers readily available to computer users. Netscape pioneered large-scale distribution of commercial software via the Web. Navigator was available for free downloads on Netscape sites and on the Web sites of many of Netscape's partners. Tens of thousands of other Web sites had links that would take users to a download site. For a fee, Netscape also licensed ISPs to distribute Navigator to their customers. Businesses could license Navigator directly from Netscape. Colleges received free licenses and the right to distribute free copies over their internal networks. Netscape also distributed Navigator through computer makers (original equipment manufacturers, or OEMs) under varying arrangements. Some paid fees, whereas others included an icon that let end users connect to a referral server where they could sign up for an ISP; Netscape gave OEMs part of the fee paid by ISPs for each new customer. Some ISPs (such as Spry) also struck deals directly with OEMs to include Navigator and a desktop icon to sign up with the ISP.[53]

Starting with the first release of Windows 95, all copies of Windows preinstalled on new computers included IE code and an IE desktop icon. Subsequent versions of IE were included along with other improvements in "service releases" that were installed on new PCs. After the first retail release, all retail copies also included IE. New versions of IE were always available free for downloading, so that anyone who wanted to update the previous version could do so. Just before IE 3 was released, only 16 percent of IE users had downloaded their copies. In the next quarter, however, following IE 3's release, 49 percent of IE users reported having downloaded their copies.[54]

Competition for distribution increased with the release of IE 3 in August 1996. Microsoft secured significant distribution when AOL and the two other large online services (OLSs) agreed to integrate Microsoft's IE browsing technologies into their subscriber software. In addition, Microsoft secured distribution through many ISPs, a channel that Netscape previously had dominated. In 1997, Microsoft entered into agreements with various Internet content providers (ICPs), such as Disney, to promote IE and to restrict their promotion and distribution of competing browsers.[55]

The Government's Line Between Competition and Predation

The government concluded that Microsoft's intense efforts to increase IE's share of browser use crossed the line from competition to predation. To understand where the government drew that line, we begin by explaining the government's theory of the case and then summarize the actions it claimed violated the Sherman Act.

The Government's Theory of the Case

The government asserted that there were two relevant markets: operating systems for Intel-compatible personal computers, in which Microsoft had a monopoly, and browsers, which constituted a separate product. Developers would write applications "first and foremost" for the most popular operating system, and consumers would use an operating system only if many applications were available for it.[56] Indeed, at times the government made it sound as if developers wrote only for the most popular operating system, and that consumers would always choose the operating system with the largest number of applications.[57] Because Windows had become very popular with both developers and users, the government contended that its monopoly was protected by an "applications barrier to entry."

Despite this barrier, the government claimed, Microsoft was concerned that the following sequence would unfold.

1. Navigator (alone or in combination with Java) would become the standard platform to which applications developers wrote software.[58]

2. This middleware platform would work with many different operating systems (and types of hardware), thereby making users less concerned with what operating system was installed on their computer.

3. This would facilitate new entry into operating systems.

4. This competition – which would "commoditize" the operating system (much as PC hardware had become a commodity in the 1980s) – would eliminate Microsoft's monopoly power.[59]

With Windows no longer an important platform, Microsoft would become one of many firms selling an operating system that controls the hardware but offers only the most basic services to applications developers. In essence, the market would shift to the middleware model shown in the center of Figure 1.

As for the browser, the government argued that it was a complement to the operating system just like any application. Consumers would have a greater demand for Microsoft's operating system if they could also use it to run a high-quality browser.[60] If Microsoft had not been trying to protect its monopoly, the government argued, it should have wanted to encourage the use of Netscape Navigator.[61] Microsoft might have wanted to compete in the browser business, but in fact it had no plans to earn money from selling browsers. According to the government, Microsoft attempted to monopolize the browser market to prevent the erosion of the applications barrier to entry and thereby to maintain its monopoly in operating systems.

This was the major theme of the government's case: Microsoft tried to prevent the "erosion" of the applications barrier to entry to avert "commoditization" of the operating system.

Distinguishing Between Competition and Predation

From this perspective, almost everything Microsoft did to popularize its browsing software – and much that it did to improve its software platform – crossed the line from competitive to predatory behavior. According to Fisher:

> ...Microsoft began devoting at least $100 million per year to developing its own browser....Microsoft also spent tens of millions of dollars a year marketing and promoting Internet Explorer....Microsoft's internal documents make it clear that Microsoft undertook its browser development not to make money from browsers...but to prevent Netscape's browser from facilitating competition with Microsoft's monopoly operating system. This is the essence of predatory monopoly maintenance.[62]

The government also claimed that Microsoft engaged in predation by compensating AOL to persuade it to use IE technologies, by offering ISPs consideration for distributing IE, and by not charging for IE.[63]

The Government's Allegations

The government claimed that Microsoft violated Section 2 of the Sherman Act by engaging in a predatory and exclusionary campaign to prevent Navigator, by itself or in combination with Java, from becoming a middleware platform. This predatory campaign included tying IE to Windows and making it harder for Netscape to distribute Navigator.[64] The government also claimed that Microsoft violated Section 1 by tying IE to Windows (a per se violation, according to the government) and foreclosing Netscape from the market.

The government also introduced several specific episodes as evidence of what the district court judge later called Microsoft's "corporate practice to pressure other firms to halt software development that either shows the potential to weaken the applications barrier to entry or competes directly with Microsoft's most cherished software products."[65] These episodes included a June 1995 meeting in which Microsoft allegedly tried to get Netscape to refrain from competing in platform-level browsing software and non-browser incidents with IBM, Apple, RealNetworks, and Intel. The facts of each episode are disputed, and the corresponding allegations have little economic content. As a result, we do not address them, except to note that in four of the five cases, Microsoft's alleged pressure came to naught: Netscape rebuffed Microsoft's overtures (whatever their nature), Apple refused to stop developing and giving away QuickTime for Windows, RealNetworks continued to develop and distribute basic multimedia streaming software, and IBM refused to reduce promotion of its competing products to obtain the lower price of Windows it wanted from Microsoft.[66] Microsoft was successful in delaying the release of native signal processing (NSP) software developed by Intel. But Microsoft's objections were based in large part on NSP's incompatibility with Windows 95, which Microsoft was about to release.[67]

OPERATING SYSTEMS, PLATFORMS, AND THE APPLICATIONS BARRIER TO ENTRY

The government's theory of the case was at war with itself throughout the trial. On one hand, government witnesses described how Microsoft was concerned that middleware would displace Windows as the leading platform and how Microsoft mounted aggressive efforts to prevent the emergence of Navigator, Java, and other middleware. The government sought Microsoft's breakup to give the newly created applications company an incentive to develop Microsoft Office into a middleware platform that could compete with Windows.[68] On the other hand, neither of the relevant antitrust markets defined by the government included middleware threats to Microsoft. The government denied that software platforms constituted the relevant market for evaluating its claims.[69] Yet it could not identify another antitrust case in which the alleged victims of the predatory behavior were not in the relevant antitrust market.[70]

The government argued that the key relevant market for evaluating its claims was that for "operating systems for Intel-compatible PCs" in which Microsoft had no serious immediate rivals.[71] It asserted that Microsoft was concerned that the success of middleware platforms would result in entry into operating systems. The value of Microsoft's Windows products, however, results primarily from their popularity as a software platform among applications software developers and computer users who want to run those applications. The government also claimed that getting software developers to write applications for Windows was mainly intended to erect a barrier to entry into operating systems. Yet any company that wants to supply a software platform must invest in supporting the applications developer side of the market as well as the end-user side of the market. The developer side of the market is an important source of value to consumers, one in which platform vendors can invest, just as they can invest in technical R&D to improve quality or in more effective distribution. Therefore, calling the availability of complementary software an "applications barrier to entry" is like saying that there is a "product-quality barrier to entry" that innovation seeks to raise.

The government's conclusion that operating systems for Intel-compatible PCs was a relevant antitrust market was based on two major mistakes in its economic analysis. First, the government's assertion that the stock of applications results in an immense barrier to entry is based entirely on a *theory* of how applications come to be written for operating systems – a theory that it did not test. Moreover, the government's theory is based on a simplistic model of network industries that assumes irrational behavior on the part of market participants. Second, the government's product market analysis assumes that the relevant competition is over *price* in a *static* market. In reality, competition in a *dynamic* market takes place largely on innovation. Incumbents are constrained not by prices charged by existing competitors, but by the prospect of displacement through drastic innovation by known and unknown competitors.

As a result of these analytic mistakes, the government based its case on the proposition that Microsoft had durable monopoly power in the market for Intel-compatible PC operating systems. As we discuss, a firm with such a durable monopoly would maximize its profits by charging many times what Microsoft charges for Windows.

The Government's Theory of How Applications Come to Be Written for Operating Systems

The government's case is based on a mechanistic model of how applications come to be written for operating systems. Software developers write "first and foremost" to the platform that has the most users.[72] Consumers use the platform that has the most attractive set of applications. There is a positive feedback loop between consumers and software developers: As more consumers use a platform, more software developers write applications; as more applications are available for a platform, more consumers want to use it. These feedbacks automatically accrue to the most popular platform and are so powerful that they lock out competitors.

The government argued that Microsoft's market position resulted from this kind of powerful feedback process. Microsoft received an early advantage over other platforms because IBM chose MS-DOS to be the operating system for its new PC in 1981.[73] Software developers wrote applications that ran on MS-DOS. By making successive generations of its platform compatible with these applications, Microsoft accumulated a large stock of applications that ran on its platforms.

In the government's model, that large stock of applications created an insurmountable barrier to entry. Consumers will not use a platform that does not have a large supply of applications. Even the 12,000 applications available for the Apple Macintosh are not enough.[74] Furthermore, software developers will not write applications for platforms that most consumers do not use. Hence the "applications barrier to entry."[75]

The government's mechanistic model does not consider the profit motives of the economic actors or other characteristics of the platform and its complementary products. Nor does it permit the economic actors to make strategic choices. Economists have recognized that such models have limited relevance. Positive feedback effects are an important aspect of competitive dynamics in the platform business, but they are only part of the story.[76]

Behavior of Platform Vendors and Software Developers

Platform vendors need to make investments that attract both consumers and software developers. Neither side of the market comes free of charge. In the case of consumers, the platform vendor must invest in making the platform reliable and easy to use. It also needs to make sure that the consumer has an adequate stock of high-quality applications that run on the platform and that perform the tasks most important to potential customers. In the case of developers, the platform vendor needs to invest in building features into the platform that reduce the cost of writing applications and that enable developers to offer attractive applications. The platform vendor also needs to invest in making sure that many consumers are using its platform so that software developers have more consumers to whom they can sell their applications. A basic element of competition among platform vendors therefore consists of attracting software developers to write applications for the platform. All platform vendors invest in developing APIs for software developers and "evangelizing" those APIs – that is, persuading software developers to use them.[77] Microsoft takes a particularly intensive and structured approach to this process.[78] Other platform vendors engage in similar activities.[79]

Contrary to the government's theory, developers do not automatically write to the platform with the most users. They care about, among other things, the characteristics of users and how much they are willing to pay. Unix applications and development tools, for example, generate three-quarters as much revenue as those for Windows even though Unix has a tiny fraction of the number of users of the Windows platform.[80]

Developers also care about the degree of competition they face. A large existing market may be much less attractive than a small emerging one if the former already has popular, high-quality incumbents in the developer's application category. If one wanted to develop and market a new personal finance application, for example, it is far from obvious that the best target platform would be Windows, where Intuit's Quicken is the leader and Microsoft Money already competes. Software developers also care about the cost of writing their software. It is cheaper to write software to a platform if the vendor has developed more APIs that the developer can use. Windows is widely acknowledged as having the most extensive set of APIs and the most complete set of developer tools to make use of those APIs in applications.[81]

The Government's Simplistic Model Versus the Facts

The government's mechanistic theory is not consistent with the facts. When MS-DOS was introduced in 1981, there were two other software platforms that had larger stocks of applications available – the Apple II OS and CP/M. One of those incumbents also offered a version (CP/M-86) that ran on the new IBM PC and that was endorsed and marketed by IBM.[82] Under the government's theory, developers and end users should have chosen CP/M over MS-DOS. They did not.

By the same reasoning, IBM's OS/2 should have beaten Windows. When Windows 95 came out, IBM's OS/2 Warp 3.0 had been on sale for almost a year. It offered full compatibility for MS-DOS and Windows 3.x applications, and over 2,000 more applications written specifically to run on OS/2.[83] Windows 95 also had backward compatibility, but it had virtually no applications written to take advantage of its new features.[84] End users and developers should all have chosen OS/2 instead of Windows 95 because OS/2 had more applications written to it.[85] Yet few did so.

Nor can the government's theory explain why Microsoft and other platform vendors invest heavily in developing and evangelizing features that will attract software developers to their platforms. That behavior is inconsistent with the model's prediction that "once ahead, always ahead." Under the government's theory, Microsoft is irrational in devoting 2,000 employees and $600 million per year to developer support, because it would automatically get the full attention of developers simply by virtue of Windows' position as leading platform.[86] The government responded that it makes sense for Microsoft to invest in order to raise the applications barrier to entry. But under the government's view, Microsoft's share of operating system sales is so high that it would be pointless to make that barrier much higher.

The government's theory is inconsistent with the fact that many firms have invested and are investing in creating platforms to challenge Windows. IBM invested substantially in OS/2, Sun and others are investing in Java, and many companies are investing in Linux.[87] It is also inconsistent with its remedy theory that splitting Microsoft would lead the new owner of Office to write a version for Linux (because Linux does not yet have many PC users).[88]

In fact, developers write applications quickly for promising platforms. Recent increases in sales of Apple computers resulted in more applications for the Mac OS.[89] Software developers are writing applications for the Windows CE and Psion operating systems for hand-held devices even though the Palm OS runs on 61 percent of hand-held computers shipped in 1999 and has more than 1,000 applications written for it already.[90] An analysis of 18,000 software firms shows that most write for multiple platforms. In 2000, 68 percent reported writing for Windows, but 48 percent wrote for Unix, 19 percent wrote for Macintosh, and a third each wrote for proprietary operating systems used in mainframes and minicomputers. Moreover, from 1996 to 2000 the proportion targeting non-Windows platforms grew, while that targeting Windows shrank.[91]

The Government's Economic Analysis of the Applications Barrier to Entry

There were three major problems with the government's claim that there was an almost insurmountable barrier to entry into operating systems. First, as we have seen above, its claim was based on a mechanistic positive-feedback model that was inconsistent with the facts of the operating system/platform business.

Second, the stock of applications could constitute an entry barrier only if it would cost more for an entrant to develop that stock of applications than it cost Microsoft. The government's economists did not attempt to demonstrate this empirically; they based their conclusion on the assertion that the stock of applications is determined by first-mover advantages and positive feedback effects.

Third, the government ignored the nature of competition in the software business. Unlike competition in traditional industries, this competition does not involve entry with a comparable ("me-too") product followed by price competition. A me-too entrant would be unlikely to recover its investment, because prices could be competed down to marginal cost (essentially zero). In the mid-1980s, for example, Microsoft focused much of its application effort on the Macintosh platform, rather than its own, more popular MS-DOS platform, where Lotus 1-2-3 dominated spreadsheets and WordPerfect was rapidly becoming the most popular word processor. Microsoft's strategy was successful: Excel and Word quickly became the most popular applications in their categories on the Macintosh platform. New platforms also need not have as broad a base of applications as older ones. One critical "killer application" that provides unique capabilities users want can make the difference, starting the "virtuous circle" that attracts users and developers to a platform. For example, Lotus 1-2-3 is sometimes credited with cementing the popularity of MS-DOS and Intel-compatible PCs.[92]

The Lack of Entry

The lack of entry into operating systems for Intel-compatible computers is consistent with at least three possible pro-competitive explanations.

One is that the threat of entry has forced Microsoft to set its prices low enough and its quality high enough to discourage entry.[93]

A second is that Microsoft has continued to prosper because of the mistakes that its rivals made. The business press provides ample discussion of mistakes that Apple and IBM made in promoting their platforms. Apple refused to license the Mac OS to other OEMs, which inflated the price of the total system. IBM's first versions of OS/2 required expensive hardware upgrades, and IBM initially ignored consumers, focusing on large business users (who were customers for IBM's larger computers). And neither has ever supported developers to the extent that Microsoft does.[94]

A third explanation recognizes that Microsoft has produced several distinct versions of its operating systems over the last 20 years: MS-DOS, Windows 3.x, Windows NT, and Windows 9x. Each new version faced entrenched incumbents (CP/M for DOS, Unix for Windows NT) or other strong contestants (OS/2 and numerous graphical user interfaces for Windows 3.x, OS/2 Warp for Windows 95). Each was a bet-the-company effort, where the winner of the race was long in doubt. Even with Windows 95, where hindsight suggests success was a foregone conclusion, many doubted at the time that Microsoft would be able to complete Windows 95 when it did, or that

Windows 95 would trump IBM's OS/2 Warp, a formidable competitor.[95]

Static Versus Dynamic Competition

The government got the economics wrong in another fundamental way. The case was mainly about dynamic competition, based on innovation, to become the leading platform vendor. Yet the government's analysis of market definitions and monopoly power relied entirely on a static model in which competition is mainly over price.[96] As a result, it did not address the questions that must be answered to determine whether Microsoft had monopoly power in any relevant market.

Types of Competition

In static competition, an identifiable group of firms vie for sales. They compete primarily over price and modest differences in product attributes. Although innovation may take place and new firms may enter the market, competition is mostly on price. In dynamic competition, on the other hand, firms attempt to leapfrog each other with significantly better products (e.g., Lotus 1-2-3 was not only a better spreadsheet than VisiCalc; it added new feature categories, including charts and macros) and in some cases totally new products that render existing products obsolete (e.g., personal computers with word-processing software made dedicated word processors obsolete). Dynamic competition may well involve innovation by previously unknown competitors. Therefore, the best any firm can do is to engage in rapid innovation in the hopes that it will remain ahead if it is the current leader or that it will leapfrog the leader if it is not.

The battle among Microsoft, Netscape, and Sun described by the government primarily involved dynamic competition. When Marc Andreessen said that Netscape would displace Windows as the leading platform, he was 23 years old and his company was only a year old. Java had been invented in 1992, but it was originally seen as a platform for consumer electronics, such as telephones and toasters; its appearance in 1995 as a "write-once, run-everywhere" platform was a brand-new role.[97] The government says each of these companies was investing in innovation to establish itself as the software platform leader. This kind of dynamic competition is particularly important in software, and in some categories it takes on a winner-take-all (or winner-take-most) character.[98] The history of PC software is full of deposed leaders, once seen as unbeatable, such as VisiCalc and Lotus 1-2-3 in spreadsheets, WordStar and WordPerfect in word processing, and dBASE in databases.[99]

Incumbents in dynamically competitive industries are constrained by the threat that another firm innovates in ways that destroy demand for the incumbent's product. These threats force firms to invest heavily in research and development and to bring out new versions of their products periodically – including versions that lead to the demise of their old products. (For example, Windows 95 largely eliminated the demand for MS-DOS.) These threats also generally constrain the prices charged by incumbents: The higher the current prices and the smaller the network of users, the more attractive an entrant will be to consumers – even if incumbents lower prices in response to that entry.[100]

Assessing Monopoly Power in Dynamically Competitive Industries

Monopoly power in dynamically competitive industries depends on actual and potential innovative threats to leading firms.[101] One cannot determine the source of these threats simply by drawing boundaries and computing shares, or even by looking at traditional barriers to entry, as such barriers concern non-innovative entry. An appropriate analysis generally requires the exercise of judgment regarding the likelihood of future races for market dominance and their probable nature. There is no guarantee that such races will continue in any dynamically competitive industry, but neither does the absence of a visible race imply that dynamic competition is at an end. Firms may be working feverishly to develop a product that will turn the industry upside down, or a product in one category may burst into another.

Examination of innovative threats also generally involves consideration of dynamic competition based on technologies and design approaches that differ radically from those used by the incumbent. An examination of IBM's position in mainframe computers in the mid-1980s, for example, would have been seriously misleading if it had not considered the emerging threats posed by networked personal computers and by powerful workstations from Sun and others.[102]

To measure the vigor of dynamic competition, one must look beyond current sales figures and examine ownership of and investment in relevant intellectual property – which may involve technologies not currently in use. If firms are making significant R&D investments to obtain and retain leadership positions, and if knowledgeable observers consider the outcome of the struggle in doubt, dynamic competition may be healthy regardless of current market concentration.

Similarly, the ability of new firms to enter into dynamic competition can impose serious constraints on the behavior of current market leaders. This constraint is likely to be particularly important in software, because capital requirements are generally small, the supply of skilled programmers is relatively deep, no capacity constraints limit production, and distribution is generally easy. In principle, of course, incumbents' intellectual property positions, capital requirements, or distribution problems may so limit the prospects of potential entrants that there is little or no effective dynamic competition. But such barriers cannot be evaluated without detailed analysis of the relevant competitive arenas.

The Government's Static Approach to Market Definition and Monopoly Power

The government defined relevant markets and measured market power through the lens of static rather than dynamic competition. That shifted the focus of its economic analysis away from issues that were relevant to assessing its allegations of anticompetitive conduct. The government claimed that Microsoft tried to prevent Netscape and Sun from producing software that would sharply reduce the value of Windows. Microsoft allegedly invested in harming these potentially competitive products through a predatory campaign involving hundreds of millions of dollars of direct costs and foregone revenues. Any sound economic analysis of such claims would have to consider the extent to which Microsoft faced dynamic competition from Netscape, Sun, and other firms with new technologies, as well as the plausibility of the assertion that eliminating Netscape and Sun as threats would free it from competition for a period long enough to recoup its alleged predatory investments.

The government declined to engage in a serious analysis of these issues.[103] Instead, it used a static market analysis approach, based on the Justice Department's *Horizontal Merger Guidelines*, and found no current competitors able to prevent Microsoft from charging more than the competitive price – a price that its economists alluded to but did not attempt to estimate or even define.[104] The traditional competitive benchmark is a price equal to marginal cost, but when marginal cost is essentially zero, no firm can survive charging that price in the long run.

The government's static approach thus divorced its economic analysis from business realities. In particular, the competitive threats – Netscape's Navigator and Sun's Java – that allegedly led Microsoft to engage in predation and other anticompetitive actions were excluded from the government's market because they were not operating systems for Intel-compatible computers.[105] For the analysis of static competition, this may have been the right approach, since they were not competing head-to-head with Windows as operating systems. For the relevant analysis of dynamic competition, this made no economic sense, since both Navigator and Java were viewed by all the parties involved as having the potential not just to take some business away from Windows at the margin but to replace it as the leading software platform.

Our point is not that Microsoft was indisputably constrained by the forces of dynamic competition. One can legitimately debate whether Microsoft's success in persuading consumers to use Windows and in persuading applications developers to write software for Windows made successful entry so improbable that Microsoft could rest secure that it would not become another Wang, a market leader eliminated by new technologies.[106] Rather, our point is that the government and its economists did not come to grips with the central issue. Instead, they declared evidence of vigorous dynamic competition to be irrelevant in an industry that was dynamically competitive according to their own version of events.

The Government's Operating Systems Market

An empirical test strongly refuted the government's theory that operating systems for Intel-compatible computers made up a relevant market in which Microsoft had durable monopoly power.[107] Under standard assumptions, it is straightforward to calculate the price that a profit-maximizing monopoly would charge for the operating system under the government's theory. The predicted price is about $900, far above the $65 actually charged by Microsoft for its operating system. The government dismissed this analysis, saying that it showed only that Microsoft was not exercising its monopoly power through its pricing.[108] However, that position does not square with the government's theory or other testimony of its economists. If a high and durable barrier to entry protected Windows, Microsoft would have no reason to charge less than the short-run profit-maximizing price. Indeed, the government's economists went so far as to say that a rational firm should earn the most it can today and lower prices only if entry actually occurs.[109]

Fisher also disputed the numerical assumptions that Schmalensee employed. Although we believe Fisher's alternative assumptions are wrong, even under those assumptions he found that the profit-maximizing price implied by the government's monopoly theory was about $265.[110] But this figure is four times the actual price and thus still inconsistent with the government's market power analysis.[111]

Microsoft might be investing in expanding the Windows network to make Windows more attractive and entry more difficult.[112] But that is inconsistent with the government's theory that an impregnable applications barrier already protects Microsoft from entry.

There may be other theories that reconcile Microsoft's pricing policy with that of a firm having durable monopoly power. To date, however, no one has proposed one. And the theory that the government relied on is not consistent with the facts.

It is important to note that the problems with the government's market definition went far beyond the ones usually associated with plaintiffs' understandable inclination to define the market narrowly, calculate the resulting high market share of the defendant, and then declare victory. These problems usually affect only the question of whether the defendant has monopoly power. In *U.S. v. Microsoft Corp.*, the government's erroneous market definition analysis infected its entire liability case. Most important, it led the government to deny that Microsoft had any "business reason" to promote its platform business or to include browsing features in its platform.

PREDATORY AND EXCLUSIONARY STRATEGIES

To analyze the government's "monopoly maintenance" claim, let us return to the difference between how the government and Microsoft viewed the browser war. The government claimed that Microsoft was afraid Navigator would become a successful middleware platform. That would eliminate the applications barrier to entry that protected Windows. As a result, Windows would face competing operating systems as this category became "commoditized," eliminating Microsoft's monopoly profits.

Microsoft agreed that it was once afraid that Netscape would become a successful middleware platform. And, as the government demonstrated at trial, Microsoft employees expressed that fear in internal e-mails. Their fear, however, was *not* that there would be more competition in operating systems, but rather that Navigator/Java would *replace* Windows as the leading *platform* around which applications developers and consumers would coalesce as a result of network effects and scale economies. And, though it reviewed hundreds of thousands of Microsoft e-mails and used many as exhibits, the government seems to have found none in which a Microsoft employee worried about Netscape's facilitating the entry of competing operating systems.[113] If the leading platform were middleware, as in the model in the center of Figure 1, the operating system business would be neither profitable nor attractive to potential entrants; the middleware platform would capture the value of network economies.

This is a distinction *with* a difference – a very important one. The government built its case on the proposition that any action Microsoft took to compete against Netscape in browsers was predatory unless Microsoft believed that it was going to make money in browsers. Thus, for example, Fisher claimed that Microsoft had "no business reason" to invest hundreds of millions of dollars in a "no-revenue product" (IE).[114] But that claim is based on the false premise that Microsoft had no business interest in remaining the software platform standard. Microsoft has earned billions of dollars by developing both sides of the two-sided demand for its software platforms – end users and software developers. *It competes in the software platforms business.*

The government's decision to rely on an unprecedented and loose definition of predation added to the analytical confusion. It argued that a business action is predatory if it is profit-maximizing only because it creates market power by harming competition. That definition sweeps up many pro-competitive actions and, in winner-take-all industries such as software platforms, necessarily convicts the winner. The problems with this loose definition were compounded by the government's failure to evaluate consumer harm. It presented no evidence that the future costs to consumers of the predation campaign, in the form of higher prices or slower innovation, were likely to outweigh the current and past benefits of lower prices and quickened innovation. Indeed, it did not seriously attempt to demonstrate that there would be any future costs at all.

The government's flawed market definition, its loose definition of predation, and its failure to examine the effect of Microsoft's actions on long-run consumer welfare led the government to claim that almost every action Microsoft took to win the browser battle was predatory and lacked any pro-competitive business justification. This was the basis for the government's "monopoly maintenance case" examined in this section.

Strictly speaking, the government's monopoly maintenance case included both "predatory" and "exclusionary" behavior. Predatory behavior included Microsoft's investment in IE and its decision not to charge a positive price for it. Exclusionary behavior included various Microsoft efforts that had the alleged effect of making it harder for Netscape to persuade end users to use its browser. However, both sorts of allegations ultimately were based on the government's theory that Microsoft had "no business reason" to be investing in the development and distribution of its browser. In the case of predatory behavior the government claimed that Microsoft's behavior was not "profit-maximizing" except as a way of maintaining monopoly power. In the case of exclusionary behavior the government claimed that Microsoft's business justifications for adopting various policies and entering into various agreements were pretexts.[115]

Defining and Testing for Predation[116]

Economic analysis led the Supreme Court to recognize several important principles in its modern decisions on predation. First, predation is seldom a rational strategy for firms because they incur significant immediate costs with uncertain future returns.[117] Second, it is difficult to distinguish predation from competition in practice because predation leads to lower prices and higher output – the hallmarks of competition.[118] Third, court decisions that erroneously condemn competition as predation could "chill the very conduct the antitrust laws are designed to protect."[119]

In the past, the Supreme Court has demanded evidence that the defendant's actions are likely to harm consumers. In *Brooke Group*, the Court required that plaintiffs establish that below-cost pricing occurred *and* that the defendant had a reasonable expectation of recouping its predatory losses through future price increases. The Court's rationale for a recoupment test was that, even if below-cost pricing by a firm may hurt some of its rivals, unless a would-be predator is able to recoup its losses, then market prices are lower on balance, consumer welfare is enhanced, and the apparently predatory pricing scheme should not be condemned.[120] In other words, although there may be harm to competitors, a court must be able to find harm to consumers to find an antitrust violation.[121] The *Brooke Group*'s recoupment test thereby reduces the risk of mistaking harm to rivals as harm to competition and consumers.[122]

The risk of such false inferences is higher in software markets than in more traditional markets because marginal costs of production are essentially zero and the result of competition is often one firm with a very large share. We show next that the standard tests for predation do not distinguish predatory from competitive behavior in such winner-take-all markets. The only way to see if consumers are likely to be injured is to examine impacts on consumers directly. We then show that the government's predation test is much more likely to punish pro-competitive behavior than the *Brooke Group* test.

Testing for Predation in Software Markets

The application of existing predation tests to the software business encounters several difficulties. On one hand, tests based on variable costs provide software firms with wide latitude for dropping prices for predatory or other reasons, because variable costs are often virtually zero, and almost always far below observed prices for successful software titles. Firms might not be able to recover their investments in predation if they priced close to zero, but a price close to zero might exceed average variable cost and thereby pass the *Brooke Group* cost screen. One could argue that letting dominant firms price in this fashion could discourage entry and reduce social welfare. On the other hand, penetration pricing, at or below variable cost, is common in many software categories as a response to network effects. Software products are often given away to build usage and affect standards by firms that plainly lack monopoly power. Thus low – or even negative – prices are likely to be rational and, so long as there is sufficient competition for the market, ultimately pro-competitive.

A more fundamental problem is that predation is not well defined in the winner-take-all competition that characterizes many software categories. Suppose two firms, an incumbent (M) and an entrant (E), are engaged in a race to develop and attract lead users for the next-generation widget. And suppose, for simplicity, that whichever firm wins the race will have a permanent widget monopoly. What does predation mean in the context of a winner-take-all race? And how would we identify it?

To answer these questions, one must be able to determine, at least in principle, how much a non-predatory M would be willing to spend on product development and attraction of lead users to win the race with E. If spending more guaranteed a win, M would be willing to spend up to the present value of the monopoly profits it would enjoy if it were to win. It would spend less if spending less would guarantee a win, and it would be better off walking away from the widget business than spending more. Of course, in the real world, it is uncertain who will win, monopolies do not last forever, and future profits can at best be roughly estimated. But the key point is that the maximum amount M would be willing to spend does not depend on whether it thinks predatory thoughts about E; an evil predator would not rationally spend more than the present value of future profits either. Thus, in principle as well as in practice, there is no cost-based test to distinguish predatory product development and marketing from non-predatory innovation in a winner-take-all setting.

In most industries, the *Brooke Group* recoupment test helps distinguish between below-cost pricing that is likely to harm consumers in the long run and below-cost pricing that is likely to benefit them.[123] Unfortunately, this recoupment test does not help in industries with winner-take-all competition. Each firm in a winner-take-all race is likely to charge low prices, possibly even below variable cost, in the expectation that it will recoup its losses by raising prices or benefiting from scale economies if it wins the race. But it does not make any sense to define the predator as whoever wins. Moreover, consumers benefit from this sort of rivalry as firms enter the race and lose money early on as they invest in attempting to win the race.

Attempting to ascertain whether M acted with predatory intent cannot shed light on the situation. Firms in winner-take-all races should be expected to generate plenty of internal memos and e-mails that talk about destroying the competition and making money after they have done so. There is no other alternative to failure. Internal memos that talk of "keeping E out of the market" have exactly the same meaning as widely distributed press releases that talk of "providing a better offering than E and doing it faster."

Ordover and Willig's discussion of "predatory innovation" is the only work in the academic literature of which we are aware that attempts to provide economic principles to guide such determinations. They propose that "the relevant question is whether the innovator anticipated positive incremental profit for the new product, given the continued viability of the rival."[124] Unfortunately, this standard is generally unworkable. Key quantities, such as the expected future profit stream over time, are not observable, and firms may invest in important new technologies without developing detailed business plans. And even when capital budgeting documents do exist, the details may not reflect consensus within top management. We suspect its impracticality is one reason the Ordover–Willig test has not been embraced by the courts or by antitrust practitioners.

In the context of winner-take-all competition, the Ordover-Willig test has a more fundamental problem. As with all the tests discussed above, there is no non-exclusion standard of comparison that makes logical sense in a winner-take-all setting. If M wins the race to attract users, it obtains a monopoly and excludes E; if it loses, it is out of the business, and its R&D costs are money down a rat hole. Success, exclusion, and monopolization are one and the same.

The Government's Test for Predation

Unfortunately, the government relied on a predation test that did not have the safety checks demanded by the Court in *Brooke Group*. It argued that actions in which a company makes less profit than it could otherwise are predatory.[125] According to Fisher:

> A predatory act, or an anticompetitive act, I should say, is an act that doesn't make sense except because of the monopoly rents to be earned when competition is driven out or hampered. ... Well, one version is it's just a deliberate money-loser. A second version says, well, you don't charge the price you could have charged. ... If it wasn't for the possibility of destroying

> competition and earning monopoly rents, you would have charged a higher price and earned higher profits. ... Actually, a seriously deep understanding of – well, I can't help it – of economics leads to the view that these are, in fact, the same thing properly considered.[126]

This definition is both non-standard and too inclusive. As Dennis Carlton and Jeffrey Perloff have observed,

> the definition used by the government's economic witness of an anticompetitive act as one that isn't profit-maximizing absent the returns from increased monopoly profits is too stringent. If applied literally, it would prevent behavior that benefits consumers.[127]

To see why the government's test can lead to false inferences, consider two situations. Suppose that company A is the only producer of widgets. It charges $10 a widget and its costs are $5 to produce each widget. (For simplicity, assume zero fixed costs.) Company B is working on an equivalent widget that will cost $8 to make and that it plans to sell for $9. Suppose Company A drops its price to $4. It loses $1 on each widget. That is unprofitable – it will only get its money back by raising prices later, after it kills off Company B. Assuming such recoupment is plausible, the government's test would correctly find that Company A's action is predatory.

Now suppose Company A drops its price to $7. That is not the most it could charge today – it could match B and charge $9. Under the government's test, the price of $7 is predatory. Company A could have charged $9 but it decided to drop the price to $7. At that lower price it is unprofitable for Company B to enter the market or to remain in business if it has already entered. Company A has forgone $2 in order to compete vigorously with B, perhaps in the hopes of driving it from the field. This is plain garden-variety competition – gasoline stations do it, dry cleaners do it, airlines do it. It is good for consumers because the threat of entry has forced prices down. The only reason B is excluded is that it is inefficient, so forcing A to raise its price to keep B afloat would plainly not benefit consumers.

Most businesses routinely invest in intellectual property and advertising to create product differentiation. They make these investments because they expect to obtain market power – that is the only way they can be compensated for their efforts. And, particularly in industries with winner-take-all competition, that market power frequently comes at the expense of existing or potential rivals. In winner-take-all competition, to succeed is to exclude rivals, and to fail is to be excluded; there is no non-exclusion baseline. The reward for success is the supra-normal profits earned from the market power that success brings. The government's test condemns this sort of pro-competitive behavior.

More specifically, the government's test necessarily condemns the winner in winner-take-all competition. Consider a counterfactual. As the incumbent, Netscape had more than an 80 percent share of browser use in early 1996 as a result of its investment in developing a browser and (generally) distributing it without charge.[128] Microsoft entered: It invested in developing and distributing its browser software and priced it at zero. Netscape dropped its price to zero for all customers and invested in improving its browser. Both companies engaged in these efforts because they expected to earn profits in later years if they were successful. But suppose Netscape had won this battle and had kept its share above 80 percent. Under the government's test, Netscape would have been guilty of predation: it sacrificed profits to maintain its dominance in browsers and possibly to attempt to obtain a monopoly in software platforms.

Improving the Quality of IE: Building the Platform or Predatory Innovation?

The government's analysis of Microsoft's investment in IE technologies shows most clearly the problems with its approach. The government took a narrow view of what sources of profit should be considered in evaluating whether Microsoft's actions were predatory. The problem originated in the government's market definition. Because it treated browsers and operating systems as separate markets, rather than as parts of a larger platform market, it focused on the fact that IE was a "no-revenue" product. As a result, almost every significant action that Microsoft took to win the browser war was labeled predatory. Microsoft might have had legitimate business reasons to compete in the browser market just as it competes in the word-processing market. However, it did not have a business model for making money in browsers. It gave them away and had announced it would always do so. Although it could have made money by driving Internet traffic to its portal site and making money from advertising revenue, it had not taken steps to do so. And, in any event, it could never have made enough money from doing so to justify the hundreds of millions of dollars it was spending to develop and distribute IE. Instead, according to the government, Microsoft was fighting the browser war to prevent Netscape from developing a middleware platform that would have opened the doors to entry into operating systems.

As we argued above, this reasoning misses the point that Microsoft was investing in browser technologies to maintain its leadership in software platforms. And changing the ending words of the preceding sentence to "maintain its *monopoly* in software platforms" does not define an antitrust violation.

Even if Microsoft had a monopoly in software platforms – a question the government refused to address, as we noted above – the antitrust laws, properly, do not prohibit it from competing fairly, by improving its product, in an attempt to maintain that monopoly.

Microsoft's Decision Not to Charge Separately for IE

IE is a "no-revenue product" only if one views it as a product, rather than as a part of the Windows platform from which Microsoft earns roughly half its annual revenues. As the brand name for several important features of that platform, IE is no more a "no-revenue product" than any other element of Windows, none of which is priced separately. Well before the trial began, all competing software platforms included "free" browsers.[129]

Microsoft's Investment in Improving, Promoting, and Distributing IE

The government never said explicitly that Microsoft engaged in predatory innovation. Yet it highlighted Microsoft's $100 million annual investment in improving IE as part of its recital of Microsoft's allegedly predatory campaign.[130] And Fisher testified that Microsoft's restrictions on OEMs did not have an anticompetitive effect until Microsoft reached rough parity in quality with Netscape following the release of IE 3.[131]

Microsoft's investment in IE made business sense as a means of competing in software platforms for at least two reasons. At the simplest level, it increased the attractiveness of Windows to consumers. If the higher quality of IE increased the number of copies of Windows sold by just 3 percent or increased the price that Microsoft could charge by as little as $1.50 per copy, that would yield more than enough extra revenue each year to cover the reported annual investment of $100 million.[132] Moreover, these calculations encompass only short-run cash flows; the intensity of expenditures on IE would probably decline once Microsoft had developed a high-quality baseline product from which to upgrade, but the incremental effect on revenues due to strengthening the platform would likely continue longer.

Broadening the analysis to include the risk of losing the platform race altogether causes the investment to make even more "business sense." In 2000, Microsoft had before-tax net operating income of $15 billion, and almost 50 percent of its sales came from "platform" products.[133] Suppose that Microsoft believed that if it ceded the Internet-related platform niche to Netscape, it ran the risk of losing that same percentage of its net income in the future. In 1995, even if it thought that the risk was five years off and that the loss would occur for only five years (i.e., from 2000 to 2004), a probability of a little over 3 percent would make it worth spending $100 million per year to avoid that risk, even if those expenditures generated no revenues from contemporary sales of Windows products.[134]

Microsoft's investment in IE was similar to many other investments it has made over the years to increase the attractiveness of the Windows platform. Microsoft invested billions of dollars during the 1990s in developing and promoting features in Windows. Virtually all of these were "no-revenue" products in the sense that they were not priced separately from Windows. Some of these features eliminated the need to purchase various system utilities (e.g., disk compression, memory management) previously sold in package bundles by third parties such as Central Point Software and Symantec. These additions increased the value of Windows to users directly. Other features eliminated the need for developers to develop or license code to support their applications. For example, any browser (including Navigator) could rely on the TCP/IP software included for the first time in Windows 95 to support those essential Internet protocols. Microsoft spent substantial sums adding and promoting these "no-revenue" products.[135]

The government claimed that Microsoft also made other investments in IE that made "no business sense." These included Microsoft's investments in persuading AOL and other OLSs to use IE technologies, investments in software that made it easier for ISPs to distribute IE, and concessions to OEMs disgruntled by Microsoft's restrictions on how they could modify the screen that appeared the first time a new computer was turned on. Yet these investments made business sense for promoting Microsoft's platform business: They helped increase the demand for Windows, increased the value of Windows to software developers, and, by making Windows a better Web-centric platform, reduced the likelihood that this product would be displaced by drastic innovation by a rival.

Raising Rivals' Cost: Pro-competitive or Anticompetitive?

The government claimed that Microsoft had taken a number of steps to make it more expensive for Netscape to distribute its browser to consumers, and that this was a type of exclusionary strategy known as "raising rivals' cost."[136] It argued that Microsoft had increased Netscape's cost of distribution by preventing Netscape from gaining access to the most efficient channels of distribution. It contended that installing two browsers resulted in additional support costs to OEMs, so OEMs would not install Navigator in addition to IE.[137] The government also claimed Microsoft's inclusion of IE in Windows had made it harder for Netscape to get customers because consumers would use whatever browser was most readily available to them.[138] The government thus concluded that Microsoft had, through its various actions, placed Netscape at a competitive disadvantage.

There are two major difficulties with the government's analysis of raising rivals' distribution cost. The first is theoretical. The government's theory cannot distinguish between pro-competitive and anticompetitive distribution efforts that make things harder for rivals. The second is empirical. The government's evidence did not show that Microsoft's actions – whether pro-competitive or not – significantly raised Netscape's cost of distribution.

Raising Rivals' Distribution Costs

The theory of raising rivals' cost developed by Steven Salop and several co-authors offers an important insight: The following chain of events is possible. (1) A firm takes actions that raise its rivals' costs disproportionately more than its own. (2) The firm's optimal output at given prices increases relative to its rivals. (3) The firm gains market power (i.e., control over prices) relative to its rivals. (4) The firm's profits increase because its gains from increased prices more than offset its losses from its own higher costs. (5) Consumer welfare falls as a result of the higher prices.[139] Examples include an alleged attempt by a capital-intensive firm to negotiate higher wages with its union, to the disadvantage of its labor-intensive rivals. The government itself can be a useful lever for raising rivals' costs; firms frequently invest in lobbying governments to impose rules that increase the relative costs of their competitors.

Salop and his co-authors have not argued that all actions by a firm with market power that raise its rivals' costs are anticompetitive. Indeed, businesses routinely engage in actions that raise their rivals' costs in ways that obviously make consumers better off. For example, if a firm increases the quality of its product, its rivals may have to spend more to market their product or to invest in their own quality improvements. Alternatively, suppose a firm makes its product conveniently available to potential customers by investing in distribution. Its rivals will need to invest more to convince potential customers to buy their products. If they do not improve their own distribution, they will have to lower their prices or improve their quality to compensate for their less convenient distribution. Competition has raised their costs.

Despite its name, "raising rivals' cost" labels as anticompetitive only actions that trigger the five-step chain described above. To apply the raising-rivals'-cost approach to distribution, the courts would have to distinguish between "pro-competitive raising rivals' cost" and "anticompetitive raising rivals' costs." That is hard to do. From the standpoint of consumers, an important characteristic of any product is the transaction cost involved in obtaining that product. Products are more desirable, all else being equal, the less time and money consumers have to expend obtaining them. Companies routinely compete by lowering transaction costs through wider distribution, easier installation, and other efforts. Because making products more conveniently available to consumers is a good thing – like lowering prices – courts interested in consumer welfare need to be extremely careful about discouraging this activity.

Perhaps for this reason, the courts have refused to condemn distribution agreements unless the agreements foreclose a significant percentage of the market. Firms with market power have been allowed to compete for exclusive distribution agreements, to lock up certain channels of distribution, and to invest in the creation of distribution methods that they do not have to make available to their rivals.[140] The courts have found distribution agreements to be anticompetitive only when they prevent rivals from gaining access to a significant fraction of the market. These are cases in which the conditions for anticompetitive raising rivals' cost are more likely to hold.[141]

The government's application of the raising-rivals'-cost theory to the Microsoft case illustrates the risks that this concept poses for the courts. The government did not attempt to establish that any of the conditions under which raising rivals' costs is anticompetitive rather than pro-competitive applied to Microsoft's efforts to win the browser war.[142] Instead, the government seemed to imply that any action Microsoft took that made it more likely that consumers would choose IE over Netscape was an anticompetitive effort to disadvantage Netscape. For example, the government seemed to claim that it was predatory for Microsoft to include a high-quality browser in Windows because consumers would not then incur the cost of seeking an alternative browser.[143]

The Effect of Microsoft's Actions on Netscape's Costs and Ability to Distribute Its Browsers

We consider the two Microsoft actions that the government claims most disadvantaged Netscape's distribution: (a) Microsoft's agreements with ISPs that allegedly restricted the ability of the ISPs to distribute Navigator;[144] and (b) Microsoft's restrictions on the ability of OEMs to modify the first screen shown after booting the computer.[145]

ISP agreements. The government attributed IE's substantial increase in share of use primarily to its allegedly anticompetitive agreements rather than improvements in IE's quality. Analyses by both of the government's economic witnesses claimed to show that absent Microsoft's agreements with OLSs and ISPs, IE's share of use would have increased by only 10 percentage points from the end of January 1997 to the beginning of August 1998, compared to its actual overall increase of about 30 points.[146] Thus, they argued, at most one-third of the increase in share could be due to quality improvements, and even that portion reflected restrictive agreements with OEMs and others, not a pure quality effect.

The impact of Microsoft's agreements with AOL and the other OLSs was not in dispute; Microsoft acknowledged that OLS subscribers generally used whatever browser their service provided in its subscriber software.[147] However, even if we eliminate all of the OLS subscribers identified in the government's data, the overall increase in IE's share was 26 percentage points over the 18-month period,[148] which implies under the government's approach that the ISP agreements resulted in a 16-percentage-point gain for IE.

The government presumes that this happened because ISPs covered by agreements with Microsoft shipped IE rather than Navigator to many users. But even among ISP subscribers, ISPs had supplied only one-quarter of the browsers in use.[149] Thus only a massive and sustained shift in ISP distribution toward IE could possibly have produced a 16-point change in share. And no such shift occurred: Survey data showed that over 80 percent of the browsers that ISP subscribers were using during this period, and which they had obtained from their ISP, were Navigator, not IE.[150] Indeed, ISP subscribers who got their browsers from their ISPs were far more likely to be using Navigator than those who obtained their browsers from other sources. Thus, it does not seem possible that the impact of the ISP agreements could have been nearly as large as the government claimed.

How did the government come to a conclusion so at odds with these facts? The government's economists derived their estimate by comparing the overall change in IE's share to its gain among subscribers to a handful of small ISPs that the government treated as a control group representative of what would have happened in the absence of Microsoft's ISP agreements.[151] However, these ISPs were not a valid control group, and the government's analysis had other serious flaws.

The government used data from AdKnowledge, a company that managed advertisements on Web sites.[152] Whenever a user visited a Web page with an ad monitored by AdKnowledge, the company registered a "hit" and recorded the browser used and the domain from which the user entered the Web. The government used one day's data from each month in question and tried to match the domain names to individual ISPs listed in a spreadsheet used by

Microsoft staff responsible for relations with ISPs. The control group was composed of hits that could be identified with ISPs that did not appear to have agreements of any sort with either Microsoft or Netscape. Overall, only about one in five hits could be matched to *any* of the ISPs listed in the spreadsheet; the other roughly 80 percent were unclassified, and hence ineligible for the control group. Although the government identified 12 ISPs as being in its control group, hits could be identified for only six of them. These hits – used as a control group for all Internet users – made up less than 0.5 percent of the total hits recorded in any month.

The most serious problem with this analysis was that the control group was self-selected. It excluded hits not only from the small number of ISPs that had agreed to limit their distribution of competing browsers in exchange for appearing on Microsoft's referral server, but also from the hundreds that had agreed to make IE their "preferred" browser. But the latter agreements entailed no restrictions on what browsers the ISPs distributed, and even the nominal requirements for promoting IE as "preferred" were never enforced.[153] Moreover, it made sense for an ISP that wanted to distribute *any* copies of IE to enter into a "preferred" agreement, which involved clicking a button on Microsoft's Web site prior to downloading a free copy of the Internet Explorer Administration Kit (IEAK), a piece of software designed by Microsoft to make it easy for ISPs and large corporate customers to customize settings in IE for their systems and to add their own logos.[154] Even if an ISP planned to specialize in Navigator, it made sense to join the "IE preferred program" if it wanted to distribute IE to at least some customers. As a result, one would expect to find in the government's control group only ISPs that had no interest in distributing IE.

After reviewing the government's study in the fall of 1998, we had researchers contact the six ISPs with hits in the control group to test this expectation. One ISP had been absorbed in a merger or acquisition, and it was not possible to identify its earlier offerings. Another ISP said it did not offer a browser because it was so easy to get free browsers from other sources. The remaining four, which accounted for 83 percent of the recorded "hits" for the group in the last month, offered Navigator exclusively.[155] This confirms the hypothesis that the control group was composed of hits from ISPs that had no interest in distributing IE.[156] We would thus expect IE's share among their customers to rise less than average, even if Microsoft's ISP contracts had no effects at all.

Even if one ignores the measurement problems in associating hits with specific ISPs and the biased nature of the control group, the government's analysis of changes in IE's share was confounded by the shifting composition of the control group. The changes in IE's share of hits from the first to the last month varied widely across the six ISPs, from 6 to 36 percentage points. Moreover, the relative numbers of hits associated with individual ISPs varied widely over time. The hits from one ISP fell from 35 percent to 15 percent of all hits in the group, while another rose from 23 percent to 39 percent. The variations observed for many ISPs were too large and abrupt to be consistent with real changes in market share; most likely they reflected variations in the sites covered by AdKnowledge-monitored ads or problems associated with the government's very limited ability to associate hits with individual ISPs.[157]

The government computed IE's share in the control group by simply dividing the total IE hits from the six ISPs by their total number of hits. Because the individual ISPs' relative shares of total hits varied widely, this approach gave radically different implicit weights to the various ISPs over the 18 months in question. The estimated change could be an artifact of the changing composition of the hits identified as coming from the group; i.e., measurement error.

To test for composition effects, we computed the change in IE's share holding constant the weights given to individual ISPs. We used three different sets of weights: (1) ISPs' shares of classified hits in the first month; (2) shares in the last month; and (3) equal weights (the simple average of the individual ISPs' changes). Using any of these fixed weights, IE's share rose substantially more (up to almost twice as much) than with the government's calculation that ignored composition effects.[158]

OEMs and the icon barrier to entry. Faced with evidence during the trial that all known commercially distributed operating systems included a "free" browser, the government eventually argued that Microsoft's predatory act in the OEM channel was not its inclusion of a "free" browser as part of Windows, but rather its refusal to allow OEMs to remove IE before delivering Windows-equipped computers to customers.[159] Even "remove" came to have a very restricted meaning after it became apparent that removing all IE code made Windows inoperable because many of IE's components supported functionality in other parts of Windows. Moreover, it became clear that IE's components provided services upon which third-party developers relied in writing applications. Thus, in essence, the government redefined "remove" to mean "hide."[160] So the problem was that Microsoft would not let OEMs delete the IE icon from the desktop and remove other easy means by which end users could browse the Internet without additional software.[161]

Microsoft did not limit the ability of OEMs to preinstall third-party software, including Navigator, or to put icons on the Windows desktop that had equal prominence with IE's. Indeed, OEMs could set Navigator as the default browser that Windows would launch automatically if the user clicked on an HTML or other Web-related file.[162] Nor did Microsoft change Windows over time to make Navigator harder to install or run than any other application.[163] In other words, it did not undertake the kinds of exclusionary tactics that most observers would condemn as harming a competitor without any pro-competitive rationale. Nonetheless, the government argued that Microsoft's actions harmed competition, based on what might be termed the "icon barrier to entry."

The government asserted that OEMs did not want to have more than one icon on the desktop for any given function, because it would create confusion among users, leading to higher support costs.[164] But several facts contradicted this claim. First, Netscape claimed to have secured good distribution through OEMs before IE 3 came out,[165] despite the prohibition on deleting IE from Windows 95. This suggests that quality, not fear of multiple icons, was the key issue. Second, many OEMs – including Apple, IBM, and Compaq – continued to ship multiple browsers throughout the period in question (though not always on the desktop). Indeed, if one includes the icons for "shell" browsers that use IE components, then a majority of new consumer PCs from the largest OEMs were shipped with more than one browser icon at the time of the trial.[166] Third, in at least some cases, OEMs' desire to delete IE appeared to be motivated more by a desire to collect higher rents for exclusive placement than by a concern about end-user confusion. For example, the Compaq episode in 1996, frequently cited by the government, started when AOL insisted that under its contract with Compaq for exclusive placement of AOL on the desktop, Compaq had to remove icons for the Microsoft Network (MSN) and Spry (an ISP that had purchased distribution with Compaq, including preinstallation of Navigator, which Spry supplied to its subscribers).[167] Finally, the facts contradict what almost anyone who had purchased a new computer in the past few years knew: OEMs were happy to clutter the desktop with any number of icons if paid to do so. That fact was illustrated by an agreement announced during the trial under which Compaq agreed to feature Netscape on the desktop of its Presario line in exchange for $700,000 in advertising credits on Netscape's Web site, a figure that implied a distribution cost of about $0.18 per copy.[169]

SECTION 1 CLAIMS: TYING AND EXCLUSION

The government accused Microsoft of violating Section 1 of the Sherman Act by tying its browser to its operating system and by foreclosing Netscape from distribution. The previous section discussed many of the factual issues surrounding these claims, which were also part of the government's Section 2 case. This section focuses on the economic evidence that supported the government's claims that Microsoft had violated the particular legal standards the courts have adopted concerning tying and foreclosure under Section 1. The evidence presented at trial showed clearly that Microsoft did not engage in tying as that term has been used by the courts and that Microsoft did not foreclose Netscape from distributing its browser – to anyone, let alone to a substantial portion of the market, as required by the case law on foreclosure.

Tying

The tying claim was the centerpiece of the case the government originally brought, and it accounted for a great deal of the testimony presented at trial.[170] Over the course of the trial, however, the scope of the conduct involved narrowed considerably. Ultimately the government contended that Microsoft did not violate tying law by integrating IE into Windows or by including it without extra charge, but only by failing to provide OEMs with the means and the right to block easy end-user access to Web-browsing functions in Windows.[171] The government asserted that it was not necessary to offer a version without browser-related code, merely to let OEMs delete the IE icon from the desktop and the Start menu and to modify various settings so that IE would not launch automatically in response to various other actions.[172] They referred to this as the "browserless" operating system, although it is in fact a "browser-disabled" operating system.

Contractual Versus Technological Ties

The case law has distinguished between contractual and technological ties. In a contractual tie a company requires that consumers purchase product B (the tied product; e.g., anesthesiology services) as a condition of purchasing product A (the tying product; e.g., surgical services). In *Jefferson Parish*, the Supreme Court found that tying violates the antitrust law when the following four-part test is satisfied:[173]

1. A substantial volume of commerce is affected.
2. Two distinguishable product markets exist (based on distinct demands

for two separate products).

3. The defendant has market power in the product market.

4. The arrangement involves the use of market power to force consumers to buy a product or service that they would not otherwise purchase.[174]

A technological tie results when a company creates a new product by integrating the features of product B (the tied product; e.g., computer hardware) into product A (the tying product; e.g., software for operating a computer time-sharing franchise). Several lower courts have ruled that technological ties are generally legal so long as they provide benefits. In *Leasco* the Fifth Circuit Court demanded the plaintiff demonstrate that "the technological factor tying the hardware to the software has been designed for the purpose of tying the products, rather than to achieve some technologically beneficial result."[175] Generally the courts have given product design decisions considerable deference in deciding whether technological ties violate the antitrust laws.[176]

Contractual Tying Analysis

In *Jefferson Parish* and other modern contractual tying cases, the concern is that consumers are denied a choice in the tied good and competitors are denied a chance to compete. Surgical patients at Jefferson Parish Hospital could not choose their anesthesiologists, and anesthesiologists not on staff could not offer their services to patients or their surgeons.[177] Similarly, in *Kodak*, consumers could not choose who installed the repair parts in their Kodak copiers, and independent service organizations thus could not compete to service those copiers.[178] Here, however, nothing prevents purchasers of Windows from ignoring IE and choosing instead to use Navigator to provide all of the browsing services it offers. Netscape's CEO testified that Navigator was "perfectly interoperable" with Windows 98.[179] At the time of trial, roughly 23 million people used Navigator as their primary browser on a computer running Windows.[180]

This case was therefore not at all like standard tying cases, where it was impossible for the consumer to choose to obtain the tied good from another provider. It is instructive how the kind of tie alleged in *Microsoft III* would apply to the products considered in *Jefferson Parish*:

> Like other area hospitals, Jefferson Parish recently included the services of its staff anesthesiologist (IE) with use of its surgical suite (Windows). As at other hospitals, there is no separate charge for the anesthesiologist, and no discount if he is not used. Also as at other hospitals, surgeons (OEMs) are free to recommend their preferred anesthesiologist (Navigator) to their patients (end-users). However, Jefferson Parish insists that surgeons inform

> patients that the hospital provides an anesthesiologist as part of its comprehensive fee (OEMs cannot delete ready access to IE). Patients are free to use an anesthesiologist provided by the surgeon or to contract with one of their own choosing. The patient can tell Jefferson Parish's anesthesiologist to stay out of the operating room (end-users can delete access to IE), but the surgeon cannot.

If these had been the facts in *Jefferson Parish*, it is hard to see how the courts could have found a restraint of trade, which Section 1 requires.

Finally, the *Jefferson Parish* test requires a demonstration that there is separate demand for the tied and untied products. In this case, that would have required showing that there is a separate demand for a browser-disabled version of Windows. As we pointed out earlier, however, all competitive operating systems include a browser. The government did not demonstrate that there was significant consumer demand for a browser-disabled operating system. It presented evidence that some companies would have preferred a version of Windows that did not include IE. However, it did not show that there were a significant number of such companies, or that "hiding" IE would have satisfied that demand in any event.[181]

Technological Tying

The D.C. Circuit Court of Appeals ruled in a related case (*Microsoft II*) that Microsoft's inclusion of IE in Windows should be considered under the technological tying cases. It stated that technological tying is presumed legal if the defendant can show a "plausible claim" of benefits from the tie. And on this basis it found that Microsoft's inclusion of IE in Windows did not violate the earlier consent decree prohibition against tying.[182]

Microsoft's inclusion of IE in Windows resulted in benefits for both sides of its two-sided market. Software developers benefited from the inclusion of IE functionality that they could use in their applications. These developers also benefited from the knowledge that all new copies of Windows included the APIs that they were using for their applications.[183] Consumers benefited from having a browser included in Windows. The browser together with other features gave consumers access to the Web immediately upon getting their computers set up. As we mentioned above, this meant consumers could download copies of Netscape or other browsers if they wanted to. The fact that all other operating system vendors included a browser in their operating systems is decisive evidence that there were actual benefits – not just plausible ones – from including a browser with the operating system.[184]

The Carlton-Waldman Analysis

The government did not present an economic analysis of how Microsoft's inclusion of IE in Windows would reduce consumer welfare. However, a recent paper claims to present a model that supports the government's case.[185] Carlton and Waldman consider a situation in which a firm has monopoly power in product A. It also produces a complementary good, product B, that could evolve into a substitute for product A and that another firm also could produce. Carlton and Waldman show that the firm with a monopoly in A may tie the sale of its version of product B to the sale of product A to discourage entry in product B. They show that whether such a tie is an effective strategy to protect or extend monopoly power depends upon the values of particular quantities that are very difficult to measure in practice.

The government did not rely on this framework and thus did not seek to demonstrate that the Carlton-Waldman conditions were satisfied in this case. In fact, two critical assumptions of this paper do not fit the facts of the Microsoft case. First, most of Carlton and Waldman's analyses assume that consumers cannot use competitor's product B with the monopolist's combined product. If they can, and the marginal cost of product B is zero, tying is never an effective anticompetitive strategy. As we noted, consumers could and did (and many still do) use Navigator with Windows/IE, and the marginal cost of another copy of Navigator is effectively zero. Second, in Carlton and Waldman's models, tying is effective only as a preemptive strategy; it is not effective if another firm already has entered and achieved wide use of its version of product B. And Netscape had done just that well before Microsoft launched IE with Windows 95. Further, the Carlton-Waldman results are fragile. In some versions of their models, tying can actually increase social welfare.[186]

Foreclosure

The courts have found that restrictive distribution agreements violate the antitrust laws if and only if they are used by a firm with market power to foreclose competitors from a significant portion of the market. For this case, it is not necessary to address how much is significant.[187] The evidence was clear that Netscape could distribute its browser to any consumer who wanted it; it was foreclosed from none of the market.

Netscape clearly had ready access to large businesses and other organizations, many of which install their own browsers and other applications using master copies obtained from the vendor or a distributor. Such customers account for about 40 percent of new PCs.[188] For example, Schmalensee's computer at MIT came with Navigator installed and without the IE icon on the desktop; like most colleges and universities, MIT also made Navigator (licensed free by Netscape to nonprofit organizations) available to students and faculty for download from its internal network. Thus, the "restrictions" discussed below were largely irrelevant to almost half the potential users.

In advising AOL about its proposed acquisition of Netscape, the investment bank Goldman Sachs criticized Netscape for its failure to market Navigator more aggressively but did not identify any serious impediments to its distribution.[189] In the fall of 1998, Goldman Sachs reported that over the past year Netscape had distributed 160 million copies of Navigator through downloading alone, 100 million of them through Web sites of its distribution partners.[190] That amounted to more than one copy for each of the 100 million or so users of the Web at the time.[191] Although the government questioned whether these downloads were successful, Goldman Sachs did not discount its estimate for failed attempts, and projections from survey data showed that millions of consumers obtained Navigator (and IE) through downloading from the Web.[192]

The evidence also showed that Netscape continued to achieve distribution through what the government said were the most "uniquely effective" channels, OEMs, OLSs, and ISPs. Fisher estimated in January 1999 that Navigator was installed on the desktops of "about half of 1 percent" of new PCs and that OEM shipments of Netscape in other forms (e.g., preinstalled but without an icon on the desktop or on a CD) total were "also quite low, although a little bit higher."[193] However, evidence introduced later showed that Netscape told Goldman Sachs in the fall of 1998 that OEMs included Navigator with 22 percent of shipments of new computers.[194] Moreover, this figure did not include the effects of Compaq's agreement in January 1999 to include Navigator on the desktops of all new models in its consumer line.[195] Similarly, with respect to ISPs, Goldman Sachs reported that Netscape was distributed by 24 percent of the top 20 ISPs.[196]

THE COURT'S DECISION, THE GOVERNMENT'S APPEAL, AND CAUSATION

The district court judge, Thomas Penfield Jackson, found Microsoft guilty on three of the government's four counts. He found that Microsoft had engaged in "predacious" behavior that violated Section 2 of the Sherman Act on two counts: maintaining Microsoft's monopoly in operating systems for

Intel-compatible computers and attempting to monopolize Web browsers.[197] He also concluded that by forcing OEMs to install IE with Windows, Microsoft had violated Section 1 tying law under criteria established by the Supreme Court in *Jefferson Parish*.[198] Finally, he found that although Microsoft's distribution restrictions on OEMs, OLSs, and ISPs were key elements in the "predacious" behavior he condemned under Section 2, there was insufficient evidence of a violation of exclusive dealing law under Section 1. The government had not shown that Netscape was excluded from at least 40 percent of the market, a criterion that he had established in a pre-trial ruling.[199]

The court's Conclusions of Law, and the Findings of Fact that preceded them, were rendered in harsh and sweeping language. But a careful reading shows that the district court did not reach Findings of Fact that would support two essential pillars of an antitrust case. First, the court did not find that the actions actually deemed illegal (as opposed to the full sweep of actions taken by Microsoft) had had a material effect on any relevant antitrust market. Second, the court's findings attributed benefits as well as costs to Microsoft's actions and made no attempt to weigh those competing factors to reach a reasoned judgment as to whether consumers were likely to be harmed on balance by those actions.

The District Court's Findings

It requires a careful reading of the district court's Conclusions of Law and the government's briefs to the appeals court to determine specifically which of Microsoft's actions ultimately were deemed illegal. The district court and the government both frequently write as if almost all of Microsoft's efforts to win the browser battle crossed the line between competitive and predatory behavior, and they rely on such sweeping indictments in arguing that Microsoft's actions caused the decline in Netscape's fortunes. They then identify a far narrower subset of those acts as having been illegal but do not analyze the incremental impacts of those acts.

This tendency is best seen in the treatment of Microsoft's investment in improving the quality of IE. Relying on the Findings of Fact, the government's appeals brief says:

> To protect the applications barrier to entry, therefore, Microsoft embarked on a multifaceted campaign to maximize IE's share of usage and to minimize Navigator's. Between 1995 and 1999, Microsoft spent more than $100 million each year and increased from five or six to more than a thousand the number of developers working on IE, even though the company has given IE away free since its initial release in July 1995.[200]

After giving the reader the distinct impression that Microsoft's substantial investment in improving the quality of IE and its pricing it at zero were important elements of Microsoft's predatory campaign, the government then fails to list them as anticompetitive acts.[201] The district court's discussion of Microsoft's actions also gives the clear impression that Microsoft's investment in developing a no-revenue product was nefarious, but it then admits that this may have been pro-competitive.[202] The district court and the government used this same rhetorical approach to Microsoft's pricing the browser at zero.[203]

So what did the district court find anticompetitive? According to the government:

> The court did not hold Microsoft liable for "improved products, increased distribution and lower prices." Rather, the court based its determination of liability on the anticompetitive conduct proved at trial ... Those anticompetitive actions include: Microsoft's constriction of Netscape's access to the OEM distribution channel through restrictions that excluded Netscape both directly and indirectly; comparable constriction of Netscape's access to the IAP [ISP and OLS] distribution channel; other actions to impede Netscape, including threats to Apple and restrictions on ICPs and ISVs [Independent Software Vendors]; and coercive and misleading actions to impede Java-based cross-platform applications.[204]

In the case of the OEM channel, the primary anticompetitive restriction was Microsoft's refusal to allow OEMs to delete the IE icon and other means of end-user access. In the case of AOL and the other OLSs, in the end the anticompetitive act was not Microsoft's winning the right to provide the browsing technology for AOL's subscriber software, but only the limitations Microsoft imposed, to which AOL agreed, on providing other browsers to AOL members who requested them. In the case of the ISPs, the only anticompetitive acts were similar (though less stringent) restrictions made on the small number of ISPs on the referral server, not free licensing of IE and the IEAK to all ISPs. With respect to versions of IE for non-Windows platforms, it was not anticompetitive to give copies away, only to pressure Apple to give IE greater prominence on the Macintosh.[205] And, in the case of Java, the actions deemed anticompetitive in the end were attempts to convince Intel to stop supporting Sun's Java efforts and the fact that Microsoft's development tools did not explicitly warn developers that the use of some of the tools would create code that would run only on Microsoft's Java Virtual Machine (JVM).[206]

The district court's Conclusions of Law on tying were similarly circumscribed. Despite a long discussion of why consumers might prefer not to have the browser built into the operating system (such as economizing on hard disk space and memory), in the end the judge found nothing illegal about the basic integration of IE into Windows. The tie occurred only when Microsoft refused to let OEMs disable end users' access to IE's functions. According to the government:

> Microsoft could provide a version of Windows without IE, which would give users all of the non-browsing features that Windows with IE provides without including browsing functionality, by simply removing the user access to browser functionality while retaining whatever code is necessary to enhance the functionality of other applications.[207]

But simply eliminating end-user access to IE's functions would not address most of the issues raised by the district court, because virtually all of the code would remain on the computer's hard drive and would be called into memory as needed by Windows itself and by applications.

The Government Did Not Show That Actions Deemed Anticompetitive Had Anticompetitive Effects

Let us recall what the government's case was all about. The government claimed that Microsoft engaged in anticompetitive *actions* that had the anticompetitive *effect* of preventing Netscape and Java from eroding the applications barrier to entry and eliminating Microsoft's monopoly in operating systems for Intel-compatible computers. For the anticompetitive actions to have had this anticompetitive effect, they had to have caused Netscape's decline in browser share,[208] and that decline had to have been the cause of Netscape's failure to emerge as a middleware platform.

Did Microsoft's Anticompetitive Actions Cause Navigator's Decline?

The district court recognized that Microsoft engaged in both pro-competitive and anticompetitive actions to win the browser war. As we have discussed above, the following *actions* were *not* anticompetitive, according to the government's reading of the district court's COL:

- Microsoft's $100 million annual investment in improving the quality of IE;
- Microsoft's annual investment of $30 million to promote and distribute IE;
- Microsoft's integration of IE 3 and IE 4 into Windows;
- Microsoft's decision not to charge for IE at a time when Netscape was charging some customers for Navigator;
- Microsoft's contract with AOL, in which AOL agreed to use IE tech-

nologies for its subscriber software;

• Microsoft's provision of free administrative software (the IEAK) and other technical support to ISPs who agreed to make IE their "preferred" browser.

Neither the government nor the district court tried to separate the impacts of these important actions, now deemed pro-competitive, from the much narrower set of acts deemed anticompetitive. As a result, there is no basis for concluding that Microsoft's anticompetitive actions had a significant effect on the decline in Netscape's share. This is not a debating point – we are not arguing that the district court failed to dot an "i" or cross a "t." An inspection of the key acts found by the district court to be anticompetitive shows that it is highly implausible – and certainly unproved – that those actions could have had significant effects on Netscape's share.

Allowing OEMs to disable end-user access to IE. Consider tying and the related predation charges. Clearly Microsoft's integration of IE into Windows and its distribution with Windows at no extra charge increased IE's share. But it seems implausible that the narrow act of denying OEMs the right to delete easy access to IE's features could have had a material incremental impact on Netscape. As we discussed earlier, the evidence of an "icon barrier to entry" was weak at best. Perhaps the most basic question is whether a significant number of OEMs would have exercised that option if given it. Suppose that Microsoft had integrated IE into Windows at no extra charge, but had let OEMs delete the IE icon and disable other ready means of access. Would that have gained Netscape significant additional distribution through OEMS once IE 3 and subsequent versions were as good as or better than Navigator?

Deleting IE 3, 4, or 5 would seem likely to generate more support calls from users trying to use a widely advertised and highly praised feature of their new operating system than it would avoid from users confused about seeing two icons for different browsers. Moreover, OEMs would not have saved any significant testing costs or hard disk space by "deleting" IE, because virtually all of the code would still have been on the hard disk, ready to be invoked by other applications.[209]

Even if OEMs decided to remove the IE icon from the desktop, why would they have shipped Navigator rather than one of the numerous "shell" browsers (such as Encompass)? Such shell browsers, available at no charge, use the IE components in Windows to do most of the work and provide a user interface that the OEM can customize to promote itself and advertisers. Because they use very little code that is not already part of Windows, they require little extra testing and take up virtually no room on hard disks. At the time of the trial, many OEMs already included a shell browser on the desktop, despite the government's claimed icon barrier to entry.[210]

AOL distribution constraint. It is clear that Microsoft's agreements with the OLSs, especially AOL, were key sources of the increase in the use of Microsoft's technology. But Judge Jackson found no indication that AOL or the other OLSs were interested in offering two versions of their software.[211] The illegal acts consisted of "the severe shipment quotas and promotional restrictions," which limited the extent to which AOL could promote the use of other (unintegrated) browsers to its members.[212] But the judge did not find that AOL was ever constrained by the agreement's 15 percent cap on shipments of other browsers, and there was little reason to believe that AOL would have actively promoted use of other browsers in place of its own access software, which helps AOL direct users to its proprietary network and to Web sites that pay promotional fees to AOL.[213]

ISP restrictions. For the reasons we discussed earlier, the government's analysis of the impacts of Microsoft's agreements with ISPs was fatally flawed. Even if one accepts that analysis, however, as the district court appears to have done,[214] it is irrelevant to the acts finally determined to be anticompetitive. The government's control group excluded hits not only from the ISPs that agreed to shipment restrictions, but also from the much larger number that did nothing more than agree to promote IE as their "preferred" browser in exchange for getting a free copy of the IEAK. To be relevant under the district court's Conclusions of Law, Fisher's analysis would have had to compare changes in IE's share among those few ISPs that agreed to restrict shipments of Navigator to the changes in IE's share among other ISPs, including the group that agreed only to promote IE as their "preferred" browser.[215]

Could Navigator Have Become a Platform Absent Microsoft's Allegedly Anticompetitive Acts?

The district court did not find that Navigator failed to become a platform because of the actions that the district court found anticompetitive. It concluded that "[t]here is insufficient evidence to find that, absent Microsoft's actions, Navigator and Java already would have ignited genuine competition in the market for Intel-compatible PC operating systems."[216]

There was no basis for it to conclude otherwise. As we discussed earlier, Netscape had no plans to become a serious middleware platform. Netscape's CEO disavowed any interest in doing so.[217] But even if Netscape had planned to turn Navigator into a platform, there was no evidence that the actions the court found anticompetitive prevented it from doing so. As we have just seen, the government did not present evidence that the relatively narrow set of actions deemed anticompetitive by the district court contributed significantly to Netscape's decline in share. Moreover, Netscape never took the most basic technological step needed to be a platform: It never componentized its browser so that it could offer APIs that let developers use those components to improve applications.[218]

The District Court's Findings Concerning Consumer Harm

Judge Jackson's Findings of Fact conclude with a section entitled "The Effect on Consumers of Microsoft's Efforts to Protect the Applications Barrier to Entry." He finds that Microsoft's efforts (a) benefited consumers directly; (b) harmed consumers directly; and (c) harmed consumers indirectly by suppressing innovation. This section of the findings reflects the tension one finds throughout that document between Judge Jackson's sweeping condemnation of Microsoft's efforts to win the browser war and his specific identification of the actions that crossed the line from competition to predation. He had found that Microsoft's substantial investment in developing a no-revenue browser helped protect the applications barrier to entry. But he did not find that those efforts had crossed the line from competition to predation. Consequently, there is no way to know whether the benefits and harms he describes in this concluding section result from pro-competitive or anticompetitive efforts. Was it Microsoft's pro-competitive investment of $100 million per year in IE that "demonstrated that [Microsoft] will use its prodigious market power and immense profits to harm any firm that insists on pursuing initiatives that could intensify competition against one of Microsoft's core products"?[219] Or was it Microsoft's anticompetitive refusal to let OEMs delete the IE icon from the Windows desktop?

It is simply impossible to reason from the highly circumscribed "bad acts" described above to the conclusion that "Microsoft placed an oppressive thumb on the scale of competitive fortune, thereby effectively guaranteeing its continued dominance in the relevant market."[220] There is no evidence that the acts deemed illegal translated into significant market effects, much less ones that could have harmed consumers.

Indeed, it is equally impossible to argue that the entirety of Microsoft's actions necessarily harmed consumers or hindered innovation, albeit for a different reason. It is clear that Microsoft's actions, taken together, reduced the likelihood that Navigator/Java would become a serious software platform. It is equally clear, however, that Microsoft's actions generated very large benefits for consumers. There is no evidence that the costs outweighed the benefits identified, or that the hindrances to innovation were more important than the spurs to innovation the judge identified. As a result, we do not see any support in Judge Jackson's findings for the proposition that Microsoft's actions – writ large or small – actually reduced consumer welfare, or would have done so in the future if left unchallenged by the government.

Direct Benefits

Judge Jackson acknowledges that Microsoft's efforts "contributed to improving the quality of Web browsing software, lowering its cost, and increasing its availability, thereby benefitting consumers."[221] The value to consumers of the reduced price alone was almost certainly in the billions of dollars. About 123 million Americans used the Web at least quarterly in 2000.[222] Prior to 1998, Netscape charged many individuals and organizations for its browsers. Prices charged on an individual basis ranged from $39 (in 1995) to $79 (for Navigator Gold) in 1996. If we accept the district court's conclusion that Microsoft "compelled" Netscape to stop charging and assume that the average browser price would have been $20 in the absence of Microsoft's actions, consumers would have saved $2.5 billion ($20 x 123 million) for the browsers they were using in 2000. Obviously, this is a very rough approximation. The actual figure would have been substantially higher if consumers had purchased several browsers between 1995 and 2000; it would have been lower if fewer consumers had used a browser at a positive price. Our point is not that the benefits were necessarily $2.5 billion – it is that under almost any plausible assumption, the benefits from a zero price were substantial.

Judge Jackson also acknowledged that Microsoft's actions spurred innovation. Competition between Microsoft and Netscape gave both incentives to improve their browsers. This is consistent with observations made in the trade press. As one article put it, "In the browser battle between Microsoft and Netscape, there has been at least one sure winner: the Internet consumer."[223] It is difficult to quantify the value of the improved product quality during this period. The browser reviews described earlier, however, suggest that both companies made tremendous improvements over a short space of time.[224]

Specific Harms Found by the District Court

Judge Jackson singled out Microsoft's refusal to offer a "browserless" (i.e., browser-disabled) operating system as a source of consumer harm worth highlighting in his concluding section. There is no evidence in the trial record, however, concerning the number of end users who would have chosen a browserless version of Windows, or how many OEMs would have chosen to distribute a browserless version of Windows. The government's evidence consisted entirely of a few statements that some corporate customers would have liked to purchase their operating system and platform separately.[225] But there is no way to infer from this evidence that any significant number of consumers would prefer a browserless operating system.[226] Two facts suggest that the overall demand for browserless operating systems was in fact not significant. First, as we have noted, all other operating system vendors include a browser. Second, the district court's injunction in *Microsoft II* had required Microsoft to allow OEMs not to put IE's icon on the desktop or the Start menu. During the several months this option was available, only Packard Bell exercised it, and only for one line of business laptops.[227] The other specific harms identified by Judge Jackson similarly are based on no evidence that could enable the district court to determine the magnitude of harm.

Innovation

Judge Jackson decided that Microsoft's actions had reduced the rate of innovation,[228] but there is no support in the trial record for his sweeping conclusion. The government did not introduce any evidence that Microsoft had reduced the rate of innovation – measured by patents, copyrights, venture capital spending, new firm starts, or any other measure – in the software, platform, operating system, or browser industry.[229] The government did not even demonstrate that Microsoft's efforts had reduced Netscape's or Sun's investments in their browsing and Java technologies, respectively.[230] As we have noted on several occasions, the evidence clearly showed that Netscape never planned to invest in becoming a platform. Finally, the district court's own Findings of Fact call its sweeping conclusions into question. Judge Jackson found that "[t]he debut of Internet Explorer and its rapid improvement gave Netscape an incentive to improve Navigator's quality at a competitive rate."[231] The district court did not report any attempt to balance these benefits of increased innovation against the cost of suppressed innovation.

CONCLUDING COMMENTS

In the early 1990s, IBM's OS/2 posed a major competitive threat to Microsoft's platform business, and Microsoft improved Windows and distributed it aggressively. A few years later, Microsoft perceived Netscape and Sun to pose another such threat, and it again competed aggressively. This time the government filed suit. At trial it condemned as predatory virtually everything Microsoft did to respond to the threat to its platform leadership. This condemnation rested on the assertion that software platforms were not the relevant antitrust market – even though the government also asserted that Windows' role as a platform was the source of most of its value and that the platform potential of Netscape's Navigator and Sun's Java was a threat to Windows. The government apparently believed that Microsoft should lose its war with Sun and Netscape. But, as Judge Learned Hand famously said, "The competitor, having been urged to compete, must not be turned upon when he wins."[232]

* This article first appeared in the *Antitrust Bulletin*. Reprinted with permission.

We thank Howard Chang and Bernard Reddy for helpful comments and discussions on the topics examined in this article. James Hunter, Melissa Long, Lauri Mancinelli, Emily Trinks, and Kirstyn Walton provided valuable research assistance. We received support from Microsoft for the preparation of this article as well as the research reported in it. The views expressed herein, however, are solely those of the authors.

[1] *Microsoft III* was the consolidation of cases brought by the U.S. Department of Justice and a coalition of 20 states (one later dropped out). *U.S. v. Microsoft Corp.*, 98 CIV. 1232 (TPJ), and *State of New York et al. v. Microsoft Corp.*, 98 CIV. 1233 (TPJ). The authors were economic consultants to Microsoft during the case, and one of us (Schmalensee) presented written and oral testimony. Schmalensee's written testimony can be found at http://www.microsoft.com/presspass/trial/mswitness/default.asp, along with transcripts of testimony by other Microsoft witnesses and Microsoft's legal filings. Court and government filings as well as testimony by the government's witnesses are available at http://www.usdoj.gov/atr/cases/ms_index.htm. The court of appeals Web site (http://ecfp.cadc.uscourts.gov/) provides links to the filings in the appeals portion of the case. The electronic versions on these sites sometimes have page or paragraph numbering that differs from the official versions because of the vagaries of automatic numbering and conversion problems from one format to another.

In this article, *U.S. v. Microsoft Corp.* and references to the "case" refer to *Microsoft III* unless noted otherwise. Similarly, citations to transcripts, written testimony, or legal filings also refer to this case unless noted otherwise. The "government" refers to the Justice Department and the state plaintiffs. *Microsoft I* (1995) resulted in a Consent Decree in which Microsoft agreed to end certain volume discounting practices and not to tie the sales of other products to Windows (*U.S. v. Microsoft Corp.*, 159 F.R.D. 318 [D.D.C.], rev'd, 56 F.3d 1448 [D.C. Cir. 1995] [hereafter *Microsoft I*]). The Justice Department claimed that Microsoft violated that Consent Decree by tying Internet Explorer to Windows (*U.S. v. Microsoft Corp.*, 980 F. Supp. 537 [D.D.C. 1997], rev'd, 147 F.3d 935 [D.C. Cir. 1998] [hereafter *Microsoft II*]). The district court granted a preliminary injunction, which the D.C. Circuit Court of Appeals then reversed. The appeals court found that Windows was an integrated product that included IE.

2 Netscape has used various other names (e.g., Communicator) for its products with Web-browser functionality. We use "Navigator" to cover all of them.

3 AOL and other online services had their own proprietary browsers until late 1996. There was considerable controversy during the trial as to which data on browser use were most reliable. The source the government relied upon did not have data prior to January 1997. Data from the University of Illinois put Netscape's share at more than 80 percent for the first half of 1996 (University of Illinois at Urbana-Champaign [UIUC], "Browser Statistics," http://www.ews.uiuc.edu/bstats/latest.html), but such "hit" data undercount activity by subscribers to AOL and other online services. Data from monthly surveys conducted for Microsoft's internal use starting in March 1996 show similarly high shares (75 to 79 percent) for most of 1996 if subscribers to OLSs are excluded. Both sources put Microsoft's share at less than 10 percent in early 1996. If OLS subscribers are included, Netscape's and Microsoft's shares decline because AOL used browsing software from Booklink. CompuServe and Prodigy also provided "other" browsing software to their members. For details, see Direct Testimony of Richard L. Schmalensee, App. D (January 3, 1999) (hereafter Schmalensee Direct).

4 This estimate is consistent with both the UIUC data cited in note 3 and with updates of the Microsoft survey data prepared for the expected remedies phase of the trial. To our knowledge, DOJ's browser data are not available past August 1998.

5 "Windows" is used here as a generic term to cover several Microsoft platform products. Most of the case focused on Windows 95 and its successor, Windows 98. However, they share a common set of APIs with the Windows NT (now Windows 2000) family of products.

6 By one estimate, 70,000 applications are available for MS-DOS and the Windows platforms compared to 12,000 for the Apple Macintosh (*see* Transcript, February 17, 1999, p.m. Session, p. 24 [Cross of John Rose]; Transcript, November 4, 1998, p.m. Session, pp. 85-87 [Cross of Avadis Tevanian]).

7 *See* Direct Testimony of Paul Maritz, Paragraph 63 (January 22, 1999) (hereafter Maritz Direct).

8 *See* DX 81, Bill Gates, "The Internet Tidal Wave," MS98 0112352 (May 26, 1995).

9 *See* Maritz Direct, *supra* note 7, Paragraph 294.

10 *See* Direct Testimony of Brad Chase, Paragraphs 23-60 (February 10, 1999) (hereafter Chase Direct).

11 Plaintiffs' Joint Proposed Findings of Fact (September 10, 1999) (hereafter PPFOF); Plaintiffs' Joint Proposed Conclusions of Law (December 6, 1999) (hereafter PPCOL).

12 Findings of Fact (November 5, 1999) (hereafter FOF); Conclusions of Law (April 3, 2000) (hereafter COL).

13 COL, *supra* note 12, pp. 9-17.

14 COL, *supra* note 12, pp. 31-32.

15 We rely heavily on the economic testimony of Schmalensee and of Franklin Fisher on behalf of the DOJ. Frederick Warren-Boulton also testified as an expert witness on behalf of the states. Since he did not offer substantial additional evidence we generally restrict our citations to Fisher's testimony.

16 The district court judge writes: "Despite the opportunity to make a substantial amount of revenue from the sale of Internet Explorer, and with the knowledge that the dominant browser product on the market, Navigator, was being licensed at a price, senior execu-

tives at Microsoft decided that Microsoft needed to give its browser away in furtherance of the larger strategic goal of accelerating Internet Explorer's acquisition of browser usage share" (FOF, *supra* note 12, Paragraph 137). But shortly thereafter he writes: "Even absent the strategic imperative to maximize its browser usage share at Netscape's expense, Microsoft might still have set the price of an Internet Explorer consumer license at zero...After all, consumers in 1995 were already demanding software that enabled them to use the Web with ease, and IBM had announced in September 1994 its plan to include browsing capability in OS/2 Warp at no extra charge. Microsoft had reason to believe that other operating-system vendors would do the same" (Paragraph 140).

[17] Some of the district court's findings have no support in the trial record. For example, see the discussion of Paragraphs 149-154 of the court's Findings of Fact during the oral arguments before the D.C. Circuit (Appeals Court Transcript, February 26, 2001, pp.132-137, 141-143 [hereafter Appeals Transcript]).

[18] For example, the district court judge has said that he wrote the document in part to shake Microsoft up – likening his findings to hitting a mule with a two-by-four (*See* Joel Brinkley and Steve Lohr, *U.S. v. Microsoft: The Inside Story of the Landmark Case* [2001], p. 278).

[19] PPCOL, *supra* note 11.

[20] The one exception was Steven McGeady, an Intel executive testifying for the government. His direct testimony was given orally (*see* Transcript, November 9, 1998 [Direct of Steven McGeady]).

[21] FOF, *supra* note 12.

[22] COL, *supra* note 12.

[23] Plaintiffs' Proposed Final Judgment, April 28, 2000. The supporting declarations were from Rebecca M. Hendersen, Paul M. Romer, and Carl Shapiro.

[24] For a critical evaluation of the remedies, see Kenneth G. Elzinga et al., "*U.S. v. Microsoft Corp.: Remedy or Malady?*" in this volume.

[25] *See* Direct Testimony of James Allchin, Paragraphs 33-36, 41-44 (January 27, 1999) (hereafter Allchin Direct).

[26] Strictly speaking, "API" refers only to the specifications, not to the code that supports the functions. Although the use of "API" to refer to the code can cause confusion in some circumstances (e.g., discussions of the extent to which vendors should document APIs), those problems do not apply to our discussion here.

[27] *See* Allchin Direct, *supra* note 25, Paragraphs 262 (Apple CyberDog), 268 (IBM Web Explorer), 272 (Sun HotJava).

[28] *See* KDE press release, *New KDE Desktop Ready for the Enterprise* (February 26, 2001; accessed April 2, 2001; November 12, 2001), http://www.kde.org/announcements/announce-2.1.html.

[29] There is an important third side to this market: hardware. In addition to software developers and consumers, Microsoft must work with hardware vendors to ensure that its platform software supports new hardware capabilities. Network externalities can be important there as well, but we omit them from our analysis because they were not central to this case.

[30] For economic analysis of these kinds of markets, see Jean-Charles Rochet and Jean Tirole, *Cooperation Among Competitors: The Economics of Payment Card Associations*, L'Institut d'Economie Industrielle (March 6, 2000); Bernard Caillaud and Bruno Jullien,

Chicken and Egg Competing Matchmakers, presented at the IDEI-R Conference on the Economics of the Software and Internet Industries, Toulouse (January 18-20, 2001); Richard Schmalensee, *Payment Systems and Interchange Fees*, MIT (December 2000) (mimeo).

[31] All major platform vendors offer tools to make it easier for developers to write to their APIs. Platform vendors also often form associations or networks for developers, and offer training, conferences, and technical assistance.

[32] Operating systems tend to be associated with particular types of microprocessors. Often versions of an operating system are also available for other microprocessors, but with a somewhat different feature set, so that applications written to run on one version need rewriting to run on a different operating system.

[33] Software written to run on middleware that works on many platforms has suffered from two weaknesses: (1) it cannot use features that are not supported on all of the hardware–software platforms and (2) it runs slower.

[34] Any software can become middleware by exposing APIs, and the government argued in its submissions on remedies that the Microsoft Office suite could become a middleware software platform (Plaintiffs' Proposed Final Judgment, *supra* note 23, Paragraph 7).

[35] *See* Allchin Direct, *supra* note 25, Section V; Direct Testimony of Daniel Rosen, Paragraphs 13, 20 (January 6, 1999).

[36] IBM, OS/2 Warp advertisement, *PC Magazine*, March 14, 1995, p. 107.

[37] Deposition of Marc Andreessen 8 (July 15, 1998).

[38] Data on Web use in 1995 are sparse and of questionable accuracy. However, one major tracker of PC industry data estimates that by the end of 1995, Netscape accounted for 78 percent of the browsers in use, while IE had less than a 4 percent share and Mosaic had 14 percent (see Schmalensee Direct, *supra* note 3, App. D, Paragraph 20, Table D-1). These figures, however, do not include the browsers built into access software from the OLSs.

[39] *See* Michael A. Cusumano and David B. Yoffie, *Competing on Internet Time: Lessons from Netscape and Its Battle with Microsoft* (1998), p. 105 (citing *Infoworld*, September 18, 1995).

[40] *See* Schmalensee Direct, *supra* note 3, Paragraph 482.

[41] *See* Transcript, October 20, 1998, p.m. Session, p. 73 (Cross of James Barksdale).

[42] Efforts to write such applications using Java technologies generally have failed. Netscape tried and failed to create a new browser using Java (see Wylie Wong, *Andreessen: Netscape's Javagator Is Dead*, CRN [July 1, 1998; accessed October 22, 2000] http://www.techweb.com/wire/story/TWB19980701S0001). Corel also failed in its attempt to write a Java version of its WordPerfect office productivity suite (see Arif Mohamed, *Corel Sidelines Office for Java, Embraces Windows*, ZDNet UK [October 22, 1997; accessed March 28, 2001] http://www.zdnet.co.uk/news/news1/ns-3030.html). Oracle and Lotus both used Java to produce application suites, but the performance limitations of both caused them to fail commercially (see Lee Copeland, *It's Official: Lotus Confirms eSuite's Demise*, CRN, [September 10, 1999; accessed March 28, 2001] http://www.techweb.com/wire/story/TWB19990910S0012; *News Briefs: Oracle's HatTrick Fnally Bites the Dust*, Infoworld [March 23, 1998; accessed March 28, 2001] http://archive.infoworld.com/cgi-bin/displayArchive.pl?/98/12/t01-12.3.htm).

[43] Michael J. Miller, "*The Web at War: The Battle for the Future of the Internet*," *PC Magazine*, May 28, 1996, p. 39.

[44] The government argued that by preventing Netscape from obtaining a dominant browser share, Microsoft could protect its monopoly in operating systems (PPFOF, *supra* note 11, Paragraphs 315, 359). The district court quotes a Microsoft employee in 1998: "We set out on this mission 2 years ago to not let Netscape dictate standards and control the browser api's [sic]. All evidence today says they don't" (FOF, *supra* note 12, Paragraph 377). Once there were two popular browsers, public standards came to dominate Web site design.

[45] *See* Maritz Direct, *supra* note 7, Paragraph 294.

[46] Nine of the magazines were chosen on the basis of paid circulation and four because they were widely read by information technology professionals. All browser reviews were identified and evaluated for each pair of versions. Where the same magazine had multiple reviews with conflicting conclusions, the researchers had rules for assigning priorities; for example, giving greatest weight to publications' "Best of" awards, followed by head-to-head comparisons of final releases of each browser. If the results were still uncertain, or the publication declared a tie, the results were recorded as "tie/mixed" (Schmalensee Direct, *supra* note 3, App. F).

[47] Netscape never released Navigator 5. The final version of Navigator 6 was not released until November 2000. Many reviewers have suggested that the version released still had many bugs that made it unreliable (see, for example, Mike Avery, *Netscape Strikes Out with Navigator 6.0*, Infoworld [November 26, 2000; accessed March 28, 2001], http://www2.infoworld.com/articles/tc/xml/00/11/29/001129tcnetscape6.xml; Rex Baldazo, *Fab Features, Solid Standards, but Still Too Slow*, CNET.com [November 14, 2000; accessed March 28, 2001] http://www.cnet.com/internet/0-3779-8-3607741-1.html).

[48] *See* Allchin Direct, *supra* note 25, Paragraphs 17, 224, 252.

[49] *See* Transcript, January 4, 1999, p.m. Session, pp. 8-12 (Cross of William Harris).

[50] *See* Cusumano and Yoffie, *supra* note 39, pp. 98-99.

[51] *See* Schmalensee Direct, *supra* note 3, Paragraph 271; Direct Testimony of James Barksdale, Paragraph 20 (October 19, 1998) (hereafter Barksdale Direct).

[52] *See* Schmalensee Direct, *supra* note 3, Paragraph 280.

[53] SpryNet had an agreement with Compaq regarding placement and promotion. This deal is mentioned in DX 2376, a 1996 letter from Ted Leonsis of AOL to Celeste Dunn of Compaq.

[54] *See* Schmalensee Direct, *supra* note 3, App. D, Table D-15.

[55] *See* Direct Testimony of William Poole, Paragraph 3 and Section V (February 4, 1999).

[56] For example, "Second, because of the economic incentives they confront, ISVs [independent software vendors] tend to write first and foremost to the operating system with the dominant share, which is Windows" (PPFOF, *supra* note 11, Paragraph 26.2); "This creates overwhelming incentives to write first and foremost for Windows because writing for Windows – the operating system with the dominant share – gives applications developers by far the highest expected return for the sunk costs incurred" (Paragraph 26.2.3).

[57] "Users will not in large numbers use an operating system other than Windows unless it supports a set of applications comparable to the set of applications available for Windows,

but ISVs will tend not to write comparable applications for other operating systems in large numbers because those operating systems lack a large number of users" (PPFOF, *supra* note 11, Paragraph 25.1).

58 The government never explicitly stated that Netscape/Java would become a platform monopolist, instead emphasizing potential competition in operating systems. However, its simplistic model of the applications barrier to entry left no room for another outcome. Developers and users would switch from Microsoft's monopoly operating system/platform to Netscape/Sun's monopoly middleware. The government implicitly recognized this fact in emphasizing the importance of Netscape's maintaining a share of browser use in excess of 50 percent (see Transcript, June 2, 1999, a.m. Session, pp. 17-18 (Franklin M. Fisher, Rebuttal, Direct); PPFOF, *supra* note 11, Paragraph 394.3).

59 The word "commoditize" was taken from one of Bill Gates's e-mails (GX 20, at MS98 01128763, Bill Gates, "The Internet Tidal Wave" [May 26, 1995]).

60 Note that the government is switching back to the operating system as software platform.

61 *See* Direct Testimony of Franklin M. Fisher, Paragraph 129.b (January 5, 1999) [hereafter Fisher Direct].

62 *See* Direct Testimony of Franklin M. Fisher, Paragraphs 122, 124.

63 PPFOF, *supra* note 11, Paragraphs 225-227, 234-236, Section V.G.

64 The government placed increasing emphasis on its predation case as the litigation progressed. Predation was not a major element of the complaint it filed, but its appeals court brief focuses almost entirely on the predation case.

The government also claimed that Microsoft attempted to monopolize the browser market in violation of Section 2. However, that effort allegedly was only to support Microsoft's maintenance of its monopoly of operating systems, so we do not address it separately. The government also made many allegations in its predation case. Those claims are discussed in Schmalensee Direct, *supra* note 3, Section X. See also David S. Evans and Richard Schmalensee, "*Be Nice to Your Rivals: How the Government is Selling an Antitrust Case without Consumer Harm in U.S. v. Microsoft*," in *Did Microsoft Harm Consumers? Two Opposing Views*, p. 45 (AEI-Brookings Joint Center for Regulatory Studies, 2000). This article focuses on the theory of the government's liability case and the government's key allegations under that theory.

65 FOF, *supra* note 12, Paragraph 93.

66 FOF, *supra* note 12, Paragraphs 91 (Netscape), 104-110 (Apple), 111-114 (RealNetworks), 116 (IBM).

67 FOF, *supra* note 12, Paragraph 98. Ironically, in light of the government's tying claims against Microsoft, the NSP software was designed to take advantage of multimedia features that Intel had integrated into its processors – thereby replacing separate chips. Moreover, the multimedia extensions were proprietary to Intel, and thus their use would have given it a major advantage over competitors that produced clones of its processors.

68 Plaintiffs' Memorandum in Support of Proposed Final Judgment 9-10 (April 28, 2000, Corrected May 2, 2000).

69 *See* David S. Evans, "*All the Facts That Fit: Square Pegs and Round Holes in U.S. v. Microsoft*," 22 (4) *Regulation Magazine* 54 (1999) for a discussion of the strategic reasons behind the government's approach.

70 The government was asked to identify a similar case at the oral arguments before the D.C.

Circuit Court of Appeals and was unable to do so (see Appeals Transcript, *supra* note 17, pp. 47, 49-50). Netscape Navigator was in the browser market that was the subject of the government's attempted monopolization claim, but not in the operating system market central to the government's claim of monopoly maintenance. Sun's Java and other alleged middleware victims were in neither relevant market.

[71] PPFOF, *supra* note 11, Paragraph 19.

[72] See Transcript, June 1, 1999, a.m. Session, p. 63 (Fisher Rebuttal, Direct); Transcript, June 3, 1999, a.m. Session, pp. 61-62 (Fisher Rebuttal, Cross).

[73] The government never alleged that Microsoft obtained its position by anticompetitive means, but much of the testimony implied that once IBM chose MS-DOS as its operating system, its rise was inevitable. Thus Judge Jackson states: "When the International Business Machines Corporation ('IBM') selected MS-DOS for preinstallation on its first generation of PCs, Microsoft's product became the predominant operating system sold for Intel-compatible PCs" (FOF, *supra* note 12, Paragraph 6).

[74] PPFOF, *supra* note 11, Paragraph 31; FOF, *supra* note 12, Paragraph 47.

[75] Given the positive feedback loop, there is conceptually no difference between referring to an "applications barrier to entry" and a "user barrier to entry." In the government's model, the stock of applications and the stock of users both prevent entry in the same way.

[76] See Schmalensee Direct, *supra* note 3, Paragraphs 100-101, 107.

[77] These efforts include identifying APIs that software developers will want for new applications, writing the code to support those APIs (the largest part of the effort), and promoting the use of those APIs by writing development tools, offering training, and holding development conferences (see Maritz Direct, *supra* note 7, Paragraph 21).

[78] See Maritz Direct, *supra* note 7, Paragraphs 136-147. A similar process goes on with hardware vendors, but we do not focus on that side of the market.

[79] Sun, for example, recently boasted that almost 2 million developers belong to its Sun Developer Connection (Sun press release, *Fourth Annual Sun Techdays 2001 Worldwide Tour Begins US Leg to Educate Developers on Latest Technologies* [January 8, 2001; accessed March 27, 2001] http://www.sun.com/smi/Press/sunflash/2001-01/sunflash.20010108.1.html.

[80] See IDC Report #22766, *Worldwide Software Market Forecast Summary, 2000–2004*, p. 171, Tables 17-18 (August 2000). The "Windows" sales include all applications written to the 32-bit Windows APIs. Unix customers pay much higher prices for Unix applications.

[81] Windows 2000 has over 5,000 APIs, compared to just over 1,000 in most versions of Unix (the number for Windows 2000 is based on a count of APIs included with the Software Development Kit; the number for Unix is for the Unix 98 specification [see The Open Group, *UNIX System Interface Tables,* 1997-1998; accessed April 5, 2001] http://www.unix-systems.org/what_is_unix/unixv2.pdf).

[82] When IBM first unveiled its Personal Computer, it endorsed and sold three operating systems: PC-DOS (its branded version of MS-DOS), CP/M-86 (from Digital Research), and the p-System (based on the UCSD Pascal interpreter). PC-DOS was not "bundled" with PCs, but it and CP/M-86 were available for separate purchase (see Paul Freiberger and Michael Swaine, *Fire in the Valley: The Making of the Personal Computer* [2000], p. 348; see also Stephen Maines and Paul Andrews, *Gates* [1994], p. 192).

[83] For IBM's comparison of OS/2 Warp 3 with Microsoft's forthcoming Windows 95 (code name Chicago), see DX 2633, "Warp vs. Chicago: A Decision Maker's Guide to 32-bit Operating System Technology," IBM Personal Software Marketing 10, 13 (September 1994). Although the government focused on OS/2 Warp 3.0, released in 1994, IBM had achieved full compatibility with Windows 3.x in OS/2 2.1, released in 1993 (see Transcript, November 17, 1998, p.m. Session, pp. 78-80 [Cross of John Soyring]). Moreover, OS/2 had been available since 1987, three years before Windows 3.0. It achieved significant sales.

[84] "There will be very few Windows 95 products available other than Microsoft Corp.'s the day the operating system ships, but more than 30 products should be out within a month of the launch and more than 100 products by year's end." "*Windows 95 Products Slow to Step up at First*," *Computer Reseller News*, August 1995, pp. 73-74.

[85] John Soyring of IBM testified for the government that OS/2 could not overcome the applications barrier to entry (Direct Testimony of John Soyring, Paragraphs 9-13 (November 17, 1998) [hereafter Soyring Direct]). However, IBM and Microsoft had equal starting points: Both had access to the source code for MS-DOS and Windows 3.x, and thus could make their systems backward compatible (as IBM did with OS/2 2.1 [see DX 2633, *supra* note 83]). Moreover, the leaders in spreadsheets and word processing, Lotus and WordPerfect, wrote OS/2 versions before they wrote for Windows (see Transcript, November 17, 1998, p.m. Session, pp. 71-72 [Soyring Cross]).

[86] See Maritz Direct, *supra* note 7, Paragraph 136.

[87] Regarding Linux, see Transcript, June 22, 1999, p.m. Session, pp. 42-44 (Schmalensee Rebuttal, Direct); regarding Java, see Schmalensee Direct, *supra* note 3, Paragraph 144; Transcript, June 22, 1999, p.m. Session, pp. 73-74 (Schmalensee Rebuttal, Direct); regarding OS/2, see Soyring Direct, *supra* note 85, Paragraph 4.

[88] See Elzinga et al., *supra* note 24.

[89] Apple recently announced that "over 20,000" applications were being developed for Mac OS X (Apple press release, *More than 10,000 Developers Working on Mac OS X Solutions* (March 21, 2001; accessed April 4, 2001), http://www.apple.com/pr/library/2001/mar/21osxdev.html; see also Apple press release, *Avalanche of New Mac Software and Peripherals Continues* (September 17, 1998; accessed March 30, 2001), http://www.apple.com/pr/library/1998/sep/17onethousand.html).

[90] For comparison, Microsoft's Windows CE platform accounted for 19 percent of 1999 handheld shipments (see IDC Report #22430, *Market Mayhem: The Smart Handheld Devices Market Forecast and Analysis 1999-2004* 28, Table 12 (June 2000); 3Com press release, *Palm Computing to Host Second Annual Worldwide Developer Conference* (September 2, 1998; accessed March 30, 2001), http://www.palm.com/pr/debconf.html).

[91] See Josh Lerner, "Did Microsoft Deter Software Innovation?" Table 2 (available at http://papers.ssrn.com/toptens/tt_jrnl_208190.html).

[92] See Manes and Andrews, *supra* note 82, pp. 217-218; Freiberger and Swaine, *supra* note 82, pp. 368-369.

[93] John Soyring of IBM testified that one reason IBM gave up on OS/2 was that "[g]iven the price [IBM or any other company] could expect to receive for each license of its operating system" (in competition with Windows), "the company would have to 'sell' tens of millions of copies of its new product to recoup its cost" (Soyring Direct, *supra* note 85, Paragraph 13). For a theoretical analysis showing why network effects can lead a firm to

set a lower current price, see Drew Fudenberg and Jean Tirole, *"Pricing under the Threat of Entry by a Sole Supplier of a Network Good,"* 48 (4) *Journal of Industrial Economics*, pp. 373-390 (December 2000).

[94] *See generally* Jim Carlton, *Apple* (1998); regarding OS/2, *see generally*, Paul Carroll, *Big Blues: The Unmaking of IBM* (1994); regarding IBM's decision to focus on large business users, see Transcript, November 17, 1998, p.m. Session, pp. 81-82 (Soyring Cross).

[95] For example, Intel did not expect Windows 95 to be released in the summer of 1995, and thus focused its native signal processing software on Windows 3.x (see Transcript, November 10, 1998, p.m. Session, pp. 21-22 [McGeady Cross]). For IBM's continued hopes regarding OS/2, see Transcript, November 18, 1998, p.m. Session, pp. 99-100 (Soyring Cross).

[96] See David S. Evans and Richard Schmalansee, "Some Economic Aspects of Antitrust Analysis in Dynamically Competitive Industries" (available at http://papers.nber.org/papers/w8268); Schmalensee Direct, *supra* note 3, Section III.

[97] See David Bank, *"The Java Saga," Wired* (December 1995; accessed April 9, 2001), http://www.wired.com/wired/archive/3.12/java.saga_pr.html.

[98] See Transcript, June 1, 1999, a.m. Session, pp. 31-32 (Fisher Rebuttal, Direct); see generally David S. Evans et al., *The Rise and Fall of Leaders in Personal Computer Software* (January 7, 1999; accessed April 5, 2001) http://www.neramicrosoft.com/NeraDocuments/Analyses/rise_and_fall.pdf.

[99] See Evans et al., *supra* note 98.

[100] See Fudenberg and Tirole, *supra* note 93.

[101] This is related to the notion of "innovation markets." See Richard J. Gilbert and Steven C. Sunshine, *"Incorporating Dynamic Efficiency Concerns in Merger Analysis: The Use of Innovation Markets,"* 63 *Antitrust Law Journal* (1995), p. 569. But it is important in the assessment of dynamic competition to look for competitive threats from alternative technologies.

[102] See Paul Carroll, *supra* note 94, pp. 325-327 (1994).

[103] Microsoft did not dispute the government's assertion that it had static market power and could set Windows prices above marginal cost. Nonetheless, the government devoted great effort to prove this assertion (see, e.g., Transcript, January 20, 1999, p.m. Session, pp. 63-66 [Schmalensee Redirect]).

[104] When asked under cross-examination for his estimate of the "competitive price" of Windows 98, which he offered as a benchmark for measuring monopoly power, Warren-Boulton answered, "significantly below whatever it is" (Transcript, November 19, 1998, a.m. Session, p. 40 [Warren-Boulton Cross]). No other estimate was ever offered.

[105] The government's market definition even excluded Apple, though it obviously is, and has been, in platform competition with Microsoft.

[106] Wang was the leader in dedicated word processors, which were supplanted by PCs with word-processing software.

[107] For details and sensitivity analysis, see Schmalensee Direct, *supra* note 3, App. B; Bernard Reddy et al., *"Why Does Microsoft Charge So Little for Windows?"* in this volume.

[108] See Transcript, June 1, 1999, p.m. Session, p. 7 (Fisher Rebuttal, Direct).

[109] See Transcript, June 2, 1999, a.m. Session, pp. 6-7 (Fisher Rebuttal, Direct); Transcript, November 19, 1998, p.m. Session, p. 33 (Warren-Boulton Cross).

110 After correcting his estimated average price of a new PC, but leaving unchanged several other implausible assumptions, Fisher testified that he could get the monopoly price within a "couple of hundred dollars" of the observed price of Windows (Transcript, June 2, 1999, a.m. Session, p. 53 [Fisher Rebuttal, Cross]). For more discussion of Fisher's analysis, see Bernard Reddy et al., "*A Monopolist Would Still Charge More for Windows: A Comment on Werden*," 18(3) *Review of Industrial Organization* (May 2001a), p. 263, and Bernard Reddy et al., "*A Monopolist Would Still Charge More for Windows: A Comment on Werden's Reply*," 18(3) *Review of Industrial Organization* (May 2001b), p. 273.

111 Economides and Hall observe that the government failed to deal seriously with this fundamental inconsistency. See Nicholas Economides, *The Microsoft Antitrust Case* (available at http://www.stern.nyu.edu/networks/papers.html); Chris E. Hall and Robert E. Hall, *National Policy on Microsoft: A Neutral Perspective, Version 2.0* (February 27, 1999; accessed April 9, 2001), http://www.netEcon.com/Neutral2.pdf. Gregory Werden, "*Microsoft's Pricing of Windows and the Economics of Derived Demand Monopoly*," 18(3) *Review of Industrial Organization* (May 2001), p. 257, and Gregory Werden, "*Microsoft's Pricing of Windows: A Reply to Reddy, Evans, Nichols, and Schmalensee*," 18(3) *Review of Industrial Organization* (May 2001), p. 269, reiterate Fisher's claims regarding parameter values and suggest that Microsoft's behavior can be explained by the existence of two distinct markets for Windows-equipped PCs, one of which is highly elastic, with a low willingness to pay. However, Reddy et al. (May 2001a, *supra* note 110), and Reddy et al. (May 2001b, *supra* note 110), show that the parameter values assumed by Fisher and Werden are inconsistent with the data and that Werden's two-segment theory cannot explain Microsoft's low price because the profit-maximizing strategy is essentially to price to sell only to the higher-value segment.

112 See, e.g., Fudenberg and Tirole, *supra* note 93.

113 One of the government's most oft-cited quotes was a Bill Gates e-mail in which he expressed concern that Netscape could "commoditize" the operating system by becoming the platform to which developers wrote (DX 81, *supra* note 8). It was clear, however, that Gates and Microsoft's other top executives all saw Windows' value as deriving from its role as the leading platform, not as an operating system narrowly defined.

114 Fisher Direct, *supra* note 61, Paragraphs 124, 127, 131-133.

115 The district court used the government's predation test to analyze the exclusionary as well as the predatory behavior, and these two types of anticompetitive actions blended together in the government's presentation. See COL, *supra* note 12, pp. 8-9; PPCOL, *supra* note 11, esp. p. 15 (noting that the Supreme Court "has used the language of 'exclusionary' or 'anticompetitive' or 'predatory'" to condemn behavior that imposes costs on the monopolist that can only make sense in the context of monopoly maintenance or acquisition).

116 This section is adapted from Evans and Schmalensee, *supra* note 96.

117 "For this reason, there is a consensus among commentators that predatory pricing schemes are rarely tried, and even more rarely successful" (*Matsushita Elec. Indus. Co. v. Zenith Radio Corp.*, 475 U.S. 574, p. 589 [1986] [hereafter *Matsushita*]). Economists have built theoretical models in which predation is a rational strategy, but there is scant evidence that the models describe any real markets (see John R. Lott, Jr., *Are Predatory Comitments Credible?: Who Should the Courts Believe?* [1999]).

118 *Cargill, Inc. v. Monfort of Colorado, Inc.*, 479 U.S. 104, fn. 17 (1986) ("...the mechanism

by which a firm engages in predatory pricing – lowering prices – is the same mechanism by which a firm stimulates competition; because 'cutting prices in order to increase business often is the very essence of competition.'" Citing *Matsushita Elec. Indus. Co. v. Zenith Radio Corp.*, 475 U.S. 574, 594 [1986]).

[119] *Matsushita*, *supra* note 117, p. 594.

[120] *Brooke Group Ltd. v. Brown & Williamson Tobacco Corp.*, 509 U.S. 209, p. 224 (1993) (hereafter *Brooke Group*).

[121] *Ibid.*, p. 225.

[122] Although the *Brooke Group* court was obviously concerned with consumer welfare, it provides a useful screen – since "predation" without recoupment is unlikely to harm consumers – not an exact test of welfare improvement. We do not believe that such an exact test is feasible.

[123] Brooke Group, *supra* note 120, p. 224.

[124] Janusz A. Ordover and Robert D. Willig, "*An Economic Definition of Predation: Pricing and Product Innovation*," 91 *Yale Law Journal*, pp. 8-53. For a finding of predation, they would also require that "the likelihood of the rival's exit must be substantially raised by the product introduction, and the additional monopoly profit that would accrue to the innovator after the exit of the rival must be sufficient to make the introduction of the new product profitable for the innovator."

[125] This interpretation is notable because it appears to be the one that the district court relied on. "Because Microsoft's business practices 'would not be considered profit maximizing except for the expectation that ... the entry of potential rivals' into the market for Intel-compatible PC operating systems will be 'blocked or delayed,' Microsoft's campaign must be termed predatory" (COL, *supra* note 12, Section I.A.2.c [internal citations omitted]).

[126] Transcript, June 1, 1999, a.m. Session, pp. 38-39 (Fisher Rebuttal, Direct).

[127] *Carlton-Perloff Companion Web Site, Student Resources, Chapter 19 – Lessons from the Microsoft Case* (accessed April 3, 2001), http://occ.awlonline.com/bookbind/pubbooks/carlton_awl/chapter19/deluxe.html.

[128] See Schmalensee Direct, *supra* note 3.

[129] The government pointed to Microsoft's free distribution of IE for platforms other than Windows as evidence of predation. But it never introduced any evidence that the foregone revenues would have been significant or that the free provision of these other platforms had a material adverse effect on Netscape. Microsoft claimed to have developed those other versions in response to demand from customers and distributors, who did not want to adopt IE unless they could provide compatible versions for their employees or subscribers who used other operating systems.

[130] See Fisher Direct, *supra* note 61, Paragraphs 122-124.

[131] Transcript, June 3, 1999, p.m. Session, pp. 46-48 (Fisher Rebuttal, Cross).

[132] See DX 2763, "Microsoft Can Break Even on IE by Realizing Small Increases in Price or Sales of Windows." In preparation for the remedies phase of the trial, two of the authors conducted surveys, described more fully in Elzinga et al., *supra* note 24, of consumers who had purchased new computers with Windows 98. The vast majority of respondents said they would prefer Windows 98 with rather than without a built-in browser. Respondents on average were willing to pay $18 to have IE included.

[133] Actual revenues for calendar 2000 from *Microsoft Corporation Quarterly Revenue* (accessed April 5, 2001), http://www.microsoft.com/msft/download/RevChanBusDiv.xls. Actual margin for calendar 2000 from *Microsoft Corporation Quarterly Income Statements* (accessed April 5, 2001), http://www.microsoft.com/msft/download/financialhistoryQ.xls. We use before-tax income because Microsoft's investments were deductible from taxable income.

[134] This calculation conservatively assumes no growth in Microsoft's income. It also assumes a discount rate of 20 percent per year and five years of investment, 1995-99. If one assumes expenditures of another $50 million per year for promotion and distribution, the break-even probability is still only 5 percent.

[135] The government distinguished Microsoft's investments in these "no-revenue" products from its investments in IE on the grounds that these other investments were not undertaken to maintain or attain a monopoly. But if those investments in "no-revenue" product actions made "business sense," there is every reason to assume that the investment in IE did also. The government sometimes seemed to argue that leading firms should not make otherwise sensible investments if those investments might harm an actual or potential competitor. Such a rule would explicitly restrict competition and would thus harm consumers.

[136] See Fisher Direct, *supra* note 61, Paragraphs 217-222; Transcript, January 11, 1999, p.m. Session, pp. 77-78 (Fisher Recross).

[137] Many people use more than one browser. Survey data showed that on average respondents who used any browser had used 1.5 different browsers during the two preceding weeks (see Schmalensee Direct, *supra* note 3, Paragraph 384).

[138] See Fisher Direct, *supra* note 61, Paragraphs 219-223.

[139] See Thomas G. Krattenmaker and Steven C. Salop, "*Anticompetitive Exclusion: Raising Rivals' Costs to Achieve Power over Price*," 96 (2) *Yale Law Journal* (December 1986); Steven C. Salop and David T. Scheffman, "*Cost-Raising Strategies*," 36 *Journal of Industrial Economics* (September 1987). For a critique in the context of this case, see Transcript, January 19, 1999, a.m. Session, pp. 52-54 (Schmalensee Cross).

[140] See *Omega Envtl., Inc. v. Gilbarco, Inc.*, 127 F.3d 1157, 1163 (9th Cir. 1997), cert. denied, 525 U.S. 812 (1998); *Roland Mach. Co. v. Dresser Indus., Inc.*, 749 F.2d 380, 393-395 (7th Cir. 1984) (Posner, J.); *Barry Wright Corp. v. ITT Grinnell Corp.*, 724 F.2d 227 (1st Cir. 1983) (Breyer, J.).

[141] The incumbent could prevent price-reducing entry if it foreclosed enough of the market to rivals. Even here, as with all predation strategies, there is an issue as to whether this is a plausible anticompetitive strategy.

[142] Fisher's entire discussion of his claim that Microsoft had used a raising-rivals'-cost strategy is at Fisher Direct, *supra* note 61, Paragraphs 133, 222; Transcript, January 11, 1999, p.m. Session, p. 78 (Fisher Redirect); Transcript, January 13, 1999, a.m. Session, pp. 56-63 (Fisher Recross).

[143] See Transcript, June 4, 1999, a.m. Session, p. 36 (Fisher Rebuttal, Redirect).

[144] We consider in detail the government's analysis of the effectiveness of the ISP agreements because: (1) it was the government's only serious attempt at quantitative analysis and (2) it was debated extensively during the trial, was referenced approvingly in the district court's FOF, and has figured in post-trial discussions by the government's economists (see Franklin M. Fisher and Daniel L. Rubinfeld, "*United States v. Microsoft: An*

Economic Analysis," in *Did Microsoft Harm Consumers? Two Opposing Views*, pp. 1, 29-33 [AEI-Brookings Joint Center for Regulatory Studies, 2000]).

[145] The government saw OEMs as a key distribution channel (PPFOF, *supra* note 11, Paragraph 213).

[146] See Fisher Direct, *supra* note 61, Paragraphs 227-229; Direct Testimony of Frederick R. Warren-Boulton, Paragraphs 144-151 (November 18, 1998).

[147] See Schmalensee Direct, *supra* note 3, App. D, Table D-19.

[148] This figure is calculated using the government's AdKnowledge data, excluding hits identified as coming from one of the OLSs. The starting and ending percentages are 20 and 46 percent, respectively.

[149] See Transcript, June 21, 1999, a.m. Session, p. 18 (Schmalensee Rebuttal, Direct).

[150] See DX 2758, "Netscape's Share Among ISP Subscribers Has Remained High." From May 1997 through April 1998, 82 percent of respondents who were ISP subscribers and received their browser from their provider used Navigator. These figures are based on the monthly surveys conducted for Microsoft starting in early 1996 (see Schmalensee Direct, *supra* note 3). These surveys were the only data introduced at trial that addressed how users obtained their browsers and were relied upon in most of the Microsoft e-mails used by the government to establish the importance of OEMs, OLSs, and ISPs as distribution channels.

[151] These six ISPs were called the "Parity" group in Fisher and Warren-Boulton's analyses.

[152] For further discussion of the AdKnowledge data and its infirmities, see Schmalensee Direct, *supra* note 3, App. D.

[153] See Transcript, February 10, 1999, p.m. Session, pp. 41-43 (Cross of Cameron Myhrvold).

[154] See Direct Testimony of Cameron Myhrvold, Paragraphs 4, 32-39 (February 8, 1999).

[155] See Schmalensee Direct, *supra* note 3, App. D, Paragraphs 115-116, Table D-10.

[156] The government claimed that such evidence was irrelevant, because it reflected the choices made by these ISPs absent contractual obligations to Microsoft or Netscape. See Transcript, June 2, 1999, a.m. Session, pp. 10-11 (Fisher Rebuttal, Direct). That argument is invalid, however, because the ISPs in the control group were self-selected, so one cannot logically ascribe the differences between their behavior and the behavior of the other ISPs to the agreements. The tiny ISPs in the control group were plainly atypical, since the vast majority of ISPs entered into agreements with Microsoft or Netscape.

[157] We discovered by chance that in at least one case an ISP in a different group had been acquired by another, and only its original subscribers continued to use the domain name identified by the government; new subscribers used a different domain. See Schmalensee Direct, *supra* note 3, App. D, Table D-11).

[158] During his redirect, Fisher presented a graph plotting results with these three sets of fixed weights (GX 1445), which he claimed showed visually that fixed weights made no difference. Transcript, January 12, 1999, p.m. Session, p. 26 (Fisher Redirect). However, he did not report the differences from the first to the last months, which can be done using the underlying data (GX 1480, "backup data for GX 1445"; GX 1445, "Microsoft's share of the Browser Market Monthly Usage by ISP Category"). They are: 19 percentage points with a simple average (equal weights), 15 percentage points with starting weights, and 13 percentage points with ending weights, compared to 10 percentage points with the government's original method.

[159] PPCOL, *supra* note 11, p. 54. The government also argued that the discounts that Microsoft offered to some OEMs for featuring IE exclusively were illegal. However, the only OEM known to have accepted Microsoft's offer was Compaq, which had numerous cross-promotional arrangements with Microsoft under its "Front-Line partnership" (see PPFOF, *supra* note 11, Paragraphs 195-203).

[160] The "Prototype Removal Program" developed by Professor Felton essentially deleted the IE icon, removed IE from the Start menu, and modified various registry settings so that IE would not launch automatically under various conditions. It removed only the "stub" of the code used to launch IE as a browser. All of the code supporting APIs was left intact. See Direct Testimony of Edward W. Felten, Paragraphs 52-67 (December 11, 1998).

[161] The OEMs act as distributors of Microsoft's products. It is common for manufacturers to limit how distributors can modify products. The government's response that other operating system vendors allowed changes is misleading. First, the government introduced no evidence that this happens much in practice. Second, many of the vendors (including Apple and Sun) act as their own OEMs. Microsoft never limited modifications that end users (or their agents, such as value-added resellers) could make to the desktop. Third, other platform vendors had not yet used their browsers to supply APIs for applications developers and therefore had less reason to care whether browser code was present in the version running on end-user machines.

[162] See Direct Testimony of Joachim Kempin, Paragraphs 20, 45 (January 6, 1999).

[163] The government cited a Microsoft e-mail saying that the company hoped to make running other browsers a "jolting" experience (PPFOF, *supra* note 11, Paragraph 129, citing GX 684, at MS6 6007119, Brad Chase, "How to get to 30% Share in 12 Months" [1996 marketing plan]), but it did not introduce any evidence that this meant more than making IE so smoothly integrated that running a separate browser application would seem "jolting" in comparison.

[164] See Fisher Direct, *supra* note 61, Paragraph 150; PPFOF, *supra* note 11, Paragraph 179.

[165] See Barksdale Direct, *supra* note 51, Paragraph 19.

[166] See Chase Direct, *supra* note 10, Paragraph 175; see also Transcript, January 5, 1999, p.m. Session, pp. 18-20 (Fisher Cross).

[167] PPFOF, *supra* note 11, Paragraph 179.

[168] See Transcript, June 21, 1999, a.m. Session, pp. 73-74 (Schmalensee Rebuttal, Direct).

[169] We do not debate the wisdom of the case law in this section. It is worth noting, however, that the per se rule against tying is not supported by the economics literature. See Keith N. Hylton and Michael Salinger, *Tying Law and Policy: A Decision Theoretic Approach,* Boston University (2000) (mimeo). On the other hand, the rules against foreclosure, properly applied, cover many actions that are probably harmful to consumers.

[170] In its complaint, the major remedy demanded by the government was that Microsoft either offer a version of Windows without IE or include Navigator in subsequent releases of Windows (see Complaint Section VIII, Paragraphs 1-2 [filed May 18, 1998]). During the trial, in addition to giving economic testimony on the tying issue, the government's two computer science experts – David Farber and Edward Felton – testified primarily on tying-related issues.

[171] The government did not object to (a) Microsoft's including APIs based on IE in Windows so that applications developers could still write to those APIs (*see, e.g.*, Transcript,

December 9, 1998, a.m. Session, pp. 63-66 [Recross of David Farber]); (b) Microsoft's charging *more* for the browser-disabled version of Windows than the regular version (see Transcript, November 24, 1998, a.m. Session, pp. 60-61 [Warren-Boulton Cross]; Transcript, November 24, 1998, p.m. Session, pp. 42-43 [Warren-Boulton Cross]).

[172] PPFOF, *supra* note 11, Paragraphs 150-194, esp. Paragraph 151.2.

[173] There is no basis for concluding that the *Jefferson Parish* test provides necessary and sufficient conditions for determining that a tie harms consumers; at best it provides necessary conditions (see Evans and Schmalensee, *supra* note 96; Hylton and Salinger, *supra* note 169).

[174] *Jefferson Parish Hosp. Dist. No. 2 v. Hyde*, 466 U.S. 2, pp. 16, 26 (1984) (hereafter *Jefferson Parish*).

[175] *Response of Carolina, Inc. v. Leasco Response, Inc.*, 537 F.2d 1307, at 1330 (5th Cir. 1976).

[176] *Microsoft II*, *supra* note 1; *Caldera Inc. v. Microsoft Corp.*, 72 F. Supp.2d 1295 (D. Utah 1999).

[177] *Jefferson Parish*, *supra* note 174, pp. 22-23.

[178] *Eastman Kodak v. Image Technical Services, Inc.*, 504 U.S. 451, p. 458 (1992).

[179] Transcript, October 22, 1998, p.m. Session, pp. 51-52 (Barksdale Cross).

[180] See Schmalensee Direct, *supra* note 3, App. D, Tables D-22-23.

[181] The government cited two types of companies: those that preferred to standardize on a different browser (such as Boeing) and those that preferred not to give some employees access to the Internet. However, the government also acknowledged that most large companies installed their own software, so what the OEMs were allowed to do did not prevent them from standardizing on another browser. For companies that did not want some employees to access the Internet, the simple solution was not to give them a connection to the Internet.

[182] *Microsoft II*, *supra* note 1, Appeals Court Decision, pp. 13-14 (June 23, 1998).

[183] The government did not dispute these benefits. However, it claimed that Microsoft could include Internet functionality for developers without also making it available to consumers. It also claimed that since some users did not benefit from the inclusion of IE, Microsoft should make a separate version of Windows available (PPFOF, *supra* note 11, Section V.B, Paragraph 93).

[184] In a brief for the district court, Professor Lawrence Lessig concluded on the trial record in *Microsoft III* that "it does not seem contested that the modularized design of IE 3.0 and later enabled independent software vendors to write to the APIs exposed by the IE components...indeed, the government's own witnesses asserted...that this feature provided 'some benefit.' Thus under the Court's test...even if part of Microsoft's motivation were anticompetitive, so long as part of what it produced was beneficial the government's Section 1 tying claim would fail" (Brief of Professor Lawrence Lessig 16 [February 1, 2000] [internal citations omitted]).

[185] The most widely circulated and cited version is Dennis W. Carlton and Michael Waldman, "The Strategic Use of Tying to Preserve and Create Market Power in Evolving Industries" (National Bureau of Econ. Research Working Paper No. 6831, December 1998; accessed April 9, 2001), http://www.nber.org/papers/w6831/ (hereafter, Carlton and Waldman). Our discussion, however, is based on a more recent version that address-

es some issues not considered in the first (Dennis W. Carlton and Michael Waldman, "The Strategic Use of Tying to Preserve and Create Market Power in Evolving Industries," George J. Stigler Center for the Study of the Economy and the State Working Paper #145 (March 2000; accessed April 9, 2001), http://gsbwww.uchicago.edu/research/cses/WorkingPapersPDF's/145.pdf).

[186] In their more recent paper (Carlton and Waldman 2000, *supra* note 185), they analyze welfare effects. In some of their models, tying may be profitable and increase social welfare (because it prevents inefficient entry).

[187] The district court had indicated early in the case that the case law had pointed to 40 percent (COL, *supra* note 12, p. 36), although how this figure was to be applied was never very clear.

[188] *See* Schmalensee Direct, *supra* note 3, Paragraph 353.

[189] *See* Transcript, June 21, 1999, a.m. Session, p. 75 (Schmalensee Rebuttal, Direct).

[190] DX 2440, "AOL and Goldman Sachs Project Odyssey Due Diligence Summaries" (November 22, 1998). See also Schmalensee Direct, *supra* note 3, Paragraphs 374-375; he based his figures on internal Netscape documents.

[191] The number of Internet users worldwide reached 100 million by the end of 1997. Lynn Margherio et al., *The Emerging Digital Economy* 2 (Washington, D.C.: U.S. Department of Commerce).

[192] The government pointed to a Microsoft e-mail on the limitations of downloads, which indicated that surveys showed that 66 percent of Web users had never downloaded a browser (PPFOF, *supra* note 11, Paragraph 366.3.1). Of course, that statement means that more than one-third had downloaded a browser. Figures reported by Schmalensee based on those same surveys (Schmalensee Direct, *supra* note 3, App. D, Tables D-15-16) show that until the end of 1997, downloading was the single most important source of copies of IE *in use* and that for Navigator it consistently ranked behind only "work/school" as the largest channel for browsers in use.

[193] Transcript, January 12, 1999, p.m. Session, p. 9 (Fisher Redirect).

[194] *See* DX 2440, *supra* note 190.

[195] *See* Transcript, January 21, 1999, p.m. Session, pp. 64-66 (Schmalensee Recross).

[196] DX 2440, *supra* note 190.

[197] COL, *supra* note 12, Section I.

[198] *Ibid.*, Section II.A.

[199] *Ibid.*, Section II.B.

[200] Plaintiffs' Appeals Brief 15 (February 9, 2001) (internal citations omitted) (hereafter Plaintiffs' Appeals Brief).

[201] This approach continued before the appeals court. The government's counsel began his presentation on monopoly maintenance by alluding to Microsoft's "extraordinary" expenditures on IE. When asked whether the government was challenging Microsoft's development expenditures, he responded "No, we are not" (Appeals Transcript, *supra* note 17, pp. 46-47).

[202] *E.g.*, contrast FOF, *supra* note 12, Paragraph 136 with Paragraph 140.

[203] For example, the government's lawyer at the oral arguments said, "In fact, an argument can be made that offering the browser for free was a form of predatory pricing. Now, we are

not arguing that here" (Appeals Transcript, *supra* note 17, pp. 78-79). See note 16 for references to the FOF in which the district court seems to take inconsistent positions on whether Microsoft's pricing was anticompetitive.

204 Plaintiffs' Appeals Brief, *supra* note 200, p. 42.

205 *Ibid.*, pp. 28-29.

206 COL, *supra* note 12, Section I.A.2.b.

207 Plaintiffs' Appeals Brief, *supra* note 200, p. 103.

208 Below 50 percent, according to the government. Transcript, June 1, 1999, p.m. Session, p. 66 (Fisher Rebuttal, Direct).

209 Jim Allchin of Microsoft testified that "[i]n fact, Dr. Felten's prototype removal program removes almost no software code at all from Windows 98. The DOJ version of Windows 98 is 99.93 percent as large as the Microsoft version of Windows 98" (Allchin Direct, *supra* note 25, Paragraph 163).

210 See Schmalensee Direct, *supra* note 3, Paragraph 358.

211 See FOF, *supra* note 12, Paragraph 293.

212 COL, *supra* note 12, p. 37. In oral arguments before the appeals court, the government's counsel stated with regard to AOL: "... they required that AOL distribute Internet Explorer as its default browser. If that alone were all that Microsoft had bargained for, that would not cause a problem" (Appeals Transcript, *supra* note 17, p. 100).

213 COL, *supra* note 12, pp. 36-37; AOL's David Colburn testified that one goal in choosing a browser was integrating it into AOL's software to make it less obvious to subscribers when they left AOL's proprietary network for the Web (Direct Testimony of David M. Colburn, Paragraph 34 [November 27, 1998]).

214 FOF, *supra* note 12, Paragraphs 370-371, appears to refer to Fisher's analysis of the AdKnowledge data. The lack of citations by the district court to the trial record makes it impossible to know exactly what the source is.

215 Although Warren-Boulton attempted to isolate the effects of Microsoft's shipment restrictions, his analysis was strongly rebutted and was not referenced even implicitly in the Findings of Fact (see Schmalensee Direct, *supra* note 3, Paragraphs 448-462 and App. D).

216 FOF, *supra* note 12, Paragraph 411.

217 Transcript, October 20, 1998, p.m. Session, pp. 72-74 (Barksdale Cross).

218 See Schmalensee Direct, *supra* note 3, Paragraph 482.

219 FOF, *supra* note 12, Paragraph 412.

220 COL, *supra* note 12, p. 20.

221 FOF, *supra* note 12, Paragraph 408.

222 See IDC Report #22216, *The Global Market Forecast for Internet Usage and Commerce,* Table 4 (May 2000).

223 Jupiter Communications, *Microsoft Internet Strategy Report*, Section IV.a (1997).

224 For more details on the evidence, see generally Schmalensee Direct, *supra* note 3, Section V, as well as Transcript, June 21-23, 1999 (Schmalensee Rebuttal, Direct).

225 In its PPFOF the government cites statements by Glenn Weadock (president of Independent Software and government witness), Joe Kanicki of Dell Computer, and

Scott Vesey of Boeing, all of which concern corporate customers (PPFOF, *supra* note 11, Paragraphs 104-108).

[226] A survey conducted in preparation for the remedies phase of the trial (see DX 2763, *supra* note 132) found that few consumers or businesses would prefer a browserless operating system. Even among respondents using Navigator, a majority preferred Windows 98 with IE.

[227] Plaintiffs' Proposed Findings of Fact mentions only Packard-Bell/NEC as a company that "took advantage of the January 1998 stipulated remedy to offer some of its PC models without Internet Explorer" (PPFOF, *supra* note 11, Paragraph 112; see also Transcript, December 16, 1998, a.m. Session, pp. 5-6 [Excerpts from John Kies' videotape deposition]).

[228] FOF, *supra* note 12, Paragraph 412.

[229] For such a study not supporting the government's assertions, see Lerner, *supra* note 91.

[230] The government highlighted Microsoft's alleged effects on innovation in its submissions on remedies, but the only specific evidence it was able to provide was that Microsoft had delayed the introduction by Intel of native signal processing (NSP) software, which the government alleged had cross-platform potential. In fact, however, Intel's NSP software was extraordinarily platform specific: It worked only on computers running Intel processors (and not AMD or other clones) and Windows 3.x. Not only did it not work with computers that had Windows 95 or Windows NT installed, a computer with NSP installed would encounter problems when upgraded to Windows 95 (see Maritz Direct, *supra* note 7, Paragraph 318; see also Transcript, November 10, 1998, p.m. Session, pp. 21, 30-31, 35-36 [McGeady Cross]).

[231] FOF, *supra* note 12, Paragraph 408.

[232] *United States v. Aluminum Company of America*, 148 F.2d 416, 430 (1945).

Section 1: *U.S. v. Microsoft Corp.*: The Economics

Essay 2

Why Does Microsoft Charge So Little for Windows?

by Bernard Reddy, David S. Evans, and Albert L. Nichols

From a conventional antitrust perspective – and certainly from the perspective of government prosecutors – Microsoft has monopoly power in the market for personal computers run with Intel-compatible microprocessors. Indeed, if it didn't possess such monopoly power, there would have been no basis for the court findings that Microsoft had abused said power.

But that raises a critical question. The market for computer hardware is highly competitive. If Microsoft is, in effect, the gatekeeper, deciding how much consumers will pay for the vital machinery of the information age, why does the company charge so little for it – typically, just a few percent of the total price of a computer system? Put it another way: If Microsoft is a monopolist, why doesn't it charge the profit-maximizing price for Windows?

This brief paper estimates the profit-maximizing price of Windows assuming that the government is right – that Microsoft has a monopoly protected by durable entry barriers. We find that if the government's theory is right Microsoft should be charging a figure that is an order of magnitude larger than the price Microsoft typically charges. No matter how you slice and dice it, the plausible price under the government's monopoly theory exceeds $1,000 – 10 or 20 times as much as the company actually charges.

The explanation, we argue, is that Microsoft is constrained by dynamic competition – in particular, the threat of innovation that makes it possible to perform the functions of a PC without a remarkably complex operating system like Windows. But whether that is the explanation or not, the more important point is that the government based its case on a theory that simply does not fit the facts.

— D.S.E.

Some observers have argued that Microsoft Windows is such an important component of most personal computers sold in the market today that computer manufacturers have no choice but to install Windows on their computers. In 1997, about 88 percent of new personal computers based on Intel x86-compatible microprocessors had a version of Windows installed; Intel x86-compatible computers in turn accounted for about 95 percent of all new personal computers.[1] These commentators claim that because Microsoft provides such an important component for personal computers, it is able to charge "high" prices for Windows. They conclude that the price of Windows is "high" based on two facts: It costs little to produce and distribute copies of Windows; and the price of Windows has not fallen as rapidly as have the prices of personal computers or computer chips.[2]

The U.S. Department of Justice (DOJ) and 20 states (plus the District of Columbia) made the same claim in an antitrust case filed in May 1998. Using the language of antitrust, they say that Microsoft has "monopoly power in the operating system market," which is defined as "the market for personal computer operating systems that are compatible with Intel x86/Pentium (or Intel-compatible) microprocessors."[3] Professor David Sibley, an economist who was scheduled to testify for DOJ at the trial, prepared a declaration and a later expert report that describe the basis for these conclusions in more detail. In part, he suggests that Microsoft is a monopolist because it could raise the price of Windows – which he says is currently in the range of \$45 to \$65[4] – by at least 10 percent and make more money.[5]

Professor Sibley and other critics of Microsoft have actually missed the most intriguing puzzle: If a hypothetical monopolist could profitably raise its operating system price by 10 percent above the levels that Microsoft charges, and if Microsoft has monopoly power in this market, then why doesn't Microsoft raise its price? Furthermore, why would a company that has an important input – the operating system – into a product used widely both in the home and in the workplace – the personal computer – charge only about \$50 for it? That is only 2.4 percent of the average price of a computer sold in 1997 (\$2,082).[6]

Those who claim that Microsoft has monopoly power have missed another paradox. The prices of Microsoft's operating systems have risen far less rapidly than the value of its operating systems. Someone in August 1989 who already had MS-DOS running on a computer would have had to spend about \$254 (in 1998 dollars) on other products to obtain just a portion of the software features that are available in Windows 98. And many features that are standard parts of Windows today simply were not available at any price in 1989.

This paper shows that Microsoft charges low prices for Windows and does not increase the price of Windows at the same rate as it enhances the capabilities of Windows for a very simple reason: competition. It is not the static competition that your college economics professor might have used to explain why wheat farmers cannot charge more for an essential food item. Rather, it is the dynamic competition noted by Joseph Schumpeter and described in the modern economics literature on innovation races and superstars.

MICROSOFT ACTS AS IF IT FACES COMPETITION, NOT AS IF IT IS A MONOPOLIST

We are going to demonstrate two implications of Microsoft's $50 price for Windows in this section. First, if Microsoft really had a monopoly in the operating system market for personal computers, under plausible circumstances it could charge at least $1,000 for Windows. Second, the fact that Microsoft only charges about $50 for Windows implies that it faces a demand curve with an elasticity whose magnitude is at least 13. That is a highly elastic demand curve and indicates that Windows faces intense competition.

Price Setting by a Monopolist

Even a true monopolist faces some constraints in setting prices – no firm can set an infinitely high price for its product and actually make sales. Prices for real-world transactions are therefore never infinitely high. In deciding how to set the price for its product, a monopolist must weigh the tradeoff between two effects: A higher price will increase the revenues per unit sold; but a higher price will also decrease the number of units sold, because consumer demand will fall, other suppliers will increase their output of (at least partially) competing products, or both. The monopolist maximizes profits when these two effects are balanced: The direct gain in revenues from a higher price would be offset by the lost net revenues due to the drop in volume caused by that higher price. This condition can be summarized in the following form:

$$\frac{P - MC}{P} = \frac{1}{E}$$

where P is the profit-maximizing price chosen by the monopolist, MC is the marginal cost for the monopolist,[7] and E is the price elasticity of demand.[8] This is a standard result in economic theory.

This equation says that a monopolist should set price so that the net margin equals the inverse of the price elasticity of demand. When demand responds sharply to price changes, the elasticity will be high, and the profit-maximizing price must therefore be close to marginal cost. When demand responds weakly to price changes, the elasticity will be small,[9] and the profit-maximizing price can substantially exceed marginal cost.

Derived Demand

Under many circumstances, the demand for one product is "derived" from the demand for another product. For example, someone who does not own a computer has no need for an operating system, and everyone who owns a computer needs an operating system. The demand for operating systems therefore depends directly on the demand for computers.

Suppose that every purchaser of a new personal computer wants exactly one operating system installed on the computer: There is no demand for "naked" machines or for machines with multiple operating systems installed, and OEMs pay for (rather than pirate) the operating systems that they install. Suppose further that the supply of personal computers is highly competitive, with many manufacturers striving to satisfy consumer demands by supplying quality products at the lowest possible prices. If so, the price that an OEM pays for an operating system will be passed on to consumers directly in the price of the computer. Under these circumstances, the demand by OEMs for any one operating system will necessarily equal the number of computers that they sell with that operating system installed (one and only one operating system for each computer).

Further, the price elasticity of demand for a given operating system will be a fraction of the price elasticity of demand for computers equipped with that operating system. That fraction will equal the price of the operating system relative to the price of the computer. If a given vendor of operating systems charges a price P_O to an OEM, who in turn charges a price P_C for the computer equipped with that operating system, then the operating system accounts for the fraction P_O/P_C of the price of the computer. If the operating system price increases by 1 percent, and that price increase is passed on in the computer price, then the computer price will rise by only (P_O/P_C) of 1 percent. Demand for computers equipped with that operating system therefore would fall by only (P_O/P_C) times the price elasticity of demand for computers equipped with that operating system. If the price elasticity of demand for personal computers is 2.0, for example, and if the operating system accounts for only 5 percent of the price of the computer, then the price elasticity of demand for the operating system is only 0.1.

Is Microsoft Maximizing Monopoly Profit?

Suppose that Microsoft were actually a monopolist – a firm that could determine its own price without regard to other competitors and could prevent entry into its market. How much would it charge for Windows?

In this hypothetical world of monopoly, every personal computer must have a copy of Windows installed. In its complaint against Microsoft, the U.S. Department of Justice states on page 1 that "PC manufacturers (often referred to as Original Equipment Manufacturers, or 'OEMS') have no commercially reasonable alternative to Microsoft operating systems for the PCs that they distribute." On the other hand, it is widely accepted that the OEM business is highly competitive. Hundreds of OEMs license operating systems directly from Microsoft, and thousands of others obtain licenses through distributors. Dataquest identified more than 30 OEMs that shipped at least 20,000 personal computers in 1997. These top firms shipped barely two-thirds of personal computers, while smaller firms accounted for over 30 percent of the total.[10]

To provide a quantitative estimate of the monopoly price of Windows, we need estimates of the price of a new personal computer, the current price to OEMs of licensing Windows, and Microsoft's marginal cost of selling another copy of Windows to OEMs:

- The average price of a personal computer is $2,000, based on 1997 industry data.[11]
- The average price paid by OEMs for licensing Windows 98 is about $50 per unit.[12]
- The marginal cost to Microsoft of licensing an additional copy of Windows to an OEM is zero. This is clearly an underestimate, as Microsoft does incur some support and other costs that vary at the margin (in general, however, OEMs are responsible for support). However, that fact reinforces the conclusions we reach, because our assumption of zero marginal cost leads to an underestimate of the true monopoly price.

With perfect competition among OEMs, the price of personal computers with Windows preinstalled (P_C) will equal the price charged by Microsoft for Windows (P_O) plus the costs of the other components. These other system costs are therefore estimated to be $1,950 ($2,000-$50).

The price elasticity of demand for the operating system (E_O) will equal the price elasticity of demand for computers (E_C) times the fraction P_O/P_C. The profit-maximizing condition presented above leads to the following derivation (substituting into this condition the expressions for the marginal cost, the computer price, and the operating system price elasticity):

$$\frac{P_o - MC_o}{P_o} = \frac{1}{E_o}$$

$$\frac{P_o - 0}{P_o} = \frac{1}{E_c\left(\frac{P_o}{P_c}\right)}$$

$$\frac{P_o}{P_o} = \frac{P_c}{E_c P_o}$$

$$1 = \frac{\$1{,}950 + P_o}{E_c P_o},$$

where the last expression follows from the assumption that on average, PC systems cost $2,000. Solving for the operating system price leads to the following expression:

Thus, the estimated monopoly price depends critically on the demand elasticity for personal computers.[13]

$$P_o = \frac{\$1{,}950}{E_c - 1}$$

We know of no reliable empirical estimates of the elasticity of demand that have been estimated specifically for personal computers. Brynjolfsson has estimated that the price elasticity of demand for computers as a whole is in the range of 1.0.[14] The price elasticity of demand for personal computers may be somewhat larger because of substitution possibilities between them and other computers. Economists generally classify the demand for a good as "elastic" or "inelastic," where the dividing line is an elasticity of 1. Estimates of elasticities for other goods show a wide range, depending on the good in question and the data and analytic structure underlying the analysis.[15] The size of the elasticity depends in part on how narrowly the good is defined; we would expect the elasticity of demand for a Toyota Camry, for example, to be much higher than that for automobiles generally, because there are many close substitutes for the Camry. If one believes that Windows is just one brand among many (as the Camry is), however, then Microsoft does not have a meaningful monopoly (just as the Camry does not). Thus, to be consistent with the assumption of monopoly that underlies this analysis, the relevant elasticity is that for the broader industry category, personal computers (or automobiles).

Many demand elasticities at the industry level are estimated to be less than 1.0, and very few exceed 2.0. For example, the demand for automobiles has an estimated elasticity of demand in the range of 0.6 to 1.2.[16] Another recent study of the demand elasticity for consumer durables found a median elasticity of demand of 1.4.[17]

We conclude that a price elasticity in the range of 1.0 to 2.0 is plausible for personal computers, with the lower end of this range agreeing with Brynjolfsson's 1.0 for computers as a whole. Thus, for most of our calculations we use 2.0 as our value for E_C, which is conservative in the sense that it gives a "low" estimate of the monopoly price.

With a demand elasticity of 2.0 for personal computers, the optimal monopoly price for the operating system is:

$$P_o = \frac{\$1{,}950}{2 - 1} = \$1{,}950$$

If the elasticity of demand is 1.5, which is still elastic by normal criteria, the monopoly price doubles, to $3,900.[18]

An operating system price in excess of $1,000 may seem high given that most copies of Windows 98 licensed through OEMs are priced at far less than $100, but such prices are not at all unheard of in the computer software business. For example, Lotus SmartSuite and Corel WordPerfect Suite, office suites that include a spreadsheet, a word processor, and other applications, sell at retail for prices in the range of $300 to $400, despite facing competition from each other and from Microsoft Office.[19] Stata, a widely used statistical program, sells for $965 for a single copy,[20] despite competing with products such as SAS, SPSS, and a variety of other, perhaps more specialized, products (EViews, TSP, LIMDEP, Shazam, S-Plus, Gauss, and other statistical or econometrics packages). AutoCAD, a professional drafting program, has a suggested retail price of $3,750.[21] Prices for other commercial operating systems that run on Intel-compatible hardware are frequently $250 or more per copy.[22]

Can Complementary Products Explain Low Prices for Windows?

In the real world, additional considerations also affect the pricing of products like operating systems. Microsoft offers many products that are complements to its consumer versions of Windows, such as Microsoft Office (word-processing software, spreadsheet software, and other office productivity applications), Microsoft Encarta (multimedia encyclopedia), and so forth. If

Microsoft succeeds in promoting one additional sale of a computer with Windows 98, it has some likelihood of making additional sales of complementary products such as these, whether through OEMs, retail suppliers, or other channels. Of course, additional sales of complementary products are not guaranteed: Not all computer users need the particular complements that Microsoft offers; and all of these complementary Microsoft products face substantial competition from products from other software vendors (Corel and Lotus, among others) – even restricting attention to competing products that still can run on Windows.

Because of the possibility of earning revenues from these complements, a monopolist over the operating system would have an incentive to temper its operating system prices. In contrast, a perfectly competitive supplier of a stand-alone operating system (a vendor of operating systems but not complementary products) would not have that incentive to keep prices low. The existence of complements can have noticeable impacts on pricing.

Suppose that net revenues (from complementary applications) equal to R are available for each unit of an operating system licensed through an OEM.[23] The profit-maximizing condition presented above leads to the following derivation:[24]

$$\frac{P_o - MC_o + R}{P_o} = \frac{1}{E_o}$$

$$\frac{P_o - 0 + R}{P_o} = \frac{1}{E_c\left(\frac{P_o}{P_c}\right)}$$

$$\frac{P_o + R}{P_o} = \frac{P_c}{E_c P_o}$$

$$1 + \frac{R}{P_o} = \frac{\$1{,}950 + P_o}{E_c P_o}$$

Solving this for the profit-maximizing price leads to the following expression:

$$P_o = \frac{\$1{,}950 - R * E_c}{E_c - 1}$$

According to Microsoft's 1997 annual report, in fiscal 1997 the firm's gross revenues from its applications group ($5.39 billion) were approximately equal to its gross revenues from its platforms group ($5.97 billion), which includes operating systems. If the "applications" group as a whole is considered a complement to the "platforms" group as a whole, then (on average)

Microsoft's complementary gross revenues per OEM unit of Windows are similar in magnitude to its average price for Windows 98. Other variations are possible, but it seems highly unlikely that complementary gross revenues per OEM unit of Windows 98 are more than a small multiple of Microsoft's average price for Windows 98.

Suppose that Microsoft could expect to earn complementary net revenues of about $100 for each unit of Windows 98 that it licenses through OEMs; this figure is roughly double the average OEM price we are using ($50 per unit) and therefore corresponds to gross revenues that are more than double the OEM price of Windows.[25] Then, with a price elasticity for personal computers of 2.0, the profit-maximizing price is $1,750 instead of $1,950.[26] Thus, the availability of revenues from sales of complementary products still cannot explain the gap between Microsoft's actual OEM prices for Windows and what the short-run profit-maximizing price would appear to be – even if the complementary net revenues are several times as large as those we have used in these calculations.[27]

Microsoft's Windows Prices Are a Small Fraction of the Price a Monopolist Would Charge

Even if we account for sales of complementary products, the price actually charged by Microsoft for Windows is more than an order of magnitude lower than a firm would charge if it had the secure monopoly that many observers (including the Department of Justice) appear to believe it has. Table 1 summarizes the prices that a monopolist would charge for Windows under several assumptions about the elasticity of demand for personal computers and the importance of complementary sales. It reports these figures for two different assumptions about the demand for personal computers – a constant elasticity of demand schedule (so that the demand elasticity is constant at all prices) and a semi-log demand schedule (so that demand becomes more elastic at higher prices). The monopoly price ranges from a low of $900 (semi-log demand, elasticity=2, complementary net revenues = $100 per unit of Windows) to a high of $7,800 (constant elasticity demand, elasticity=1.25, zero complementary net revenues).

Microsoft's Prices Are Consistent With Its Facing a High Elasticity of Demand

If one had to place the $50 price of Windows somewhere along the spec-

***Table 1.* Monopoly Operating System Price Depends on Elasticity of Computer Demand, Complementary Net Revenues, and Shape of Demand Curve**

	CONSTANT ELASTICITY DEMAND			SEMI-LOGARITHMIC DEMAND		
Elasticity	**R=0**	**R=$50**	**R=$100**	**R=0**	**R=$50**	**R=$100**
1.25	$ 7,800	$ 7,550	$ 7,300	$ 1,600	$ 1,550	$ 1,500
1.50	$ 3,900	$ 3,750	$ 3,600	$ 1,333	$ 1,283	$ 1,233
1.75	$ 2,600	$ 2,483	$ 2,367	$ 1,143	$ 1,093	$ 1,043
2.00	$ 1,950	$ 1,850	$ 1,750	$ 1,000	$ 950	$ 900

Note: R is the net revenue from complements per unit of operating system; for the semi-logarithmic demand, the elasticities are assumed at a computer price of $2,000 and increase as the computer price gets higher.

Source: As noted in text.

trum of prices that could emerge from the usual static economic models, it would fall far closer to the price that would emerge from perfect competition (roughly marginal costs plus average development costs plus a return on those costs that compensates for the fact that most software investments do not pan out) than the price that would emerge from perfect monopoly (roughly $1,000 or more). As discussed in more detail in the fourth section, we believe that the answer to this apparent inconsistency – a "monopolist" who charges relatively low prices – is that Microsoft in fact faces a great deal of competition, from existing firms and from potential new entrants. Clearly it does not make sense to think of the demand elasticity for Windows as being derived entirely from the demand elasticity for personal computers. Microsoft prices Windows as low as it does because of several types of substitution, not just the substitution of other devices for personal computers: the substitution of personal computers that are not Intel-compatible for those that are; the substitution of other operating systems for Windows on Intel-compatible computers; continued use of existing computers (and their operating systems) by users forgoing the purchase of new units (with new operating systems); and piracy of Microsoft's operating systems.

Economists often use the elasticity of demand as a proxy for how much competition a firm faces. A higher elasticity of demand indicates that consumers have more substitution possibilities and that the firm's ability to raise prices is limited. It is possible to take the mathematical apparatus presented above and use it to answer the following question: At what elasticity of demand is the profit-maximizing price for Windows $50? With a constant-elasticity demand schedule, the demand elasticity equals:

$$E_c = \frac{P_o + C_c}{P_o + NR} = \frac{P_c}{P_o + NR}$$

where NR equals the average net revenues available from complements for every copy of Windows that Microsoft licenses. Inserting $50 for P_O and $2,000 for P_C yields an elasticity of demand of 40 when net revenues from complements are not available. Assuming that net revenues from complementary products are $100 per unit yields an elasticity of demand of 13. The elasticity of demand for Windows is similar to that for many narrowly defined brands for which there are many substitutes. For example, Tay and McCarthy found that price elasticities for particular types of vehicles ranged from 0.5 to 6.1;[28] Berry, Levinsohn, and Pakes found price elasticities for individual makes of cars in the range of about 3.1 to 6.8.[29] It therefore appears that Microsoft sets its prices as if it believes that it faces the kind of highly elastic demand curve that characterizes firms that produce products for which there are many readily available substitutes.

THE QUALITY-ADJUSTED REAL PRICE OF WINDOWS' CAPABILITIES HAS FALLEN

Microsoft therefore charges a "low" price for its operating system relative to the monopoly price. Moreover, its price is "low" taking into account the features that have been added to Windows. When Windows 1.0 was released in 1985, it was a limited operating environment that ran in conjunction with an operating system such as MS-DOS or its IBM-labeled twin, PC-DOS. Both Windows and MS-DOS were improved over the years through 1993, when Windows for Workgroups 3.11 and MS-DOS 6.2 were released; these were the last major products in the Windows 3.x and MS-DOS lines. Windows 95, released to great fanfare in August 1995, essentially combined the operating system underpinnings formerly provided by MS-DOS (and enhanced by Windows 3.x) with the graphical user interface formerly provided by Windows 3.x into a unified whole, with both the operating system and the GUI greatly improved. In this regard, Windows 95 became like other operating systems such as the Apple Macintosh operating system, IBM's OS/2 (for Intel-compatible hardware), and Microsoft's own Windows NT. Windows 95 went through several interim upgrades (installed by OEMs on new computers or [for most components] available as free downloads directly from Microsoft) and was replaced by Windows 98.

We compare the current OEM price for Windows 98 with the price that consumers would have had to pay in 1989 (before Windows 3.0 was released) for a fraction of the capabilities provided by Windows 98. This comparison is complicated by several factors:

• Until August 1995, a copy of MS-DOS (or a clone of MS-DOS) was needed to boot a system in order to run Windows. Windows 95 and its successor, Windows 98, are stand-alone operating systems. As a result, comparisons over time must include the price of the companion booting operating system, when relevant.

• Microsoft at various times has licensed new copies of Windows and MS-DOS to OEMs for installation on new computers, upgrades to end users for older versions of Windows and MS-DOS, and (at least for Windows) new copies (not upgrades) for end users who did not have an older version of Windows. In general, however, Microsoft has not licensed full MS-DOS products at retail to end users.

• Prices for OEM products are generally not available.

• Retail prices for various products vary in their availability.

• There is no obvious way to control for changes in product quality over time.

We deal with each of these problems in the following analysis.

Changes in Product Quality

The first popular version of Windows was 3.0, released in May 1990, typically running in conjunction with MS-DOS 4. When Windows 3.1 was released in April 1992, it typically ran in conjunction with MS-DOS 5. Versions of Windows for Workgroups (3.1 and 3.11) and MS-DOS (6.0, 6.2, 6.21, and 6.22) were released between October 1992 and June 1994. Windows for Workgroups was a full-fledged member of the Windows 3.x family of products, but it was priced slightly higher than Windows 3.1 and provided peer-to-peer networking. The staggered releases of MS-DOS and Windows 3.x provided an opportunity for Microsoft to ship improved MS-DOS components that were useful for Windows, such as disk caching software and memory managers.[30] Windows 95 simultaneously replaced MS-DOS and Windows 3.x when it was released in August 1995.[31] Windows 98 replaced Windows 95 in June 1998.

Important release dates and notable new capabilities of these products are summarized in Table 2. In general, capabilities that were introduced in one version of MS-DOS or Windows were retained in future versions, unless they were made obsolete.[32]

In some cases, the new capabilities of a given release of MS-DOS or Windows could have been provided with stand-alone utilities that were previously available. For example, PC Tools for DOS was a collection of utilities that, as of 1989, provided menu capabilities, file undelete, disk unformat, disk caching, a DOS shell for file management, disk backup, disk defragmenting, and communications; later versions added even more utilities. Its "desktop manager" included notepads, calculators, an appointment scheduler, and a cut-and-paste utility that could be used to transfer information from one DOS program to another. Other vendors in 1989 marketed utilities either singly (e.g., PC-KWIK for disk caching) or in combination (e.g., Norton Utilities, which partially overlapped the capabilities of PC Tools, other than the desktop manager). QEMM was a memory manager available in 1989, when MS-DOS had no such capabilities; later versions of QEMM enhanced the memory management capabilities of the memory managers built into even the last versions of MS-DOS and Windows 3.x. Also available in 1989, DESQview was a highly regarded, multitasking, windowed environment for running DOS-based programs. Various fax programs existed for DOS (such as BitFax); later fax programs for Windows 3.x (such as WinFax) made faxing from within Windows 3.x little more difficult than printing to a standard printer. Stacker was perhaps the best-known of the disk-compression packages, becoming available around the beginning of 1991. TCP/IP software for DOS and Windows 3.x became available from a number of vendors. Lantastic provided peer-to-peer networking for DOS and Windows 3.x computers.[33]

A number of other capabilities, however, could be duplicated only with great difficulty, if at all, before being integrated into Windows. The direct operating system support for printers, fonts, modems, and sound cards introduced in various versions of Windows all greatly simplified the prior state of affairs. Every DOS program that wanted to allow for printing with other than the plainest of text had to provide printer drivers for every popular printer, taking into account the fonts and other capabilities of each printer. The printer drivers installed with Windows 3.x took care of that for Windows-based programs. Much the same was true for communications packages, fax software, remote-control utilities, and other programs that needed to control modems; rather than develop drivers for every popular modem, the software vendors could rely on the modem drivers in Windows 95 and Windows 98. The same is true of games and, increasingly, mainstream business applications that use sound. Before sound cards became directly supported by Windows, these applications had to provide their own drivers for every popular sound card.

TrueType fonts fall into a slightly different category. To some extent, font-scaling utilities could be used in Windows 3.0. In practice, however, no application program could rely on the assurance that such a utility would be avail-

Table 2. **Release Dates and Summary of New Features of Major Versions of MS-DOS and Windows, 1990-1998**

Product	Date	New Capabilities
Windows 3.0	5/22/90	3D scroll bars Program Manager, File Manager, and Control Panel Improved memory management; Multitasking Printer support Desktop accessories (Recorder, etc.)
MS-DOS 5	6/11/91	Memory manager, task swapping, shell Undelete and unformat Full-screen editor Online help
Windows 3.1	4/6/92	TrueType fonts for screen and printers OLE for linking documents Drag and drop Start-up program launcher Sound-card support; multimedia functionality Improved disk caching, network support, print manager
Windows for Workgroups 3.1-3.11	10/27/92- 11/8/93	Peer-to-peer networking 32-bit file access; 32-bit disk access MSMail and Schedule+ clients
MS-DOS 6.0-6.22	3/30/93- 6/14/94	Improved memory management and optimization Disk compression, disk defragmentation Improved backup Antivirus utility
Windows 3.11	2/15/94	"Refresh release" – updated drivers, etc.
Windows 95	8/24/95	32-bit in most operations Improved GUI: Desktop, Start button, Taskbar, etc; Windows Explorer, Internet Explorer File viewing from within Explorer Long file names Dial-up networking TCP/IP Modem support MAPI mail client; fax Plug and play Peer-to-peer networking; network client support Preemptive multitasking
Windows 98	6/25/98	USB and other new hardware support Web TV support Multiple monitor support Vastly improved Internet capabilities (compared with first release of Windows 95) Automatic update features Greatly improved system diagnostic and repair utilities

Source: Various product manuals, reviews in the trade press, and *Computer Desktop Encyclopedia*.

able on a given computer, or on what fonts would be installed if such a utility were available.[34] The inclusion of TrueType font technology with Windows 3.1 finally guaranteed that a font-scaling utility would be available on every Windows 3.1 desktop, that some set of fonts (e.g., Times New Roman, Arial, Symbol, Courier New) would be available on those desktops, and that the fonts on the screen would match the fonts on the printed page. This helped cause an explosion of interest in Windows applications that could make use of these capabilities.

The capabilities of object linking and embedding (OLE), a method to link information between documents, were impossible to duplicate with DOS or Windows applications before they were supported in Windows 3.x. OLE permitted users to copy information from one Windows application and paste it into another – with a live link that would permit the target document to automatically reflect changes in the source document.

Value to Users of These Product Improvements

There probably do exist users of Windows 95 or Windows 98 who have little or no need for these enhancements to Windows that have been implemented over the years and who would have had no need for related capabilities before they were added to Windows. A person with no need for any of these capabilities, however, would not do *any* of the following:

- connect to a network (peer-to-peer networking, direct network support);
- use a modem (direct modem support, communications software, fax software, dialup networking);
- access the Internet (TCP/IP, FTP, and browsing support);
- print formatted documents (direct printer support, scalable fonts);
- play modern, multimedia games (direct sound card support, direct video support);
- link information between two documents (OLE);
- run multiple applications or large single applications (memory managers, task switching and/or multitasking);
- perform basic file and hard disk maintenance – including recovering deleted files, defragmenting hard disks, marking bad clusters (undelete, defragmenting, and disk-scanning capabilities);
- compress a disk to postpone the need to purchase a larger hard disk (disk compression).

In contrast, a substantial number of users of Windows 95 or Windows 98 – perhaps even a majority – are likely to need most of these capabilities. Disk compression is perhaps the least important; with rapidly falling prices for hard disks, it may be easier (but not cheaper) to install a second hard disk than to activate the disk compression software in Windows 98. Quite commonly, however, a user in a corporate setting needs many of these capabilities, even sound card support – modern business applications are increasingly using sound. Quite commonly, a small office or home business user would need most of these capabilities. And also quite commonly, a home non-business user would need most of these capabilities (with the various network capabilities being used to connect to the Internet or to office networks).

Trying to develop a year-by-year, quality-adjusted price index for Windows appears to be impossible. It is possible, however, to take some snapshots of the prices for Windows, DOS, and various utilities needed in the past to provide some semblance of the capabilities available in Windows 98. Table 3 summarizes the combinations of non-Windows products as of 1989 (before Windows 3.0 was released) needed to provide some of the useful features of Windows 98. In 1989, many important capabilities of Windows 98 were either unavailable (e.g., file linking) or not readily available (e.g., cross-application support for scalable fonts, printers, modems, and sound cards). Some other capabilities would have been either irrelevant (e.g., Web browsing) or less widely useful (e.g., TCP/IP support) in 1989 than in 1998.

In 1989, many of the capabilities of Windows 98 could have been obtained by using a combination of MS-DOS 4.01, PC Tools 5.5, QEMM386, and DESQview, although with much reduced ease of installation and ease of use compared with Windows 98. Table 4 summarizes what these combinations of products would have cost at retail in 1989 and 1998. These comparisons are complicated by the fact that Microsoft never sold MS-DOS at retail, and prior to 1991 (with the release of MS-DOS 5) it never sold MS-DOS upgrades at retail.[35] They are also complicated by the fact that Microsoft's OEM prices for MS-DOS and Windows are not publicly available.

Based on an estimated price of $50 for copies of Windows 98 licensed through OEMs, we see that the capabilities included in Windows 98 cost the user far less than did even a small fraction of those capabilities in 1989. Even ignoring inflation, the $50 price for Windows is less than half the 1989 price for DESQview 386 (see note 36) alone. In August 1989, the combined prices of DESQview 386 and PC Tools totaled $194. This total excludes any implicit price for MS-DOS. Public data on average OEM prices for MS-DOS are not available, but the prices were substantially less than the price of Windows 98. The consumer price index[37] rose approximately 31 percent between August 1989 and August 1998. In order for the older prices to be made comparable

Table 3. **Operating Systems and Utilities Needed in 1989 and 1998 for Similar Capabilities**

Capabilities	1989 Product	1998 Product
Booting system	MS-DOS 4.01	Windows 98
Memory management	QEMM386	Windows 98
File management	PC Tools Deluxe 5.5	Windows 98
Backup	PC Tools Deluxe 5.5	Windows 98
Disk utilities (e.g., defragment, scan, undelete)	PC Tools Deluxe 5.5	Windows 98
Multitasking	DESQview	Windows 98
Scalable fonts, printer support, modem support, sound card support	None (generally not available)	Windows 98
TCP/IP, network support, dialup networking, browsing, other Internet capabilities	None (generally not relevant)	Windows 98
Disk compression	None	Windows 98
File linking	None	Windows 98
Communications software	PC Tools Deluxe 5.5	Windows 98

Sources: Various product manuals, reviews in the trade press, and *Computer Desktop Encyclopedia.*

Table 4. **Prices of Products Needed for Comparable Capabilities: 1989 and 1998**

Product	August 1989	August 1998
MS-DOS (OEM)	?	NA
DESQview 386[36] 1.0	$115	NA
PC Tools Deluxe 5.5	$79	NA
Windows 98 (OEM)	NA	$50
Total in Nominal Dollars	$194+MS-DOS	$50
Total in 1998 Dollars	$254+MS-DOS	$50

Sources: OEM price for Windows 98 assumed to be $50. All other prices are for mail-order purchases from PC Connection, a major mail-order vendor for over a decade. August 1989 prices from advertisement in that month's issue of *PC Magazine.*

with the 1998 prices, the August 1989 figure should be multiplied by 1.31. In 1989, it would have cost consumers $254 (in 1998 dollars), plus the cost of MS-DOS, to obtain a fraction of the capabilities that later cost $50 with Windows 98.

One might argue that only so-called power users of personal computers would actually have spent over $200 per computer for utility software in the days before Windows 3.0 became popular (despite the fact that many people did indeed purchase these and other utilities, some similar and others not). If so, then the comparisons presented here might be considered to be biased in favor of Windows 98 – they include too much software for 1989. An opposing argument, however, seems more likely to be valid: the non-power users are the ones who gained most from the emergence of Windows. The gains in ease of use, in configuring and using modems, sound cards, and printers, in connecting to the Internet, and in using screen fonts that match printer fonts – these are the gains that probably matter most to people who are not power users. And these gains are not reflected in any way in the price comparisons presented here.

The inescapable conclusion to be drawn from these figures is that the quality-adjusted, real price of obtaining the capabilities reflected in Windows 98 has fallen sharply since 1989. This is true for capabilities that were reasonably available as of 1989. It would be even more true if the comparison could reflect capabilities that were not available in 1989 but would have been highly valued had they been available (e.g., printer, modem, sound card, and scalable font support).

Comparing Operating System and Hardware Prices

As mentioned above, some observers have attempted to compare pricing over time for Windows with pricing over time for personal computers or microprocessors. Such comparisons are meaningless. The products have different cost structures and different rates of technological change. There is no more reason for the prices of software and computers to behave similarly over time than there is for the prices of gold and *Golden Books* to behave similarly.

Microprocessors and personal computer hardware embody tremendous advances in technology for semiconductors and electronics. As a result, there is good reason for the prices of personal computers (holding quality constant) to have fallen markedly over, say, the last decade. Alternatively put, there is good reason for a $3,000 computer today to be much more powerful than a $3,000 computer a decade ago.

Writing computer software, whether today or a decade ago, takes time and effort on the part of computer programmers. Technological change in programming is quite different from technological change in hardware. Programming tools have certainly improved over the past decade, but so have user expectations for computer programs. Programs like operating systems have, on average, gotten much larger over the past decade. Whether programming tools have improved programmer productivity faster than user demands have increased program complexity and size is not self-evident. In general, however, there is no reason to believe that the costs of writing an operating system today are less than the costs of writing an operating system a decade ago – today's operating system is much more complex than that of a decade ago. (The marginal costs to Microsoft of licensing an operating system through an OEM are approximately the same today as they were a decade ago: close to zero.)

In general, then, there is no cost-based reason for the price of Windows today to be less than the price of Windows a decade ago. The "Windows" of today is far more capable than the "Windows" of 1993 and the "Windows" of 1988. In contrast, there do exist cost-based reasons for personal computer hardware to have gotten both less expensive and more powerful over time.

MICROSOFT HAS FACED, AND CONTINUES TO FACE, COMPETITION

Microsoft charges low prices for Windows and has steadily improved the quality of its operating system not because it is benevolent: Vigorous competition has forced Microsoft to behave this way. Microsoft has faced competition since it released its first operating system in 1981, and it continues to face competition today. This competition has occurred at many levels, involving the speed, power, and ease of use of operating systems. The discussion below concentrates on major products visible to the public. It ignores numerous other products (e.g., OS-9, Theos, CTOS, QNX, and PTS-DOS) that run on Intel-compatible hardware.[38]

Entry in the Past[39]

Microsoft has faced operating system competition at all times since its first operating system was released. When IBM started to ship its first personal computer, in 1981, it announced the availability of three operating systems: PC-DOS (written by Microsoft for IBM); CP/M-86 (from Digital Research), and the UCSD p-System (from Softech Microsystems). CP/M-86 had the advantage of being a rewrite of the most popular operating system for Intel's 8-bit microprocessors (8080 and 8085) and related CPUs from other vendors (Zilog's Z80). The p-System had the advantage of running on multiple hardware platforms (such as the Apple II and the 8080/8085/Z80 computers that typically could run CP/M). PC-DOS had the advantages of being much cheaper than CP/M-86 ($40 instead of $240), immediately available with applications (CP/M-86 was not immediately available and had no immediately available applications from IBM), and much faster than the p-System. PC-DOS won the early race for popularity on the IBM PC. Of course, the early IBM PC faced competition from the Apple II and the many brands of computers running CP/M, such as Osborne, Kaypro, Xerox, Radio Shack, Cromemco, IMSAI, Morrow, and many others.[40]

When Microsoft began licensing its operating system to OEMs under its own branded name (MS-DOS), it faced competition not only from CP/M-86 and the p-System but also from its near-twin, PC-DOS. IBM sold its version of the operating system at retail. As a result, consumers could purchase a copy of PC-DOS and run it on a "clone" of the IBM-PC, unless the manufacturer of the clone had customized its hardware so that a generic operating system would not run properly.[41] An OEM that did not like the license terms offered by Microsoft could always tell its customers to pick up a copy of PC-DOS. Even after PC-DOS and MS-DOS stopped being virtually identical (beginning with version 6 in 1993, they had different utilities for memory management, for example), a consumer could purchase a copy of PC-DOS for use on non-IBM computers. Microsoft's MS-DOS therefore faced competition from the essentially identical PC-DOS.

In the early to mid-1980s, Microsoft had to weather several other attacks. Digital Research continued to produce new products, such as its Concurrent DOS. Various vendors began porting operating systems from other hardware platforms to the IBM PC. Microsoft itself had developed a 16-bit version of Unix (Xenix), but other vendors were active as well. Pick ported its operating system from larger computers to the IBM PC.

Competition arose on other fronts as well. Apple's Lisa (1983), followed by its Macintosh (1984), introduced a graphical user interface (GUI) to the general public. Several vendors became interested in developing interfaces for the IBM PC that would provide some combination of windowing, multitasking, and a GUI. VisiCorp, publisher of VisiCalc, showed its integrated software system VisiOn at the fall Comdex show in 1982. This integrated operating system/applications package introduced windows technology to the IBM-PC world of hardware. Unfortunately, it could not run DOS programs, it was slow and buggy, and it was expensive. In September 1984, Digital Research announced GEM (Graphics Environment Manager), which provided a graphical interface but no multitasking; this product made at least some headway when Tandy (Radio Shack) announced that it would offer the product for its computers. Quarterdeck Office Systems developed a highly regarded product that could multitask standard DOS programs in windows, although its interface was not graphical. Originally called DESQ, it later became DESQview.

In February 1985, IBM released TopView, a multitasking program that also provided windows but not graphics. Microsoft announced Windows in November 1983 and finally shipped it in November 1985.

GEM Desktop, TopView, DESQview, and the first release of Windows all differed fundamentally from the failed VisiOn: all were run after a computer had been booted with MS-DOS or PC-DOS. All provided windows for different applications. GEM and Windows provided a graphical interface, whereas TopView and DESQview did not. DESQview excelled at multitasking DOS programs. The other three programs provided a platform for which software developers could write new applications; several GEM applications were available from Digital Research. GEM could run standard DOS applications, but not in a window; nor could it multitask or switch between DOS applications. In a review of these programs in their infancy, an article in *PC Magazine* presciently predicted that at most one would prosper:

> Consequently, it seems likely that only one of these alternative operating environments will survive. If none of them makes it, then something else will. The Macintosh proved that a command line interface is unnecessary and antiquated. The once-ubiquitous DOS prompt may be a dying breed.[42]

TopView was withdrawn from the market in mid-1987. GEM eventually found a home as the operating environment for Atari computers. DESQview attracted a dedicated group of followers until the capabilities and growing popularity of Windows 3.0 (released in 1990) eliminated the need for a program whose strength was multitasking DOS programs. Microsoft kept developing and enhancing its Windows product. At the end of 1987, Microsoft started shipping Windows 2 – and its own first high-quality Windows application, Excel for Windows.

The operating system wars continued on other fronts. IBM and Microsoft had cooperated in developing a new operating system called OS/2. Designed to be more powerful and stable than MS-DOS, it was initially released (without a graphical front end) in December 1987, but met with little success. The first version of OS/2 with a GUI (1.1) shipped October 31, 1988 – but still with relatively poor support for DOS applications and relatively few device drivers to support hardware other than IBM's.

In mid-1988 came DR DOS, the latest operating system product from Digital Research. This time, however, Digital Research released a product that attempted to be compatible with MS-DOS, much as PC-DOS was, but without the advantage of relying on the same underlying operating system code as MS-DOS. It provided some additional utilities and capabilities, but it also attempted to run DOS programs in exactly the same ways that MS-DOS did.

Subsequent releases by Digital Research of improved products put pressure on Microsoft to improve MS-DOS, with MS-DOS 5 shipping in 1991 and MS-DOS 6 in 1993. Under the terms of the agreements between IBM and Microsoft, IBM also released new versions of PC-DOS in the same time period.

In May 1990, Microsoft began to ship Windows 3.0, the first truly successful version of the product. Some of the remaining major gaps in capabilities were addressed two years later with the release of Windows 3.1, which provided true what-you-see-is-what-you-get capabilities to Windows applications (along with other features). These improvements finally moved Windows ahead of a host of other products that for the most part merely ran on top of DOS: GEOS, a graphical windowing environment running on top of DOS, released to substantial praise in late 1990; various multitasking environments, including DESQview 386, VM/386 MultiTasker, Omniview 386, and Vmos/3; and task-switching programs such Software Carousel, HeadRoom, and other products.

About the time that OS/2 1.1 shipped in late 1988, Microsoft began work on its own advanced operating system – what eventually became Windows NT. In late 1990, the Joint Development Agreement between IBM and Microsoft, which had led to the development of OS/2 (among other products) unraveled. Microsoft emerged with control of the NT work, and IBM emerged with OS/2. The first version of Windows NT finally was released in July 1993 – more than a year after OS/2 2.0, which finally won praise for support of DOS and Windows applications. IBM promoted this version of OS/2 as a "Better DOS than DOS" and a "Better Windows than Windows."[43]

After its agreement with Microsoft was dissolved, IBM formed an alliance (Taligent) in 1991 with Apple to develop an object-oriented operating system (based on Apple's Pink) that would run on future computers to be built by each firm. That partnership was essentially dissolved when Taligent became an IBM subsidiary in 1996, with no operating system emerging from the joint venture.

Meanwhile, Unix had not disappeared; to the contrary, it was thriving. In 1988, NeXT introduced its computer running a Unix-based operating system with a GUI, NeXTStep. When NeXT later gave up on the hardware business, it ported its operating system to other platforms, including Intel-compatible computers. NeXT has since been purchased by Apple; originally, Apple expected NeXTStep to form the basis for future operating systems for Apple's computers, but those plans have since changed. Also in 1988, the Open Software Foundation was founded by a consortium of seven companies, including IBM, to promote standards in the fractured world of Unix. Work undertaken by the OSF eventually led to Motif, a standard GUI for use with different versions of Unix. This work built on the X-Windows development performed earlier at MIT to produce a windowing environment for Unix. Several vendors (such as SCO and Sun) currently sell versions of Unix that run on Intel-compatible computers, and yet more versions (e.g., from Sun, IBM, Hewlett Packard, and other firms) run on other computers that compete with Intel-compatible computers to varying degrees.

Microsoft has continued to release improved versions of its operating systems. Major milestones were the releases of Windows 95 (August 1995), Windows NT 4.0 (July 1996), Windows 98 (June 1998), and Windows XP (November 2001). IBM has also continued to improve OS/2, with major new releases in 1994 (version 3) and 1996 (version 4).

In summary, Microsoft's operating systems for Intel-compatible computers have faced competition since they were first released. This competition has occurred at various levels: from operating systems that were not compatible (e.g., CP/M-86, Unix); from alternative operating environments (e.g., TopView, DESQview, GEOS, GEM) that ran on DOS; from compatible operating systems (e.g., DR DOS); from advanced, compatible operating systems with a GUI (e.g., OS/2 2.0 and later); and from other hardware platforms that compete with Intel-compatible computers (e.g., the Macintosh and PowerPC, NeXT). And Microsoft's MS-DOS had to compete against a near-twin: PC-DOS.

Entry Today

Microsoft faces competition from existing operating systems that run on Intel-compatible hardware (and often other hardware as well), such as OS/2, BeOS, Linux, Unixware, Solaris, and so forth. Microsoft also faces competition from operating systems running on other hardware, such as the Macintosh and proprietary hardware from other firms. Besides the Macintosh operating system, this includes BeOS (running on Apple hardware), Linux (running on various hardware), and Solaris (running on Sun's hardware), as well as other proprietary versions of Unix running on proprietary hardware. Microsoft also faces competition from new and emerging technologies, some of which are currently visible and others of which are not.

The flurry of interest in the "network computer," an example of a new or emerging technology, has posed a threat to Microsoft, at least for some computer uses. Objectives for the network computer included low initial cost and ease of administration – with standardized hardware, no local storage (e.g., no hard or floppy disks), a simple operating system not based on Windows, and a browser as a user interface.[44] Widespread acceptance of the network computer could have substantially cut into sales of personal computers running Windows. To date, the network computer has not succeeded in capturing large numbers of desktops. It did, however, encourage computer manufacturers to release low-cost computers and Microsoft to reduce the administration costs (initial setup, software maintenance, and so forth) for networked computers running Windows.

Currently Linux and the BeOS may provide the biggest near-term competition to Microsoft, although the threat of the network computer has not disappeared. Both are currently available for Intel-compatible hardware (and other hardware as well). Both are Posix-compliant,[45] with Linux essentially being a flavor of Unix and the BeOS sometimes described as Unix-like.[46] Linux is a freeware product that is available (with technical support and various utilities and applications) from commercial vendors such as Red Hat and Caldera. Linux is already popular for Web servers and file servers. Commercial software firms (such as Netscape, Oracle, and Informix) have plans to port applications to Linux. If desktop applications follow (such as Corel's announced port of WordPerfect Suite), Linux could displace Windows on a substantial number of both servers and desktops. The BeOS is a commercial product developed and marketed by Be, Inc., with initial applications targeted at video and audio processing involving multiple processing threads and huge file sizes. If its file handling proves superior to that of other operating systems, it could become a desirable platform for other applications software as well.

The Palm OS, EPOC, and similar operating systems for hand-held computers currently provide a different, perhaps more distant, type of competition for Microsoft's desktop operating systems. The Palm OS is used in 3Com's PalmPilot series of hand-held computers, and EPOC is used in Psion's line. Hand-held computers with these operating systems currently compete directly with other models running Microsoft's Windows CE; product reviews to date have generally rated the Palm and Psion products as superior to those running Windows CE. At present, none of these operating systems (including Windows CE) will run on a desktop (or laptop) computer. In principle, however, there is no reason why the vendors of these products could not do the reverse of what Microsoft has attempted: Microsoft has tried to write a scaled-down, Windows-style operating system that can run within the current hardware limits of the hand-held personal computers; these other operating systems could in principle be scaled up to run on low-cost desktop personal computers. Psion has agreements with major cellular phone manufacturers

(Ericsson, Nokia, and Motorola) for a joint venture (Symbian) to develop and market versions of its operating system for devices with cellular phone capabilities. Microsoft has announced that hardware vendors are developing the AutoPC, a computer running Windows CE that would handle various tasks in automobiles. And Microsoft's Windows CE 2.1 runs on mini-notebook computers that are larger than the current class of hand-held computers. Given that these operating systems already are being ported to various hardware platforms (including the movement of CE to the mini-notebook), it seems plausible that they could be ported to desktop computers as well.

CONCLUSIONS

Based solely on market share, it would be easy to conclude that Microsoft has a near-monopoly in operating systems for personal computers. Yet, as we have shown, Microsoft's price for Windows is a small fraction of what a monopolist would charge. Furthermore, that price is much less than what consumers would have had to pay in the past for even a fraction of the current capabilities of Windows. The answer to this apparent puzzle is that although Microsoft has what would appear to be great market power based on traditional static measures of competition, it has faced, and continues to face, substantial dynamic competition from a host of competitors or potential competitors. Some of these competitors (e.g., IBM, Sun) currently sell products that run on the same hardware as Microsoft's products. Others sell products that run on other hardware (e.g., Sun, 3Com, Apple). Others could arise from the vast pools of highly mobile and talented programmers and venture capitalists who could be persuaded to back the next software superstar. Entry into operating systems for personal computers has occurred repeatedly over the two decades of the industry's existence. There is no reason to believe that entry has suddenly come to a halt.

In typical manufacturing industries, firms with high market shares arise because of high barriers to entry. They own key patents, have exclusive access to essential natural resources, own highly specialized and expensive physical capital that has large economies of scale, or have government-granted exclusive franchises. Microsoft has none of these barriers working in its favor. In the short run, it benefits from "network effects." Users care not only about the quality of the operating system and its price but also about the availability of a rich set of applications software that will run on the operating system. These effects mean that at any time, one operating system is likely to capture most of the market. That position, however, is not protected in the "longer" run, which in the computer industry is measured in months or a few years, not the decades that may be required for capital turnover in other industries.

The market for operating systems is best seen as an overlapping series of races or contests to become the "superstar." The odds against any one contestant are long, but the rewards are sufficiently great – and the factors of production sufficiently mobile and readily supplied – that a steady stream of contestants is guaranteed. The firm that rests on its success and fails to innovate will quickly be overtaken by other firms that seize the opportunity to take advantage of advances in hardware that open up new possibilities. The firm that tries to exploit its ostensible monopoly through high prices will quickly find that lower-priced clones claim the market, or that users will switch to a new platform with its own set of applications. Only through a combination of frequent innovation and relatively low prices can the leader in such a race maintain its position.

[1] According to data from International Data Corporation, in 1997 shipments of Windows NT, Windows 95, and Windows 3.x accounted for 87.5 percent of "worldwide PC/client operating environment shipments," excluding shipments of operating systems from Apple. In principle, these shipments include "new systems and competitive upgrades" but exclude "upgrades and updates." International Data Corporation, *1998 Worldwide Markets and Trends*, Report C2348, May 1998, Table 2.

[2] Michael Moeller, "Pegging the Cost of an OS," *PC Week*, May 4, 1998, p. 19; Mark Boslet, "Microsoft Keeps Pricing Steady for Its Windows 95 Software," *The Wall Street Journal Interactive Edition*, March 23, 1998.

[3] David S. Sibley, "Declaration of David S. Sibley," *U.S. v. Microsoft Corp.*, May 15, 1998 (redacted), p. 5. Sibley also asserts (p. 7) that "even if the product market were more broadly defined to include desktop operating systems for all PCs, such as those offered by Apple and UNIX that do not use Intel (or Intel-compatible) microprocessors, Microsoft's market share would fall only slightly ... and its monopoly power would remain." Sibley is an economist who was scheduled to testify for the U.S. Department of Justice in this lawsuit. He was withdrawn as a witness before the start of trial. The other economist scheduled to testify at trial on behalf of the Department of Justice, Franklin Fisher, states in his declaration (p. 13) that he reviewed Sibley's declaration and was "in agreement with its contents."

[4] According to Sibley, $65 is the royalty that Microsoft most commonly charges computer manufacturers for copies of Windows 95 installed on new personal computers; this excludes up to about $20 in discounts that computer manufacturers can earn "for meeting all of the conditions specified in Microsoft's Market Development Agreement" (p. 6).

[5] Professor Sibley does not say this exactly. He says that operating systems for Intel x86-compatible computers constitute a market because a hypothetical monopolist could profitably raise the price of the operating system in such a market by 10 percent. This method for defining a market is based on the DOJ *Horizontal Merger Guidelines*. He then concludes

that Microsoft has a monopoly over operating systems because its share of operating systems for the Intel x86-compatible computers exceeds 90 percent and because he believes that entry barriers are high for operating systems.

[6] In his analysis, Sibley uses $1,500 as a representative price for a personal computer. According to data from IDC, the average price of a personal computer sold in 1997 was $2,082 (International Data Corporation, *Worldwide PC Forecast Update, 1997-2002*, Report R1560, May 1998, Table 3).

[7] A number of issues can complicate the real-world calculation of marginal cost. In general, marginal cost can be thought of as the amount by which a firm's total cost would increase if output were to increase by one unit. In the case of Microsoft's licensing of operating system software to OEMs (computer manufacturers) for installation on new computers, the marginal cost to Microsoft is typically very low, approaching zero. For large computer manufacturers, Microsoft's licensing arrangements are pure intellectual property agreements; generally, no physical goods change hands, and the computer manufacturer bears the costs of duplicating disks, printing manuals, and supporting customers. In making retail sales of upgrades, Microsoft incurs substantial marginal costs due to these factors as well as packaging and distribution costs. This section concentrates on Microsoft's pricing for OEM licenses, which account for the vast majority of units of Windows distributed.

[8] For convenience, the price elasticity of demand is treated here as a positive number. It can be thought of as the percentage by which the quantity demanded will fall when price increases by 1 percent. When the price elasticity of demand equals one, the revenue gain per unit from a small price increase would be exactly offset by the revenue loss from the lower volume due to that price increase. The price elasticity of demand for a given product may be approximately constant over substantial ranges for price. In general, however, the price elasticity of demand is expected to rise eventually as price rises.

[9] Under the conditions for which this profit-maximizing condition is valid, a monopolist will never set prices such that the price elasticity of demand is smaller than one. If the elasticity were smaller than one, a monopolist could increase revenues by increasing the price; an increase in revenues, with output constant or falling, will always increase profits.

[10] Dataquest, *Personal Computers Worldwide: Market Statistics*, April 20, 1998, Table 2-1.

[11] The average personal computer price was $2,082 in 1997, according to International Data Corporation, *Worldwide PC Forecast Update, 1997-2002*, May 1998, Table 3.

[12] According to Sibley (p. 6), "the licensing fee for the vast majority of the operating systems currently licensed by Microsoft to OEMs is approximately $65," but available discounts can bring that down to as little as $45. The midpoint of this range is $55. Articles in the press have suggested that "Windows 95 sells for about $45 a copy to computer makers who buy in quantity," and that Windows 98 is similarly priced. Mark Boslet, "Microsoft Keeps Pricing Steady for Its Windows 95 Software," *The Wall Street Journal Interactive Edition*, March 23, 1998. We use a price of $50 as representative of the average price paid by OEMs for licensing Windows.

[13] This equation is valid only when the elasticity is greater than one; for Ec less than one, the monopoly price is infinite.

[14] Erik Brynjolfsson, "Some Estimates of the Contribution of Information Technology to Consumer Welfare," *MIT Sloan School Working Paper* 3647-094, January 1994.

[15] In addition to our own professional experience, we have looked at a variety of economics textbooks and review articles on the subject. For a classic study on the subject, see Hendrik S. Houthakker and Lester D. Taylor, *Consumer Demand in the United States: Analyses and Projections* (Cambridge: Harvard University Press), 1970.

[16] Patrick McCarthy, "Market Price and Income Elasticities of New Vehicle Demands," *Review of Economics and Statistics*, 78(3), August 1996, pp. 543-547.

[17] P. M. Parker and R. Neelamegham, "Price Elasticity Dynamics over the Product Life Cycle: A Study of Consumer Durables," INSEAD Working Paper 96/71/MKT, Table 3.

[18] These calculations assume that the price elasticity of computer demand would remain constant as the operating system price (and therefore the computer price as well) rises to the monopoly level. If the price elasticity of demand for personal computers is proportional to the price (as is true for one popular form of demand equation, the semi-logarithmic), then the profit-maximizing operating system price would be $1,000 if the price elasticity of personal computer demand is 2.0 at a computer price of $2,000.

[19] As of August 28, 1998, PC Connection (a major mail-order firm) was offering Windows 95/NT versions of Corel WordPerfect Suite 8 Professional for $350 and Lotus SmartSuite Millenium for $400.

[20] Volume discounts can bring the price down to as low as $245 for extra copies after the first 50. Pricing information obtained directly from Stata, Inc.

[21] Information Access Company, *Computer Select* (CD-ROM), August 1998.

[22] For example, the retail price of IBM's OS/2 Warp 4.0 was $250 (PC Connection, http://www.pcconnection.com, August 5, 1998); the price of Sun's Solaris 2.6 was $318 (Access Micro, http://www.accessmicro.com, August 5, 1998); and the price of SCO's Unixware V2.1.2 Personal Edition was $497, while that of its OpenServer Desktop was $582 (Insight, http://www.insight.com, August 5, 1998).

[23] These revenues are like marginal costs that are negative rather than positive.

[24] We are assuming here that prices of applications software are determined by competition among applications software vendors. The operating system vendor takes as given the price of applications and does not simultaneously choose the price of applications software and the operating system.

[25] For example, suppose that the variable costs for the complementary revenues amounted to one-third of the gross revenues. If so, then gross complementary revenues of $150 per copy of Windows (three times the OEM price we are using here) would lead to net revenues of $100.

[26] Assuming that the price elasticity of demand for personal computers is proportional to the price of those computers, revenues from complementary products reduce the profit-maximizing price for the operating system by the amount of those revenues.

[27] One alternative approach to the one presented here would be to assume that the demand for computers depends not just on the computer price but on the sum of that price plus the prices of the applications software that will be used with the computer. This approach yields the same general conclusion: Complements cannot explain the low price for Windows.

[28] Richard S. Tay and Patrick S. McCarthy, "Demand Oriented Policies for Improving Market Share in the U.S. Automobile Industry," *International Journal of Transport Economics* 18 (1991), pp. 151-166.

[29] Steven Berry, James Levinsohn, and Ariel Pakes, "Automobile Prices in Market Equilibrium," *Econometrica*, July 1995, pp. 841-890.

[30] For example, Windows 3.1 shipped with a new version of Smartdrive, which performed disk caching.

[31] A substantial fraction of computer buyers continued to purchase computers equipped with MS-DOS and Windows 3.x through the end of 1996; Microsoft did not discontinue Windows 3.1/3.11 until the end of 1997. "Microsoft Pulls Last Plug on Windows 3.1 Sales," *PC Week*, September 1, 1997, p. 51.

[32] Exceptions do exist, however. For example, the unformat and antivirus utilities provided with MS-DOS 6.x were eliminated from Windows 95. The Recorder utility that came with Windows 3.0 was also dropped from Windows 95.

[33] Either at home or in the office, one of the authors installed (often painfully) and used almost every non-Windows product mentioned in this paragraph – and more – except Lantastic and TCP/IP software. He waited until Windows for Workgroups was available to install a home network, and he didn't need TCP/IP software until after Windows 95 was available.

[34] Some late DOS and Windows 3.0 applications shipped with font-scaling utilities, such as Adobe's Type Manager and Bitstream's FaceLift.

[35] Users who wanted MS-DOS upgrades had to get them through the manufacturers of their computers.

[36] DESQview 386 was a bundle of QEMM386 and DESQview, with a price for the bundle that was less than the sum of the component prices.

[37] Urban consumers, all items.

[38] These are among the many bootable operating systems that the software product System Commander claims to support on Intel-compatible hardware. If a user installs multiple operating systems on a computer, System Commander is a product that lets the user choose, at boot time, which of those operating systems to run.

[39] This section draws from many sources, particularly the following: Stephen Manes and Paul Andrews, *Gates* (New York: Touchstone), 1993; Ken Polsson, *Chronology of Events in the History of Microcomputers*, http://www.islandnet.com/~kpolsson/comphist.htm, August 30, 1998; David R. Brousell, "MS-DOS, CP-M, Unix Battle for Domination in Market Demanding Multi-tasking, Multi-User Capability," *Electronic News*, September 26, 1983; Frank Delaney, "The Deal of the Century," *History of the Microcomputer Revolution*, 1995, http://exo.com/~wts/mits0013.HTM, August 30, 1998; *Computer Desktop Encyclopedia*, 1998 (as distributed by Information Access Company, *Computer Select* [CD-ROM], August 1998); *Newton's Telecom Dictionary* (as distributed by Information Access Company, *Computer Select* [CD-ROM], August 1998); "The History of Computing," Lexikon Services, 1998; "The History of Windows," *PC Magazine*, June 25, 1998; Brian Carr, "Making DOS Work Overtime," *PC Magazine*, October 16, 1990, pp. 196-227.

[40] One Web site offers conversion services for files stored on floppy disks for approximately 150 different CP/M-based computers. Trio Company of Cheektowaga, "CP/M File & Document Conversions," http://www.triousa.com, accessed September 7, 1998.

[41] In the early 1980s, some OEMs (such as DEC) introduced computers that were not perfectly compatible with IBM's. Microsoft developed customized versions of MS-DOS for these firms. Even some OEMs that produced what were widely regarded as "clones,"

such as Compaq, sometimes contracted with Microsoft for customized versions of MS-DOS. For example, the first Compaq Deskpro was an 8086-based computer that was much faster than a standard IBM PC. Some programs, however, did not operate properly at that higher speed. The MODE command in Compaq-DOS could be used to toggle the computer between high-speed and standard-speed operation.

[42] Charles Petzold, "Operating in a New Environment," *PC Magazine*, February 25, 1986, p. 115.

[43] Joe Salemi, "OS/2 2.0: Does It Fulfill the Promise?" *PC Magazine*, April 28, 1992, p. 165.

[44] The network computer has been designed for network settings. The computer would load all of its applications software from a network server and save all files to a network server. In a corporate setting, the network server would be connected to the corporate network. In a home setting, the network setting would be connected to the home user's Internet service provider.

[45] Posix is an acronym for "Portable Operating System Interface for Unix, a set of IEEE and ISO standards that define an interface between programs and operating systems. By designing their programs to conform to Posix, developers have some assurance that their software can be easily ported to Posix-compliant operating systems. This includes most varieties of Unix as well as Windows NT." Source: http://www.pcwebopedia.com/POSIX.htm, August 4, 1998. Linux is fully Posix-compliant, and the BeOS is partially compliant and as of this writing is moving toward full compliance. The Be Operating System, http://www.be.com/products/beos/beos_ds.html, August 6, 1998.

[46] Peter Wayner, "The Be-All-You-Can-Be OS," *Byte*, December 1997.

References

AccessMicro, http://www.accessmicro.com, accessed August 5, 1998.

Alsop, Stewart. 1992. "Intelligent Life Discovered at IBM: OS/2 to Be Bundled," *Infoworld*, May 4, p. 4.

Anthony, Robert S. 1998. "The Ultimate Personal Peripheral," *PC Magazine*, March 10.

Barr, Christopher. 1993. "Stacker 3.1 for Windows & DOS," *PC Magazine*, September 14, p. 124.

Be, Inc., "Be Product Price List," 1998, http://www.be.com/purchase/price_lists/index.html, accessed August 6, 1998.

Be, Inc., "The BeOS Features: Is BeOS Similar to Unix?" 1998, http://www.be.com/support/faqs/, accessed August 6, 1998.

Be, Inc., "The BeOS Features: Is BeOS Unix-Based (or Mach-Based)?" 1998, http://www.be.com/support/faqs/, accessed August 6, 1998.

Be, Inc., "The Be Operating System," 1998, http://www.be.com/products/beos/beos_ds.html, accessed August 6, 1998.

Berry, Steven, Levinsohn, James, Pakes, Ariel. 1995. "Automobile Prices in Market Equilibrium," *Econometrica*, July, pp. 841-890.

Bertolucci, Jeff. 1993. "WinFax Pro 3.0: Sophisticated Fax Software," *PC World*, January, p. 86.

Boslet, Mark. 1998. "Microsoft Keeps Pricing Steady for Its Windows 95 Software," *The Wall Street Journal Interactive Edition*, March 23.

Bournellis, Cynthia. 1998. "Software Platforms Lead to New Products," *Electronic News*, January 19, p. 58.

Brousell, David R. 1983. "MS-DOS, CP-M, Unix Battle for Domination in Market Demanding Multi-tasking, Multi-User Capability," *Electronic News*, September 26.

Brown, Bruce. 1998. "The Handheld that Beams," *PC Magazine*, May 5.

Brynjolfsson, Erik, "Some Estimates of the Contribution of Information Technology to Consumer Welfare," *MIT Sloan School Working Paper* 3647-094, January 1994.

Caldera, "OpenStore," http://www.caldera.com/openstore/index.html, accessed August 30, 1998.

Carr, Brian. 1990. "Making DOS Work Overtime," *PC Magazine*, October 16, pp. 196-227.

Central Point Software. 1989. *PC Tools Shells 5.5 Manual.*

The Computer Language Co. Inc., *Computer Desktop Encyclopedia*, Computer Select, CD-ROM. July 1998.

Dataquest. 1998. *Personal Computers Worldwide: Market Statistics*, April 20, Table 2-1.

Datasources. "SCO OpenServer Desktop System (Rel.5.0.4)," Computer Select, CD-ROM. July 1998.

Datasources, "SCO UnixWare Personal Edition (V.2.1)," Computer Select, CD-ROM. July 1998.

Delaney, Frank. 1995. "The Deal of the Century," *History of the Microcomputer Revolution*, http://exo.com/~wts/mits0013.HTM, accessed August 30, 1998.

Fox, Steve. 1995. "Windows 95: The Verdict Is In," *PC Magazine*, August, pp. 86+.

Goodman, John M., Eva, Elizabeth. 1994. "MS-DOS Version 6.22," *Infoworld*, August 29, pp. 87+.

Information Access Company, *Computer Select*, CD-ROM. August 1998.

Insight, http://www.insight.com, accessed August 5, 1998.

International Data Corporation. 1998. *Client Operating Environments: 1998 Worldwide Markets and Trends, C2348*, May, Table 2.

International Data Corporation. 1998. *Worldwide PC Forecast Update, 1997-2002, C2346*, May, Table 3.

Jones, Mitt. 1991. "GeoWorks Ensemble Lays the Foundation for a Brave New OS," *PC Magazine*, February 12.

Lexikon Services. 1998. *The History of Computing*.

Libes, Sol. 1995. "The Gary Kildall Legacy," *Amateur Computer Group of New Jersey*, http://www.acgnj.org/newslett/newsx011.html, accessed August 28, 1998.

Kildall, Gary, "CP/M: A Family of 8-and 16-bit Operating Systems," http://www.maxframe.com/gary&cpm.htm, accessed August 28, 1998.

Informix Corporation, "Informix Goes Linux," *Informix Cyber Planet*, September 1, 1998, http://www.informix.com/cyb-cgi/Webdriver?Mival=cyberzine_view_Story&ID=1634.

Manes, Stephen, Andrews, Paul. 1994. *Gates* (New York: Touchstone).

McCarthy, Patrick. 1996. "Market Price and Income Elasticities of New Vehicle Demands," *Review of Economics and Statistics*, 78(3), August, pp. 543-547.

Mendelson, Edward. 1994. "When All You Need Is the Fax," *Computer Shopper*, December, p. 552.

Microsoft Corporation. 1997. *Microsoft Annual Report, 1997 Fiscal Year.*

Microsoft Corporation. 1998. *Getting Started: Microsoft Windows 98.*

Microsoft Corporation. 1995. *Introducing Microsoft Windows 95*, pp. 56-57.

Microsoft Corporation. 1991. *Microsoft MS-DOS: User's Guide and Reference for the MS-DOS Operating System Version 5.0.*

Microsoft Corporation. 1992. *Microsoft Windows Version 3.1 User's Guide: For the Microsoft Windows Operating System.*

Microsoft Corporation. 1988. *MS-DOS Operating System Version 4.01 User's Guide: Gateway 2000 Edition.*

Microsoft Corporation. 1990. *Microsoft Windows: User's Guide for the Windows Graphical Environment Version 3.0, Gateway 2000 Edition.*

Microsoft Corporation. 1988. *MS-DOS Operating System Version 4.01 User's Guide.*

Microsoft Corporation. 1994. "Concise User's Guide: Microsoft MS-DOS 6.22," *User's Guides Microsoft MS-DOS and Microsoft Windows for Workgroups Operating Systems.*

Microsoft Corporation. 1994. "User's Guide: Microsoft Windows," *User's Guides Microsoft MS-DOS and Microsoft Windows for Workgroups Operating Systems*, pp. 15-21.

Miller, Michael J. 1995. "The Big Picture," *PC Magazine*, September 26, p. 108.

Mills, Elinor, Schwartz, Ephraim. 1998. "WordPerfect 8 for Linux Targets Corporate IT Users," *Infoworld*, May 25.

Moeller, Michael. 1998. "Pegging the Cost of an OS," *PC Week*, May 4, p. 19.

Nerney, Chris. 1998. "TCP/IP Stack Vendors Reborn," *Network World*, August 17, p. 28.

Newsbytes, "PC Briefs," July 23, 1998, p. NEW07230018.

Newsbytes, "Ericsson, Motorola, Nokia & Psion Create Symbian Alliance," June 24, 1998, p. NEW06240039.

Newton, Harry, "*Newton's Telecom Dictionary*," Computer Select, CD-ROM, Information Access Company, July 1998.

Parker, P. M., Neelamegham, R., "Price Elasticity Dynamics over the Product Life Cycle: A Study of Consumer Durables," INSEAD Working Paper 96/71/MKT, Table 3.

PC Connection, http://www.pcconnection.com.

PC Magazine. 1998. "The History of Windows," June 25.

PC Magazine. 1990. "Pipeline," October 30, pp. 65+.

PC Magazine. 1998. "Hot Technology," April 21.

PC Webopedia, "POSIX," 1998, http://webopedia.internet.com/TERM/P/POSIX.html, September 1, 1998.

PC Week. 1998. "A Linux World?" July 31.

PC Week. 1997. "Microsoft Pulls Last Plug on Windows 3.1 Sales," September 1, p. 51.

Petzold, Charles. 1986. "Operating in a New Environment," *PC Magazine*, February 25, p. 115.

Polsson, Ken. 1998. *Chronology of Events in the History of Microcomputers*, August 4. http://www.islandnet.com/~kpolsson/comphist.htm, accessed August 30, 1998.

Red Hat, "Red Hat Linux/Intel (Software)," http://www.redhat.com/products-details.phtml?id=rhl-intel, accessed August 5, 1998.

Rigney, Steve. 1993. "Lantastic," *PC Magazine*, May 25, p. 215.

Rosch, Winn L. 1991. "The Better Operating System?" *PC Magazine*, February 12, p. 245.

Salemi, Joe. 1992. "OS/2 2.0: Does It Fulfill the Promise?" *PC Magazine*, April 28, p. 165.

SCO, "SCO UnixWare Personal Edition," http://www.sco.com/unixware21/perserver/, accessed August 5, 1998.

Sibley, David S., "Declaration of David S. Sibley," *U.S. v. Microsoft Corp.*, May 15, 1998.

Spooner, John G. 1998. "'Jupiter's Handhelds Seek out IT Space," *PC Week*, August 4, http://www.zdnet.com/pcweek/news/0727/3lejupit.html.

Stata Corporation, "Stata Single-User and Volume-Purchase Pricing," (e-mail) August 24, 1998.

Stone, M. David. 1990. "Task Switchers: The Hot Key to Fast Application Access," *PC Magazine*, October 30, pp. 175+.

Stone, M. David. 1986. "DESQview," *PC Magazine*, February 25, pp. 115-117.

Sun, "Sun Solaris Operating Environment Version 2.6," http://www.sun.com/software/white-papers/wp-solaris2.6, accessed August 5, 1998.

Tay, Richard S., McCarthy, Patrick S. 1991. "Demand Oriented Policies for Improving Market Share in the U.S. Automobile Industry," *International Journal of Transport Economics* 18, pp. 151-166.

Theos Software, "The THEOS Operating System," http://www.theos-software.com/products/t32_os.htm, accessed August 28, 1998.

Theos Software, "THEOS 32 Version 4," http://www.theos-software.com/products/t32_development.htm, accessed August 28, 1998.

Trio Company of Cheektowaga, "CP/M File & Document Conversions," http://www.triousa.com/, accessed September 7, 1998.

United States of America, Department of Justice, "Complaint," *U.S. v. Microsoft Corp.*, May 18, 1998, p. 1.

Van Arsdale, Steve, Sisk, Johnson. 1984. "Choosing the Pick of the Litter," *PC Magazine*, April 17, p. 321.

Wayner, Peter. 1997. "The Be-All-You-Can-Be OS," *Byte*, December, pp. 137-138.

ZDNN, "What is Linux?" July 23, 1998, http://www.zdnet.com/zdnn/stories/zdnn_display/0,3440,2120842,00.html, August 19, 1998.

Section 1: *U.S. v. Microsoft Corp.*: The Economics

Essay 3

U.S. v. Microsoft Corp.: Remedy or Malady?*

by Kenneth G. Elzinga, David S. Evans, and Albert L. Nichols

The government, it is fair to say, had little difficulty convincing the district court judge presiding in the Microsoft trial that the software maker had a monopoly in operating systems for PCs, and that Microsoft had abused its monopoly power with the goal of protecting Windows dominance as a platform of applications software. But that victory, it is also fair to say, left the prosecutors with the problem of devising a remedy that would prevent a recurrence of the alleged abuses.

In the government's view, the sustained pattern of abuses made a "go and sin no more" solution ineffective: Limited behavioral remedies would leave Microsoft free to make an end run around the proscribed behavior in efforts to sustain its alleged monopoly. A group of economists sympathetic to the government's position led by Robert Litan of Brookings Institution proposed a full-frontal attack on the monopoly itself – a division of the company into two or three competitive entities, each of which would have the right to produce operating systems based on the Windows code. Yet even a casual consideration of so bold a stroke pointed to the pitfalls: Adding to the number of companies with the right to use Windows technology could shatter the de facto standard in operating systems on which both consumers and software developers have come to depend.

The government's Solomon-like alternative, which the district court rubber-stamped, was to divide Microsoft into one company making operating systems and another making applications software. The appeals court's subsequent decision, limiting Microsoft's liability in some areas and forcing the

prosecutors to show that consumers had been adversely affected in others, led the Bush administration to abandon the breakup initiative. But it is still worth exploring the likely consequences of the original plan, if only as a cautionary tale in the consequences of "don't just stand there, do something" antitrust activism. For it is difficult to imagine a punishment that less fits the alleged crime – or one that so obviously would leave consumers worse off.

There is another reason to look at the proposed split. Microsoft's competitors have been advocating a breakup since the early 1990s and continued to advocate this remedy vigorously even after the appeals court threw cold water on the idea. There is no reason to believe that they will cease prodding the government to investigate Microsoft, or stop advocating this "solution" to their problems. — *D.S.E.*

INTRODUCTION

> Accepting [competitors'] invitation to restructure the computer industry more to their liking through sweeping remedies such as dismembering Microsoft very well might advance [their] private interests…; but such remedies would not necessarily benefit competition and would … act against the public interest.
>
> U.S. Department of Justice, January 1995.[1]

Did the punishment fit the crime in what has been dubbed the antitrust trial of the century? In *U.S. v. Microsoft Corp.*, the U.S. Department of Justice (DOJ) and 19 state attorneys general argued that Microsoft illegally tied its operating system software for PCs (Windows) to a major new application (Internet browsing) and entered into exclusionary contracts with various computer service providers. The purported goal: to prevent browsers and other software from becoming commercially viable alternatives to Microsoft's monopoly in operating systems.[2]

Judge Thomas Penfield Jackson held for the DOJ and the 19 states (hereafter the "government") and accepted their recommendation to break Microsoft into two tightly regulated companies selling Microsoft operating systems and Microsoft software applications, respectively. Although an appeals court subsequently reduced Microsoft's liability and the government responded by dropping its efforts to break up the company, the government's initial demands arguably represent a high-water mark in activist antitrust enforcement. The mismatch between the alleged violation and that proposed remedy is the subject of this article.

The government's breakup remedy was not a solution for the antitrust violations alleged by the government and found by the district court. Indeed, the economic theories behind the government's remedy contradicted the economic theories that formed the basis for the government's liability theory and the court's findings. We reach several conclusions in analyzing the potential consequences of this mismatch and how it came about. First, the remedies adopted by the district court were out of proportion to the same court's findings of minimal consumer harm. Second, the government's structural and conduct remedies would have resulted in higher prices for consumers and deterred innovation. Finally, breaking up Microsoft was the remedy long sought by Microsoft's competitors and the one that would have benefited them most.

The first and second sections chronicle the government antitrust investigations of Microsoft from the early 1990s through the current litigation. The third section lays out basic economic concepts for designing antitrust remedies. The final four sections provide a critique of the remedies proposed by the government and adopted by the district court.

PRIOR ANTITRUST PROCEEDINGS INVOLVING MICROSOFT

The Microsoft trial capped a decade of investigation into and litigation over Microsoft's business practices. As we discuss below, prior to the court proceedings that led the district court to order the division of Microsoft, the antitrust enforcement agencies had (a) accepted that Microsoft became the market leader in operating systems software for personal computers through lawful behavior; (b) recognized that the emergence of a dominant PC operating system was explicable in the context of a competitive market; (c) found no basis for prosecuting Microsoft for leveraging its success in operating systems into software applications; and (d) rejected a 1995 proposal by Microsoft's competitors to break up the company.

The FTC's Abortive Investigation

The FTC began an investigation of Microsoft in 1990. The impetus was a concern that Microsoft and IBM had agreed to limit the functionality of Windows in order to promote sales of OS/2, an operating system that IBM was developing with Microsoft for its PCs.[3] Although this concern faded, the FTC broadened its investigation to other issues.[4] These included an allegation that Microsoft had hidden application programming interfaces (APIs) – the specifications for how applications software can call up services from the operating system – in MS-DOS and Windows. This purportedly allowed Microsoft's own developers to take advantage of operating system features not available to other applications developers.[5] There also were allegations that Microsoft used "vaporware" – misleading new product announcements intended to discourage customers from buying a competitor's product – and that Microsoft added features to Windows for the sole purpose of creating incompatibilities with non-Microsoft versions of DOS.[6]

By late 1992, the commission was focused primarily on Microsoft's contracts with computer manufacturers (known as original equipment manufacturers, or OEMs); the other charges had largely been dismissed by the staff. Several aspects of Microsoft's OEM contracts were examined as to whether they obstructed sales to OEMs by competing operating systems like DR DOS.[7] The particular contractual options investigated by the FTC included: (1) per-processor licenses, which based royalties on the number of PCs (rather than the number of copies of Microsoft operating systems) shipped by an OEM; (2) minimum commitments, which were the annual payment commitments that OEMs made to secure volume discounts; and (3) contract lengths, which typically were for two years, although some were longer.[8]

Within the FTC, there was a difference of opinion about whether to proceed against Microsoft. The Bureau of Competition recommended that the commission challenge Microsoft's use of per-processor licenses and minimum commitments. But the Bureau of Economics refused to endorse this recommendation. Neither bureau recommended action on claims that Microsoft leveraged its position in operating systems to gain advantages in applications software. The FTC's general counsel, however, recommended further investigation of this issue, but the commission decided to end the inquiry.[9]

The commission deadlocked on whether to proceed with the contractual issues by a two-to-two vote in February 1993, with one commissioner recused.[10] The tie meant the FTC would not file suit. However, the commission did ask the Bureau of Competition to further investigate alleged incompatibilities between Windows 3.1 and DR DOS. Microsoft's competitors, particularly Novell, continued to lobby for action.[11] Novell was the owner of both DR DOS and Netware; Netware was the most popular operating system for network server computers but faced competition from Microsoft's new Windows NT Server operating system. Once again, the Bureau of Competition recommended action, the Bureau of Economics dissented, and the commission deadlocked in July 1993.[12] In August 1993, the commission voted to suspend the investigation. Neither the two FTC bureaus, nor the FTC itself, ever recommended an antitrust action against Microsoft based on "hidden" APIs or other claims of "leveraging" from operating systems to applications software.[13]

The 1995 Consent Decree with the U.S. Department of Justice

In the summer of 1993, the antitrust division of the DOJ decided to pursue the investigation the FTC had dropped. In addition to reviewing the FTC files, the DOJ issued subpoenas of its own and took depositions of Microsoft executives. The DOJ revisited not only the OEM contract issues, but also the "hidden API" matter. Shortly after the DOJ launched its investigation, representatives from three of Microsoft's competitors met with antitrust division officials to present their arguments as to which of Microsoft's practices were anticompetitive. The three companies were Novell, WordPerfect (which owned what had been the leading word processor, but which was losing market share to Microsoft's Word), and Lotus (whose 1-2-3 spreadsheet software was losing market share to Microsoft's Excel after having been the most popular spreadsheet since its release 10 years earlier).[14]

In July 1994, the DOJ ended its investigation of Microsoft by filing a complaint and entering into a consent decree with Microsoft to settle the charges in that complaint.[15] The complaint did not allege that Microsoft's integration of operating systems and applications software was anticompetitive. Rather, the consent decree focused on Microsoft's OEM contracts: eliminating per-processor licenses and minimum commitments, and limiting contracts to one year. In addition, the settlement prohibited Microsoft from tying operating system licenses to any other products, with the caveat "that this provision in and of itself shall not be construed to prohibit Microsoft from developing integrated products."[16] Microsoft also agreed not to condition its licenses with OEMs on any hardware manufacturers' agreement *not* to license a competitor's product.[17]

In September 1994, the consent decree draft was submitted to Judge Stanley Sporkin of the U.S. District Court for the District of Columbia for what the parties expected to be routine approval under the *Tunney Act*. Instead, Judge Sporkin questioned the scope of the settlement, relying in part on *Hard Drive*,[18] a book that claimed Microsoft used "vaporware" practices to harm competitors. Judge Sporkin refused to approve the settlement without additional proceedings.[19]

Microsoft's competitors submitted additional material for the judge to consider. The most prominent example was a 96-page *amicus* brief submitted by Silicon Valley attorney Gary Reback (who had also been active in lobbying the FTC to act against Microsoft) on behalf of "certain clients that prefer to retain their confidentiality." The brief, which listed two economists – Garth Saloner and Brian Arthur of Stanford University – as having provided "extensive consultation," argued that Microsoft used its "monopoly in the operating systems market... to leverage its installed base to dominate the markets for applications and other software products."[20] The brief further argued that Microsoft was extending its dominance over successive "layers" on both client computers and servers by creating "technological linkages between layers within the same market."[21]

The brief's economic section highlighted network effects such as tipping and lock-in, and noted the danger that markets subject to such effects might experience. First, markets subject to these effects could end up dominated by inferior technologies. Second, these markets were particularly susceptible to anticompetitive actions by a monopolist in one market moving into a market for a complementary product. The brief predicted that the inclusion of software for Microsoft Network (MSN) in the then-forthcoming Windows 95 would "instantly displace existing on-line competition."[22] Although the brief itself did not call for specific remedies, it urged Judge Sporkin to require that the government submit additional materials, including statements from economic experts analyzing whether divestiture of Microsoft's applications software might be necessary to provide a "level playing field" in software markets.[23] It appears this was the first public proposal to break up Microsoft. The Computer Communications Industry Association (CCIA), whose leading members included Sun and other Microsoft competitors, also filed a brief urging a tougher decree.[24]

The DOJ responded with a declaration from Kenneth Arrow, a Nobel Prize–winning economist also from Stanford, and a submission that rejected the idea of dividing Microsoft:

> Accepting amici's invitation to restructure the computer industry more to their liking through sweeping remedies such as dismembering Microsoft very well might advance the private interests of the anonymous amici; but such remedies would not necessarily benefit competition and would, in Professor Arrow's view, act against the public interest.[25]

Furthermore, the DOJ argued that, "[n]either the government nor the amici contend that Microsoft achieved monopoly power unlawfully."[26] Arrow concurred, saying, "For the most part, Microsoft appears to have achieved its dominant position in its market as a consequence of good fortune and possibly superior product and business acumen."[27] He went on to conclude that the licensing practices "made only a minor contribution to the growth of Microsoft's installed base."[28] Thus, after four years of continuous government investigation, Microsoft's only significant business practice that the DOJ found to be anticompetitive was its licensing provisions with OEMs.[29]

Judge Sporkin again refused to approve the settlement, whereupon both sides appealed. The D.C. Circuit Court of Appeals disqualified Judge Sporkin and remanded the matter to the district court with directions to enter an order implementing the settlement.[30] Judge Thomas Penfield Jackson issued the final order in August of 1995.[31]

The Consent Decree Contempt Litigation

In 1996, the DOJ launched a new investigation of Microsoft, focusing its attention on Internet browsing software.[32] Netscape, the leading vendor of Internet browsers, prodded this investigation from the beginning.[33] In June 1995, two days after Microsoft met with Netscape representatives to discuss possible areas of business collaboration, Reback sent a letter to the DOJ claiming that Microsoft asked Netscape to "divide markets" and threatened to punish Netscape if it did not agree to do so.[34] This episode became a central dispute in *U.S. v. Microsoft Corp*. In July 1996, Reback submitted a lengthy "white paper" on behalf of the Netscape Corporation.[35] The document urged the DOJ to force Microsoft to separate its browser, Internet Explorer (IE), from Windows and to offer IE only on a stand-alone basis. It also urged the DOJ to forbid Microsoft from giving away IE, except during a brief introductory promotion, and to compel Microsoft to stop including its Web-server software at zero price with Windows NT Server, its server operating system.[36]

In the fall of 1997, the DOJ asked Judge Jackson to declare Microsoft in contempt of the 1994 consent decree's prohibition on tying. The government argued that Microsoft was forcing OEMs to license IE as a condition for licensing Windows. Microsoft replied that IE was an integrated feature of Windows, not a separate product; consequently, it came under the "integrated product" exemption in the consent decree. Judge Jackson decided in December 1997 that Microsoft was not in contempt of the decree. But on his own initiative, he began a more extensive review of the integration issue.[37]

In the interim, Judge Jackson required Microsoft to offer OEMs the option of licensing a version of Windows that did not include the IE files. Microsoft responded that removing IE files from the then-current version of Windows would disable the operating system because the code that enabled Internet browsing was tightly integrated into Windows and supported other key operating system services. Judge Jackson then pointed to the "uninstall" capability offered by Windows and ordered Microsoft to let OEMs exercise it on IE.[38]

Microsoft complied, noting that the procedure was more akin to "hiding" than "removal," as it left virtually all of the code intact while disabling the two most convenient methods for Windows users to activate Internet browsing.[39] Microsoft appealed the district court's ruling. In June 1998, the D.C. circuit reversed Judge Jackson, finding that IE was "integrated" into Windows, not "tied."[40]

There are two important backdrops that set the stage for the Microsoft case. First, Microsoft had been under antitrust scrutiny even prior to the success of Windows and its Office suite of productivity applications. But in the original investigations by the FTC and the DOJ, Microsoft's conduct with regard to its APIs was never put forward as a plausible source of anticompetitive behavior. By the same token, neither enforcement agency recommended that Microsoft be divided into two or more software companies. Indeed, the DOJ and its expert economist specifically recommended against breaking up Microsoft, noting the adverse effect a breakup would have on consumer welfare.

Second, Microsoft's competitors lobbied the antitrust authorities to take action against Microsoft. Competitors may have an indirect interest in seeing competition restored, but they always have a direct interest in seeing a rival weakened. The companies that urged the DOJ to pursue Microsoft all had experienced significant losses in sales because Microsoft offered competitive products with more features at lower prices.

THE INTERNET EXPLORER TYING LITIGATION

A month before the D.C. circuit handed down its June 1998 decision, the DOJ filed a new complaint against Microsoft.[41] This section briefly reviews the procedural history of this case and describes the district court's remedies and the rationale the government presented for these remedies.

Procedural Background

The complaint charged that Microsoft had attempted to maintain its monopoly in a relevant market comprising operating systems for Intel-compatible PCs, and endeavored to *obtain* a monopoly in browsing software for those computers by (1) tying IE to Windows and (2) contracting with OEMs to exclude Netscape from important channels of distribution.[42] The DOJ sought an injunction that would require Microsoft (a) to offer OEMs a version of Windows without IE, or to include copies of Netscape's browser with Windows, giving OEMs the option of installing only one, and (b) to cease entering into exclusive contracts with OEMs.[43] Attorneys general from 20 states and the District of Columbia also filed a complaint that paralleled the DOJ's in most respects.[44] However, their complaint also alleged that Microsoft used its monopoly in operating systems to obtain a monopoly in office productivity applications, such as word processors and spreadsheets.[45] The states' amended complaint, filed after Judge Jackson joined the cases for trial, dropped this allegation.[46]

Instead of ruling on the government's request for a preliminary injunction, the district court decided to have an expedited and abbreviated trial.[47] The summer of 1998 was left for further fact and expert discovery and the trial was scheduled for the fall of 1998.[48] By the time the trial started in October 1998, the government's case included additional allegations that went beyond the browser-related complaints. These allegations focused on several instances in which Microsoft allegedly bullied other firms (e.g., Intel) in efforts to stop them from developing software that would compete with Windows as a platform for applications software.[49] But even with this expansion of the case, Microsoft's joint production of operating systems and applications was, at most, a peripheral issue.[50]

The trial on liability issues concluded in June 1999. The district court then announced its findings in two stages. The Findings of Fact (FOF), issued in November 1999, adopted most of the evidence submitted by the government's witnesses and rejected, or ignored, much of the evidence submitted by Microsoft's witnesses.[51] At this point, with the consent of the parties, the district court appointed Judge Richard Posner of the U.S. Court of Appeals for the Seventh Circuit to act as a mediator in settlement negotiations.[52] Negotiations broke down at the end of March 2000, and the district court entered its Conclusions of Law (COL) shortly thereafter.[53]

Judge Jackson found that Microsoft sought to maintain its monopoly in operating systems and sought to obtain a second monopoly in browsing software. The judge ruled that this "predacious behavior" violated Section 2 of the Sherman Act.[54] He also found that Microsoft illegally tied its operating system to its browser in violation of Section 1 of the Sherman Act.[55] The parties were ordered to submit their recommendations for remedies.

The government submitted a proposed remedy at the end of April 2000, which included splitting Microsoft into operating system and applications companies, along with numerous conduct remedies.[56] The proposal was supported by declarations from three economists who had not participated in the trial: Professors Rebecca Henderson, Paul Romer, and Carl Shapiro.[57] The government also submitted declarations from two investment bankers, who concluded that the split was feasible and that it should not cause "a material decrease in the market value of the current Microsoft shareowners' holdings."[58] A declaration was also submitted by Professor Edward Felten,[59] a computer scientist, who had testified during the liability phase on the feasibility of removing access to IE from Windows.

Microsoft was given 10 days to submit a preliminary reply and recommendations for further proceedings on remedies. Microsoft argued for summary dismissal of the government's structural remedy and proposed much less restrictive conduct measures.[60] On May 24, 2000, the district court heard oral arguments by attorneys from both sides and announced that it had decided not to accept further expert submissions or evidence concerning remedies.[61]

Thus, this landmark case was to include no serious inquiry into the remedy. Judge Jackson requested that the government prepare a final proposal and gave Microsoft five days to respond to its form and wording, but not its substance.[62] On June 7, after the government made minor changes in response to Microsoft's brief, the district court issued its decision.[63] Judge Jackson adopted the government's proposed remedies with no substantive changes. In an accompanying memorandum, the judge in part justified the use of a structural remedy by citing Microsoft's refusal to admit its guilt, and remarking that "Microsoft has proved untrustworthy in the past."[64] He added, "Plaintiffs won the case and for that reason alone have some entitlement to a remedy of their choice."[65] Judge Jackson also expressed doubt that additional evidence would yield "any significantly greater assurance that it will be able to identify what might be generally regarded as an optimum remedy." In subsequent press interviews the judge said that he had ordered Microsoft's breakup as "a last resort" because of Microsoft's "intransigence."[66]

Microsoft appealed to the D.C. circuit.[67] The D.C. circuit announced that all seven judges would hear the case on an expedited schedule.[68] The DOJ, however, requested that Judge Jackson certify the case for direct appeal to the Supreme Court, which he did, at the same time staying all of the remedies. On September 26, 2000, the Supreme Court in an 8-1 vote remanded the case to the appeals court for initial review.[69] The D.C. circuit held two days of oral hearings at the end of February 2001.[70] The appeals court's ruling, made after the initial publication of this article, reversed some of Judge Jackson's findings of liability, modified others, and removed Judge Jackson from further proceedings.[71]

The District Court's Remedies

The district court adopted both structural and conduct remedies. The centerpiece of the remedies was a division of Microsoft into two companies: one ("Ops Co") would have the rights to Microsoft's operating systems (Windows 98, Windows 2000, Windows CE, and their successors); the other ("Apps Co") would own all its remaining products, including its Office suite of business productivity applications; its server software for Web sites (IIS), large databases (SQL Server), and e-mail and collaboration software (Exchange); its programming languages and developer tools; and its consumer software.[72] A key exception to this division between Ops Co and Apps Co was the code in the Windows operating system that supports Web-browsing functions, known as Internet Explorer (IE). Apps Co would get custody of the code and the right to develop it in the future. Ops Co would have a perpetual license to use existing versions of IE, but would not be allowed to modify it.

The remedy also included detailed constraints on Microsoft's conduct that would apply until the division took place and would continue to apply to Ops Co for three years thereafter. These conduct remedies included requirements that Microsoft deal uniformly with other firms – OEMs, independent software developers, and others – and that it make the source code underlying Windows available to what amounts to all comers.[73] Moreover, Microsoft was told to allow OEMs to customize the Windows platform (and, indeed, give them a discount if they choose to delete parts of it), while continuing to allow OEMs to use Microsoft's logos and other symbols of its brand.

Under the Final Judgment, Microsoft would have been required to offer identical sales terms to the 20 largest OEMs, with prices allowed to vary only according to "reasonable volume discounts."[74] Microsoft would have been able to price new versions of its operating systems as it wished, but would have to offer OEMs the option of buying an older version at the previous price for at least three years. OEMs would be permitted to make extensive changes to Windows, including substitution of components from other vendors. To facilitate such substitution, Microsoft would be required to make all "middleware products" removable.[75] OEMs that took advantage of this provision would be entitled to a discount, proportional to the amount of code removed.

Microsoft would also have been required to provide information to all software and hardware vendors on equal terms and to establish a "secure facility" where software companies, including competitors, would be allowed to review source code for Microsoft's operating systems for purposes of "enabling their products to interoperate effectively with Microsoft Platform Software."[76] If Microsoft had made changes in its operating systems that would negatively affect the operation of other companies' middleware, it would have had to notify those companies, explaining the reason for the change, and suggesting ways to solve the problem.[77] The Microsoft Ops Co would also have been prohibited from offering any consideration (including early technical information or assistance) to software or hardware vendors for distributing or promoting a product.[78]

Government's Rationale for Its Remedies

To understand the rationale for the government's proposed remedies, one must turn to the memorandum the government submitted and the declarations of its economists.[79] The government advanced two rationales for splitting Microsoft, both of which focused on Microsoft's Office suite of applications. First, an independent Apps Co would be more inclined to offer versions of Office for other platforms, such as Linux, because Apps Co would not have a direct stake in the success of Windows.[80] This purportedly would help reduce the "applications barrier to entry" and create new opportunities for competing operating systems.[81] Second, Apps Co would be inclined to expand the existing APIs in Office, transforming it into a new middleware threat to the applications barrier to entry that allegedly protects Windows from competition.[82] Thus, the government and its economists argued, the split would reduce the dominance of Windows by creating popular software that would run on other platforms and by transforming Microsoft's own popular applications software into full-fledged middleware that would allow applications written to it to run on other operating systems.

The government and its experts placed great emphasis on the role that the structural and conduct remedies would play in promoting innovation. Professor Henderson, for example, concluded her declaration as follows:

> The remedies proposed will prevent Microsoft from crippling competition and will release a flood of innovative energy. Rapid action is vital to ensure that innovation and consumer choice in this particularly important sector of the economy are preserved.[83]

Professor Shapiro also invoked "innovation" to support the government's remedies, concluding that there are "strong reasons" to believe that splitting Microsoft "will lower entry barriers, encourage competition and promote innovation."[84] He claimed that separating Office from Windows would give each of the new companies incentives to foster competition in the other's realm, arguing that "[w]hile network monopolies can be very strong, they are most vulnerable to attack by firms with a strong position in the provision of a widely-used *complementary product*."[85] Professor Shapiro also supported the requirement that Microsoft give other firms access to its source code, arguing this would "prevent Microsoft from using its Windows monopoly power to gain control of complementary applications and middleware."[86] Like Professor Henderson, he concluded with an endorsement of divestiture that emphasized innovation:

> As explained above, there are strong reasons to believe – based on economic principles and based on the experience of this and other industries – that the proposed reorganization of Microsoft into separate applications and operating systems businesses will lower entry barriers, encourage competition and promote innovation.[87]

Three things are noteworthy about the remedies proposed by the government and accepted by the district court. First, they are unrelated to the remedies proposed in the complaint. Originally, the government sought only to force Microsoft to unbundle Windows and IE and to cease entering into certain kinds of contracts (most of which Microsoft had already abandoned before the court ruled on remedies and which, for the most part, Judge Jackson found not to violate the Sherman Act).[88] The second noteworthy aspect of the Final Judgment's breakup remedy is its similarity to the proposals promoted by Microsoft's competitors since 1994, when Reback filed his brief on behalf of the "anonymous amici." Those remedies were urged as the solution to very different alleged problems.

The third noteworthy characteristic of the remedies is how radical they are compared to remedies in past antitrust cases. Court-ordered breakups of companies have been a rarity in Sherman antitrust litigation. Dr. Robert Crandall's survey of antitrust remedies over the last century found only one case – *United Shoe Machinery* – in which the courts ordered the breakup of a company that had not been created through mergers and acquisitions. The other breakups (including the two most celebrated, Standard Oil in 1911 and AT&T in 1984) all involved corporations that had preserved the original companies as separate enterprises with clear geographic or functional boundaries. In each of these breakups, the companies were split according to those obvious boundaries.[89]

Two questions spring from this chronicle of Microsoft and its antitrust involvement. First, did the remedies imposed in the Microsoft case – in particular the breakup – address the problem that the government complained about and for which the district court found supporting evidence? Second, did the remedies solve the newly discovered problem – inadequate innovation – that is the focus of the government's remedy submissions? The answer to both questions is "no." To understand why, it is useful to review the principles on which antitrust remedies are traditionally based.

ECONOMIC PRINCIPLES FOR ANTITRUST REMEDIES

The primary goal of an antitrust remedy in a monopolization case is to end anticompetitive behavior.[90] But in achieving this goal, the court must ensure that the cure is not worse than the disease – that the remedy's costs do not exceed its benefits to consumers.[91] All else being equal, the court should avoid remedies that require extensive or prolonged oversight by the judiciary, as well as remedies that impose large or prolonged compliance costs on the defendant.[92] There are two types of antitrust remedies in monopolization cases, conduct remedies and structural remedies.

• *Conduct Remedies* are injunctive decrees that proscribe a firm's behavior or require that it undertake an action it has previously refused to undertake, often with regard to its marketing practices.[93] Typically, conduct remedies in antitrust are "Thou shalt not" proscriptions or "Thou must" prescriptions.[94]

• *Structural Remedies* involve dissolution, divorcement, and divestiture – the "three Ds" of antitrust. Historians call this "trustbusting." A vertical structural remedy requires a firm to divest a downstream subsidiary in order to rectify a foreclosure-of-competition problem. A horizontal structural remedy breaks a firm into components that are in head-to-head competition with each other.

Conduct Remedies

Conduct remedies vary in duration and complexity. A remedy may be in force for only a brief period (e.g., directing a firm to sell 25 percent of its output to a designated customer base for six months) or may apply over the long term (e.g., a 10-year ban on acquisitions of specified types). It is important during the design phase that attention be given to limiting a remedy's intrusiveness and duration so as not to: (a) generate high compliance costs for the court; (b) impose high compliance costs upon the defendant; or (c) prevent the defendant from being a vigorous competitor.

Conduct remedies bear an uneasy relationship with the economic foundation of antitrust. If an antitrust remedy requires an enforcement agency or court to set prices, dictate output, regulate profits, choose market entrants, or approve market exits, the remedy violates the core principle that the enforcement agency is a referee rather than a regulator.[95] Indeed, the potential for intrusive regulation is the primary strike against most conduct remedies. Making matters worse, a conduct remedy may gain a life of its own as competitors petition the court for relief from the defendant's alleged noncompliance. Prolonged monitoring potentially perverts antitrust enforcement, as regulatory directives replace market forces.

Structural Remedies

The remedy of structural relief has been applied infrequently in the history of the Sherman Act.[96] Typically structural relief has not involved the dissolution of trusts under Section 2 of the Sherman Act (the antimonopoly provision) but rather the divestiture of *mergers and acquisitions* under Section 7 of the Clayton Act (the antimerger provision). Structural relief via the divestiture of acquired assets is more common for several reasons: (1) more Section 7 antimerger cases are brought than Section 2 monopolization cases; (2) past mergers usually offer a "seam" so that rending the corporation is less intrusive to business operations; (3) Section 7 requires only a prophylactic standard with regard to liability, in contrast to the Section 2 higher standard, thereby making Section 7 antimerger lawsuits more likely to be filed and won; and (4) structural relief can be an effective prescription when the antitrust offense itself was the result of a merger or acquisition. But even in the realm of antimerger cases, structural remedies via divestiture of a firm's acquisition(s) are infrequent.[97]

Antitrust analysts generally do not consider structural remedies to be successful. For example, Crandall shows that the breakup of the Standard Oil trust in 1911, the paradigmatic illustration of trustbusting in U.S. history textbooks, had no measurable effect on petroleum output and prices.[98] The petroleum trust's market position centered on its operations in Pennsylvania and Ohio and was undercut by new producers from the West.[99] Crandall also illustrates how structural remedies can reduce consumer welfare, as occurred in the vertical dissolution of production and distribution of motion pictures in the *Paramount* case.[100]

The most recent antitrust breakup of a major corporation was the 1982 dissolution of AT&T.[101] The structural remedy in AT&T is sometimes compared to the Microsoft case, the argument being that the breakup of AT&T

enhanced consumer welfare, so the breakup of Microsoft will do the same. Crandall shows that any comparison between the breakup of AT&T and Microsoft is inapposite. AT&T was a regulated enterprise operating in a government environment that constrained price and new entry. Moreover, Crandall argues that the consumer benefits generated by the breakup of AT&T could have been secured more efficiently without a mandated structural remedy had the FCC required equal access by competing phone service providers as a regulatory policy.[102] As he points out, Canada required access, but did not require divestiture, and it reaped equal or greater benefits despite a later start than the United States.[103]

Antitrust Remedies and Error Costs

In antitrust, "false positive" errors are serious because less efficient firms will benefit and consumers will be harmed as a result of legal intervention. The probability is high that the proposed remedies in the Microsoft case would have raised prices and reduced the pace of innovation.[104] If our analysis is correct, the expected harm from a false positive is significant. On the other hand, the U.S. software industry is roiling with technological change, making monopoly rents difficult to capture for long.[105] This suggests that the expected cost of a false negative is low in *U.S. v. Microsoft Corp.*

The breakup of Microsoft, as proposed by the government and its post-trial remedy economists, contains no appraisal of expected error costs. This leaves a serious gap in the analysis. An analysis of the remedy proposed by the government, endorsed by economists Henderson, Romer, and Shapiro, and accepted by Judge Jackson, must begin by asking whether it addresses the problems identified by the district court in its Findings of Fact and Conclusions of Law.

THE REMEDIES AND INNOVATION

The first step in fashioning a remedy is to define the problem. There are two ways of reading Judge Jackson's Findings of Fact and Conclusions of Law. At a formal level, he found that Microsoft had (1) illegally tied IE to Windows and (2) engaged in predatory behavior. Tying and predation are standard fare in antitrust and generally do not lead to anything more than injunctions (e.g., untie) or limited conduct remedies (e.g., cease entering into exclusive contracts).[106]

At a visceral level, Judge Jackson asserted that Microsoft's behavior had sweeping (though ill-defined and largely unspecified) negative effects on innovation and the future of the software industry. Microsoft had "placed an oppressive thumb on the scale of competitive fortune, thereby effectively guaranteeing its continued dominance in the relevant markets."[107] In his remarks to the press, he expressed a belief that Microsoft needed a severe remedy because it was "intransigent"[108] (i.e., it would not admit that it had violated the law) and "untrustworthy."[109]

The government's proposed structural remedies followed from the visceral aspects of Judge Jackson's findings, focusing almost exclusively on the district court's finding that Microsoft had suppressed innovation. This is a weak foundation for two reasons. First, Judge Jackson's statements concerning suppressed innovation are rhetorical flourishes unsupported by his own findings; they are in fact undermined by the findings and by the evidentiary record on which the findings purport to be based.[110] Second, there is no basis in the government's submissions or in the district court's findings to conclude that the government's remedies would increase innovation or stimulate middleware competition.

Microsoft's Alleged Impact on Innovation

Judge Jackson concluded his Findings of Fact with this sweeping statement: "Microsoft's past success in luring such companies and stifling innovation deters investment in technologies and businesses that exhibit the potential to threaten Microsoft. The ultimate result is that some innovations that would truly benefit consumers never occur for the sole reason that they do not coincide with Microsoft's self-interest."[111]

This finding is referenced three times in the government's accompanying memorandum on remedies, as well as in the declarations of two of the three economists.[112] It is the cornerstone of the government's remedy. But, it is not consistent with the record of software innovation in the U.S. and with Judge Jackson's Findings of Fact.

The District Court's Acknowledgment of Innovation Due to Microsoft

Judge Jackson acknowledged that Microsoft's actions in the browser war *increased* the rate of innovation of both Microsoft *and* Netscape since both companies improved their Web browsers throughout the period in question and sought to surpass the other's performance. He found several concrete benefits from Microsoft's efforts to overtake Netscape:

> The debut of Internet Explorer and its rapid improvement gave Netscape an incentive to improve Navigator's quality at a competitive rate. The inclusion of Internet Explorer with Windows at no separate charge increased general familiarity with the Internet and reduced the cost to the public of gaining access to it, at least in part because it compelled Netscape to stop charging for Navigator. These actions thus contributed to improving the quality of Web browsing software, lowering its cost, and increasing its availability, thereby benefiting consumers.[113]

A study of reviews in 13 major computer magazines reveals the trajectory of progress.[114] For versions 1 and 2 of Netscape Navigator, Netscape was the clear winner in the view of all of the magazines. However, with the release of IE 3 in August 1996, the tide began to turn.

IE 3 was based on new code and was more tightly integrated with Windows than previous versions. Reviewers' preferences were split between IE 3 and Navigator 3, with half of the evaluations declaring a tie and a quarter each declaring Navigator or IE to be the best browser. When IE 4 was released in October 1997, the weight of favorable opinion shifted almost entirely to the Microsoft browser.[115] IE has continued to be rated above Netscape's offerings, with 75 percent of the reviews choosing IE 5 over Navigator 4.5. (Netscape never released a version 5 and its version 6 was not released until November 2000).[116]

Judge Jackson acknowledged that Microsoft improved its browsing software more rapidly than did Netscape, to the point where "the number of reviewers who regarded it as the superior product was roughly equal to those who preferred Navigator."[117] The district court's Findings of Fact thus support the position that Microsoft enhanced, rather than suppressed, innovation in browsing software.

Microsoft's integration of IE into Windows, using what software engineers call "components," also boosted software innovation. This improvement in IE 3 helped other software vendors develop products that could exploit seamless access to the Internet. AOL used this feature to add browsing capabilities to its proprietary network software, while other independent software developers used it to access information from the Web without exiting their own programs.[118] Intuit's Quicken, for example, uses IE components to go to the Web to update security prices;[119] IBM/Lotus Notes uses IE components in Windows in similar ways.[120] Netscape, in contrast, did not release a final componentized version of its browser until November 2000,[121] despite requests from potential partners dating back to AOL in early 1996.[122]

The District Court's Examples of Suppressed Innovation

The Findings of Fact discuss six specific instances in which the district court found that Microsoft suppressed, or attempted to suppress, innovations by other firms that involved competing platforms or middleware.[123] The first instance occurred at the June 1995 meeting of Microsoft and Netscape executives. Judge Jackson accepted Netscape's interpretation of that meeting – specifically, that Microsoft pressured Netscape to stop developing platform-level software and to rely instead on Microsoft's platform for basic software services.[124] Microsoft employees who attended the meeting described a very different set of discussions. But nobody claims that the meeting led Netscape to change its development plans or strategy.

Microsoft also failed to achieve its purported goals in three other instances Judge Jackson cited as evidence of Microsoft's inclination to pressure other firms to halt software development that "shows potential to weaken the applications barrier to entry or competes directly with Microsoft's most cherished software products."[125] IBM asked Microsoft for favorable pricing and a marketing partnership similar to the one Microsoft had with Compaq. When Microsoft set as a condition for the partnership that IBM soft-pedal promotion of its competing operating system and office productivity software, IBM refused.[126] When Microsoft tried to get Apple to stop developing and giving away QuickTime for Windows, Apple also refused.[127] When Microsoft asked RealNetworks to defer to the multimedia software Microsoft built into Windows, RealNetworks refused.[128] The outcome of each of these episodes does not square with claims that Microsoft had the ability to suppress innovation or wield monopoly power. In each case Microsoft offered inducements, but was turned down. And in each case, the product involved was not hurt. RealNetworks continues to be the leader in streaming media players and Apple claimed to be number 2 in June 2000.[129] Netscape Navigator continued to have a majority of browser use for three more years, until 1998, despite widespread agreement that Microsoft had caught up in quality in 1996.[130]

The Findings of Fact describe only two cases in which Microsoft apparently succeeded in its attempts to "suppress innovation," and neither involved significant software innovation. The first was Microsoft's 1996 "Windows experience" restrictions on OEMs.[131] Microsoft found that some OEMs were setting up system software to run their own programs between the time that Windows started loading and the time the Windows 95 "desktop" first appeared on the screen. Some OEMs even substituted their own "shells" on top of Windows. Under its Windows copyright, Microsoft believed it had the right to insist that OEMs let Windows 95 load as intended and be presented to users as Microsoft had designed. To that end, Microsoft required that OEMs not install any programs that would run automatically after Windows started loading for the first time on a new computer.

OEMs, however, remained free to install software that would launch automatically before Windows started loading. They also were free to add as many icons for programs or services to the Windows desktop as they wished. Moreover, OEMs were free to give users the opportunity of having any programs chosen by the OEM (including shells or Navigator) launch automatically every time Windows started loading on subsequent boots. Few OEMs chose to offer customers that choice, apparently deciding that customers were not interested enough to choose the OEMs' shells.

In any event, Microsoft's 1996 "Windows experience" was irrelevant for large buyers, who account for close to half of all new PCs purchased.[132] Such customers typically install their own selection of software or have OEMs do it for them. Hence they were free to install shells or other programs and have them launch automatically.

The only other case in which the district court found that Microsoft succeeded in suppressing software innovation was the 1995 conflict with Intel over native signal processing (NSP) software.[133] In the spring of 1995, Intel released a beta version of its NSP software and started promoting it to OEMs. This software was designed to integrate some multimedia functions with other functions performed by the central (Intel) processor, rather than have them performed by specialized, inexpensive processors on accessories like sound cards.[134] However, it worked only with Microsoft Windows 3.x operating systems. It did not work with Windows NT. More important, it was incompatible with Windows 95, the major new operating system that Microsoft was set to release later that summer. Indeed, if NSP software was installed on a computer using Windows 3.1 that was subsequently upgraded to Windows 95, the system was likely to crash.[135]

In addition to being concerned about NSP's incompatibility problems with Windows NT and Windows 95, Microsoft was concerned that Intel had not tested the software sufficiently. As Microsoft officials pointed out to Intel, users who encountered problems were likely to blame Microsoft.[136]

Microsoft executives were unsuccessful in persuading the Intel officials in charge of NSP to stop promoting it, and asked Bill Gates, Microsoft's CEO, to talk directly to Intel's CEO, Andy Grove.[137] Gates met with Grove in July and again in early August, a few weeks before Windows 95 was to be released. They agreed that Intel would not promote NSP to OEMs (in part because Intel had a strong interest in promoting Windows 95) and that Microsoft would work with Intel to implement many of the features in the NSP software in software developer kits and in Windows 95. The district court noted, however, that "[e]ven as late as the end of 1998, though, Microsoft still had not implemented key capabilities that Intel had been poised to offer consumers in 1995."[138]

In its proposed Findings of Fact, the government argued that Microsoft's concerns about incompatibilities were not important: OEMs would install the software only on systems shipped with Windows 3.x and Microsoft could add features to upgrades of Windows 95 that would detect NSP software and take steps to avoid the compatibility problems.[139] However, the idea that Microsoft could make such changes a few weeks before the public release of Windows 95, when the upgrade versions were already being manufactured, is not credible and has no support in the record.

There is no evidence in the record that NSP software represented a significant innovation that OEMs would have adopted or from which consumers would have gained value via its early adoption. In an October 1995 article in *Byte* magazine, a senior product manager at a major manufacturer of dedicated processors expressed skepticism about the value of NSP, even if it worked properly: "The functions that NSP can provide by using the host [CPU]," he explained, "a few dollars' worth of hardware can provide."[140] In light of its incompatibilities with Windows 95, it is hard to imagine that many OEMs would have installed NSP software. Users interested in multimedia were unlikely to choose to buy computers with Windows 3.1 once Windows 95 became available, and problems with upgrades would have caused support problems for OEMs as well as Microsoft. Moreover, the strongest demand for multimedia features comes from video-game players, and using NSP software actually slowed down the performance of games compared to the alternative of using a separate processor for sound and leaving the central processor free for the intensive calculations required by games.[141]

The interaction between Intel and Microsoft on the NSP issue illustrates the complexity of their business relationship. Cooperation is clearly important to both – virtually all versions of Windows (other than Windows CE) run on Intel chips or clones thereof, and the vast majority of Intel chips are used in systems shipped with Windows operating systems. Intel benefits if Microsoft's operating systems take advantage of new features in its chips, and support of new hardware features creates more sales of Windows.

At the same time, each firm has an incentive to encourage the other's competitors in order to reduce its dependence on the other and to drive down the other's prices: the lower the price of Intel chips, the more copies of Windows will be sold, and vice versa. As a result, Intel encourages competition to Windows by investing in Linux vendors and BeOS, and Microsoft works with other chip vendors.[142] In much of the computer industry, there is no potential for such conflict because the same company makes the hardware and the operating system. Sun, IBM, Hewlett Packard, and the other Unix system vendors follow this vertically integrated model, as does Apple.

In summary, the trial record provided little evidence to support the district court's sweeping statements regarding Microsoft's impact on innovation. Most of the purported attempts failed, and those that succeeded involved "innovations" of ambiguous value. If the government planned to justify draconian remedies on the basis of the need to stimulate more innovation in the software industry, its experts in the remedy phase should have bolstered the record with new, more rigorous analyses.

The Government's Remedy Economists Added No New Evidence of Suppressed Innovation

The declarations submitted by the government's three experts in the remedy phase are notable for their lack of specificity regarding Microsoft's alleged harm to software innovation. All three claim that Microsoft's actions impeded innovation and applaud the potential effects of the remedies on innovation. Yet none systematically compares the records of innovation in areas where Microsoft is "dominant" to areas in which it is not.[143] Instead, the three experts simply adopt the district court's story about suppressed innovation.[144]

The claims made by Professors Henderson, Romer, and Shapiro can be summarized as four implicit assertions:

- The rate of new product development for important classes of software has been slowed by actions of Microsoft. Examples include "middleware" and applications software.
- The greatest progress in the software industry occurs when firms face "market-based" competition. When a single firm – or small set of firms – dominates an industry, progress is retarded.
- Microsoft's control of the personal computer operating system market has allowed it to exclude new platforms.
- Fears of predatory actions have deterred small and new companies from introducing products that compete directly with Microsoft products.

To evaluate these claims, one must examine the available evidence.

Evidence of Innovation in Software During Period of Alleged Suppression

Absent demonstration to the contrary, which neither the government nor its experts provided, claims that Microsoft's actions impeded innovation in the software industry are contradicted by the rapid pace of innovation in this industry. These claims were not systematically analyzed during the trial or by the remedy experts thereafter. Rather, the arguments that Microsoft deterred innovation are thin and anecdotal.

One indicator of the implausibility of Microsoft's conduct having harmed software innovation during the 1990s is the industry's remarkable record of new firm formation. New entrants in the software industry typically introduce new products rather than mimic existing products. Consequently, the pace of new entry is a proxy for the pace of innovation in the industry. Table 1 highlights the record of entry in the industry during the 1990s. The table shows the number of active firms in the U.S. software industry for even-numbered years during the 1990s.[145] It shows that there was substantial new firm formation in the software industry over this period.

Table 1. **Number of Active Software Firms in CorpTech Database**

Year	Number of Firms
1990	6,970
1992	7,617
1994	8,143
1996	9,972
1998	10,236
2000	11,061

Note: Number of firms at start of calendar year.

Source: Corporate Technology Information Services, CorpTech Database, unpublished tabulation (2000).

Much of the entry activity took place in the application service provider (ASP) segment, which Microsoft allegedly targeted for monopolization. Norma Leong identified approximately 300 new firms that entered the ASP market between 1997 and early 2000 alone.[146]

Recently Josh Lerner has used data from the same source used to create Table 1 to test how segments in the software industry that Judge Jackson found to be targets of Microsoft's anticompetitive actions had fared compared to other segments. He found no evidence that firms in those segments allegedly targeted by Microsoft had attracted less venture capital or had grown more slowly.[147] Contrary to the implications of the government's claim of an applications barrier to entry, he also found that during the late 1990s firms increasingly were writing software for Unix and other non-Microsoft platforms.[148]

There is another empirical challenge to the government's claims about the suppression of innovation: The level of venture capital investment in software firms has increased in recent years. Not only do venture capitalists respond to innovative advances by funding new firms, but their investments in turn stimulate innovation.[149] Estimates by the National Venture Capital Association indicate that funding in computer software and services, the category most likely to encompass Microsoft's competitors, enjoyed a steady increase during the period Microsoft engaged in its allegedly anticompetitive behavior. The total venture capital investment rose more than 10-fold, from $459 million in 1991 to $7.50 billion in 1999.[150] These tabulations do not include investments in firms specializing in online products and services, which also grew explosively.[151] The number of companies receiving venture capital financing for the first time also rose steadily. Many other technology sectors, notably biotechnology, experienced less growth in venture investment over the same period.[152]

An indirect test of the assertion that Microsoft has reduced innovation is found in the work of Bittlingmayer and Hazlett.[153] They explore the effects on Microsoft's rivals of antitrust enforcement against Microsoft. Their hypothesis: If an antitrust intervention fulfills its stated objectives, a broad spectrum of publicly traded firms should benefit. As a result, stock market reactions to enforcement "events" should be positive for firms that produce *complements* to Microsoft operating systems (e.g., computer hardware, semiconductors, microprocessor chips, peripheral equipment, network systems, and applications software).

However, a review of share-price reactions to antitrust enforcement actions by the FTC and the DOJ during the 1991-97 period shows that returns for a computer industry index of 159 firms (excluding Microsoft) were negatively correlated with antitrust enforcement events. Antitrust measures against Microsoft appear to depress equity values in the software sector. Thus, financial market evidence leans against the joint hypothesis that (a) Microsoft engages in anticompetitive conduct, and (b) antitrust policy is likely to impose remedies producing net efficiency gains.

The Government's Claims that the Remedy Would Increase Innovation

The government and its three economists all asserted that the proposed remedies would, in the words of Professor Henderson, "release a flood of innovative energy,"[154] but there is no evidence in the trial record or in the scholarly literature that Microsoft suppressed significant innovations. Nor is there evidence that innovation in the computer industry in general and PC software in particular has been sluggish. Nor is there evidence that software entrepreneurs with promising ideas are denied financing.

The government's economists based their opinions on a conjecture that breaking up Microsoft would trigger more platform competition among operating systems and various types of middleware.[155] In particular, they conjectured that Apps Co would focus its independent energy on developing office productivity software for Linux and promoting Office as a platform for other software applications. Yet, there is no direct or indirect evidence that Apps Co would try to turn Office into a platform, let alone succeed.

The software industry seems to be moving toward systems that use the Web as a platform. The notion that Apps Co's Office platform would be Windows' main competition, instead of Web-based computing, is dated. Neither is there evidence that Apps Co would be more likely than an integrated Microsoft to write a version of Office for Linux. As discussed later, the premise that Apps Co would have sufficient incentive to compete with Windows as a platform, or to write applications for a new platform like Linux, contradicts the government's liability case.

Economists generally agree that there is no simple relationship between market structure and the level of innovative activity.[156] Innovation comes from unexpected places at unexpected times, often for unexpected reasons. Competition makes firms race to introduce the next product improvement, but incentives are curtailed if competitors can ride free on their efforts.[157] Monopolies, by contrast, capture scale economies in research and development, and have more protection from poaching by "fast second" competitors.[158] In commenting on the government's proposed remedy, Professor Krugman summarized the problems with the economic analysis put forward by the government and its economists:

> My point is not that it is wrong to consider the impact of policy on innovation; it is that because the determinants of innovation are not well understood, clever advocates can invoke technological progress as an all-purpose justification for whatever policy they favor ...In short, the promise of technological benefits has become the universal policy justification. Does a proposal seem to cost taxpayers billions or raise prices to consumers? Never mind – it will promote innovation! And maybe it will; or maybe in the 21st century, technology, not patriotism, has become the last refuge of a scoundrel.[159]

CONTRADICTIONS BETWEEN THE GOVERNMENT'S THEORIES IN THE REMEDY AND LIABILITY PHASES

The arguments used by the government to support the proposed remedy contradict arguments made by the government in the liability phase of the case – arguments that were endorsed by the court's Findings of Fact and Conclusions of Law. If one believes the theories used to support liability, many of the remedies proposed by the government make little sense. Conversely, if one accepts the theories used to support the remedies, it is far from clear that Microsoft was guilty in the first place. At a minimum, these contradictions point to the need for a careful and reflective remedies phase in which Microsoft would have had the opportunity to confront these contradictions through cross-examination and to present its own evidence and expert testimony. The two main contradictions between liability and remedy involve the "applications barrier to entry" and the arena of competition for analyzing Microsoft's market power.

The centerpiece of the government's case against Microsoft was the "applications barrier to entry."[160] This was the supposed source of Microsoft's durable monopoly power and the asset Microsoft allegedly wanted to protect at all costs. The government claimed that Netscape was uniquely positioned to erode the applications barrier.[161] Other actual and potential Windows competitors – Apple's MacOS, IBM's OS/2, and Linux – were dismissed by the government on grounds that they could never generate enough software development activity to attract large numbers of consumers to use them.[162] This argument appeared over and again in the district court's Findings of Fact.[163]

In contrast to the dreary prospects for entry portrayed by the government at trial, the experts in the remedies phase conjure a porous applications barrier to entry. Now it is stated that Microsoft's is a market environment in which Apps Co would create a version of Office for Linux and possibly other operating systems that previously were dismissed as potential competitors to Windows.[164]

The government also shifted its view of how the relevant market is to be understood. For purposes of finding that Microsoft has monopoly power, the government insisted that the relevant market was narrow, consisting of operating systems for Intel-compatible personal computers. Arguments at trial by Microsoft and its expert that the relevant arena of competition was *platforms* for applications software – including other types of computers and the burgeoning array of programs that run on the Web and can be used by a variety of computers linked to the Web – were rejected by the court.[165]

Many of the arguments made by the government in support of its remedies, however, hinged on that broader arena of platform competition. Whereas in the liability phase the government portrayed Netscape's Navigator browser combined with the Java run-time environment as a uniquely powerful threat to Microsoft, the structural remedy in the government's remedy phase rested on the prospect that a single popular application could evolve into a platform that challenges Windows' hegemony.

In most respects, the government's theories about the market for software at the remedy stage are more plausible than the theories the government put forward at the liability stage. The applications barrier to entry is indeed quite porous. Software developers flock to promising computing platforms. They once flocked to Microsoft DOS from CP/M and AT&T's Unix. Now they flock to Linux.[166]

The Applications Barrier to Entry: Impenetrable or Porous?

The district court found that the economic characteristics of operating system software give the "first mover" a significant advantage.[167] On the supply side, there are scale economies in operating system software. Although it is expensive to develop and promote an operating system, it costs very little to produce additional copies of the finished product. Indeed, the marginal cost to Microsoft of licensing its operating systems to OEMs is virtually zero because OEMs bear the cost of buying CDs and documentation from authorized replicators.[168] There also are substantial economies on the demand side through "network effects." Consumers value operating systems that run more applications, and applications developers value operating systems that have more consumers, creating a positive feedback loop in which success begets success.[169]

Adopting the government's claims, the district court found that network effects in operating system software were so strong that they essentially bestowed a monopoly on the first firm that got its product in the hands of consumers and software developers. According to the district court, there is an

> intractable "chicken-and-egg" problem: The overwhelming majority of consumers will only use a PC operating system for which there already exists a large and varied set of high-quality, full-featured applications, and for which it seems relatively certain that new types of applications and new versions of existing applications will continue to be marketed at pace with those written for other operating systems.... [S]oftware developers generally write applications first, and often exclusively, for the operating system that is already used

> by a dominant share of all PC users. Users do not want to invest in an operating system until it is clear that the system will support generations of applications that will meet their needs, and developers do not want to invest in writing or quickly porting applications for an operating system until it is clear that there will be a sizeable and stable market for it.[170]

This reasoning led the district court to embrace the term "applications barrier to entry" and to find that "[t]his barrier ensures that no Intel-compatible PC operating system other than Windows can attract consumer demand . . .."[171]

Judge Jackson focused in particular on potential entrants that produced middleware, in his words software that "relies on interfaces provided by the underlying operating system while simultaneously exposing its own APIs to developers."[172] A middleware program could thus compete with an operating system as a platform for applications software. The court claimed that the applications barrier to entry makes it unlikely that middleware could succeed in becoming a competitive alternative to the dominant operating system:

> As the Court finds above, however, it remains to be seen whether server- or middleware-based development will flourish at all. Even if such development were already flourishing it would be several years before the applications barrier eroded enough to clear the way for the relatively rapid emergence of a viable alternative to incumbent Intel-compatible PC operating systems.[173]

Although the district court found that Netscape's wide distribution gave it an advantage over other possible entrants, it found that the applications barrier to entry made it unlikely that Netscape or Sun could ever provide commercially viable middleware.

> ... the collaboration of Netscape and Sun also heralded the day when vendors of information appliances and network computers could present users with viable alternatives to PCs themselves. Nevertheless, these middleware technologies have a long way to go before they might imperil the applications barriers to entry. Windows 98 exposes nearly ten thousand APIs whereas the combined APIs of Navigator and the Java class libraries, together representing the greatest hope for the proponents of middleware, total less than a thousand.[174]
>
> It is not clear whether, absent Microsoft's interference, Sun's Java efforts would by now have facilitated porting between Windows and other platforms enough to weaken the applications barrier to entry.[175]
>
> There is insufficient evidence to find that, absent Microsoft's actions, Navigator and Java already would have ignited genuine competition in the market for Intel-compatible PC operating systems.[176]

Judging the applications barrier to entry to be impenetrable, the court found that it would be "several years" at best before successful middleware technologies could imperil Windows' monopoly.

If the district court were correct in its pessimism, there would be no remedy that could create enduring competition in software platforms.[177] Even the dissolution of Microsoft's operating systems into multiple companies would cause only temporary competition (and confusion). Eventually one of them would gain a slight but decisive lead, which would propel the leader to a new monopoly. During the interim, consumers would be denied the benefits of network effects and economies of scale.[178]

In defending the government's proposed remedy, its post-trial economists contradicted the testimony of the government's trial economists and the district court's findings. During the trial, the government's experts presented a simplistic theory that users would choose the platform for which the most applications were available.[179] For example, the court rejected Apple's Macintosh as a viable competitor because there are "only" 12,000 applications available to run on it, including Microsoft Office.[180]

The government's remedy experts, however, assume that having the handful of applications in Microsoft Office available for Linux would make Linux a breakthrough competitor. As Professor Henderson put it, "the availability of the world's most popular office productivity suite on alternative platforms would serve to reduce the barriers to entry protecting Microsoft's monopoly, which will, in turn, increase the potential for competition in the PC operating systems market."[181] But if having Office is critical to overcoming the applications barrier to entry, what accounts for the Macintosh's relative failure?[182] Similarly, Professor Shapiro attributes Linux's limited success on desktop computers to its unfriendly user interface and the fact that "many of the most popular applications on Windows, including especially Microsoft Office, are not available on the Linux platform."[183] Like Professor Henderson, he makes no reference to the government's theory of an applications barrier to entry driven by overwhelming numbers of compatible applications.

Judge Jackson accepted the government's claims that software applications developers generally write only for the dominant operating system.[184] Further, he concluded that "the porting of applications from one operating system to another is a costly process,"[185] one that leads "ISVs [independent software vendors] that do go to the effort of porting frequently [to] set the price of ported applications considerably higher than that of the original versions written for Windows."[186]

But if this is true, Apps Co is unlikely to port a version of Office to Linux. This is even less likely to happen if the Linux threat to Windows is so remote as to be "a joke," as it was called by Professor Franklin Fisher, the government's chief economic witness in the liability phase.[187] "Office for Linux" would face the additional hurdle that one of Linux's key attractions is its low cost, and many Linux users are predisposed to using free, open-source software.[188]

The government's remedy experts are correct to say that the "applications barrier to entry" is not the "intractable" problem that Judge Jackson found it to be and that Linux is more than "a joke."[189] Operating systems need applications to be successful, but the key measure is the quality and coverage of those applications, not their sheer number. Platform vendors can influence the number and quality of applications written to run for them by the amount of support they provide to developers. As Professor Shapiro quotes from a Microsoft document, the company devotes about 10 percent of its employees to supporting developers, and "[n]o other computer company provides anything like this level of support to the developer community."[190] Those efforts are pro-competitive, because they have fostered the development of more and better software applications.

Professor Arrow, the DOJ's economist for the 1994-95 *Tunney Act* proceedings, is correct that scale economies on the supply side and network effects on the demand side do create a "natural barrier" and confer an advantage on the leading software vendor.[191] As Arrow noted, such natural barriers exist in many other software categories as well. Entry into categories where natural barriers emerge can be accomplished only by software developers who market superior products. The previous research of Professors Henderson and Shapiro supports this view. Professor Henderson suggests that entrants dominate radical innovations and that incumbent firms have difficulty in making transitions to new technologies in high-tech industries.[192] Professor Shapiro makes the point that to succeed, new applications must "provide sufficiently great improvements in performance to justify the switching costs users would have to incur to adopt them."[193] In a paper with Michael Katz, Professor Shapiro pointed out that although market forces may lead to too much inertia in the presence of network effects, they also may lead to insufficient inertia, as purchasers of new systems do not account for the lost network benefits of owners of older (no longer compatible) systems.[194]

The government's economic experts on remedies implicitly acknowledge that Linux, or various types of middleware, could dethrone Windows. Likewise, Arrow recognized that it would have been possible in the early 1990s for IBM's OS/2 to have beaten Windows in the contest to become the new PC operating system standard.[195] This contrasts sharply with testimony during the trial by Professor Fisher and Dr. Frederick Warren-Boulton that the applications barrier to entry is virtually impenetrable.

As a matter of economic logic, the government cannot have it both ways. Once it has "proved" its thesis that there is an applications barrier to entry that gives Microsoft durable monopoly power – an essential predicate for the district court's finding of liability – it cannot reverse course and support its proposed remedy on the antithesis. If the government's remedy theory is right, its liability theory is wrong, and conversely.

The "Relevant Market:" Intel-Compatible Operating Systems or Platforms?

The government's elastic view on the applications barrier to entry is related to its malleable definition of the relevant market. In the liability phase, the government insisted there was a "market" delineated as operating systems for Intel-compatible computers.[196] Microsoft's economic expert, Professor Schmalensee, argued that this definition was too narrow because it excluded products that constrain Microsoft's pricing. [197] He argued that the key competition was not in operating systems narrowly construed, but in "platforms" for applications, which include not only operating systems for different types of small computers, but also middleware that could attract developers away from Windows and toward the Web as a platform.[198] With Web-based applications, software is written to run on server operating systems, a line of business in which Microsoft is far from dominant.[199] The operating system on the desktop PC is irrelevant to most of these applications, as long as it contains a browser that meets industry standards.

In its Findings of Fact and Conclusions of Law, the district court sided with the government in determining that the relevant market was limited to "Intel-compatible PC operating systems."[200] Judge Jackson rejected applications running on servers as relevant competition.[201] With such a narrow market definition, coupled with the undisputed fact that Microsoft operating systems run more than 90 percent of all PCs, Judge Jackson's conclusion that "Microsoft enjoys monopoly power in the relevant market" was hardly surprising.[202]

In contrast to the narrow market definition used to declare Microsoft a monopolist, the arguments made by the government's remedy economists center on platforms, not operating systems. For example, whereas in the liability phase, Judge Jackson rejected applications running on servers as relevant competition,[203] in the remedy phase, Professor Henderson devotes substantial attention to allegations concerning the security protocol used in Microsoft's new Windows 2000 Server operating system. Professor Henderson notes that "[s]erver operating systems, other platform software running on servers, or other technology running on devices other than the PC, could increasingly threaten to lower the entry barriers protecting [Microsoft's] monopoly."[204]

The number of potential platform threats accorded significant roles by the government's remedy phase experts contradicts the starring roles assigned to Netscape's browser and Java in the liability phase. In the liability phase, the government asserted that Netscape and Java were unusually strong threats, justifying predatory expenditures by Microsoft and making their defeat a major blow to competition.[205] However, if there were several potential platform threats to Microsoft, then it is not evident that defeat of Netscape/Java would be a major blow to competition. Moreover, since rational predation requires recoupment after the challenger is driven from the market,[206] the fact that there are multiple challengers casts doubt on the viability of Microsoft's engaging in predatory actions against just one of them. There can be no recoupment if defeated challengers can be replaced by new ones that put competitive pressure on the incumbent firm.

THE DISPROPORTIONATE REMEDY

The district court adopted one of the most far-reaching antitrust remedies ever imposed. The possibility that this remedy might be upheld by the Supreme Court sent Microsoft's stock price plummeting.[207] Although some of the drop was the consequence of other forces, the proposed breakup and resulting uncertainty about the company's prospects was surely a major factor.[208] One study estimated that higher prices for operating systems and applications as a result of the breakup of Microsoft would cost U.S. consumers at least $50 billion over three years.[209] This article has not attempted to conduct a benefit–cost analysis of the proposed remedy, nor has the government or its economists. However, this section addresses a narrower question: Did the court establish harm to competition and consumers of such significance that one would logically consider a drastic remedy to prevent harm in the future? The district court's own Findings of Fact demonstrate that Microsoft's actions did not impose significant harm to competition or to consumers. Indeed, a fair reading of the Findings of Fact demonstrates that Microsoft's actions provided overall benefits to consumers and offers no basis for believing that these benefits would have been outweighed by future costs.

Lack of Evidence of Significant Harm to Competition

In his Findings of Fact, Judge Jackson concluded "there is insufficient evidence to find that, absent Microsoft's actions, Navigator and Java already would have ignited genuine competition in the market for Intel-compatible PC operating systems."[210] He also found that the applications barrier to entry made it unlikely that any middleware technologies would succeed in displacing Windows.[211]

In his Conclusions of Law, Judge Jackson asserted that "Microsoft's campaign succeeded in preventing – for several years, and perhaps permanently – Navigator and Java from fulfilling their potential to open the market for Intel-compatible PC operating systems to competition on the merits."[212] There was no evidence submitted at trial, however, that Netscape had taken the necessary steps to develop its browser as a platform for Internet-related applications, let alone as a broad software platform. (Indeed, as explained below, Netscape's CEO denied on the stand that Netscape ever intended such a course.) Nor was evidence offered that Java's problems in gaining widespread usage were due to Microsoft's actions. To whatever extent Netscape and Java were ever potential platform competitors of Microsoft, they remain so today. Events since the trial confirm that Netscape's and Java's potential to emerge as significant competitive platforms has not diminished.

Netscape

In early 1995, Marc Andreessen, the founder of Netscape, made public statements about developing Netscape's Navigator browser as a platform that would reduce Windows to a set of "slightly buggy device drivers."[213] Although Microsoft was concerned that Netscape would transform Navigator into a competing platform, there is no evidence from the trial or elsewhere that Netscape ever seriously planned to do so.[214] Netscape's CEO, Jim Barksdale, testified that Andreessen's comments reflected his youth and a "spirit of jocularity and sometimes sarcasm that have gotten us in trouble."[215] Throughout the pre-trial period, Netscape never developed a "componentized" version of Navigator that would enable other applications to use it as a platform. Without componentization, other applications could do little more than launch Netscape's browser.[216]

Netscape's share of browser use (though not its total number of users) declined after the release of IE 3 and AOL's decision to use IE.[217] If AOL-branded versions of IE are included in the reckoning, Microsoft probably passed Netscape in usage in 1998.[218] Nonetheless, AOL purchased Netscape in

March 1999 for AOL stock valued at $10 billion.[219] Navigator continues to capture a significant share of browser users. The University of Illinois Engineering Labs, which the DOJ cited as a reliable source of information on browser use, reported Netscape's share at 29 percent when the district court issued its final order in June 2000.[220] Netscape/AOL has since released Navigator 6. If AOL uses the browsing features of Navigator 6 to replace IE in the software provided to AOL's 23 million subscribers, Netscape could once again claim more users than Microsoft.[221]

Java

Similarly, Microsoft's actions caused no anticompetitive harm to Sun Microsystems' Java programming and run-time environment. The primary issue concerning Java during the trial was Microsoft's competition with Netscape, which reduced distribution of Netscape's version of the software needed to run Java programs on Windows and other platforms.[222] However, Microsoft developed its own "Java Virtual Machine" (JVM), which it included with all new copies of Windows until the release of Windows XP in November 2001. Although Sun sued Microsoft for implementing an approach different from Sun's to calling Windows-specific code from Java programs, Microsoft's actions did not delay the development of "pure," platform-independent Java.

Nor did Microsoft undermine the versatility of Java. In each of the two years preceding the trial, the leading computer magazine rated Microsoft's JVM as the best available for running "applets" (small applications) written to and certified by Sun as meeting "pure" Java specifications. In tests with 20 such applications, Microsoft's JVM ran more applications than JVMs provided by either Netscape or Sun – even when Sun's JVM ran on its own hardware and its own Solaris operating system.

The problems inherent in Java were illustrated by the experiences of several Sun allies and Microsoft competitors – including Netscape, Corel, and Lotus/IBM – that tried to write major applications in pure Java and failed. Corel and Netscape never were able to finish Java versions of WordPerfect or Navigator, respectively.[223] Lotus/IBM's *eSuite* achieved minimal commercial success, and that only after it was rewritten to take advantage of new features added by Microsoft to its Windows JVM.[224] It has since been withdrawn from the market.[225] As an editor of *PC Magazine* summarized the situation: "Java hasn't succeeded, as some hoped, simply because it isn't all it was once cracked up to be... And despite Sun's complaints about Microsoft, the problem doesn't appear to have much to do with Microsoft's interpretation of Java."[226]

Most developers have abandoned the vision of running major Java applications on desktop computers. But this reflects performance problems that are inherent in any cross-platform approach. Java developers have focused their energies on using Java as a language for writing server applications, with Java running on networked PCs providing an interface to the server applications.

Java continues to grow. All commercially significant operating systems include a JVM to run Java applications.[227] Sun lists 19 Java "partners" on its Web site, including IBM, Apple, Oracle, and Hewlett Packard.[228] Sun promotes "Java Beans" as the best option for writing applications that run partly on servers and partly on remote computers linked to the network.[229] IDC projects that the percentage of professional developers using Java will triple from 1998 to 2003.[230] Microsoft has not driven Java from the field of competition or neutralized it as a platform competitor of Windows. There has been no harm to competition here.

Lack of Evidence of Significant Harm to Consumer Welfare

Judge Jackson never found that Microsoft harmed consumers by suppressing competition in the market for PC operating systems. He did find a "dangerous possibility" that Microsoft's conduct would "allow it to attain monopoly power in a second market," namely, the browser market.[231] In this market, the court found that Microsoft's actions created benefits for some consumers and costs for others.[232]

Benefits of Microsoft's Actions

As noted earlier, Judge Jackson found that Microsoft conferred concrete benefits on consumers in terms of higher-quality and lower-priced browsers.[233] This finding is a tribute to Microsoft, not a finding of the dead hand of monopoly. Indeed, all consumers who used Web-browsing software enjoyed the benefits identified by the court.

It is impossible to determine the precise dollar savings to consumers from the way Microsoft chose to market its browser. Netscape's strategy with its browser involved what Professors Michael Cusumano and David Yoffie have called "free but not free."[234] Netscape distributed millions of copies of Navigator, many at zero price, but also charged some customers (notably businesses) prices ranging from $40 in 1995 to as much as $79 in 1996.[235] The district court found that Microsoft's competition made it increasingly difficult for Netscape to charge customers.[236] Without Microsoft's zero-price strategy,

Netscape might have been able to hold its prices steady (or increase them) while increasing the fraction of customers who were charged.

IDC estimated that, by the end of the year 2000, 123 million Americans would access the Web on at least a quarterly basis, using 184 million devices.[237] If each of the 123 million users would have paid $50 for a browser, total browser cost to consumers would have been over $6 billion. If the average user paid only $20 (about half of the lowest price that Netscape ever charged individual users who paid), the total cost would have been over $2 billion. Thus, under Judge Jackson's own assumptions, Microsoft's pricing strategy generated consumer savings of $2 billion to $6 billion. It is no exaggeration to claim a figure of this magnitude as a benefit conferred on users by Microsoft's aggressive promotion of IE.

Free browsers are not the only benefit that consumers received as a result of Microsoft's competition with Netscape. According to the district court, Microsoft gave AOL and other Internet access providers valuable services (and in a few cases, bounties) for distributing IE rather than Navigator. According to Judge Jackson, Microsoft:

• developed "an Internet sign-up program that made it simple for users to download access software from, and subscribe to any IAP appearing on a list assembled by Microsoft;"[238]

• created the Online Services Folder, which reduced the cost of signing with online service providers;[239]

• gave online service providers reduced referral fees if they upgraded subscribers to IE;[240] and

• offered the Internet Explorer Access Kit (IEAK) to Internet access providers, which made the process of installing and distributing IE easier.[241]

In addition, Microsoft granted MCI a $5 credit for distributing IE and granted AOL a $2 credit for each new subscriber who used IE.[242] The benefits that Microsoft offered these companies reduced their cost of providing customers with Web-browsing software.[243]

Harm from Microsoft's Actions

The court also held that Microsoft's actions in browsers harmed some consumers:[244]

• Microsoft forced OEMs to ignore consumer preferences for a browserless version of Windows.

• Microsoft increased confusion and support costs for users who wanted to have only one browser (Netscape's) installed on their computers.

• Microsoft deprived consumers of helpful aids and increased support costs by denying OEMs the right to automatically launch their own "shells" and tutorials when computers were first turned on.

• Microsoft deprived consumers of software innovation by pressuring Intel to drop the development of its platform-level NSP software.

It has already been noted why the last two claims did not result in significant losses. Here the focus is on the users the court claimed were "forced" to accept copies of Windows that included browsing capabilities.

The "evidence" of harm to consumers from the inclusion of IE in Windows consisted of a handful of anecdotal reports and speculation by government witnesses (and the district court). In preparation for expected remedies testimony, National Economic Research Associates developed surveys to obtain empirical data on this issue. In telephone surveys conducted in the late spring of 2000, home and business PC users were asked about their preferences with respect to browsing capabilities built into Windows.[245] Respondents qualified for the survey if they had purchased a PC with Windows since 1998. To qualify, they did not have to use their computers to access the Internet, although the overwhelming majority did.[246] These questions included a series on respondents' preferences between two otherwise identical new computers: one with the current version of Windows with Internet Explorer "built in," the other without. Among home users, only 11.6 percent preferred "without," 79.0 percent preferred "with," and 9.4 percent did not express a preference.[247] Even users of Netscape's browser preferred the built-in option by a three-to-one margin, apparently not experiencing the "confusion and frustration" that concerned Judge Jackson.[248]

Moreover, when asked how much extra they would be willing to pay to get their preferred version, most of those who preferred "without" were unwilling to pay anything, whereas a majority of those who preferred "with" were willing to pay extra for that version. Only 2 percent placed any monetary value on having a browserless copy of Windows. Overall, those who wanted IE built in were willing to pay more than 15 times more than what those who did not want IE built in were willing to pay.[249] This result is striking because of the current wide availability of browsers at no cost.

Among business managers responsible for selecting their companies' computers, 66.5 percent preferred Windows with IE built in, whereas 25.5 percent preferred without, and 8.0 percent did not express an opinion.[250] As with the home sample, a majority of those who used Netscape still preferred the version of Windows with IE built in. As with the home users, those who preferred "with" were more likely to be willing to pay extra for their preferred version than were those who preferred "without." The total amount they were willing to pay was more than five times higher than what those who preferred "without" would pay.[251]

On average, business users were not willing to pay as much as home users, presumably because they could readily download free copies and then install them on all of the machines in their companies; 71 percent of those who preferred "with" but would not pay anything extra indicated they would download a free copy of IE if one were not included with Windows.[252] The preference for having IE installed was strongest among officials from companies that do not routinely install additional software on new computers. Conversely, the smallest majority preferring IE built in occurred among officials from companies that routinely "wipe" the hard disks of new computers and install the company's standard set of software.

These survey results show that Judge Jackson's concerns about harm to users who did not want IE built in were misplaced, or at least swamped by the benefits accruing to those users who have found it valuable. Even among users who prefer Netscape's browser and use it regularly, a majority would choose to buy the version of Windows with IE built in. Moreover, the survey results understate the overall benefits of IE to consumers because respondents were answering the questions in mid-2000, when competition from Microsoft already had driven the price of browsers to zero and free browsers were easy to obtain. Presumably, respondents would have been willing to pay more had the alternative been purchasing a browser at prices in the neighborhood of the $50 or so that Netscape charged customers before IE caught up in quality.

The overwhelming majority of computer users gained from Microsoft's actions with respect to Web-browsing software. Quality rose, prices fell, and large majorities of both home and business users prefer to have browsing capabilities built into Windows. Judge Jackson's concerns about the integration of IE causing "confusion and frustration" among users who wanted a different browser, or none at all, are not borne out by the data.

HARM TO CONSUMERS FROM THE COURT'S REMEDIES

Is there any basis for concluding, then, that consumer welfare would be improved if the district court's remedies were imposed? The district court suggested that the only way to answer that question is to try the remedies and see what happens:

> There is little chance that those divergent opinions will be reconciled by

> anything short of actual experience. The declarations (and the "offers of proof") from numerous potential witnesses now before the Court provide some insight as to how its various provisions might operate, but for the most part they are merely the predictions of purportedly knowledgeable people as to effects that may or may not ensue if the proposed final judgment is entered. In its experience the Court has found testimonial predictions of future events generally less reliable even than testimony as to historical fact, and cross-examination to be of little use in enhancing or detracting from their accuracy.[253]

Notwithstanding the court's speculation about the aftermath of its remedies, they are likely to impose significant costs on consumers without generating offsetting benefits. Using an economic model presented by the government's economist during the liability trial, we calculate that consumers could pay roughly three times as much for an operating system as they paid before, because the Ops Co and Apps Co would no longer have an incentive to increase sales of Microsoft applications software. Also, consumers could expect a slowdown in innovation as a result of the breakup and the restraints on the successor companies.

Divestiture and Higher Prices as a Result of Double Marginalization

One direct consequence of splitting Microsoft along the lines proposed would have been an increase in the price of the operating system. The reason is simple, and it is not speculative. When Microsoft sets its price for Windows today it takes into account the fact that selling additional copies of Windows affects the demand for Office and other Microsoft applications as well. If Microsoft raises the price of Windows, it will sell fewer copies of Office and other applications and therefore earn less revenue from a product that costs almost nothing at the margin to produce.[254] This is an example of the double marginalization problem.[255] As Professor Paul Krugman explained: "The now 'naked' operating-system company would abandon its traditional pricing restraint and use its still formidable monopoly power to charge much more. And at the same time applications software that now comes free would also start to carry hefty price tags."[256]

The magnitude of the double marginalization effect can be inferred using the analysis employed by both sides during the liability phase of the trial. Schmalensee, testifying for Microsoft,[257] and Fisher, testifying for the DOJ, both used a model of monopoly pricing in which:

$$P^* = \frac{P_0}{E} - R$$

where P^* is the profit-maximizing price of the operating system, P_0 is the price of the PC observed in the market today, E is the elasticity of demand for PCs at the current price, and R is the complementary revenue received from sales of other products.[258] For each \$1 reduction in complementary revenue, the operating system monopolist's profit-maximizing price would rise by \$1. Fisher used a value of R = \$160.[259] If Microsoft were broken up by the Final Judgment, most of those complementary revenues would go to Apps Co, inducing Ops Co to raise the price of Windows by an equal amount. If one assumes that only three-fourths of the complementary revenues (\$120) would go to Apps Co, the profit-maximizing price of Windows would increase by \$120. Thus, under the government's theory of Microsoft's pricing, Windows would roughly triple in price from its current average of about \$65.[260]

Schmalensee's model was not intended to be an analysis of how Microsoft actually behaves, but rather a demonstration that Microsoft's prices are less than what it would charge if it acted like a monopolist. However, because finding that Microsoft has a monopoly in PC operating systems was a predicate to the finding of liability, the remedies proposed by the government and imposed by the court cannot ignore the implication of their own analysis: the prospect that Windows prices could triple under divestiture.

Divestiture and Lost Economies of Scope

The government and its remedy economists euphemistically referred to the proposed breakup of Microsoft as a "reorganization."[261] But splitting Microsoft into two companies would have significant repercussions for its operational efficiency and for consumer welfare. The government's breakup proposal is oddly disconnected from economic analysis of the business enterprise and from the realities of how Microsoft is organized.

The Economic Theory of the Firm

The economic theory of the firm explains which economic activities will be conducted *inside* a firm and which will be organized *outside* the firm – i.e., made available to the firm via markets.[262] A theme that runs through the economic analysis of the business firm is that the boundaries of firms, and the internal organization of their activities, are designed to minimize costs.[263] This analysis has important implications for using structural remedies because structural relief alters the boundaries. The remedy economists treat Microsoft as a collection of independent divisions that can be reshuffled at will, with few impacts on efficiency other than those driven by the incentives of changes in ownership. They treat the firm as a black box, where it does not matter whether a transaction takes place within a firm or at arm's length in the market. The reality of corporate organization, however, is much more complicated.

Professors Milgrom and Roberts observe that coordination *within* firms is especially important for firms whose products have what they call "design attributes."[264] An example would be the software industry. The theory of the firm also suggests that design attributes in "knowledge-intensive" industries often will be organized internally within a firm rather than through external markets. This is because of the public goods characteristic of intellectual assets.[265]

In "old economy" manufacturing industries that depend on large amounts of physical capital,[266] company boundaries and internal organizations are relatively stationary. In the software industry, firms' capital is more intellectual than physical, so boundaries and organizations are fluid. As a result, firms evolve continually and adapt to changing market forces. Further, stages of production in the software industry are not readily distinguished as they are in traditional industries.[267]

In the software industry, production, inventory management, and distribution of output are secondary activities. There is little or no scope for establishing cost-based transfer prices between successive vertical stages of production as there would be, for example, between the sequential stages of producing virgin ingot, product fabrication, inventory, and distribution of finished products in the aluminum industry. In contrast to vertically organized industrial sectors, software firms are rarely divisible into stand-alone units.

Historically, virtually all of the firms that have been the objects of structural relief in antitrust were themselves the product of growth by merger. Significantly, their acquisition pattern itself generated a blueprint for their breakup – i.e., the divestiture of earlier acquisitions. Where growth to market dominance has been accomplished by acquiring competitors, the defendant firm normally is organized along reversible lines that are a vestige of that growth. The remnants of the acquisitions remain recognizable and therefore separable by function or geography or both.

For example, refineries acquired by the Standard Oil trust that were located in Ohio remained in Ohio after their acquisition. When the trust was dissolved, they became the basis of the new Standard Oil of Ohio; in the same way, acquired refineries in Indiana became the basis for the new Standard Oil of Indiana. When AT&T broke itself up to avoid further antitrust proceedings, the seven Regional Bell Operating Companies were formed by combining the preexisting local Bell operating companies. What remained as "AT&T" consisted of the former Long Lines Division, Western Electric, and Bell Labs.[268]

In his classic treatise on antitrust, Robert Bork wrote, "Advocates of large firm dissolution must demonstrate that the process will not destroy significant amounts of efficiency. Otherwise, they ask us to risk doing consumers more harm than good."[269] One weakness of proposals to break up Microsoft is a failure to consider the potential harm to consumers in destroying the organic unity of knowledge-based firms like Microsoft that did not grow by acquisition. Having multiple firms is not an end in itself – particularly if it leads to higher prices, lower quality, or less innovation.

Disruption of Microsoft's Organization

Microsoft does not offer clear lines along which to divide the company. Microsoft is defined more by its organizational capabilities than by its current portfolio of products.[270] Of Microsoft's almost 40,000 employees, about 22,000 work at the Redmond, Washington, campus, including virtually all of the software developers.[271] Regional offices in the U.S. and foreign subsidiaries are organized primarily around sales, which cut across all product lines. Within the Redmond campus, sales are organized by channel rather than by product – OEMs versus corporate accounts, for example. Similarly, support services such as accounting and human resources are not organized by product.

Dividing these departments between the two new companies would require increased staffing as a result of lost economies of scale and scope. Where there may be a need for just one account manager to deal with an OEM now, the Ops Co and Apps Co both would need an account manager for that OEM. The same problem would arise with foreign subsidiaries; a single Microsoft subsidiary in the United Kingdom would be replaced by two.

The lost economies of scale and scope would also extend to Microsoft's highest executive levels: Each company would require its own board, chairman, president, chief financial officer, and so forth. Microsoft's founder, Bill Gates, has continued to play a key role throughout Microsoft's quarter-century of existence. He and the current CEO, Steve Ballmer, whose working relationship developed over decades, bring complementary skills to the company. If Microsoft were divided, either that pairing would be split or one of the new companies would have to recruit new top leadership.

The technical teams that design, develop, and test software are organized along product lines. Here the division might appear not to affect costs significantly. However, in the past there has been considerable movement of personnel across the dividing line that was proposed. In some cases, this has occurred when code components are shifted from an application to the operating system. In other cases, when a project is completed, developers or testers join projects in a division that would have been part of a different company under the Final Judgment. Dividing the company would have made such movement more costly to the companies and, ultimately, consumers.

It takes little effort, then, to imagine the diversion of managerial energy that would have resulted from dividing what had hitherto been a unified company. It is no surprise to an economist that Microsoft's competitors want *structural* relief: It would be enormously draining for Microsoft's management and would confer advantages upon present and future Microsoft rivals. In the meantime, antitrust uncertainties may cause Microsoft to be a less vigorous competitor. The historical parallel would be the DOJ's investigation of IBM that some observers believe led to its diminution as a player in information technology markets.[272]

Throughout the transition years, Ops Co and Apps Co would have been extremely vulnerable to the loss of key personnel. It would not have been surprising if many of Microsoft's executives and senior technical employees had decided that the headaches of a breakup, followed by additional years of being hobbled by cumbersome product-design limitations, made it an opportune time to retire or move to a less fettered environment.

Lost Synergies between Operating Systems and Applications

In many vertically integrated firms, not only are the boundaries between layers distinct, they stay that way for good reasons. In a vertically integrated steel firm, the iron ore mines will never be blast furnaces; blast furnaces will never become mines. But the line between operating systems and applications software changes with time. When the government called for "separation of the Operating Systems Business from the Applications Business," it assumed a line can be drawn cleanly between the two. But throughout the company's history, Microsoft has added features to its operating systems, features that often had been separate "applications."[273] Microsoft has not been alone in shifting the line; other operating systems have added new features as well.[274] Imposing a corporate structure based on the current dividing line could only hinder future innovation and cost reductions through integration of features into the operating system.

Microsoft and consumers reap numerous economies of scope from the company's unified structure. In several instances, for example, innovations that started in Office have been moved to Windows and exposed as APIs that outside developers can use to improve the functionality of their own software. One of the more important examples of such movement is the development of Object Linking and Embedding (OLE), which makes it possible for one program to embed information from another (e.g., an Excel spreadsheet embedded as a table or a graph in a Word document). This technology started in the group working on Office, as a means to integrate various components of the software suite more closely. The technology was then moved to the operating system so that applications from third parties could use it as well, and has become the standard way for one application to link material from another (e.g., a Lotus 1-2-3 spreadsheet can be linked to a WordPerfect document).

If Office and Windows had been owned by different companies in the early 1990s, it is improbable that the relevant technology would have been transferred for use by Office's competitors. Indeed, if such a development were to occur during the period in which the proposed conduct remedies would have applied, Apps Co would not be allowed to make such a transfer.

More recently, the Office group at Microsoft started a project in response to requests from corporate customers who were concerned about managing multiple versions of files ("DLLs") that support various APIs. The goal was to make Office easier to manage in corporate networks, with automated installation and self-repair. Once the technology was developed, the project was moved to Windows and renamed Windows Installer; it exposes APIs to all developers and allows them to better manage the components they include with their applications. A separate Apps Co probably would not have offered this service to competitors. In any case, it would not have been allowed to license the technology for three years to Ops Co under the proposed conduct remedies.

The synergies lost in splitting Microsoft would not be limited to Office and Windows. Other divisions of Microsoft would have been likely to sustain damage, in particular because operating systems would have been separated from developer tools and server software that are closely integrated with Windows 2000. Of all companies, Microsoft is widely credited with having created and maintained the most extensive set of tools and support services for developers to use in creating software.[275]

Microsoft also offers unparalleled support services to developers. During the liability phase of the trial, Paul Maritz testified that Microsoft devoted 2,000 employees and $630 million in fiscal year 1999 to working with developers.[276] One reason that Microsoft's operating systems have been successful is that the company provides so much assistance to outside developers, who have generated a rich array of applications. Developer support has played a key role in generating the vast array of applications available, thus providing benefits to other software vendors and consumers.

Although Microsoft sells many of its tools and services, they are not a direct source of profit. If ownership had been severed from the operating systems, Apps Co would not have provided the same level of support because it would not have reaped the same benefits that the integrated company does now. Indeed, Apps Co probably would have refocused the tools and support services toward its own applications, rather than supporting ISVs writing to the Ops Co platform. Such a change would not have benefited ISVs or consumers. It also would have placed Ops Co at an artificial disadvantage. All vendors of commercial operating systems devote resources to providing tools to developers and to "evangelizing" new applications software. Ops Co would have been forced to replace at least some of the capability lost as a result of the split.

The split also would have hobbled Microsoft's pro-competitive activities by artificially separating its server operating systems from its "back office" software, including the Internet Information Server, SQL Server, and Exchange. Microsoft has built its business strategy around close integration of these various components. Although its operating systems provide the external "hooks" (APIs) needed to interoperate with other systems, the company coordinates the introduction of new features at different levels (server operating system, server middleware such as SQL server, client). Without such connections, these innovations could not be implemented as quickly as they are now, if at all.[277]

There are, of course, alternative strategies that rely less on close integration, and some companies have adopted such strategies. Presumably Apps Co and Ops Co would have had to adopt such strategies, too. They would have been at a disadvantage, however, because Microsoft's software has been designed to match its strategy, not that of others.

In a recent paper, Professor Bresnahan (the DOJ's chief economist during the remedy phase) provided an insightful discussion of these issues in connection with competition for the enterprise market in heavy-duty server-based database software, the database systems that underpin large corporations and e-commerce Web sites.[278] In this segment of the software industry, Oracle, and to a lesser degree IBM, are the successful incumbents, and Microsoft is the challenger. Microsoft offers an approach different from that of the incumbents, one that emphasizes integration and standardized software (as opposed to the more service-oriented, customized approaches of Oracle and IBM). Bresnahan's conclusions merit quoting:

> From a societal perspective, it is hard to see a better epochal competition situation than this. The events of recent years make it clear that there will be considerable market power in server DBMS [database management software]. It seems nearly certain that there will be a dominant firm. But there is a real contest for dominant position at this point.
>
> Perhaps I may have surprised you with my remark that this situation is excellent. Many analysts will say that the proposed replacement of separate DBMS and server OS firms with a unified, more proprietary structure is bad. They will favor the continuation of the incumbent Oracle against entrant Microsoft on this industry structure argument. This is an error. The reason I am so sure it is an error is that I trust the customers in the server DBMS market to make their own decisions. Customers, spending their own money, will choose between two very different structures. They may choose integration over flexibility and choice, and choose Microsoft. Or they may make the opposite choice and stay with Oracle and Unix. It would be the height of arrogance on our part to tell them to prefer the current situation to its possible replacement.[279]

The proposed split would have prevented this type of competition because it would have vitiated Microsoft's strategic option.[280]

The Conduct Remedies and Lost Innovation

The structural portion of the district court's aborted remedies in *U.S. v. Microsoft Corp.* has been the focus of most discussion. The conduct remedies, however – remedies that, as of this writing, are still on the table – are themselves draconian, and several pose a threat to continued innovation by Microsoft or its successor companies. For example, OEMs would be free to remove significant blocks of code from Windows and to receive a discount for doing so.[281] That would reduce the uniformity of the Windows platform, leaving software developers without the certainty that the particular elements of Windows that their applications relied upon would be present on customers' systems. Microsoft (and Ops Co following the split) also would be required to provide voluminous technical information beyond documentation and support services for developers to every software vendor (including competitors) at the same time that it became available to its own personnel.[282]

In addition, Microsoft would have to "create a secure facility where qualified representatives of OEMs, ISVs, and IHVs shall be permitted to study, interrogate and interact with relevant and necessary portions of the source code and any related documentation of Microsoft Platform Software...."[283] Although the Final Judgment states that visitors to the facility would use the information for "the sole purpose of enabling their products to interoperate effectively with Microsoft Platform Software," guaranteed access would make it extremely difficult to prevent the misappropriation of Microsoft's intellectual property. Competitors could send developers to learn precisely how Microsoft has designed new features (even before the product is released) and then implement these features in their own products. With this provision in place, Microsoft's incentives to innovate would be reduced because it would be less able to capture the returns.

The conduct remedies also would make it difficult for Microsoft (or Ops Co after the split) to enter into alliances common in the computer industry and essential for products that must interact with one another. Such alliances often include exchanges of confidential information and agreements for joint promotion. Microsoft, however, would be barred from treating allies differently from other companies, including direct competitors.

CONCLUSIONS

As in medicine, antitrust remedies must be considered in the context of their side effects. The antitrust parallel to the Hippocratic oath's "do no harm" is "don't make it worse." Antitrust remedies – in particular, breaking up a large company and imposing detailed restrictions on its successors' conduct – should be based on more than sweeping assertions about "unleashing" innovation. As Professor Paul Krugman has pointed out, we know very little about what promotes innovation.[284] Nonetheless, it has become fashionable to wrap one's position in the flag of innovation, as if the assertion of more innovation trumps any other consideration.[285]

The government's remedies would raise prices, not lower prices, and, as another consequence, probably reduce innovation in software, not increase it. The inefficiencies that would have followed from Microsoft's breakup would have swamped the few tangible harms identified by Judge Jackson. The Microsoft case began as a case about tying and predation with respect to the operating system and browsers. The Final Judgment's remedy focused on applications and forced disclosure of source code. That is the remedy that Gary Reback has been seeking on behalf of Microsoft's competitors for the better part of a decade. As the DOJ said of that remedy in 1995, it "might advance the private interests" of Microsoft's competitors but "would act against the public interest." The DOJ had it right in 1995. The DOJ got it wrong in 2000.

* Elzinga was preparing testimony concerning the government's remedies on behalf of Microsoft when the district court terminated the remedies proceedings. Evans and Nichols conducted economic analyses concerning the government's remedies on behalf of Microsoft. The authors thank Lena Andrews, Tim Estes, Josh Lerner, David E. Mills, Belinda Morris, Steven S. Reinemund, Emily Trinks, and Kirstyn Walton for their assistance. This article originally appeared in the *George Mason Law Review* (Volume 9, Issue 3). Reprinted with permission.

1 Memorandum of the United States of America in Support of the Motion to Enter Final Judgment and in Opposition to the Position of IDE Corporation and Amici, *U.S. v. Microsoft Corp.*, Civil Action No. 94-1564, January 18, 1995.

2 For a detailed analysis of the economics of the government's liability claims in this case, see David S. Evans, Albert L. Nichols, and Richard Schmalensee, "An Analysis of the Government's Economic Case in *U.S. v. Microsoft Corp.*," in this volume.

3 Memorandum of Microsoft Corporation in Support of Proposed Final Judgment, *U.S. v. Microsoft Corp.*, Civil Action No. 94-1564 (SS), December 5, 1994, pp. 3-4.

4 Concerning the successful release of Windows 3.0 in mid-1990 and the bitter public "divorce" of IBM from Microsoft in 1991, see Paul Carroll, *Big Blues* (New York: Crown Trade Paperbacks), 1993, pp. 261-262, 288-292.

5 Brian Livingston, "Undocumented Windows Calls: Deciphering the Charges Leveled at Microsoft," *InfoWorld*, November 16, 1992, pp. 98-103.

6 Memorandum of the United States, *supra* note 1, pp. 37-38.

7 DR DOS was a clone of MS-DOS developed by Digital Research, which Novell acquired in 1991.

8 See generally Memorandum of the United States, *supra* note 1.

9 Memorandum of Microsoft Corporation, *supra* note 3, p. 9.

10 United States Response to Public Comments, *U.S. v. Microsoft Corp.*, Civil Action No. 94-1564 (SS), October 31, 1994, p. 4.

11 "Novell has reportedly been quietly lobbying the FTC to act against Microsoft while also soliciting support in the industry for a class-action suit should the FTC fail to act." (Lindquist, Christopher, "FTC Decides Not to Decide [Yet]," *ComputerWorld*, July 26, 1993, p. 4; see also Pitta, Julie, "Microsoft's Dark Shadow," *Forbes*, March 1, 1993, pp. 106-107).

12 Memorandum of Microsoft Corporation, *supra* note 3, p. 11; United States Response, *supra* note 10, p. 4.

13 Several of Microsoft's competitors made submissions to the FTC during its investigation. Among these were: Novell, which owned DR DOS and faced competition from Microsoft in server operating systems, and Taligent, the IBM-Apple joint venture to develop a new operating system that would run on IBM's Power PC chip and compete with Windows running on Intel chips. See Memorandum of Microsoft Corporation, *supra* note 3, p. 7.

14 Richard McKenzie, *Trust on Trial: How the Microsoft Case is Reframing the Rules of Competition* (Cambridge: Perseus Publishing), 2000, pp. 197-198.

15 The consent decree was the result of joint settlement discussions between Microsoft and both the Justice Department and the European Commission, which had been investigating a complaint filed by Novell against Microsoft.

[16] Final Judgment, *U.S. v. Microsoft Corp.*, Civil Action No. 94-1564 (SS), July 15, 1994, p. 7.

[17] *Ibid.*, p. 6.

[18] James Wallace and Jim Erickson, *Hard Drive* (New York: Wiley), 1992.

[19] Sporkin discussed this in a status conference on September 24, 1994. For discussion, see Brief for the Defendant-Appellant, *U.S. v. Microsoft Corp.*, on Appeal from the United States District Court for the District of Columbia, Civil Action Nos. 95-5037, 95-5039, March 7, 1995.

[20] Memorandum of Amici Curiae in Opposition to Proposed Final Judgment, *U.S. v. Microsoft Corp.*, Civil Action No. 94-1564 (SS), January 10, 1995, p. 2.

[21] *Ibid.*, p. 33.

[22] *Ibid.*, p. 67. MSN access software was included, but attracted few users. Five years later, MSN had 3.5 million members compared with over 24.6 million for AOL. Dominic Gates, "Raising the White Flag," *The Standard*, October 23, 2000; http://www.thes-tandard.com/article/display/0,1151,19569,00.html (accessed October 24, 2000).

[23] *Ibid.*, p. 95.

[24] Laton McCartney, "Microsoft Takes Lessons in Lobbying," *Upside*, June 1998, pp. 89-94; Oral Argument, *U.S. v. Microsoft Corp.*, Civil Action Nos. 95-5037, 95-5039, April 24, 1995; http://www.usdoj.gov/atr/cases/f0200/0200.htm (accessed November 17, 2000).

[25] Memorandum of the United States, *supra* note 1.

[26] The "amici" refers to three computer companies that sought to intervene in the Tunney Act proceedings. See Revised Joint Brief of Amici Curiae, *U.S. v. Microsoft Corp.*, on Appeal from the United States District Court for the District of Columbia Nos. 95-5037, 95-5039, April 6, 1995.

[27] Declaration of Kenneth Arrow, *U.S. v. Microsoft Corp.*, Civil Action No. 94-1564 (SS), January 17, 1995, p. 11.

[28] *Ibid.*, p. 12.

[29] Complaint, *U.S. v. Microsoft Corp.*, Civil Action No. 94-1564 (SS), July 15, 1994.

[30] Opinion of the Court by Circuit Judge Silberman, *U.S. v. Microsoft Corp.*, Civil Action No. 94-1564, June 16, 1995.

[31] Consent Decree, *U.S. v. Microsoft Corp.*, Civil Action 94-1564, August 21, 1995.

[32] See Microsoft's Memorandum in Response to the DOJ Petition Seeking to Hold Microsoft in Contempt of the Consent Decree, *U.S. v. Microsoft Corp.*, Supplemental to Civil Action No. 94-1564, November 10, 1997, Section V.

[33] By way of reference, Netscape's share of U.S. browser use was above 80 percent throughout most of 1996. This figure is based on both internal tabulations maintained by Netscape, which were obtained as part of the discovery process, and tabulations from the University of Illinois site later cited by the government. See Transcript in *U.S. v. Microsoft Corp.*, Civil Action No. 98-1232 (TPJ), *State of New York ex rel., et al. v. Microsoft Corp.*, Civil Action No. 98-1233 (TPJ) (hereafter Transcript), June 1, 1999, p.m. Session, pp. 19-20 (Fisher Rebuttal, Direct); Plaintiff's Exhibit 1955; and http://www.ews.uiuc.edu/bstats/latest.html for the latest browser statistics. Data collected through telephone surveys showed Netscape with a lower share, primarily because many individuals were still using an older browser that AOL packaged with its system access

software, which was not based on either IE or Navigator. (Direct Testimony of Richard L. Schmalensee, *U.S. v. Microsoft Corp.*, Civil Action No. 98-1232 (TPJ), *State of New York ex rel., et al. v. Microsoft Corp.*, Civil Action No. 98-1233 (TPJ), January 3, 1999, Paragraph 276 (hereafter Schmalensee Direct).

[34] See Transcript, October 26, 1998, a.m. Session, pp. 21-28 (Cross of James Barksdale) and Plaintiffs' Exhibit 1259.

[35] Gary Reback and Susan Creighton, *White Paper Regarding Recent Anticompetitive Conduct of Microsoft Corporation* (submitted to the U.S. Department of Justice on Behalf of Netscape Corporation), July 1996.

[36] The 1996 Reback document also called for Microsoft to provide its competitors with the same access to APIs in its operating systems and applications that Microsoft's own developers had.

[37] Memorandum and Order, *U.S. v. Microsoft Corp.*, Supplemental to Civil Action No. 94-1564, Civil Action 94-1564, December 11, 1997.

[38] See, for example, Jeri Clausing, "Federal Judge Confronts Microsoft Over Browser," *New York Times*, January 14, 1998; http://www.nytimes.com/library/cyber/week/011498microsoft-day.html (accessed October 26, 2000).

[39] Stipulation and Order in *U.S. v. Microsoft Corp.*, Civil Action No. 94-1564 (TPJ), January 21, 1998.

[40] *U.S. v. Microsoft Corp.*, 147 F.3d 935 (D.C. Cir. June 23, 1998) (Nos. 97-5343, 98-5012).

[41] Complaint in *U.S. v. Microsoft Corp.*, Civil Action No. 98-1232 (TPJ), May 18, 1998 (hereafter Complaint).

[42] Complaint, Paragraphs 13-22.

[43] *Ibid.*

[44] One state, South Carolina, withdrew in December 1998. See Statement of South Carolina's Attorney General Charles Condon Re: Withdrawal of South Carolina from Microsoft Antitrust Suit, http://www.techlawjournal.com/courts/dojvmsft2/81207.htm (accessed April 16, 2001).

[45] Complaint, Paragraph 103.

[46] Plaintiff States' First Amended Complaint, *State of New York ex rel., et al. v. Microsoft Corp.*, Civil Action No. 98-1233 (TPJ), July 17, 1998.

[47] Order in *U.S. v. Microsoft Corp.*, Civil Action No. 98-1232 (TPJ), *State of New York ex rel., et al. v. Microsoft Corp.*, Civil Action No. 98-1233 (TPJ), May 22, 1998.

[48] Judge Jackson limited each side to 12 witnesses, who were to file written direct testimony, with two (later increased to three) additional witnesses able to testify during a rebuttal phase.

[49] "Platform" traditionally has referred to the combination of hardware and systems software on which applications run. For example, the "WinTel" platform refers to the combination of Intel-compatible processors and Windows operating systems. "Platform," however, also is used sometimes to refer to "middleware" that runs on top of the operating system and that provides APIs for applications. The Java run-time environment, for example, is a software platform that lets "pure Java" programs run on any hardware-operating system combination for which a Java Virtual Machine (JVM) and program libraries are available.

[50] The only time that Office is mentioned in the court's Conclusions of Law is in connection with Microsoft's threat to stop developing Office for the Macintosh if Apple did not accede to its wishes, including promotion and placement of IE over Navigator on new Apple computers (Conclusions of Law, *U.S. v. Microsoft Corp.*, Civil Action No. 98-1232 (TPJ) and *State of New York, ex rel., et al. v. Microsoft Corp.*, Civil Action No. 98-1233 (TPJ), April 3, 2000, Paragraph 17; hereafter COL). The states originally included claims related to Office, but dropped them in their amended complaint (Complaint in *State of New York, ex rel., et al. v. Microsoft Corp.*, Civil Action No. 98-1233 [TPJ], May 18, 1998 and Plaintiff States' First Amended Complaint, *supra* note 46). Moreover, even those claims were directed not at allegations that Microsoft used Office to maintain a barrier to entry in operating systems, but rather in the opposite direction – that owning the dominant operating system gave Microsoft's applications an unfair advantage. Neither of the government's economic experts testified about alleged anticompetitive acts related to Office (or to applications more generally) other than the Apple episode (Direct Testimony of Franklin Fisher, *U.S. v. Microsoft Corp.*, Civil Action No. 98-1232 [TPJ] and *State of New York, ex rel., et al. v. Microsoft Corp.*, Civil Action No. 98-1233 [TPJ], October 14, 1998, Paragraphs 153-154; hereafter Fisher Direct).

[51] Findings of Fact, *U.S. v. Microsoft Corp.*, Civil Action No. 98-1232 (TPJ) and *State of New York, ex rel., et al. v. Microsoft Corporation*, Civil Action No. 98-1233 (TPJ), November 5, 1999 (hereafter FOF).

[52] Order of Reference for Mediation, *U.S. v. Microsoft Corp.*, Civil Action No. 98-1232 (TPJ) and *State of New York, ex rel., et al. v. Microsoft Corp.*, Civil Action No. 98-1233 (TPJ), November 19, 1999.

[53] COL.

[54] *Ibid.*, pp. 8-9.

[55] *Ibid.*

[56] Plaintiffs' Proposed Final Judgment in *U.S. v. Microsoft Corp.*, Civil Action No. 98-1232 (TPJ) and *State of New York, ex rel., et al. v. Microsoft Corp.*, Civil Action No. 98-1233 (TPJ), April 28, 2000 (hereafter PPFJ).

[57] Declaration of Paul Romer, *U.S. v. Microsoft Corp.*, Civil Action No. 98-1232 (TPJ) and *State of New York, ex rel., et al. v. Microsoft Corp.*, Civil Action No. 98-1233 (TPJ), April 27, 2000 (hereafter Romer); Declaration of Rebecca Henderson, *U.S. v. Microsoft Corp.*, Civil Action No. 98-1232 (TPJ) and *State of New York, ex rel., et al. v. Microsoft Corp.*, Civil Action No. 98-1233 (TPJ), April 28, 2000 (hereafter Henderson); Declaration of Carl Shapiro, *U.S. v. Microsoft Corp.*, Civil Action No. 98-1232 (TPJ) and *State of New York, ex rel., et al. v. Microsoft Corp.*, Civil Action No. 98-1233 (TPJ), April 28, 2000 (hereafter Shapiro).

[58] Declaration of Robert F. Greenhill and Jeffery P. Williams, *U.S. v. Microsoft Corp.*, Civil Action No. 98-1232 (TPJ) and *State of New York, ex rel., et al. v. Microsoft Corp.*, Civil Action No. 98-1233 (TPJ), April 28, 2000.

[59] Declaration of Edward Felten, *U.S. v. Microsoft Corp.*, Civil Action No. 98-1232 (TPJ) and *State of New York, ex rel., et al. v. Microsoft Corporation*, Civil Action No. 98-1233 (TPJ), April 28, 2000.

[60] Microsoft Corporation's Proposed Final Judgment, *U.S. v. Microsoft Corp.*, Civil Action No. 98-1232 (TPJ) and *State of New York, ex rel., et al. v. Microsoft Corp.*, Civil Action No. 98-1233 (TPJ), May 10, 2000.

[61] Microsoft submitted an "Offer of Proof," which summarized the testimony that it would present if given adequate time. Kenneth G. Elzinga, a co-author of this paper, was one of the experts whose potential testimony was summarized.

[62] This decision is one of the principal elements of the controversy over whether Microsoft was denied due process. See Jurisdictional Statement, *Microsoft Corp. v. United States of America*, No. 00-139, July 26, 2000 and Brief for the United States in Response to the Jurisdictional Statement, *Microsoft Corp. v. United States of America*, No. 00-139, August 2000.

[63] *Ibid.*

[64] Memorandum and Order, *U.S. v. Microsoft Corp.*, Civil Action No. 98-1232 (TPJ) and *State of New York, ex rel., et al. v. Microsoft Corp.*, Civil Action No. 98-1233 (TPJ) June 7, 2000, p. 4.

[65] *Ibid.*, p. 5.

[66] "Judicial intervention – forcible application of law – became a last resort," Jackson said. "And in my judgment, Microsoft's intransigence was the reason." James Grimaldi, "Microsoft Judge Says Ruling at Risk on Appeal," *The Washington Post*, September 29, 2000, p. E1.

[67] Notice of Appeal, principal elements of the controversy over whether Microsoft was denied due process. See Jurisdictional Statement, *Microsoft Corp. v. United States of America*, No. 00-139, July 26, 2000 and Brief for the United States in Response to the Jurisdictional Statement, *Microsoft Corp. v. United States of America*, No. 00-139, August 2000.

[68] *Ibid.*

[69] Decision of the Supreme Court of the United States, *Microsoft Corp. v. United States et al.*, 530 U.S. 00-139 (2000) and *New York v. Microsoft Corp.*, 530 U.S. 00-261 (2000), September 26, 2000.

[70] The transcripts for the hearings on February 26 and 27 of 2001 are available at http://www.microsoft.com/presspass/trial/transcripts/feb01/02-26.asp and http://www.microsoft.com/presspass/trial/transcripts/feb01/02-27.asp, respectively (accessed April 16, 2001).

[71] United States Court of Appeals for the District of Columbia, Opinion, *U.S. v. Microsoft Corp.*, June 28, 2001, http://ecfp.cadc.uscourts.gov/MS-Docs/1720/0.pdf.

[72] Final Judgment, *U.S. v. Microsoft Corp.*, Civil Action No. 98-1232 (TPJ) and *State of New York, ex rel., et al. v. Microsoft Corp.*, Civil Action No. 98-1233 (TPJ), June 7, 2000, pp. 2-3 (hereafter Final Judgment).

[73] *Ibid.*, pp. 3-12.

[74] *Ibid.*, Section 3.a.ii.(2).

[75] Middleware is a vaguely defined term that could cover many of the newer components in Windows that facilitate the use of applications software. Schmalensee Direct, Paragraph 136.

[76] Final Judgment, Section 3b.

[77] *Ibid.*, Section 3c.

[78] *Ibid.*, Section 3e.

[79] *See* generally Shapiro, Romer, Henderson.

[80] Plaintiffs' Reply Memorandum in Support of Proposed Final Judgment, pp. 14-15.

[81] See Henderson, Paragraphs 21-22; Shapiro, p. 5.

[82] See Henderson, Paragraphs 23-25.

[83] Henderson, Paragraph 126.

[84] Shapiro, p. 29.

[85] *Ibid.*, p. 7 (emphasis in original).

[86] Shapiro's declaration supported all of the individual remedies with the exception of the requirement that OEMs be entitled to discounts in proportion to the size of the Windows components they chose not to install (none of the experts mentioned that provision).

[87] Shapiro, p. 29.

[88] Complaint, Paragraphs 130-137.

[89] See Robert W. Crandall, "The Failure of Structural Remedies in Sherman Act Monopolization Cases," in this volume (hereafter Crandall). During the recent oral hearings before the appeals court, the judges pressed the government's counsel to name any cases in which the Supreme Court had ordered the breakup of a unitary company; he was unable to do so. U.S. Court of Appeals, D.C. Circuit, *Microsoft v. U.S.* (No. 00-5212), and *Microsoft v. State of New York et al.* (No. 00-5213), Transcript, February 27, 2001, pp. 274-276.

[90] Robert H. Bork, *The Antitrust Paradox* (New York: The Free Press), 1978, pp. 178-79.

[91] Put differently, the remedy should recognize expected error costs. Taking account of expected error costs means balancing the probable effects on consumer welfare if the remedy imposed on Microsoft were inefficiently harsh (i.e., harmed consumers because it shackled pro-competitive behavior by Microsoft) versus probable effects on consumer welfare if the remedy were inefficiently weak (i.e., harmed consumers because it did not restore competition).

[92] An enormous amount of research has been conducted regarding antitrust enforcement. Very little of it is devoted to antitrust remedies and penalties. This is puzzling because an antitrust violation that harms consumers but that is not then followed by an appropriate remedy results in a Pyrrhic victory for the antitrust plaintiff – and for consumers. But see William Breit and Kenneth G. Elzinga, *The Antitrust Penalties: A Study in Law and Economics* (New Haven: Yale University Press), 1976; Richard Posner, *Antitrust Law*, Chapter 5 (Chicago: The University of Chicago Press), 1976; Crandall.

[93] An example of a conduct remedy would be prohibiting a seller from charging different prices for a product to different customers during a designated period.

[94] The antitrust arsenal also contains penalties such as *fines* and *jail sentences*. These are reserved for criminal cases in which the enforcement goal is *deterrence*. The scholarly literature in antitrust is tilted more to the analysis of fines and incarceration than structural and conduct remedies.

[95] In Section 7 remedies studied by one of the authors, it was shown that when the government used conduct rather than structural relief, it often ended up serving as a regulator rather than as a referee. Kenneth G. Elzinga, "The Antimerger Law: Pyrrhic Victories?" 12 *Journal of Law and Economics* 43 (1969).

[96] Early prominent cases of literal trustbusting relief include *Standard Oil Company of New Jersey v. U.S.*, 221 U.S. 1 (1911); *U.S. v. American Tobacco Co.*, 221 U.S. 106 (1911). Since World War II, two prominent examples of applying antitrust's "three Ds" would be

U.S. v. E. I. DuPont, 353 U.S. 586 (1957) (ending DuPont's partial stock ownership in General Motors) and *U.S. v. AT&T, 552 F. Supp.* 131 (D.D.C. 1982) (the breakup of AT&T into the so-called Baby Bells or regional operating companies).

[97] See "The Antimerger Law: Pyrrhic Victories?" *supra* note 95 and Federal Trade Commission, "A Study of the Commission's Divestiture Process," Staff Report of the Bureau of Competition, 1999.

[98] Crandall, pp. 13-21.

[99] Crandall shows that the breakup of American Tobacco, also in 1911, had no discernible effect on tobacco prices or on the returns to shareholders.

[100] The cases Crandall studies in detail are: *Standard Oil of New Jersey, American Tobacco, Alcoa, Paramount, U.S. Shoe Machinery, the Television Network Cases*, and *AT&T*. Crandall's conclusion that market processes, including unexpected changes in market conditions, do more to reinvigorate competition than structural remedies is consistent with Elzinga's finding that the market as a force for antitrust relief often is faster and more effective than structural relief in antimerger enforcement.

[101] Crandall, pp. 70-76.

[102] *Ibid.*, p. 89.

[103] *Ibid.*, pp. 102-103.

[104] See Harm to Consumers From the Court's Remedies, p. 164.

[105] For example, the U.S. software industry has not lagged behind the Europeans', in contrast to the U.S. steel industry, or behind the Japanese, in contrast to the U.S. automobile industry.

[106] Crandall, Table 1.

[107] COL, p. 20.

[108] Grimaldi, *supra* note 66.

[109] Memorandum and Order, *supra* note 64, p. 3.

[110] Although everything that Judge Jackson said in his Findings of Fact is technically a "finding," there is an important distinction between (a) findings that are tied to verifiable facts (e.g., Netscape has a y percent share) that could in principle be verified by going to the portion of the trial record that deals with those facts and (b) findings that are simply conclusions (e.g., Microsoft suppressed innovation) that have weight only insofar as there are verifiable facts that support them. Some of the district court's findings have no support in the trial record. For example, see the discussion of Paragraphs 149-154 of the court's Findings of Fact during the oral arguments before the D.C. circuit. Appeals Transcript, *supra* note 89, February 26, 2001, pp. 132-137, 141-143.

[111] FOF, Paragraph 412.

[112] Plaintiffs' Memorandum in Support of Proposed Final Judgment (once on p. 1, twice on p. 23). Henderson, Paragraph 80; Romer, Paragraph 11.

[113] FOF, Paragraph 408.

[114] In preparation for Richard Schmalensee's testimony, researchers systematically gathered reviews from 13 major computer magazines. They then classified the magazines' recommendations for the various versions of Netscape's browsers and Microsoft's IE. See Schmalensee Direct, Paragraphs 255-268, Table 6, and Appendix F. In preparation for the anticipated remedies phase in May 2000, NERA staff updated the survey to include

comparisons of IE 5 and Navigator 4.5 (the newest version then available).

[115] Seventy-three percent of the magazine reviewers found it better than Navigator 4, and 27 percent called it a tie or made selective recommendations according to types of users.

[116] "Netscape Launches Groundbreaking Netscape 6 Browser," Netscape press release, November 14, 2000; http://home.netscape.com/newsref/pr/newsrelease821.html (accessed November 16, 2000).

[117] FOF, Paragraph 135.

[118] FOF, Paragraph 288.

[119] Intuit's William Harris testified for the government, but agreed on cross-examination that Intuit would have chosen to use IE independent of Microsoft's alleged pressure because Intuit engineers found it a better solution than Navigator. (Transcript, January 4, 1999, p.m. Session [Cross of William Harris]).

[120] FOF, Paragraph 324; Schmalensee Direct, Paragraphs 229, 481.

[121] Even Navigator 6 does not appear to be componentized in the way that IE is. Netscape's Web site focuses on how Navigator's source code may be adapted and incorporated into other programs, rather than the APIs it exposes. ("Netscape Gecko Developer Central," http://devedge.netscape.com/tech/gecko/gecko.html, accessed April 16, 2001).

[122] FOF, Paragraph 282.

[123] FOF, Paragraphs 68-78.

[124] FOF, Paragraphs 82, 87. See also Direct Testimony of Daniel Rosen, *U.S. v. Microsoft Corp.*, Civil Action No. 98-1232 (TPJ) and *State of New York, ex rel., et al. v. Microsoft Corp.*, Civil Action No. 98-1233 (TPJ), January 1999, Paragraphs 76-108.

[125] FOF, Paragraph 93.

[126] FOF, Paragraph 120.

[127] FOF, Paragraph 109.

[128] FOF, Paragraph 114.

[129] Mary Jo Foley, "Real-Apple: Can You Say Monopoly?", *ZDNet News*, June 12, 2000; http://www.zdnet.com/zdnn/stories/news/0,4586,2586491,00.html (accessed November 16, 2000).

[130] Saul Hansell, "Revamped Netscape to Challenge Microsoft," *Star Tribune* (Minneapolis, MN), March 21, 2000; Philip Michaels, "No Truce Yet in Browser Wars," *Macworld*, July 2000, p. 25; Paula Rooney, "AOL, Gateway Tackle Net Appliances," *Computer Reseller News*, June 5, 2000, p. 20.

[131] FOF, Paragraph 213.

[132] IDC PC Tracker data show that in 1999 52 percent of U.S. PCs were sold outside of the home and small office segments.

[133] FOF, Paragraphs 94-103. This episode is mentioned once in the district court's Conclusions of Law (p. 18) and twice in the DOJ's memorandum in support of its proposed Final Judgment (pp. 16, 20). Two of the government's remedy experts also use this incident as their evidence that Microsoft suppressed innovation (Romer, Paragraph 4; Henderson, Paragraph 61).

[134] "Semiconductors: An Industry in Transition," *Red Herring*, September 1995; http://www.redherring.com/mag/issue23/transition.html (accessed November 16, 2000); FOF, Paragraph 95.

[135] Direct Testimony of Paul Maritz, *U.S. v. Microsoft Corp.*, Civil Action No. 98-1232 (TPJ), *State of New York ex rel., et al. v. Microsoft Corp.*, Civil Action No. 98-1233 (TPJ), January 6, 1999, Paragraph 317.

[136] FOF, Paragraph 98.

[137] The Intel official most directly responsible for NSP software, Steven McGeady, testified for the government at trial. He claimed that the software his group had created was valuable. More senior Intel officials, however, were silent or skeptical. Ronald Whittier, McGeady's boss, had in mind a more general definition of NSP in his deposition, of which the particular NSP software was only a small part. Thus, the following exchange: "Q. 'Do you have an estimate as to how many engineers worked on the [NSP] project?' A. 'You are using a past tense. It's not a past tense... We used this NSP nomenclature for a while, but the concept, you know, we had done forever. So anything that can be done in terms of computing on a platform, you try to do it on a central host processor to reduce the cost of the system. It has been an ongoing program to try to do as many things as well as possible on the central processor.'" (Whittier deposition, pp. 44-45)

[138] FOF, Paragraph 101.

[139] Plaintiffs' Joint Proposed Findings of Fact, Paragraph 355.4.3, *U.S. v. Microsoft Corp.*, Civil Action No. 98-1232 (TPJ) and *State of New York, ex rel., et al. v. Microsoft Corp.*, Civil Action No. 98-1233 (TPJ), August 10, 1999 (hereafter PPFOF).

[140] Tom R. Halfhill, "The New PC: Four New Technologies Will Usher Your Next PC into the '90s," *Byte*, October 1995; http://www.byte.com/art/9510/sec6/art1.htm (accessed November 16, 2000).

[141] Transcript, February 23, 1999, p.m. Session, pp. 48-49 (Cross of Eric Engstrom).

[142] Shapiro, pp. 11-12.

[143] For example, one might compare the innovations in Windows operating systems to innovations by Apple, IBM, or the many Unix vendors. Or one might ask whether innovation has been more rapid (or prices lower) in the many types of applications outside the business productivity category where Microsoft's Office is "dominant." Alternatively, one could examine the impact of Microsoft's entry into specific software categories, such as the rise in popularity of Word and Excel in the early 1990s when they displaced WordPerfect and Lotus 1-2-3, respectively. Or one might have examined the impact of Windows NT Server on innovation and pricing of server software when it was introduced in a crowded market in 1993.

[144] The closest they come to new "evidence" concerning Microsoft's impact on innovation is Professor Romer's assertion (without citations) that "some types of applications forecast by the advocates of the browser and the Java virtual machine are finally emerging" and that "in the absence of Microsoft's actions, it is likely that this class of applications would be farther down its development path" (Romer, Paragraph 11). The fact that such applications have appeared less rapidly than originally predicted by their proponents, however, is hardly unusual for a new technology.

[145] The source of these data is Corporate Technology Information Services (CorpTech), which employed a rigorous and consistent survey methodology over this period.

[146] Norma Leong, "Application Service Providers: A Market Overview," Los Altos, Internet Research Group, 2000.

[147] Josh Lerner, "Did Microsoft Deter Software Innovation?" Harvard Business School Working Paper, 2001.

[148] *Ibid.*, Table 2.

[149] Samuel Kortum and Josh Lerner, "Assessing the Impact of Venture Capital on Innovation," *Rand Journal of Economics*; available through http://www.rje.org.

[150] National Venture Capital Association Yearbook, Newark, Venture Economics 2000.

[151] See Lynn Margherio, et al., *The Emerging Digital Economy*, Washington, D.C.: U.S. Department of Commerce, April 1998, p. 9; http://www.ecommerce.gov/emerging.htm (accessed November 6, 2001).

[152] National Venture Capital Statistics, http://www.velocityholdings.com/PV-web.nsf/pages/nationalstatistics (accessed April 13, 2001).

[153] George Bittlingmayer and Thomas W. Hazlett, "DOS Kapital: Has Antitrust Action Against Microsoft Created Value in the Computer Industry?" This volume.

[154] Henderson, Paragraph 126.

[155] Henderson, Paragraphs 19-25; Romer, Paragraph 6.

[156] *See, e.g.*, Jean Tirole, *The Theory of Industrial Organization* (Cambridge: The MIT Press), 1988, Chapter 10, esp. pp. 390-394; Dennis Carlton and Jeffrey Perloff, *Modern Industrial Organization*, 3rd ed. (New York: Addison-Wesley), 2000, pp. 532-541; F.M. Scherer, and David Ross, *Industrial Market Structure and Economic Performance*, 3rd ed. (Boston: Houghton Mifflin Co.), 1990, pp. 630-660.

[157] Tirole (1988), *supra* note 156, pp. 390-399; Jennifer F. Reinganum, "The Timing of Innovation: Research, Development, and Diffusion," *Handbook of Industrial Organization*, Vol. 1, Chapter 14, pp. 849-908; Carlton and Perloff (2000), pp. 505-513, 536-540; Scherer and Ross (1990), *supra* note 156, pp. 630-651.

[158] Tirole (1988), *supra* note 156, pp. 390-394; Scherer and Ross (1990), *supra* note 156, pp. 651-660.

[159] Paul Krugman, "*The Last Refuge*," *The New York Times*, June 11, 2000, section 4, p. 17. Microsoft, too, has waved the innovation flag in the Microsoft case.

[160] Franklin M. Fisher and Daniel L. Rubinfeld, "*United States v. Microsoft*: An Economic Analysis," presented at the AEI-Brookings Joint Center on Regulatory Policy, Washington D.C., February 11, 2000; Transcript, January 13, 1999, a.m. Session, pp. 5, 55-57 (Fisher Recross, Redirect); PPFOF, Paragraphs 31-56.

[161] As one of the authors has discussed, the government never presented a coherent explanation of how Netscape could erode that barrier while others could not. See David S. Evans, "All the Facts that Fit: Square Pegs and Round Holes in *U.S. v. Microsoft*," *Regulation*, November 1999.

[162] PPFOF, Paragraphs 25-31.

[163] FOF, Paragraphs 36-52.

[164] In effect, the availability of office productivity applications would hurdle the heretofore inconsequential operating systems over the barrier posed by the 70,000 applications that run on Windows.

[165] Schmalensee Direct, Paragraphs 183-187, 340; FOF, Paragraphs 18-32. For further discussion of antitrust policies in dynamically competitive industries such as software, see David Evans and Richard Schmalensee, "Some Economic Aspects of Antitrust Analysis in Dynamically Competitive Industries," National Bureau of Economic Research Working Paper, 2001.

[166] Indeed, Professor Lessig, whom Judge Jackson asked to file an amicus brief on the tying issue, has written that "by 1998 it had become apparent to all that Linux was an important competitor to the Microsoft operating system." Lawrence Lessig, *Code and Other Laws of Cyberspace*, 1999. The Web site http://www.linuxapps.com lists all the applications currently available to the Linux platform. As of December 1999, there were over 2,500 applications available for Linux. IBM, Compaq and Dell, among others, offer to install Linux on computers they sell. See, for example, "Linux at IBM" at http://www-4.ibm.com/software/is/mp/linux (accessed October 20, 2000); "Support Your Linux Enterprise with Compaq Expertise" at http://www5.compaq.com/services/software/ss_linux.html (accessed October 20, 2000); "Dell Likes Linux, They Really Do" (June 20, 2000) at http://www.wirednews.com/news/business/0,1367,37104,00.html (accessed October 20, 2000). Oracle and other major enterprise vendors offer Linux versions of their software. See, for example, "Oracle Beats IBM in Offering the First Enterprise-Class Application Server for Linux" (August 9, 2000) at http://www.oracle.com/corporate/press/index.html?266652.html (accessed October 20, 2000). Corel offers a Linux version of its WordPerfect software. See http://linux.corel.com/products/wpo2000_linux/index.htm (accessed October 20, 2000) for details. Intel, among others, has directly invested in companies that distribute Linux operating system software. See, for example, "Linux Looms Large: Intel, Netscape Slap NT, Will Invest in Red Hat" (September 25, 1998) at http://www.zdnet.com/zdnn/stories/zdnn_smgraph_display/0,4436,2142107,00.html (accessed October 20, 2000); "IBM, Compaq, Novell and Oracle Invest in Red Hat" (March 9, 1999) at http://www.linuxworld.com/linuxworld/lw-1999-03/lw-03-redhat.html (accessed October 20, 2000).

[167] FOF, Paragraph 42.

[168] FOF, Paragraph 38.

[169] FOF, Paragraph 39. More generally, see Kenneth G. Elzinga and David E. Mills, "PC Software," 44 *Antitrust Bulletin*, pp. 739, 753-763 (1999).

[170] FOF, Paragraph 30.

[171] COL, p. 5.

[172] FOF, Paragraph 28.

[173] FOF, Paragraph 32.

[174] FOF, Paragraph 77.

[175] FOF, Paragraph 407.

[176] FOF, Paragraph 411.

[177] The liability case is internally inconsistent as well, as one of us has pointed out elsewhere. If Microsoft is indeed protected by the applications barrier to entry, it has no rational motivation for investing in predation to eliminate entrants who are so foolish as to try the impossible. See David S. Evans and Richard Schmalensee, "The Economics of the Microsoft Antitrust Case: A Post-Trial Primer," presented at the *AEI-Brookings Joint Center on Regulatory Policy*, Washington D.C., February 11, 2000.

[178] These concerns apparently helped persuade the government to avoid the more extreme divestitures proposed in the amicus brief filed by Dr. Robert Litan and Professors Roger Noll, William Nordhaus, and F.M. Scherer. Robert E. Litan, Roger G. Noll, William D. Nordhaus and Frederic Scherer, *Remedies Brief of Amicus Curiae*, April 27, 2000.

[179] Fisher Direct, Paragraph 66; Direct Testimony of Frederick M. Warren-Boulton, *U.S. v. Microsoft Corp.*, Civil Action No. 98-1232, 98-1233, November 18, 1998, Paragraph 53

(hereafter Warren-Boulton Direct); Transcript, January 7, 1999, a.m. Session, pp. 28-29 (Fisher Cross).

[180] Indeed, Microsoft Office, and its key components, Word and Excel, were available for the Macintosh before they were available for Windows. Word and Excel were huge successes on the Macintosh when character-based WordPerfect and Lotus 1-2-3 dominated the MS-DOS world.

[181] Henderson, Paragraph 22.

[182] In its Findings of Fact, the district court hints at another problem the Macintosh operating system has faced – relatively high prices for the hardware–software combination in which it is sold (FOF, Paragraphs 351-353) – but then ignores that issue in ascribing the Macintosh's problems to the applications barrier to entry (FOF, Paragraphs 36-52).

[183] Shapiro, p. 3.

[184] FOF, Paragraph 30.

[185] FOF, Paragraph 30.

[186] FOF, Paragraph 38.

[187] Transcript, January 12, 1999, p.m. Session, p. 78 (Fisher Cross). Professor Fisher testified for DOJ. Dr. Frederick Warren-Boulton testified for the states.

[188] This preference for free, open-source software often takes on a quasi-religious air. Many supporters of GNOME, for example, disparaged a competing graphical user interface for Linux, KDE, because although it was free and open source, some elements were not covered by the GPL license. "GNOME in 60 Seconds (or so)," Chapter 2, *Red Hat Linux 6.2: The Official Red Hat Linux Getting Started Guide*; http://www.redhat.com/support/manuals/RHL-6.2-Manual/getting-started-guide/ch-gnome60.html (accessed October 23, 2000); "Interview: KDE Developers Answer Your Questions," *Slashdot* (November 26, 1999); http://slashdot.org/interviews/99/11/26/1126252.shtml (accessed October 23, 2000).

[189] Sun has purchased Star Office, an applications suite that covers most of the functions of Microsoft Office, and distributes it at no cost for Linux (and other platforms). "Sun Microsystems Open Sources StarOffice Technology," press release, July 19, 2000; http://www.sun.com/smi/Press/sunflash/2000-07/sunflash.20000719.1.html (accessed October 23, 2000).

[190] Shapiro, p. 14.

[191] Arrow declaration, *supra* note 27, p. 10.

[192] See Rebecca Henderson and Kim Clark, "Architectural Innovation: The Reconfiguration of Existing Product Technologies and the Failure of Established Firms," *Administrative Science Quarterly* 35 (March 1990), p. 9; and Rebecca Henderson, "Underinvestment and Incompetence as a Response to Radical Innovation: Evidence from the Photolithographic Alignment Equipment Industry," *RAND Journal of Economics* 248 (Summer 1993), p. 24.

[193] Carl Shapiro, "Antitrust in Network Industries," speech before the American Law Institute and the American Bar Association, January 7, 1996; http://www.usdoj.gov/atr/public/speeches/shapir.mar.htm (accessed October 26, 2000).

[194] See Michael Katz and Carl Shapiro, "Systems Competition and Network Effects," 8 *Journal of Economic Perspectives* 93 (1994), and Michael Katz and Carl Shapiro (1992), "Product Introduction with Network Externalities," 40 *Journal of Industrial Economics*,

55 (March 1992).

195 Arrow declaration, *supra* note 27.

196 Complaint, Paragraphs 2, 54.

197 It does not include operating systems for the Apple Macintosh or Unix workstations from Sun, IBM, and other vendors, because they run on different processors. It also excludes the very products – Netscape and Java – the government alleged Microsoft found so threatening that it engaged in a predatory campaign to defeat them. If the operating system on Apple's desktop computers is not in competition with Microsoft's operating system, one wonders in what market Apple is positioned – and has it monopolized that market?

198 Schmalensee Direct, Paragraphs 93-94.

199 Microsoft had just 14 percent of revenues from operating systems for servers/host computers in 1999. IDC, *Server Operating Environments Market Forecast and Analysis*, Report #22347, June 2000, Table 1.

200 FOF, Paragraphs 33, 176-187.

201 FOF, Paragraphs 19-21.

202 FOF, Paragraph 33.

203 FOF, Paragraphs 19-21.

204 Henderson, Paragraph 13.

205 Fisher Direct, Paragraph 133; Warren-Boulton Direct, Paragraph 16.

206 See Frank H. Easterbrook, "Predatory Strategies and Counterstrategies," 48 *University of Chicago Law Review* 201 (1981); Kenneth G. Elzinga and David E. Mills, "Testing for Predation: Is Recoupment Feasible?" 34 *Antitrust Bulletin* 869 (1989).

207 Since the breakdown of the settlement negotiations in late March 2000, Microsoft's stock price had fallen more than 34 percent by November 15, 2000, resulting in a loss of capital value of more than $190 billion.

208 See, for example, Robert McGough and Rebecca Buckman, "Heard on the Street – Microsoft Investors Worry About 'Conduct Remedies'," *The Wall Street Journal*, June 7, 2000; Alex Berenson, "The Markets: Market Place, Investors Find Vulnerability in Microsoft," *The New York Times*, April 25, 2000, for discussions of the litigation's impact on the stock market.

209 Stan J. Liebowitz, "An Expensive Pig in a Poke: Estimating the Cost of the District Court's Proposed Breakup of Microsoft," Association for Competitive Technology (September 21, 2000); http://www.actonline.com/pubs/remedies3.pdf (accessed October 20, 2000). Professor Liebowitz also examined the potential for reduced competition in database and game console markets, increased development costs for software developers due to the balkanization of "middleware," the reduced incentives to improve Windows, and the costs to consumers of collecting information about which OEM's version of Windows would be best for them. Some of these effects would directly raise costs to consumers, and others would raise costs to software developers, indirectly harming consumers.

210 FOF, Paragraph 411.

211 The district court does add that, "[i]t is clear … that Microsoft has retarded, and perhaps altogether extinguished, the process by which these two middleware technologies could have facilitated the introduction of competition into an important market" (FOF,

Paragraph 411). But given its other statements and its view of the "intractable chicken-and-egg problem," this can only mean that Microsoft interfered in the process by which these technologies could have attempted to become alternative software platforms even though it is not likely they would have succeeded. The district court also found that Netscape and Sun had exposed too few APIs to provide a viable alternative to Windows (COL, p. 9).

212 COL, p. 9.

213 Michael A. Cusumano and David B. Yoffie, *Competing on Internet Time* (New York: The Free Press), 1998, p. 40 (hereafter Cusumano and Yoffie).

214 See generally Cusumano and Yoffie, who conducted intensive interviews with Netscape employees.

215 Transcript, October 20, 1998, p.m. Session, pp. 72-73 (Barksdale Cross).

216 For example, in contrast to Microsoft's IE 3 and subsequent versions of Microsoft's browser, Netscape Navigator could not be used to display data extracted from the Web within an independent application. When Netscape competed with Microsoft to provide a browsing engine to AOL, it promised it would build a componentized version. However, after it lost that initial competition, Netscape never followed through, despite continued urging from AOL and others (FOF, Paragraph 282); see also discussion in Cusumano and Yoffie, pp. 183-185.

217 FOF, Paragraphs 296, 298.

218 The government and Microsoft used different types of data for measuring browser use, but both put the crossover point sometime between the late spring and late summer of 1998. The government's "hit" data showed Microsoft passing Netscape in August 1998 (Fisher Direct, Paragraphs 225-234), whereas the survey data used by Microsoft showed the crossover occurring in the second quarter of 1998 (Schmalensee Direct, Table 7).

219 See Transcript, June 21, 1999, p.m. Session, p. 32 (Schmalensee Rebuttal, Direct); "America OnLine, Inc. Completes Acquisition of Netscape Communications Corporation," March 17, 1999; http://media.web.aol.com/media/press_view.cfm? (accessed October 25, 2000).

220 See http://www.ews.uiuc.edu/bstats/latest-month.html for statistics.

221 Dominic Gates, "Raising the White Flag," *The Standard*, October 23, 2000; http://www.thestandard.com/article/display/0,1151,19569,00.html (accessed October 24, 2000). See also Saul Hansell, "Revamped Netscape to Challenge Microsoft," *The Star Tribune* (Minneapolis, MN), March 21, 2000; Philip Michaels, "No Truce Yet in Browser Wars," *Macworld*, July 2000, p. 25; Paula Rooney, "AOL, Gateway Tackle Net Appliances," *Computer Reseller News*, June 5, 2000, p. 20.

222 FOF, Paragraphs 395-400.

223 See, for example, Arif Mohammed, "Corel Sidelines Office for Java, Embraces Windows," ZDNet UK (October 22, 1997); http://www.zdnet.co.uk/news/news1/ns-3030.html (accessed November 17, 2000); Ellis Booker, "Java Client Brews in Limbo," *InternetWeek* (March 2, 1998); http://www.techweb.com/wire/story/TWB19980302S0010 (accessed November 17, 2000).

224 Joe Wilcox and Lee Pender, "Outlook for Lotus Java eSuite is a Mixed Bag," *Computer Reseller News*, January 5, 1998.

225 Christa Degnan, "Lotus Pulling the Plug on eSuite," ZDNet UK (September 10, 1999); http://www.zdnet.co.uk/cgi-bin/printnews.cgi (downloaded October 25, 2000).

[226] Michael J. Miller, "Why Java Still Matters," *PC Magazine*, April 7, 1998.

[227] Under the terms of a civil suit settlement with Sun that limited its ability to update its JVM, Microsoft chose not to install a JVM in Windows XP. However, a JVM can be downloaded at no cost from a Microsoft Web site.

[228] Sun lists 19 partners on its Web site, including Apple Computer, Inc., Corel Corporation, IBM Corporation, Netscape Communications Corporation, Novell, Inc., and Oracle Corporation. See generally http://java.sun.com/products/javabeans/partners.html.

[229] See generally http://java.sun.com/products/javabeans.

[230] IDC, *1999 IDC Worldwide Professional Developer Model*, Report #21268, December 1999, Table 2.

[231] "The Court is nonetheless compelled to express its further conclusion that the predatory course of conduct Microsoft has pursued since June of 1995 has revived the dangerous probability that Microsoft will attain monopoly power in a second market" (COL, p. 24).

[232] FOF, Paragraphs 173-174, 186.

[233] FOF, Paragraph 408.

[234] Cusumano and Yoffie, p. 99.

[235] Greg Pastrick, "Netscape Navigator 1.1 Sails Around the World-Wide Web," *PC Magazine*, July 1995; Information Access Company, "Netscape Navigator Gold (V.2.01)," *Computer Select*, August 1996.

[236] FOF, Paragraph 136.

[237] IDC, *The Global Market Forecasts for Internet Usage and Commerce: Based on Internet Commerce Market Model, Version 6*, Report # 22216R, May 2000, Table 4.

[238] FOF, Paragraph 244.

[239] FOF, Paragraph 245.

[240] FOF, Paragraph 246.

[241] FOF, Paragraph 248.

[242] FOF, Paragraphs 260, 295.

[243] The district court found that Internet content providers such as Disney would have paid $10 million for placement in the Channel Bar – a benefit that Microsoft offered at no charge. (FOF, Paragraph 316).

[244] FOF, Paragraph 410.

[245] These surveys were planned and initially conducted in anticipation of testimony during the remedies phase that the district court elected not to schedule. The surveys were developed by NERA in conjunction with Professor Eugene Ericksen of Temple University, a specialist on surveys. They were conducted by a survey firm during May and June 2000. The home survey had a total of 500 respondents, as did the business survey. However, the business survey was administered in two questionnaire versions that had slightly different wording. The differences in results from the two versions were not statistically significant. However, we report results only from the second version (200 respondents), which were slightly less favorable to Microsoft.

[246] Ninety-four percent of home respondents and more than 95 percent of business respondents.

[247] See discussion of surveys, *supra* note 245.

[248] FOF, Paragraph 410.

[249] The 380 respondents who preferred Windows with IE built in were willing to pay $27.71 on average. The 58 who preferred "without" were willing to pay only $11.64 on average. The ratio of the total amounts is 15.6.

[250] See discussion of surveys, *supra* note 245.

[251] Among the 127 preferring "with," the average amount they were willing to pay was $16.52. Among the 46 preferring "without," the average amount they were willing to pay was $8.28. Thus, the ratio of the two totals is 5.5.

[252] See discussion of surveys, *supra* note 245.

[253] Memorandum and Order, *supra* note 64.

[254] Schmalensee Direct, Paragraph 163.

[255] Among economists, there does not seem to be much doubt that the government's proposed remedy – at least in the first instance – would result in an increase in price for precisely this reason. Dr. Litan and Professors Noll, Nordhaus, and Scherer commented on this problem in the amicus brief they filed with the district court in support of a further breakup of the operating system company. (Remedies Brief of Amici Curiae, *U.S. v. Microsoft Corp.*, 98-1232, April 27, 2000, p. 49). In Microsoft's *Offer of Proof* on remedies, Schmalensee and Murphy also concluded that the government's remedy would increase operating system prices. (Offer of Proof, *U.S. v. Microsoft Corp.*, Civil Action No. 98-1232, May 24, 2000.) Aside from a dismissive statement by Shapiro in his declaration (p. 16), we are not familiar with any economist who has questioned this price effect.

[256] Paul Krugman, "Reckonings: Microsoft: What Next?" *The New York Times*, April 26, 2000.

[257] Schmalensee Direct, Paragraph 162. The prices paid by individual OEMs vary and are considered highly confidential by both them and Microsoft. All detailed discussions of pricing issues were in closed sessions, with sealed transcripts and exhibits. Both sides agreed to use "less than $65" as a rough figure in public sessions of the trial.

[258] Government Exhibit 1960 shows this formula. Professor Fisher discusses it in his rebuttal testimony (Transcript, June 1, 1999, p.m. Session, pp. 6-12 [Fisher Rebuttal, Direct]).

[259] Transcript, June 1, 1999, p.m. Session, p. 17 (Fisher Rebuttal, Direct). For further discussion of the model and Fisher's assumptions, see Bernard Reddy et al., "A Monopolist Would Still Charge More for Windows: A Comment on Werden," and "A Monopolist Would Still Charge More for Windows: A Comment on Werden's Reply," 18 (3) *Review of Industrial Organization*, 263, 273 (May 2001).

[260] In the remedies phase, the only government expert to comment on this issue, Professor Shapiro, dismissed it as a "theoretical possibility," one that would be offset by lower prices from increased competition (Shapiro, p.14-15).

[261] *See e.g.* PPFJ. At Microsoft's request, the Final Judgment referred to it more accurately as divestiture.

[262] The questions addressed would be in the realm of: Why might a brewing firm elect to integrate into can production but not malt production? Why might the firm hire regional sales reps as employees but contract for the services of regional advertising and promotion? The *locus classicus* of this analytical approach is Ronald H. Coase, "The Nature of the Firm," 14 (n.s.) *Economica* 386 (1937).

[263] Note that this perspective stands in opposition to that of Berle and Means and of Galbraith,

who claimed that the main force behind the boundaries and organization of firms was the acquisition and exercise of market power. See Adolf A. Berle, Jr. and Gardiner C. Means, *The Modern Corporation and Private Property* (New York: MacMillan), 1934; John Kenneth Galbraith, *The New Industrial State* (Boston: Houghton-Mifflin), 1967.

264 P. Milgrom and J. Roberts, *Economics, Organization and Management* (Englewood Cliffs, N.J.: Prentice-Hall), 1992, pp. 90-92.

265 Note that these principles of firm boundaries and organization apply apart from the "network effects" and "positive feedback loop" described in the FOF, Paragraphs 39-40. On network effects generally, in addition to the earlier reference to Carl Shapiro and Hal Varian, see Daniel Rubinfeld, "Competition, Innovation, and Antitrust Enforcement in Dynamic Network Industries," Address before the Software Publishers' Association, March 24, 1998; http://www.usdoj.gov/atr/public/speeches/1611.htm (accessed October 23, 2000); David Evans and Richard Schmalensee, "A Guide to Antitrust Economics of Networks," *Antitrust* (Spring 1996).

266 In the sense of factories, machinery, production equipment, and parts inventory.

267 For an exposition of this point, see Timothy F. Bresnahan and Franco Malerba, "Industrial Dynamics and the Evolution of Firms' and Nations' Competitive Capabilities in the World Computer Industry," in David C. Mowery and Richard R. Nelson (eds.), *Sources of Industrial Leadership: Studies of Seven Industries* (New York: Cambridge University Press), 1999.

268 See "A Brief History of AT&T" at http://www.att.com/history/history3.html.

269 Bork, *supra* note 90, p. 181.

270 See generally D. Teece, "Towards an Economic Theory of the Multiproduct Firm," 3 *Journal of Economic Behavior and Organization* 39 (1988).

271 See "Microsoft Fast Facts," at http://www.microsoft.com/presspass/fastfacts.asp. Current employment headcount as of October 2, 2001: 48,958 are total; 24,210 are in the Puget Sound area.

272 Franklin M. Fisher, John J. McGowan, and Joen E. Greenwood, *Folded, Spindled, and Mutilated: Economic Analysis and U.S. v. IBM* (Cambridge: The MIT Press), 1983, pp. 11-19.

273 Schmalensee Direct, Paragraphs 170-173.

274 *Ibid.*, Figure 11.

275 In fact, Microsoft began as a company specializing in computer languages, and that heritage is reflected in the diverse software development kits that it offers.

276 Maritz, *supra* note 135, Paragraph 136. In preparation for hearings on remedies (which never occurred), we reviewed the underlying data and discovered that the actual level of support was even higher because Mr. Maritz's figures were incomplete. At the time this was written Microsoft had close to 4,000 employees devoted to products and support services for third-party developers, with total annual expenditures of $1.5 billion.

277 For example, Windows 2000 Server software includes an improved directory system called Active Directory. In the past, Microsoft's Exchange Server included its own directory of users, forcing network administrators to maintain two separate directories. The newest version relies on Active Directory. It is difficult to imagine how that integration could take place as readily if Exchange Server were owned by the Apps Co.

278 Timothy F. Bresnahan, "New Modes of Competition: Implications for the Future Structure

of the Computer Industry," in Jeffrey A. Eisenach and Thomas M. Lenard (eds.), *Competition, Innovation and the Microsoft Monopoly: Antitrust in the Digital Marketplace* (Boston: Kluwer), 1999, pp. 155-208.

[279] *Ibid.*, p. 183.

[280] We also note Professor Bresnahan's conclusion regarding a (then-hypothetical) structural remedy that would split the operating systems from the rest of Microsoft: "It is flat-out picking winners" (p. 206). Picking winners (or causing losers) is not an appropriate role for antitrust to play.

[281] Final Judgment, Section 3.g.ii.

[282] *Ibid.*, Section 3.b.

[283] *Ibid.*, section 3.b.

[284] Paul Krugman, *supra* note 256.

[285] Microsoft has followed this same strategy in its public relations efforts, framing the case as being about its right to innovate.

Section 1: *U.S. v. Microsoft Corp.*: The Economics

Essay 4

DOS Kapital: Has Antitrust Action Against Microsoft Created Value in the Computer Industry?*

by George Bittlingmayer and Thomas W. Hazlett

At the heart of the government's 1994 case against Microsoft was the allegation that the big software maker provided discounts and other incentives to computer manufacturers agreeing to contracts that put Microsoft's rivals at a disadvantage. Such marketing practices, the government claimed, would ultimately lead to less competition and higher prices.

If this was, in fact, Microsoft's strategy, the effects ought to show up in the stock market's expectations of profitability for companies that produce both complements and substitutes for Microsoft products, as well as for such large customers of Microsoft products as computer makers. Thus a pro-enforcement "event" – one that increased the prospect that Microsoft's practices would be limited by government action – should reduce Microsoft's stock price and raise the stock prices of other firms in the information technology industry that either compete with Microsoft or buy its products in very large quantity. Conversely, a setback to enforcement should reduce the market capitalization of these other IT firms.

Thomas Hazlett of the American Enterprise Institute and George Bittlingmayer of the University of Kansas Business School test this proposition using 54 antitrust enforcement "events" involving Microsoft, starting in 1991 and ending in December 1997. For example, the Justice Department's August 9, 1995 announcement that it would not try to block the sale of Windows 95 is classified as an anti-enforcement event, whereas a request by three senators on June 30, 1997 that the Federal Trade Commission reopen the FTC's Microsoft investigation is classified as pro-enforcement. The authors' statistical analysis should be no comfort to the view that enforcement has served competition.

*The 159 computer firms in the study actually experienced an average collective loss of more than $1 billion on the three days surrounding each of 29 pro-enforcement events. A possible explanation for this positive relationship between the interests of Microsoft and other firms in the IT industry is that the market recognizes the need for a dominant platform standard – one that allows other software companies to write applications at lower cost and increases the demand for software in general by making it easier to use. Or perhaps the market sees the attack on Microsoft as part of a broader government policy of "punishing winners" that would ultimately limit the profitability of other successful technology companies.** Either way, it's clear that investors did not find merit in the rationale underlying government efforts to clip Microsoft's wings.* — *D.S.E.*

THE VALUE OF ANTITRUST

> Microsoft's sway over operating systems and applications puts everyone else in the industry at a disadvantage, said Alan C. Ashton, president of WordPerfect Corp., Orem, Utah. They are a threat to everybody in the industry.
>
> —*The Wall Street Journal*, December 11, 1992

Since the advent of the personal computer in 1981, Microsoft's operating systems and application programs have claimed impressive shares of a rapidly expanding market for PC software. This success has attracted attention not only within the industry but also from state and federal antitrust enforcers, the private antitrust bar, and the public at large. Since 1990, federal authorities – first at the Federal Trade Commission (FTC) and then at the Department of Justice's Antitrust Division (DOJ) – initiated a series of antitrust investigations of Microsoft. These inquiries resulted in a 1995 consent decree between Microsoft and the DOJ, and a 1997 DOJ suit alleging that Microsoft had violated the decree. In 1998, the DOJ and 20 states filed a new suit on broader charges.

Is Microsoft "a threat to everybody in the industry?" If so, does that harm consumers? Will antitrust policy help alleviate that threat? For some analysts, Microsoft's high market share, coupled with certain of the firm's aggressive marketing practices, implies predatory conduct.[1] For others, Microsoft's success in the highly competitive and rapidly growing computer sector offers a classic example of a "good monopoly," one that garners market share by offering popular products at low prices.[2]

Whatever Microsoft's intent or success in monopolizing PC software, it is unclear what kind of policy would promote lower prices for consumers, the goal championed by Bork (1978) and other antitrust analysts. A policy that corrects an identified market failure improves welfare only if the value created exceeds the policy's cost. Even Microsoft's foes fear that intervention by the government and the courts will result in net losses.[3]

In this paper we ask: Have antitrust enforcement initiatives increased the stock market value of Microsoft's alleged victims? The Microsoft case seems especially suited for a stock price study. First, the long history of investigations, filings, court decisions, and other antitrust announcements offer a substantial number of policy events. Second, a large number of computer industry firms will prosper if the market for operating systems and major desktop applications becomes more competitive. This study exploits these circumstances by examining share price reactions for both Microsoft and a portfolio of 159 other computer firms around the times of 54 antitrust enforcement announcements involving Microsoft over the seven years 1991-97.

THE MICROSOFT QUESTION AND THE STOCK MARKET

The basic facts are straightforward, but interpretations vary. Microsoft has a large market share in desktop operating systems and in several important lines of PC software. It has also earned a high rate of return on its past investments. Additionally, the firm's stock boasts a very high P/E ratio, indicating that investors anticipate unusually high earnings growth in the future. Finally, Microsoft employs aggressive business practices.

To Microsoft's critics, these facts are consistent with the view that Microsoft gained a monopoly through predation and that the stock market expects this strategy to produce an even larger flow of monopoly rents in the future. The critics claim that quality-adjusted prices of operating systems, software, and related products are higher now – or will be higher in the future – because of Microsoft's actions. To Microsoft's supporters, these same facts are consistent with the view that Microsoft out-competes rivals by expanding output and lowering prices for consumers and that stock investors expect continued competitive superiority in a rapidly growing industry. The supporters claim Microsoft's practices might have hurt competitors, but not consumers.

Specific aspects of the Microsoft debate demonstrate the difficulty of relying on economic theory alone. For example, after initially giving away its browser, Netscape began to charge $49 per copy. Soon afterward, Microsoft incorporated its browser, Internet Explorer, into Windows 98, essentially charging a price of zero. Microsoft also required computer manufacturers installing Windows 98 to place an IE icon on the opening screen (Nash, 1996; Quittner and Slatalla, 1998). Did Microsoft's "tie-in" and/or zero pricing hurt Netscape? Would its actions ultimately hurt consumers by eliminating a rival? It seems clear that prices for browsers were lower in the short run, but the elimination of a rival might mean higher prices in the long run. As a matter of economic theory, the ultimate effects are unclear.

Another line of controversy concerns "network effects" in operating systems and applications software. Network effects arise when a product becomes more valuable as more people use it. Telephones and fax machines provide classic examples. When a single firm controls the underlying standard, the result may be a "winner-take-all" outcome. Economic analyses[4] and popular treatments[5] of the Microsoft case have highlighted network effects. However, network effects cut both ways. By one journalist's reckoning, "the theory of increasing returns is crucial to the case against Microsoft... [but] increasing returns are equally crucial to the case *for* Microsoft – as a reason why trying to break it up would be a bad thing."[6] Again, theory is inconclusive. Such ambiguity plagues nearly every other aspect of the decade-old discussion about Microsoft and monopoly.

We will attempt to break this deadlock with the help of some evidence. We turn to the verdict of the financial markets, examining the stock returns of firms allegedly hurt by Microsoft's anticompetitive behavior. The use of financial data to study the effects of regulation is summarized by Schwert (1981). Three types of studies are relevant. One type, pioneered by Eckbo (1983) and Stillman (1983), examines the effects of mergers or merger policy by examining the stock prices of competitors. Prager (1992) looks at competing firms in the celebrated 1904 *Northern Securities* decision (which brought mergers under the Sherman Act). Mullin et al. (1995) examine the stock prices of competing and vertically related firms in the *U.S. Steel* divestiture suit. Banerjee and Eckard (1998) look at the prices of competitors of merging firms during the 1897-1903 merger wave.

The second group of event studies examines the stock price effects for firms that are actual or potential targets of regulation. Jarrell and Peltzman (1985) investigate the direct and the indirect spillover effects of product recalls. Mitchell and Netter (1989) implicate anti-takeover legislation as a precipitating factor in the 1987 stock crash by looking at returns of "in-play" stocks, and Schipper and Thompson (1983) analyze securities and tax law changes by looking at the stock price movements of frequent acquirers. In the case of Microsoft, antitrust action may have had legal implications for other firms. In fact, the FTC has investigated both Intel and Cisco since the Department of Justice filed its most recent charges against Microsoft. America Online (AOL) has been the target of litigation by state attorneys general.

The third group of studies focuses on litigation between private parties. It turns out that the stock gains accruing to a successful litigant are often more than offset by the losses to other firms. Cutler and Summers (1988) look at the Pennzoil-Texaco litigation, as do Hertzel and Smith (1993), who specifically note "the importance of evaluating industry effects when drawing conclusions about the social costs of litigation."[7] Similarly, Bizjak and Coles (1995) report that financial distress, behavioral constraints, and the costs of follow-on suits result in a net decline in the total value of the opposing parties in a private suit. In the case here, the government suit may represent litigation carried out on behalf of Microsoft's rivals.

One point deserves emphasis. The stock market will not render a verdict on whether Microsoft's behavior was anticompetitive. Rather, it will reflect investors' judgments about the marginal effect of antitrust enforcement on the expected profitability of firms allegedly victimized by monopolization. If stock values in the computer sector decline with enforcement actions, this could reflect a belief that antitrust enforcement will impose losses, but not that Microsoft's practices helped the rest of the industry. Fortuitously, this focuses on the proper margin for policy analysis, comparing not an existing market structure to a theoretically improved alternative, but what exists before policy intervention to what is expected afterward.

TESTING ANTITRUST POLICY EFFECTS

Under anyone's theory of antitrust – the pro-consumer view that antitrust enforcement lowers quality-adjusted prices for consumers (Buchanan and Lee, 1992) or the "capture theory" view that antitrust protects competitors (Baumol and Ordover, 1985; Gilligan et al., 1989; Wolf, 1993) – Microsoft share prices should fall with unexpected enforcement. Formally stated, the expected abnormal return to Microsoft shareholders will be negative during "pro-enforcement" news windows: $E(R_{MS}) > 0$, where R_{MS} is the return to Microsoft stock during the event window, adjusted for market-wide returns.

Conversely, either view predicts that setbacks to antitrust actions directed against Microsoft will imply rising share prices: $E(R_{MS}) < 0$ during "anti-enforcement" event windows. Antitrust prosecution brings no benefits, while entailing the following: litigation costs, diverted managerial attention, constraints on operations (due to antitrust liability), lost monopoly profits, and civil penalties levied by a court or agreed to in a consent decree. Although Microsoft's stock price reactions do not distinguish between the two views of antitrust policy, they do identify the enforcement actions that matter to investors.

Under the pro-consumer view, effective antitrust action against Microsoft should produce three types of beneficiaries. First, firms that buy Microsoft products will directly benefit (through lower input costs). Second, firms that produce complementary products will indirectly benefit (through an outward shift in demand for their products). Third, according to the predation and vertical foreclosure arguments central to the case against Microsoft, effective antitrust enforcement will ease barriers to entry for Microsoft's rivals. This implies that, during pro-enforcement event windows, $E(R_{NMS}) > 0$, where R_{NMS} is the abnormal return to non-Microsoft computer companies, and that during anti-enforcement event windows, $E(R_{NMS}) < 0$. Under the pro-consumer view, setbacks in enforcement produce the opposite results. Microsoft's customers, the producers of complementary products, and its rivals should all lose.

Under the capture view of antitrust, enforcement could hurt consumers by imposing substantial litigation costs by deterring efficiency-enhancing behavior, by implicitly putting other successful firms at risk of becoming targets of antitrust, or by increasing the uncertainty of investment. Stock prices of firms in the computer industry could in fact fall, especially the stock prices of customers and producers of complements. Retreats or setbacks in enforcement will have opposite effects, which would be reflected in rising computer industry stock prices.

ANTITRUST EVENTS AND THE COMPUTER PORTFOLIO

News of a Federal Trade Commission investigation of Microsoft first leaked to the press in March 1991. That investigation led the FTC to vote on a preliminary injunction against the firm in February 1993, when it deadlocked (hence, filing no action). It deadlocked a second time in July 1993 on whether it would file a case. In an unusual policy twist, the Department of Justice immediately began its own investigation utilizing the FTC files. This inquiry resulted in a July 1994 agreement between Microsoft and the DOJ, finalized as a consent decree in August 1995.

In the interim, a series of court actions took place, including rejection of the proposed consent decree by District Court Judge Stanley Sporkin (who found the agreement too lenient toward Microsoft), and then reinstatement of the decree by the D.C. circuit. The DOJ filed a suit against Microsoft on October 21, 1997 accusing the firm of violating the 1995 consent decree. Legal skirmishing, including a much broader antitrust suit filed by the DOJ in May 1998, continued into 1999. We end our study, however, at December 31, 1997.

Table 1 provides details of the 54 events used in this study. The list was created from the *Wall Street Journal Index*, and consists of every breaking news story concerning Microsoft and antitrust. Table 1 includes the returns, net of the market, for both Microsoft and an equally weighted index of computer industry firms over the one- and three-day windows surrounding publication dates. These are the net returns to Microsoft and to the equally weighted index of other computer firms based on the market model. This index is described in more detail below. Stock return data used throughout this study are from the Center for Research in Security Prices at the University of Chicago. Table 1 also lists other news stories in the *Wall Street Journal* that could have had a major effect on Microsoft share prices on or near event dates.

Table 1 classifies three event groups. "Pro-enforcement" events (Pro) report stricter antitrust enforcement against Microsoft; "anti-enforcement" events (Anti) entail clear setbacks for, or withdrawal from, vigorous antitrust enforcement. "Ambiguous" events (?) involve either (1) enforcement actions with unclear implications or (2) another major contemporaneous event likely to substantially affect Microsoft's stock price.

To illustrate, the March 12, 1991 revelation that Microsoft was the target of an investigation had straightforward negative implications for Microsoft shareholders, and no possibly offsetting *Journal* stories appeared simultaneously.[8] Hence the event is classified as pro-enforcement. In contrast, the April 15, 1991 article announcing that the FTC was broadening its investigation (clearly pro-enforcement) was followed by an April 17 report that Microsoft earnings increased 65 percent. This event is placed in the ambiguous category.

Table 1 lists 29 pro-enforcement events. These stories report antitrust investigations, inquiries proceeding or expanding, pressure on antitrust authorities for stricter enforcement, signals implying a collapse of the negotiated

Table 1. **One- and three-day residual returns for Microsoft and the computer industry (excluding Microsoft) around dates with Wall Street Journal news articles involving Microsoft and antitrust, 1991-1997.** The "news summary" column includes a short description of the event and any other story published, with date of publication, that could have influenced returns. "Pro"' events are categorized as pro-enforcement, "anti" are categorized as anti-enforcement, and those assigned a question mark are ambiguous either because of the nature of the enforcement action or because of a contaminating event.

	Published Date	Residual Return 1-Day Microsoft (%)	Residual Return 1-Day Industry (%)	Residual Return 3-Day Microsoft (%)	Residual Return 3-Day Industry (%)	News Summary	Category
1.	3/12/91	-2.30	-0.80	-1.54	-0.94	Microsoft is target of FTC investigation.	Pro
2.	4/15/91	5.69	-1.60	-2.61	-1.57	FTC is broadening its investigation. 65% increase in earnings (4/17).	?
3.	10/21/92	2.14	0.52	1.69	1.37	FTC has subpoenaed data from Microsoft.	Pro
4.	12/11/92	-2.77	-0.79	-4.53	-1.84	FTC staff lawyers sent report on 12/4 requesting injunction against Microsoft.	Pro
5.	2/8/93	-3.44	-0.58	0.18	-3.98	FTC splits 2-2, no preliminary injunction against Microsoft.	?
6.	7/15/93	-0.66	-0.72	-1.36	-1.85	FTC ends its two-year probe of Intel, to take up Microsoft allegations.	?
7.	7/22/93	-0.93	0.48	-3.46	1.07	FTC unable to reach a conclusion.	?
8.	8/2/93	-2.40	0.61	-7.82	0.98	DOJ is reviewing documents from Microsoft.	Pro
9.	8/23/93	1.11	0.99	0.74	-0.11	DOJ reported 8/20 it will launch a formal investigation of Microsoft.	Pro
10.	6/6/94	3.00	0.20	2.06	-2.23	DOJ investigation intensifying, taking depositions. No other reports.	Pro
11.	7/1/94	-3.41	-1.24	-4.51	-0.97	Information-gathering portion of DOJ investigation is over.	?
12.	7/18/94	3.49	0.02	2.52	-1.85	Microsoft signed consent decree.	Anti
13.	10/17/94	-1.44	0.02	-1.17	-0.14	Microsoft acquisition likely to spur antitrust probe.	?
14.	10/24/94	0.27	0.45	1.77	0.59	DOJ will examine agreement to purchase Intuit.	?
15.	11/22/94	0.37	-0.30	-0.22	-0.80	Microsoft's proposed acquisition of Intuit is facing continuing scrutiny.	?
16.	1/11/95	0.63	-0.03	1.20	1.30	Competitors file brief, try to unravel consent decree.	Pro
17.	1/16/95	0.89	0.06	2.34	0.43	Sporkin invites Jacobovitz and Reback to present oral arguments.	Pro
18.	1/20/95	-2.24	-0.29	-1.98	-1.13	Sporkin asks DOJ and Microsoft to explain why changes should not be made in consent decree.	Pro
19.	1/23/95	1.92	-0.78	-1.99	-0.87	Sporkin at loggerheads with Bingaman and MS attorney; Apple appeals case to Supreme Court. Sony and MS agree on partnership, free upgrades on Word 6.0.	Pro
20.	2/1/95	-0.73	0.58	-1.80	0.73	DOJ has issued subpoenas in Microsoft/Intuit investigation.	Pro
21.	2/15/95	-2.63	0.01	-2.85	0.04	Sporkin rejects government's consent as too lenient.	Pro
22.	2/23/95	-0.59	-0.34	0.66	-1.41	Apple alleges Microsoft threatened it.	Pro
23.	2/24/95	-0.94	-0.65	0.43	-1.15	Story about antitrust chief Bingaman calling Gates Saturday night.	?
24.	3/8/95	4.44	0.52	6.03	1.19	DOJ and Microsoft ask federal appeals court to reverse Sporkin's decision.	Anti
25.	4/25/95	2.95	-0.07	4.67	1.40	Three-judge appeals panel voices concerns that Sporkin may have exceeded his authority.	Anti

26.	4/28/95	3.64	0.09	2.47	0.08	DOJ files suit against Intuit deal. Microsoft is pressing to complete the deal.	?
27.	5/1/95	0.52	-0.57	0.70	-0.50	DOJ unveils key documents in unusual move.	?
28.	5/22/95	0.99	-0.18	1.95	0.01	Microsoft says it is ending its plan to acquire Intuit.	?
29.	6/9/95	1.94	1.11	-0.11	2.61	DOJ racing to finish an investigation aimed at MS plan to bundle access to its new software.	?
30.	6/12/95	-2.17	0.06	-1.62	1.14	DOJ looking at Microsoft stipulation against patent infringement suits.	Pro
31.	6/19/95	1.75	0.73	5.24	1.79	Appeals court reinstates consent decree Sporkin rejected.	Anti
32.	6/22/95	-0.26	-0.35	-1.74	0.26	DOJ issues subpoenas to publishers, others.	Pro
33.	7/14/95	3.65	0.18	8.35	1.22	DOJ unveils antitrust arguments. Net income increase (7/18).	?
34.	7/24/95	0.60	1.51	-2.27	2.26	DOJ withdraws broad subpoenas.	Anti
35.	7/31/95	-2.24	-0.64	-6.24	-0.79	DOJ extends investigation to new area – bundling of software.	Pro
36.	8/9/95	3.11	0.96	0.63	0.83	DOJ says it will take no action prior to Windows 95 shipment.	Anti
37.	8/22/95	4.75	0.83	1.03	0.80	Judge formalizes consent.	Anti
38.	2/6/96	-1.78	-0.17	1.20	-0.51	DOJ takes interest in Microsoft acquisition of Vermeer Technologies, Internet tools.	Pro
39.	9/20/96	-0.58	0.00	-0.10	0.93	DOJ has launched an investigation of Microsoft's Internet software business.	Pro
40.	2/12/97	-1.01	-0.32	-2.40	-2.59	State of Texas has launched an antitrust investigation of Microsoft.	Pro
41.	5/20/97	2.00	0.18	2.32	0.44	DOJ requests additional information about Microsoft's planned acquisition of WebTV networks. MS has signed up more than a dozen business-information providers (5/22).	Pro
42.	6/30/97	-0.87	0.77	-4.23	-0.29	At the urging of competitors, three senators have asked the FTC to once again investigate Microsoft's business practices, including compliance with the 1994 consent decree.	Pro
43.	7/14/97	4.33	0.68	4.08	2.08	Netscape tries to convince government that Microsoft plans to use new Internet software to lock out rivals. MS to announce that it will link up with Disney and Warner Bros. (7/15); net income announcement (7/18).	?
44.	8/4/97	0.10	0.21	0.87	2.82	Microsoft closes its purchase of WebTV after DOJ ends its lengthy review without taking action.	Anti
45.	8/19/97	1.44	-0.35	-0.05	-1.63	DOJ is reviewing Microsoft's minority stake in Apple as well as three unrelated investments.	Pro
46.	10/7/97	-0.45	-0.90	1.17	-0.06	Microsoft under investigation by European officials.	Pro
47.	10/17/97	0.70	-0.68	-0.74	-2.21	Four more states join investigation by European officials.	Pro
48.	10/21/97	1.96	-0.52	-1.35	-0.40	U.S. sues Microsoft over PC browser – move to restrict bundling with Windows 95 hits key market strategy. MS profit tops analysts' forecasts.	?
49.	11/3/97	-0.49	-0.58	-1.66	0.13	Senate Internet panel to probe Microsoft's power.	Pro
50.	11/10/97	-0.33	-0.18	1.40	-1.01	Texas sues Microsoft, alleging licenses impede state's probe.	Pro
51.	12/8/97	1.90	1.09	0.48	-0.74	Microsoft, DOJ face off, but hearing ends without decision.	?
52.	12/12/97	-1.29	-2.75	-2.65	-5.46	Microsoft is dealt a blow on Internet plans – judge orders firm to stop bundling software with Windows operating systems.	Pro
53.	12/18/97	-1.94	-0.93	-4.90	0.93	U.S., Microsoft clash on court-order compliance.	Pro
54.	12/30/97	0.30	-0.55	1.06	-0.24	Microsoft is again assailed by DOJ, which says firm thwarts court order.	Pro

Table 2. **Means, Medians, and Standard Deviations of Residual Returns for Microsoft and the Rest of the Computer Industry at Announcements of Enforcement Actions in *The Wall Street Journal.***

		1-Day		3-Day	
		Microsoft (%)	**Industry (%)**	**Microsoft (%)**	**Industry (%)**
Pro-enforcement	Mean	-0.45	-0.26	-1.16	-0.53
n=29	Median	-0.58	-0.29	-1.54	-0.24
	SD	1.60	0.73	2.73	1.48
Ambiguous	Mean	0.85	-0.13	0.33	-0.26
n=17	Median	0.52	-0.18	0.18	-0.40
	SD	2.57	0.76	2.99	1.55
Anti-enforcement	Mean	2.65	0.59	2.34	1.15
n=8	Median	3.03	0.63	1.77	1.29
	SD	1.70	0.53	2.82	1.40
All events	Mean	0.42	-0.09	-0.16	-0.18
n=54	Median	0.29	-0.05	0.06	-0.09
	SD	2.23	0.75	2.99	1.57
All days	Mean	0.00	0.00	0.00	0.00
n=1771	SD	1.75	0.87	2.92	1.72

consent decree, and state-level antitrust investigations of Microsoft. Table 2 reports the summary statistics for the event dates and all days in the sample. Average abnormal returns over the 29 pro-enforcement dates for Microsoft equal -0.45 percent on the day of publication and -1.16 percent over three days (t – 1, t, t + 1). The computer industry portfolio also declines: Average abnormal returns are -0.26 percent over the one-day window and -0.53 percent over the three-day window. On average, both Microsoft and other computer firm stocks decline in value when antitrust measures directed against Microsoft are announced in the press.

Table 1 reports eight anti-enforcement events (i.e., positive events for Microsoft shareholders). Four involve the joint struggle of Microsoft and the DOJ with Judge Sporkin over the proposed consent decree. Table 2 reports Microsoft's mean abnormal return on those eight news dates as 2.65 percent. The three-day return is 2.34 percent. Average abnormal returns for the rest of the industry are 0.59 percent and 1.15 percent over one and three days, respectively. Microsoft and other computer firm stocks generally increase in value when antitrust enforcement declines.

Table 2 shows that the 17 ambiguous events are accompanied by a positive one-day return for Microsoft (0.85 percent) and a much higher standard deviation. Microsoft's median one-day return (0.53 percent) is substantially closer to zero. Over three days, Microsoft's mean and median returns are even closer to zero (0.33 percent and 0.18 percent, respectively). Industry returns are negative, especially over three days.

Note that Microsoft's returns provide a barometer for our choice of event dates. Three facts support our a priori classification and suggest that the associated publication dates mark events of importance for Microsoft shareholders. First, Microsoft's one-day return is higher on the eight anti-enforcement dates than on the 29 pro-enforcement dates (t = 4.74). Second, Microsoft's one-day return is statistically indistinguishable from zero on the ambiguous dates (t = 1.36) and much more volatile. Third, the standard deviation of Microsoft's returns are higher on the 54 event dates than for the sample as a whole.

To construct a portfolio of non-Microsoft computer-sector stocks, we included all firms in *Hoover's Guide to Computer Companies 1995* that were publicly traded in the U.S. and operated primarily in the computer industry. We allocated the resulting 159 firms to one of nine industry segments based on their description in *Hoover's*. We excluded two product lines – electronic content and mainframes – because each had only two firms.

Not all firms were publicly listed throughout the sample period. The Appendix (not included here) lists the nine industry segments, their representative products, and the names of the firms in each. We calculated the simple mean return in each segment and then calculated the simple mean return across segments. We also utilized an index with equal weighting for each firm in the industry (save Microsoft), and the results for that model are reported as well. They do not vary substantially from the results based on equally weighted segments, which are the results we discuss below. Either method avoids having a handful of large-capitalization firms such as Intel, Hewlett Packard, and Compaq dominate a value-weighted portfolio.

EMPIRICAL RESULTS

This paper estimates the marginal effect of Microsoft antitrust enforcement news on equity values in each of nine segments of the computer industry. We employ the multivariate regression model used extensively in stock market studies of regulation. Binder (1985) discusses the use of the multivariate regression model in event studies and credits the method to Gibbons (1980, Appendix D).[9]

Define Dt as a [0, 1] variable that equals unity if a given event occurs on day t; let R be the return for an index, segment, or firm i on day t, and let Mt be the return on the market on day t. We estimate the following regression:

$$R_{it} = a_i + b_i M_t + \sum_{k=-5}^{5} c_{i,t+k} D_{i,k} + \varepsilon_{it}.$$

The term b_i is the coefficient of the market model. The $c_{i,t+k}$ coefficients yield estimates of the daily leading, simultaneous, or lagging effects of an event, and the summed values of the estimated $c_{i,t+k}$'s over $k = [-5, 5]$ yield the cumulative effect. The discussion of results will focus on the three-day window, $k = [-1, 1]$.

Antitrust Events Signed A Priori

Table 3 presents estimates from Equation 1 for eight anti-enforcement and 28 pro-enforcement events.[10] During the latter, Microsoft shares decline by an average of 1.20 percent over three days ($t = 2.06$), while the rest of the industry declines 0.71 percent per event ($t = 2.45$). Manufacturers of components and network products, as well as distributors, experience statistically significant declines of 1 percent or more. The other sectors are all negative over three days. The top panel of Figure 1 shows the comparatively strong negative effects for Microsoft over these 28 events and substantially weaker, though still negative, effects for the computer industry portfolio.

Also seen in Table 3 are mirrored results during the eight anti-enforcement events. Microsoft's stock increases by 2.36 percent on average over the three-day windows ($t = 2.19$), while the equally weighted nine-segment portfolio experiences three-day returns of 1.18 percent ($t = 2.21$). Firms making components, network products, PC software, and semiconductors witnessed three-day returns in excess of 1 percent. No industry segments exhibit negative three-day returns, and the few negative returns over one- or 11-day windows are statistically insignificant. The bottom panel of Figure 1 graphs the cumulative returns indicating that the anti-enforcement events have strong positive effects on Microsoft shares and positive, although smaller, effects on other computer stocks.

The dollar values implied by these estimates are of interest. The 159 computer firms used in this study had an aggregate market capitalization of $141 billion in January 1991 and $754 billion in December 1997.[11] The mean three-day return per event of -0.59 percent for the average of all computer firms implies a loss of several hundred million to several billion dollars per event. In fact, this group experiences mean market-adjusted declines in value of $1.2

Table 3. **Computer Sector Returns During Microsoft Antitrust News Windows**

Coefficients and t-statistics for regressions of firm or industry segment returns on lagging and leading dummy variables that are coded as shown in Table 1. Coefficients for the constant and the market return are calculated but not reported. One pro-enforcement event is omitted due to insufficient data for estimation of the lagging terms.

Firm or Segment	8 Anti-Enforcement Events			28 Pro-Enforcement Events		
	11-Day [-5,5]	3-Day [-1,1]	1-Day [0]	11-Day [-5,5]	3-Day [-1,1]	1-Day [0]
Microsoft	-0.0039	0.0236	0.0265	-0.0194	-0.0120	-0.0049
	(-0.019)	(2.19)	(4.280)	(-2.01)	(-2.06)	(-1.45)
Average of computer firms	0.0149	0.0117	0.0060	-0.0029	-0.0059	-0.0028
	(1.45)	(2.19)	(1.94)	(-0.60)	(-2.04)	(-1.70)
Average of computer segments	0.0131	0.0118	0.0060	-0.0035	-0.0071	-0.0036
	(1.29)	(2.21)	(1.94)	(-0.74)	(-2.45)	(-2.07)
Component	0.0271	0.0198	0.0147	-0.0121	-0.0184	-0.0036
	(1.57)	(2.20)	(2.83)	(-1.51)	(-3.79)	(-1.28)
Computer	0.0181	0.0085	0.0072	-0.0045	-0.0064	-0.0050
	(1.21)	(1.09)	(1.60)	(-0.65)	(-1.52)	(-2.06)
Corporate	-0.0075	0.0022	-0.0065	-0.0060	-0.0092	-0.0052
	(-0.42)	(0.24)	(-1.23)	(-0.73)	(-1.86)	(-1.81)
Distributor	-0.0153	0.0079	0.0027	-0.0052	-0.0111	-0.0005
	(-0.89)	(0.88)	(0.53)	(-0.66)	(-2.31)	(-0.18)
Network	0.0072	0.0124	0.0104	-0.0117	-0.0108	-0.0062
	(0.44)	(1.45)	(2.10)	(-1.53)	(-2.34)	(-2.33)
PC software	0.0201	0.0143	0.0057	0.0003	-0.0023	-0.0022
	(1.31)	(1.73)	(1.21)	(0.05)	(-0.52)	(-0.87)
Peripheral equipment	0.0180	0.0072	0.0025	0.0014	-0.0003	-0.0071
	(0.92)	(0.69)	(0.42)	(0.15)	(-0.06)	(-2.22)
Semiconductor	0.0308	0.0258	0.0188	0.0049	-0.0043	-0.0005
	(1.49)	(2.39)	(3.02)	(0.51)	(-0.73)	(-0.14)
Non-PC software	0.0189	0.0085	-0.0007	0.0010	-0.0007	-0.0007
	(1.51)	(1.28)	(-0.19)	(0.18)	(-0.19)	(-0.36)

billion on the three days surrounding each of 29 pro-enforcement events.

The cumulative decline is $35 billion. Conversely, the same group of firms has a mean increase in value of $8.8 billion on the three days surrounding each of the eight anti-enforcement events. The cumulative increase is $70 billion. Clearly, in view of the large standard errors attached to these estimates, they should be taken with a grain of salt. The fact that the cumulative increase is greater than the cumulative decline might only reflect the possibility that good news for Microsoft came as more of a surprise than bad news.

Figure 1. **Cumulative residual returns for Microsoft, equally weighted average of all computer firms in the sample (excluding Microsoft), and equally weighted average of all segments (excluding Microsoft).** The upper panel shows the cumulative residual returns from day -5 through day 5 around 28 "pro-enforcement"' antitrust event dates involving Microsoft. The solid line shows the cumulative returns for Microsoft, the long dashes for an equally weighted portfolio of all other firms in our sample, and the short dashes for a portfolio of equally weighted segments (themselves equally weighted averages). The lower panel shows similar cumulative returns for eight "anti-enforcement" antitrust events dates involving Microsoft. The list of dates appears in Table 1. (a) Pro-enforcement events (n=28), (b) Anti-enforcement events (n=8).

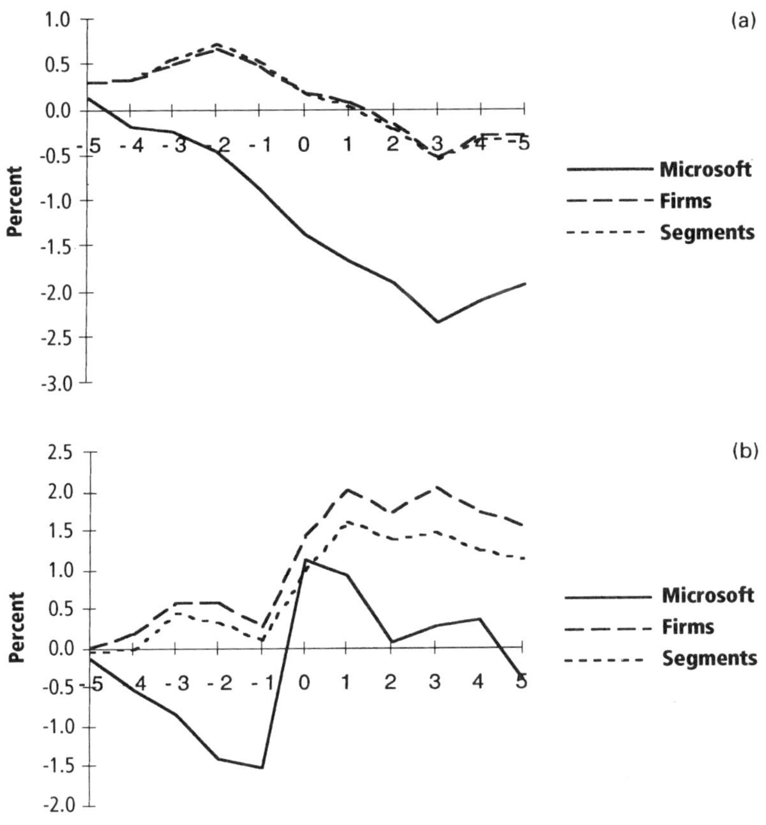

Still, these dollar estimates offer some idea of the importance for the computer industry as a whole of policies directed against Microsoft.

Antitrust Events Defined by Microsoft Stock Price Reactions

As an alternative to a classification system that relies on the investigator's judgment, we allow Microsoft stock price movements themselves to identify announcements as good or bad news for Microsoft. A positive event for Microsoft, which we classify as anti-enforcement, occurs on one of the 54 dates in Table 1 when either (a) Microsoft's cumulative residual return exceeds 2 percent over the five-day interval [-4, 0] or (b) Microsoft's daily residual return exceeds 2 percent on any day of the three-day interval [-2, 0].

The longer, five-day criterion based on cumulative returns is intended to capture slow releases of information, and the shorter, three-day criterion is intended to capture sudden releases of information. We define a negative (pro-enforcement) event symmetrically. For the 1,771 days in the sample, Microsoft's cumulative five-day residual excess returns exceed 2 percent 26.7 percent of the time and fall below -2 percent 28.9 percent of the time. Microsoft's daily excess returns exceed 2 percent with probability of 16.6 percent, and fall below -2 percent with probability of 11.7 percent.

Twenty-four of the 54 events are accompanied by increases in Microsoft stock as defined here; of these, six are among the eight defined a priori as anti-enforcement events in Table 1. We eliminate the July 14 and July 24, 1995 events because they coincide with a sharp increase and then collapse of Microsoft's stock price that was linked with shifting earnings expectations in connection with the July 18 publication of earnings news. The two event dates are separated by only five trading days. Twenty-three of the 54 events in Table 2 are flagged by threshold declines in Microsoft stock; of these, 15 are among the 29 defined as pro-enforcement events in Table 1.

The results in Table 4 show that negative movements of Microsoft stock at the time of enforcement actions coincide with negative returns for the rest of the industry. Not surprisingly, Microsoft stock declines by 2.18 percent over three days (t = -3.49) and by 4.52 percent over 11 days (t = -3.89). However, the industry as a whole declines by 0.62 percent over three days (t = -2.00) and by 1.05 percent over 11 days (t = -1.83). Figure 2 shows this pattern and that both Microsoft and other computer stocks continue to decline after the event dates.

On news accompanied by positive Microsoft stock movements, the rest of the industry prospers. Microsoft's stock price increases an average of 1.49 percent during the three-day windows. Note that the cumulative return over the longer 11-day interval is only 0.76 percent. Figure 2 shows that for this cluster of events, Microsoft stock declines after day zero, largely reversing earlier gains.[12] The average of all computer segments (and the average of all firms) experiences returns that are statistically indistinguishable from zero around these "positive" events. As seen in Figure 2, cumulative industry returns move up about 1 percent in the four days prior to the event dates.

Table 4. **Computer Sector Returns During Microsoft Antitrust News Windows Accompanied by Increases or Decreases in Microsoft Stock Price**

Coefficients and *t*-statistics for regressions of firm or industry segment returns on lagging and leading dummy variables equal to unity if (a) an antitrust event listed in Table 1 occurred and (b) Microsoft's cumulative residual return increased by more than 2 percent over the five days [-4,0] or increased by 2 percent on any day [-2,0] (to identify implied anti-enforcement events), or Microsoft's cumulative residual return declined by more than 2 percent over the five days [-4,0] or declined by 2 percent on any day [-2, 0] (to identify implied pro-enforcement events).

Firm or Industry	Antrust News & Microsoft Increases (*n*=24)			Antrust News & Microsoft Decreases (*n*=23)		
	11-Day [-5,5]	3-Day [-1,1]	1-Day [0]	11-Day [-5,5]	3-Day [-1,1]	1-Day [0]
Microsoft	-0.0076	0.0149	0.0167	-0.0452	-0.0218	-0.0066
	(0.73)	(2.48)	(4.60)	(-3.89)	(-3.49)	(-1.81)
Average of computer firms	0.0053	0.0000	0.01	-0.0105	-0.0056	-0.0025
	(1.02)	(0.01)	(0.53)	(-1.83)	(-1.81)	(-1.38)
Average of computer segments	0.0065	-0.0004	0.0006	-0.0105	-0.0062	-0.0029
	(1.26)	(-0.12)	(0.33)	(-1.83)	(-2.00)	(-1.61)
Component	-0.0001	-0.0039	0.0031	-0.0073	-0.0112	-0.0027
	(-0.01)	(-0.78)	(1.02)	(-0.75)	(-2.13)	(-0.87)
Computer	0.0038	-0.0024	-0.0033	-0.0105	-0.0082	-0.0049
	(0.51)	(-0.55)	(-1.23)	(-1.24)	(-1.82)	(-1.85)
Corporate	0.0033	-0.0001	-0.0029	-0.0130	-0.0078	-0.0047
	(0.37)	(-0.01)	(-0.94)	(-1.30)	(-1.46)	(-1.51)
Distributor	-0.0122	-0.0010	-0.0006	-0.0197	-0.0038	0.0028
	(-1.41)	(-0.20)	(-0.21)	(-2.04)	(-0.73)	(0.91)
Network	-0.0011	-0.0024	0.0002	-0.0171	-0.0037	-0.0052
	(-0.13)	(-0.51)	(0.06)	(-1.85)	(-0.75)	(-1.79)
PC software	0.0102	0.0001	0.0009	-0.0100	-0.0078	-0.0048
	(1.28)	(0.14)	(0.32)	(-1.12)	(-1.63)	(-1.70)
Peripheral equipment	0.0184	0.0008	-0.0023	-0.0156	-0.0065	-0.0064
	(1.84)	(0.14)	(-0.66)	(-1.40)	(-1.10)	(-1.83)
Semiconductor	0.0324	0.0022	0.0079	0.0089	-0.0024	0.0001
	(3.10)	(0.36)	(2.18)	(0.76)	(-0.39)	(0.01)
Non-PC software	0.0039	0.0029	0.0025	-0.0106	-0.0043	-0.0005
	(0.61)	(0.77)	(1.11)	(-1.50)	(-1.12)	(-0.22)

A Fishing Expedition

The results in Tables 3 and 4 offer no support for the view that investors expect antitrust enforcement to improve efficiency. Events implying an

Figure 2. **Cumulative residual returns for Microsoft, equally weighted average of all computer firms in the sample (excluding Microsoft), and equally weighted average of all segments (excluding Microsoft).** The upper panel shows the cumulative residual returns from day -5 through day 5 around 23 antitrust event dates involving Microsoft and marked by threshold declines in Microsoft's residual returns. The solid line shows the cumulative returns for Microsoft, the long dashes for an equally weighted portfolio of all other firms in our sample, and the short dashes for a portfolio of equally weighted segments (themselves equally weighted averages). The lower panel shows similar cumulative returns for 24 antitrust event dates involving Microsoft and marked by threshold increases in Microsoft's residual returns. The list of dates appears in Table 1. Enforcement actions accompanied by Microsoft stock price (a) declines (n=23), (b) increases (n=24).

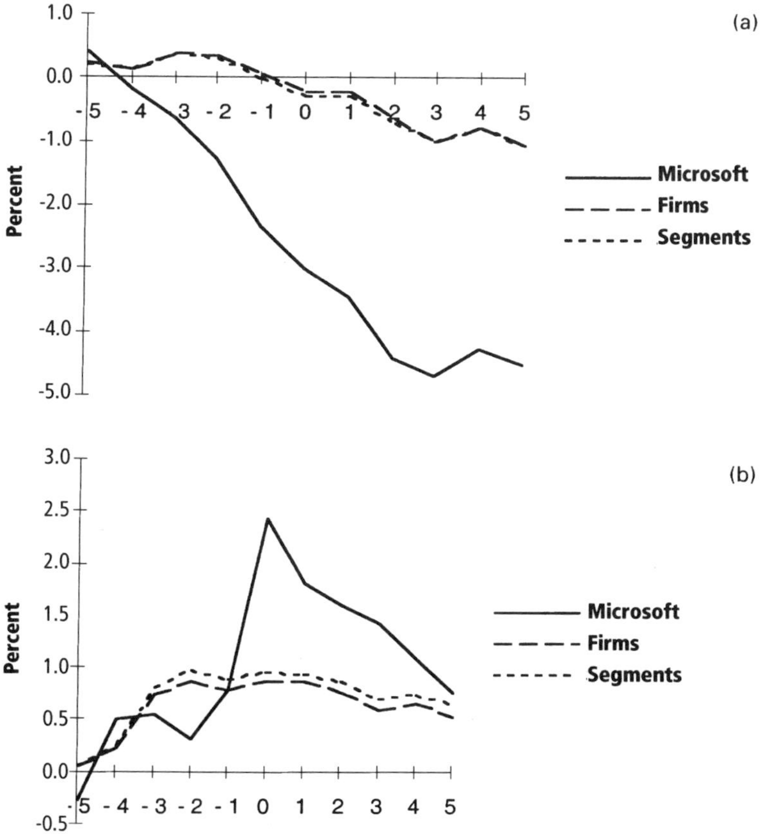

antitrust victory for Microsoft do not harm the industry, and actions hurting Microsoft do not help. Yet perhaps we have overlooked financial market evidence that supports the pro-consumer view of antitrust. To investigate this possibility, we reverse our method. Instead of testing abnormal returns around event dates to determine whether the pattern suggests that investors expect antitrust policy to enhance efficiency, we cull the data for windows displaying the pattern consistent with pro-consumer policy expectations – specifically, a negative correlation between Microsoft and computer sector returns. What sorts of events generate these results, and, specifically, do policy interventions play a role?

We identify one-day and three-day periods over which either Microsoft's abnormal return declines by at least 1.5 standard deviations while the abnormal return of the computer portfolio increases by at least one standard deviation, or the inverse occurs (Microsoft up, computer industry down). Table 5 shows the relevant dates, one- and three-day returns, and possible causative events for the Microsoft stock price movement and/or the large opposing movement in other computer firm stocks. The flagged dates occur in 19 clusters, numbered at the left. The bold percentages pass the respective hurdles (one- or three-day). Typically, the related news stories deal with earnings news, product announcements, or other non-antitrust litigation (e.g., Apple's "look-and-feel" suit, March 7, 1991).

Of the 54 antitrust news events in the 1991-97 periods, only three coincide with substantial capital losses for Microsoft and capital gains for the non-Microsoft computer sector, or the reverse. The first is the April 15, 1991 announcement that the FTC was broadening its investigation. However, the signs of the one-day returns (Microsoft positive, industry negative) are opposite from those implied by the pro-efficiency theory of antitrust, whereas the three-day returns for both Microsoft and the industry are negative. The second date is February 5, 1993, when the FTC's vote on issuing a preliminary injunction split 2-2. While the one-day price movements are consistent with the pro-efficiency view of antitrust (Microsoft up, computer sector down), the three-day returns for both Microsoft and the industry are strongly negative.

The third and final event involves the July 31, 1995 story that the DOJ was planning to examine Microsoft's bundling practices. This was preceded by a decline in Microsoft's shares and positive returns for the rest of the industry on the three days centered on July 27. However, other events – such as the July 26 announcement that Microsoft had settled a California consumer protection lawsuit and a July 27 announcement that Oracle, Apple, and IBM were teaming up against Microsoft – are more closely linked in time. Overall, the small number of instances in which Microsoft and computer industry shares react in substantial opposition around the announcement of antitrust enforcement news concerning Microsoft, as well as examination of the few episodes showing the appropriate correlation, lend little support to the pro-efficiency view of antitrust.

***Table 5.* One- and Three-Day Periods with Large Negative (Positive) Microsoft Returns and Large Positive (Negative) Returns for the Rest of the Industry**

The table shows excess returns for day t or the compounded returns for days t-1 through t+1 on which Microsoft's excess return exceeded 1.5 standard deviations and the return for the industry fell below 1.0 standard deviations, or the reverse. *The Wall Street Journal* news stories at or near each cluster of dates involve either antitrust or related legal action or otherwise could explain the inverse movement of Microsoft and the rest of the industry. Boldface indicates the returns that pass the hurdle for inverse movements. Returns clustered by groups of event dates.

	Dates	1-Day Return (t)		3-Day Return (t-1, t, t+1)		Story and Date
		Microsoft (%)	Industry (%)	Microsoft (%)	Industry (%)	
1.	3/6/91	-3.71	-0.68	**-5.59**	**1.99**	A federal judge boosts Apple's chances of profiting from
	3/7/91	**-3.11**	**1.36**	-7.84	1.27	GUI by striking down key defense arguments in its case against MS, H-P, 3/7.
2.	4/15/91	5.69	-1.60	-2.61	-1.57	FTC broadening investigation, 4/15; Microsoft reports increased earnings, 4/17.
3.	1/17/92	-1.23	0.80	**-5.46**	**1.83**	Net income figures, 1/20.
4.	2/5/93	**5.08**	**-2.18**	-3.37	-4.65	FTC splits 2-2 against injunction, administrative action still possible, 2/8.
5.	2/23/93	**3.56**	**-1.71**	3.06	-4.04	Patent office rejects MS rights to "Windows"
	2/24/93	**3.28**	**-0.98**	**6.86**	**-2.05**	trademark. 2/25.
6.	2/8/94	**-2.65**	**1.09**	-3.44	2.49	No stories.
7.	4/18/94	-0.99	-0.44	**6.31**	**-1.75**	Earnings report, 4/19.
	4/19/94	**6.54**	**-1.60**	**7.73**	**-4.30**	New OS "Chicago," 4/25
	4/20/94	2.12	-2.31	**8.67**	**-2.68**	
8.	4/18/95	-0.42	-0.54	**6.44**	**-2.33**	Earnings report, 4/14; reports on pending Intuit deal, 4/21.
9.	7/27/95	-0.62	1.27	**-5.04**	**2.10**	MS settled Calif. lawsuit, 7/26; Oracle, Apple, and IBM team up against MS, 7/27; DOJ to look at bundling of Web software, 7/31.
10.	12/6/95	**4.98**	**-1.27**	2.76	-2.95	MS announces NBC pact, 12/7; MS announces flurry of new Internet products, 12/7.
11.	12/20/95	**-3.43**	**1.04**	1.42	3.81	No stories.
12.	1/16/96	**3.05**	**-1.24**	-1.77	-4.28	Microsoft to buy Vermeer (Web software co.), 1/16.
13.	9/25/96	-1.25	1.38	**-4.97**	**2.24**	Bingaman recuses herself from MS case, 9/23.
14.	12/17/96	**3.29**	**-1.73**	2.82	-2.21	Story on MS issue of preferred stock, possible raid on
	12/18/96	2.07	0.54	**5.61**	**-3.49**	competitors, 12/16.
15.	4/4/97	**-2.77**	**1.32**	1.02	2.24	MS, Intel, and Compaq initiative on digital TV standards, 4/4; MS to buy WebTV, 4/7.
16.	4/17/97	-0.05	0.68	**8.68**	**-2.89**	
	4/18/97	**8.94**	**-1.54**	**10.40**	**-2.13**	Earnings report, 4/18.
	4/21/97	1.39	-1.27	**11.08**	**-4.95**	
	4/22/97	0.57	-2.22	**6.07**	**-3.95**	
17.	5/2/97	**-3.28**	**0.98**	**-7.52**	**3.13**	No stories.
	5/5/97	-3.99	0.86	**-8.87**	**2.50**	
	5/6/97	-1.86	0.64	**-5.63**	**3.17**	Borland sues MS, 5/8.
18.	7/18/97	**-3.95**	**1.08**	-5.12	0.87	Java announcement, 7/18.
19.	7/22/97	**2.92**	**-1.23**	-2.23	-1.15	MS to acquire Progressive networks, 7/22; MS to increase sales, marketing efforts, 7/24.

Antitrust Enforcement and the Correlation Between Microsoft and Computer Industry Returns

A final test is again generated by the negative correlation between Microsoft's residual return and the residual return of the computer sector that is implied by a pro-efficiency antitrust regime. Successes and failures of such a regime should lower the typical positive correlation between Microsoft's residual returns and the residual returns of the rest of the industry. In fact, the correlation increases on the 54 event dates ($r = 0.3258$) compared to the 1,717 non-event dates ($r = 0.2578$). An analysis of the algebraic signs of residual returns yields a similar result. Victories for effective antitrust should result in more negative Microsoft residual returns accompanied by positive rest-of-industry residual returns. In fact, the frequency of that combination declines on the 54 event dates compared to the rest of the sample, from 23.6 percent to 14.8 percent. That decline is statistically significant at the 5 percent level ($t = 1.75$). Similarly, setbacks for effective antitrust should result in more positive Microsoft residual returns accompanied by negative rest-of-industry returns. However, that pattern occurs at roughly the same rate on the 54 event dates, 18.9 percent rather than 20.4 percent of the time.

Summary of Empirical Results

We have been unable to find evidence that antitrust initiatives against Microsoft created expected gains for the rest of the computer industry. Policy measures affect Microsoft share prices, which decline in response to pro-enforcement news and increase with the release of anti-enforcement news. On average, however, the pro-enforcement (anti-enforcement) actions are accompanied by declines (increases) in the rest of the computer industry. Even a deliberate search for effects that would yield opposing price movements fails to find evidence that antitrust efforts have helped the industry. Indeed, investors appear to believe that antitrust enforcement *increases* the link between the fortunes of Microsoft and those of other computer firms.

THE POLITICAL ECONOMY OF *U.S. V. MICROSOFT*

If antitrust enforcement against Microsoft produces zero or negative returns for allegedly victimized computer firms, why does it occur? We offer three possible explanations warranting further study.

Private Use of Antitrust

Clearly, some of Microsoft's competitors have an economic interest in government action. This possibility is recognized in the "raising rivals' costs" literature (Krattenmaker and Salop, 1986) and in work that emphasizes the use of antitrust to constrain competitors' strategies (Baumol and Ordover, 1985; Baron, 1998). Attacks on Microsoft can be profitable even for firms that benefit from Microsoft products generally. Netscape's browser competes with Microsoft's Internet Explorer, for instance, but is complementary with ("dependent on" in the antitrust allegation) Microsoft's operating systems MS-DOS, Windows 95, Windows 98, NT, Windows 2000, and Windows XP.

In fact, managers of several computer firms have actively promoted the case against Microsoft. Netscape cooperated with the 1998 Department of Justice case, and retained former Judge Robert Bork to write a "white paper" for public dissemination and to argue the case in television debates and op-ed page articles.[13] Sun Microsystems and Oracle executives have also endorsed the case against Microsoft. Sun CEO Scott McNealy comments, "I think the government is doing all the right things. Government has to come in and discipline (Microsoft) until the rest of the world catches up."[14]

Similar sentiments have been expressed by Oracle CEO Larry Ellison.[15] Novell prevailed upon Orrin Hatch (R-UT), its home state senator and powerful head of the Judiciary Committee, to hold hearings on the problem of monopoly in the computer industry, and to pressure the Department of Justice to take sterner enforcement measures against Microsoft. A trade association has been established to pressure policymakers to increase regulatory scrutiny of Microsoft. The Project to Promote Competition and Innovation in the Digital Age (ProComp) is "funded by Microsoft's competitors including Sun Microsystems and Netscape."[16]

We examine the returns of individual firms and find no systematic evidence that the likely beneficiaries (e.g., Netscape, Sun, Novell, Apple) realize higher returns when antitrust enforcement measures are taken against Microsoft. In specific instances, however, antitrust enforcement actions did seem to benefit Netscape shareholders. For example, the December 12, 1997 court order that kept Microsoft from bundling its software was accompanied by negative returns for both Microsoft and the industry as a whole, but a 6.2 percent increase in Netscape's price. (This gain was quickly reversed.)

If the expected benefits to competing firms are in fact scant, managerial support for antitrust in this instance could reflect a principal-agent problem. The specter of Microsoft could provide a rationalization for managerial shortcomings. As shown, such distractions do not come cheaply. Companies producing goods highly complementary to Microsoft stand to incur the largest capital losses from inefficient antitrust interventions. Consistent with shareholder interests revealed in the financial market data examined above, they have opposed the case. This anti-antitrust group includes the major computer makers (Compaq, Dell, Hewlett Packard), the major chipmaker (Intel), and the major computer retailers (CompUSA and Vanstar). In fact, the CEOs of 26 major computer industry firms signed a letter sent to the Department of Justice in May 1998 requesting that the government refrain from filing additional antitrust charges against Microsoft.[17]

The behavior of individual states also sheds light on the political support for action against Microsoft. The May 1998 suit filed by the DOJ was accompanied by a suit filed by 20 states. As has been widely observed in the press, these states appear to have been the subject of intense lobbying pressure from locally based computer companies. California, home to important Microsoft competitors such as Sun, Oracle, and Netscape, filed; Texas, home to important Microsoft complement suppliers such as Compaq, Dell, and CompUSA, did not, despite the fact that the Texas attorney general had originally begun the states' investigation of Microsoft.[18]

Bureaucratic Self-Interest

Government agents may themselves gain from legal action. Top-level antitrust officials typically enjoy short tenure and receive much of their compensation in human capital (Wilson, 1980). At the state level, attorneys general often use high-visibility litigation to enhance their political stature. The Microsoft case is "the type of case attorneys general dream about, regardless of how deeply it affects – or fails to directly affect – their states' consumers or businesses... It's also true that a number of the AGs (the letters are sometimes said to stand for 'aspiring governors') involved in the suit are seeking higher office."[19]

In the case of Microsoft, antitrust officials have also received substantial favorable publicity. Tellingly, rival agencies have fought over federal jurisdiction, and the Federal Trade Commission initiated what some dub "copycat" investigations of Intel and Cisco.[20]

Political Extraction

The rent-seeking literature points out that policymakers exploit the competition between interest groups for government favors. Policymakers may also extract rents from private parties. In this framework, political officeholders are not entirely passive. They achieve some degree of market power and exploit this incumbency to demand payments from various economic actors with rents at risk (McChesney, 1997). Transfers can take the form of campaign contributions, non-monetary political support, or public cooperation on a policy issue (including a consent decree in an antitrust case).

According to some accounts, the government took action against Microsoft at least in part because it lacked a "Washington presence." Compared to other large firms, Microsoft historically contributed only small sums to political campaigns. It only recently opened a Washington office to represent its interests. Policymakers might have been attempting to "correct" this "underinvestment" in political goodwill with heightened antitrust scrutiny.[21]

CONCLUSION

In what *The Economist* identifies as "the biggest antitrust case in a generation,"[22] a large number of firms have products that are tied to the success of the allegedly monopolized product, desktop operating systems. These firms will prosper if actions are taken – by Microsoft or the DOJ – to make operating systems cost less, function better, or provide a more convenient platform for popular products. Policy actions that are expected to effectively constrain Microsoft's market power should simultaneously increase economic efficiency and improve profitability for firms throughout the sector.

This study turns to the stock market evidence. Have repeated antitrust initiatives against Microsoft increased the expected earnings of (non-Microsoft) firms in the computer industry? The answer is a decisive "no." In fact, government action against Microsoft appears to inflict capital losses on the computer sector as a whole. Retreats in antitrust enforcement offer symmetric confirmation: withdrawals from policy enforcement have been accompanied by positive shareholder returns throughout the computer sector.

These results deserve attention for three reasons. First, the burden of proof ought to be on policy intervention. A case of this magnitude generates clear costs to the government (i.e., taxpayers) and to Microsoft. In fact, each enforcement action lowered Microsoft's stock by 1.2 percent, roughly $3 billion at May 1998 share prices. It should produce visible gains in the form of positive returns to the large number of other firms in the computer sector. That such gains fail to be in evidence is the key finding of this study. Moreover, rather than generating offsetting gains, each enforcement action decreased a broad index of other computer stocks by 0.7 percent, equivalent to an additional loss of $5 billion in May 1998.

The second reason these results demand attention is that they suggest that antitrust policy has lowered returns to investments in the computer sector and discouraged capital inflows. Policy risk increases the cost of capital across an entire industry when intervention occurs at a key point within that sector. Pindyck (1991) and Dixit and Pindyck (1994) model the investment-reducing effect of public policy uncertainty.

Third, stock market data produce a bottom-line evaluation of public policy. Rather than narrowly focusing on alleged abuses of market power, financial markets also consider likely policy outcomes. When actual markets are compared to hypothetical alternatives in traditional antitrust analysis, policymakers run the risk of "fanciful reasoning [wherein] much mischief and little useful purpose is served by pronouncing failure if no clearly superior feasible alternative can be described and implemented with expected net gains."[23] Financial markets set asset prices by utilizing the best available predictions as to what the full spectrum of antitrust enforcement actions will achieve. The verdicts rendered by "courts of investor opinion" constitute reliable economic evidence compared to the available alternatives.

* This article originally appeared in the *Journal of Financial Economics*, Volume 55 (2000). Reprinted with permission.

** See Josh Lerner, "The Returns to Investments in Innovative Activities," in this volume.

1 DOJ, 1998; more generally, see Gilbert and Williamson, 1998.

2 "A case built on speculation, dubious theories," *Wall Street Journal*, May 19, 1998, op-ed page; Liebowitz and Margolis, 1999.

3 "Supporters and critics of the case both dread the same doomsday scenarios of the technology industry: that the suits will ultimately lead to much broader government intervention in the software business," *The Wall Street Journal Interactive Edition*, May 14, 1998.

4 Declaration of Kenneth J. Arrow, *U.S. v. Microsoft Corp.*, January 17, 1995.

5 "The Force of an Idea," *The New Yorker*, January 12, 1998.

6 "The Legend of Arthur," *Slate Magazine*, January 14, 1998; see also "Soft Microeconomics: the Squishy Case Against You-Know-Who," *Slate Magazine*, April 23, 1998.

7 p. 442.

8 The closest was a March 20 report on insider sales.

9 Also see Salinger (1992). Papers using this method include Schipper and Thompson (1983), Rose (1985), Smith et al. (1986), Binder (1988), Karafiath and Glascock (1989), Cornett and Tehranian (1990), and Alexander and Spivey (1994).

[10] Although 29 news stories are assigned pro-enforcement status, the last event date, December 30, 1997, occurs too late to allow estimation of lagging effects.

[11] This increase reflects the growth in value of the firms as well as an increase in the number of firms.

[12] The decline over days two through five is not statistically significant.

[13] "Culture Clash," *National Journal*, May 16, 1998, p. 1102; "Book Bork, Browser Bork," *Slate Magazine*, December 10, 1998; "Browser Bork Replies,"' *Slate Magazine*, Dec. 29, 1998; "What Antitrust Is All About," *The New York Times*, May 4, 1998, op-ed page; "The Most Misunderstood Antitrust Case," *The Wall Street Journal*, May 22, 1998, op-ed page; Full text of Bork's "White Paper" on DOJ v. Microsoft, ZDNN, July 29, 1998, online at www.zdnet.com.

[14] "Microsoft Antitrust Case Splits Valley," *San Jose Mercury News*, October 12, 1998.

[15] "In Parts of Silicon Valley, Muted Applause," *The New York Times* online edition, May 19, 1998.

[16] "Microsoft, Foes Square Off Over Windows 98," *San Jose Mercury News*, May 6, 1998.

[17] "Microsoft Seeks Allies to Halt Antitrust Move," *The Wall Street Journal Interactive Edition*, May 1, 1998; "PC Makers, Despite Microsoft Suit, Aren't Clamoring to Control Screen," *The Wall Street Journal Interactive Edition*, May 19, 1998.

[18] "Microsuits," *Slate Magazine* online, May 22, 1998; "Politics Play a Role in States' Status in Antitrust Action Against Microsoft," *The Wall Street Journal Interactive Edition*, May 28, 1998.

[19] "Politics Play a Role in States' Status in Antitrust Action Against Microsoft," *The Wall Street Journal Interactive Edition*, May 28, 1998.

[20] "The Main Event: 'Browser' Bill Gates vs. Joel 'The Trustbuster' Klein," *Time Magazine* online, June 1, 1998; "Wrestling for Glory in the Antitrust Arena," *The Washington Post*, June 12, 1998, p. F1; "Justice Department and FTC Battle to Bust the Biggest Antitrust Prizes," *The Wall Street Journal Interactive Edition*, June 11, 1998.

[21] "Culture Clash," *National Journal*, May 16, 1998, p. 1102.

[22] "At War with Microsoft," *The Economist*, May 23, 1998.

[23] Gilbert and Williamson, 1998, p. 7.

References

Alexander, J., Spivey, M. 1994. "CEBA of 1987 and the Security Returns and Market Risk of Savings and Loan Institutions: a Note," *Journal of Banking and Finance* 18, pp. 1205-1215.

Banerjee, A., Eckard, W. 1998. "Are Mega-mergers Anticompetitive? Evidence from the First Great Merger Wave," *Rand Journal of Economics* 29, pp. 803-827.

Baron, D. 1998. "Integrated Market and Nonmarket Strategies in Client and Interest Group Politics." Paper presented at the Positive Political Theory of Business Strategy Conference, Haas School of Business, University of California at Berkeley, October 15-17.

Baumol, W., Ordover, J. 1985. "Use of Antitrust to Subvert Competition," *Journal of Law and Economics* 28, pp. 247-266.

Binder, J. 1985. "On the Use of the Multivariate Regression Model in Event Studies," *Journal of Accounting Research* 23, pp. 370-383.

Binder, J. 1988. "The Sherman Antitrust Act and the Railroad Cartels," *Journal of Law and Economics* 31, pp. 443-468.

Bizjak, J., Coles, J. 1995. "The Effect of Private Antitrust Litigation on the Stock-Market Valuation of the Firm," *American Economic Review* 85, pp. 436-461.

Bork, R. 1978. *The Antitrust Paradox*. New York: Basic Books.

Buchanan, J., Lee, D. 1992. "Private Interest Group Support for Efficiency Enhancing Antitrust Policies." *Economic Inquiry* 30, pp. 218-224.

Cornett, M., Tehranian, H. 1990. "An Examination of the Impact of the Garn-St. Germain Depository Institutions Act of 1982 on Commercial Banks and Savings and Loans," *Journal of Finance* 45, pp. 95-111.

Cutler, D., Summers, L. 1988. "The Costs of Conflict Resolution and Financial Distress: Evidence from the Texaco-Pennzoil Litigation," *Rand Journal of Economics* 19, pp. 157-172.

Dixit, A., Pindyck, R. 1994. *Investment Under Uncertainty*, Princeton, NJ: Princeton University Press.

Department of Justice (DOJ). 1998. "U.S. Department of Justice Complaint in United States v. Microsoft (May 18)," online at http://interactive.wsj.com/edition/resources/documents/mssuit0518-1.htm.

Eckbo, B. 1983. "Horizontal Mergers, Collusion, and Stockholder Wealth," *Journal of Financial Economics* 11, pp. 241-273.

Gibbons, M. 1980. "Econometric Models for Testing a Class of Financial Models – an Application of the Nonlinear Multivariate Regression Model," Ph.D. dissertation, University of Chicago, IL.

Gilbert, R., Williamson, O. 1998. "Antitrust Policy," In: Newman, P. (Ed.), *New Palgrave Dictionary of Economics and the Law*, pp. 3-9. New York: Stockton Press.

Gilligan, T., Marshall, W., Weingast, B. 1989. "Regulation and the Theory of Legislative Choice: the Interstate Commerce Act of 1887," *Journal of Law and Economics* 32, pp. 35-62.

Hertzel, M., Smith, J. 1993. "Industry Effects of Inter-Firm Lawsuits: Evidence from *Pennzoil v. Texaco*," *Journal of Law, Economics and Organization* 9, pp. 425-444.

Jarrell, G., Peltzman, S. 1985. "The Impact of Product Recalls on the Wealth of Sellers," *Journal of Political Economy* 93, pp. 512-536.

Karafiath, I., Glascock, J. 1989. "Intra-Industry Effects of a Regulatory Shift: Capital Market Evidence from Penn Square," *Financial Review* 24, pp. 123-134.

Krattenmaker, T., Salop, S. 1986. "Anticompetitive Exclusion: Raising Rivals' Costs to Achieve Power over Price," *Yale Law Journal* 96, pp. 209-293.

Liebowitz, S., Margolis, S. 1999. *Winners, Losers and Microsoft: Competition and Antitrust in High Technology*. Oakland, CA: *Independent Institute*.

McChesney, F. 1997. *Money for Nothing: Politicians, Rent Extraction, and Political Extortion*. Cambridge, MA: Harvard University Press.

Mitchell, M., Netter, J. 1989. "Triggering the 1987 Stock Market Crash: Anti-takeover Provisions in the Proposed House Ways and Means Tax Bill," *Journal of Financial Economics* 24, pp. 37-68.

Mullin, G., Mullin, J., Mullin, W. 1995. "The Competitive Effects of Mergers: Stock Market Evidence from the U.S. Steel Dissolution Suit," *Rand Journal of Economics* 26, pp. 314-330.

Nash, K. 1996. "Netscape Warns Investors of Threat from Microsoft," *Computerworld*, Nov. 11 Online via Computer Magazine Archive (http://cma.zdnet.com/texis/cma/cma/).

Pindyck, R. 1991. "Irreversibility, Uncertainty and Investment," *Journal of Economic Literature* 29, pp. 1110-1152.

Prager, R. 1992. "The Effects of Horizontal Mergers on Competition: the Case of the Northern Securities Company," *Rand Journal of Economics* 23, pp. 123-133.

Quittner, J., Slatalla, M. 1998. *Speeding the Net: The Inside Story of Netscape and How It Challenged Microsoft*. New York: Atlantic Monthly Press.

Rose, N. 1985. "The Incidence of Regulatory Rents in the Motor Carrier Industry," *Rand Journal of Economics* 16, pp. 299-318.

Salinger, M. 1992. "Standard Errors in Event Studies," *Journal of Financial and Quantitative Analysis* 27, pp. 39-53.

Schipper, K., Thompson, R. 1983. "The Impact of Merger-Related Regulations on the Shareholders of Acquiring Firms," *Journal of Accounting Research* 21, pp. 184-221.

Schwert, G. 1981. "Using Financial Data to Measure Effects of Regulation," *Journal of Law and Economics* 24, pp. 121-158.

Smith, R., Bradley, M., Jarrell, G. 1986. "Studying Firm-Specific Effects of Regulation with Stock Market Data: An Application to Oil Price Regulation," *Rand Journal of Economics* 17, pp. 467-489.

Stillman, R. 1983. "Examining Antitrust Policy Towards Horizontal Mergers," *Journal of Financial Economics* 11, pp. 225-240.

Wilson, J. 1980. *The Politics of Regulation*. New York: Basic Books.

Wolf, C. 1993. *Markets or Governments? Choosing Between Imperfect Alternatives*, 2nd Edition. Cambridge, MA: IT Press.

Section 1: *U.S. v. Microsoft Corp.*: The Economics

Essay 5

The Price of Unanimity: The D.C. Circuit's Incoherent Opinion in *U.S. v. Microsoft Corp.*

by John E. Lopatka and William H. Page

To many of us involved in Microsoft's defense, the antitrust trial seemed closer to a stage production of Alice in Wonderland than a landmark judicial proceeding. The government's case was, at best, confused. Its leading cross-examiner seemed as interested in embarrassing witnesses as in establishing Microsoft's legal liability. And the trial judge's behavior was at times off the wall, betraying a mix of impatience with due process, contempt for higher courts, and enthusiasm for media attention.

So when the D.C. Circuit Court of Appeals, a court well regarded for its expertise in economics and regulation, agreed to review the judgment, we were relieved. And when, during two days of oral argument, the appellate judges made no secret of their skepticism about the government's case and their disgust with Judge Thomas Penfield Jackson's behavior in court and out, we were delighted.

Weighed objectively, the appeals court's decision amounted to a victory on points for Microsoft. The most damning findings of law were reversed or remanded with instructions that made it very difficult to reestablish liability. The judge's breakup order was reversed. And the trial judge was removed from further proceedings on grounds that he had repeatedly violated the canon of judicial ethics.

But as John Lopatka and Bill Page, of the University of South Carolina Law School and University of Florida Levin College of Law, respectively, show here, the D.C. circuit's opinion was itself no model for legal reasoning.

It is in places incoherent – or worse, inconsistent – making its use as a guide for the new trial judge fashioning remedies or as a source of precedent for antitrust case law highly problematic.

Just how so experienced and professional a court could have produced such a document is a matter of speculation. Lopatka and Page argue that, in the process of negotiating a unanimous decision that carried the full weight of the court, the judges simply – or, rather, not so simply – lost their way. Thus, instead of a "a majority analysis (with perhaps an insightful concurrence and a trenchant dissent)" the court produced "an inscrutable per curiam opinion that gives us only a result and confusion." — *D.S.E.*

INTRODUCTION

The D.C. circuit's long-awaited decision in the *Microsoft* case[1] should disappoint anyone concerned about the integrity of antitrust law. Surprisingly, the opinion was not only "per curiam,"[2] but unanimous.[3] Most per curiam opinions reach an obvious result by straightforward reasoning;[4] this one reaches a controversial result by convoluted reasoning. Indeed, it strains credulity to believe that all members of the court agreed with every portion of this opinion. Maybe the court thought the per curiam strategy would avoid a confusing welter of opinions, and thus give its pronouncement greater authority and less likelihood of reversal. If that was its intent, the result is the opposite: The suppressed divisions on the court are manifest in a host of inconsistencies that undermine the opinion's significance and dilute its doctrinal implications. That the members of the court were willing to sign such a document suggests that the court's paramount goal was to reach a particular result, regardless of the collateral damage to antitrust policy.

Perhaps this highly political act will induce a settlement – at the time of this writing, Microsoft and the government are attempting to find a mutually acceptable compromise. In the wake of the opinion, the Department of Justice did give up its demand for a breakup of the company and its explicit tying claim.[5] But the incoherence of the opinion may yet make both sides optimistic that they can achieve more complete victories in a remedial order and encourage them to press on to a final decision.

In this essay we highlight some of the opinion's many inconsistencies, focusing on the court's treatment of (1) the role of the "browser market" in proof of anticompetitive effects, and (2) the role of efficiency concerns in evaluating the integration of the browser and the operating system. Although we disagree with many of the court's holdings on their own terms, we save for another day any extended analysis of the court's treatment of specific issues. Here, we critique the court's rulings and statements only on grounds of incoherence or opacity. Moreover, we limit our consideration of inconsistencies to the substantive rulings. The appellate court, of course, also reversed the structural remedy – a breakup of the company – ordered by the district court and, because of Judge Jackson's misconduct, remanded the case to a new judge.[6] We express no view on these actions.

ANTICOMPETITIVE EFFECTS AND THE BROWSER MARKET

The browser market played a central role in the appeals court's disposition of the claims of monopoly maintenance, attempted monopolization, and tying. The court held (1) that Microsoft monopolized the operating system market mainly by its actions in the browser market; (2) that the government failed to prove attempted monopolization of the browser market because it failed to prove that such a market exists; and (3) that the government must prove an anticompetitive effect in the browser market in order to establish the tying claim. These conclusions are contradictory.

In the first section of the opinion, the court affirmed most of the district court's findings and conclusions in holding that Microsoft illegally maintained its OS monopoly by integrating its browser with the operating system; entering into restrictive agreements with Apple and other computer makers, Internet access providers, independent software vendors, and Internet content providers; and interfering with the development of Sun Microsystems' Java programming language.[7] In doing so, the court endorsed the district court's adoption of the government's theory of anticompetitive effect. Under that theory, Microsoft used the various exclusionary practices to prevent the emergence of software platforms – Netscape's browser and Java – that could undermine the Windows monopoly. Because the emerging platforms would allow developers to write software applications that could run regardless of the underlying operating system, they threatened the OS market's "applications barrier to entry" – the strong tendency of users to buy (and developers to write programs for) the operating system for which the most applications are available.[8] The court wrote that the government was not required to prove actual anticompetitive effect or harm to consumers – only that the acts had a reasonable likelihood of preserving Microsoft's OS monopoly.[9]

The court explained how "market share in the browser market affects market power in the operating system market" by observing that:

> Microsoft's efforts to gain market share in one market (browsers) served to meet the threat to Microsoft's monopoly in another market (operating systems) by keeping rival browsers from gaining the critical mass of users necessary to attract developer attention away from Windows as the platform for software development.[10]

The critical point to note here is that the anticompetitive effect in the OS market *depends entirely on Microsoft's acquisition of market share in the browser market*. Only if Microsoft achieved a certain usage share could it convince developers to write to Windows application programming interfaces (APIs) rather than to Netscape's (or some other firm's) cross-platform APIs.

The court confirmed this dependence again and again in its discussion of particular exclusionary practices, using terms like "market share"[11] and "usage share"[12] in connection with browsers in ways that presupposed the existence of a browser market. For example, it stated "Microsoft reduced rival browsers' usage share not by improving its own product but, rather, by preventing OEMs[13] from taking actions that could increase rivals' share of usage"[14] and "a monopolist's use of exclusive contracts, in certain circumstances, may give rise to a Section 2 violation even though the contracts foreclose less than the roughly 40% or 50% share usually required in order to establish a Section 1 violation."[15] These statements assume that, for there to be a Section 2 violation, there must be foreclosure of *some* share of *something*. An antitrust lawyer would be forgiven for assuming that something was a market.

But in the next section of the opinion, we learn that there is no browser market. The government alleged that Microsoft, in addition to monopolizing the OS market, had attempted to monopolize the browser market using many of the same tactics alleged in support of the monopoly maintenance claim, and by its famous offer to "divide" the browser market with Netscape. But the court short-circuited any consideration of this conduct as attempted monopolization, holding that the plaintiff had failed "to prove a dangerous probability of achieving monopoly power in the putative browser market," as required by *Spectrum Sports*.[16] To prove a dangerous probability of success, the plaintiff must "define the relevant market and ... demonstrate that substantial barriers to entry protect that market."[17] On the first point, the plaintiff must offer:

> a detailed description of the purpose of a browser – what functions may be included and what are not – and an examination of the substitutes that are part of the market and those that are not. ... The District Court never engaged in such an analysis nor entered detailed findings defining what a browser is

> or what products might constitute substitutes. In the Findings of Fact, the District Court (in a section on whether IE and Windows are separate products) stated only that "a Web browser provides the ability for the end user to select, retrieve, and perceive resources on the Web." ... Furthermore, in discussing attempted monopolization in its Conclusions of Law, the District Court failed to demonstrate analytical rigor when it employed varying and imprecise references to the "market for browsing technology for Windows," "the browser market," and "platform-level browsing software."[18]

The district court's failure was apparently so complete that the court of appeals foreclosed any reconsideration of the issue on remand. The court pointed to:

> plaintiffs' failure to articulate and identify evidence before the District Court as to (1) what constitutes a browser (i.e., what are the technological components of or functionalities provided by a browser) and (2) why certain other products are not reasonable substitutes (e.g., browser shells or viewers for individual internet extensions, such as Real Audio Player or Adobe Acrobat Reader).[19]

The court went on to rule that, even if the browser market had been properly defined, a reversal would be required because the government had failed to offer any evidence that the browser market was subject to entry barriers, particularly an applications barrier to entry like the one found to protect the OS market.[20]

The court's rejection of the district court's finding of the existence of a relevant browser market is strange given its deference to the district court's delineation of a market for OSs for personal computers with Intel-compatible processors. That definition excluded other platform software, including browsers, because of the special characteristics of OSs, and the lack of reasonable interchangeability within a foreseeable time.[21] Although the court of appeals stated that the district court's findings on the browser market "pale by comparison" with its findings on the OS market, it is difficult to see why the record is sufficient to define a market for one and not the other. Moreover, the court's insistence on "analytical rigor" in the definition of a browser market is inconsistent with its deference to other important findings of the district court. And it seems peculiar that the court of appeals would accuse the district court of lack of analytical rigor without even citing, much less discussing, the district court's most relevant findings (in Paragraphs 199-201) that there is a market for Web-browsing functionality.[22]

More important than any of this is the inconsistency between the court of appeals' reversal of the district court's finding that there is a browser market and its affirmance of the holding that Microsoft monopolized the OS market by building its share of the browser market. The lynchpin of the government's theory of anticompetitive effect was the idea that Microsoft prevented the emergence of a platform threat by Netscape and Java by denying Netscape usage share in the *browser market.* Although the court insisted that attempted monopolization requires "an analysis wholly independent of the conclusions and findings on monopoly maintenance,"[23] the factual bases for the two claims are inseparable. If there is no market for browsers, then the usage share numbers on which the court relied in finding monopolization are meaningless because they fail to account for usage of other reasonable substitutes. And if there is no market for browsers, then the weakening of a single firm would do nothing to reinforce Microsoft's OS monopoly, because there would be countless other platform threats that would remain. If there are no entry barriers in the browser market, particularly if there is no applications barrier to entry attributable to network effects, then the strategy of acquiring greater share in the browser market would be a vain effort – new entrants would quickly take the place of any firm at whose expense Microsoft had increased its browser usage.

It is not enough to respond that the browser threat was "nascent."[24] The court rejected Microsoft's argument that the government's theory of anticompetitive effect was inconsistent with the district court's exclusion of browsers from the market for Intel-compatible operating systems, stating that "[n]othing in section 2 of the Sherman Act limits its prohibition to actions taken against threats that are already well-developed enough to serve as present substitutes."[25] According to the court, then, the browser can be a nascent competitive constraint on an OS monopolist, without actually being in the OS market. Whatever the merits of that proposition, the court's theory of competitive harm in the OS market requires at least that Microsoft and Netscape were competitors in a browser market. We need *some* evidentiary basis for concluding that harm to a firm constitutes harm to competition in a particular case.[26] Even if the law prohibits harm to "nascent" competitors, we at least must have some coherent theory to support the inference of anticompetitive effect from the injury of a particular firm. In *U.S. v. Microsoft Corp.*, the entire theory rested on Microsoft's building of usage share in a browser market. If there is a reasoned economic argument why the absence of a browser market does not undermine the theory of monopolization of the OS market, the court failed to provide it.

But it gets worse. In the third section of the opinion, the court of appeals reversed the district court's holding that Microsoft illegally tied the browser to the operating system, requiring that the district court on remand apply a newly minted rule of reason. Most important here, the court insisted that under its rule of reason for tying, any anticompetitive effect from the tie must be in the tied product market – the market for browsers. Both law[27] and economics[28] require the plaintiff in a tying case to define the market for the tied product. Just as "[i]t is impossible to monopolize a market that does not exist,"[29] it is impossible to reduce competition in a market that does not exist. Nevertheless, the court precluded the government on remand from proving that a browser market exists:

> [O]n remand, plaintiffs must show that Microsoft's conduct unreasonably restrained competition. Meeting that burden "involves an inquiry into the actual effect" of Microsoft's conduct on competition in the tied good market, the putative market for browsers. To the extent that certain aspects of tying injury may depend on a careful definition of the tied good market and a showing of barriers to entry other than the tying arrangement itself, plaintiffs would have to establish these points. ... But plaintiffs were required – and had every incentive – to provide both a definition of the browser market and barriers to entry to that market as part of their section 2 attempted monopolization claim; yet they failed to do so. ... Accordingly, on remand of the section 1 tying claim, plaintiffs will be precluded from arguing any theory of harm that depends on a precise definition of browsers or barriers to entry (for example, network effects from Internet protocols and extensions embedded in a browser) other than what may be implicit in Microsoft's tying arrangement.[30]

So the government must prove harm in the market for browsers, but will be precluded from proving that there is a market for browsers. Reason totters on her throne. No wonder the government chose not to pursue the tying claim on remand.[31]

BUNDLING THE BROWSER AND THE OPERATING SYSTEM

Almost as confused as the D.C. circuit's treatment of the role of the browser market in evaluating competitive effects is its treatment of the integration of the browser and the operating system. In June of 1998, a panel of the same court had reversed Judge Jackson's preliminary injunction enforcing a 1995 consent decree by requiring Microsoft to permit OEMs to remove Internet Explorer functionality from Windows 95.[32] The panel majority announced the standard that IE and Windows 95 were "integrated" if Microsoft could offer "facially plausible"[33] evidence that bundling "combines functionalities .... in a way that offers advantages unavailable if the functionalities are bought separately and combined by the purchaser."[34] It reasoned that because of "the limited competence of courts to evaluate high-tech product designs and the high cost of errors,"[35] a "court's evaluation of a claim of integration must be narrow and deferential"[36] to a firm's design decisions. The court concluded the government had failed to show a probability of success on the merits,[37] because "[o]n the facts before us,"[38] Microsoft had met the criteria for integration, although that conclusion was "subject to reexamination on a more complete record."[39]

Two years later, however, the court of appeals was far less clear in its treatment of integration under Sections 1 and 2 of the Sherman Act. The government alleged that the bundling of the browser and the operating system constituted both monopoly maintenance and illegal tying. In resolving both of these claims the court expressed concerns about efficiency and judicial competence, but the implications of those concerns for doctrine in the two contexts were quite different. Indeed, the standards that emerged from the court's analysis were similar mainly in their opacity.

Two types of bundling constituted monopoly maintenance: (1) Microsoft's imposition of license restrictions precluding OEMs from "removing any desktop icons, folders, or 'Start' menu entries,"[40] and (2) Microsoft's physical integration of the code of the browser and the operating system.[41] The issues were closely related: The first addressed Microsoft's *contractual* preclusion of OEMs from removing IE;[42] the second addressed Microsoft's *technological* preclusion of OEMs from removing IE. Both were found to be anticompetitive because of their effect on browser usage share.

Interestingly, however, "IE" means different things in the different contexts. In the licensing discussion, the court addressed only Microsoft's failure to allow OEMs to delete "*visible means of user access to IE*."[43] That was anticompetitive because including two browsers would have created consumer confusion and increased support costs. But in the commingling discussion, the court addressed Microsoft's failure to allow OEMs to delete any of *the actual code that constitutes IE*. By mixing IE code with OS-specific code, Microsoft made it harder to delete IE code without harming the underlying OS:

> [H]aving the IE software code as an irremovable part of Windows meant that pre-installing a second browser would "increase an OEM's product testing costs," because an OEM must test and train its support staff to answer calls related to every software product preinstalled on the machine; moreover, pre-installing a browser in addition to IE would to many OEMs be "a questionable use of the scarce and valuable space on a PC's hard drive."[44]

The court affirmed the district court's conclusions that Microsoft's "commingling" of browser code in the same files with OS code and its prevention of removal of IE from Windows (by not providing a "remove" function) were anticompetitive because the actions reduced rival browsers' usage share.[45]

Moreover, the court held that integration of IE and the OS, with the exception of one design feature, lacked any business justification.[46] In reaching this conclusion, it affirmed the district court's acceptance of the testimony of two government witnesses – contradicted by Microsoft's witnesses – that the files containing IE code and shared code also contain OS-specific code.[47] The critical point here is that the court gave no special weight to concerns about interfering with Microsoft's design of Windows. It did express an abstract reluctance to interfere with design decisions,[48] but did not on that account hold the government to any higher standard of proof. The issue of integration is to be considered in the context of the defendant's proffered business justifications and the plaintiff's proffered rebuttals as an ordinary issue of fact. Thus allegations of predatory innovation, unlike claims of predatory pricing, are apparently to be viewed with no particular skepticism. Efficiency concerns have no doctrinal implications, even when the court applies what it concedes is an "edentulous" standard of anticompetitive effects.

The court did conclude that Microsoft's design of Windows to override the user's default browser in a few instances – launching IE unexpectedly – was supported by business justifications that the government had failed to rebut.[49] This holding, however, only confuses matters, in two important respects. First, the court's statement of the plaintiff's rebuttal burden here conflicts with its own statement of the burden earlier in the section. In its discussion of integration, the court stated that, if the plaintiff establishes a prima facie case of anticompetitive effect and the defendant responds by offering a pro-competitive justification for the conduct, the plaintiff must "not only rebut the proffered justification, but also ... demonstrat[e] that the anticompetitive effect of the challenged action outweighs it."[50] Earlier in the monopoly maintenance section, however, the court stated that the plaintiff may prevail *either* by rebutting the justification or by showing the anticompetitive effect outweighs it.[51] The inconsistency did not affect the outcome, because on the one issue for which the court found Microsoft had offered a justification, the government failed to either rebut it or show that it was outweighed by the anticompetitive effect. Nevertheless, the court has created the potential for future confusion on this critical point.

Second, for purposes of remand in the case, this holding greatly complicates the task of determining exactly what Microsoft must allow OEMs to remove. Apparently, Microsoft must allow deletion of all of the means of "readily accessing" IE, but it need not allow deletion of IE technologies necessary to launch IE where an override of the default browser was shown to be justified. But the condemnation of commingling code, combined with the court's holding that unjustified use of disk space is anticompetitive, would seem to suggest that any code specific to IE, apart from what is necessary for the default overrides, must be capable of being removed. None of this has yet been specified.[52]

More important, the court's treatment of integration in the monopoly maintenance section is inconsistent with its treatment of the same issue in the tying section. In the latter context, the court of appeals held that the district court applied an incorrect standard in evaluating the legality of Microsoft's tying of the browser to the OS.[53] The district court had refused to apply the standard for tying that the court of appeals announced in the 1998 consent decree case, instead applying a version of the per se rule drawn from the Supreme Court's decision in *Jefferson Parish*.[54] The court of appeals reversed, but not (as one might expect) because Judge Jackson had dodged its 1998 standard. Indeed, the full court of appeals dismissed the panel's 1998 standard, somewhat disingenuously, as limited to the consent decree context.[55] Instead, the court held that an unspecified "rule of reason" inquiry was necessary because of the special efficiency concerns associated with the integration of functionality in platform software.[56]

The court recognized that there are potential harms to consumer choice from combining applications with the operating system and preventing their removal. But Microsoft had asserted important efficiencies that, according to the court, the conventional test did not allow to be considered adequately. Although the requirement that there be two products for there to be a tie (even under the per se rule) is a proxy for an efficiency analysis, according to the court it is too crude a test to address the efficiencies adequately. Consequently, the court remanded for consideration under a rule of reason, which "more freely permits consideration of the benefits of bundling in software markets, particularly those for OSs, and a balancing of these benefits against the costs to consumers whose ability to make direct price/quality tradeoffs in the tied market may have been impaired."[57] The court emphasized that in the tying inquiry the plaintiff must establish an anticompetitive effect in the market for the *tied* product – browsers.[58]

First of all, we note the absurdity of a tying rule created specifically to address "technological integration of added functionality into software that serves as a platform for third-party applications."[59] The move is particularly suspect because it is unnecessary, even if we grant that platform competition has unique aspects. There is ample precedent for considering pro-competitive justifications under current tying law.[60]

More important, however, the court's invocation of efficiency as the basis for its concoction of a special test for platform tying is inconsistent with its indifference to efficiency in the context of monopoly maintenance. The court asserted that a new test for tying is necessary to allow adequate consideration of productive efficiency and thus to avoid deterring beneficial integration. But the same efficiency concerns apply with equal force in the monopoly maintenance context. The court gave lip service to a concern about interfering in design decisions in that context. But, far from creating any special test, it simply affirmed the district court's conclusory findings that Microsoft's commingling code and prevention of removal of IE were anticompetitive and lacked any pro-competitive justification. In the process, it addressed none of the concerns about efficiency that it found so compelling in the tying section.

Another puzzle is worth noting. The court declared that, if the plaintiffs pursue a tying claim on remand, the district court "must also consider" a theory not addressed in its analysis of monopoly maintenance, something called "price bundling."[61] Describing the "core concern" in tying law, the court explained that competition on the merits of the tied product "is foreclosed when the tying product either is sold only in a bundle with the tied product or, though offered separately, is sold at a *bundled price*, so that the buyer pays the same price whether he takes the tied product or not."[62] The court here appears to divide the universe of tying arrangements sensibly into two groups, one in which a buyer is forced to purchase two products because of contractual or physical constraints, and one in which the buyer is permitted to purchase the tying product alone but has no economic incentive to do so because the price is no lower than the price charged for the package of products.[63] One would assume that the latter sort of tie is what the court calls "price bundling."

But the government did not allege "price bundling" in this sense, because Microsoft did not offer a version of Windows without IE. In the court's typology, the government's case alleged only the first kind of tying arrangement – one created by contractual or physical binding. Why, then, would the district court need to consider price bundling? The court of appeals required the district court to compare Microsoft's charge for Windows and IE together with the amount that "its charge *would have been* for Windows alone."[64] But under the court's typology, a *hypothetical* price of Windows without IE (however that might be determined) is irrelevant to price bundling, which occurs when the tying product is *in fact* offered separately, but at a price that represents no discount from the price of the bundle.

Apparently, the court is employing a different (but unstated) definition of price bundling from the one it had suggested earlier in its opinion. The price bundling claim the court would have the lower court resolve is whether Microsoft charged a price *increment* for IE in Windows.[65] If Microsoft charged no higher price for the combination of Windows and IE than it would have charged for Windows without IE, then Microsoft did not engage in price bundling. Under this definition, price bundling is charging a higher price for the package of tying and tied products than for the (hypothetical) tying product alone. In other words, if Microsoft gave IE away at no cost – a question on which the court finds conflicting record evidence[66] – it did not price bundle. One might think that if a seller gave away a valuable product it would face condemnation for predatory pricing. But the court sidesteps this implication by noting "there is no *claim* of price predation."[67]

Thus, apparently Microsoft may have committed a tying offense by charging more for the combination of IE and Windows than it would have charged for Windows alone. Why such a practice should be given a name, much less the misleading term "price bundling," is obscure. Perhaps the court meant to say that contractual or physical tying is okay if the seller charges no increment in price for the tied good, because the practice does not harm consumers. Thus, if and only if the seller charges a price increment will the seller have to prove that it has procompetitive justifications for the contractual or physical tie.[68] But this interpretation of the court's analysis conflicts with its conclusion in the monopoly maintenance section that OEMs incurred a cost in pre-installing a second browser because of customer confusion and that end users incurred an opportunity cost in installing a second browser by wasting space on their hard drives. If these effects are taken seriously, tying could be anticompetitive despite a zero price increment.

CONCLUSION

The D.C. circuit's bizarre disposition of the Microsoft case is a missed opportunity. One would have hoped that a court with such expertise in antitrust and regulatory matters would have produced a majority analysis (with perhaps an insightful concurrence and a trenchant dissent) that pointed the way for antitrust law in the information age. Instead, we are left with an inscrutable per curiam opinion that gives us only a result and confusion. The most important monopolization case of the information age deserved better.

[1] *U.S. v. Microsoft Corp.*, 253 F.3d 34 (D.C. Cir. 2001).

[2] In this context, *per curiam* means "not attributed to any one member of the court." *A Dictionary of Modern Legal Usage* 125 (2d ed. 1995), quoted in R. Perry Sentell, Jr., "*The Peculiarity of Per Curiam: The Georgia Supreme Court*," 52 *Mercer. L. Rev*. 1, 2 (2000).

[3] Some controversial opinions are decided per curiam, but with numerous partial concurrences and dissents. *See, e.g., Buckley v. Valeo*, 424 U.S. 1 (1976). Whatever else may be said for that use of the per curiam device, it does not submerge the divisions on the court.

[4] One study of the Supreme Court's per curiam practice concluded that per curiam opinions, among other functions, "decide less controversial cases in a cost-effective manner; provide prompt direction to lower courts to follow recent decisions; rapidly answer obvious legal questions that, nonetheless, represent important issues; and extend major decisions incrementally." Stephen L. Wasby et al., "*The Per Curiam Opinion: Its Nature and Functions*," 76 *Judicature* 29, 38 (1992).

[5] John R. Wilke and Ted Bridis, "*Regulators Won't Seek Microsoft Breakup*," *The Wall Street Journal*, Sep. 7, 2001, p. A3.

[6] The court disqualified the judge "retroactive only to the date he entered the order breaking up Microsoft," *U.S. v. Microsoft Corp.*, 253 F.3d, p. 111. Even though the court found "fair room for argument that the District Court's factfindings should be vacated *in toto*," p. 119, it declined to set aside the entire decision because there was no evidence of actual bias. Microsoft challenged the consistency of this ruling with the appellate court's decision to affirm the trial court's findings on the merits, Petition for Writ of Certiorari, *U.S. v. Microsoft Corp.*, No. 1-236 (U.S., filed Aug. 7, 2001), http://www.microsoft.com/presspass/trial/appeals/08-07petition.asp, but the Supreme Court denied certiorari.

[7] *U.S. v. Microsoft Corp.*, 253 F.3d, pp. 58-80.

[8] *Ibid*., p. 60.

[9] *Ibid*., p. 79.

[10] *Ibid*., p. 60.

[11] *See, e.g., U.S. v. Microsoft Corp.*, 253 F.3d, p. 60 ("The reason market share in the browser market affects market power in the operating system market is complex, and warrants some explanation."); *ibid*. ("Microsoft's efforts to gain market share in one market [browsers] served to meet the threat to Microsoft's monopoly in another market [operating systems]"); *ibid*., p. 69 ("Following *Tampa Electric*, courts considering antitrust challenges to exclusive contracts have taken care to identify the share of the market foreclosed."); *ibid*., p. 72 ("Microsoft's exclusive deals with the ISVs had a substantial effect in further foreclosing rival browsers from the market.").

[12] *Ibid*., p. 60 ("The restrictions Microsoft places upon Original Equipment Manufacturers are of particular importance in determining browser usage share"); *ibid*., p. 62 ("Microsoft reduced rival browsers' usage share not by improving its own product but, rather, by preventing OEMs from taking actions that could increase rivals' share of usage."); *ibid*., p. 65 ("Because Microsoft's [commingling code] through something other than competition on the merits, has the effect of significantly reducing usage of rivals' products and hence protecting its own operating system monopoly, it is anticompetitive."); *ibid*., ("Because the [default] override [of users' choice of browsers] reduces rivals' usage share and protects Microsoft's monopoly, it too is anticompetitive."); *ibid*., p. 67 ("Plaintiffs plainly made out a prima facie case of harm to competition in the operating system market by

demonstrating that Microsoft's [commingling code] increased its browser usage share and thus protected its operating system monopoly from a middleware threat."); *ibid*., p. 71 ("By ensuring that the 'majority' of all IAP subscribers are offered IE either as the default browser or as the only browser, Microsoft's deals with the IAPs clearly have a significant effect in preserving its monopoly; they help keep usage of Navigator below the critical level necessary for Navigator or any other rival to pose a real threat to Microsoft's monopoly."); *ibid*., pp. 73-74 ("Because Microsoft's exclusive contract with Apple has a substantial effect in restricting distribution of rival browsers, and because (as we have described several times above) reducing usage share of rival browsers serves to protect Microsoft's monopoly, its deal with Apple must be regarded as anticompetitive.")

13 OEM stands for "original equipment manufacturer," industry jargon for companies that assemble, brand, and sell computers.

14 *U.S. v. Microsoft Corp*., 253 F.3d, p. 63. The court did not explain why the relevant measure of the browser market is *usage*, rather than *installation*. The court's analysis focused on the reluctance of OEMs to install a rival browser. See, e.g., p. 61. But we put this point aside.

15 *Ibid*., p. 70.

16 *Spectrum Sports, Inc. v. McQuillan*, 506 U.S. 447, 456 (1993).

17 *U.S. v. Microsoft Corp*., 253 F.3d, p. 81.

18 *Ibid*., p. 81 (citations omitted).

19 *Ibid*., pp. 81-82 (citations omitted).

20 *Ibid*., pp. 82-84.

21 *Ibid*., pp. 53-54. See *also Ibid*., pp. 79-80.

22 *U.S. v. Microsoft Corp*., 65 F. Supp. 2d 1, pp. 49-50 (D.C.C. 1999).

23 *Ibid*., p. 81.

24 *Ibid*., p. 54.

25 *Ibid*.

26 Economic harm is typically not anticompetitive if the injured firm is not a competitor of the defendant. *NYNEX Corp. v. Discon, Inc*., 525 U.S. 128, 138 (1998); *Intergraph Corp. v. Intel Corp*., 195 F.3d 1346, 1355-56 (Fed. Cir. 1999). In theory, a firm could be on the verge of entering its first market yet represent such an unusual and promising competitive force that its foreclosure would work a cognizable injury to competition. But this theory would not apply here, because Netscape was indeed supplying a product commercially and the methods used to exclude it related to the distribution of that product.

27 *Brokerage Concepts, Inc. v. U.S. Healthcare, Inc*., 140 F.3d 494, 519 (3d Cir. 1998) ("Before we can determine whether there was harm to competition in the tied market, that market must be defined."); *Virtual Maintenance, Inc. v. Prime Computer, Inc*., 11 F.3d 660 (6th Cir. 1993) (holding that plaintiff failed to establish a threat to competition in "most narrowly defined tied product market"); *Town Sound and Custom Tops, Inc. v. Chrysler Motors Corp*., 959 F.2d 468, 493 (3rd Cir. 1992) (finding that plaintiff improperly defined the tied product market too narrowly).

28 Edmund H. Mantell, "*Antinomies in Antitrust Law: Tying and Vertical Integration*," 7 *J.L. & Commerce* 23, 58 (1987): "Thus, in order to determine what fraction of the aggregate market for the tied product has been 'foreclosed' to other sellers of that product, one must define the scope of that market. This requirement of market definition, considered

purely as a question of economics, constitutes essentially the same requirement of market definition as in a Section 2 monopolization case. The issues which arise are the same, and the depth of the economic analyses are essentially the same."

[29] *Collins v. Associated Pathologists, Ltd.*, 844 F.2d 473, 480 (7th Cir. 1988).

[30] *U.S. v. Microsoft Corp.*, 253 F.3d, p. 95 (citation omitted). The court's reference to "the tying arrangement itself" apparently as implicit evidence of a browser market and entry barriers is obscure. It is reminiscent of the proposition that a tying arrangement itself may prove market power in the tying product market. See *Fortner Enterprises, Inc. v. United States Steel Corp.*, 394 U.S. 495 (1969); *Northern Pacific Ry. Co. v. United States*, 356 U.S. 1 (1958). That proposition has since been repudiated. See *United States Steel Corp. v. Fortner Enterprises, Inc.*, 429 U.S. 610 (1977).

[31] Joint Status Report, p. 2, *U.S. v. Microsoft Corp.*, No. 98-1232 (CKK) (filed Sept. 20, 2001), http://www.usdoj.gov/atr/cases/f9000/9085.htm.

[32] *U.S. v. Microsoft Corp.*, 147 F.3d 935 (D.C. Cir. 1998), *rev'g* 980 F.Supp. 537, 541 (D.D.C. 1997). The preliminary injunction barred Microsoft from "forcing OEMs to accept and preinstall the software code" of IE 3. *Ibid.*, p. 940.

[33] *Ibid.*, p. 950.

[34] *Ibid.*, p. 948. The court continued that the bundle "must be different from what the purchaser could create from the separate products on his own" and the combined form must "be better in some respect.... The concept of integration should exclude a case where the manufacturer has done nothing more than to metaphorically 'bolt' two products together." *Ibid.*, p. 949.

[35] *Ibid.*, p. 950, n.13.

[36] *Ibid.*, pp. 949-950.

[37] *Ibid.*, p. 953.

[38] *Ibid.*, pp. 950, 952.

[39] *Ibid.*, p. 952.

[40] *Ibid.*, p. 61.

[41] *Ibid.*, pp. 64-67.

[42] *Ibid.*, p. 61.

[43] *Ibid.*, p. 61. The court confirmed this interpretation by stating "because an OEM's altering the appearance of the desktop or promoting programs in the boot sequence *does not affect the code already in the product*, the practice does not self-evidently affect either the 'stability' or the 'consistency' of the platform." *Ibid.*, pp. 63-64.

[44] *Ibid.*, p. 64 (quoting the district court).

[45] *Ibid.*, p. 65 ("Because Microsoft's conduct, through something other than competition on the merits, has the effect of significantly reducing usage of rivals' products and hence protecting its own operating system monopoly, it is anticompetitive."). *See also* p. 66 (asserting that "commingling deters OEMs from pre-installing rival browsers, thereby reducing the rivals' usage share and, hence, developers' interest in rivals' APIs as an alternative to the API set exposed by Microsoft's operating system").

[46] *Ibid.*, pp. 66-67.

[47] *Ibid.*, p. 66.

[48] *Ibid.*

[49] *Ibid.*, p. 67.

[50] *Ibid.*

[51] "If the monopolist asserts a procompetitive justification ... then the burden shifts back to the plaintiff to rebut that claim.... *[I]f the monopolist's procompetitive justification stands unrebutted*, then the plaintiff must demonstrate that the anticompetitive harm of the conduct outweighs the procompetitive benefit." *Ibid.*, p. 59. Thus, if the plaintiff rebuts the pro-competitive justification, the finding of anticompetitive effect stands, and the plaintiff prevails; only if the plaintiff *fails* to rebut the pro-competitive justification must it prove that the anticompetitive harm outweighs the pro-competitive benefit.

[52] Perhaps more important, the court says nothing about whether Microsoft can pay OEMs to leave IE on the desktop if, for example, Netscape/AOL offered a bounty for deleting IE. The court's failure to address these issues, and provide instructions for remand, will undoubtedly cause difficulties in framing remedies.

[53] *U.S. v. Microsoft Corp.*, 253 F.3d, pp. 84-97.

[54] *U.S. v. Microsoft Corp.*, 87 F. Supp. 2d 30, 47-51 (D.D.C. 2000), applying *Jefferson Parish Hosp. Dist. No. 2 v. Hyde*, 466 U.S. 2 (1984).

[55] *U.S. v. Microsoft Corp.*, 253 F.3d, p. 92. The panel had explicitly stated that the rule it announced was "consistent with tying law." *U.S. v. Microsoft Corp.*, 147 F.3d, p. 950. The full court said that "[t]o the extent that the [panel] decision completely disclaimed judicial capacity to evaluate 'high-tech product design,' ... it cannot be said to conform to prevailing antitrust doctrine (as opposed to resolution of the decree-interpretation issue then before us)." *U.S. v. Microsoft Corp.*, 253 F.3d, p. 92. It is hard to see how the court's institutional competence to evaluate product design is dependent upon the legal theory under which the design is challenged.

[56] *U.S. v. Microsoft Corp.*, 253 F.3d, pp. 89-95.

[57] *Ibid.*, p. 94.

[58] *Ibid*, p. 95 (proving a reduction in competition "involves an inquiry into the actual effect of Microsoft's conduct on competition in the tied good market, . . . the putative market for browsers") (internal citations and quotation omitted).

[59] *Ibid.*, p. 84.

[60] *See, e.g.*, *PSI Repair Services, Inc. v. Honeywell, Inc.*, 104 F.3d 811, 815 n.2 (6th Cir. 1997) following the Areeda treatise in interpreting Kodak as "provid[ing] for an inquiry into whether the defendant's [tying] conduct has procompetitive effects").

[61] *U.S. v. Microsoft Corp.*, 253 F.3d, p. 96.

[62] *Ibid.*, p. 87 (emphasis added). The court continued, "In both cases, a consumer buying the tying product becomes entitled to the tied product; he will therefore likely be unwilling to buy a competitor's version of the tied product even if, making his own price/quality assessment, that is what he would prefer."

[63] The latter would be the limiting case of an economic tying arrangement. In theory, a seller could offer a discount for the tying product alone, but such a small one that a buyer would generally find purchase of the tied product from an alternative seller to be uneconomical.

[64] *U.S. v. Microsoft Corp.*, 253 F.3d, p. 96 (emphasis added).

[65] *Ibid.* The court implies that Microsoft engaged in "price bundling" if "there is a positive price increment in Windows associated with IE. ..."

[66] *Ibid.*

[67] *Ibid* (emphasis added).

[68] See *U.S. v. Microsoft Corp.*, 253 F.3d, p. 96 ("If there is a positive price increment in Windows associated with IE [we know there is no claim of price predation], plaintiffs must demonstrate that the anticompetitive effects of Microsoft's price bundling outweigh any procompetitive justifications the company provides for it.").

Section 1: *U.S. v. Microsoft Corp.*: The Economics

Essay 6

Judicial Misconduct and the Microsoft Case

by Leonard Orland*

During the Microsoft trial, presiding judge Thomas Penfield Jackson was touted as a folk hero by media desperate for ways to make coverage of complex and often tedious legal proceedings interesting to the public. What only a few people knew at the time, though, was that Judge Jackson was flagrantly breaking the judicial canon of ethics by holding secret briefings for numerous reporters. And his remarks at those meetings – a bizarre mix of country humor and rude comments about the defendants – were almost as shocking as his disregard for the rules against ex parte conversations. Indeed, it is hard to imagine what the judge thought he was doing, since the violations were bound to be made public by reporters with articles and books to write.

The violations became a serious legal and political problem for the D.C. Circuit Court of Appeals judges, who made no secret of their disgust with Judge Jackson but did not want to force the government to make its case again from scratch. So they compromised, merely disqualifying Judge Jackson from future proceedings and handing Microsoft a fistful of tactical legal victories virtually guaranteed to spare the company from the death sentence earlier pronounced by the trial judge.

Here, Leonard Orland, an expert on judicial ethics who teaches law at the University of Connecticut, makes the case that the appeals court was on very shaky ground in allowing any of Judge Jackson's decisions to stand. "No judge wants to disqualify fellow judges, to require painstaking work by judge and litigants to be redone," he writes. "But our society depends on just such an investment in the rule of law." — *D.S.E.*

INTRODUCTION

The appeals court decision in the Microsoft antitrust case put the consequences of judicial misbehavior front and center. In a 7-0 decision, the U.S. Court of Appeals for the D.C. Circuit concluded that most of the violations found by the trial court did not withstand scrutiny[1] and vacated the harsh remedies – including a corporate breakup – ordered by the trial judge.[2] Nevertheless, Microsoft asked the U.S. Supreme Court to overturn what remained of the trial court's decision, thereby throwing out all of the judge's findings. In October 2001 the Supreme Court declined to review this relatively narrow appeal, but effectively reserved judgment on the question of whether the justices later would revisit the issue as part of a broader appeal.

Microsoft was, in essence, asking the Supreme Court to consider what should happen when a judge breaks the rules.[3] Should the answer turn on when during the proceedings you discover that the judge has violated the judicial code of ethics? The implications for litigants are every bit as important as the substantive antitrust issues raised by the Microsoft case.

The court of appeals found that District Judge Thomas Penfield Jackson's comments – made in secret meetings with reporters while the case was pending before him – at a minimum gave the appearance that the judge was biased against Microsoft. Judge Jackson's conduct violated the federal judiciary's canon of ethics as well as a federal law. Indeed, the appeals court found that the violations were "deliberate, repeated, egregious, and flagrant."[4] Judge Jackson violated the code of judicial ethics merely by discussing the case, but the substance of what he said created a separate problem by indicating animus toward Microsoft and its officers. Together, the court of appeals said, these statements "called into question the integrity of the judicial process."[5]

Had these conversations come to light immediately, the judge would have been removed from the case on the spot. As one appellate judge noted, "had he not placed that embargo, he would have been off that case in a minute."[6] But because Judge Jackson insisted that the conversations not be disclosed until after he decided the case and announced the remedies, the appeals court was faced with a different problem. The judge's conduct was doubly troubling – he both broke the rules and, by delaying the discovery of that fact, raised the cost of fixing things.

The appeals court could not simply put another judge in charge to finish a trial and decide the case. Instead, it had to choose between vacating voluminous factual and legal determinations in a very complex case, thereby forcing a costly duplication of effort, or crediting decisions of a judge who at least appeared to be biased against a defendant.

The appeals court thus tried to steer a middle course. It vacated the judge's decision on remedies at least in part in response to his misconduct, and it removed him from further proceedings in the case. But the court also gave deference to many of Judge Jackson's Findings of Fact. The court did not have the opportunity to engage in a probing examination of Judge Jackson's actual bias, but it did find that on the surface it did not seem that "actual bias infected his factual findings."[7] And, since most of Judge Jackson's disclosed contacts with the press occurred closer to the end of the proceeding than the beginning, the appeals court let Judge Jackson's liability decisions stand despite the ethics violations.

This paper explores the implications of Judge Jackson's misconduct and the way appellate courts should respond in these circumstances. I argue that fairness to litigants and the integrity of the judicial process should outweigh concerns about practical difficulties of retracing steps of the litigation. The courts should not treat judicial misconduct in the same manner as judicial mistake (for example, erroneous rulings on evidence or improper instructions to the jury). The best course to follow in addressing the sorts of problems associated with Judge Jackson's actions is to vacate all decisions from the time of the judge's initial violation of the rules.

JUDGE JACKSON'S BEHAVIOR

From its inception, it was plain that the government's antitrust suit against Microsoft involved more than adversaries with very different interests. It also involved starkly different views of the facts and the law. During a 76-day trial, heard by Judge Jackson without a jury, witnesses for the company and the government described different products, different market conditions, different conduct, and different motivations. At the outset, neutral observers (as well as participants in the drama) were uncertain how Judge Jackson would react to the cases being presented by the government and by Microsoft. When he issued his Findings of Fact in November 1999, however, Judge Jackson left no one in doubt.[8] Though lacking any references to the trial record, the findings make clear that the judge believed the government witnesses – and rejected the testimony of Microsoft witnesses – on nearly every disputed factual issue. Even though his findings did not always point in the direction of liability for Microsoft, they plainly laid the groundwork for concluding that Microsoft violated the antitrust laws.

Four months later, following the failure of settlement negotiations, Judge Jackson dropped the other shoe. He ruled that Microsoft was, indeed, liable for tying under Section 1 of the Sherman Act and both attempted monopolization and monopoly maintenance under Section 2.[9] In a surprise move, he rejected Microsoft's request for hearings on the consequences of the government's proposed remedy – a corporate breakup combined with disclosure of proprietary information about Microsoft software and strict ongoing regulation of software design and marketing. Judge Jackson then accepted the government's remedy almost intact.

What Microsoft did not know at the time – and could not know because the journalists in question had been sworn to secrecy – was that Judge Jackson had been speaking to reporters covering the trial. He gave interviews about the case and the parties to reporters from *The Washington Post*, *The Wall Street Journal*, *The New York Times*, *The New Yorker*, and *The Financial Times*, among others. Some reporters were privy to many hours of discussion with the judge over a period of months, some to only one session. These secret meetings started during the trial, before the judge had issued his Findings of Fact. They continued through the end of the trial, through his deliberations about the disposition of the charges against Microsoft, through his decision on remedy, and in the period immediately following as well.[10]

The reporters' descriptions of these conversations paint a remarkably consistent picture of Judge Jackson's comments. All agree that Judge Jackson was consistently hostile to Microsoft and its officers, while praising the government and its representatives. In interviews with Ken Auletta of *The New Yorker*, Judge Jackson opined that Microsoft Chairman Bill Gates "has a Napoleonic concept of himself and his company, an arrogance that derives from power and unalloyed success ..."[11] Referring to a photo he had seen in the press of Gates dating from the 1970s, Judge Jackson said that he looked like "a smart-mouthed young kid ... who would be better off if he finished Harvard."[12] And Judge Jackson explicitly compared Microsoft's protestations of innocence to those of a Washington, D.C., street gang that had appeared before his court on charges of first-degree murder and drug trafficking. "On the day of the sentencing," Judge Jackson recalled, "the gang members [like Microsoft executives] maintained they had done nothing wrong."[13]

Not only did Judge Jackson find Microsoft's officers unappealing; he also disliked the way the corporation did business. The judge told reporters he did not like product integration – a central issue in the case – using the example of cameras and light meters. Judge Jackson explained that some consumers might like the convenience of having the light meter built in, but ventured that cameras "should also serve the needs of photographers who want a separate light meter..."[14]

In contrast, the judge said that the lawyers from the Department of Justice and the state attorneys general suing Microsoft were "genuinely concerned about the public interest."[15] He disparaged Microsoft's approach to the remedy question, but said that the government lawyers had "studied all the available options" and "consulted with some of the best minds in America over a long period of time."[16] He said he couldn't do better than the government lawyers at designing a remedy and noted that Microsoft's "intransigence" (in insisting that it had not violated the law) had made a breakup inevitable.[17]

The judge explained the decision to break Microsoft in two with a story about a "North Carolina mule trainer" who only managed to get an animal to do tricks by hitting it on the head with a two-by-four: "You just have to get his attention."[18] On his unwillingness to hold evidentiary hearings on the sanctions to be imposed on Microsoft, Judge Jackson rhetorically asked a reporter for *The Financial Times,* "Were the Japanese allowed to propose the terms of their surrender?"[19]

Judge Jackson insisted that, as a condition for granting interviews, the reporters not reveal these conversations until after he issued his final order in the case.[20] As a result, there was never an opportunity for an evidentiary hearing on the degree to which the judge was biased against Microsoft, on the source of the bias, or on its effect on the disposition of the case. The comments were disclosed after the judge decided that Microsoft had behaved pretty much as the government alleged, had determined that that behavior violated the antitrust law, and had ordered Microsoft to be broken up along with other remedial measures.

LEGAL ISSUES: JUDICIAL ETHICS AND THE LAW

The rules governing judicial conduct are sensitive to both the reality and the appearance of impartiality. They are a cornerstone of the rule of law and supplement the "floor established by the Due Process Clause," which, Chief Justice Rehnquist reminds us in *Bracy v. Gramley* (1997), "clearly requires a 'fair trial in a fair tribunal,' before a judge with no actual bias against the defendant."[21]

Several provisions of the Code of Conduct for U.S. judges regulate what federal judges can say about judicial proceedings, when they can say it, and what to do if they cross the line. Canon 3A(6) requires federal judges to "avoid public comment on the merits of ...pending or impending" cases.[22] That covers cases before other judges as well as cases that are before the commenting judge or that might come before that judge. Canon 3A(4) forbids judges to initiate or consider *ex parte* communications on the merits of pending or impending proceedings.[23] And Canon 2 admonishes judges to "avoid impropriety and the appearance of impropriety in all activities."[24] Section 455(a) of Title 28 of the U.S. Code (the title of federal law relating to courts) requires judges to recuse themselves (to step down from a particular proceeding) whenever their "impartiality might reasonably be questioned."[25]

The court of appeals in the Microsoft case concluded on the basis of the published reports that Judge Jackson had violated all of these provisions. If Judge Jackson's comments had been known during the trial, Microsoft would have moved to have the judge disqualified. If the judge rejected that motion, the company would have been able to take the matter to the appeals court. And it certainly would have prevailed. The court of appeals decision says as much: "Given the extent of the Judge's transgressions in this case, we have little doubt that if the parties had discovered his secret conversations with the press, he would have been disqualified, voluntarily or by court order."[26]

The court of appeals firmly rejected the argument that secrecy had served the public interest in having court proceedings appear impartial. The appellate judges declared, "Far from mitigating his conduct, the judge's insistence on secrecy – his embargo – made matters worse.[27] The appeals court added: "Concealment of the interviews suggests knowledge of their impropriety. Without any knowledge of the interviews, neither the plaintiffs nor the defendant had a chance to object or to seek the judge's removal before he issued his Final Judgment."[28]

The court of appeals noted that the problem is not simply one of appearances. By holding out-of-court conversations about a case, the judge does more than impart his views to people who are not properly privy to the information. He also risks being influenced by what they say to him. Canon 3A(4) predicates its ban on *ex parte* comments with the observation that a "judge should accord to every person who is legally interested in a proceeding, or to the person's lawyer, full right to be heard according to law..."[29] The appeals court remonstrated that the questions reporters pose and the comments they make during interviews reflect their views of the people and issues involved. Interview subjects often feel subtle pressure to agree with the interviewer, especially if the interviewer represents a powerful news organization. The pressure is particularly sinister because those who respond to it are almost never aware that they are doing so. The parties have the right to a hearing before judges who are as free as possible of influences that cannot be tested in the courtroom by procedures prescribed by law. This is the reason that judicial codes are so sensitive to the vice of judges engaging in extrajudicial discussion of pending cases.

Having demonstrated considerable discomfort over Judge Jackson's behavior, the court of appeals faced the problem of addressing his misconduct. The issue did not come before the court in a petition to sanction Judge Jackson, but in an appeal of his decision. Ordinarily, appellate courts give considerable deference to a trial judge's determinations of fact. The trial judge has seen and heard the witnesses and has spent time assessing the evidence. Here, however, the judge's behavior was not ordinary and put large question marks on the way his misbehavior interacted with ordinary judicial functions.

How much of Judge Jackson's decision in this case reflected merely his own evaluation of witness credibility and his own weighing of competing testimony? How much of the decision was colored by bias against Microsoft? How much of that bias was the product of discussions with reporters? Without answering these hard questions, an appellate court cannot know whether Judge Jackson's decisions were within the bounds of impartial decision making – adverse to Microsoft because the judge found the other side's case more compelling – or were products of improper bias, the result of unethical judicial behavior.

In an ordinary case of alleged bias, the parties can challenge the judge before he or she has spent months drafting decisions, before the public has seen hundreds of pages of judicial findings and conclusions, before securities markets have reacted to the ups and downs in a case with enormous financial implications. Of course, in an ordinary case, the judge cannot successfully hide the evidence of bias until those thresholds have been passed.

ADDRESSING JUDICIAL MISCONDUCT

This left the appeals court without an easy choice. Reviewing the case without giving any deference to the trial judge's fact-finding would pose extraordinary problems for the appellate court, which relies on trial judges to make the sort of judgment calls about evidence that cannot effectively be made by judges who have not seen the evidence firsthand. Throwing out the entire case after so many months and so much work – sending it back for entirely new fact determinations by a judge who clearly was free of improper bias – would also present considerable practical difficulties. It would involve substantial additional legal costs, and it would allow Microsoft's possibly illegal conduct to continue for months or years in the fast-moving information technology business. Failing to address the judge's misconduct, however, would have serious implications also – not only for Microsoft, but for the notion of impartial justice as well.

The court of appeals seemed to recognize this last point when it compared Judge Jackson's comments to other instances of judicial misconduct:

> The public comments were not only improper, but also would lead a reasonable, informed observer to question the District Judge's impartiality. Public confidence in the integrity and impartiality of the judiciary is seriously jeopardized when judges secretly share their thoughts about the merits of pending cases with the press. Judges who covet publicity, or convey the appearance that they do, lead any objective observer to wonder whether their judgments are being influenced by the prospect of favorable coverage in the media. Discreet and limited public comments may not compromise a judge's apparent impartiality, but we have little doubt that the District Judge's conduct had that effect. Appearance may be all there is, but that is enough to invoke the Canons and Section 455(a)...
>
> Members of the public may reasonably question whether the District Judge's desire for press coverage influenced his judgments, indeed whether a publicity-seeking judge might consciously or subconsciously seek the publicity-maximizing outcome. We believe, therefore, that the District Judge's interviews with reporters created an appearance that he was not acting impartially, as the Code of Conduct and 455(a) require.[30]

The appeals court went on to remove Judge Jackson from further proceedings in the case, and vacated his breakup order, leaving it to another trial judge to decide on remedies. But the appeals court concluded that Microsoft's lawyers had not demonstrated sufficient actual bias affecting specific factual determinations to disqualify Judge Jackson retroactive to the point of his initial misconduct. It found that the most serious misconduct had occurred around the time Judge Jackson was contemplating the remedy to be imposed on Microsoft. Consequently, the appellate judges concluded that they could address that misconduct adequately by a limited retroactive disqualification, one tied to his remedial decision only.

This was a public slap on Judge Jackson's wrist without any real consequence. After all, the appeals court listed several independent reasons for vacating Judge Jackson's decision on remedy. His retroactive disqualification merely put an exclamation point behind that part of the appellate decision. And it is not clear how hard one must slap Judge Jackson to have an impact. Judge Jackson, after all, had been scolded by the court of appeals previously for his public comments to reporters in a prior high-profile case.[31]

The appeals court judges may have concluded that even if Judge Jackson was biased, there was little harm from that bias at the end of the day. The court of appeals had discarded much of Judge Jackson's decision on liability already. It threw out one major claim in its entirety, sent another back for retrial under a radically different standard than Judge Jackson had used, and significantly pared back the ground on which it affirmed the sole liability determination to survive appeal.[32] Further, the appeals court said, much of what Judge Jackson said would not have been clear grounds for disqualification if he had said the same things in open court.

Yet the appeals court also gave the answer to why this was different. Because Judge Jackson's comments came in conversations with reporters, we cannot know how much his animus toward Microsoft was affected by what reporters said to him, from the cues they gave about what would play well in the press.

This is not a mere debating point. It is critical to the outcome of the case. All of the liability determination against Microsoft rests on decisions with respect to contested facts. The appellate court found in each instance in which they accepted one of Judge Jackson's Findings of Fact that there was sufficient evidence on the record to choose the interpretation Judge Jackson selected. He could have made a different determination, but the evidence did not contradict what he did. Microsoft may disagree, but the court of appeals defers to trial judges' fact-finding decisions if they are not clearly wrong.

The appellate court, however, underscored more than once the difficulty of deferring to a judge whose views might be colored by improper conversations: "Deference to a District Court's factfindings presumes impartiality on the lower court's part." The appeals court asked, "When impartiality is questioned, how much deference is due?" It then answered the question this way: "The question implies that there is some middle ground, but we believe there is none. As the rules are written, district court factfindings either receive full deference under the clearly erroneous standard or they must be vacated."[33]

The government urged the Supreme Court to deny Microsoft's certiorari petition because there was no proof of actual bias on Judge Jackson's part and because the prosecutors were as much innocent victims of the judge's deception as Microsoft was. Indeed, this seemed very much on the minds of the appeals court judges as they wrestled with the question of remedying the trial judge's misbehavior. But other courts looking at similar issues in cases far less compelling have decided that the bigger concern comes from the possibility of blessing the judgments of a biased decision maker.

In a key 1988 decision, *Liljeberg v. Health Services Acquisition Corp.*, the Supreme Court gave an appellate court wide latitude in dealing with Findings of Fact by a judge who presents the appearance of bias. In affirming the appeals court decision vacating the judge's findings, conclusions, and judgment in *Liljeberg*, the court declared that the law "neither prescribes nor prohibits any particular remedy for a violation of that duty. Congress has wisely delegated to the judiciary the task of fashioning the remedies that will best serve the purpose of the legislation."[34]

But the exercise of that discretion should be especially sensitive to the prospect that parties receive a fair hearing and that the public agrees that the proceedings were impartial. In *Liljeberg*, the judge had a modest financial interest in the case, but was not aware of that fact until the trial was over and his decision had been rendered. Nonetheless, the verdict was overturned and a new trial ordered. As the Supreme Court emphasized in another judicial misconduct case, *Liteky v. United States* (1994), "what matters is not the reality of bias or prejudice but its appearance."[35] In *Liljeberg*, the Supreme Court added, "The guiding principle is that the administration of justice should appear to be disinterested as well as be so in fact."[36]

Recent appeals court decisions follow a similar route. For example, in *United States v. Cooley*, the Court of Appeals for the Tenth Circuit disqualified a judge because of a single television appearance in the midst of judicial proceedings.[37] The court stated that even one appearance would cause a reasonable observer to "harbor a justified doubt as to his impartiality."[38] Reversal was required even though the record disclosed no actual bias, the evidence establishing the defendants' guilt was "overwhelming," and the judge was "courteous to the defendants and sedulously protected their rights."[39]

More recently, in *In re Boston's Children First*, the Court of Appeals for the First Circuit disqualified a judge for publicly responding to statements by lawyers comparing one case with another.[40] The lawyers' statements were carried in the press, and the judge responded to press inquiries by explaining that one case was more complex than the other. The appeals court found that enough for disqualification, despite the fact that there was no evidence of bias. The judge's statements were "sufficiently open to misinterpretation so as to create an appearance of partiality."[41] In a world in which impartiality is critical if litigants are to be treated fairly, the court decided that it was the better course to err on the side of too-ready disqualification.

Traditionally, appellate courts have enjoyed considerable discretion to address accusations of judicial misconduct. The trend, however, has been one of increasing unwillingness to tolerate judges' breaking the rules, or even seeming to do that. Not because the appellate judges believe that actual bias infected most of the decisions they set aside, but because the appellate judges believe that any plausible question about judicial impartiality is corrosive of our system.

The judges' relatively bland statements in *Cooley and Boston Children's First* seem most readily and reasonably construed as innocent and unbiased. Yet the cases were overturned because of concern for the integrity of the judicial system. The decisions of the first and tenth circuits in these cases no doubt will lead to the disqualification of judges who are almost certainly impartial. But the appellate judges looking at these cases decided that the risk of disqualifying unbiased judges poses less of a problem for our system of justice than the risk that we will fail to disqualify judges who are not impartial.

The calculation courts have made in looking at judicial disqualification is the same kind of calculation we make in our criminal justice system, where we give much more weight to the risk of convicting the innocent than to the risk of acquitting the guilty.[42] In both cases, the rules have been slanted to protect those against whom the power of the government is deployed. Constraint of that power is the essence of the rule of law. Faith in that constraint sustains our legal system and our system of governance.

It is a fragile faith. As the Supreme Court, in *Liljeberg*, declared, "people who have not served on the bench are often all too willing to indulge suspicions and doubts concerning the integrity of judges."[43]

In the *Microsoft* case, there is more than mere "suspicions and doubts." A judge who has held secret meetings with the press, covered up his misconduct during the time that it best could have been addressed, and made clear his love of the limelight hardly can be credited with the sort of impartiality litigants deserve and our system of justice requires. Ultimately, it is the system and people of the United States as a whole who are the beneficiaries of an impartial judiciary and the victims of misconduct that undermines that crucial element of the rule of law. No judge wants to disqualify fellow judges, to require painstaking work by judge and litigants to be redone, but our society depends on just such an investment in the rule of law.

* Leonard Orland is a consultant to Microsoft.

[1] "[S]ome – indeed most – of the findings of remediable violations do not withstand appellate scrutiny." United States Court of Appeals for the District of Columbia, Opinion, *U.S. v. Microsoft Corp.*, June 28, 2001, http://ecfp.cadc.uscourts.gov/MS-Docs/1720/0.pdf, p. 102. Hereafter, Appeals Court Decision.

[2] The appeals court vacated the remedies because it had "drastically altered the scope of

Microsoft's liability"; the district court had failed to hold evidentiary hearings on remedies, the district court to explain the basis for its remedies; and, as discussed in detail below, the district court judge was disqualified from determining remedies as a result of judicial misconduct.

[3] Microsoft's Petition for Writ of Certiorari, *U.S. v. Microsoft Corp.*, August 7, 2001, http://www.microsoft.com/presspass/trial/appeals/08-07petition.asp, p. 2. The question presented in the Certiorari petition is: "Whether the court of appeals erred in not disqualifying the district judge as of the date of his earliest known violation of 28 U.S.C. Section 455(a) and the Code for Conduct of United States Judges, thus requiring that his findings of fact and conclusions of law be vacated."

[4] Appeals Court Decision, p. 106.

[5] Appeals Court Decision, p. 7.

[6] Oral Argument in *U.S. v. Microsoft Corp.*, February 27, 2001, transcript, p. 310.

[7] Appeals Court Decision, p. 122.

[8] Judge Thomas Penfield Jackson, Findings of Fact, *U.S. v. Microsoft Corp.*, November 5, 1999, http://www.usdoj.gov/atr/cases/f3800/msjudge.pdf.

[9] Judge Thomas Penfield Jackson, Conclusions of Law, *U.S. v. Microsoft Corp.*, April 3, 2000, http://www.usdoj.gov/atr/cases/f4400/4469.pdf.

[10] Ronald Rotunda, "Judicial Comments on Pending Cases: The Ethical Restrictions and the Sanctions – A Case Study of the Microsoft Litigation," 2001 *U. Ill. L. Rev.* 611, p. 622. "After these series of interviews were published, and after receiving criticism from lawyers and academics for granting these interviews about a pending case, in late October, 2000, the Microsoft trial judge engaged in extrajudicial comments yet again....He spoke while his rulings were pending in the D.C. Circuit." (footnote omitted).

[11] Ken Auletta, *World War 3.0* (New York: Random House), 2001, p. 397. Hereafter Auletta.

[12] Auletta, p. 169.

[13] Auletta, pp. 369-370.

[14] Joel Brinkley and Steve Lohr, *U.S. vs. Microsoft – The Inside Story of the Landmark Case* (New York: McGraw-Hill), 2000 (hereafter, Brinkley and Lohr), p. 263.

[15] Joel Brinkley and Steve Lohr, "U.S. vs. Microsoft: Pursuing a Giant; Retracing the Missteps in the Microsoft Defense," *The New York Times*, June 9, 2000.

[16] *Ibid.*

[17] Brinkley and Lohr, p. 315.

[18] *Ibid.*, p. 278.

[19] Peter Spiegel, "Microsoft Judge Defends Post-Trial Comments," *Financial Times*, October 7, 2000.

[20] Appeals Court Decision, p. 107.

[21] *Bracy v. Gramley*, 520 U.S. 899, 905 (1997).

[22] Canon 3A(6) of the Code of Conduct for U.S. Judges as cited in appeals court decision, p. 106.

[23] Canon 3A(4) of the Code of Conduct for U.S. Judges as cited in appeals court decision, p. 106.

[24] Canon 2 of the Code of Conduct for U.S. Judges as cited in Appeals Court Decision, p. 116.

[25] 28 U.S.C. Section 455(a) as cited in Appeals Court decision, p. 117.

[26] Appeals Court Decision, p. 115.

[27] Appeals Court Decision, p. 115.

[28] Appeals Court Decision, p. 115.

[29] Canon 3A(4) of the Code of Conduct for U.S. Judges as cited in appeals court decision, pp. 115-116.

[30] Appeals Court Decision, pp. 119-120.

[31] *In re Barry*, 946 F.2d 913 (D.C. Cir. 1991). Chief Judge Edwards dissented from the denial of mandamus and an emergency stay based on Judge Jackson's public remarks made after sentencing, but while the case was pending on appeal: "In this case, a reasonable person confronted with the facts, i.e., that a trial judge appeared in a public forum during the pendency of a criminal case to discuss the merits of the case and to criticize the jury and the defendant who had appeared before him in the criminal trial, would question whether the judge could sentence the defendant with impartiality." 946 F.2d, pp. 916-917.

[32] David S. Evans, "*The Disposition of Claims Against Microsoft by the District Court and the Appeals Court*," August 13, 2001, unpublished paper excerpted in part in the introduction to this volume.

[33] Appeals Court Decision, p. 123.

[34] *Liljeberg v. Health Services Acquisition Corp.*, 486 U.S. 847, 862 (1988).

[35] *Liteky v. United States*, 510 U.S. 540, 548 (1994).

[36] 486 U.S., pp. 869-870.

[37] *United States v. Cooley*, 1 F.3d 985 (10th Cir. 1993).

[38] 1 F.3d, p. 995.

[39] 1 F.3d, p. 996.

[40] *In re Boston's Children First*, 244 F.3d 164 (1st Cir. 2001).

[41] 244 F.3d, p. 170.

[42] "The principle that there is a presumption of innocence in favor of the accused is the undoubted law, axiomatic and elementary, and its enforcement lies at the foundation of the administration of our criminal law." *Coffin v. United States*, 156 U.S. 432, 453 (1895). "The *Coffin* Court traced the venerable history of the presumption from Deuteronomy through Roman law, English common law, and the common law of the United States." *Taylor v. Kentucky*, 98 S.Ct. 1930, 1934 (1978).

[43] *Liljeberg v. Health Services Acquisition Corp.*, 486 U.S. 847, 864-865 (1988).

Section 2: Antitrust Policy and the New Economy

Essay 7

Antitrust and the New Economy

by David S. Evans*

While the idea that a New Economy exists has been called into question in the wake of the collapse of technology stocks, the concept is alive and well in the context of antitrust analysis.

In this article, I define New Economy industries in terms of a variety of attributes that make it difficult to analyze markets in traditional fashion. They are often characterized by network effects that may, in themselves, create barriers to entry. They often have high fixed costs and low marginal costs, implying that to be profitable, they must charge much more than marginal cost. They are often created on very high risk business plans, implying that the expected return to capital necessary to attract investors is also very high. Most important, competition in New Economy markets is dynamic rather than static, largely working through product-defining innovation rather than through marginal changes in cost, marketing strategy, or product design.

Notice that, even in highly competitive New Economy markets, one might expect to find dominance by single firms that charge far more than marginal cost and earn what one might on first glance assume are excess profits – all benchmarks of market power and potential harm to consumers in traditional markets. How, then, is one supposed to know whether New Economy markets are working properly?

The somewhat unsatisfying answer is that the old rules of thumb don't apply, and that satisfactory alternatives don't yet exist – and may never. Antitrust still has a place in the New Economy. But to serve the spirit of modern antitrust policy, enforcement agencies and courts must refrain from apply-

ing inapt rules developed for old-economy industries and carefully evaluate whether intervention will likely serve the interests of consumers. —*D.S.E.*

Can century-old antitrust laws, created in the days when the public was concerned about robber barons controlling entire industries, serve economic policy in an era in which the Next Big Thing regularly wipes out fortunes made from the Last Big Thing?

Actually, the question can be answered only by filling in a bit of history. Two inventions, each about a quarter-century old, launched a new industrial revolution – the birth of what has come to be known as the New Economy. The first personal computer, the Altair 8800, was introduced in 1975 as a mail-order kit for electronic hobbyists. A year later, two young entrepreneurs named Bill Gates and Paul Allen released the first programming language for the Altair. Two years after that, Apple delivered the first computer for home use that could be purchased in stores.

Meanwhile, in 1972, the Internet was born. Forty terminals were hooked up to a dozen computers, creating a network of users in 20 cities across the United States. This primitive network evolved into the physical backbone for connecting computers around the world.

Figure 1. **The Convergence of PCs and the Internet Has Launched a Third Industrial Revolution Built on Information Technology**

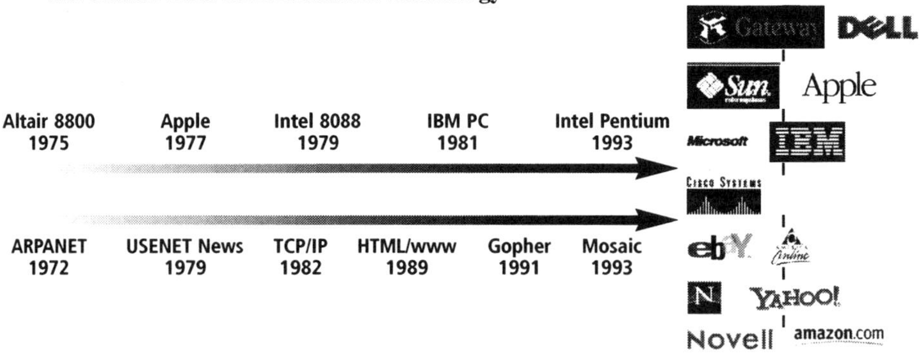

Sources: "A Brief History of Computing," http://ox.compsoc.net/~swhite/timeline.html and http://www.pbs.org/internet/timeline.

Three other developments accelerated the commercialization of these new technologies. First, the cost of computer processing and storage declined sharply. Second, the cost of sending electronic information over physical networks fell in tandem. Third, by the early 1990s, the invention of easy-to-use software for viewing, editing, and sending documents on the Internet made this meta-network a much more powerful tool for distributing information.

This resulting industrial revolution is our third. The first revolution, in the 18th century, was responsible for widespread innovations ranging from steam engines to iron production. The second brought electricity, telephones, and the internal combustion engine. Both revolutions promoted changes in industrial technology and organization by expanding physical capital. The third revolution, built on technology for processing and distributing information electronically, is more ethereal. Indeed, many of the gains in productivity linked to this third industrial revolution are based on the rapid creation of intellectual, rather than physical, property.

To see how much the economic landscape has changed as a result, compare the companies with the highest market values at the beginning of the year 2000 with the most valuable companies just 30 years earlier (see Table 1).

So many of the faces are new. And most of them are at the forefront of the third industrial revolution – Microsoft, Cisco Systems, Intel, Nokia, and Sun, to mention a few. Others, like AT&T and IBM, have been trying with some success to turn themselves into New Economy companies. And virtually all of them allocate the lion's share of their investment budgets to R&D.

NEW ECONOMY INDUSTRIES DIFFER FROM OLD ONES

The new industries that are emerging from the third industrial revolution differ from older industries in a number of ways.

• Many produce for markets that exhibit "network effects" – that is, their products are more valuable to all if more people use them. I enjoy AOL more if you also subscribe to AOL's Internet service because we can be on each other's "buddy list" and exchange messages instantly online. Most old economy industries, by contrast, don't have substantial network effects: I don't enjoy Coke more because you drink it, too.

• Many have high fixed costs and low marginal production costs. New Economy firms often have to invest a great deal to develop their products, either because they must make substantial investments in research and development, or because they must invest in a physical or virtual network to create and deliver the product. But once they make this initial investment, it's cheap to create additional units. It doesn't cost much to produce another copy of, say, the Microsoft Office software package; nor does it cost much to add another subscriber to the AOL network. Thus, material and selling expenses represent less than 20 percent of revenues in software. By contrast, outlays for material

Table 1. **Top 25 Companies Ranked by Market Value as of January 1 (in Billions of Dollars)**

	1970		2000	
Rank	**Company Name**	**Market Value**	**Company Name**	**Market Value**
1	Intl. Business Machines Corp.	$38	Microsoft Corp.	$506
2	AT&T Corp.	$26	General Electric Co.	$438
3	General Motors Corp.	$18	Cisco Systems Inc.	$377
4	Eastman Kodak Co.	$12	Intel Corp.	$329
5	Exxon Mobil Corp.	$12	Exxon Mobil Corp.	$290
6	Sears Roebuck & Co.	$9	Wal-Mart Stores	$244
7	Xerox Corp.	$7	Nippon Telegraph & Telephone	$240
8	Texaco Inc.	$6	AT&T Corp.	$235
9	General Electric Co.	$6	Nokia Corp.	$214
10	Minnesota Mining & Mfg. Co.	$5	Deutsche Telekom AG	$210
11	Gulf Corp.	$5	Intl. Business Machines Corp.	$200
12	Royal Dutch Petroleum	$4	Citigroup Inc.	$191
13	Coca-Cola Co.	$4	Merck & Co.	$183
14	Du Pont (El) De Nemours	$4	Lucent Technologies Inc.	$176
15	Avon Products	$4	BP Amoco Plc	$174
16	Proctor & Gamble Co.	$4	Toyota Motor Corp.	$164
17	BP Amoco Plc – Ads	$4	American International Group	$161
18	Ford Motor Co.	$4	Ericsson (LM) Tel.	$145
19	Mobil Corp.	$3	SBC Communications Inc.	$145
20	Chevron Corp.	$4	Coca-Cola Co.	$141
21	Lilly (Eli) & Co.	$3	Oracle Corp.	$140
22	ITT Industries Inc.	$3	Pfizer Inc.	$139
23	Polaroid Corp.	$3	Sun Microsystems Inc.	$137
24	American Home Products Corp.	$3	France Telecom	$135
25	Atlantic Richfield Co.	$3	Proctor & Gamble Co.	$132

Source: FactSet Research Systems, Inc., CompuStat Monthly Database, July 2000.

and selling expenses in manufacturing exceed 60 percent of revenues.

• New Economy firms are also much more labor-intensive and much less capital-intensive than old economy industries. That's because the fixed costs incurred by New Economy firms are mainly from the labor used to develop their products. They don't need many plants or equipment. For example, labor cost represents 46 percent of revenues in software manufacturing, compared to just 9 percent in manufacturing overall.[1] By the same token, New Economy industries generally employ better-educated workers than their old economy counterparts.

• In the third industrial revolution, competition often consists of a series of races. In the first race, firms invest to develop a product that creates a new category – the Palm Pilot, Visicalc's pioneering spreadsheet for Apple computers, AOL's Instant Messaging Service. Winners get huge market shares. In subsequent races, firms invest heavily to displace the leader by leapfrogging the leader's technology. Lotus 1-2-3 displaced Visicalc. Microsoft Excel, in turn, displaced Lotus 1-2-3.

• As with a host of endeavors in which many try but few succeed, the winners are assured enormous profits as long as they stay ahead of their rivals. These "prizes" for the winner serve the same purpose as prizes in tennis tournaments, huge salaries for movie stars, and enormous earnings for best-selling authors; they maintain the flow of contenders. Because the path of successful innovation is so difficult to lay out in advance, it serves the interests of society to encourage a lot of entrepreneurs to try to blaze their own.

• Competition is dynamic. The contest is not about which widget producer can sell widgets for the lowest price today, but which inventor can come up with something so much better that no one wants widgets anymore. Many decades ago the great economist Joseph Schumpeter prophetically described this dynamic competition as a "perennial gale of creative destruction" that "strikes not at the margins of the profits of the existing firms but at their foundations and their very lives."[2] Andy Grove, the former CEO of Intel, summarized business life for those in the path of these uprooting events: "Only the paranoid survive."[3]

These differences change the logic underlying antitrust policy. The "first take" on market economics presented in most undergraduate economics courses is built on a model of static competition – one in which there is no past and no future. Economists have long used this static model to describe an ideal state known as perfect competition, which becomes the benchmark for measuring the losses associated by the inevitable departures from this blissful world. And this way of thinking has heavily influenced the practice of antitrust over the last century. Departures from the pre-conditions of perfect competition signal a breakdown and invite the courts to intervene.

Compare this static model of competition so often used to analyze firms in economics textbooks and antitrust courtrooms with the dynamic model that better describes markets in the New Economy (see next page).

Antitrust practitioners have known for a long time that the textbook model of static competition is not relevant for many industries. In fact, that's one reason the courts have been clear all along that it is all right for firms to become monopolies as a result of superior efficiency and foresight. What's more, we have known that using the textbook model of competition as the standard of comparison can lead to error in judging the consequences for consumers. The

Static Versus Dynamic Competition

STATIC	DYNAMIC
Competition takes place **in** the market. Firms vie with each other to offer the lowest prices and best features.	Competition takes place **for** the market. Firms compete through innovation to dominate the market. Those firms that succeed may be thought of as "fragile monopolists" because they can retain their position only if they continue to innovate.
With many firms and few barriers to entry, competition minimizes costs to consumers and eliminates the ability of any firm to earn above-normal profits.	Scale economies in production together with network effects result in a single firm with lowest costs and a large share of the market. Consumers benefit from lower prices and greater standardization.
Competition ensures that prices equal the marginal cost of production. Prices in excess of marginal cost are evidence that sellers have some degree of monopoly power.	To succeed, firms must charge more than marginal cost. That's the only way firms can be compensated for both their fixed costs and the high risk inherent in the investment.
Competition ensures there is only one price for a product. Firms that charge different prices to different customers must have some degree of monopoly power.	Charging different customers different prices is common. It is the most efficient way to earn back fixed costs.
Firms get just a normal return, adjusted for risk, on their invested capital. Persistent high profits indicate that firms have some degree of durable monopoly power.	The return to competitors, in aggregate, consists of normal profits adjusted for risk. But winners receive huge profits that offset the huge losses incurred by losers. The fact that firms are very profitable is not an indication that competition is failing.

Supreme Court has made that point clearly in the line of cases beginning with *BMI v. CBS, Inc.*[4] These cases recognize that in certain industries, price fixing actually serves the interests of consumers.

Nevertheless, there is still a reflexive tendency to compare all industries and all marketing practices to the textbook model of competition. That creates serious problems for New Economy industries because the textbook model of competition can never work in many of these industries. If, for example, we restructured these industries to create a large number of small firms, or if we forced them to price their products at marginal cost, consumers would be worse off.

HOW THE ECONOMICS OF THE THIRD INDUSTRIAL REVOLUTION AFFECT KEY ANTITRUST CONCEPTS

Market Power

The analysis begins with the issue of how to determine whether firms have market power. Antitrust experts typically look at one or more traditional indicators, all of which would suggest that third-industrial-revolution industries are antitrust cases waiting to be prosecuted. But that's because static standards of competitive behavior ignore the discipline that the dynamic process of competition places on the fragile monopolists that dot the New Economy landscape.

Market Share

The most common antitrust indicator is whether a firm has a large share of a relevant market. But in third-industrial-revolution industries, the incumbent typically has a large market share because competition is often a matter of "winner-take-most." A better test of market power is contestability. Imagine what Intel's market share would be two years from now if it left the innovation to AMD, IBM, Compaq, or any of a dozen other firms with the technical capacity to create faster, more flexible microprocessors.

Price Versus Marginal Cost

Another common indicator of market power, which simply doesn't work in New Economy industries, is whether a firm is charging a price that exceeds marginal cost. To highlight the problem, let me share one of my favorite lines of testimony from the Microsoft case. One of the government's economists, Frederick Warren-Boulton, testified that the price of Windows was higher than the competitive level. When asked on cross-examination what the competitive price of Windows was, he replied that it was "significantly below whatever it is."[5]

Comparing price with the marginal cost of production doesn't make sense for companies that have very low marginal costs and very high fixed costs. No firm would enter the competitive races that characterize third-revolution industries if they had to charge marginal cost. All software companies charge more than marginal cost, even though this industry is intensely competitive. Most other third-industrial-revolution companies do the same.

Predatory Behavior

Another antitrust concept that doesn't travel well from a world of static competition to one of dynamic competition is predatory behavior. In the usual story, the predator tries to eliminate its rivals from the market so that it can raise prices above competitive levels. Now, the courts have taken a pretty jaundiced view of predation theories, even in cases regarding old economy industries. That's because, in practice, it's hard to distinguish predation from competition where the essence of competition is harming one's rivals.

The Recoupment Test

As a result, the courts have developed stringent tests to distinguish predation from competition. Roughly speaking, the plaintiff must demonstrate that the alleged predator incurred economic losses to drive its rivals out of business and that it did so because it could plausibly expect to recoup those losses after it vanquished them.

Even by this relatively stringent test, however, all successful firms subject to dynamic competition are predators. Think about it for a moment. You and I engage in competition for a market that is likely to end in a winner-take-all result because of a combination of scale economies in production and network effects in demand. We both invest a lot of money to come up with the next-generation product. We're losing money now, and the only way either of us can earn our money back is by winning the innovation race. Yet under the courts' recoupment test, I'm the predator if I win and you're the predator if you win.

Evidence of Intent

The courts also look to intent to determine whether a firm is engaging in predation. Whatever you think this kind of evidence is worth for cases involving older industries, it doesn't help at all in companies involved in dynamic competition. If I intend to survive a winner-take-all race, I must intend for you to fail. And if you intend to survive, you must intend for me to fail. So if antitrust authorities looked hard enough, one would expect them to find plenty of evidence – e-mails, memos, and so forth – that each competitor wants to bury the other.

WHERE'S THE CONSUMER HARM?

Not surprisingly, the Department of Justice and the Federal Trade Commission have become quite interested in third-revolution industries. In a January 1998 speech, Joel Klein, the head of the Justice Department's antitrust division, noted: "The economic qualities that tend to characterize market behavior in high-tech industries are such that we will almost certainly see companies come to enjoy very significant market power, which in turn is likely to lead to antitrust scrutiny...."[6]

A few months later Mr. Klein's chief economist further explained that "allegations of anticompetitive behavior need to be treated quickly and seriously"[7] in these industries. In the second term of the Clinton administration, the Justice Department adopted the view that not only are New Economy industries different from old economy industries, but they are different in ways that require even closer antitrust scrutiny than old economy industries.

This view reflects a fundamental misunderstanding of how competition works in the New Economy. Mr. Klein takes a snapshot of these industries through the lens of static competition and sees market failure. The fact that successful firms have high market shares, charge prices that exceed marginal cost, and earn enormous profits tells him something is wrong. But the dynamic view of the same facts tells a different story – one that shows how fragile this market power is and how hard successful firms must compete to stay on top of the heap.

Recent high-profile antitrust cases have all used the static competitive model as their foundation, in particular the Federal Trade Commission's case against Intel along with the Justice Department's cases against Microsoft and Visa–MasterCard. In each, the crack in the foundation appears when the enforcement agency gets to what's supposed to be the bottom line in an antitrust case, demonstrating how consumers have been harmed. In none of these cases did the enforcement agencies offer direct evidence of consumer harm.

• In the Intel case, the Federal Trade Commission settled after F.M. Scherer, an economist at Harvard and the government's expert witness, acknowledged in pre-trial testimony that no tangible harm could be identified.[8]

• In the Microsoft case, Frank Fisher, the government's chief economic witness, responded to a question of whether consumers had been harmed by saying, "that's hard to know... I would think the answer was no, up to this point."[9]

• In the Visa–MasterCard case, Michael Katz, the government's chief economic witness, acknowledged that he had "not come up with specific numerical or – numerical quantification of the harm to competition and consumers."[10]

Lacking tangible evidence of damage to consumers in the form of higher prices or lower quality, the government concluded each of these cases with the claim that the defendants had harmed consumers indirectly by inhibiting innovation. But that's a very difficult claim to prove. After all, the essence of innovation is that it is unpredictable, often coming from unanticipated sources at unanticipated times. As Professor Paul Krugman of Princeton University put it in a column in *The New York Times* expressing his skepticism about the harsh remedies prescribed in the Microsoft case:

> My point is not that it is wrong to consider the impact of policy on innovation; it is that because the determinants of innovation are not well understood, clever advocates can invoke technological progress as an all-purpose justification for whatever policy they favor...[11]

There are instances, of course, when it is possible to show cause and effect in technological innovation – or lack thereof. But, in spite of the judge's assertions to the contrary, there is nothing in the Microsoft trial record showing that innovation was suppressed. And in the other two major New Economy cases discussed here, the government's experts admitted as much in sworn testimony.

> *Question to F.M. Scherer regarding Intel:*
>
> "...Has it [Intel's conduct] adversely affected research and development expenditures by any microprocessor competitor?"
>
> *Answer:*
>
> "We've gone through this before, and I've not found evidence in effect."[12]
>
> *Question to Michael Katz regarding Visa–Mastercard:*
>
> "Would it be correct to say that you don't know whether and to what extent any suppressed innovation, if it existed, harms consumers?"
>
> *Answer:*
>
> "...I have not attempted to come up with a quantitative estimate."[13]

CONCLUSIONS

Despite obvious misgivings, I believe antitrust still has a place in promoting competition. The basic principles of antitrust apply just as well to the New Economy as to the old. Agreements to fix prices or to restrict output are surely as bad in the information age as they were when John D. Rockefeller was making it almost impossible for rivals to move oil to market. Unless there are the kinds of extenuating circumstances identified in *BMI v. CBS, Inc.* and *State Oil Co. v. Khan*,[14] such agreements probably harm consumers and should be banned; the per se rule provides clear guidance for businesses. Most other practices require the courts to take a closer look at the facts to figure out whether they impose significant harm to competition and consumers. And so the rule-of-reason inquiry remains the practical approach to antitrust.

There is certainly plenty of controversy over the application of the basic principles. And there are still instances in which the courts condemn practices that economists consider pro-competitive – price discrimination and tying come to mind. Yet, all in all, these basic principles have served to maintain competition without the sorts of government regulations that undermine innovation and risk-taking.

The real problem is how those principles are applied to specific industries and specific sets of facts. So long as the courts keep two things in mind, there's no reason why the sound antitrust principles that have fostered competition in the United States for the last century can't do so for the next. The first is: "one size does not fit all." Antitrust analyses must be tailored to the realities of contemporary markets. In particular, the courts need to alter their benchmarks for what constitutes healthy competition in light of the characteristics of New Economy industries outlined above.

The second thing to keep in mind is that the true clients of antitrust are consumers. Before determining that a practice is illegal, the courts should always insist on sound evidence that, on balance, it harms consumers. What they really need to resist is efforts by plaintiffs to sidestep the question of consumer harm by claiming there is harm to rivals or harm to competition in the abstract. Behavior widely perceived as anticompetitive in the context of the old economy can be benign in the New, where corporate success often means failure for rivals.

[*] David S. Evans is a senior vice-president of National Economic Research Associates and a consultant to both Microsoft and Visa. This paper is adapted from a presentation to the American Law Institute–American Bar Association, Sept. 14, 2000, in New York City.

[1] U.S. Bureau of the Census, Current Population Survey Labor Extracts, Outgoing Rotations (1997-1999).

[2] Joseph A. Schumpeter, *Capitalism, Socialism and Democracy* (1942), currently available from HarperCollins Publishers (1984).

[3] Andrew S. Grove, *Only the Paranoid Survive* (Bantam), 1999.

[4] *Broadcast Music, Inc., et al. v. Columbia Broadcasting System, Inc., et al.*, 441 U.S. 1, 1979.

[5] Excerpt from cross-examination of Frederick Warren-Boulton taken November 19, 1998, in *U.S. v. Microsoft Corp.*, 98 CIV.1232.

[6] Joel Klein, "The Importance of Antitrust Enforcement in the New Economy," Address Before the New York State Bar Association Antitrust Law Section Program, Jan. 29, 1998.

[7] Daniel L. Rubinfeld, "Competition, Innovation, and Antitrust Enforcement in Network Industries," Address Before the Software Publishers Association Spring Symposium, March 24, 1998, http://www.usdoj.gov/atr/public/speeches/1611.htm.

[8] Arik Hesseldahl, "Intel, FTC Settle Case," *Electronic News*, March 15, 1999.

[9] Excerpt from testimony of Franklin Fisher taken June 12, 1999, in *U.S. v. Microsoft Corp.*, 98 CIV.1232.

[10] Excerpt from cross-examination of Michael Katz taken June 11, 2000, in *U.S. v. Visa*, 98 CIV.7076.

[11] Paul Krugman, *The New York Times*, June 11, 2000, p. A17.

[12] Excerpt from testimony of Frederic M. Scherer taken February 4-6, 1999, in the matter of Intel Corporation, Docket No. 9288.

[13] Excerpt from cross-examination of Michael Katz taken June 12, 2000, in *U.S. v. Visa*, 98 CIV.7076.

[14] *BMI, et al. v. CBS, Inc., et al.*, 441 U.S. 1, 1979, *State Oil Co. v. Khan*, 93 CIV.1372, 1993.

Section 2: Antitrust Policy and the New Economy

Essay 8

The Rise and Fall of Leaders in Personal Computer Software

by David S. Evans, Albert L. Nichols, and Bernard Reddy*

For some years, economic policymakers have been struggling to formulate strategies with respect to industries in which "network effects" have the potential of trapping consumers into using technologies that ultimately prove inferior to alternatives.

The classic example cited in the technical literature is the battle between the early videocassette recording formats, Betamax and VHS. Betamax was widely considered superior to VHS. But VHS was the first to introduce technology that made it possible to record an entire movie on a single cassette. Video stores, loath to stock both versions, opted for VHS. And although Betamax quickly caught up with a two-hour cassette, the damage was done. With more rental movies easily available on VHS, consumers were inclined to buy VHS players. And with more VHS players around, both film distributors and video rental stores chose the VHS format.

There is, in fact, some doubt that the triumph of VHS actually generated net losses in welfare for consumers. The technical superiority of the Betamax format is not as certain as is generally represented. Even if it were, it is possible that the costs to consumers in waiting until Betamax caught up would have outweighed the benefits of the earlier introduction of long-playing cassettes in a different format. But the illustration is clear enough: One can imagine circumstances in which network feedbacks create substantial barriers to entry. And antitrust authorities already inclined toward interventionist policies therefore had a rationale for looking closely at barriers in software –

products that often exhibit network effects.

But as Evans, Nichols, and Reddy (all economists at National Economic Research Associates in Cambridge, Massachusetts) show here, what makes sense in theory doesn't have much relevance in fact. In major areas of software development – including operating systems for personal computers – leadership has been contested and has changed hands. More important, software that is viewed by independent reviewers as better than the competition has succeeded in toppling the incumbent.

This doesn't prove – or even suggest – that antitrust enforcement is unnecessary in key industries like software where network effects are significant. But it does imply that concerns to date about network effect–based barriers to entry have been overwrought. — *D.S.E.*

This paper documents the sequence and timing of leadership by various microcomputer software packages in different product categories. We review when products were released, when they became leaders in their categories, and when they lost their leadership positions. We examined the sequence of leadership in the following microcomputer software categories: operating systems; word processors; spreadsheets; personal finance; databases; and presentation graphics. These have been among the most widely used categories of microcomputer software over the past 20 years.

DATA SOURCES

We relied primarily on market research reports from International Data Corporation (IDC), a well-known market research firm in the microcomputer industry. As a secondary source, we used market research reports from Dataquest (part of the Gartner Group). Data from these two firms are widely used in the industry. Of course, like all market research data, these are imperfect. For example, these firms sometimes change their reporting methods, so data may not be perfectly comparable over time. Nonetheless, the data are sufficiently accurate for our purposes in showing trends and changes in relative shares. We also considered articles from the trade press, including product reviews, and journalistic accounts (including a variety of books) of the microcomputer hardware and software industries.

We have observed two phenomena that are characteristic of the software industry. First, products that become category leaders are usually considered by industry reviewers to be the best or among the best available. Second, products that become category leaders are usually displaced when a significantly better one emerges. We have come to these conclusions in large part through the examination of product reviews in popular trade magazines. These reviews rate the quality of competing software applications. To document our findings systematically, we gathered reviews from every issue of *PC Magazine* going back through the early 1980s. *PC Magazine* is ranked first in paid circulation and is one of few publications whose reviews consistently cover the last two decades of software development. Although we have gathered and studied reviews from various publications, limited resources have kept us from performing an exhaustive search of more than one magazine. In four software categories (word processors, spreadsheets, databases, and personal finance software), we have used direct quotes from *PC Magazine* to support our conclusions.

RISE AND FALL OF CATEGORY LEADERS

The microcomputer industry and the microcomputer software industry have grown together in fits and starts, feeding off each other in the process. Advances in hardware have spurred the development of new software; advances in software have spurred the adoption of new hardware. The microcomputer hardware and software industries both began in the mid-1970s, based on 8-bit microprocessors. Since then, three important developments have affected both hardware and software:

1. *The shift to 16-bit computing*. Because the 16-bit microprocessors were not fully backward compatible with the older microprocessors, new software had to be developed for the new computers.

2. *The shift to 32-bit computing*, which finally made graphical user interfaces sufficiently fast that they were adopted widely.

3. *Networks, including the Internet*, which have shifted the focus of many business and home users.

Operating systems and applications have had to adapt to each of these changes, with major opportunities for new products arising with each.

Operating Systems

A general-purpose computer, such as a personal computer, typically runs an *operating system* as well as *applications software*. From an economic and commercial perspective, the dividing line between the two types of software is at best fuzzy; it may not even exist. In general, an application is a program that a user runs to accomplish a task that is unrelated to the computer itself, such as writing a letter. Sometimes a computer user wants to perform actions that are related to the computer itself, such as locating and copying a file. An operating system will frequently provide these capabilities to the user. But also frequently, specialized applications programs (called "utilities") can provide some of these capabilities. Here, we take the practical view that an operating system is software marketed as an operating system.

The first operating system for personal computers was arguably CP/M, written by Gary Kildall around 1974 for use on computers running Intel's 8080 microprocessor[1]. It began to be used widely in 1977 on machines from several manufacturers. It was one of two early operating systems that were available for a number of different computers, the other being the UCSD p-System. Computers in the late 1970s that did not run CP/M, such as the Apple II, typically ran a proprietary operating system. The most common computers for business applications in the late 1970s were the Apple II (for which VisiCalc was first written) and those running CP/M.

CP/M has frequently been described as an industry standard.[2] CP/M was an operating system standard in two senses: It ran on multiple brands of computers; and computers running CP/M accounted for a large fraction (possibly a majority, although that is not clear) of personal computers used by business. Even the Apple II could run CP/M – when equipped with Microsoft's Z-80 SoftCard, released in 1980 and bundled with CP/M.[3]

IBM's Personal Computer (PC), announced in August 1981, was based on a 16-bit cousin of Intel's 8080 microprocessor, the 8088. Software that ran on an 8080 computer could be converted to the 8088, but the new microprocessor was not backward compatible with the old. When IBM announced its new PC, it offered four options for an operating system:[4]

• "Cassette BASIC" for computers without a floppy disk drive. This version of Microsoft BASIC loaded from ROM and could control an audiocassette; it was not a "disk" operating system.

• The IBM Disk Operating System, which eventually became known widely as PC-DOS. Microsoft developed this product from an operating system purchased from Seattle Computer Products.[5] PC-DOS was a newly developed operating system that used syntax partially patterned after that of CP/M.

• CP/M-86 from Digital Research, which was not available until April 1982.

• The UCSD p-System from SofTech Microsystems.

A buyer of a new IBM PC who wanted to use a floppy disk drive (hard disks for the IBM PC were not yet available) therefore faced a choice: an unknown operating system (PC-DOS) that was immediately available and inexpensive ($40); a direct descendant (CP/M-86) of the industry standard (CP/M) that was not immediately available and was expensive ($240); or the UCSD p-System, a known product whose interpreted programs executed slowly. The choice at the time between PC-DOS and CP/M-86 was not an obvious one: "Analysts expected CP/M-86 to knock DOS off the moment it became available – despite the fact that it would not ship for months."[6] Further, "when MS-DOS was released, nine out of ten programs on the *InfoWorld* best-seller list for 1981 ran under CP/M-80, and CP/M-86, which became available about six months later, was the operating system of choice to most writers and reviewers in the trade press."[7] Even the choice between PC-DOS and the p-System was not obvious: At least one major early integrated application (Context MBA) was written for the p-System – and died in part due to its slow execution speed.[8]

The period from the introduction of the IBM PC in 1981 through the end of 1983 was one of transition. CP/M, the early industry standard, continued to thrive with shipments exceeding those of the IBM PC. But by the end of 1983 the eventual success of 16-bit computers became clear. Computers based on the Intel 8086/8088 chips were pulling ahead of those based on other 16-bit chips, and the ever-changing near-twins, PC-DOS and MS-DOS, collectively were winning out over CP/M-86 in the 8086/8088 world. With their continued improvements in new versions, PC-DOS/MS-DOS were emerging as the new standard. According to Microsoft, "by the end of 1983 the technical superiority of MS-DOS (bolstered by the introduction of such products as Lotus 1-2-3) carried the market."[9]

MS-DOS/PC-DOS was not designed for running multiple programs simultaneously. And it had difficulties managing memory in the mid-1980s, due to limitations in the Intel microprocessors of the day and the design of the IBM PC. Several other software vendors attempted to "port" operating systems to the Intel-compatible platform, but none succeeded in making substantial inroads. Microsoft and IBM cooperated in developing a would-be successor for DOS, OS/2. Designed to be more powerful and stable than MS-DOS, OS/2 was initially released (without a graphical user interface) in December 1987, but met with little success. OS/2 1.1, the first version of OS/2 with a graphical user interface (GUI), called Presentation Manager, shipped October 31, 1988. But it offered relatively poor support for DOS applications and relatively few device drivers to support hardware other than IBM's.

Given poor backward compatibility, poor support for non-IBM hardware, and the memory and other resources that it required, these early versions of OS/2 attracted little interest from users or independent software vendors (ISVs). One critic has noted that "not a single Presentation Manager application was ready on the day of the PM announcement."[10] The first major application available for Presentation Manager was actually Microsoft Excel, released a year later – two years after Excel had first shipped for Windows and four years after it had first shipped for the Macintosh.

The first version of OS/2 to win wide praise was the 32-bit version 2.0, released in early 1992, about the same time as Windows 3.1. This version was highly compatible with applications written for either MS-DOS or Windows 3.0. Many analysts were unsure at the time whether it or Windows 3.1 would ultimately dominate. Later versions of OS/2 added compatibility with Windows 3.1 applications.

On the DOS front, competition heated up in the late 1980s and early 1990s. IBM became more aggressive in marketing its version of DOS. Digital Research released DR DOS, an operating system that attempted to be compatible with MS-DOS. Reviews of DR DOS generally praised its utilities (such as the memory manager that it began to include with version 5), but some questioned the compatibility of the product. DR DOS made little headway with original equipment manufacturers (OEMs). Other MS-DOS clones were also developed and marketed in this period, but they met with little commercial success.

Another limitation of early operating systems was ease of use. The Xerox Star (1981), Apple Lisa (1983), and Apple Macintosh (1984) demonstrated that a graphical user interface could be easier to use, although the Star and the Lisa were prohibitively expensive for most users. Microsoft tried to develop a companion operating system to work in conjunction with MS-DOS, announcing Windows in late 1983 and shipping it in late 1985.

Windows did not become popular until after version 3.0 was released in May 1990. But its popularity was sustained by the release of Windows 3.1 in April 1992. By that time Windows applications, including Microsoft's own Word, Excel, and PowerPoint, were becoming available. Around the end of 1992, Windows passed DOS in popularity. A majority of new computers with DOS installed also had Windows installed.

In 1995, Windows 95 began to replace both MS-DOS and earlier versions of Windows. Within about one year of its release, it had surpassed Windows 3.x in popularity on new computers. Windows 95 was seen as a great improvement over its predecessors. Nonetheless, versions of DOS and

Windows for Workgroups were still available in 1999.[11]

In mid-1993, Microsoft released Windows NT, its first fully 32-bit operating system. It had the same graphical user interface as Windows, but like OS/2, it was less prone to failure than DOS.

In summary, CP/M was the popular "standard" operating system on 8-bit computers. MS-DOS/PC-DOS replaced it on 16-bit computers. CP/M-86 was late and expensive, and neither software developers nor users waited until it became available before purchasing the IBM PC with PC-DOS. Shortcomings in PC-DOS/MS-DOS were evident in the 1980s. Microsoft and IBM released OS/2 with the intent of solving those problems, but the shortcomings of OS/2 (e.g., poor backward compatibility) meant it gained little support from software developers or users.

Microsoft Windows, a companion to MS-DOS that provided a GUI and multitasking, also gained little support in the five years after the release of its first version in 1985. The 3.0 and 3.1 releases in 1990 and 1992, however, were more popular. In part, advances in hardware (such as computers based on Intel's 486 microprocessor) gave the product enough speed to be useful. Around the end of 1992, new computer shipments with Windows installed finally outnumbered computers with DOS but without Windows. Advanced features of Windows 95 (and later Windows 98) led to its rapid replacement of Windows 3.x.

Word Processors

Released in June 1979, MicroPro's WordStar was not the first word-processing program for microcomputers; products including Electric Pencil on CP/M computers and EasyWriter on the Apple II preceded it. But WordStar soon became the standard on computers running the CP/M operating system, which was used by most business-oriented non-Apple microcomputers. It also ran on Apple II computers that were equipped with the Microsoft SoftCard.

When the IBM PC first began shipping in 1981, EasyWriter was available for PCs running PC-DOS as the operating system. Other companies came out with word-processing software for the PC, but none was overwhelmingly popular until MicroPro released WordStar 3.3 for PC-DOS. In its first year for the PC, WordStar sold roughly three times as many copies as its nearest competitor, MultiMate (originally underwritten by an insurance company looking for software that would minimize retraining costs for typists switching from dedicated Wang word processors to PCs). Within a short period, many other firms began marketing word-processing software; a 1984 article in *PC Magazine* noted that "the number of word processing packages on the market today is staggering" and went on to review the 19 most popular.[12] WordStar 3.3's features and speed quickly won over corporate users and ushered in the era of word processing on the PC. The trade press spoke highly of MicroPro's product. In 1984, for example, *PC Magazine noted that "WordStar* has given its users enormous capabilities right from the beginning, and few word processing programs have carried the art further."[13]

In late 1984, MicroPro came out with its intended replacement for WordStar, WordStar 2000. Although it offered many new features, this product was slow and replaced the familiar WordStar interface with an entirely different one. *PC Magazine* described the program as "slower than *WordStar*, clumsier to use, and more limited in some ways."[14] The result pleased neither reviewers nor existing users, opening the door for competitors.[15]

WordPerfect was originally released in 1980 for Data General minicomputers and was ported to PC-DOS for the IBM PC in 1983, after WordStar's release. Fueled in part by good reviews of later versions,[16] sales of WordPerfect passed WordStar around 1987, a year after *PC Magazine* declared the product an Editor's Choice. The magazine recognized WordPerfect as a "finely engineered piece of software that not only does what's intended but goes much further." They went on to note, "It's hard to imagine a better and more powerful word processor than this one...."[17] Later versions continued to earn good reviews, and WordPerfect comfortably maintained its lead through about 1990.

With the release of Windows 3.0 in 1990, public attention began to turn to Windows. WordPerfect Corporation did not have a Windows version under development at the time; its first Windows version was not released until November 1991. Moreover, the user interface of WordPerfect 5.2 for Windows was an uneasy compromise between that of WordPerfect for DOS and the standard Windows interface. Versions 6.0 and 6.1 (released in October 1993 and November 1994, respectively) were received more favorably, but generally were seen as inferior to Microsoft Word.

Word was first released in a DOS version in late 1983, about a year after WordPerfect's DOS release. A version for the Macintosh followed in 1985 and for Windows in early 1990. Word was not the first word processor available for Windows; Samna's Ami was released in late 1988.[18] At about the same time WordPerfect shipped its first Windows-based word processor, Microsoft shipped its second major release. Reviews of Word for Windows generally deemed it the best of the Windows word processors. A year after it became the category leader, Microsoft Word 6.0 for Windows won distinction for its technical excellence. *PC Magazine* named the product "an example of the best trends in current software...[that] raises the word processing species to a new plateau."[19]

Around 1993, shipments of Word exceeded shipments of WordPerfect for DOS and Windows combined. Word's popularity rose further with the emergence of office "suites," in which a word processor, a spreadsheet, and other applications were sold in a bundle at a substantial discount from the stand-alone prices. Microsoft had strong applications in each of the categories included in its suite, Microsoft Office, while other would-be suite vendors did not.

In summary, WordStar was a big hit on 8-bit computers and the early years of 16-bit computers, but its publisher failed to come out with a successor product that could maintain its leadership. WordPerfect was very successful in the late 1980s, but failed to manage the transition to the graphical user interfaces that 32-bit computing made possible. Word took 10 years from its initial release to become a category leader and remains the leader today. Based on our analysis, each of the category leaders received strong reviews for the years in which they led their category. Although there have been many products in the word-processing category that have received strong reviews at different times, the three applications that have led the category seem to have received the consistently highest reviews for their category during the reign of their lead.

Spreadsheets

The spreadsheet category came into existence in late 1979 with the release of VisiCalc for the Apple II. Clones quickly followed, but VisiCalc remained the preeminent spreadsheet for microcomputers for several years.[20] When IBM announced its PC in August 1981, it also confirmed that VisiCalc would be available for it. Several other companies that already marketed spreadsheets also ported them to the IBM PC, including Sorcim's (later Computer Associates') SuperCalc (a popular spreadsheet in the CP/M world) and Microsoft's Multiplan. In 1982 – the first year in which we were able to obtain *PC Magazine* reviews for spreadsheets – the magazine noted that VisiCalc "has set the standard against which other worksheet programs are measured." Nevertheless, SuperCalc by this time was also highly regarded, and *PC Magazine* awarded both applications "A Split Decision."[21]

Despite this formidable competition from "established" companies and the fact that it had "high" memory requirements (256 kilobytes [KB] of memory[22] at a time when many machines had only 64 KB), Lotus Corporation's 1-

2-3 program was an almost immediate hit when it was introduced in early 1983. Lotus 1-2-3 went beyond its competitors in both performance and features. In addition to spreadsheet functions, it included charting, simple database operations, various disk utilities, keyboard macros to automate tasks, and primitive word-processing abilities. It passed VisiCalc in sales in 1984 to become the category leader. In that year *PC Magazine* noted, "For power and ease of use, 1-2-3 spreadsheet is hard to beat. Other programs do some things that 1-2-3 can't, but none seems to have been designed with comparable attention to detail and care for the user."[23]

Lotus faced competition from several directions in the 1980s, including other full-featured spreadsheets (primarily SuperCalc), low-priced clones like VP-Planner, Twin, and Farsight, and spreadsheet alternatives like Javelin. Borland's Quattro, introduced in 1987 (later called QuattroPro), posed a more serious challenge, offering excellent compatibility and some extra features at less than half the price. Quattro continued to be Lotus's low-priced competitor for several years. Later purchased by Novell and then Corel for bundling into a suite with WordPerfect, Windows-based versions of Quattro were still on sale in 1999.

The year 1987 also marked the introduction on the IBM PC of Lotus 1-2-3's ultimate successor as category leader, Microsoft Excel.[24] Excel was designed to use Microsoft Windows' graphical interface, although it could be run without installing Windows. A reviewer in *PC Magazine* hailed it as making "1-2-3 look like a rough draft."[25] Compared to Lotus 1-2-3, the PC version of Excel offered greater ease of use, better graphing capabilities, and more built-in functions. It also included file translation from 1-2-3, as well as special help for 1-2-3 users making the switch. After 1987, either Excel or Quattro generally bested 1-2-3 in reviews. Release 3 of 1-2-3 (in 1989), however, did offer one extremely useful feature that was not available until much later in the other products: three-dimensional spreadsheets.

After the release of Windows 3.0 in 1990, Excel began to gain rapidly on 1-2-3, pulling ahead in 1993. Lotus did not release a Windows version of 1-2-3 until late 1991, by which time Excel was already in its second major release for Windows. Moreover, the first Windows version of 1-2-3 suffered from a variety of problems.[26] As a result, Lotus almost immediately released 1.0a for Windows with numerous bug fixes and came out with Version 1.1 in April 1992.[27] Although 1.1 was a considerable improvement, in the meantime Microsoft had released Excel 4.0 (its third release for Windows), which received rave reviews. And although the latest products offered by Lotus and Borland were highly regarded, *PC Magazine* noted in 1992 that "Excel still has plenty of qualities that are unmatched by another spreadsheet in any operating environment."[28]

Personal Finance

Personal financial software comes in many guises; here, we refer to software that at minimum includes the ability to track a checkbook but not to software that is intended to be used for full-blown accounting systems. Some programs (either as stand-alone products or packaged with checkbook tracking) have provided for tracking of investment portfolios, paying bills online, downloading credit card statements, and financial planning. At heart, a personal finance program consists of a specialized database that must be easy to use in order to appeal to its intended audience, home users. It must compete with alternative means of accomplishing financial management tasks – such as electronic spreadsheets or (perhaps most commonly) paper, pencil, and calculator for balancing checkbooks.

In contrast to word-processing documents or spreadsheets, people seldom want to exchange personal financial information with others. As a result, direct network externalities seem to be absent. Complementary products like training courses and books seem less important as well.

Home computers had been used to track personal finances since the early days of computers. But the first "modern" personal finance packages began to arrive around 1983 and 1984, when early versions of Managing Your Money, Dollars and Sense, and Quicken[29] began to ship. Early versions of personal finance software were often considered unacceptable.[30] By 1986, Managing Your Money and Dollars and Sense were each accounting for about 40 percent of retail sales of personal finance software.[31] These programs seem to have earned their popularity: A 1986 reviewer chose Dollars and Sense (the Macintosh version) as his favorite, despite the fact that it was not quite as powerful as Managing Your Money;[32] the headline for a 1987 review described Managing Your Money as "still the best personal financial tool."[33]

Although Quicken had not won overwhelming praise in the 1986 review referred to above, by 1987 and 1988 newer versions of it began to be considered as the best of the low-end financial packages (in contrast with Managing Your Money, which was still considered the best or among the best of the high-end programs). By 1989, Quicken was accounting for 70 percent of unit sales of personal finance software and was still receiving excellent reviews for both its DOS and its Macintosh versions; a 1988 review of the Macintosh version described it as "the industry standard."[34]

In 1991, Microsoft released its first version of Microsoft Money, a Windows-based personal finance program. At about the same time, Intuit released its first Windows version of Quicken. Over the next several years, Quicken generally won comparison reviews over Money, although Money sometimes was viewed as on par with or slightly better than Quicken. Intuit itself claims that Quicken currently has 75 percent of sales of personal finance software.[35] While both Money and Quicken garnered strong reviews from *PC Magazine* over the years, a "First Looks" by *PC Magazine* noted in 1992, for example, that "Quicken 5.0 was the best personal finance package around, and Version 6.0 is a noticeable, evolutionary improvement."[36] Quicken Basic 98 and Quicken Basic 99 offered far more than did the first releases of Quicken that gained positive reviews. New features included online bill payment, home banking, downloading of credit card statements, and extensive tracking of loans and investments. Quicken Deluxe added even more features.

The personal finance software category has an unusual history of leaders for a software category in which network effects should be minimal: In the early years, two high-end products became widely used within a year or two after their release, accounting for a large majority of product sales. Quicken, which was released at about the same time as the original leaders but was initially considered a low-end product, surpassed the early leaders after approximately two more years and accounted for a large majority of product sales. And with continual improvements, including migrating from the DOS and Macintosh platforms to Windows, it has maintained (and possibly extended) that lead for 14 years.

Databases

The first serious database product for personal computers, dBASE II from the Ashton–Tate Corporation, was released in 1981 for CP/M computers. It was an instant success. Ported to MS-DOS, its file formats became an industry standard.[37] dBASE II was considered a high-end database with a programming language that could be used to write accounting systems and the like. Simpler databases were also popular in the early 1980s, and some people relied on the modest database capabilities of products like 1-2-3. This section concentrates on the high-end databases.

The programming language for dBASE may have created noticeable network effects. Companies that wanted to use dBASE needed programmers; programmers needed training in dBASE. So training courses and books proliferated,[38] and computer consulting firms provided custom dBASE programming. Articles in the trade press pointed out that the size of the dBASE installed base gave developers incentives to write applications that worked with dBASE.[39]

dBASE II and its successors (including dBASE III, dBASE III Plus, and dBASE IV) were the leading high-end database products for personal computers for over a decade until about 1992, although their share of shipments fell over much of that period. They sometimes received high marks in product reviews, but so did some competitors. As noted by *PC Magazine* in 1983, "Since its inception, dBase II has been regarded as a high-quality product... there are very few things that dBASE II cannot do."[40] Competitors in the same niche included clones as well as products (like R:BASE and Paradox) that were substantially different.

In the fall of 1988, the release of dBASE IV turned into a disaster; a 1989 article described dBASE IV as "floundering in a sea of bad publicity wrought by delivery delays and performance problems."[41] Although much more powerful and easier to use than its predecessors, the product was riddled with bugs that were not fixed for two years. Even the 1990 bug fixes in dBASE IV 1.1 did not stem the decline. Nevertheless, dBASE held onto its lead for several years after the release of version 1.1. Although competition was growing strongly in its wake, dBASE IV was a solid and well-regarded product. *PC Magazine* noted in 1991 that "While dBASE IV, Version 1.1, doesn't leave FoxPro or Paradox in the dust, Ashton-Tate's long nightmare is over. It has reestablished its prominent role in the PC database market, and its staff seems committed to gaining back the place that dBASE once held."[42]

Microsoft released its new Windows database, called Access,[43] in late 1992 with a very low initial price ($99, at a time when comparable databases cost $400 or more). Its ease of use and praise from reviewers quickly made it popular. Two other Windows databases, Paradox (descended from an older DOS product) and Approach, a less powerful but easier-to-use database, also won praise. Paradox briefly pulled ahead of both dBASE and Access in sales, but calling it a "category leader" seems questionable. By 1994, however, Access had emerged as the leader and remains the leader today. Early in its development, *PC Magazine* stated, "The product's polished technology and user-friendly Wizardry are a major step ahead of currently shipping competitors..."[44] Reviews in the late 1990s generally called it the best all-around end-user database, but Approach also received excellent reviews.

To some extent, however, the apparent replacement of dBASE by Access as a category leader may be illusory. It is true that dBASE has collapsed while Access has grown, but the two events may not be closely related. The low-end database packages that were so popular in the past (like Q&A or PFS:File) seem almost to have disappeared. Some databases that in the past would have used these low-end products are now probably being implemented in Access; others are probably being handled in spreadsheets, such as Excel;[45] and simple phone lists have to some extent migrated to products like Outlook. As a result, part of the success of Access has been in replacing these low-end products, not dBASE. At the high end, some database applications that in the past might have been written in dBASE are now probably being written in one of the very high end databases, such as those from Oracle and Informix. Access has no doubt gained some popularity from the decline of dBASE, but dBASE has no doubt lost some popularity to more powerful products.

Presentation Graphics

Graphics programs of one kind or another date back to the early days of microcomputers: The Apple II offered color graphics capabilities. Modern presentation graphics programs date back to about 1986, when Software Publishing Corp. released the first version of Harvard Graphics (then known as Harvard Presentation Graphics), which "the firm billed as the first presentation graphics program to include text, graphs and charts in one program."[46] The predecessor to Lotus's Freelance product was released at about the same time. PowerPoint, a similar program for the Macintosh, was released in 1987 and acquired by Microsoft in the same year.

Many similar products were released over the next few years. All of these programs attempted to make it easy for people to put together presentations with text slides, charts based on numeric data, and graphics drawn with various tools. In the early years of these applications, the results were typically sent to a slide printer or a color plotter to use in making transparencies. Over time, capabilities were added to present slide shows from the program itself.

The first versions of Harvard Graphics and Freelance were DOS-based applications. In their early years, Harvard Graphics and Freelance generally took turns getting top honors in reviews of presentation graphics programs for Intel-compatible computers. No product, however, was a category leader – none ever had a category share that reached 25 percent in the 1987-1994 period for which we have consistent data.

Around 1991, Harvard Graphics and Freelance were ported to Windows;[47] PowerPoint had arrived a year earlier. Reviews of all three products were generally positive, with PowerPoint being considered the easiest to use and Harvard Graphics often being considered the most powerful. Reviews in the last few years have tended to favor PowerPoint, but Freelance has also been highly regarded.

Presentation graphics are a category in which network effects are likely to have been minimal for many years. In contrast with word processors and spreadsheets, users were not likely to share files.

Summary of Case Studies

Some of our results are summarized in Table 1. For each category (except presentation graphics), this table lists each product that ever led its category. For this purpose, we have defined a product as a "category leader" if it had the highest share of shipments and its share was at least 25 percent. The table also shows the introduction date for each product, the date at which it became a leader, how many years it took to become a leader, and how many years it spent as a leader. The table also shows (except for operating systems) the median share of each product when it was a category leader, as well as the shares of the second- and third-place products over that time period.

Products such as CP/M, dBASE, and VisiCalc essentially defined their categories – they became leaders immediately. Other products took varying time to become leaders, ranging from one year for 1-2-3 and WordStar to 10 years for Microsoft Word. Omitting the instant leaders, the median time needed to become a leader was about three years.

The number of years spent as a leader also varies widely. Managing Your Money and Dollars and Sense were co-leaders only briefly (firm data are not available) before being displaced by Quicken; Paradox was a leader for only a single year, if it can be considered a true leader. As discussed above, the presentation graphics category had no leader over the 1987-1994 period for which we had consistent data. Both Quicken and dBASE were leaders for more than a decade, with Quicken still leading today. The median number of years spent as a leader has been about five (with some products extending their leadership).

The table does not show how many revisions the products went through over time. For example, MS-DOS was in its second major version when it passed CP/M to become a leader. By the time it, in turn, was passed by Windows 3.1 at the end of 1992, it had gone through version 3 (of which there were several releases), version 4, and version 5, with version 6 still to come Windows was in its third major release before it became a leader. Initially released for the Macintosh, Excel went through three major releases fo Windows before becoming a category leader in 1993; it has gone through fou

Table 1. **Summary of Category Leaders for Microcomputer Software through 1997**

	Introduction Date	Leadership Start Date	Years to Leadership	Years Spent as Leader	Approximate Shares[1] (percent)		
					Leader	Second	Third
Word Processors: 1979-1997							
WordStar	1979	1980	1	5	na	na	na
WordPerfect[2]	1980	1987	7	6	41	21	10
MS Word	1983	1993	10	5+	62	26	9
Spreadsheets: 1979-1997							
VisiCalc	1979	1979	0	5	na	na	na
Lotus 1-2-3	1983	1984	1	9	51	20	12
MS Excel[3]	1985	1993	8	5+	69	26	5
Database: 1981-1997							
dBASE	1981	1981	0	12	59	9	8
Paradox	1985	1993	8	1	28	25	16
MS Access	1992	1994	2	4+	56	30	5
Personal Finance: 1985, 1989-1997							
Managing Your Money	1984		na	na	na	na	na
Dollars and Sense	1983		na	na	na	na	na
Quicken	1984	1987 (?)	3+	11+	67	11	7
Operating Systems: 1977-1997							
CP/M 4[4]	1974	1977	na	7			
MS-DOS/PC-DOS	1981	1984	3	9			
Windows (16-bit)	1985	1993	8	3			
Windows 95	1995	1996	1	2+			

Notes: Presentation graphics had no consistent leader in the 1987-1994 period.
[1]Median share for first-, second-, and third-placed competitors over the tenure of the leader.
[2]WordPerfect was released first for Data General in 1980 and for DOS in late 1982.
[3]Excel was released for the Macintosh in 1985 and for Windows in 1987.
[4]CP/M was developed circa 1974, but its first major OEM deals were in 1977.

Source: International Data Corporation. See references for specific titles.

more since then. Although it was not always true, Quicken is now updated on an annual basis. No product has remained a leader while staying unchanged.

CONCLUSIONS

Economists interested in network industries have sometimes asserted that "tipping can occur very rapidly"[48] to an outcome that may or may not be socially desirable. Our six case studies provide no evidence that "tipping can occur very rapidly" in these software categories, except in the case of products that essentially defined their categories (CP/M, dBASE, VisiCalc). It seems highly unlikely that social welfare would have been improved if would-be users of these products had been asked to wait for a competing product to come along to see which was better. The shifts from existing products to WordStar and 1-2-3 were fairly rapid, but these products were widely considered superior to their predecessors.

Economists interested in network industries have sometimes asserted that consumers can get "locked in" to a product, and that network effects can make it difficult for consumers to switch when a better product comes along. Our six case studies provide no evidence that such lock-in has occurred. The products with the greatest longevity are dBASE and Quicken, which would appear to be at the top and the bottom of the range of network effects. Although dBASE was a leader for about 12 years, no single version of dBASE lasted more than a few years as a leader. Major releases included dBASE II, dBASE III, dBASE III Plus, and dBASE IV. Users were not locked in – they kept switching from one version of dBASE to another (or to other products, as the combined share of the dBASE products fell continually after 1983). But, as noted above, changeover was never instantaneous. Excel was considered superior to 1-2-3 for several years before passing it.

There is no evidence that any product became a category leader without providing substantial new benefits to users. That is obviously true for the instant leaders in new categories (CP/M, VisiCalc, dBASE). In each of the other cases, however, products that gained the lead did so because the public (at least as represented by reviewers in the trade press) viewed them as superior. Besides instant leaders in new categories, no software application has come to lead a category without being rated the best or among the best products available. Additionally, no category leader has been able to maintain its lead for a significant time without remaining among the top picks of software reviewers.

* We would like to thank Cary Elliott, Terrence Kontos, and Matthew Leder for research help on this paper and Microsoft for financial support.

[1] It was later adapted for similar microprocessors, the Intel 8085 and the Zilog Z-80.

[2] Robert Slater, *Portraits in Silicon* (Cambridge, MA: MIT Press), p. 257.

[3] According to Manes and Andrews (p. 201), "Eventually the SoftCard would become the single most popular platform ever to run CP/M."

[4] Stephen Manes and Paul Andrews, *Gates* (New York: Touchstone), p. 192.

[5] The version of the operating system that Microsoft licensed to other computer manufacturers (OEMs) was known as MS-DOS.

[6] Manes and Andrews, p. 192.

[7] Ray Duncan, ed., *The MS-DOS Encyclopedia*, p. 26.

[8] Robert X. Cringely, *Accidental Empires* (HarperBusiness), 1996, pp. 154-155.

[9] Ray Duncan, ed., *The MS-DOS Encyclopedia*, p. 28.

[10] Manes and Andrews, p. 375.

[11] PC-DOS can be purchased from IBM. DR DOS can be purchased from the Lineo Corporation.

[12] Barbara Krasnoff, "The Word on Word Processors," *PC Magazine*, September 4, 1984, p. 112.

[13] George D. Hughes, Jr., "A MicroPro Family Portrait," *PC Magazine*, May 1, 1984, p. 271.

[14] M. David Stone, "WordStar 2000: Laden with Luxury," *PC Magazine*, April 16, 1985.

[15] W.E. Peterson, *Almost Perfect* (Prima Publishing), 1993, 1998, Chapter 5.

[16] Peterson, Chapter 6.

[17] Dawn Gordon, "The Business of Words," *PC Magazine*, January 28, 1986.

[18] Polsson. Lotus eventually acquired Ami, renaming it first AmiPro and then WordPro.

[19] "Technical Excellence," *PC Magazine*, December 20, 1994.

[20] In 1982, *Byte* magazine reported that there were 24 different spreadsheets available.

[21] "Calc Wars," *PC Magazine*, August 1982.

[22] Cringely, *Accidental Empires*, p. 156.

[23] "Thumbing Through the Spreadsheets," *PC Magazine*, April 17, 1984.

[24] A Macintosh version had been released in 1985; the initial Windows release was called version 2.0.

[25] Jared Taylor, "Excel: Microsoft's Second-Generation Spreadsheet," *PC Magazine*, November 10, 1987.

[26] Craig Stinson, "Lotus 1-2-3 for Windows," *PC Magazine*, December 31, 1991.

[27] Clifton Karnes, et al., "Test Lab: Spreadsheets," *Compute!*, May 1992.

[28] "Spreadsheets," *PC Magazine*, November 10, 1992.

[29] According to Intuit's Web site, "At the time of its release in 1984, Quicken was the 43rd personal finance software package on the market." http://www.intuit.com/corporate/history.html (accessed September 26, 1998).

[30] Don Crabb, "Packages Prove You Get Your Money's Worth," *InfoWorld*, April 14, 1986.

[31] Scott Mace, "Home Banking Helps Drive Growing Market," *InfoWorld*, April 14, 1986.

[32] Don Crabb, "Packages Prove You Get Your Money's Worth," *InfoWorld*, April 14, 1986.

[33] Loren Amsden, "Managing Your Money: Still the Best Personal Financial Tool," *PC Magazine*, February 10, 1987.

[34] Ken Landis, "Quicken: Personal Finance Software from Intuit," *MacUser*, November 1988.

[35] http://www.intuit.com/company/press_releases/2001/fact_sheet_02_Q1.pdf.

[36] "Quicken 6.0 Adds Electronic Credit Card Statements," *PC Magazine*, November 10, 1992.

[37] Excel 97 can save data in DBF formats.

[38] A search of Amazon.com for books with the term "dbase" in the title turned up 879 books.

[39] Glenn Hart, "Power Add-Ons for dBASE," *PC Magazine*, July 1986, p. 27.

[40] "dBASEing," *PC Magazine*, June 1983.

[41] Scott Mace, "Paradox Moves Ahead in Database Market," *InfoWorld*, September 18, 1989, p. 13.

[42] Richard Hale, "dBASE IV, Version 1.1 A New Beginning," *PC Magazine*, January 29, 1991.

[43] Microsoft recycled the name Access from an entirely different program it had released in the mid-1980s – a communications program. M. David Stone, "Microsoft Access: Power Offset by Slow Response," *PC Magazine*, November 26, 1985, p. 46.

[44] Sal Ricciardi, "End User Databases Balance of Power," *PC Magazine*, June 24, 1994.

[45] Excel 97 has excellent capabilities for handling simple queries and cross-tabs.

[46] Cyndi Privett, "Software Firm Launches New Line to Revive Sales," *The Business Journal–San Jose*, February 10, 1986.

[47] Peter Jackson, "Harvard v. Freelance: Now It's War!" *PC User*, November 6, 1991, p. 44.

[48] Daniel Rubinfeld, Deputy Assistant Attorney General for Antitrust, "Competition, Innovation, and Antitrust Enforcement in Dynamic Network Industries," speech before the Software Publishers Association, March 24, 1998; http://www.usdoj.gov/atr/public/speeches/1611.htm.

References

Amsden, Loren. 1987. "Managing Your Money: Still the Best Personal Financial Tool," *PC Magazine*, February 10.

Crabb, Don. 1986. "Packages Prove You Get Your Money's Worth," *Infoworld*, April 14.

Cringely, Robert X. 1996. *Accidental Empires*. HarperBusiness.

Dataquest. 1994. *Personal Computing Software Vendor Shipment and Revenue Data; Market Statistics 1994*, June.

Dataquest. 1995. *Personal Computing Software Vendor Shipment and Revenue Data; Market Statistics*, May.

Dataquest. 1989. *SWIS Worldwide Shipments and Forecasts*, July.

Duncan, Ray, ed. 1988. *The MS-DOS Encyclopedia* (Redmond, WA: Microsoft Press).

Gordon, Dawn. 1986. "The Business of Words," *PC Magazine*, January 28.

Hale, Richard. 1991. "dBase IV, Version 1.1 A New Beginning," *PC Magazine*, January 29.

Hart, Glenn. 1986. "Power Add-Ons for dBASE," *PC Magazine*, July, p. 27.

International Data Corporation. 1995. *Applications and Information Access – Cross-Industry View; PC Accounting and Personal Finance 1995 Software Review and Forecast*, September.

International Data Corporation. 1994. *Applications and Information Access: PC Accounting and Personal Finance Software Market Analysis, Review and Forecast, 1993-1998*, September.

International Data Corporation. 1997. Bulletin: *PC Word Processor Market Review and Forecast, 1996-2001*, May.

International Data Corporation. 1998. Bulletin: *PC Word Processor Market Review and Forecast, 1997-2002*, April.

International Data Corporation. 1998. *Client Operating Environments 1998 Worldwide Markets and Trends.*

International Data Corporation. 1993. *Desktop Database Review and Forecast, 1992-1997: The Windows Migration Has Begun*, June.

International Data Corporation. 1990. *PC Software, Graphical User Interfaces*, October.

International Data Corporation. 1991. *Graphical User Interfaces.*

International Data Corporation 1996. *IDC Flash: 1996 Preliminary Desktop Database Market Year in Review*, July.

International Data Corporation. 1997. *Operating Environments Review and Forecast, 1996-2001.*

International Data Corporation. 1993. *PC Accounting and Personal Finance Software Market Analysis, Review and Forecast, 1992-1997*, May.

International Data Corporation. 1989. *PC Database Management Systems Software*, September.

International Data Corporation. 1991. *PC Database Management Systems Software Market Analysis Review and Forecast, 1989-1994*, March.

International Data Corporation. 1989. *PC Operating Systems*, June.

International Data Corporation. 1991. *PC Operating Systems*, March.

International Data Corporation. 1991. *PC Operating Systems: Market Analysis, Review and Forecast, 1990-1995*, October.

International Data Corporation. 1996. *PC Operating Systems Market Review and Forecast, 1995-2000.*

International Data Corporation. 1995. *PC Operating Systems Market Review and Forecast, 1994-1999.*

International Data Corporation. 1991. *PC Operating Systems Outlook, 1990-1995.*

International Data Corporation. 1995. *The PC Single-User Database Market Review and Forecast, DOS, Windows, OS/2, and Macintosh, 1994-1999*, March.

International Data Corporation. 1992. *PC Software – Microsoft Windows Five-Year Forecast*, June.

International Data Corporation. 1989. *PC Spreadsheet Software: Market Review and Forecast, 1988*, November.

International Data Corporation. 1991. *PC Spreadsheet Software*, March.

International Data Corporation. 1992. *PC Spreadsheet Software 1991 Spreadsheet Report*, February.

International Data Corporation. *PC Spreadsheet Software Market Review and Forecast, 1992-1997.*

International Data Corporation. *PC Spreadsheet Market Review and Forecast, 1997-2002.*

International Data Corporation. 1989. *PC Windowing Software*, April.

International Data Corporation. 1995. *The Spreadsheet Software Market Review and Forecast: DOS, Windows, OS/2 and Macintosh, 1994-1999*, September.

International Data Corporation. 1998. *Word Processing Software: A Research Report Prepared for IDC Continuous Information Services Clients*, November.

International Data Corporation. 1991. *Word Processing Market Review and Forecast, 1990*, August.

International Data Corporation. 1992. *Word Processing Market Review and Forecast, 1991*, July.

International Data Corporation. 1990. *Word Processing Software, 1989*, December.

International Data Corporation. *PC Software: The Word Processing Software Markets Review and Forecast - DOS, Windows, OS/2, and Macintosh, 1994.*

International Data Corporation. 1995. *The Word Processing Software Market Review and Forecast, 1994-1999: DOS, Windows, OS/2, and Macintosh*, September.

International Data Corporation. 1998. *Worldwide Desktop Database Market Review and Forecast, 1997-2002*, April.

Intuit Inc., "Company History," 1998; http://www.intuit.com/corporate/history.html (accessed September 26, 1998).

Jackson, Peter. 1991. "Harvard v. Freelance: Now It's War!" *PC User*, November 6, p. 44.

Karnes, Clifton, et al. 1992. "Test Lab: Spreadsheets," *Compute!*, May.

Krasnoff, Barbara. 1984. "The Word on Word Processors," *PC Magazine*, September 4, p. 112.

Landis, Ken. 1988. "Quicken: Personal Finance Software from Intuit," *MacUser*, November.

Libes, Sol. 1982. "Spreadsheets Proliferate," *Byte*, June.

Mace, Scott. 1989. "Paradox Moves Ahead in Database Market," *Infoworld*, September 18, p. 13.

Mace, Scott. 1986. "Home Banking Helps Drive Growing Market," *Infoworld*, April 14.

Manes, Stephen, Andrews, Paul. 1994. *Gates*. New York: Touchstone.

Peterson, W.E. 1993, 1998. *Almost Perfect*. Prima Publishing.

Polsson, Ken. 1998. *Chronology of Events in the History of Microcomputers*, August 4. http://www.islandnet.com/~kpolsson/comphist.htm, accessed August 30, 1998.

Privett, Cyndi. 1986. "Software Firm Launches New Line to Revive Sales," *The Business Journal–San Jose*, February 10.

Ricciardi, Sal. 1994. "End User Databases Balance of Power," *PC Magazine*, June 24.

Slater, Robert. 1987. *Portraits in Silicon*. Cambridge, MA: MIT Press.

Stinson, Craig. 1991. "Lotus 1-2-3 for Windows," *PC Magazine*, December 31.

Stone, M. David. 1985. "Microsoft Access: Power Offset by Slow Response," *PC Magazine*, November 26, p. 46.

Taylor, Jared. 1987. "Excel: Microsoft's Second-Generation Spreadsheet," *PC Magazine*, November 10, pp. 33-34.

Section 2: Antitrust Policy and the New Economy

Essay 9

The Failure of Structural Remedies in Sherman Act Monopolization Cases

by Robert W. Crandall*

Antitrust problems, especially those created by the anticompetitive behavior of big corporations, demand bold structural solutions. This, at least, is the conventional wisdom within the interventionist school of antitrust policy – one that helps to explain why the Justice Department and 19 state attorneys general asked district court Judge Thomas Penfield Jackson to break Microsoft in two, and why the judge readily agreed.

Later, the D.C. Circuit Court of Appeals effectively removed divestiture from the roster of possible fixes. But the notion that major structural change has been an effective pro-competitive remedy in the past lives on.

Robert Crandall, an economist specializing in regulatory issues at the Brookings Institution, debunks this sturdy myth by analyzing the consequences of structural remedies – notably in the cases of Standard Oil, American Tobacco, Alcoa, Paramount, United Shoe Machinery, and AT&T, each of which was found liable under Section 2 of the Sherman Act.

In the most celebrated of the cases, the 1911 dissolution of John D. Rockefeller's Standard Oil trust into 38 separate companies, Crandall finds that the remedy had little effect because the expansion of the oil patch beyond the trust's reach had already eroded its market power. More recently, the "voluntary" breakup of AT&T did come at the cusp of an era of increasing competition and collapsing prices in telecommunications. But Crandall argues that the dissolution generated substantial inefficiencies – and that the benefits could have been had by regulatory changes that opened AT&T's markets without radical structural change. In three other cases he examined closely – American Tobacco (1911), Alcoa (1945), and Paramount (1948) – structural changes did not pay off in the form of greater price competition. Indeed, in the Paramount case, the evidence suggests that the changes led to higher prices.

"The important lesson," Crandall writes, "is that the government often lags the market in finding ways to increase competition, rendering antitrust cases redundant. In other cases, the government failed to formulate relief that resulted in any meaningful change in competition because it failed to grasp the essentials of the market that led to concentration in the first place. ... Given the rapid pace of technical progress that we are now encountering, there is little prospect that Section 2 will be employed more productively in the future than it has been in the past." — *D.S.E.*

INTRODUCTION

On June 7, 2000, Judge Thomas Penfield Jackson ordered that Microsoft be broken into two separate companies as the remedy for its monopolization of the market for PC operating system software.[1] This ruling marked the first major antitrust divestiture since the 1982 consent decree that broke AT&T into seven operating companies and a long-distance/manufacturing company.[2] It was also one of only a handful of examples of the breakup of a firm whose growth had not been the result of mergers. Given the size of Microsoft, its position in the U.S. economy, and the drastic nature of the relief ordered by the judge, this remedy could have had a major impact on American consumers if an appeals court had not reversed the judge. Is there any evidence on the likelihood that such relief can work? In this paper, I look at the historical record for clues.

Among the best-known U.S. antitrust cases are those that have been brought by the government under Section 2 of the Sherman Act, alleging that a firm has "monopolized" an industry. Actions in which the government prevailed include *Standard Oil*,[3] *American Tobacco*,[4] *Alcoa*,[5] *Paramount*,[6] *United Shoe Machinery*,[7] and *AT&T*.[8] The prevailing conventional wisdom is that in most of these cases the remedies were at least partially successful in restoring competition. However, there is a surprising lack of evidence to support such a view, in part because scholars have not attempted counterfactual analyses of the relevant industries.

Given the passage of time and the dearth of data for cases litigated decades ago, this review cannot always provide dispositive conclusions. However, there is sufficient evidence to question whether the government's victories and the structural relief it obtained had a beneficial effect on competition and economic welfare. Because the resources expended by the government and defendants on lengthy litigation and the ensuing structural relief are substantial, the long-run gains must also be substantial to justify restructuring. But in most cases the evidence does not support the conclusion that the court-imposed relief had its intended effect.

Identifying "Monopolization"

An essential part of any Section 2 Sherman Act case is identifying monopoly power and its sources. Under the case law, monopoly power is the power to exclude competitors and to raise prices. Determining whether a firm has such power requires inferences from data on market concentration, ease of entry, price-cost margins, and rates of return on capital. Even if a firm appears to possess monopoly power by any or all of these measures, however, it may not be guilty of "monopolizing." Monopoly power may have evolved naturally through economies of scale or scope, or because of patents or other intellectual capital. To prove monopolization, the government must demonstrate that this power was obtained by decisions whose intent was to exclude competition.[9]

Anecdotal evidence on the causes of rivals' failures will often suggest that predation was involved, but such evidence rarely withstands scrutiny. The defendant may have been innovative in developing products, distribution channels, marketing strategies, or backward integration into the supply of requisite inputs. If such strategies allowed it to price its products or services below those of its rivals or to otherwise offer a more attractive package to its customers, such a strategy could hardly be considered predatory. Nevertheless, the government may argue and the court may accept the argument that the practices are exclusionary. If so, the government may seek relief that limits the "bundling" of attractive features or that requires vertical divestiture.[10]

Remedies in Antitrust Cases

If the government has advanced an incorrect theory of how the defendant has achieved a monopoly position, its proposed remedies are likely to prove ineffective. For instance, the dissolution of the Standard Oil trust in 1911 had no discernible effects on output and prices in the petroleum industry after 1911 because Standard's market power was already eroding because of the success of entrants in the booming oil patches outside Standard's strongholds in Pennsylvania and Ohio. Establishing 38 independent companies by dissolving the trust thus had little impact on industry expansion in Oklahoma, Texas, or California. The alleged sins visited on Standard's early competitors in Pennsylvania or Ohio had nothing to do with the state of competition in Missouri, Kansas, Oklahoma, Texas, or California a decade later.

An antitrust decree may even be counterproductive by establishing an inefficient market structure. For example, the decree ordering vertical dissolution in the *Paramount* case broke the essential bonds between production, distribution, and exhibition arguably required for efficient production and distribution of motion pictures.[11] If this is true, the decree reduced consumer welfare until vertical integration was reestablished by downstream integration into cable television 30 years later or into Internet delivery more than 40 years later. Whether it was counterproductive or not, I show that the decree had no discernible effect on output and may have increased consumer prices.

A decree may also be ineffective because the government and the court fail to anticipate changes in technology or customer demand. In 1969, the government charged IBM with monopolizing the computer industry.[12] The case was dropped in 1982 when the assistant attorney general for antitrust acknowledged that the industry had changed drastically in the 1969-1982 period. Any theory that purportedly explained IBM's dominance of the market for 360 or 370 mainframe computers was not likely to provide a useful guide to establishing competition in an era in which IBM was struggling to compete with Apple in personal computers.[13] Surely, this should have been a warning to those who advocated a structural decree in the Microsoft case.

These problems are particularly acute in markets that have been regulated as monopolies for decades. For example, the Federal Communications Commission began to admit entrants into interstate telecommunications in 1969. By the mid-1970s, the FCC had lost control of this liberalization process and actually attempted to *block* the entry of MCI into ordinary long-distance services. When rebuffed by the courts, the FCC was forced to regulate inter-carrier connections to facilitate competition. Not surprisingly, it failed, and MCI struggled to take market share from AT&T. MCI and others eventually persuaded the government to bring a Section 2 Sherman Act suit against AT&T,[14] but a co-defendant in this suit should have been the FCC. As I demonstrate below, the FCC could have achieved at least as good a result without the costly disruption associated with the dissolution of AT&T.

Structural Versus Behavioral Relief

Remedies in Section 2 cases generally take one or both of two forms:

structural remedies and behavioral relief. With structural remedies, the court orders some change in the firm's or industry's organization. These changes may involve a horizontal divestiture through which two or more companies are created from the assets of the defendant. The dissolution of the Standard Oil trust created several quasi-independent refining companies simply by requiring that the various companies in the trust be spun off to Standard's stockholders. Or the relief may require vertical divestiture, the creation of separate companies at different stages of production. The *Paramount* case led to five decrees that divested the major film distributors' theater chains from their production–distribution operations.

Behavioral relief generally proscribes firm behavior that the government identified as anticompetitive, such as tying arrangements, collusive agreements to exclude competitors, and predatory pricing. Such prohibitions obviously require monitoring and are likely to result in numerous issues that have to be resolved by the courts.

Finally, relief may involve the compulsory licensing of intellectual property that is the source of the monopoly power. There have been a large number of such decrees, involving such diverse products as copying machines, motion picture film, glass, and oil well equipment.[15]

The ongoing costs of enforcing antitrust decrees can be very large. If an industry is changing rapidly, structural remedies may be difficult to enforce. For instance, it may be difficult to determine the demarcation point between stages of production. When television exhibition replaced theatrical exhibition of feature films, for example, would the *Paramount* defendants be allowed to own television stations, but not theaters? Could the divested Bell operating companies provide Internet service through *local* Internet service providers if the latter sent data packets across long-distance boundaries? What if the Bell-owned ISP connected with another entity within its own region, which in turn sent the data packets to the Internet backbone?

Most of the antitrust decrees analyzed here continued in effect for years, even decades. In many cases, these decrees required continual supervision. The *AT&T* decree, in particular, involved scores of hearings before the district court and created a backlog of unresolved disputes that had become very large when the decree was finally vacated by 1996 legislation. Approximately 35 to 40 waiver requests were filed per year in the first eight years of the decree, and by 1993 the average age of pending waiver requests had grown to four years.[16] This caseload was due in no small part to the changing nature of the telecommunications industry.

STRUCTURAL RELIEF IN MONOPOLIZATION CASES

I exhaustively reviewed antitrust remedies that were imposed as the result of government victories or consent decrees in monopolization cases brought by the government between 1890 and 1996. The goal was to determine the frequency and types of cases in which structural remedies were imposed.

To construct the database, I assembled all the relevant cases from the CCH Abstracts from 1890 to 1996. Of the more than 4,000 entries, I found 423 cases for which sufficient information was available and that met the initial criterion – a finding against the defendants or a consent decree in a monopolization case brought by the government.[17]

Of the 423 monopolization cases, 87 were criminal cases and 336 were civil cases. All 87 criminal cases resulted in monetary fines. As shown in Table 1, of the remedies in the 336 civil cases, 172 were behavioral remedies (51 percent), 69 involved compulsory licensing (21 percent), and 95 were structural remedies (28 percent).

Table 1. **Monopolization Cases That Resulted in Structural Remedies**

Case Name	Date Case Initiated	Violation	Type of Activity Involved	Relief
Standard Oil Co. of N.J.	11/15/06	Monopolization	Coordination between Firms	Dissolution
American Tobacco Co.	07/10/07	Monopolization	Mergers & Acquisitions	Divestiture
Du Pont de Nemours & Co.	07/30/07	Monopolization	Mergers & Acquisitions	Dissolution
Lake Shore Ry. Co.	08/04/11	Monopolization	Coordination between Firms	Limits on Business Activity
International Harvester Co.	04/30/12	Monopolization	Mergers & Acquisitions	Divestiture
Corn Products Co.	03/01/13	Monopolization	Mergers & Acquisitions	Dissolution
American Coal Products Co.	03/03/13	Monopolization	Mergers & Acquisitions	Dissolution
New Departure Mfg. Co.	05/27/13	Monopolization	Coordination between Firms	Dissolution
Eastman Kodak Co.	06/09/13	Monopolization	Mergers & Acquisitions	Divestiture
American Telephone & Telegraph Co.	07/24/13	Monopolization	Coordination between Firms	Limits on Business Activity
Reading Co.	09/02/13	Tying & Monopolization	Coordination between Firms	Dissolution
Lehigh Valley R.R. Co.	03/18/14	Monopolization	Mergers & Acquisitions	Dissolution
New York, New Haven & Hartford R.R. Co.	07/23/14	Monopolization	Coordination between Firms	Dissolution
New England Fish Exchange	06/21/17	Monopolization	Coordination between Firms	Dissolution
Grant F. Discher	12/04/17	Monopolization	Coordination between Firms	Dissolution
Ironite Co.	12/17/19	Monopolization	Coordination between Firms	Dissolution
Swift & Co.	02/27/20	Monopolization	Coordination between Firms	Limits on Business Activity
Sumatra Purchasing Corp.	04/13/20	Monopolization	Coordination between Firms	Dissolution
Barbers' Supply Dealers Ass'n.	05/07/20	Monopolization	Coordination between Firms	Dissolution

Case Name	Date Case Initiated	Violation	Type of Activity Involved	Relief
Goodwin-Gallagher Sand & Gravel Corp.	01/18/21	Monopolization	Mergers & Acquisitions	Dissolution
Oscar Kern	03/08/21	Monopolization	Coordination between Firms	Dissolution
Cement Securities Co.	01/10/22	Monopolization	Coordination between Firms	Dissolution
National Enameling & Stamping Co.	02/14/22	Monopolization	Coordination between Firms	Dissolution
Wickwire Spencer Steel Corp.	03/20/22	Monopolization	Coordination between Firms	Dissolution
Flower Producers Cooperative Ass'n.	12/15/25	Monopolization	Coordination between Firms	Dissolution
Ward Food Products Corp.	02/08/26	Monopolization	Mergers & Acquisitions	Dissolution
Lay Fish Co.	05/12/26	Monopolization	Coordination between Firms	Dissolution
Leibner & Co.	07/02/26	Monopolization	Coordination between Firms	Divestiture
Maine Co-Operative Sardine Co.	10/04/27	Monopolization	Coordination between Firms	Dissolution
Foster & Kleiser Co.	04/22/30	Monopolization	Mergers & Acquisitions	Limits on Business Activity
Radio Corp. of America	05/13/30	Monopolization	Coordination between Firms	Limits on Business Activity
Kansas City Ice Co.	06/05/34	Monopolization	Coordination between Firms	Dissolution
Aluminum Co. of America	04/23/37	Monopolization	Coordination between Firms	Limits on Business Activity
Paramount Pictures, Inc.	07/20/38	Tying & Monopolization	Coordination between Firms	Divestiture
Schine Chain Theatres, Inc.	08/07/39	Tying & Monopolization	Coordination between Firms	Divestiture
Crescent Amusement Co., Inc.	08/11/39	Monopolization	Coordination between Firms	Limits on Business Activity
The Pullman Co.	07/12/40	Monopolization	Mergers & Acquisitions	Divestiture
Washington Wholesale Grocers Ass'n.	07/01/42	Monopolization	Coordination between Firms	Dissolution
Auditorium Conditioning Corp.	08/19/43	Monopolization	Coordination between Firms	Dissolution
National Lead Co.	06/24/44	Monopolization	Coordination between Firms	Limits on Business Activity
Borax Consolidated Ltd.	09/14/44	Monopolization	Mergers & Acquisitions	Divestiture
Market Truckmen's Ass'n. of New York	04/19/45	Monopolization	Coordination between Firms	Dissolution
Libbey-Owens-Ford Glass Co.	05/23/45	Monopolization	Coordination between Firms	Limits on Business Activity
Pacific Greyhound Lines	10/24/45	Monopolization	Coordination between Firms	Divestiture
Scophony Corp. of America	12/18/45	Monopolization	Coordination between Firms	Limits on Business Activity
General Instrument Corp.	07/17/46	Monopolization	Coordination between Firms	Dissolution
A.B. Dick Co.	07/22/46	Tying & Monopolization	Coordination between Firms	Limits on Business Activity
North Coast Transportation Co.	11/20/46	Monopolization	Coordination between Firms	Divestiture
United Shoe Machinery Corp.	12/15/47	Tying & Monopolization	Mergers & Acquisitions	Divestiture
The Liquid Carbonic Corp.	06/24/48	Monopolization	Coordination between Firms	Divestiture
H.P. Hood & Sons, Inc. et al.	09/27/48	Monopolization	Mergers & Acquisitions	Divestiture
Inter-Island Steam Navigation Co. Ltd	12/17/48	Monopolization	Coordination between Firms	Limits on Business Activity
Besser Manufacturing Co.	04/28/49	Monopolization	Coordination between Firms	Limits on Business Activity
E.I. Du Pont de Nemours and Co.	06/30/49	Monopolization	Mergers & Acquisitions	Limits on Business Activity

Case Name	Date Case Initiated	Violation	Type of Activity Involved	Relief
New York Great Atlantic & Pacific Tea Co., Inc	09/15/49	Monopolization	Coordination between Firms	Dissolution
Food Machinery and Chemical Corp.	11/21/49	Tying & Monopolization	Coordination between Firms	Dissolution
Harry F. Stern	12/16/49	Monopolization	Coordination between Firms	Dissolution
The Davis Co.	12/28/49	Monopolization	Coordination between Firms	Dissolution
Ass'n. of American Battery Mfrs.	02/06/50	Monopolization	Coordination between Firms	Dissolution
Lee Shubert	02/21/50	Monopolization	Coordination between Firms	Divestiture
General Outdoor Advertising Co., Inc.	06/30/50	Tying & Monopolization	Mergers & Acquisitions	Limits on Business Activity
Kobe, Inc.	04/10/51	Monopolization	Coordination between Firms	Limits on Business Activity
Allied Florists Ass'n. of Illinois	06/29/51	Monopolization	Coordination between Firms	Dissolution
International Business Machines Corp.	01/21/52	Tying & Monopolization	Single Firm	Divestiture
International Boxing Club of New York Inc.	03/17/52	Monopolization	Coordination between Firms	Dissolution
Alliance Theatre Corp. et al.	04/02/52	Monopolization	Coordination between Firms	Limits on Business Activity
National Ice and Cold Storage Co. et al.	06/11/52	Monopolization	Coordination between Firms	Dissolution
The Kansas City Star Co. et al.	01/06/53	Tying & Monopolization	Single Firm	Divestiture
Standard Oil Co. (N.J.) et al.	04/21/53	Monopolization	Coordination between Firms	Divestiture
Liberty National Life Insurance Co., et al.	06/29/54	Monopolization	Coordination between Firms	Limits on Business Activity
United Fruit Co.	07/02/54	Monopolization	Mergers & Acquisitions	Divestiture
Seafarers Sea Chest Corp. et al.	08/20/54	Monopolization	Coordination between Firms	Limits on Business Activity
National Linen Service Corp.	04/25/55	Monopolization	Mergers & Acquisitions	Divestiture
Maryland and Virginia Milk Producers Ass'n., Inc.	11/21/56	Monopolization	Coordination between Firms	Divestiture
True Temper Corp.	06/30/58	Monopolization	Coordination between Firms	Limits on Business Activity
American Cynamid Co. et al.	10/05/60	Monopolization	Coordination between Firms	Divestiture
Greater Buffalo Press, Inc. et al.	01/06/61	Monopolization	Mergers & Acquisitions	Limits on Business Activity
The Grinnell Corp	04/13/61	Monopolization	Mergers & Acquisitions	Limits on Business Activity
American Optical Co. et al.	12/29/61	Monopolization	Coordination between Firms	Limits on Business Activity
Greater New York Roll Bakers Ass'n. Inc. et al.	06/07/62	Monopolization	Coordination between Firms	Dissolution
MCA Inc.	07/13/62	Tying & Monopolization	Mergers & Acquisitions	Dissolution
Blue Chip Stamp Co. et al.	12/26/63	Monopolization	Coordination between Firms	Divestiture
Philadelphia Ass'n. of Linen Suppliers	02/26/64	Monopolization	Coordination between Firms	Dissolution
E. W. Scripps Co.	05/27/64	Monopolization	Mergers & Acquisitions	Limits on Business Activity
Chrysler Corp. and Mack Trucks, Inc.	07/30/64	Monopolization	Mergers & Acquisitions	Limits on Business Activity

Case Name	Date Case Initiated	Violation	Type of Activity Involved	Relief
Broadcast Music, Inc.	12/10/64	Monopolization	Coordination between Firms	Limits on Business Activity
The Citizen Publishing Co. et al.	01/04/65	Monopolization	Mergers & Acquisitions	Limits on Business Activity
Pittsburgh Brewing Co. et al.	12/28/65	Monopolization	Mergers & Acquisitions	Limits on Business Activity
Mid-America Dairymen, Inc.	12/27/73	Monopolization	Coordination between Firms	Divestiture
American Telephone & Telegraph Co.	11/20/74	Monopolization	Single Firm	Divestiture
CBS, Inc.	12/10/74	Monopolization	Coordination between Firms	Limits on Business Activity
American Broadcasting Companies, Inc.	12/10/74	Monopolization	Coordination between Firms	Limits on Business Activity
National Broadcasting Co., Inc.	12/10/74	Monopolization	Coordination between Firms	Limits on Business Activity
Hospital Affiliates International	09/25/80	Monopolization	Mergers & Acquisitions	Divestiture
GTE Corp.	05/04/83	Monopolization	Mergers & Acquisitions	Limits on Business Activity

Of the 95 cases in Table 1, 63 resulted in a divestiture or dissolution and 32 in restrictions on business activities. In the latter cases, a firm might be barred from offering certain goods or services or be required to sell as well as lease its products. I distinguish these prohibitions from outright divestiture or dissolution, which requires the separation of a firm's assets, the sale of certain divisions, or the dissolution of an entire trade association. For example, the line-of-business restrictions imposed on the Bell Operating Companies in the 1982 AT&T decree would be classified as a *structural* remedy, not as a behavioral remedy. If these restrictions required the sale or spinoff of assets, as the AT&T decree surely did, it would be defined as a "divestiture."

For each of the cases in Table 1, I created three separate subcategories reflecting the activities that led to the firm(s) being charged with monopolization: (1) cases in which *mergers and acquisitions* were central to the government's case, (2) cases involving *coordinated price behavior* among defendants, and (3) cases in which neither mergers and acquisitions nor coordinated price behavior were central elements (*single-firm* cases). Note that a very large share of the divestiture cases involved either price coordination (i.e., price-fixing or market-sharing conspiracies) or mergers and acquisitions that led to monopoly power.

Singling out the cases that resulted in structural relief is important because the problems in effecting such relief are likely to be very different across the three categories. First, divestiture in cases involving pricing coordination is generally quite simple because dissolution of a trade association is straightforward and does not necessarily imperil the viability or efficiency of the independent firms involved. Similarly, divestiture of recently merged entities is much more easily accomplished than the breakup of a firm that is not a combination of recently independent companies. However, divestiture of a single organic firm can be much more problematic in terms of lost output or producer efficiency. And courts are understandably reluctant to order relief that may not be sustainable in the marketplace.

For example, Judge Wyzanski resisted divestiture in *United Shoe Machinery* because of the difficulty in dividing up a company with only one plant.[18] Similarly, the court left intact the Standard Oil companies that comprised the trust, fearing the effects of a more drastic divestiture.[19]

Of the 63 cases in which divestiture or dissolution was imposed, 17 involved mergers and acquisition(s), 43 resulted from coordinated price behavior, and only three were single-firm divestitures in which neither conspiracy nor acquisitions were involved. Another three cases in the coordination category, the three network television cases brought in the 1970s, resulted in less drastic structural relief. Table 2 lists the cases that did not allege coordinated price behavior or mergers and acquisitions, but resulted in divestiture or dissolution.

To summarize, of the 95 monopolization cases that resulted in structural relief, only three led to divestiture when a single firm was charged with monopolization without resort to mergers and acquisitions or coordinated pricing

Table 2. **Monopolization or Tying Cases Involving Firms Not Involved in Conspiracies or Acquisitions that Resulted in Divestiture or Dissolution**

Case	Year Filed	Violation	Relief Provisions
International Business Machines Corp.	1952	Monopolization & Tying	Divestiture
The Kansas City Star Co. et al.	1953	Monopolization, Tying & Exclusive Dealing	Divestiture
United Shoe Machinery (See text)	1947	Tying & Monopolization	Behavioral in Initial Phase: Divestiture 15 Years Later
American Telephone & Telegraph Co.	1974	Monopolization	Divestiture

behavior. In addition, I include *United Shoe Machinery* in this list in Table 2 because it was eventually required to spin off assets 15 years after the trial judge refused to order such relief. In another of the "landmark" monopolization cases, *Alcoa* (filed in 1937), a single-firm monopoly was not broken up despite having been found in violation of Section 2 of the Sherman Act. The trial judge held that sale of government-owned assets would provide sufficient structural "relief."[20]

THE LEADING CASES

The essence of monopoly power is the ability to raise prices through the control of output and entry. Therefore, for a Section 2 decree to have a beneficial effect, it should lead to greater output and lower prices. In addition, entry or the increased threat of entry should increase innovation. Where possible, I provide some evidence of changes in market shares, the profitability of the defendant(s) before and after the decree, and the returns to stockholders. These measures are used to develop tentative conclusions about the success of the relief that was built into the decree.[21]

Standard Oil

John D. Rockefeller and associates formed the company in Ohio in 1870.[22] In its early years, Standard Oil refined and marketed oil produced in Pennsylvania, Ohio, and Indiana. Over time, however, it expanded to a large number of surrounding states and developed transportation and production facilities for processing crude oil from a number of states. From its beginning, Standard Oil was controversial because of its aggressive conduct, particularly in negotiating contracts for transporting its oil on eastern railroads and in its alleged use of predatory pricing. It was the subject of numerous state and federal actions, culminating in a Sherman Act suit in 1906.[23] The Trust was eventually broken up in 1911 after the government prevailed.

Oil Production

Crude oil was discovered in Pennsylvania in 1859. Production rose steadily in Pennsylvania and then on the Ohio–Indiana border in the 1870s. In 1899, production in the Mid-Continent (Kansas–Oklahoma), Gulf (Texas–Louisiana), and California fields accounted for just 7 percent of total U.S. output.[24] The oil boom in Texas, Kansas, California, and Oklahoma began in earnest in 1901-02, and by 1909 these areas accounted for nearly two-thirds of U.S. crude production.[25] As Figure A-1 shows, crude oil production grew slowly for 17 years after 1883, but began to accelerate in 1901-1910 because of the exploitation of these western fields. Surprisingly, production growth slowed somewhat from 1910 until 1919 despite growth in the economy stimulated by World War I.[26]

Figure A-1. **U.S. Oil Production Versus Real GNP, 1870-1925**

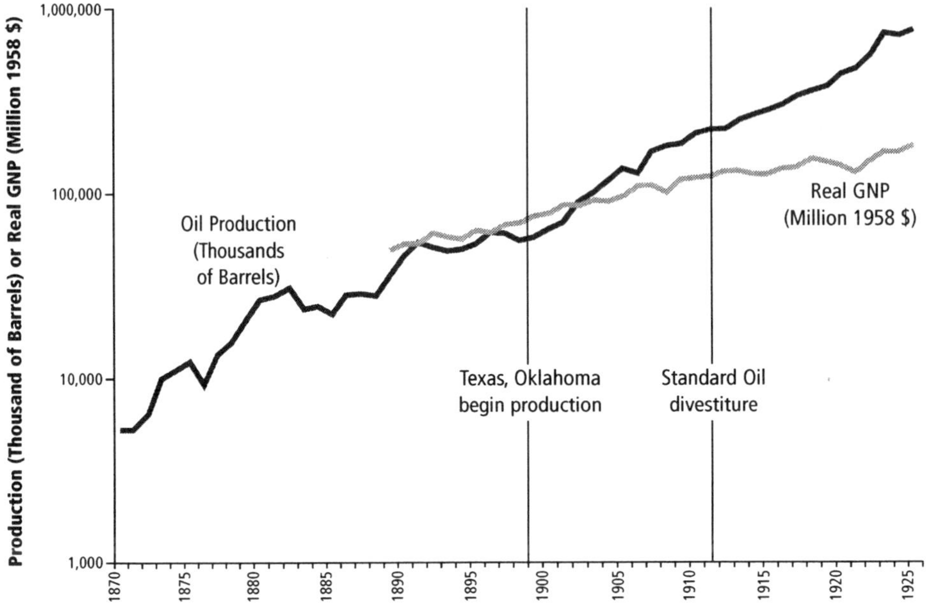

Source: U.S. Bureau of the Census, *Historical Statistics of the United States, Colonial Times to 1970, Bicentennial Edition* (U.S. Department of Commerce), 1975, pp. 593-594.

The rapid growth in oil output in the 1900-1910 period is clearly attributable to a dramatic shift in supply, not simply to the introduction of the automobile. There were only 190,000 motor vehicles registered in the U.S. as late as 1910, and gasoline production accounted for less than 25 percent of the domestic shipments of refined petroleum products as late as 1914.[27]

Most refined oil was used as lubricant, as fuel to power industry and heat commercial and residential buildings, or for illumination. The prices of these latter refined products fell in the first decade of the 20th century, but the price of gasoline did not because of technological constraints on gasoline production.

Industry Structure

In its formative years, Standard Oil purchased crude oil from Pennsylvania and Indiana–Ohio producers and arranged for transportation to its refineries. With time, an ever-larger share was transported through Standard's own pipelines, which it used to control output.[28] When the Mid-Continent and Gulf fields opened, however, Standard was unable to achieve a similar dominant position through controlling pipelines. Gulf Oil, the Texas Company, Sun Oil, and a host of independents prospered throughout the 1901-1910 period.[29]

Refining evolved because of changing product demand and improvements in technology. The share of gasoline in total output rose steadily in the early 20th century as the stock of motor vehicles increased. The development of new technologies, such as cracking, was required to increase the yield of gasoline and other volatile compounds.

The Standard companies and their large competitors, Union Oil, the Texas Company, Pure Oil, Cudahy, and Gulf Oil, built terminals for wholesale distribution of fuel oil, kerosene, gasoline, and lubricating oils. But the shift away from kerosene toward fuel oil and gasoline required major new investments in distribution facilities that opened the door for Standard's competitors in the 12 years leading up to the 1911 dissolution. In 1899, Standard's competitors accounted for only 15 percent of the domestic market for all refined products. By 1911, they supplied nearly 70 percent of the country's fuel oil, 34 percent of the gasoline, and one-quarter of the kerosene.[30] For the most part, these products were sold by the integrated (i.e., refiner-owned) and independent wholesalers to an independent retail sector and directly to large industrial users.

Oil Prices

Crude oil prices fell sharply in real terms during the formative years of Standard Oil and continued their decline until 1892.[31] For the rest of the 1890s, the real price of crude rose as production growth slowed. However, from 1900 until 1911 real prices fell once again in response to the sharp increase in production from the newly developed Mid-Continent, Gulf, and California fields (See Figure A-2). Standard Oil was scrambling to build new refineries to compete with Sun Oil, Gulf Oil, and the Texas Company. As it expanded its refinery output and distribution, it would reduce prices selectively to compete with the non-Standard companies. In response, Standard's competitors – including the smaller local refineries – pressed a number of states to pass "antidiscrimination" laws preventing any company from reducing its prices in one part of the state without reducing them everywhere.

Perhaps as a result of these antidiscrimination laws, the price of refined products did not decline with the sharp decline in crude-oil prices between 1900 and 1910 (See Figure A-2). The widening price gap between crude and refined products was an issue in a series of legal actions against the Standard Oil trust that were to culminate in the Sherman Act case in 1906. One of the reasons for this gap, however, was the shift toward gasoline at a time when refinery output of gasoline was constrained by technology.

The spread between gasoline and kerosene prices widened from 3.9 cents in 1909 to a peak of 17 cents in 1917. During this period, the price of kerosene

Figure A-2. **Real U.S. Oil Prices, 1870-1925**

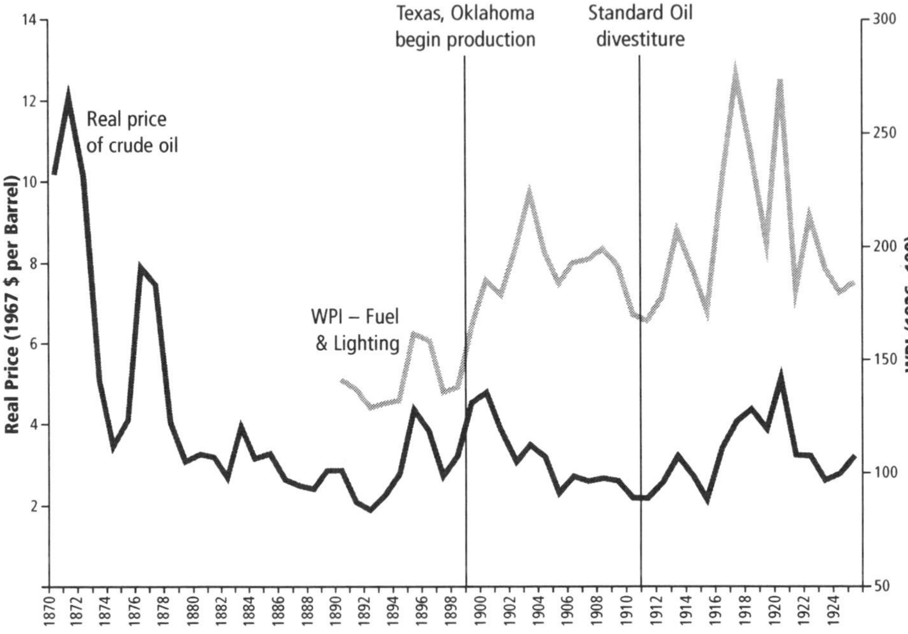

Note: The Wholesale Price Index for Fuel & Lighting and the Real Price of Crude Oil are deflated by the Consumer Price Index for all urban consumers.

Sources: U.S. Bureau of the Census, *Historical Statistics of the United States, Colonial Times to 1970, Bicentennial Edition*, (U.S. Department of Commerce), 1975, pp. 200, 593-594; and the Bureau of Labor Statistics Internet site (http://www.bls.gov/).

was relatively stable, declining from 9.5 cents per gallon to 6 cents per gallon between 1909 and 1911, then returning to 9 cents per gallon for virtually all of the 1913-17 period. By contrast, gasoline prices nearly doubled between 1909 and 1917, rising from 13.4 cents per gallon to 26 cents per gallon.[32]

The domestic demand for gasoline was increasing rapidly because of the increase in the number of motor vehicles, but the demand for kerosene – used largely for illumination – was rising more modestly. With constraints on the proportion of refined output that could be produced as gasoline, this increase in the demand for gasoline relative to the demand for other products placed pressure on gasoline prices relative to the prices of other refined products. In addition, the onset of World War I led to a sharp increase in gasoline exports while kerosene exports declined. As a result, the spread between real gasoline prices rose dramatically in the 1914-17 period (See Figure A-3).

The Antitrust Case and Its Antecedents

Complaints about Standard Oil's business practices took a number of

Figure A-3. **Real Petroleum Prices, 1899-1925**

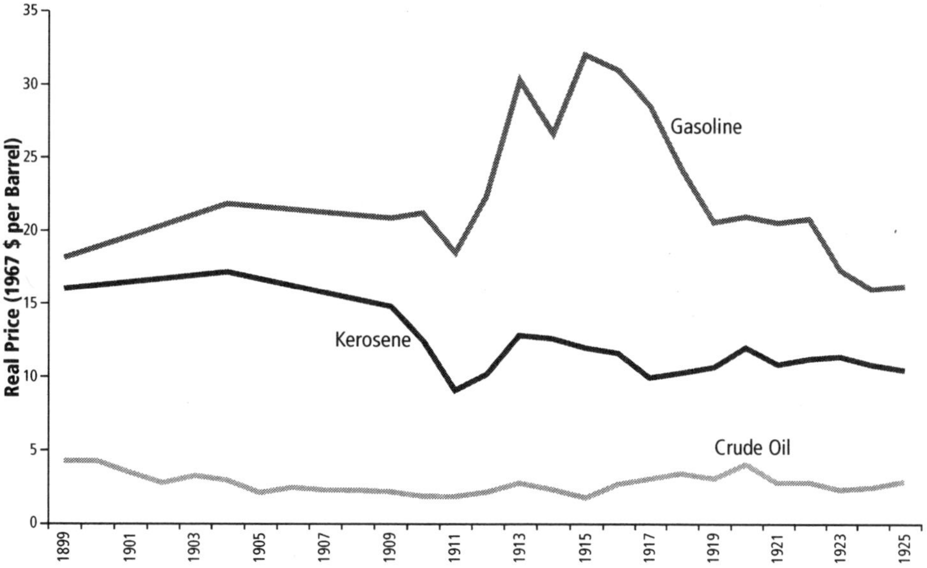

Note: Gasoline and kerosene prices are deflated by the Consumer Price Index for all urban consumers. Crude oil prices are deflated by the GNP deflator.

Sources: Williamson et al., *supra* note 23, pp. 172, 457; U.S. Bureau of the Census, *Historical Statistics of the United States, Colonial Times to 1970, Bicentennial Edition* (U.S. Department of Commerce), 1975, pp. 224, 593-594; Bureau of Labor Statistics Internet site (http://www.bls.gov/).

forms. First, it was alleged that Standard Oil used ruthless practices in negotiating transportation contracts with railroads through its South Improvement Company and later in denying independents access to its own pipelines. Second, Standard Oil was alleged to have used selective price cuts to drive rivals from the market.[33] Third, the public feared that Standard Oil's secretive organization – the Standard Oil "trust" – gave it unspecified market power. Finally, it was alleged that Standard Oil used its organization to create a price-fixing conspiracy, complete with profit "pools."[34]

The lower court ruled that Standard had violated Sections 1 and 2 of the Sherman Act by engaging in a massive restraint of trade by monopolizing interstate commerce in petroleum products.[35] The lower court decision was handed down in St. Louis on November 20, 1909 and was upheld by the Supreme Court on May 15, 1911, with Justice White writing the opinion.[36] At the time of the trial, the Standard companies controlled 72 percent of Appalachian crude oil supplies, 95 percent of the Ohio–Indiana supply, and 100 percent of the Illinois supply. However, they controlled only between 10 and 45 percent of the Mid-Continent, 10 percent of Gulf Coast, and 29 percent of California supplies, which collectively accounted for two-thirds of U.S.

supply by the time Chief Justice White penned his opinion. In the first 12 years of the 20th century, Standard's refinery capacity fell from 82 percent to 64 percent of the U.S. total.[37]

Although substantial, Standard's shares of the refined-products market were also in decline before the antitrust case was finally decided. Its share of the kerosene market had fallen from 85 percent to 75 percent from 1899 to 1906-1911. In the more rapidly growing fuel oil and gasoline markets, Standard's average shares were lower and also falling. By 1906-1911, its share of fuel oil sales had declined to just 31 percent from 85 percent in 1899. In gasoline, Standard accounted for 66 percent of sales in 1906-1911, down from 85 percent in 1899.[38]

The courts found that Standard's aggressive behavior in transporting oil and pricing refined products constituted sufficient evidence of a willful strategy to monopolize the country's petroleum industry. But they also found that the manner in which Standard reconstituted its trust in New Jersey, after an Ohio court had invalidated the earlier Ohio trust, to be particularly offensive. Clearly, the federal circuit court and the Supreme Court saw the New Jersey trust as a set of potentially competing companies that had been brought together for the purpose of restraining trade.

The relief decree was rather simple in design. It required that the New Jersey trust be dissolved and that the stock in each of the constituent companies be spun off to Standard's stockholders. As a result, 38 separate companies were established as independent entities, albeit with common ownership. However, the Court was explicit that no single entity was to control these companies henceforth. The company complained that the dissolution created a set of uneconomic companies, many of which had insufficient upstream or downstream integration to compete successfully, and that the pipeline companies would be deprived of the essential network economies for which they were mutually designed. Its complaints were rejected by the Court.

The Effect of the Dissolution

The enormous discoveries of oil in Oklahoma, Texas, and California and the rapid shift to gasoline from other refined products after 1910 would have made it difficult for the Standard Oil trust to maintain its position even without the dissolution mandated by the court. To estimate the effect of the dissolution on the output and price of crude oil, I estimated two reduced-form regression equations in which the exogenous variables are real GNP, total U.S. automobile registrations, total U.S. electricity production, two time trends for the period prior to 1901 and the period thereafter, and a dummy variable equal

Table A-1. **The Determinants of U.S. Crude-Oil Production and Price, 1889-1917 (t-statistics in parentheses)**

Dependent Variable	Time Period	Constant	Time Trend (89-00)	Time Trend (01-17)	Real GNP	Automobile Registrations	Electricity Production	Dissolution Dummy (1912-1917=1)	R^2
U.S. Production	1889-1917	67270 (4.34)	656.6 (0.71)	9590 (4.25)	-407.6 (-1.27)		3.4779 (4.36)	-11485 (-1.79)	0.995
U.S. Production	1900-1917	75418 (2.72)		12350 (2.68)	-464.8 (-1.30)	1.4711 (0.21)	2.3464 (0.90)	-12668 (-1.85)	0.994
Real U.S. Crude Oil Price	1889-1917	1.9874 (1.45)	0.1248 (1.54)	-0.5636 (-2.83)	0.007368 (0.26)		0.000197 (2.80)	0.4975 (0.88)	0.560
Real U.S. Crude Oil Price	1900-1917	2.465 (1.52)		-0.7986 (-2.97)	0.0208 (1.00)	-0.000206 (-0.50)	0.000300 (1.97)	0.4492 (1.13)	0.756

Note: For each of the four regressions, standard tests for the presence of heteroscedasticity or autocorrelation were conducted. In each case, there was no evidence of these problems at standard confidence levels.

to zero prior to 1912 and one thereafter to capture any effects of the decree.[39] These variables capture the effects of aggregate demand and other influences on the demand for petroleum as well as the supply shift that occurred just after the turn of the century due to the opening up of the new western fields. The period of estimation is 1889-1917, which includes the era before the antitrust case and six years after the decree. The results are exhibited in Table A-1 for both the entire period and for 1900-1917, a shorter period for which data on all variables are available.[40]

These results generally confirm the effect of new discoveries after 1900, but do not suggest any influence of automobile registrations in the period through 1917. The coefficients for the dummy variable for the period following the dissolution of Standard Oil are not statistically significant. The oil production estimates suggest a perverse effect of the decree – the coefficient for the 1912+ dummy variable is marginally significant and *negative* in the total production equation, suggesting that output fell after the dissolution.[41] Thus, the most conservative interpretation of these results is that the dissolution had, at best, no effect.

Indeed, it appears that the stock market had discounted these possibilities in advance. Despite the apparently drastic remedy, the price of the Standard Oil of New Jersey stock and its successor companies rebounded in 1911 after the Supreme Court decision and soared in 1912. Burns has found that this rebound was greater than the decline in the value of Standard's stock in 1906 when the government's complaint was announced.[42] He suggests that this was the result of recognition by the market of the "benign" nature of the decree.[43]

An alternative explanation is that the decree could not reduce Standard's market power in markets where it had none.

I have confirmed Burns's basic results using monthly data on the returns to holding Standard Oil (NJ) common stock and on the Dow Jones Average in the standard Capital Asset Pricing Model.[44] The announcement of the antitrust suit initially depressed Standard's equity price – i.e., created a negative excess return – by 10.9 percent in the month it was announced, but the stock partially recovered. Five months after the announcement of the suit, the cumulative negative excess return had been reduced to 5.8 percent (See Table A-2). In the month that the trial court's decision was announced, November 1909, Standard shareholders once again suffered a negative excess return of 3.8 percent, but this entire loss was recovered within the next five months. Finally, the Supreme Court decision of May 1911 reduced shareholder excess returns by about 4 percent through August 1911, the last month in which the old Standard company remained intact. If one uses a six-month "window" after the first two events to assess the stock market's reaction to antitrust developments, the overall effect on shareholders is only an 8 percent negative excess return. Over the entire period from November 1906 to the end of the old Standard Oil in August 1911, however, the cumulative excess returns from the capital asset pricing model are very large and positive. Overall, these results confirm that investors did not expect the adverse antitrust ruling to have negative repercussions for Standard Oil shareholders.

Table A-2. **The Excess Returns to Stockholders of Standard Oil (NJ) During Major Antitrust Events, 1906-1911**

Event	Excess Return in Same Month	Cumulative Excess Returns Over Six Months
Antitrust Case Filed (November 1906)	-10.9%	-5.8%
Lower Court Decision and Decree (November 1909)	-3.8%	+1.6%
Supreme Court Decision (May 1911)	-2.0%	-4.1%*

* Cumulative return for the only four months of available data for old equity shares of Standard Oil (NJ).

The decree established 10 refining companies, but these companies were separated by substantial distances and were unlikely to begin competing against each other very soon after the decree. All were simply set free with their assets. Some, such as Standard of California and Standard of New Jersey, had extensive pipeline and marketing facilities. Others, such as Standard of Kansas, had none. Ohio Oil and Prairie Oil and Gas were crude oil producers with pipelines, but South Penn Oil was left as a crude oil producer without pipelines.[45] In short, the post-dissolution structure of the industry was largely an accident of Standard's pre-1911 corporate organization.

The erstwhile Standard companies' share of output of refined products continued to fall after the decree, but the decline was simply an extension of the 1899-1911 trend (See Table A-3).

Table A-3. **Standard's Share of Refined Output, 1899-1920 (Percent)**

Region	1899	1911	1920
Eastern	87	80	78
Mid-Continent and Gulf	NA	39	33
Rocky Mountain	NA	NA	95
California	NA	29	29
Total U.S.	82*	64*	50**

* Percent of "control" over refinery capacity

** Percent of crude oil "consumed" by refineries

NA = Not available

Source: Williamson et al., *supra* note 23, pp. 7, 16-17 and 166.

Indeed, the rate of decline in the Standard companies' share of refined output, as measured by capacity of crude oil consumed, increased only from -2.0 percent per year to -2.7 percent per year after 1911.[46] Of course, the Standard companies were independent only in theory after the 1911 dissolution because independence was constrained for a time by common stock ownership.

Since the Standard companies were the major purchasers of crude oil, if their alleged monopoly – and monopsony – position had been damaged by the dissolution, one might have expected crude oil prices to rise sharply after 1911. But as Figure A-2 shows, real crude oil prices rose only slightly between 1911 and 1913, and then fell for two years. Thereafter, spurred by strong demand during World War I, they rose sharply and then receded to 1911 levels by 1923. Moreover, oil production actually grew more rapidly in the decade prior to the 1911 decree than in the decade that followed (Figure A-1).

It would be difficult to ascribe any of these price movements to the antitrust decree. Indeed, as we have seen, Standard companies controlled less than one-third of the total output from the three new oil-producing regions when the decree was entered, and their share of crude oil purchases in these regions had been falling. The regions in which the Standard companies continued to be dominant accounted for just 12.7 percent of oil production by 1919. It is difficult to see how separating the various Standard pipeline or refining-pipeline companies from each other would have increased competition for crude materially in the newer oil-producing regions if there was already aggressive competition from large, well-capitalized independents such as Gulf Oil, Union Oil, the Texas Company, Sun Oil, Phillips, and Cities Service.[47]

Nor is there evidence that the dissolution had any effect on refined product prices. Figure A-3 shows that real kerosene prices rose slightly after the decree – particularly during the first few years of World War I – but then receded to their 1911-12 levels. Gasoline prices, on the other hand, had been declining prior to 1911, but then soared with rising demand during World War I. Technological change in refining processes eventually narrowed the gap between kerosene and gasoline prices, but the gap remained above its 1911 level until the 1920s.

Concluding Assessment

There is simply no evidence that the *Standard Oil* decree, which created 38 quasi-independent companies by dissolving the Standard Oil trust – had much effect on output or prices in the U.S. oil industry. Whatever the merits of the government's case for the pre-1900 industry, it appears that the case had already been made moot by competitive developments in the early 1900s. The decree might have worked to restore competition prior to 1900, but by 1911 the oil industry was very different and the decree was not needed.

American Tobacco

Like Standard Oil, the American Tobacco Company was organized as a trust. It was first incorporated in 1890, and by 1909 the trust had grown to include 86 companies in the United States, Cuba, and Puerto Rico and 33 others in other parts of the world.[48]

Market Position

The company dominated production of all U.S. tobacco products other than cigars, accounting for between 76 percent and 96 percent of the output of such products as plug tobacco, smoking tobacco, snuff, and cigarettes in 1910 (See Table B-1).

This market position was obtained through acquisitions, including the Union Tobacco Company and the Continental Tobacco Company, and extremely aggressive pricing, allegedly including sales at prices below manu-

Table B-1. **American Tobacco's Share of U.S. Output, 1910 (Percent)**

Product	American Tobacco Trust Share
Cigarettes	86.1
Plug	84.9
Smoking	76.2
Fine Cut	79.7
Snuff	96.5
Little Cigars	91.4
Cigars	14.4

Source: Richard B. Tennant, *The American Cigarette Industry: A Study in Economic Analysis and Public Policy* (Yale University Press), 1950, p. 27.

facturing costs.[49]

Between 1890 and 1910, U.S. production of cigarettes increased fourfold, from 2.5 billion to 10 billion cigarettes. Although it lost market share to new "Turkish" brands of cigarettes in the early 1900s, the American Tobacco trust's share of domestic output recovered to approximately 85 percent by 1910. Throughout this period, its overall rate of return on tangible assets varied substantially, declining from about 54 percent in 1890 to only 16 percent in 1899, but rising thereafter to more than 35 percent in 1903.[50]

The Antitrust Suit

The American Tobacco trust was challenged in numerous state antitrust actions in the 1890s, but the trust generally prevailed in these actions. The 1904 *Northern Securities*[51] decision forced a reorganization of the Tobacco trust, but it was not until 1908 that the government filed its major Sherman Act case against the tobacco producers, seeking to dissolve the trust entirely. This case was decided in favor of the government, and an injunction was entered against American Tobacco that barred it from operating in interstate commerce until the conditions that existed prior to the formation of the trust were restored.[52] The Supreme Court found this remedy too drastic, ordering instead that the lower court hold hearings to determine a "plan or method for dissolving the combination."[53]

The lower court subsequently approved a dissolution that divided cigarette production into three parts. American kept assets that accounted for approximately 37 percent of cigarette production, P. Lorillard had 15 percent, and a new company, Liggett and Myers, received the assets to produce brands that accounted for 28 percent of cigarette output.[54] There were similar divisions of assets for plug tobacco, smoking tobacco, and cigars. Restrictive covenants provided by firms and individuals that had sold out to the trust were declared invalid.

Although individual stockholders' control of the voting rights in the new companies were somewhat reduced, the large stockholders continued to hold important positions in all three major companies that emerged from the decree. This ongoing control by the former owners of the trust was very controversial at the time of dissolution, as was the three-firm oligopoly structure established by the decree. The lower court rejected objections based on these concerns, asserting that it was a court of law, not a commerce commission.[55]

The Effect of the Decree

The dissolution of the American Tobacco trust occurred very quickly. The court's decree was entered in November 1911, and the changes were effected by February 1912. According to Tennant, the immediate practical effect was to unleash a battle for market share, carried out largely through advertising.[56] The three-firm oligopoly did not engage in vigorous price competition. With the incredibly successful introduction of the Camel brand, Reynolds became the industry's price leader.

Cigarette prices were essentially stable in the 1909-1913 period (See Table B-2). The average real price of the "domestic and blended brands" that accounted for the overwhelming share of sales fell between 1909 and 1910, but then rose after imposition of the decree.[57] The real price of the "Turkish" brands fell between 1909 and 1910 and continued to fall, albeit at a somewhat reduced rate, after the decree. Thus, one can hardly conclude that the immediate effects of divestiture were to reduce cigarette prices to consumers. Thereafter, prices became somewhat more volatile as Reynolds introduced and began promoting Camel (See Figure B-1). Wholesale prices rose much more rapidly in the 1917-1920 period in response to increases in tobacco excise taxes.[58] Throughout this period, the industry avoided price competition and the price wars that had accompanied the ascendancy of the trust.

***Table B-2.* Cigarette Prices, 1909-1913 (Dollars per Thousand)**

Year	Domestic & Blended (Nominal Price)	Domestic & Blended (Real Price)	Turkish (Nominal Price)	Turkish (Real Price)
1909	2.36	26.22	6.93	76.84
1910	2.41	25.74	6.93	74.12
1912	2.67	27.56	7.17	74.04
1913	2.81	28.30	6.92	69.71

Note: Prices deflated by Consumer Price Index.

Source: Derived from Tennant, *supra* note 48, p. 71, Table 12.

Figure B-1. **Net Real Price to Manufacturer (Dollars per 1000), Chesterfield and Camel Cigarettes**

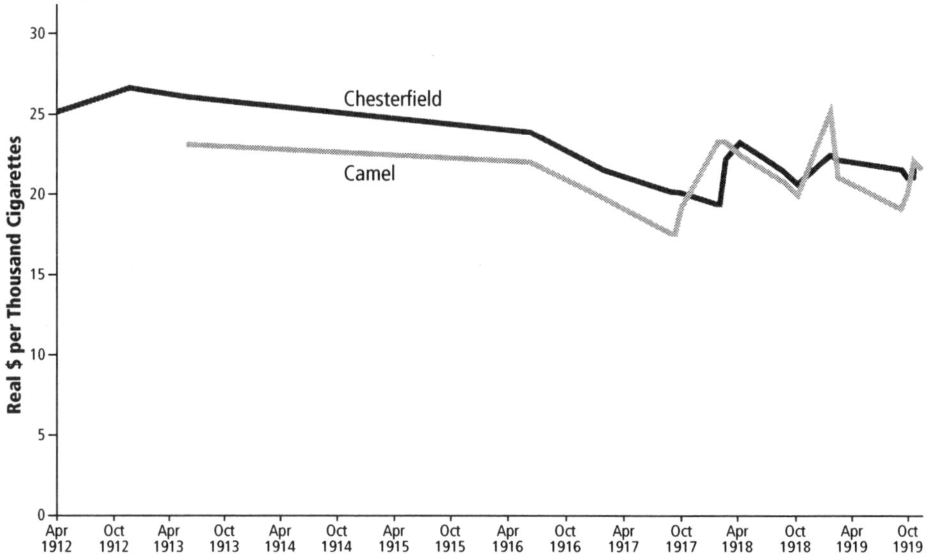

Notes: Prices are deflated by the Consumer Price Index (1982-1984=100). Monthly CPI was used except for 1912, where annual CPI was used.

Source: William Nicholls, *Price Policies in the Cigarette Industry*, pp. 46-47; Bureau of Labor Statistics Web site; *Historical Statistics of the United States Bicentennial Edition*, pp. 210-211.

Had prices fallen after the decree, one would have expected the value of the industry's output to fall relative to GNP because cigarette demand is price-inelastic. But the share of cigars, cigarettes, and tobacco fell only slightly – from 1.29 percent of GNP in 1911 to 1.20 percent in 1912 – and then fluctuated between 1.04 and 1.30 for the next eight years.[59] The higher advertising expenses eroded unit profits in the early post-decree period. However, the return on assets remained high throughout the next 15 years. Indeed, Tennant calculated that operating profits averaged 17.5 percent on tangible net worth between 1912 and 1949 for the four major companies, about the same profit rate as that earned by the trust in 1898-1908.[60]

There is also no evidence that the dissolution of American Tobacco affected the price of raw tobacco. It averaged 9.8 cents per pound in 1906-1910 and 10.3 cents in 1911-15.[61] This increase of 5 percent was less than the rate of inflation.[62]

Given these results, it is hardly surprising that the returns to stockholders were largely unimpaired by the dissolution of the trust. The prices of American Tobacco stocks and bonds recovered in late 1911 and 1912 from the earlier declines that had resulted from the filing of the suit in 1907 and the

Supreme Court's June 1911 decision. Using the capital asset pricing model, Burns finds that the excess returns generated by the announcement of the dissolution plan and the subsequent declaration of dividends and interest by the successor companies essentially wiped out the negative excess returns caused by the adverse news.[63]

Conclusion

The limited data available suggest that real cigarette prices were little affected by the decree in the first two years. In fact, immediately after the 1911 decree, real prices actually rose. The principal effect of the decree appears to have been the development of oligopolistic rivalry that diverted substantial resources to advertising while having little effect on cigarette prices. Thus, it is difficult to conclude that the decree improved consumer welfare. The stability of the industry's profit rate and the absence of any decided break in prices after 1911 inevitably leads to the conclusion that this major Section 2 case contributed very little to developing meaningful competition.

Alcoa

The manufacture of aluminum consists of four distinct phases: (1) mining aluminum ore, usually bauxite, (2) refining the ore to extract alumina (aluminum oxide), (3) reducing the alumina into aluminum ingot, and (4) fabricating the ingot into mill products like sheet, tube, and wire. Vertically integrated producers of primary aluminum generally make their own alumina and refine it into aluminum. The fabrication process, however, has always consisted of a mix of independents and integrated producers.

Early History

The aluminum industry was born in the 1880s when America's Charles M. Hall and France's Paul L.T. Héroult separately developed patents for a cheap electrolytic process of reducing aluminum from alumina. Hall's patent application won over Héroult's in the United States due to Héroult's failure to file a "Preliminary Statement" with the U.S. Patent Office.[64] The Pittsburgh Reduction Company (PRC) was formed in 1888 to apply Hall's patent, and soon faced legal challenges from Alfred and Eugene Cowles, who also used Hall's process to make pure aluminum. The Cowles brothers had secured rights to a patent by Charles Bradley for internal heating of the electrolytic bath, which the PRC used in its aluminum production process. The PRC and the Cowles brothers sued and countersued for patent infringement, and separate decisions upheld the claims of both sides. With neither party able to produce aluminum without the patent of the other, the PRC and Cowles brothers came to an agreement. PRC paid for a license to use the Bradley patent, and the Cowleses agreed not to reenter the aluminum production business.

This allowed PRC to extend its exclusive rights to aluminum production to 1909 (the Bradley patent had been granted three years after the Hall patent). When the patent expired, the economy had entered a recession, and entry into aluminum production proved difficult for would-be competitors. PRC changed its name to Aluminum Company of America ("Alcoa") in 1907, and by 1909 it had already integrated backward into ore and electricity production and had begun "to roll sheet and fabricate sundry articles."[65]

The aluminum market was very small until World War II. Primary aluminum output in the United States peaked at 65,000 tons per year during World War I and did not exceed 200,000 tons until 1940.[66] By contrast, U.S. steel production peaked at 50 million tons in World War I and was only marginally higher in 1940, rising to 67 million tons[67] (See Figure C-1). The small size of the aluminum market prior to World War II made entry very difficult because of economies of scale in alumina production. Through the 1930s, Alcoa produced its entire output of alumina from a single plant in East St. Louis. Germany had but one alumina plant, the French had three or four, and

***Figure C-1.* U.S. Production of Raw Steel and Primary Aluminum, 1900-1960**

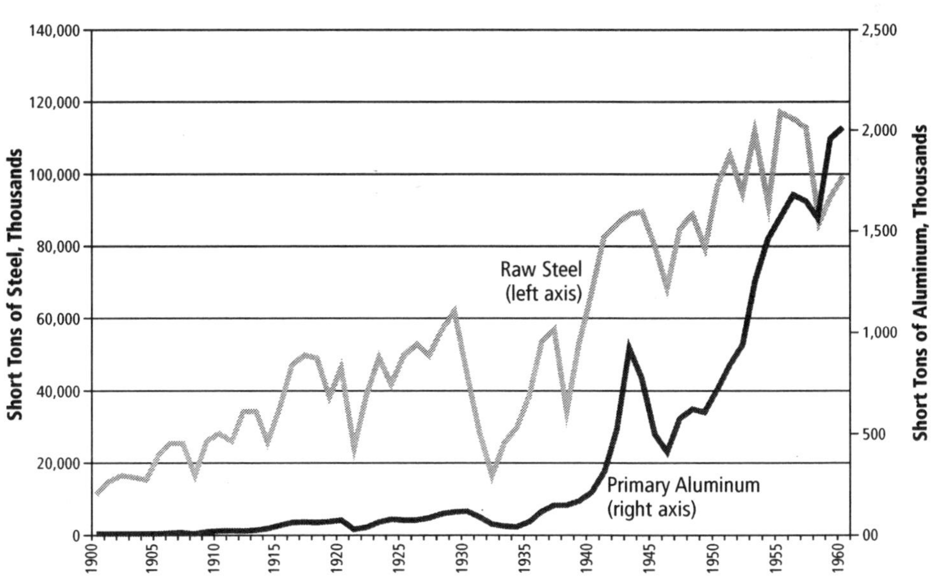

Source: U.S. Geological Survey.

the British one.[68]

In 1912, the Southern Aluminum Company was formed by French interests to construct a hydropower plant and a reduction plant in North Carolina, but it could not complete the projects because of a lack of capital during World War I. In 1915, the plants were sold to Alcoa. Other facilities were bought by Alcoa in the 1920s, including a Dutch mining operation in South America and the power facilities of the Quebec Aluminum Company founded by J.B. Duke. Alcoa also built considerable reduction capacity in Canada to go along with the Quebec Aluminum Company assets. Alcoa assigned these properties, along with its holdings in Europe, to Aluminum Limited ("Limited"). Limited was legally independent of Alcoa, but the same 11 stockholders who held half of Alcoa also held half of Limited.

Much of the Justice Department's early interest in aluminum centered on Alcoa's control of bauxite reserves and hydropower sites. But it seems unlikely that entry would have occurred in a market this small. The failure of the French attempt prior to World War I is often ascribed to poor timing, but it might not have succeeded anyway given the economies of scale in alumina production and the small size of the market. During the Great Depression, aluminum output fell to less than 40,000 tons per year. If the East St. Louis alumina plant could supply Alcoa's smelters when output was at 115,000 tons per year, its excess capacity in the 1930s would loom menacingly over any entrant's nascent operation. Moreover, Alcoa's return on invested capital between World War I and 1935 hardly suggested that a bonanza awaited a successful entrant. According to Wallace, Alcoa's average return over this period was just over 6 percent after taxes.[69]

By the late 1930s, Alcoa's primary production and imports constituted 90 percent of the total American supply, with the rest imported by others. This did not include "secondary" aluminum, which was processed by independent smelters and competed with primary aluminum. The 90 percent share included aluminum fabricated by Alcoa as well as ingot sold in the market.[70]

The Antitrust Cases

In 1912, the Department of Justice charged Alcoa with restraining trade and monopolizing the aluminum industry.[71] Alcoa signed a consent decree through which it gave up its Canadian subsidiary, dropped a contract with two chemical firms whose bauxite it had purchased, agreed not to enter any collusive agreements or mergers, and agreed not to discriminate against any competing fabricator in the sale of ingot. Neither of the two chemical firms subsequently entered the business despite the advantages the consent decree gave them.

The Federal Trade Commission subsequently brought two suits against Alcoa. The Cleveland Products Company had built a small rolling mill in 1915, but found it difficult to make money because of the wartime price ceiling for sheet. Alcoa agreed to invest in the plant in exchange for a controlling stock interest. The commission challenged the stock purchase under Section 7 of the Clayton Act and was sustained by the Third Circuit Court of Appeals.[72] Alcoa sold its interest to the other stockholder, but Cleveland Products encountered severe financial difficulties. When Alcoa bought the property at a sheriff's sale, the commission again objected, but the circuit court overruled.[73] In any case, the mill was soon closed because it had become obsolete.

In 1924, the Federal Trade Commission charged that Alcoa had violated the 1912 consent decree.[74] The Department of Justice cleared Alcoa in 1926.[75] The commission also charged Alcoa with delaying shipments of materials to competitors and with price discrimination, but dismissed the charges in 1930.[76]

In 1937, three years after beginning an investigation of Alcoa, the Department of Justice filed a Sherman Act civil suit, charging Alcoa with monopolizing the aluminum market and restraining trade. District Judge Francis Caffey found no evidence of a current attempt to monopolize.[77] He also rejected the government's argument that the power to fix prices and to exclude others from the market was monopolization.[78] The government appealed Judge Caffey's decision to the Supreme Court, but so many justices had to disqualify themselves because of their prior work in the Department of Justice against Alcoa that a quorum of six could not be achieved. As a result, legislation was enacted to allow the three senior judges of the Circuit Court of Appeals with territorial jurisdiction to serve as the ultimate appellate court in such cases. Judge Learned Hand issued the decision of the Second Circuit Court of Appeals in Alcoa in March 1945. He sustained Judge Caffey's decisions on almost all of the charges, but ruled that the power to exclude and the power to fix prices constituted monopolization in violation of Section 2 of the Sherman Act.[79] Alcoa was thus found guilty of monopolizing the market for primary aluminum.

The court's ruling generated substantial controversy. Secondary aluminum, produced from aluminum scrap, was excluded from the relevant product market because it could not be made without primary aluminum, whose production was controlled by Alcoa. Even though secondary aluminum would not enter the market for five to 25 years after its primary source was fabricated, Judge Hand concluded that a company would account for the effect of secondary products when pricing the primary product.[80]

Whereas Alcoa had argued that its profits on primary aluminum sales were not extravagant, Judge Hand ruled that the level of profits was irrelevant to the determination of monopolization and price fixing. The court also found that Alcoa had created a price squeeze on downstream customers from 1925 to 1932 by selling some aluminum sheet at prices that were too close to the price of primary aluminum ingot to allow independent fabricators to achieve adequate margins on their sales. Judge Hand did not rest his opinion on this violation, but prohibited this practice in the future. Neither Judge Caffey nor Wallace could provide a motive for the price squeeze, but it was likely motivated by a desire to engage in price discrimination without the fear of arbitrage.[81]

Postponement of Relief

Judge Hand postponed the implementation of major remedies until the war ended because of changes in the industry's structure created by the war emergency. Because of the need for aluminum in the national defense effort, the government had constructed plants for alumina reduction, aluminum smelting, and fabrication.[82] By 1944, the government plants accounted for approximately 50 percent of the domestic aluminum reduction capacity. The Defense Plant Corporation, a subsidiary of the Reconstruction Finance Corporation (RFC), owned these plants. Alcoa, Reynolds Metals Company, and Olin Corporation operated the government plants under management contracts. The Surplus Property Act, passed a year before Judge Hand's decision, directed that these plants be sold in a manner consistent with the development of competition. Therefore, although Alcoa had leases on several wartime plants that were effective through 1947 and 1948, the RFC canceled them on August 30, 1945.[83]

Since there were only two government alumina plants, there could be only two new competitors to Alcoa in the primary aluminum market if the new firms were to be vertically integrated. Given that Alcoa remained vertically integrated, the Surplus Property Board (SPB) decided the new competitors should also be vertically integrated. The board approached over 200 metals companies as possible purchasers of the wartime plants, but only Reynolds Metals and Kaiser (then Permanente Metals Corporation) were willing to make the large financial outlays required to become vertically integrated producers. With the exception of an extrusion plant and a smelter, which attracted no bidders and were thus granted to Alcoa, all of the government's wartime aluminum properties were assigned to Reynolds and Kaiser in 1946, 1947, and 1948.[84]

From these government-owned assets, Reynolds received one of the two large alumina plants, two smelters, two sheet mills, two extrusion plants, and one forge shop. Kaiser received one of the two large alumina plants, two smelters, and one sheet mill. The government also induced Alcoa to allow the new competitors to use its alumina patents, free of royalties, conditional on a "grant-back" to Alcoa of any improvement patents obtained by the competitors.

Had Judge Hand ordered the vertical dissolution of Alcoa in his ruling rather than leaving the SPB to act without knowing the government's final decision, the SPB might have been able to sell its aluminum production facilities to more than two companies. It cannot be known whether a vertically fragmented industry structure would have improved market performance, although some economists criticized the court for preventing such a result.[85]

The Final Decree

In 1947, Alcoa asked the court to rule that it no longer monopolized the market for primary aluminum. After the government moved to dismiss the petition, the district court was directed to find whether further remedies were needed. Judge John Knox ruled against divestiture in 1950, but required that the court retain jurisdiction over the case for five years in the event that the new competitors were unable to provide sufficient competition. In addition, the court ordered each of the 11 major Alcoa stockholders to sell their interest in either Alcoa or Limited within 10 years. The grant-back provision of the license agreements between Alcoa and the two new competitors was also eliminated, but Judge Hand's invocation against price squeezes remained.

In 1956, the Department of Justice argued that Reynolds and Kaiser had not proven an ability to compete and thus petitioned for another five-year test. District Judge Cashin dismissed the government's petition.[86]

The Effects of the Decree

The disposition of the government's aluminum properties created two viable competitors in Reynolds and Kaiser. Three other companies entered the primary aluminum market between 1950 and 1955, once again with government assistance. In 1950, another government program was launched to expand aluminum capacity because of the onset of the Korean War. The government issued each participating company an accelerated five-year amortization certificate for 85 percent of the cost of the new production and provided for government purchase at list prices of all the new plants' output that the producers could not sell commercially. The government also had the option to buy any aluminum from the new facilities at the list price.[87]

Three new entrants into primary aluminum production were funded from this Korean War program: Harvey Aluminum Company, Anaconda Aluminum Company, and Ormet, a joint venture between Olin Mathieson and Revere

Copper and Brass. In addition, the program funded capacity expansions by the three existing producers, Alcoa, Kaiser, and Reynolds.

Olin had managed one of the government's plants during World War II, and Revere was an established aluminum fabricator. Both companies had initially planned to produce primary aluminum. However, Olin experienced financing problems and Revere had been denied an accelerated amortization certificate from the government to build its own reduction plant. Thus, Olin and Revere formed Ormet, which constructed an aluminum reduction plant in 1958. Olin and Revere signed a 25-year agreement to purchase the ingot produced by Ormet at full manufacturing cost. Each would sell the output in either ingot or fabricated form. Thus, the joint venture resulted in one additional primary aluminum producer, but two primary aluminum sellers.[88]

The Korean War drove aluminum production to more than 1.25 million tons, or nearly nine times its level when the antitrust case was filed (See Figure C-1). As a result, even though Alcoa's share had fallen to 40 percent by 1955, its output was more than four times its "monopoly" level in 1937.

The increase in the size of the market clearly facilitated entry, even without two government programs to build new facilities. By 1958, even Ormet had the capacity to produce the entire U.S. pre-World War II output (See Table C-1). With demand fluctuating between 34,000 and 102,000 metric tons in the 1930s, entry had not been likely, with or without government assistance. Once output rose to more than 900,000 tons, the environment was quite different.

***Table C-1.* Installed Primary Aluminum Capacity in the United States**

	1949		1955		1958	
	Tons	Percent	Tons	Percent	Tons	Percent
Alcoa	294,000	45	706,500	43	798,250	36
Reynolds	227,000	35	440,000	27	601,000	27
Kaiser	133,000	20	428,200	26	537,000	24
Anaconda	0	0	60,000	4	60,000	3
Harvey	0	0	0	0	54,000	2
Ormet	0	0	0	0	144,000	7
Total	654,000	100	1,634,700	100	2,194,250	100

Source: Aluminum Association, *Aluminum Industry Annual Statistical Review* (1965), pp. 12-13.

The price of aluminum ingot had fallen steeply during the Depression, and it continued to decline through World War II. After 1947, the price of primary aluminum stabilized. It appears that the antitrust case and government-funded entry did not lead to lower aluminum prices (See Figure C-2). A regression analysis of real aluminum prices over the period 1926-1950 confirms this conclusion. This analysis includes a time trend for technical change in aluminum production, real GNP, the price of hot-rolled steel bars (a substitute), the real price of electricity, the real price of imported bauxite, a dummy variable for the World War II years (1942-45), and a dummy variable for the postwar years to reflect the effect of the government's structural "relief" – the increase in the number of sellers of primary aluminum from one to three.[89]

The results are in Table C-2 for 1926-1950 and for an extended period, 1926-1965. In general, they show that the real price of aluminum is positively related to the cost of an important input, electricity, and to the price of a substitute, steel. The trend rate of prices is negative in all four of the equations, but the time trend and Real GNP are statistically significant only in the linear equations. There is no discernible impact of World War II on the real price of aluminum.

***Table C-2.* Regression Results for the Real Price of Primary Aluminum (t-statistics in parentheses)**

Period	Constant	Real GNP	Time Trend	World War II Dummy	Real Price of Steel	Real Price of Electricity	Real Price of Imported Bauxite	Post-1945 Dummy	R^2
1926-50 (linear)	-0.175 (-1.04)	0.0006 (1.51)	-0.0081 (-2.88)	-0.00917 (-0.38)	0.00157 (2.51)	0.0845 (6.00)	0.00179 (0.42)	0.0360 (0.85)	0.986
1926-50 (log-linear)	-2.98 (-1.77)	-0.0430 (-0.19)	-0.00782 (-1.36)	-0.0155 (-0.24)	0.340 (2.74)	0.778 (3.10)	-0.112 (-1.35)	-0.0764 (-0.64)	0.989
1926-65 (linear)	-0.209 (-2.76)	0.000417 (4.19)	-0.00547 (-2.28)	0.00879 (0.34)	0.00282 (4.89)	0.0894 (8.11)	-0.0055 (-1.81)	0.02539 (0.70)	0.984
1926-65 (log-linear)	-4.682 (-2.68)	0.169 (0.72)	-0.00383 (-0.49)	-0.0575 (-0.97)	0.442 (2.64)	0.719 (2.86)	-0.0212 (-0.17)	-0.0966 (-0.98)	0.611

Note: All continuous independent variables in logarithmic form in log-linear regressions. The linear regressions for 1926-1950 and 1926-1965 were corrected for heteroscedasticity by computing robust standard errors consistent in the presence of heteroscedasticity. The log-linear regression for 1926-1965 was corrected for autocorrelation. The original model's Durbin–Watson test rejected the null hypothesis of no positive autocorrelation. The model was corrected for autocorrelation with the maximum likelihood iterative procedure. The new model's Durbin–Watson test is inconclusive for positive autocorrelation and does not reject the null hypothesis of no negative autocorrelation at the 5% level of significance.

For our purposes, the important result is the absence of a shift in real aluminum prices after the imposition of the decree in 1945. The coefficient of the post-1945 dummy variable is statistically insignificant in all equations.

Moreover, as Figure C-2 shows, the relationship between the wholesale price of aluminum extrusions and the price of primary aluminum did not change perceptibly between 1947 and 1960. (Earlier data on wholesale prices of aluminum products are unavailable.) Thus, it would appear there was no change in the markup over primary aluminum and, therefore, no apparent effect of the decree on price "squeezes."

Figure C-2. **Average Annual Real Price of Primary Aluminum and Producer Price Index for Aluminum Mill Shapes**

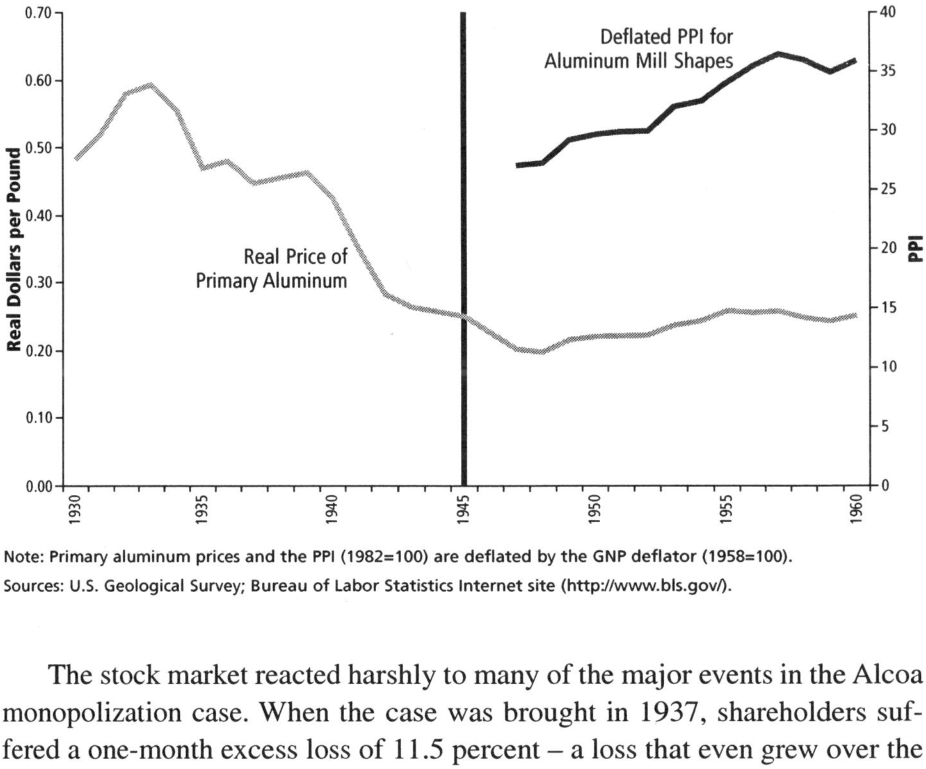

Note: Primary aluminum prices and the PPI (1982=100) are deflated by the GNP deflator (1958=100).
Sources: U.S. Geological Survey; Bureau of Labor Statistics Internet site (http://www.bls.gov/).

The stock market reacted harshly to many of the major events in the Alcoa monopolization case. When the case was brought in 1937, shareholders suffered a one-month excess loss of 11.5 percent – a loss that even grew over the next five months to a cumulative 13.3 percent negative excess return (see Table C-3). When the lower court issued its Findings of Fact and Conclusions of Law in September–October 1941, stockholder excess returns were -1.2 percent in September but rebounded to a cumulative + 4.6 percent at the end of the fifth month thereafter. The lower court's decision dismissing the complaint in July 1942 was greeted by the stock market favorably at first, generating an excess return of 7.8 percent in July but declining to a cumulative -8.0 percent five months thereafter. Judge Hand's appellate court opinion in March 1945, reversing the lower court and finding that Alcoa had monopolized, generated negative returns of -0.3 percent in the first month, growing to a cumulative negative excess return of -3.4 percent five months later. Finally, Judge Knox's decision in June 1950 not to grant the government structural relief resulted in a positive excess return of 6.8 percent in the first month, increasing to a cumulative 7.9 percent five months later. Overall, when we use a six-month window to gauge the effect of these five decisions, Alcoa stockholders appear to have lost about 12 percent relative to the overall market. However, when we use only the contemporaneous month, the excess returns are slightly positive.

The last event shown in Table C-3, the final decision regarding Alcoa's forced disposition of its stock in Alcan, resulted in very large negative returns for stockholders. This event, occurring at about the same time as the introduction of the government's Korean War subsidy program that led to the entry of Anaconda, Harvey, and Ormet, appears to have had a substantial effect on Alcoa shareholders. But it is difficult to attribute this effect to any belief that competition might break out along the Canadian border.

Table C-3. **Excess Returns to Alcoa Stockholders During Major Antitrust Events, 1937-1951**

Event	Excess Return in Same Month	Cumulative Excess Returns Over Six Months
Complaint Filed (April 1937)	-11.5%	-13.3%
Lower Court Findings of Fact and Law (September 1941)	-1.2%	+4.6%
Lower Court Decision (July 1942)	+7.8%	-8.0%
Judge Hand's Decision (March 1945)	-0.3%	-3.4%
Lower Court Rejects New Plea for Divestiture (June 1950)	+6.8%	+7.9%
Final Court Judgment on Stock Disposal (January 1951)	-13.1%	-15.1%

Conclusion

With hindsight, it appears that the failure of the 1912 decree to erode Alcoa's monopoly derived from the small and even declining market for aluminum in the early and mid-1930s. When demand grew in the 1940s and 1950s, entry would probably have occurred without government assistance. The government's decision to bring a Section 2 case in the middle of the Depression when demand would not have supported more than one supplier must surely be questioned. Demand soared as the case was being litigated, and the federal government funded an expansion of capacity for the war effort. As in *Standard Oil*, changes in the market rendered the monopolization case irrelevant. In the end, the antitrust suit served little purpose other than to ignite controversy over the proper method for defining the relevant market and for determining the market-share threshold for establishing monopoly power.

Paramount

The motion picture industry's origins derive from a series of patents obtained by Thomas Edison and others in the late 19th century.[90] One company controlled a large share of production and distribution of feature films through its ownership of patents until 1912-18 when it lost a series of antitrust cases and a major case involving a key patent. New entry soon followed with the antecedents of many of today's major film distributors – Universal, Fox, and Paramount – emerging as major producer–distributors.

The exhibition of feature films was consolidated into a number of "circuits," many of which formed First National Exhibitors' Circuit. First National soon began to finance and distribute the films exhibited in its theaters. After World War I, theater owners integrated into distribution to avoid the market power of distributors, and distributors countered by entering the exhibition business. By 1931, six of the firms that would subsequently be defendants in the Paramount case controlled nearly 2,500 theaters across the country. By this time, many of the distributor practices that allegedly constituted violations of the Sherman Act – such as block booking – emerged. As a result, the distributors were repeatedly involved in antitrust suits long before the *Paramount* litigation.

Industry Structure

The Paramount case was brought in 1938, and the complaint was amended in 1940. The defendants were the five "major" distributors – the ones owning theater chains – and three "minor" distributors. These eight firms apparently controlled 95 percent of total film rentals in the early 1940s and accounted for roughly two-thirds of all feature film releases.[91] National distribution of feature films was managed through a large number of "exchanges" in urban centers that monitored and enforced rental agreements with theaters. No major distributor was so integrated into distribution as to be able to exhibit its films solely in its own theaters. As a result, each major realized substantial rentals from the theaters of its four integrated rivals.

A large number of independent theaters also exhibited the films distributed by the eight *Paramount* defendants. Indeed, these independent theaters and theater circuits accounted for about half of all theatrical rentals in the early 1940s. While several major distributors often owned theaters in the same town, these holdings were often operated jointly as a "pool," and these pooling arrangements extended to independent theaters as well.

At the time the Paramount case was brought, seven of the distributor defendants owned production facilities and had extensive long-term agreements with talent – actors, directors, etc. By the time that the trial had begun, however, the "studio" system of long-term, exclusive contracts was in decline. Independent producers existed, but these producers were forced to distribute their films through one of the 11 national distributors. Because production was fragmented, the government was unable to argue successfully that the defendants had monopolized this stage of production.

Antitrust

Antitrust actions against distributors and theater chains were common before World War II. Many of these cases involved allegations of conspiracies to fix theatrical admission prices or rental terms or to restrict output to competing theaters.[92] However, the complaint in the Paramount case, as amended in November 1940, went much further. The eight defendants were charged with fixing license terms for feature films, excluding independently produced films, controlling first runs of films in their own theaters, and even pooling profits in territories where two or more of the five majors operated theaters.

These charges were quickly followed by a consent decree that limited the defendants' ability to engage in various tying or "block booking" practices and provided for arbitration of disputes with unaffiliated theater owners who felt they had been unfairly denied access to the defendants' films. Most of these disputes involved clearances – the timing of licensing films to different theaters in the distribution chain. These clearances were employed to enforce a system of price discrimination.

In 1944, the government moved to modify the 1940 decree, arguing that this decree had not eliminated the anticompetitive abuses. A full-blown trial ensued in 1945-46, resulting in a government victory in the district court in December 1946.[93] The court found that a large number of practices violated Sections 1 and 2 of the Sherman Act, including:

- The fixing of uniform admission prices – both among the defendants and between the distributors and their theater licensees;
- The system of uniform length or runs and clearances among theaters;
- "Formula deals" between distributors and entire theater chains or circuits;
- Block booking – that is, tying arrangements;
- Pooling agreements.

The district court refused to order divestiture of theaters, but prohibited a large number of the offenses alleged to be anticompetitive by the government. Agreements to maintain uniform admission prices and clearances among theaters were banned. Clearances had to be reasonable and could not be granted against theaters not in substantial competition with each other. The court required that competitive bidding among theaters for each run of a feature film replace these collusive practices. Various restrictions on block booking and circuit-wide formula deals were also decreed.

In 1948, the Supreme Court upheld the lower court in most respects, but it found the system of competitive bidding unworkable.[94] Instead, it ordered the lower court to reconsider divestiture. Interestingly, the Court's reversal of the competitive bidding relief was based on its fear that such a mechanism would require the federal courts to be involved in the day-to-day operations of the industry. As it developed, however, the structural remedy itself required substantial ongoing enforcement as distributors devised new approaches to exhibiting their films.

As a result of the Supreme Court decision, two of the major distributors entered into consent agreements divorcing their theaters and even divesting some of their theaters before the divorcement. The other three majors were ordered to divest their theater chains by the lower court in 1950-52.[95] Stock ownership of the divorced theater circuits and the major distributors were to be kept totally separate. All eight defendants were still subject to the injunctive relief in the original decree except for the competitive bidding requirement.

The Effect of the Decrees

The primary objective of the *Paramount* decrees was to prevent collusive, joint-profit-maximizing activities among the eight defendants. Absent collusion in the licensing of films to one another's theater circuits and in licensing and exhibiting films, distributors would have to compete for theater space by offering attractive rental terms. These terms, in turn, would be available to large numbers of theater owners who would decide which films to bid for and how long to run them. Independent distributors would have better access to theaters, and the independents would be able to take market share away from the eight defendants. Entry of new distributors might also occur, further reducing the defendants' market shares.

If this scenario had played out, we might have expected the share of theatrical revenues obtained by the distributors to fall, admission prices to decline, and the number of distributors and annual film releases to increase. In fact, none of these events occurred.

A major complication in analyzing the motion-picture industry after the *Paramount* decision was the sudden change in the entertainment habits of U.S. households after 1948. The introduction of television as a mass medium led to a dramatic decline in theater admissions. Total theater admissions fell by more than two-thirds between 1948 and 1958, and by another 50 percent between 1958 and 1967.[96] As a result, large numbers of theaters closed, but substantial excess theater capacity remained in 1967.[97] As in Standard Oil and Alcoa, unanticipated changes in market conditions had enormous impacts that the designers of the decrees could not foresee.

Despite these negative trends, the average real price of a movie ticket actually rose over the two decades following *Paramount*. The Consumer Price Index (CPI) for Indoor Theaters rose by 36.4 percent between 1948 and 1958, a period in which the overall CPI rose just 20.1 percent. This trend continued over the 1958-1967 period, with the CPI for indoor theaters rising by 68.9 percent while the overall CPI rose by just 15.5 percent[98] (See Figure D-1). In a sharply contracting industry, one might have expected substantial downward pressure on prices, particularly if the Justice Department had just succeeded in breaking a cartel of distributor–exhibitors. Instead, real theatrical admission prices rose substantially.[99]

The objectives of the *Paramount* decrees were broader than the elimination of price-fixing in admissions. Another goal was to open the theaters to competing producer–distributors, thereby breaking the grip of the eight large Hollywood distributors. However, there was little entry into distribution in the years following the *Paramount* decision. RKO declined rapidly and exited the industry in 1957 because of internal problems deriving from Howard Hughes's ownership of the company. The remaining seven defendants actual-

Figure D-1. **Consumer Price Index for Indoor Movie Admissions and All Urban Consumers, 1947-1967 (1967 = 100)**

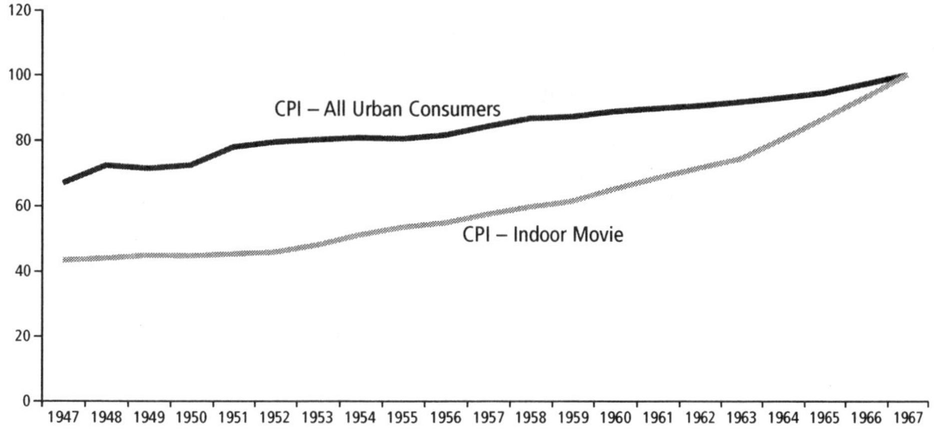

Sources: U.S. Department of Labor, Bureau of Labor Statistics (BLS), *Handbook of Labor Statistics* (1978), p. 426; and the BLS Internet site (http://www.bls.gov/).

ly experienced an increase in their collective share of motion-picture rentals between 1948 and 1954. Thereafter, their share fell for a few years due to a disastrous set of releases, but then rebounded by 1966-67 to between 70 and 72 percent of U.S. rental revenues – only slightly less than their 1948 share of 76 percent.[100] During the 1948-1967 period, the major distributors steadily reduced the number of feature film releases from 248 to about 150, and U.S.-produced independents also contracted supply. Thus, the *Paramount* decrees did not introduce new competition or new competitors in distribution. After 20 years, the seven survivors of the *Paramount* litigation continued to account for nearly three-fourths of all U.S. theatrical rentals.[101]

Given the sharp decline in demand for theatrical admissions and the dissolution of the cartel, one might have expected Hollywood distributors to be more aggressive in attempting to market their films to a declining number of U.S. theaters. In fact, they reduced supply and held the line on prices through the 1948-67 period. As real admission prices rose, the distributors were successful in capturing most of the additional revenues for themselves. Their share of theatrical admission receipts rose from 30.4 percent in 1948 to 45.8 percent in 1967. Thus, the distributors absorbed approximately two-thirds of the real increase in theater ticket prices. Surely, this is not the result one would have expected from an end to collusion.

Estimating the effect of the Paramount case on the defendant companies' stockholders is complicated by the large number of court decisions and the number of defendant companies. The announcement of the filing of the case in July 1938 had a large negative impact on the common equities of the larger, integrated defendants, but the opposite effect on the minor unintegrated distributors, Universal and Columbia (See Table D-1). However, the amended complaint and the subsequent consent decree in November 1940 were followed by enormous positive excess returns for both the majors and the minor distributors. When the government reopened the case in August 1944, the stockholder excess returns were understandably negative for all but one of the major distributors, but positive for one of the two minor distributors that had no theaters to divest. Finally, the Supreme Court decision in 1948 generated very large negative returns for the majors as well as both of the minor distributors. In short, the market does not appear to have foreseen the devastating effect of television, reacting very badly to the forced divestiture of theaters!

What Went Wrong?

Why did the decrees not achieve their goal? There are at least two possible reasons.

Table D-1. **Cumulative Six-Month Excess Returns to Paramount Defendants' Stockholders During Major Antitrust Events, 1937-1951**

Event	Paramount	RKO	20th-Century Fox	Warner Bros.	Loews	Columbia	Universal
Case Filed (July 1938)	-12.3%	-25.1%	-14.8%	-31.4%	-10.0%	+8.4%	+58.7%
Complaint Amended and Decree Issued (November 1940)	+64.0%	+27.9%	+0.7%	+42.4%	+32.4%	+11.6%	+104.7%
Gov't Files to Modify Decree (August 1944)	-13.2%	-14.3%	-3.0%	-13.6%	+5.6%	+19.5%	-8.9%
Lower Court Ruling (December 1946)	-26.0%	-33.1%	-35.0%	-20.9%	-22.1%	-14.1%	-25.4%
Supreme Court Opinion (May 1948)	-23.6%	-13.6%	-27.0%	-32.0%	-24.3%	-16.0%	-39.5%

First, the government may have erred in charging the defendants with violating the Sherman Act. If the conduct of these companies was not collusive prior to 1948, or if their actions did not result in a reduction of output or higher theater admission prices, the suit should never have been filed. DeVany and Eckert argue that the practices assailed by the government – the agreement on clearances and length of runs – were required to provide a stable environment for the exploitation of feature films and to provide information on the demand for each film.[102] Barring such practices or breaking the ownership ties between distributors and theaters would thus reduce the efficiency of the distribution system. The result was higher costs, higher rental rates, and fewer feature film releases.

A second possibility is that the collusive arrangements among distributors and exhibitors were successful in reducing output and raising prices, but that the decrees were not successful in ending such collusion. After decades of agreeing on clearances and lengths of runs, the seven remaining *Paramount* defendants would still be able to collude tacitly by reporting their revenues from each theater to the trade press, thereby allowing the detection of deviations from the implicit cartel agreement. If a theater dropped a film earlier in its run than expected, distributors would be able to infer that the distributor of the film that replaced it had cut its rental rate to obtain the clearance.

It is even possible that elements of both theories are correct. The decrees might have made it more expensive to distribute films without facilitating new entry and without stimulating enhanced competition. The result could have been higher prices and lower output than would have existed without the decrees. Whatever the explanation, it seems clear that the motion picture industry did not become more competitive as a result of vertical divestiture of theaters from distributors.

The Paramount case once again illustrates the difficulty in designing a decree that is effective when market conditions are changing. Like *American Tobacco*, it also demonstrates that structural relief may not create the conditions for aggressive competition.

United Shoe Machinery

United Shoe Machinery Corp. (USM) began operations in 1899 with the acquisition of five shoe machinery manufacturers.[103] These acquisitions provided USM with a prominent position in the major segments of shoe machinery manufacturing. The company grew rapidly thereafter, acquiring a number of other companies, and it eventually centralized its manufacturing operations in one plant in Massachusetts.[104]

As early as 1911, USM faced a civil suit charging it with combination in restraint of trade and monopolizing in violations of Sections 1 and 2 of the Sherman Act.[105] USM won the suit, but was faced with another in 1915, charging that USM's equipment leasing practices violated Section 3 of the Clayton Act because of tying and exclusive-use provisions in its contracts.[106] This suit was won by the government, resulting in a court decree requiring USM to modify the terms of its leases.[107] The third major antitrust case against USM was brought in 1947, charging USM with violations of Section 1 and Section 2 of the Sherman Act. The district court ruled against USM in 1953 and was upheld by the Supreme Court in 1954.[108] Although the 1953 decree did not result in divestiture, a review of the case in 1964 led to a Supreme Court decision that instructed the lower court to consider divestiture. And in 1969, a substantial share of USM's assets were divested.[109] The company was purchased by Emhart Industries five years later.

USM's Products and Services

USM manufactured a full line of specialized machines to produce shoes. By the 1940s, it offered more than 300 types of machines, of which a shoe manufacturer might need as many as 100 to produce a shoe.[110] These included clicking machines, lasting machines, eyeleting machines, outsole stitching machines, and heel-attaching machines, to name only a few.

USM's customer base consisted of shoemakers across the United States. These were typically small enterprises (although several were very large, and one or two were nearly the size of USM). In 1947, there were approximately 1,650 shoe factories in the United States operated by some 1,460 firms.[111] The number of factories and the volume of shoe production increased rapidly between 1915 and 1947, but declined after 1958.[112]

USM offered its shoe machines through a combination of sale and lease programs. Shoe machines were extremely complex and often experienced technical problems. As a result, in addition to offering machines for sale or lease, USM provided repair and advisory services for both its own machines and others. Factories that were engaged in the manufacture of shoes often needed advice on the selection and layout of machines and timely repair services. As a result, USM employed forces of roadmen who could be dispatched quickly to the shoe factories for such advice and repair services.[113]

Market Shares

USM had a very large share of the sale or lease of major shoe machines, and a slightly smaller proportion of the market with respect to minor machines. Table E-1 shows USM's share of the outstanding major and minor machines in shoe manufacturing plants in 1949 and the share of the market held by its competitors.[114]

Table E-1. **Share of Major and Minor Machines by Manufacturer, 1949**

Company	Share of Major Machines (percent)	Share of Minor Machines (percent)
United	91.0	64.0
Boston Machine Works	–	6.0
Compo	3.4	5.5
International	0.6	–
20 Other Competitors	5.0	–
81 Other Competitors	–	24.5

Source: Kaysen, *supra* note 104, pp. 52-53.

USM was dominant in large machines; its principal rivals competed by offering a more limited line of machines. None of the rivals was a large manufacturing enterprise. As a result, Kaysen concluded that: "[t]hey are essentially shoe machinery or machinery-and-supplies businesses, and their small scale in the machine field indicates their overall smallness and weakness relative to USM."[115]

The Government's Case Against USM

The government claimed that USM had monopolized the shoe machinery market through the use of leases that impeded the purchase or lease of competitors' machines. Specifically, the government charged that several provisions of USM's leases were exclusionary. Among the most important were: (a) the 10-year terms of the leases; (b) the return charges or deferred payments due upon early termination of a lease; (c) the minimum monthly usage charges on machines subject to per-unit payments; and (d) the "full-capacity" clause that required lessees to use the machine to the fullest extent possible in producing all shoes for which the machine was capable of being used.[116]

USM would also waive the monthly rental and minimum-usage balances due on unexpired leases when machinery returns were made for reasons other than the substitution of a competitor's machine. USM would charge the shoe manufacturers with violating the full-capacity clause only in cases in which a competitor's machine was used. Penalties were waived when the full capacity clause was not met as a result of changes in demand, conversion to manual operations, or replacement with another United machine.[117]

USM's market power was allegedly enhanced by a number of other factors. First, USM offered a full line of machinery, which gave it the ability to use tying practices and to employ price discrimination against its rivals, charging low markups for machines that faced competition and high markups for those without competition.[118] Second, USM held a large number of patents, which made it difficult for a potential rival to develop machines or techniques that did not infringe on a USM patent.[119] Kaysen conceded that he could not fully dismiss the theory that USM was a natural monopoly because of the small size of the shoe machinery market. However, his observations on the small lot size for parts and machine manufacturing in USM's Massachusetts plant led him to conclude that USM was probably not a natural monopolist.[120]

The Government's Victory and Proposed Relief

In February 1953, the district court found that USM had violated Section 2 of the Sherman Act by illegally monopolizing the shoe machinery market and the market for some shoe machinery supplies.[121] USM appealed the decision, but the Supreme Court upheld it.[122] The government requested the division of USM into three full-line manufacturers and the separation of all supply activities from the machinery business. The major obstacle was the fact that USM produced its entire output in a single plant. In addition, the government sought an end to USM's reliance on leasing and the dissolution of USM's outstanding leases. This remedy, in conjunction with modifications in

USM's patent policies and a ban on expansion of USM through acquisitions, was intended to reduce barriers to entry.[123]

The court declined to dissolve USM, but did take aim at USM's leasing policy. Under the decree, USM was forced to offer its machines for sale as well as lease, but it could not structure the lease and sales terms in a fashion that would make it more advantageous to lease. In addition, the duration of all new leases had to be reduced to five years or less with an option to return machines after one year. Return charges and deferred payments were banned. USM was barred from acquiring any shoe machinery factory or shoe supply business, or stock in such business, for more than $10,000. USM was also severely restricted with respect to the acquisition of patents.[124]

The decree was intended to stimulate competition in at least three ways. First, by stimulating the purchase of machines, the decree might create a vibrant secondhand market. These secondhand machines would limit USM's market power in the sale or lease of new machines and provide potential entrants with valuable information about USM's technology. Second, by limiting the term of the leases and limiting discriminatory termination fees, the decree might induce shoe manufacturers to choose more competitors' products. Third, by creating a secondhand market and stimulating incremental sales of competitive machines through a relaxation of USM's leasing terms, the decree might stimulate the growth of an active independent repair sector, freeing shoe manufacturers from reliance on USM's technical staff.

The Effect of the Decree

After 10 years, the lower court held hearings on the effectiveness of the decree and concluded that the decree was generally working as expected. Specifically, Judge Wyzanski found that:[125]

- USM's market share of lease and sales revenue fell from 85 percent in 1953 to 62 percent in 1963.
- USM's lease and sales revenue fell from $32 million in 1953 to $24 million in 1963.
- The number of new entrants had increased, and machinery shipments of USM's principal competitors had increased substantially.
- USM shipped only 51.7 percent of all shoe machines sold in 1963.
- A secondhand market had been established.
- Approximately 54 percent of machines in shoe factories in 1963 were made by USM, but only 47 percent had been obtained from USM.
- In 1963, only 17 percent of leased machines in shoe factories were leased from USM.

• Between 1953 and 1963, shoe factories purchased approximately 53,000 previously leased machines from USM.

Table E-2 shows the decline in USM's share of shoe machinery lease and sales revenues between 1947, the year the case was brought, and 1963, the year before the review of the decree in the district court.[126] No single firm attained a very large market share, but USM nevertheless lost about one-quarter of its preexisting share because the rate of entry increased following the decree. According to Waldman, "[i]n three-year segments of the period from 1955 to 1965, the number of entries into shoe machinery manufacture increased, respectively, by 11, 19, and 26."[127] However, Waldman offers no evidence that such entry was atypical of the pre-decree period, or that the entrants provided much competition for USM. The "other" competitors' share of industry revenues, shown in Table E-2, rose by only 8.9 percentage points in 16 years.

Table E-2. **Shoe Machinery Revenue Shares, 1947 vs. 1963 (percent)**

Company	1947	1963
USM	85	62
Compo	2.0	7.2
International	0.5	9.4
Other Competitors	12.5	21.4

Source: Waldman, *supra* note 126, p. 47.

Although there were substantial increases in the total revenue of USM's competitors in the nine years following the decree (See Table E-3),[128] USM's revenue gains were about double the sum of the four major competitors combined.

The market for secondhand machinery also grew following the decree. Used machinery dealers sold 35.2 percent of the shoe machines leased and sold in 1963,[129] and they offered machines in 108 of 177 separate operations identified by a USM consultant."[130]

In the two years after the decree, USM's net income reached an all-time high, apparently because of the sale of USM machines that had low book value and because of an increase in lease prices.[131] Waldman argues that the high prices following the decree may have been a result of USM's attempting to placate the court, but such behavior is hardly consistent with Waldman's view that USM suffered a reduction in market power.[132] Moreover, USM's rate of return on equity was little affected by the decree (See Figure E-1). In the first two years, as explained above, USM's return on equity rose, but thereafter

Table E-3. Total Revenue (in Thousands of Dollars)

Year	United	Compo	Schwabe	International	Boston Machine
1954	80,480	5,230	712	1,022	1,591
1963	95,928	8,671	2,316	5,656	1,578
% Change	+19.2	+65.8	+224.8	+453.4	-0.8

Source: Parrish, *supra* note 125, p. 97.

***Figure E-1.* USM's Profit Margin and Rate of Return on Equity, 1944-1961**

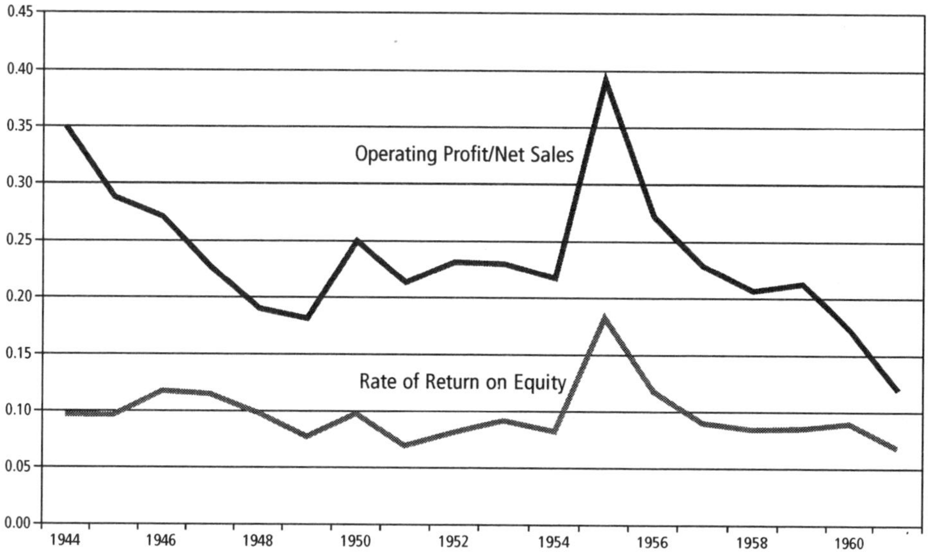

Sources: Waldman, *supra* note 126, p. 48; *Moody's Manual of Industrial Securities* (Moody's Investors Service, various years).

it returned to the levels of 1945-1953.

Given the heterogeneity of shoe machinery, there is no index of shoe machinery prices. Therefore, an indirect test of the effect of the decree on prices is required. If the decree had succeeded in reducing machinery prices, shoe manufacturers should have incurred lower machinery expense relative to the value of shoes produced. In the short run, a lower price on shoe machines probably would not result in much substitution of machines for labor. Yet, the ratio of shoe machinery shipments to shoe shipments declined from 0.014 in 1947 to 0.012 in 1954, then remained constant at 0.012 in 1958, 1963, and 1967[133] (See Figure E-2). In 1972, this ratio rose sharply – perhaps in response to machine sales following the revision of the decree in 1968, but then declined equally as sharply in 1977.[134] The average ratio was 0.015 for the

Figure E-2. **Value of Shipments of Shoe Machinery Divided by Value of Shipments of Shoes, 1947-1967, and Shipments of Footwear**

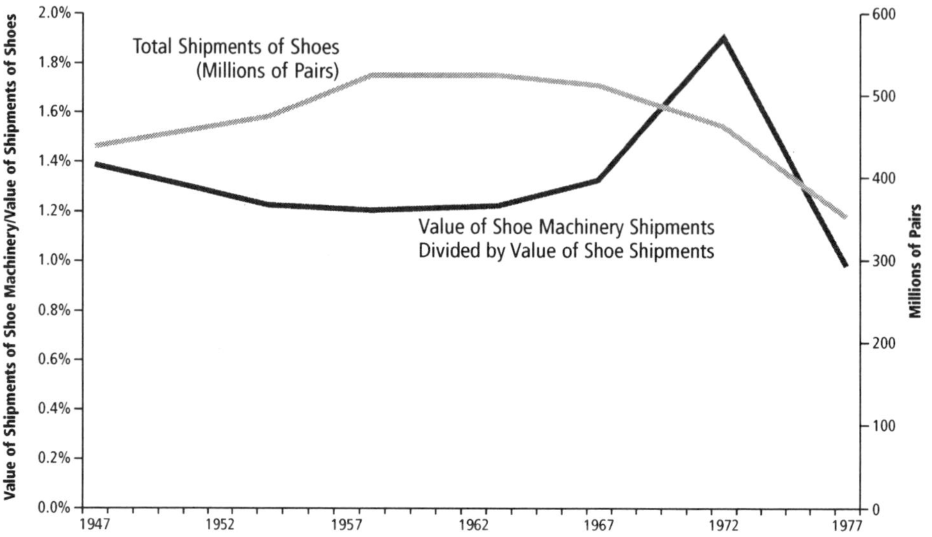

Note: Shipments of shoes includes shipments of all footwear excluding rubber and slippers, and including interplant transfers.

Source: *Census of Manufactures.*

1972-77 years combined, or approximately its value in the year the case was filed. That suggests the decree had little effect on shoe machinery prices.

The court's decision also had several other less quantifiable effects on USM and the shoe machinery industry in general. USM's ability to combat free riding was reduced, as was USM's incentive to commit resources to new technology. In addition, rentals increased. The share of imports rose, from a very small fraction before 1950 to 25 percent by 1964, and continued to rise thereafter.[135] Finally, the U.S. shoe industry began to decline in the late 1950s following the decree (which may or may not have been related to the decree).[136]

Stockholders anticipated the mild effect of the decrees on USM's fortunes. When the initial complaint was filed in 1947, the stock market reacted modestly (See Table E-4). Even the adverse ruling by Judge Wyzanski in 1953 is associated with only a -0.3 percent decline in the price of the stock in the same month, and the excess returns were actually positive over the six-month window. In total, the complaint and the lower court decision are associated with less than a 2 percent negative excess return to stockholders. However, when the government lost its appeal on the lack of structural relief in the Supreme Court in 1954, these negative excess returns were wiped out. Over the three event windows, the excess returns to stockholders were positive.

Table E-4. **Excess Returns to USM Stockholders During Major Antitrust Events, 1947-1954**

Event	Excess Return in Same Month	Cumulative Excess Returns Over Six Months
Complaint Filed (December 1947)	-1.6%	-0.2%
Lower Court Decision (February 1953)	-0.3%	+5.9%
Supreme Court Decision (May 1954)	+11.3%	+27.5%

The 1964 Review of the Decree

After the 1964 review of the evidence, the lower court ruled that sufficient competition had been introduced and that the decree should stand "unmodified."[137] On review, however, the Supreme Court recommended that the lower court consider "more definitive means" to achieve competition.[138] As a result, the company was forced to divest itself of approximately one-third of its remaining shoe machinery manufacturing operations in 1969.[139] Thus, structural relief was finally obtained by the government 22 years after first filing its case at a time when – much as in the case of Paramount – the U.S. shoe industry began a steep decline.

Conclusion

There is at least a modicum of evidence that the antitrust action against USM succeeded in creating a more competitive shoe machinery market after 1953. Entry occurred, USM lost market share, and the secondhand market blossomed. On the other hand, there is no evidence that the prices of machines fell or that innovation flourished.

The Television Network Cases

For several decades, the Federal Communications Commission's spectrum allocation policy limited the number of television broadcast stations in major metropolitan areas. As a result, there were only three commercial broadcast networks in the United States because a fourth network could not assemble a large enough roster of affiliates to compete.[140] The inevitable result of this market concentration was public concern over the networks' power in several arenas. In the 1960s, the FCC conducted an inquiry into network program procurement practices that led to limits on network "ownership" of programming, including participation in the marketing of reruns of their network series, referred to as "syndication."[141] At about the same time, the Justice Department launched an inquiry into network programming practices that would eventually result in antitrust cases filed in 1972 against each of the three networks[142] and in three antitrust consent decrees.

Network Television

The commercial television networks developed as organizations to distribute mass entertainment programming across the country through hundreds of independent and network-owned local broadcast stations. The exploitation of mass entertainment programming requires national distribution. But because the FCC limits the number of local stations that any single entity may own, a national broadcasting company cannot reach its audience solely through its own stations. It is forced to negotiate affiliation agreements with broadcast stations throughout the country.

Network programming is produced by the networks themselves and by hundreds of entities generally involved in the theatrical motion picture business.[143] Because programs are expensive to produce, few are developed without a network contract. Networks often provide development funding for "pilot" productions before committing to a year's output of a series.

Popular network television series have value in foreign markets and in further exhibition as "reruns" in domestic markets. As a result, the seller of a series will not generally recover its full production costs from the network run alone. The talent – the actors, producers, directors, etc. – are able to command salaries that reflect the series' market value in all of these markets. Thus, when a network purchases a new network series, its payments for these programs will not fully defray the supplier's costs.

Early on, networks shared the risk in developing series with their program suppliers by purchasing the rights to distribute the program as reruns in the domestic market or to the foreign market or by sharing in the profitability of such "syndication." In the 1960s, the major program suppliers, principally the large motion picture companies, argued that this network participation in reruns was being demanded from them at non-compensatory prices and therefore should be forbidden by the FCC.[144]

The Antitrust Suits

When the networks entered the motion picture business in the late 1960s, the Justice Department also began to investigate network program "ownership" and the market power of the networks in programming. In 1970, the FCC enacted its financial interest and syndication rules,[145] and the Justice Department's inquiry languished. The FCC rules barred the networks from the syndication market and forbade them to acquire interests in the financial returns in reruns. The rules did not, however, bar the networks from producing their own programs or syndicating them in foreign markets.

The Justice Department inexplicably renewed its interest in network programming in 1972 and brought suits charging each network with attempting to monopolize the prime-time programming on its own network. These curious charges implied that each network's prime-time programming was a separate antitrust market.

The case was never fully litigated, and therefore the absurdity of this theory was never exposed to the adversary process. Instead, the networks each negotiated consent decrees, which included the provisions of the FCC's financial interest and syndication rules and further provisions to limit the amount of programming that network could produce for itself.[146] These decrees thus drove a greater wedge between distribution and production, requiring the network to purchase a minimum amount of programming from outside companies – mostly the motion picture companies. They also provided greater assurance to the motion picture companies that the FCC could not, by itself, repeal the rules that barred the networks from the syndication market and from the purchase of financial interests in these programs.

The Decrees and Related FCC Regulations

From the outset, the case against network program "ownership" was one of monopsony power.[147] The networks allegedly used this power to depress the total price of their programming – the price for the initial network run less the expected returns from their right to syndicate it (if they obtained it) and any interest they obtained in the profits from subsequent distribution of the programming. The popular version of this theory, advanced by the movie studios, was that the networks used their power to force their suppliers to accept non-compensatory prices, but that is obviously incorrect. The networks could not force the Hollywood studios to provide them programming at a loss. To the extent that the monopsony theory had any merit, such power must have been exercised through a reduction in the number of programs purchased each year. If the networks had monopsony power – an unlikely possibility – it was because FCC spectrum-allocation policies limited the number of broadcast networks to three.

The irony of the network cases is that the originator of the theory of network dominance over programming – the FCC – subsequently ruled that the networks must reduce their prime-time programming by one half-hour per day on weekdays. This "Prime Time Access Rule" was promulgated in 1972 to introduce more distributors into national television by the same agency that had constrained the number of distributors through its limitation on the number of broadcast stations in each market.[148] The FCC now asserted that it wished to increase program diversity by simply changing the identity of the three distributors for this one half-hour per day. Unfortunately, the Prime Time Access Rule did not create new "networks," but spawned a large number of inexpensive game shows that typically carried more advertising minutes than the network series they displaced.

Curiously, the three national television networks supported the Prime Time Access Rule a few years after it was promulgated. They saw the rule as beneficial as long as it reduced the supply of high-quality programming and increased advertisers' demand for commercials in their reduced output – particularly in periods of economic recession. Subsequently, the networks agreed to limit their own program production in the antitrust consent decrees.[149] They were being forced to reduce programming hours anyway and did not view the threat of self-supply as an important source of bargaining power in procuring programs from the Hollywood studios.

The Result of the Decrees

The decrees and the FCC syndication rules could not have eliminated network monopsony power, even if such power had existed. The number of buyers of programming was unaffected by these interventions because they did not increase the number of networks. The three networks had to continue to bid for programming against motion picture producers, the live theater, and other media that employed actors, directors, camera operators, film-tape editors, etc. However, the decrees and the FCC rules did reduce the number of firms in the syndication market and the number of large companies that could finance risky programming series by obtaining a share of their downstream returns.

Prior to the FCC rules, each network had about 6 percent of national program syndication revenues. In 1971, before the FCC rules began to have an effect on syndication markets, the seven major motion picture studios' domestic syndication accounted for just 23 percent of the total viewer hours of nationally syndicated programs. In 1981, the year after the consent decree was negotiated, this share had risen to 37 percent. By 1989, the seven motion picture companies accounted for 41 percent of viewer hours from national syndication and 59 percent of the viewer hours from syndicating network reruns.[150] This increase in concentration was the direct result of banning three of their major competitors from the syndication market.

Equally important, the FCC rules (and the network decrees that incorporated them) affected risk sharing in programming development. In the 1969-1970 television season, the four largest suppliers of network programming accounted for 34 percent of revenues from network program purchases. By 1988-89, this four-firm share had risen to 47 percent because the networks could no longer share in the risk of programming by purchasing syndication interests in these programs.[151] Smaller producers were forced to seek other sources of capital, and the large motion picture companies were the obvious alternative.

Because the networks were uniquely positioned to bear program risk, denying them the right to acquire financial interests in programming and limiting their ability to produce their own programs changed the composition of their new program series. The risk of innovative programming had to be borne by others who were less well positioned to bear it. As a result, the variance in network program ratings declined after 1972, reflecting a program acquisition process that resulted in less daring new program series.[152] Further evidence of this decline in risk taking may be found in the variance in the average number of years that prime-time network shows were kept on the air. Between 1963 and 1972, this variance in the length of run of new series increased. But after 1972 it decreased steadily, reflecting the fact that network programming was less innovative and thus less subject to early cancellation after the antitrust consent decrees were promulgated.[153]

The FCC rules would have had adverse effects on innovation in network programming by themselves, but the consent decrees' limitation on the networks' ability to supply their own programs surely exacerbated this unfortunate result. The networks could not underwrite the risks themselves through self-supply, and were thus increasingly dependent on the Hollywood studios for programming. The result was less innovative, risky programming.

A Concluding Assessment

The network antitrust cases, like the 1970 FCC Financial Interest and Syndication Rules, were based on a faulty analysis of the program acquisition process. The networks purchased programs from a large number of suppliers and had to compete with other media to attract such programming and the talent required for its production. Barring the networks from owning rights or profit shares in syndication and limiting their ability to supply their own programming led to an increase in concentration in program supply. It also reduced the efficiency of bearing the risk of innovative new programming. By the time the FCC rules were repealed and the network antitrust decrees were vacated, these results were widely acknowledged.[154] Nevertheless, it was not until cable television had decimated the networks' share of viewers that the regulators and the Justice Department could agree to end these unfortunate restrictions.

AT&T

The *AT&T* case is often cited as an overwhelming antitrust policy success because long-distance competition grew substantially after the breakup of AT&T in 1984. In fact, it was not the vertical divestiture in the decree but a seemingly small change in one regulatory requirement that propelled competition. Federal regulators could have enacted this provision 10 years earlier and avoided the breakup.

Origins of Telephony

The telephone industry in the United States has been tightly regulated for much of the past century. Although it was often assumed to have many of the characteristics of "natural monopoly," the telephone industry did not evolve naturally through market forces. Instead, its structure was heavily influenced and even dictated by regulatory and antitrust authorities.

The telephone sector began to develop in the late 19th century as the result of several patents, the most important of which were registered by Alexander Graham Bell. Telephone exchanges were developed to route calls among these patented devices. In the U.S., exchanges were developed by the Bell and related companies almost exclusively until the expiration of the original patents in 1893. Thereafter, "independent" local telephone companies began to proliferate in major cities.[155]

At first, telephony was local. Later, the development of the vacuum tube allowed calls to be transmitted over increasing distance. The Bell companies – under the parentage of the American Telephone and Telegraph Company (AT&T) – began to patent and deploy this technology, but they often refused to allow the independent telephone companies to interconnect with their "long-distance" service. As a result of this handicap and the intense price competition with the Bell companies, many of the independents eventually chose to sell their companies to AT&T. These practices (and others) placed AT&T in the crosshairs of the antitrust authorities in the early part of the 20th century. To avoid a suit, AT&T agreed to cease its acquisition of independent telephone companies, to provide interconnection, to sell certain assets, and to submit to federal regulation.

Industry Structure Before 1974

After World War I, AT&T was permitted to resume its acquisition of independent telephone companies.[156] By the 1930s, it controlled approximately 80 percent of local exchange lines in the country. AT&T was also the country's only national long-distance company. It produced most of its own transmission, switching, and terminal equipment through its Western Electric subsidiary, much of which was developed from ideas that originated in its Bell Laboratories.

Throughout the interwar period, AT&T and the independent telephone companies were regulated by state commissions and by federal authorities. The 1934 Federal Communications Act established the FCC as the regulator of interstate services, but it was not active in regulating telephony until after World War II. During the interwar period, most of the regulatory and antitrust concern about AT&T centered on its ownership of Western Electric and the effect of such ownership on the prices charged to AT&T's operating divisions.

After World War II, the states and the FCC responded to a court decision that required the joint (non-traffic-sensitive) costs of local networks to be recovered in part from interstate long-distance services. This ultimately led to long-distance calls that were priced far above long-run incremental cost, allowing the states to keep the price of residential connections low, particularly in high-cost rural areas.[157]

In the 1960s, the FCC began to consider more liberal policies toward entry of competitors in interstate services. In 1969-1971, it opened dedicated "private-line" business services to competition. But it did not extend competition to ordinary interstate long-distance services, whose rates were far above long-run incremental cost. The new entrants into private-line services could easily extend their operations into the interstate long-distance market if they obtained the FCC's permission to do so and could arrange for the local phone companies to deliver their calls. Alternatively, they could do so surreptitiously by leasing connections that would deliver such services while pretending to offer only dedicated private-line service.

MCI availed itself of the latter opportunity in 1974, offering ordinary switched long-distance service without FCC authority. The FCC responded by attempting to bar MCI from this service, but it was rebuffed by the federal courts.[158] In this rather unusual manner, long-distance competition was born.

The FCC was altogether unprepared to deal with it. The entire long-distance network had evolved as a monopoly of AT&T, whose network was connected to those of the monopoly local carriers, including AT&T's own Bell companies. MCI could not obtain equivalent connections because AT&T's

switches were not designed to offer equal access to competitive long-distance carriers.

Telephone service was offered under state rules that did not allow customers to connect their own equipment. A series of legal challenges to these restrictive provisions of the tariffs narrowed the ability of the companies to limit non-interfering customer attachments, but it was not until the mid-1970s that the FCC tried to open all terminal equipment to competition. By 1976, the courts had rebuffed state regulators' challenges to the FCC's terminal equipment policy, allowing competitors to sell telephone handsets, answering machines, and other devices as long as they posed no threat to the network.[159]

The 1974 Antitrust Case and the 1982 Decree

Antitrust investigations had dogged AT&T for much of its existence. In 1913, AT&T avoided antitrust prosecution through the Kingsbury Commitment, in which AT&T agreed to dispose of certain assets, to cease its aggressive acquisition policy, and to interconnect its long-distance network with independent telephone companies. A 1938 FCC report that was never released eventually led to a 1949 Sherman Act case whose objective was divestiture of Western Electric. This case was settled in 1956 without divestiture, but with a requirement that AT&T confine its activities to "common carrier communications services."[160]

Two decades later, as the FCC moved slowly to open interstate services and terminal equipment to competition, the incumbent carriers – particularly AT&T and its Bell operating companies – were far from cooperative with the new competitors. AT&T used every opportunity to argue in regulatory and legislative proceedings against competition. At the same time, it often denied the nascent competitors interconnection with its network facilities, or delayed such interconnection through aggressive exploitation of the regulatory processes. These actions invited private antitrust suits[161] and renewed scrutiny from the Department of Justice.

The private antitrust suits brought by AT&T's new long-distance competitors were winding their way through the federal courts when the government filed a Section 2 Sherman Act suit against AT&T on November 20, 1974.[162] The complaint alleged monopolization of long-distance services and telecommunications equipment by AT&T and its subsidiaries. The case languished for four years until reassigned to Judge Harold H. Greene, who began to guide it toward trial in 1981. After the government presented its case, Judge Greene decisively rejected AT&T's motion for summary judgment, and the parties quickly moved to negotiate a settlement decree.[163]

The government's case relied heavily on the theory that AT&T's ownership of local operating companies had provided it with the incentive and the ability to exclude competitors in long-distance services and telecommunications equipment manufacture by denying them interconnection with the local Bell companies. As a result, the central provision of the decree was a total divestiture of the local operating companies. This separation of local monopolies – which were not likely to be threatened by competitive entry anytime soon – from the rest of AT&T's businesses would allow competitors to invade these latter businesses and compete with AT&T on an even footing since the divested Bell companies would no longer have any incentive to exclude competitors.

Technically a "Modification of Final Judgment" (MFJ) from the 1949 antitrust case against AT&T, the 1982 decree barred the divested Bell companies from offering long-distance services outside "Local Access and Transport Areas" (LATAs), which were drawn around each Bell company's major service areas. In some cases, the LATAs were only as large as a metropolitan area; in less populous regions, one LATA might include a whole state, such as South Dakota. In addition, the divested Bell companies were barred from manufacturing telecommunications equipment and from offering "information" services without the prior approval of the court. The most important provision was a requirement that the Bell companies modify their switching facilities to provide equal access to all long-distance competitors, a requirement the FCC subsequently extended to the independent local companies.

Administering the Decree – Regulation from the Bench

The decree became a major enterprise for Judge Greene's court and the staff of the Antitrust Division of the Justice Department. Many initial decisions had to be made over the design of the LATAs, the number of Regional Bell Operating Companies (RBOCs) to be established, and the method of separating AT&T's local assets from other assets. Part of Bell Labs was spun off as Bellcore, a research organization to be owned jointly by the divested RBOCs. Disputes arose over who should own the inside wiring in a customer's premises, how the costs of conversion to equal access should be funded, and who should offer Yellow Pages directories.

In the 12 years in which the decree was in force, Judge Greene's court was essentially a third regulator of the telecommunications sector, along with the state regulators and the FCC, and many of his decisions were appealed to the federal appellate courts. Judge Greene was very reluctant to cede control over RBOC entry into advanced information services, even though the antitrust suit did not involve allegations of anticompetitive Bell practices in information services. His rulings were eventually reversed by the court of appeals, which ruled that the decree could not restrain RBOC information-services offerings.[164]

Equally important, the trial court wrestled with the definition of "manufacturing." At issue was whether basic research and engineering of new equipment or software were to be included in the proscribed Bell activities. The court eventually allowed the Bell companies to develop or modify software that is integral to the operation of hardware designed to deliver local services. But it was always difficult to delineate R&D in such a manner.[165]

Clearly, the most contentious issue in the 12 years after divestiture involved the restriction on long-distance service. The divested Bell companies could offer such services over their wireless networks, but not from their wired networks. Many enhanced services might require the downloading of traffic across LATA boundaries even though the service itself was local. As the Internet developed, the distinctions between local, intra-LATA, and long distance became blurred. Was an Internet connection that communicated with a server across the same city different from one that communicated with a server across the country? Could the Bell companies offer basic Internet service to their customers, but not provide the "backbone" services that connected their ISP to the Internet "cloud"?

The premise of the decree was that long-distance service and manufacturing were to be separated from the delivery of local service as long as the latter remained a monopoly. But how much competition would be required to permit the court to allow a Bell company entry into inter-LATA services? Given the rapid growth of competition in central business districts from new fiber-optic competitive access providers (CAPs), would the Bell companies be permitted to offer long-distance service to large business customers? Would wireless competition alleviate the local monopoly problem sufficiently to assuage the fears of the court about the ability of the Bell companies to frustrate long-distance competition?

Many of the questions lingered before the court. Eventually, frustrated Bell companies petitioned to vacate the entire line-of-business provisions of the decree, a petition that was still pending when Congress interceded. It passed the Telecommunications Act of 1996,[166] which vacated the 1982 AT&T decree and substituted rules that the Bell companies must satisfy on a state-by-state basis in order to offer long-distance service. Nearly five years later, only two companies – Verizon and SBC – have succeeded in satisfying regulators that they have met these requirements, and then for only two states – New York and Texas.

Evaluating the Decree

It is now commonplace to conclude that the AT&T decree led to a substantial increase in competition in long-distance services. Customer-premises equipment had become very competitive before 1984; hence, there is little attempt to link increased competition in the manufacture of terminal equipment to the decree. But was the decree responsible for increasing long-distance competition, and – more particularly – was *vertical divestiture* essential to promote competition?

At the dawn of divestiture in 1984, AT&T had more than 90 percent of all long-distance carrier revenues.[167] Indeed, in the first year of divestiture, there were only two national competitors for AT&T's services: MCI and GTE-Sprint (Table F-1). This was fully a decade after MCI began offering switched interstate service and the FCC began wrestling with what to do about it. Over the next five years, AT&T would lose another 22.6 percentage points of market share to new rivals, including several new entrants, many of which would eventually become part of Worldcom. Thus, the decree appears to have worked much better than FCC regulation in promoting entry. But what accounts for this acceleration?

It is possible that the vertical divestiture in the decree is, by itself, responsible for the acceleration of long-distance competition. But if this is true, the

Table F-1. **Revenue Shares of U.S. Long-Distance Carriers (Percent of Total Revenues)**

Year	AT&T	MCI	Sprint	WorldCom	Others
1984	90.1	4.5	2.7	–	2.6
1985	86.3	5.5	2.6	–	5.6
1986	81.9	7.6	4.3	–	6.3
1987	78.6	8.8	5.8	–	6.8
1988	74.6	10.3	7.2	–	8.0
1989	67.5	12.1	8.4	0.2	11.8
1990	65.0	14.2	9.7	0.3	10.8
1991	63.2	15.2	9.9	0.5	11.3
1992	60.8	16.7	9.7	1.4	11.5
1993	58.1	17.8	10	1.9	12.3
1994	55.2	17.4	10.1	3.3	14.0
1995	51.8	19.7	9.8	4.9	13.8
1996	47.9	20.0	9.7	5.5	17.0
1997	44.5	19.4	9.7	6.7	19.8

Note: Excludes local-exchange carriers' long-distance revenues, but includes both intrastate and interstate revenues of long-distance carriers.

Source: James Zolnierek, Katie Rangos, and James Eisner, Long Distance Market Shares: Fourth Quarter 1998, Industry Analysis Division, Common Carrier Bureau, Federal Communications Commission (Mar. 1999).

U.S. should be enjoying the most rapid advance in long-distance competition of any country in the world. No other country has chosen to divorce its long-distance companies from their local operations. Canada, Australia, New Zealand, and the EU countries have opened long-distance services to competition without requiring such divestiture. The EU required all countries to open their markets on January 1, 1998, but the United Kingdom began much earlier – in 1985 – by allowing Mercury (Cable & Wireless) to enter the long-distance market. Canada followed much later, opening long distance to competition in 1992. Neither required vertical divestiture, but Canada mandated equal access for all carriers, whereas the United Kingdom did not. The differences in the rate of growth of entrants in Canada, the United Kingdom, and the U.S. are quite remarkable.

The United Kingdom privatized British Telecom (BT) in 1984 and opened the long-distance market to competition shortly thereafter. It subsequently licensed cable television companies to offer telephone service, both local and long distance. However, the UK has never required British Telecom to modify its switches to offer equal access to its rivals in long distance. As a result, competition in long distance has increased steadily but not dramatically. Fourteen years after Mercury's entry, BT still had about 73 percent of the long-distance market.[168]

By contrast, Canada did not allow entry into switched long-distance services until late 1992. Though not requiring the incumbent long-distance carrier, Bell Canada, to divest its local operations in the most populous two provinces, Ontario and Quebec, the Canadian Radio–Television and Telecommunications Commission (CRTC) did require all local companies to convert their switches to equal access. The result has been quite striking (see Table F-2). In less than seven years, entrants have amassed a larger share of the long-distance market than new entrants have obtained in the UK in twice the time. Indeed, Canadian entrants have the same market share as entrants had in the U.S. in

Table F-2. **Canadian Long-Distance Market Shares, 1995-98 (Percentage of Minutes)**

Company	1995	1996	1997	1998	1999 (Q2)
Former Stentor (Incumbent) Companies	78	71	66	64	65
AT&T Canada	8	11	12	10	–
Sprint Canada	8	11	14	12	–
Others	6	6	7	14	–
Total Non-Incumbents	22	28	33	36	35

Source: 1995: Stentor Hearings Evidence in CRTC Forbearance Proceeding; 1996-98 Call-Net Interrogatory Responses in CRTC 99-5.

1990, fully 16 years after MCI's entry into switched long distance.

The European Union liberalization regime has much more extensive interconnection requirements than the provision of equal access. Entrants are able to lease network elements from the incumbent carriers and to obtain interconnection in a variety of ways, much as in the post-1996 U.S. environment. As a result, entry into long-distance services has led to a substantial erosion of the incumbent national company's long-distance market shares in some countries in just one year, even though the incumbents have not been required to divest any operations. In Germany and Sweden, for example, the incumbents lost 15 to 20 percent of their long-distance market in just one year.[169]

These data suggest that the vertical divestiture provisions in the AT&T decree were necessary to reduce concentration in the long-distance market. Indeed, barring the divested Bell companies from inter-LATA services probably increased market concentration. All that is required to develop a more competitive long-distance market is the guarantee of interconnection with local carriers on an equal basis. A vertically integrated local carrier apparently cannot engage in any "subtle" discrimination that really impedes long-distance competition as long as its switches originate and terminate its rivals' calls in the same fashion.[170]

Data on average transaction prices in the long-distance market are difficult to obtain for liberalized national markets. Comparisons of undiscounted posted peak or off-peak prices can be misleading when numerous discount plans are offered. To demonstrate this, I reproduce in Figure F-1 two examples of tariffed rates offered by AT&T and Sprint: a daytime rate for AT&T and a lower, off-peak rate for Sprint. Note how these declined from the early 1980s to 1990-91, but stabilized thereafter.[171] However, the average interstate long-distance revenues per minute as estimated by the FCC continued to decline slowly after 1990.

Note that rates in both the United States and Canada have fallen since 1992 when Canada initially liberalized, but that Canadian rates have fallen much more rapidly. Indeed, by 1998 Canadian carriers realized *less* per minute than their counterparts in the United States. A likely reason for the lower Canadian rates is that *local* carriers are not quarantined as in the United States, but are free to compete with the new long-distance carriers, AT&T and Sprint Canada. These local carriers have every incentive to expand output as long as their marginal returns are above incremental cost, and the incremental cost of long-distance service plus local connections is very low even relative to 1998 rates. Therefore, we should expect Canadian rates to fall even farther in the post-1998 period.

Figure F-1. **Real Long-Distance Rates in the U.S. and Canada, 1980-1998**

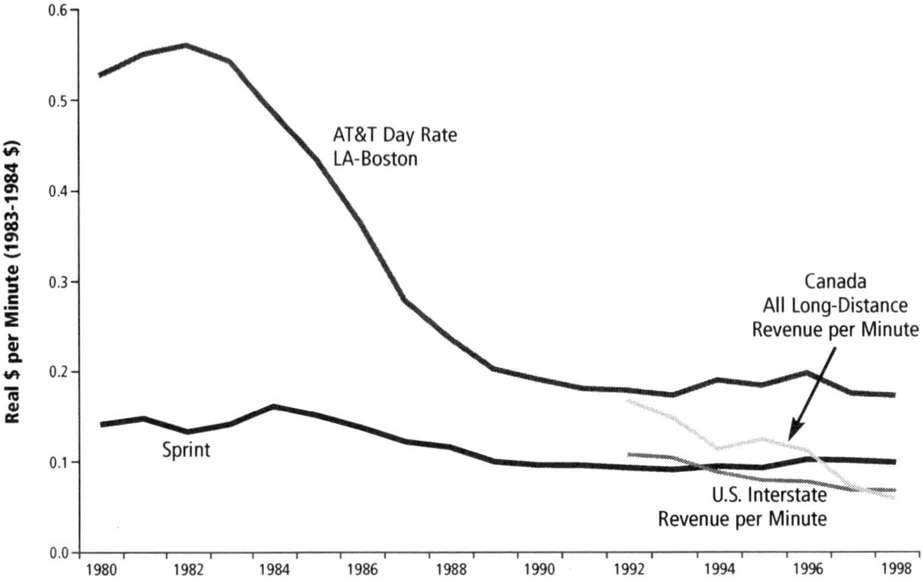

Note: Canadian rates have been converted to U.S. dollars at the exchange rate of US $0.68 = Canadian $1. All rates are deflated by the Consumer Price Index.

Sources: FCC's *Statistics of Communications Common Carriers*, annual editions; CRTC 99-5; Bureau of Labor Statistics.

Lessons for the Future

Vertical divestiture was not required in order to unleash competition. The imposition of equal-access arrangements – and deregulation of prices – was all that was necessary. Nor was vertical divestiture needed to stimulate productivity growth. Competition for AT&T from MCI, Sprint, Qwest, Worldcom, and numerous others would surely have sufficed. AT&T subsequently realized that vertical integration between local and long-distance operations is necessary in the modern telecommunications era. As a result, it has spent $110 billion to acquire two of the country's largest cable-television companies.

Just as revealing is the *voluntary* divestiture of manufacturing from AT&T's operations. In 1998, AT&T spun off Lucent's manufacturing division because it felt that Lucent would be more valuable if freed from AT&T's patronage. The antitrust authorities had left manufacturing with AT&T, but divested it of its local operating companies. The market is now reversing those decisions in a much more competitive era. Similarly, in Canada, Bell Canada is keeping its operating companies but *voluntarily* divesting itself of Nortel, its manufacturing company. Competition in manufacturing and long distance is thriving on both sides of the border, even if the U.S. now appears to be lagging in the

Figure F-2. **Average Long Distance Revenue: Canada Versus United States, 1992-98**

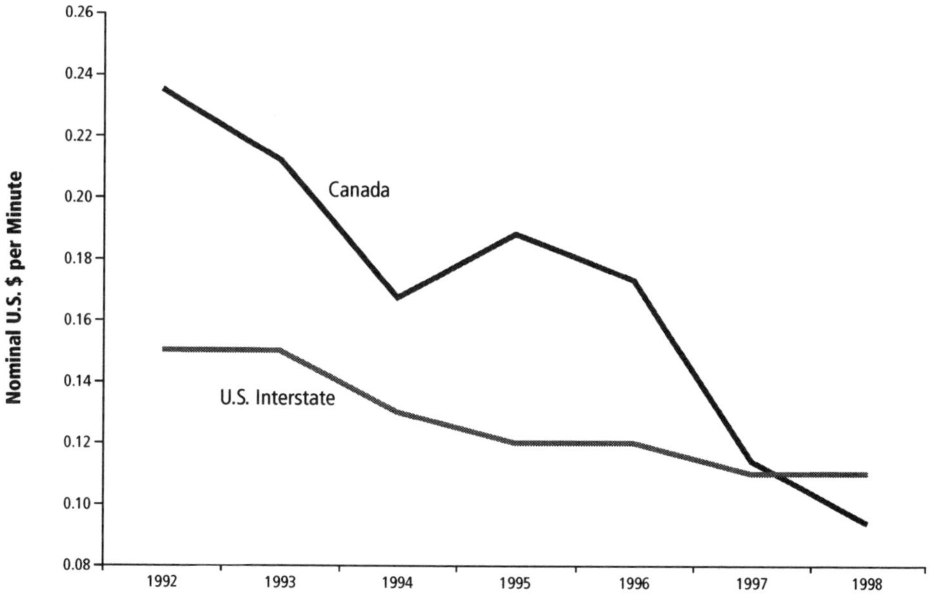

Sources: FCC's *Trends in Telephone Service*, March 2000, Table 14.5; Midland Walwyn, CRTC 99-5.

growth of competition in long distance. Had antitrust authorities focused their attention on the actions of state or provincial authorities years ago, competition in local services might also be a reality today.

Two Other Single-Firm Cases

Of 423 Section 2 cases in which the government imposed a consent decree or a court found against the defendants, only three or four involved single-firm monopolization not achieved through mergers. Of these, I have extensively reviewed only *United Shoe Machinery* and *AT&T*, leaving *IBM* (1952) and *Kansas City Star* (1953). Neither of these cases would qualify for "landmark" status, and there is very little in the economics literature about them.

IBM

The 1952 Section 2 case against IBM has many similarities to the *United Shoe Machinery* case. IBM dominated the "tabulating machine" business and the related business of tabulating cards, or "punch cards," long before the commercial development of the computer. The Justice Department filed the suit against IBM in 1952, alleging that it had achieved monopoly power in tabulating machines through its lease-only policy and a restrictive patent policy. In addition, IBM allegedly enjoyed monopoly power in tabulating cards, which it maintained in part through discriminatory pricing.

IBM settled the case in 1956, agreeing to sell some rotary presses and to end its discriminatory pricing. It was also required to divest some of its card manufacturing capacity in order to reduce its market share to 50 percent by 1962. In addition, IBM was required by the decree to set up a separate "service bureau" through which it offered service to customers who did not lease or own tabulating machines. This service bureau was subsequently sold to Control Data Corporation to settle a private suit.

Although the decree led to greater competition in tabulating cards, at least one student of the decree claims that it was a failure because the new firms did not make sustainable profits.[172] In any case, there is little evidence that this antitrust action had any favorable effects on competition in the computer industry, which was already beginning to replace tabulating machines when the decree was signed.[173] Indeed, IBM quickly vaulted to a dominant position in mainframe computers during this period, leading the Justice Department to file another Section 2 case against it in 1969. This latter case was eventually dropped in 1982, in no small part because the market had changed once again.[174]

If there is a lesson in these IBM cases, it is that federal antitrust actions were far behind market developments. The replacement of tabulating machines by computers was under way when IBM settled the first case, and IBM was losing its market power to upstart firms offering minicomputers and personal computers in the 1969-1982 period. Competitive forces eroded IBM's position, leaving antitrust at the gate.

Kansas City Star

The Kansas City Star case involved both criminal and civil complaints under the Sherman Act in 1953 alleging monopolization and attempts to monopolize the news and advertising markets in Kansas City.[175] Most of the charges involved exclusive dealing, tying arrangements, and discriminatory pricing across the Star's newspapers in the 1930s. However, the government also alleged tying arrangements between the Star's newspapers and its local broadcasting stations, WDAF and WDAF-TV. Cross-ownership of media has been a major issue at the Federal Trade Commission for decades, but the Kansas City Star case antedates even the Commission's lengthy record on the issue.

The Kansas City Star newspapers obtained a dominant position in news and advertising in the Kansas City area through a variety of pricing policies and acquisitions throughout the first half of the 20th century. By 1953, the Star's three newspapers – one daily morning edition, one daily evening edition, and a single Sunday newspaper – averaged about 360,000 in circulation. The nearest competitor, across the river in Kansas, had less than 28,000 in daily circulation. The lower court refused to admit evidence on the degree to which national publications or newspapers in adjacent markets competed for readership and advertising with the Star's papers. Therefore, the data on Kansas City dailies' circulation provided un-rebutted evidence of the Star's market power.[176]

The government alleged that earlier competitors had been vanquished through a variety of anticompetitive practices. In particular, advertisers were required to purchase "combination" advertising in the Star's morning and evening papers. Television advertisers were required to advertise in the Star's newspapers to gain access to WDAF-TV. Predatory pricing – "depression discounts" – drove the Star's principal newspaper rival from the market. And once this rival exited, prices were raised.

The case was developed and filed during the last days of the Truman administration, but litigated during the Eisenhower administration. Allegations of political influence surrounded the case, especially when the criminal charges against the Star's president were dropped on the eve of trial. The government won the criminal case against the Star and one of its executives, but the judge levied fines of only $7,500 against the two defendants.

The civil case was never litigated because the Star and the government entered negotiations to settle the case shortly after the Star lost its appeals of the criminal case.[177] Five months later, a consent decree was entered that forbade discrimination in advertising, tying arrangements in advertising or subscription sales, and discrimination in credit policies with advertisers. Although the government had asked that the Star's broadcast licenses be revoked, the consent decree simply required the Star to sell them and transfer the licenses. Thereafter, the Star was forbidden to acquire any other newspaper or broadcaster in the Kansas City area.

There is very little evidence available on the decree's effect on the newspaper business in Kansas City. The 1950s began a lengthy period of consolidation of the newspaper industry throughout the country as consumers turned increasingly to television for news. The consent decree had little apparent effect on the concentration in local newspapers in Kansas City, but it is probably naive to have expected such an effect in this period of rapid growth of television. Four years after the decree was entered, the three Star newspapers still averaged about 348,000 in circulation, and the other dailies totaled just

43,000. Between 1957 and 1961, the Star newspapers' circulation declined from 348,000 to 339,000, while their competitors' had fallen from 47,000 to 43,000.[178]

The price of a subscription to the Star papers remained constant in real terms between 1953 and 1960, but increased thereafter. The Star's combined daily advertising rate rose by 52 percent and its Sunday rate rose by 54 percent between 1953 and 1969, compared to a 37 percent increase in the consumer price index.[179] These increases do not constitute convincing evidence that the Star's market power was unaffected by the decree, given the likely changes in costs and the availability of competitive media. However, the data certainly do not suggest that the decree improved competition among news and advertising media in Kansas City.

CONCLUSION

Beginning with Arnold Harberger's seminal work,[180] a number of empirical studies have suggested that the total cost of monopoly is very small. Harberger found that the social cost of monopoly is only 0.1 percent of gross national product. More recent studies place the loss between 0.02 percent and 13.1 percent, but the higher-end numbers include estimates of the costs of advertising that allegedly result from monopoly power. Without including advertising as a source of the loss of economic welfare due to monopoly, the estimates of the social cost of monopoly are 4 percent of GDP or less.[181]

This review of the major Section 2 Sherman Act cases won by the government or ending in consent decrees provides remarkably little evidence that these cases and the relief that emanated from them had a positive effect on competition and consumer welfare. In some cases, such as *Standard Oil* (1911) or *IBM* (1956), this was due to the fact that markets were changing rapidly, thereby reducing the defendant firms' market power anyway. In at least three others, *American Tobacco* (1911), *Alcoa* (1945), and *Paramount* (1948), the relief simply did not generate an increase in price competition. In *American Tobacco* and *Alcoa*, the substitution of a three-firm oligopoly for a single firm did not have a measurable effect on prices. In *Paramount*, prices actually rose after the forced vertical divestitures, but this result is clouded by the enormous changes wrought by the substitution of television for movie admissions that occurred in the 1950s. Similarly, the relief obtained by the government in *United Shoe Machinery* (1953) over more than 15 years was surely overwhelmed by the development of foreign competition in shoe manufacturing, but there is no evidence that shoe machinery prices were reduced very much by the first decree. Nor can one find evidence that the vertical divestiture in *Kansas City Star* (1958) or the limitations on television network program "ownership" and production in the 1980s had any beneficial effects on competition. Indeed, the network decrees appear to have reduced competition by eliminating three competitors from the syndication market.

The exception in this analysis is the *AT&T* (1982) decree that broke up AT&T, a monopoly created by government regulation. However, the vertical divestiture could have been avoided through a simple regulatory policy requiring equal access to local networks. Therefore, this antitrust success in correcting a market failure was, in reality, the correction of an earlier government failure.

The important lesson from this review of Section 2 cases is that the government often lags the market in finding ways to increase competition, rendering antitrust cases redundant. In other cases, the government failed to formulate relief that resulted in any meaningful change in competition because it failed to grasp the essentials of the market that led to concentration in the first place. This is particularly true for markets driven by rapid technological change, such as computers and the distribution of video programming. Given the rapid pace of technical progress that we are now encountering, there is little prospect that Section 2 will be employed more productively in the future than it has been in the past.

* The author is indebted to Hal Singer, Bruce M. Owen, J. Gregory Sidak, and Clifford Winston for comments and suggestions. Research assistance was provided by Jeffrey West, Ana Kreacic, and Kristin Jaeger. The author has been a consultant to Microsoft in its current Sherman Act litigation. This article originally appeared in the *University of Oregon Law Review*. It is reprinted with permission.

[1] Tom Foremski, Christopher Grimes, and Richard Wolfe, "*Judge Jackson Orders Break-up Order to Microsoft*," *Financial Times*, June 8, 2000, p. 1.

[2] *United States v. AT&T*, 552 F. Supp. 131 (D.D.C. 1982) *aff'd sub. nom., Maryland v. United States*, 460 U.S. 1001 (1983).

[3] *Standard Oil Company of New Jersey v. United States*, 221 U.S. 1 (1911).

[4] *United States v. American Tobacco*, 221 U.S. 106 (1911).

[5] *United States v. Aluminum Company of America*, 148 F.2d 416 (2d Cir. 1945).

[6] *United States v. Paramount Pictures*, 334 U.S. 131 (1948).

[7] *United States v. United Shoe Machinery*, 110 F. supp. 295 (D.Mass. 1953), aff'd. 347 U.S. 521 (1954).

[8] *United States v. AT&T*, 552 F. Supp.131 (D.D.C. 1982), *aff'd sub. nom.*; *Maryland v. United States*, 160 U.S. 1001 (1983).

[9] Philip Areeda, *Antitrust Analysis* (Little, Brown), 1988.

[10] *United States v. United Shoe Machinery*, 110 F. Supp. 295 (D.Mass. 1953), aff'd. 347 U.S. 521 (1954).

[11] See third section below.

[12] *United States v. IBM*, 69 Civ. 200.

[13] For a discussion of the futility of the government's case, see Franklin M. Fisher, Joen E. Greenwood, and John J. McGowan, *Folded, Spindled, and Mutilated: Economic Analysis and U.S. v. IBM* (MIT Press), 1983.

[14] *United States v. AT&T*, 552 F. Supp. 131 (D.D.C. 1982).

[15] See F.M. Scherer, *Innovation and Growth: Schumpeterian Perspectives* (MIT Press), 1984, Chapter 10.

[16] See Paul H. Rubin, "*What Do Economists Think About Antitrust? A Random Walk Down Pennsylvania Avenue*," in *The Causes and Consequences of Antitrust: The Public-Choice Perspective* (Fred McChesney and William F. Shughart II, ed., University of Chicago Press), 1995, p. 30.

[17] Another 34 met the criterion, but there was insufficient information in the Abstracts to complete the categorization of them.

[18] See Carl Kaysen, *United States v. United Shoe Machinery Corporation: An Economic Analysis of an Antitrust Case* (Harvard University Press), 1956, pp. 272-275.

[19] Malcolm R. Burns, "*The Comparative Effects of Trust Busting*," 85 *Journal of Political Economy* 717 (1977).

[20] I examine this case in detail below.

[21] Ideally, an analysis of the effects of a decree should include the effects on the productive efficiency of the defendant firm and others in the industry. If the decree causes a sacrifice of economies of scale, the reduced productive efficiency should be weighed against any improvement in consumer welfare due to lower prices. In this survey, I do not attempt to conduct such an analysis of every case, focusing instead on whether the decrees had any measurable beneficial impact on prices and output.

[22] Harold F. Williamson and Arnold R. Daum, *The American Petroleum Industry: The Age of Illumination 1859-1899* (Northwestern University Press), 1959, p. 302.

[23] Harold F. Williamson, Ralph L. Andreano, Arnold R. Daum, and Gilbert C. Klose, *The American Petroleum Industry: The Age of Energy 1899-1959* (Northwestern University Press), 1963, p. 9. (A "partial list" of state suits against Standard includes 20 actions filed in 1904-06.)

[24] *Ibid.*, p. 17.

[25] *Ibid.*

[26] U.S. Bureau of the Census, *Historical United States, Colonial Times to 1970, Bicentennial Edition* (U.S. Department of Commerce), 1975, pp. 593-594; Williamson et al., *supra* note 23, p. 168.

[27] Williamson et al., *supra* note 23.

[28] Among the charges in the 1906 *Standard Oil* case was that Standard denied common carriage on its pipelines to small independent refiners.

[29] Williamson et al., *supra* note 23, pp. 64-109.

[30] *Ibid.*, p. 7.

[31] U.S. Bureau of the Census, *Historical United States, Colonial Times to 1970, Bicentennial*

Edition (U.S. Department of Commerce), 1975, pp. 593-594.

[32] Williamson et al., *supra* note 23, p. 172.

[33] John S. McGee, "*Predatory Price Cutting: The Standard Oil (N.J.) Case*," 1 *Journal of Law and Economics* 137 (1958). (Provides a cogent argument that Standard did not attain its market position through predatory prices, but rather through simply acquiring rivals in large numbers. McGee does not dispute, however, that Standard may have used exclusionary practices with respect to its transportation facilities.)

[34] It is not clear why such "profit pools" were viewed with such hostility if they were indeed simply the pooling of profits within a single entity – the Standard Oil trust.

[35] *United States v. Standard Oil*, 173 F. 177 (1909).

[36] *Standard Oil Co. of New Jersey v. United States*, 221 U.S. 1 (1911).

[37] All of these data are from Williamson et al., *supra* note 23, p. 7.

[38] *Ibid.*

[39] All prices are deflated by the GNP deflator (1958=100). Data for crude oil production and prices are available in U.S. Bureau of the Census, *Historical Statistics of the United States, Colonial Times to 1970, Bicentennial Edition* (U.S. Department of Commerce), 1975, p. 593. Crude oil production is in thousand barrel units. Crude oil prices per barrel are in units of 1958 dollars. Real GNP and the GNP deflator are available from the *Historical Statistics of the United States*, p. 224. Real GNP is in billion 1958 dollars. Automobile registrations are in thousand units and are available from the *Historical Statistics of the United States*, p. 716. Electricity production is in units of million kilowatt-hours and is available from the *Historical Statistics of the United States*, p. 821. Missing values for electricity production were interpolated by fitting a power function to the existing data points from 1902 to 1934.

[40] A similar analysis of the determinants of gasoline and kerosene prices would have been informative, but annual data on these prices are not available for the requisite time period.

[41] These coefficients are statistically significant when electricity capacity is substituted for electricity production in these two equations.

[42] Malcolm R. Burns, "*The Comparative Effects from Trust Busting: A Portfolio Analysis*," 85 *Journal of Political Economy*, pp. 717-739 (1977).

[43] *Ibid.*

[44] In this analysis and those reported below for the other cases, I estimate a standard capital asset pricing model of the form $r_{it} = a + ßR_t + u_{it}$ where r_{it} is the return to stockholders of the *i*th company's equity (capital gains plus dividends divided by the value of the common equity at the beginning of the period) in period t, R_t is the return to the entire market (Dow Jones Average) in period t, and u_{it} is a random error term. The CAP model is estimated for the period prior to the filing of the case, and the estimate of ß from this regression is used to generate predicted values of r for the event windows in the case. The residuals are simply the actual return less the predicted return.

[45] Williamson et al., *supra* note 23, pp. 12-13.

[46] Derived from Williamson et al., *supra* note 23, pp. 7, 166.

[47] One historian, Joseph A. Pratt, advances the theory that it was Texas antitrust law that prevented Standard from expanding its market power into the Gulf area. ("*The Petroleum Industry in Transition: Antitrust and the Decline of Monopoly Control of Oil*," 40 *Journal of Economic History*, pp. 815-837 (1980). I do not address his theory in this

paper because it is not germane to my inquiry into the effects of federal antitrust actions. However, Pratt does not explain how Texas antitrust law could have affected Standard's behavior in other Gulf, Mid-Continent, and Western states.

[48] Richard B. Tennant, *The American Cigarette Industry: A Study in Economic Analysis and Public Policy* (Yale University Press), 1950, p. 27.

[49] Tennant, *supra note* 48, pp. 28-29.

[50] Tennant, *supra note* 48, pp. 28-29.

[51] *Northern Securities v. United States*, 193 U.S. 197 (1904).

[52] *United States v. American Tobacco*, 164 F. 700 (1908).

[53] *United States v. American Tobacco*, 221 U.S. 106 (1911).

[54] Tennant, *supra note* 48, p. 61.

[55] *United States v. American Tobacco*, 191 F. 371 (1911), as quoted in Tennant, *supra* note 48, p. 65.

[56] Tennant, *supra note* 48, p. 70.

[57] Tennant, *supra note* 48, p. 71, Table 12.

[58] Tennant, *supra note* 48, p. 85.

[59] U.S. Bureau of the Census, *Historical Statistics of the United States, Colonial Times to 1970, Bicentennial Edition* (U.S. Department of Commerce), 1975, pp. 224, 699.

[60] Tennant, *supra* note 48, pp. 96, 346.

[61] U.S. Bureau of the Census, *Historical Statistics of the United States, Colonial Times to 1970, Bicentennial Edition* (U.S. Department of Commerce), 1975, p. 517.

[62] *Ibid.*, p. 211.

[63] Malcolm R. Burns, "*An Empirical Analysis of Stockholder Injury Under #2 of the Sherman Act*," 31 *Journal of Industrial Economics*, p. 333 (1983).

[64] This description of the early aluminum industry is derived mainly from Merton J. Peck, *Competition in the Aluminum Industry 1945-1958* (Harvard University Press), 1961; Simon Whitney, *Antitrust Policies: American Experience in Twenty Industries, Volume II* (The Twentieth Century Fund), 1958; and Margaret B.W. Graham and Bettye H. Pruitt, *R&D for Industry: A Century of Technical Innovation at Alcoa* (Cambridge University Press), 1990.

[65] Donald H. Wallace, *Market Control in the Aluminum Industry* (Harvard University Press), 1937, p. 24.

[66] U.S. Bureau of the Census, *Historical Statistics of the United States, Colonial Times to 1970, Bicentennial Edition* (U.S. Department of Commerce), 1975, p. 605.

[67] *Ibid.*, p. 695.

[68] Wallace, *supra* note 65, p. 194.

[69] Wallace, *supra* note 65, p. 226.

[70] Whitney, *supra* note 64, p. 90.

[71] *United States v. Aluminum Company of America*, Eq. 159 (W.D. Pa. 1912), decree in *Decrees and Judgments in Federal Antitrust Cases* (U.S. Department of Justice), 1918, pp. 341-350, and in Wallace, *Market Control in the Aluminum Industry*, pp. 547-555, as cited in Simon N. Whitney, *Antitrust Policies* (The Twentieth Century Fund, Inc.), 1958, p. 86.

[72] *Aluminum Company of America*, Docket 248, 3 FTC 302 (1921); *Aluminum Company of America v. FTC*, 284 Fed. 401 (3d Cir. 1922), *certiorari denied* 261 U.S. 616 (1923).

[73] *Aluminum Company of America v. FTC*, 299 Fed. 361 (3d Cir. 1924).

[74] Federal Trade Commission, "*Kitchen Furnishings and Domestic Appliances*," in *Report on House Furnishings Industry*, Vol. 3, p. xxxii (1924).

[75] *Aluminum Company of America*, S. Doc. 67, 69th Cong., 1st sess. (1926).

[76] *Aluminum Company of America*, Dkt. 1335, 13 FTC 333 (1930).

[77] *United States v. Aluminum Company of America*, 44 F. Supp. 97 (S.D. N.Y. 1942).

[78] *United States v. Aluminum Company of America*, 44 F. Supp. 97, 152 (S.D. N.Y. 1942).

[79] *United States v. Aluminum Company of America*, 148 F.2d 416 (2d Cir. 1945).

[80] A lively literature developed over this issue. See Darius W. Gaskins, Jr., "*Alcoa Revisited: The Welfare Implications of a Second-Hand Market*," 7 *Journal of Economic Theory*, pp. 254-271 (1974); Franklin M. Fisher, "*Alcoa Revisited: Comment*," 9 *Journal of Economic Theory*, pp. 357-359 (1974).

[81] Whitney, *supra* note 64, p. 93.

[82] Germany had become the world's largest producer of aluminum when World War II began in 1939. By itself, Alcoa could not afford to sufficiently expand its operations to meet the emergency demands of the Allied powers. See George David Smith, *From Monopoly to Competition: The Transformation of Alcoa 1888-1986* (Cambridge University Press), 1988, pp. 191-192.

[83] Whitney, *supra* note 64, p. 95.

[84] Whitney, *supra* note 64, pp. 97-98.

[85] Whitney, *supra* note 64, p. 98, note 48.

[86] *United States v. Aluminum Company of America*, 153 F. Supp. 132 (S.D.N.Y. 1957).

[87] Peck, *supra* note 64, pp. 148-150.

[88] Peck, *supra* note 64, pp. 176-178.

[89] All prices are deflated by the GNP deflator (1958=100). Data for the prices of primary aluminum and imported bauxite were obtained from the Minerals Information Team of the U.S. Geological Survey. Prices of primary aluminum are in units of 1958 dollars per pound. Prices of imported bauxite are in units of 1958 dollars per short ton. Real GNP and the GNP deflator are from U.S. Bureau of the Census, *Historical Statistics of the United States, Colonial Times to 1970, Bicentennial Edition* (U.S. Department of Commerce), 1975, p. 224. Real GNP is in billion 1958 dollars. Steel prices are from U.S. Geological Survey, *Metal Prices in the United States through 1998*, p. 63 (available at http://minerals.usgs.gov/minerals/pubs/metal_prices/). Steel prices are in units of 1958 dollars per short ton. Electricity prices are from U.S. Bureau of the Census, *Historical Statistics of the United States, Colonial Times to 1970, Bicentennial Edition* (U.S. Department of Commerce), 1975, p. 827, and are in units of 1958 cents per kilowatt-hour.

[90] The information in this section is derived from Michael Conant, *Antitrust in the Motion Picture Industry* (University of California Press), 1960.

[91] *Ibid.*

[92] *United States v. Interstate Circuit*, 20 F. Supp. 868, 874 (N.D. Texas, 1937); *United States v. Crescent Amusement*, 323 U.S. 173 (1944); *United States v. Griffith*, 334 U.S. 100

(1948); *Schine Chain Theatres v. United States*, 334 U.S. 110 (1948).

[93] *United States v. Paramount Pictures*, 70 F. Supp. 53, 72-76 (S.D.N.Y. 1946).

[94] *United States v. Paramount Pictures*, 334 U.S. 131 (1948).

[95] *United States v. Loew's*: Warner Consent Decree, 1950-51 CCH Trade Cases Paragraph 62,765 (S.D.N.Y. 1951); Twentieth Century-Fox Consent Decree, 1950-1951 CCH Trade Cases Paragraph 62,861 (S.D.N.Y. 1951); Loew's Consent Decree, 1952-1953 CCH Trade Cases Paragraph 67,228 (S.D.N.Y. 1952), as cited in Conant, *supra* note 90, p. 103.

[96] *Census of Service Industries* (U.S. Bureau of the Census), 1958, 1967.

[97] Much of the discussion of the motion-picture industry after *Paramount* is derived from Robert W. Crandall, "*The Postwar Performance of the Motion Picture Industry*," 20 *Antitrust Bulletin* pp. 49-88 (1975).

[98] *Ibid.*; U.S. Bureau of the Census, *Historical Statistics of the United States, Colonial Times to 1970, Bicentennial Edition* (U.S. Department of Commerce), 1975, p. 210.

[99] Crandall, *supra* note 97.

[100] Crandall, *supra* note 97.

[101] All of these data are from Crandall, *supra* note 97.

[102] Arthur DeVany and Ross D. Eckert, "*Motion Picture Antitrust: The Paramount Cases Revisited*," in *Research in Law and Economics* (Richard O. Zerbe, Jr., and Victor P. Golberg, eds.), 1991.

[103] Carl Kaysen, *United States v. United Shoe Machinery Corporation* (Harvard University Press), 1956, p. 6.

[104] Kaysen, *supra* note 103, p. 9.

[105] Kaysen, *supra* note 103, p. 3.

[106] Kaysen, *supra* note 103, p. 3.

[107] Kaysen, *supra* note 103, p. 3.

[108] *United States v. United Shoe Machinery*, 110 F.Supp. 295 (D.Mass. 1953), *affd.* 391 U.S. 244.

[109] *United Shoe Machinery*, 1969 U.S. Dist. LEXIS 13280, *1.

[110] Scott E. Masten and Edward A. Snyder, "*United States versus United Shoe Machinery Corporation: On the Merits*," 36 *Journal of Law and Economics* (1993), p. 38.

[111] Kaysen, *supra* note 103, p. 27.

[112] *Ibid.*

[113] Masten and Snyder, *supra* note 110, p. 35.

[114] Several different analyses were performed to determine the market share of USM and its competitors. The results here are taken from Kaysen, *supra* note 103, p. 6. [Kaysen served as a special "law clerk" to Judge Charles E. Wyzanski, Jr. for the USM trial, even though Kaysen was an economist.] The specific results cited by Kaysen are from the Government's *Summary* of Depositions, which included a study of 45 shoe manufacturers canvassed in 1949. (See Kaysen, pp. 45, 52.) Also note that the percentage of market share for "Other Competitors" was found by subtracting the sum of the market shares of major machines for United, Compo, and International from 100 percent. For minor machines, the market shares of United, Boston Machine Works, and Compo were summed

and subtracted from 100 percent to determine the market share of other competitors.

[115] Kaysen, *supra* note 103, p. 53.

[116] Masten and Snyder, *supra* note 110, p. 57.

[117] *Ibid.*

[118] Kaysen, *supra* note 103, p. 74.

[119] *Ibid.*, p. 89.

[120] *Ibid.*, p. 92.

[121] *United States v. United Shoe Machinery*, 110 F. Supp. 295 (1953).

[122] *United States v. United Shoe Machinery*, 347 U.S. 521 (1954).

[123] Kaysen, *supra* note 103, pp. 272-273.

[124] *United Shoe Machinery v. United States*, 347 U.S. 521 (1954).

[125] Gordon Parrish, *The Experience with Antitrust Relief in Shoe Machinery* (Ph.D. Dissertation, Washington State University, 1973, p. 142).

[126] Don E. Waldman, *Antitrust Action and Market Structure* (D.C. Heath and Company), 1978, p. 47; *United States v. United Shoe Machinery*, 391 U.S. 244 (1968), Supreme Court decision, Finding of Fact No. 2.

[127] Waldman, *supra* note 126.

[128] Parrish, *supra* note 125, p. 107 (citations omitted).

[129] Parrish, *supra* note 125, p. 97.

[130] Parrish, *supra* note 125, p. 138.

[131] Parrish, *supra* note 125, p. 161.

[132] Waldman, *supra* note 126, p. 47.

[133] *Ibid.*

[134] Data from the quinquennial *Census of Manufactures*.

[135] See the next section.

[136] Masten and Snyder, *supra* note 110, pp. 66-67.

[137] Masten and Snyder, *supra* note 110, p. 66.

[138] 266 F. Supp. 328 (D.Mass. 1967).

[139] 391 U.S. 244 (1969).

[140] See Robert W. Crandall, "The Economic Case for a Fourth Commercial Television Network," 22 *Public Policy*, pp. 513-536 (1974).

[141] Federal Communications Commission Office of Network Inquiry, Television Network Program Procurement., H.R. Rep. No. 88-281 (1st Sess. 1963); Federal Communications Commission Office of Network Inquiry, Television Network Program Procurement, Part II, Washington, 1965.

[142] The cases were *United States v. American Broadcasting*, *United States v. Columbia Broadcasting*, and *United States v. National Broadcasting*, Civil Complaints (C.D. Cal. 1972).

[143] A thorough discussion of network program production, acquisition, and distribution may be found in Federal Communications Commission, Network Inquiry Special Staff, New Television Networks: Entry, Jurisdiction, Ownership, and Regulation (October 1980). (Hereafter FCC, Special Staff Report.)

[144] FCC, Special Staff Report, *supra* note 143, Vol. II.

[145] For details of these rules, see FCC, Special Staff Report, *supra* note 143, Vol. II.

[146] NBC entered into a decree in 1976, and CBS and ABC both followed in 1980.

[147] Critical analyses of the assumption that networks had monopsony power may be found in Robert W. Crandall, "*FCC Regulation, Monopsony, and Network Television Program Costs*," 3 *Bell Journal of Economics and Management Science*, pp. 483-508 (1972), and Franklin M. Fisher, "*The Financial Interest and Syndication Rules in Network Television: Regulatory Fantasy and Reality*," in *Antitrust and Regulation: Essays in Memory of John J. McGowan*, pp. 263-298 (Franklin M. Fisher, ed., 1985).

[148] See FCC, Special Staff Report, *supra* note 143, Vol. II, pp. 736-741.

[149] *United States v. National Broadcasting*, 449 F.Supp. 1127 (C.D. Cal. 1978), *aff'd*, 603 F.2d 227 (9th Cir. 1979), *cert. denied*, 444 U.S. 991 (1979); *United States v. American Broadcasting*, 45 Fed. Reg. 58,442 (1980); *United States v. CBS*, 45 Fed. Reg. 34,464 (1980).

[150] These data are derived from Robert W. Crandall, "The Economic Case Against the FCC's Television Network Financial Interest and Syndication Rules," submitted in the Federal Communications Commission's *In the Matter of the Syndication and Financial Interest Rules*, MM Docket No. 90-162, 1990, Table V.2.

[151] *Ibid.*, Table V.1.

[152] *Ibid.*, p. 31.

[153] Bruce M. Owen and Steven S. Wildman, *Video Economics* (Harvard University Press), 1992, Ch. 5.

[154] See, for example, the analysis of the FCC on Network Inquiry Special Staff in FCC, Special Staff Report, *supra* note 143, and Owen and Wildman, *supra* note 153.

[155] This discussion of the early history of the U.S. telephone industry is based principally on Gerald W. Brock, *The Telecommunications Industry* (Harvard University Press), 1981.

[156] The Willis-Graham Act of 1921 exempted telephone mergers from the antitrust laws.

[157] Robert W. Crandall and Leonard Waverman, *Who Pays for Universal Service? When Telephone Subsidies Become Transparent* (Brookings), 2000.

[158] *MCI Telecommunications v. FCC*, 561 F.2d 365 (D.C. Cir. 1977), *cert. denied*, 434 U.S. 1040 (1978); *MCI Communications v. FCC*, 580 F.2d 590 (D.C.Cir. 1978), *cert. denied*, 439 U.S. 980 (1978).

[159] *North Carolina Utility Commission v. FCC*, 537 F.2d 787 (4th Cir, 1976).

[160] *United States v. Western Electric*, Civil Action No. 17-49, C.A. 82-0192 (D.N.J. Jan. 24, 1956).

[161] These cases included *MCI Communications v. AT&T*, 708 F.2d 1081 (7th Cir. 1983); *Southern Communications v. AT&T*, 556 F. Supp. 825 (D.D.C. 1983); and *Mid-Texas Communications Systems v. AT&T*, 615 F.2d 1372 (5th Cir. 1980).

[162] *United States v. AT&T*, Civil Action No. 74-1698 (D.D.C. Nov. 20, 1974).

[163] *United States v. AT&T*, 552 F. Supp. 131 (D.D.C. 1982).

[164] *United States v. Western Electric*, 951 F.2d 1324 (D.C. Cir. 1991).

[165] See Michael K. Kellogg, John Thorne, and Peter W. Huber, *Federal Telecommunications Law* (Little, Brown & Co.), 1992, Section 6.5, for a thorough discussion of these problems.

[166] 47 U.S.C. Section 271.

[167] Long-distance carrier revenues do not include the long-distance revenues of local exchange companies, but the local Bell companies did not compete outside their LATAs because of the decree, and other local companies did not offer interLATA service to any major extent. Thus, the concentration of long-distance carrier revenues provide a good measure of market concentration in the interLATA market, which accounts for about three-fourths of all long-distance service.

[168] *Fifth Report on the Implementation of the Telecommunications Regulatory Package: Communication from the Commission to the European Parliament, the Council, the Economic and Social Committee and the Committee of the Regions*, COM (99) 537 final, p. 151, Annex 4.2.

[169] European Commission, *supra* note 168.

[170] B. Douglas Bernheim and Robert D. Willig make this argument in *The Scope of Competition in Telecommunications*, Draft (American Enterprise Institute), 1996.

[171] All rates are taken from the FCC's *Statistics of Communications Common Carriers*, annual editions. They are residential rates deflated by the overall Consumer Price Index.

[172] Waldman, *supra* note 127, p. 141.

[173] See Ronald P. Wilder, "*The Electronic Data Processing Industry: Market Structure and Policy Issues*," *Antitrust Bulletin*, pp. 25-47 (1975). Wilder views the service-bureau provision of the decree as a mild success.

[174] For a scathing critique of the government's 1969 case, see Franklin M. Fisher, John J. McGowan, and Joen E. Greenwood, *Folded, Spindled, and Mutilated: Economic Analysis and U.S. v. IBM* (MIT Press), 1983.

[175] *United States v. Kansas City Star*, Criminal No.18444 and Civil No. 7989 (W.D. Mo. Jan. 6, 1953).

[176] These data are from Lorry E. Rytting, *United States of America v. Kansas City Star: An Antitrust Case Study* (Ph.D. Dissertation, Department of Mass Communications, University of Wisconsin, 1969).

[177] *Kansas City Star v. United States*, 240 F.2d 643 (1957); cert. den., 354 U.S. 923 (1957).

[178] Rytting, *supra* note 176, p. 194.

[179] *Ibid.*, pp. 296-300; Bureau of Labor Statistics, Consumer Price Index, 1953-1969.

[180] Arnold Harberger, "*Monopoly and Resource Allocation*," *American Economic Review*, papers and proceedings, pp. 77-87. (1954).

[181] For a review of these estimates, see Paul R. Ferguson and Glenys J. Ferguson, *Industrial Economics: Issues and Perspectives*, 2d ed. (NYU Press), 1988, p. 94.

Section 2: Antitrust Policy and the New Economy

Essay 10

Economic Perspectives on Software Design: PC Operating Systems and Platforms

by Steven J. Davis, Jack MacCrisken, and Kevin M. Murphy

The legality of Microsoft's decision to integrate an Internet browser with its Windows operating systems was, arguably, the key issue in the antitrust case. The government charged that this integration amounted to "tying" – that is, using its monopoly power in one product (Windows) to extend power to a second product (Internet Explorer). Moreover, the government asserted that Microsoft's failure to charge more for Windows when Internet Explorer was included in the package was "predatory," with the alleged goal of driving Netscape's Navigator browser from the market.

Microsoft countered with a variety of legal and economic arguments, which did not sway the trial court judge but did convince the D.C. appeals court. Although the appeals court left open the door to a charge of tying, it set tough standards for proving liability under a "rule of reason." Implicitly acknowledging the difficulty of meeting the appeals court's test – that is, showing that the harm of integration to consumers exceeded the benefits – the Department of Justice dropped the charge.

In this paper, two economists from the University of Chicago Graduate School of Business (Davis and Murphy) and a consulting software engineer (MacCrisken) examine the economic incentives driving design decisions by software companies – in particular, software that can serve as a platform for other software. And although their analysis does not prove that Microsoft did not integrate new features into Windows in order to create or defend market power, it strongly buttresses the appeals court's logic in applying a rule of rea-

son. The three researchers demonstrate that there are clearly strong pro-competitive reasons that vendors are inclined to add ever-more functions to operating systems.

The need to keep pace with technological change in hardware, the need to simplify the use of computers, and the desire to stimulate the production of complementary software all play a role. So, too, do demand-side considerations: The economics of bundling functions are especially compelling with software, where the marginal cost of manufacturing another unit of the product is close to zero. *— D.S.E.*

INTRODUCTION

This paper considers a multitude of economic forces that shape the design of commercial software products. We focus on "operating systems" that provide basic management functions for computer hardware as well as platforms for running software applications and interfaces for computer users. Prominent examples include the Apple Mac OS, IBM OS/2, and Microsoft Windows. But much of our analysis also applies to the design of applications and other software that coordinates many interacting components of a larger system.

One reason to study the economic forces that shape the design and evolution of operating systems is to better understand the spectacular growth and productivity performance of the personal computer industry. Over the last two decades, the PC has evolved from a costly, clunky device with a narrow range of applications into an inexpensive technological marvel used by hundreds of millions of people. The PC has become ubiquitous in data storage, information processing, communication, and entertainment activities at the workplace and in the home. It is now a major business and consumer product and a key complement to many types of creative activity. Improvements in operating system software, broadly defined, have played a major role in this transformation.

A second reason is to build a sounder analytic basis for the treatment of product design issues under antitrust law. The design of Microsoft Windows was a key issue in *U.S. v. Microsoft Corporation*, the most prominent antitrust case in a generation.[1] According to the government, Microsoft engaged in various anticompetitive actions, including the illegal "tying" of its Web browser to Windows. The presiding trial judge concurred, ordering that Microsoft be split in two and placing tight restrictions on the design of the companies' respective software products.[2] We do not explicitly assess legal tying doctrine, but our analysis suggests that product integration and bundling are often highly beneficial for consumers.[3]

Third, software is inherently malleable in ways that bring product design issues to the fore. Software code can be expanded, modified, and combined to add functions, bundle features, and redraw the boundaries between product categories. Moreover, design changes in software often have minimal impact on marginal costs. Extra features do not alter the (extremely low) cost of stamping a CD-ROM that contains the code for a software product. By the same token, consumers can often dispose of unwanted features in software: The relevant code can reside unused on a computer disk indefinitely without significant cost. All told, these characteristics lead to an extraordinary degree of design flexibility.

Fourth, and not coincidentally, competition in many software products is mainly exhibited through innovation rather than price.[4] Thus the consumer benefits from competition largely take the form of product improvements, new product introductions, and, occasionally, the creation of whole new product categories rather than price changes.

Finally, the PC operating system is the prime example of a product that derives most of its value from its capacity to function as a platform for other products. And because it is a platform, the demand for PC operating systems is influenced by what economists call "network effects." Easy file sharing, widespread familiarity with the user interface, and the compatibility of software applications across computers and computer users are examples of direct network benefits from the use of a common software platform. Network efforts work from the supply side, too: The greater the number of users of a platform, the greater the incentive for software developers to invest in new applications. Thus design characteristics – in particular, the ability to create a common standard and to elicit the development of complementary applications – are critical determinants of market outcomes for platform products.

The second section of the paper highlights the declining cost and growing power of personal computing. The third section identifies three basic forces that propel the evolution of commercial operating system products: the need to keep pace with advances in computer-related technology, the need to simplify computer use, and the desire to stimulate new applications for the operating system-as-platform. The fourth section elaborates on design flexibility in software and discusses alternative concepts of software integration. The fifth section describes "componentized" design architectures for complex software products, analyzes the costs and benefits of componentization, and explains its role in managing the evolution of a software platform. The sixth section explains how the need to manage the interacting components of a PC system drives the ongoing integration of new features into operating systems. This section also sketches a theory of how and when operating systems evolve in order to simplify end-user experience with the computer system, facilitate applications development, and reduce customer support costs for software vendors. The seventh section discusses demand-based motives for the bundling of software applications and utilities with operating system products, and the implications of bundling for economic efficiency and consumer welfare.

Our study draws on a variety of sources for factual background and analysis. The discovery and trial record in *U.S. v. Microsoft Corp.* brought forth a wealth of testimony related to the economic and technological forces that shape the design of operating systems and other software. Several senior executives and software developers at Microsoft answered our questions about software design issues and the evolution of the PC operating system.[5] We also draw on previous research in economics and related fields, especially in our analysis of demand-based motives for software bundling.

FACTUAL BACKGROUND

Operating Systems and Platforms

Every computer requires a central processing unit (CPU) and an operating system (OS). The CPU is hardware, typically one or more microprocessors, that performs basic operations. The OS is software that manages the CPU and other hardware such as the keyboard, monitor, storage media, and communication devices. Hardware management functions are often combined with an interface between the user and the computer. The interface allows the user to access and manipulate files, run programs, and operate the hardware, either directly or through instructions generated by applications software. In turn, the hardware management and user interface functions are often combined with a software platform into a single "operating system" product.

A software platform contains application programming interfaces (APIs) that specify how a software developer can access useful modules of code built into the platform. The APIs, and the underlying code modules, enable a software developer to economize on writing new code for applications software. Essentially, the applications software calls on the processing functions built into the platform, reducing the need for applications developers to write code that performs routine functions. Microsoft Windows, for example, contains literally thousands of APIs that can be accessed by software applications and that are relied upon by developers to simplify the creation of everything from word processors to spreadsheets to games.[6]

Expanding Functionality of OS Products

A striking aspect of the evolution in commercial OS products is the continual integration of new features, many of which began as stand-alone applications. Examples include graphical user interfaces, disk management and data compression utilities, memory management utilities, fax and e-mail utilities, support for local area networks, integrated multimedia support, and Web-browsing functions. Software that cost thousands of dollars in the early 1990s is now routinely included with operating system products, and at a small fraction of the original cost.

Why this process has been so relentless – and what it means for competition – is controversial and important. Indeed, the questions received a great deal of attention in *U.S. v. Microsoft Corp.*[7] Undeniably, though, the continual integration of new features into OS products predates the coming of age of Microsoft Windows, circa 1992. All commercially successful OS products aimed at the general computer user in recent decades have expanded functionality over time. This suggests that the impulse to include ever more functions reflects fundamental economic and technological forces.

We identify and discuss three such forces in the next section. To set the stage, we first review the breathtaking pace of technological advance and cost reduction during the PC era.

The Growing Power and Declining Cost of Personal Computing

It is hard to exaggerate the pace of technological change – and the resulting collapse in the cost of computing power – that have transformed the structure of the computer industry several times in two decades.

Start with microprocessors. When IBM introduced the first PC in 1981, its Intel processor contained 29,000 transistors; Pentium III processors, now standard on low-end PCs, contain 9.5 million transistors. Processing power rose commensurately: The Intel Pentium II 450 MHz chip (released in late 1998) performs roughly 4,000 times as many instructions per second as the Intel 8086-5 chip that did the number-crunching for the IBM PC-XT, a popular PC in the mid-1980s. The price for mid-range Intel processors fell from $12.12

Figure 1. **The Price of Processors in Personal Computers, 1993-2001, Intel Processor MIPS**

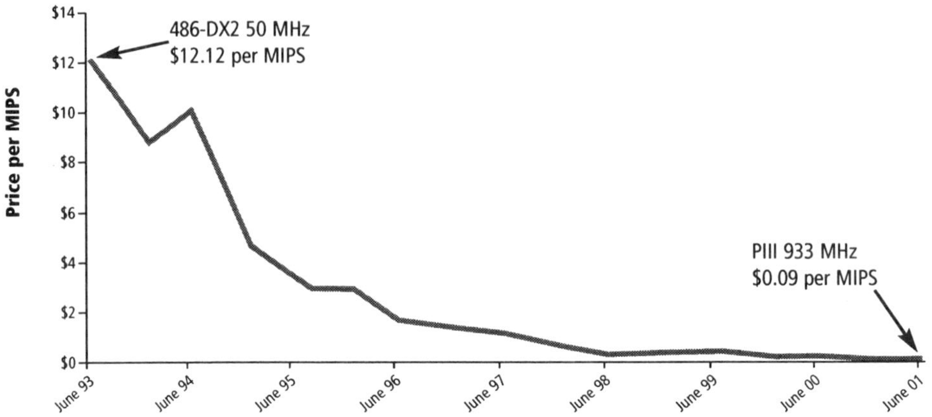

per MIPS (millions of instructions per second) in 1993 to $0.09 per MIPS in 2001 (Figure 1).[8]

Or consider random access memory (RAM), the memory on a chip that can be accessed in billionths of a second. PCs using DOS, the leading OS until the early 1990s, could not utilize more than 640,000 bytes of memory at a time. Today, 64 million bytes of RAM is viewed as a bare minimum in a desktop PC. The price per megabyte of RAM fell from $880 in January 1984 to just 38 cents in June 2001 – an average rate of decline of 44 percent annually (Figure 2).

Much the same has happened with "hard drive" storage. In the late 1980s, 20-megabyte drives were widely viewed as adequate for the typical home or office desktop. By mid-1999, even cheap PCs came with drives that held at least 4,300 megabytes and that offered much faster data access than a decade earlier. The price per megabyte of storage fell from $199 in January 1983 to a

Figure 2. **The Price of Random Access Memory (RAM) in Personal Computers, 1984-2001, Log Scale**

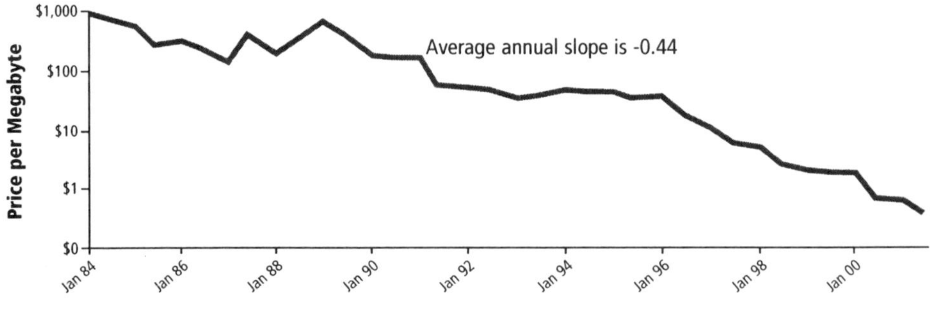

Figure 3. **The Price of Hard Disk Storage in Personal Computers, 1983-2001, Log Scale**

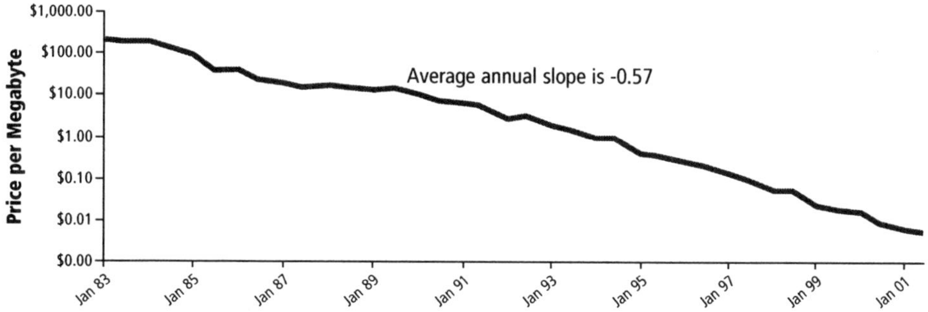

mere half-penny in June 2001 – an average annual rate of decline of 57 percent (Figure 3).

Alternative forms of storage have proliferated, even as prices plummeted (Figure 4). "Floppy" disk drives, once the only form of storage for PCs, used 5¼-inch disks that held a mere 160 kilobytes in 1981.[9] By 1983, floppy capacity had increased to 360 kilobytes at a cost of $708 per megabyte for the drive unit. The next big advance in secondary storage was a 1.2-megabyte disk at a cost of $145 per megabyte for the drive unit. CD-ROM drives, introduced in 1990, hold over 600 megabytes, and the "read only" storage capacity costs a mere 76 cents per megabyte. Storage capacity for DVD-ROM devices, introduced on PCs in 1998, cost less than a penny per megabyte. Over the 1983-1999 period, the price per megabyte in secondary storage devices fell at an average rate of 62 percent annually.

The ongoing revolution in printer technology has been equally dramatic,

Figure 4. **The Price of Secondary Storage Devices for Personal Computers, 1983-2001**

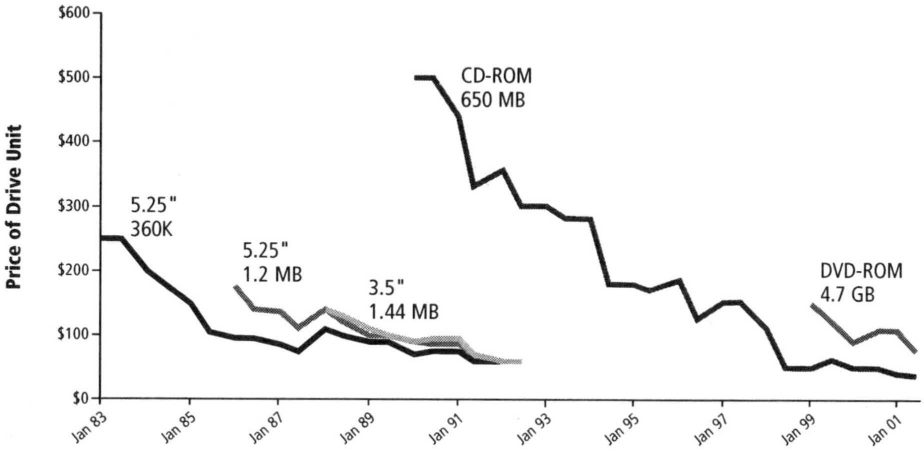

if harder to quantify. In 1984 a slow, noisy, low-resolution "dot-matrix" printer cost about $600 and, as a practical matter, printed only text. The black-and-white laser printers of the early 1990s were much sharper and printed graphics – but were far more expensive. But in recent years color printers using "inkjet" technology have overwhelmed other technologies in low-end printers. They produce fine color at high resolution – and slower models now cost less than $100. (Table 1.)

Modems, too, have come of age. In the early 1980s, the typical home or office modem could transfer data at 300 bps (bits per second) and was effectively limited to transmitting text. Today, the standard modem on PCs is capable of 57,600 bps. Cable modems and DSL service can transfer data at several million bps. Prices, and this is no surprise, have fallen sharply. In 1985 the price for a modem device amounted to roughly 27 cents per bps transfer rate, more than 1,000 times the corresponding price for cable modem and DSL devices 15 years later (Figure 5).

All told, this onslaught of technology has put incredible power in the hands of anyone with a thousand dollars to spend.[10] In early 1986, a "high-end" PC with a 286 processor running at 8 megahertz (MHz), half a megabyte of RAM, and 20 megabytes of hard drive storage cost about $2,800. As of September 2001, $708 bought a Gateway V667C PC system with a 667 MHz processor, 64 megabytes of RAM, and 10,000 megabytes of disk storage, a 15-inch high-resolution color monitor, a 56K modem, a 48x CD-ROM, Microsoft Windows ME and a color ink-jet printer with a resolution of 1200 x 1200 dpi.[11]

The incredible pace of technological change and cost reduction on the hardware side of PC systems has driven many of the developments on the software side. Market leadership in commercial OS and other software categories

Figure 5. **The Price of Modem Devices for Personal Computers, 1983-2001**

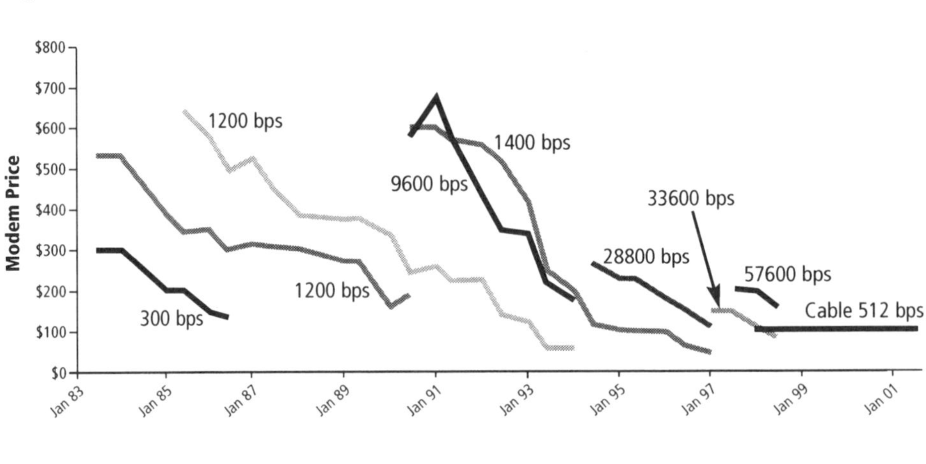

Table 1. **Printers for Personal Computers, Prices and Characteristics, 1984-2001**

Debut Year	Category	Product	Specifications	Price	Date
	B&W Dot Matrix	Epson FX-80	160 characters/sec., 9 pin dot matrix	$589	Jan-84
		Epson FX-80		$429	Jan-85
		Epson LX 80	100 characters/second, letter quality	$232	Jun-86
1984	B&W Ink Jet	ThinkJet	300x300 dpi, 1-2 minutes per page	$495	Oct-84
	B&W Ink Jet	ThinkJet		$445	Oct-84
	B&W Ink Jet	ThinkJet		$435	Jan-85
	B&W Ink Jet	ThinkJet		$388	Jan-86
1984	B&W Laser	LaserJet	300x300 dpi, 8 pages per minute		
	B&W Laser	LaserJet		$2,995	Jan-85
	B&W Laser	LaserJet		$2,376	Jan-86
	B&W Laser	LaserJet		$2,289	Jan-87
	B&W Laser	LaserJet IIIsi	300 dpi, 17 pages per minute	$3,525	Jan-92
	B&W Laser	LaserJet	4600 dpi, 8 pages per minute	$1,435	Jan-93
	B&W Laser	LaserJet 4L	300 dpi, 4 pages per minute	$669	Jan-95
	B&W Laser	LaserJet 5L	600 dpi, 4 pages per minute	$527	Jan-96
	B&W Laser	LaserJet 5si	600 dpi, 24 pages per minute	$2,449	Jan-98
	B&W Laser	LaserJet 1100se	600 dpi, 8 pages per minute	$399	Jun-99
	B&W Laser	LaserJet 2100M	1200 dpi, 10 pages per minute	$629	Jun-00
	B&W Laser	LaserJet 1100xi	600 dpi, 8 pages per minute	$349	Dec-00
	B&W Laser	LaserJet 1200	1200 dpi, 15 pages per minute	$377	Jul-01
1991	Color Ink Jet	Color DeskJet 500C	300 dpi, 4 minutes per page color	$1,059	Oct-91
	Color Ink Jet	Color DeskJet 500C		$719	Jan-92
	Color Ink Jet	Color DeskJet 500C		$699	Jun-92
	Color Ink Jet	Color DeskJet 500C		$619	Jan-93
	Color Ink Jet	Color DeskJet 500C		$396	Jan-94
	Color Ink Jet	Color DeskJet 500C		$299	Jan-95
	Color Ink Jet	Color DeskJet 560C	300 dpi, 3 minutes per page color	$479	Jan-95
	Color Ink Jet	Color DeskJet 660C	300 dpi, 3 minutes per page color	$388	Jan-96
	Color Ink Jet	Color DeskJet 680C	300 dpi, 1.5 pages per minute color	$292	Jan-97
	Color Ink Jet	Color DeskJet 672C	300 dpi, 1.5 pages per minute color	$199	Jun-98
	Color Ink Jet	Color DeskJet 420C	300 dpi, 4 minutes per page color	$119	Feb-99
	Color Ink Jet	Color DeskJet 420C	300 dpi, 4 minutes per page color	$99	Jun-99
	Color Ink Jet	Color DeskJet 812C	600 dpi, 3 pages per minute	$149	Jan-00
	Color Ink Jet	Color DeskJet 930C	1200 dpi, 2 pages per minute	$199	Jun-00
	Color Ink Jet	Color DeskJet 930C	1200 dpi, 2 pages per minute	$177	Jul-01
1994	Color Laser HP	Color LaserJet	300 dpi, 1-2 pages per minute	$6,000	Sep-94
	Color Laser HP	Color LaserJet		$5,929	Jan-96
	Color Laser HP	Color LaserJet 5	300 dpi, 2-3 pages per minute	$5,829	Jan-97
	Color Laser HP	Color LaserJet 5		$3,939	Jun-98
	Color Laser HP	Color LaserJet 4500	600 dpi, 4 pages per minute	$2,499	Feb-99
	Color Laser	Tektronix Phaser 740/N	600 dpi, 5 pages per minutes	$1,850	Jun-99
	Color Laser	QMS Magicolor 330	600 dpi, 4 pages per minute	$1,849	Jan-00
	Color Laser HP	Color LaserJet 4550	600 dpi, 4 pages per minute	$1,888	Jul-01

has undergone several shifts in recent decades, even though the Microsoft Windows family of operating systems has held the leading position since 1993. As emphasized by Evans, Nichols, and Reddy (1999), major shifts in the leadership of software categories have often been closely linked to technological developments in hardware. This fact has not been lost on suppliers of OS software, and largely explains why they have integrated new features that keep OS products abreast of technological developments in hardware.

THREE KEY FORCES THAT PROPEL THE EVOLUTION OF OS PRODUCTS

Keeping Pace with Technological Advances

Rapid innovation in computers is plainly one of the great technological wonders of our age. And the resulting changes in what users expect from computers compel frequent upgrades in complementary products – especially ones as central to computer performance as operating systems.

By the early 1990s, exponential advances in speed and functionality had made PCs a staple on virtually every desk in the corporate enterprise, while advances in the efficiency and miniaturization of chips, batteries, hard drives, and other components made computers easily portable. New innovations in data sharing and interconnectivity, led by Novell and 3Com, gave rise to an entire new industry in PC networks and servers.

In the mid-1990s the face of computing was again changed by technology – this time by the Internet. The Internet powered a surge in the demand for both PCs and network server computers and created an entirely new computing environment in the form of the Web browser. Even more recently, handheld computing devices such as the Palm Pilot have come of age, providing still another hardware platform for data manipulation and communication.

This explosive growth in memory, processing muscle, and versatility has created powerful incentives to add capabilities and features to OS products. For example, Microsoft made PC-DOS 1.0 to specifications set for the original IBM PC in 1981. When IBM added a hard drive to the PC a year later, version 2.0 was enhanced to support the additional storage medium. DOS 3.1 adapted the PC for use on local area networks. DOS 3.2 and DOS 3.3 supported the new 3½-inch, 720-kilobyte and 1.44-megabyte floppy disks, respectively. And when the 386 microprocessor arrived, DOS version 3.3 supported it.[12]

By no coincidence, leadership in the market for OS products has often been up for grabs since the mainframe era of the 1960s. Microsoft emerged as the preeminent producer of PC operating system products in the early 1990s. As late as 1992, though, some knowledgeable observers touted IBM's OS/2 as likely to become the dominant general-purpose OS for PCs.[13]

Consider the ongoing impact of printer technology on operating systems. In the mid-1980s the only high-quality printers for home and office use were very expensive black-and-white laser printers. But color ink-jet printers, introduced in 1991, are now nearly as ubiquitous as microwave ovens. They have opened desktop printing of cards, brochures, and the like to a mass market. And, in tandem with the advent of low-cost digital still cameras, they are making the PC an integral part of photography. To accommodate the plethora of sophisticated new printers from a half-dozen major manufacturers, operating systems have incorporated ever-larger numbers of ever-more-complex printer "drivers." Windows XP, the newest version of Windows, incorporates basic software for manipulating and printing photo images.

More generally, so long as the cost of processing power, random access memory, and data storage fall at 40 to 60 percent a year, the practical uses of personal computers will continue to expand rapidly. The ability to manage huge amounts of data and display complex graphics has decentralized publishing from the factory to the desktop. Rapid number crunching and super-cheap memory have transformed the spreadsheet into an all-purpose tool for business, finance, and science. The Internet gives PCs access to avalanches of data. And with the expansion of functionality, of course, come new demands on operating systems to manage more hardware and more software with more sophisticated user interfaces.

Simplifying Computer Use

A second key force behind OS integration is the need to make computers easier to use. Just as standard features on the automobile evolved from bare necessities to include gas gauges, heaters, defrosters, and other "extras," computer operating systems have evolved to accommodate consumer tastes and to facilitate computer use. For example, the Unix operating system, used on a substantial share of engineering and scientific workstations, gradually added a full-screen editor, virtual memory, terminal independence, job control capability, and a networking API called "sockets."[14]

And because of the tremendous popularity of Internet applications among today's computer users,[15] Web browsers are now routinely integrated into (or bundled with) OS products. Internet Explorer, the Web-browsing technology developed by Microsoft, is integrated into Windows 98 and later versions of Windows. But Microsoft is hardly alone in packaging a browser with an OS. IBM led this trend, developing its own browser for OS/2. Sun Microsystems' Solaris and Java OS, SCO's UnixWare and Open Server all provide browsing by bundling Netscape Navigator with the OS. In addition to bundling its OS products with Netscape Navigator, Sun also supplies the HotJava Web browser.

PCs of the past were notoriously frustrating to end users. Walter Mossberg's *Wall Street Journal* column on personal technology debuted in 1991 "with the contention that personal computers are too hard to use, and that the blame lies not with the people trying to use them but with the supposed geniuses who design the machines and the software that runs on them." Mossberg later lamented, "even rocket scientists are baffled by personal computers. I once got e-mail from a scientist at NASA who works on giant supercomputers all day with aplomb but goes home at night and finds to his great frustration that he can't get the family IBM-compatible PC to run multimedia software correctly."[16]

As the market for PCs has widened, the market pressure to make them easier to use has intensified. Weekend tinkerers may revel in the intricate workings of the PC. For their part, science labs, graduate schools, and businesses with sophisticated information management departments may tolerate – even take pride in their ability to control – the PC's eccentricities. But those early markets for computers were long ago saturated. Much of the growth in demand now comes from untutored users – small businesses and households – who expect to plug and play (or work).

One much-welcomed response to this changing market reality has been the expansion of the PC operating system to include elements that previously stood alone, such as software "drivers" to run peripherals ranging from scanners to DVD players. Likewise, the addition of TCP/IP communications software has simplified the once absurdly complicated task of linking computers to network servers, effectively opening the Internet to the untutored.[17]

Attracting Software Developers

A third key force behind integration is the desire to encourage software developers to create new applications for the operating system-as-platform, thereby enhancing the operating system's value to consumers and giving it a leg up in the market. Platform vendors compete by making it cheap and easy for independent software vendors to develop applications. They accomplish this goal in part by providing software building blocks (APIs) that lower the cost of developing complementary software applications.[18, 19] These building blocks include support for sound cards, integrated audio, extended memory, object linking and embedding, scalable fonts, and the like.

The desire to support software developers also explains why commercial OS products incorporate Web-browsing support and other Internet functionality.[20] The integration of IE into Windows ensures software developers that a browser with known functionality and specifications is available with Windows. And this, in turn, facilitates the development of simpler, yet more powerful, software applications.

Microsoft's own word processor, Word 97 (and later versions), uses Internet Explorer (or another default browser) to automatically convert any typed-in Web address (URL) into a live link. Clicking on the address brings up the Web page in the browser if the user is connected to the Internet. A stand-alone browser can be used to achieve comparable functionality – indeed, many operating system products work this way. But integration ensures the availability of specific browser services for any software application running on the OS. And this, in turn, encourages the development of applications that rely on browser functionality. The designers of Quicken financial-planning software, for example, can be confident that every PC user who runs Windows 98 (or later versions) has access to built-in code that enables rapid, automatic information retrieval from the Web.

SOFTWARE DESIGN FLEXIBILITY AND INTEGRATION CONCEPTS

The Inherent Flexibility of Software Design

Several witnesses in *U.S. v. Microsoft Corp.* emphasized the remarkable flexibility of software. Professor David Farber neatly describes this flexibility in his written direct testimony:

> [S]oftware modules are then "knitted together" into unified programs. That is, each software product is built up from simple low-level routines that are then called by routines at a higher level of composition. Routines at each level are called by yet higher level routines until the desired functionality of the end product is achieved. In this manner, all software is built up layer by layer through the use of often-large numbers of routines, but each with limited complexity. As a result of this layering, software has an inherently malleable and modular structure that gives software developers broad freedom in

> combining (i.e., bundling) different functions into software products. This malleability also gives a software developer two related types of design freedom: (1) to integrate two separate CD-ROM's because the functions on one particular CD-ROM can be integrated by an OEM or retail end user with functions on another CD-ROM and (2) to determine which functions to include within software sold as one product and which to separate and sell as a different product, whether produced by the same or different software developer, for installation and use together by the retail end user. (p. 7)

In short, the same functionality can be achieved in many ways – and, in particular, with more or less tightly integrated code.[21]

Flexibility and choice in software design work against efforts to define the boundary between OS and applications software, or between the operating system, narrowly conceived, and the broader notion of an operating environment. Indeed, the inherent flexibility of software design underscores the arbitrary nature of definitions of what is part of the operating system and what isn't.[22]

Several other factors confound attempts to fix these boundaries.[23] First, there is no consensus as to which functions belong within the domain of the operating system.[24] Second, most knowledgeable observers agree that the functions of the PC operating system, however narrowly defined, have grown and will continue to grow. Third, while experts have proposed a variety of tests for whether a particular set of files is actually integrated into the OS, these tests are ambiguous, inconsistent – and often in conflict with common-sense views about the functional boundaries of the operating system.[25]

The flexibility of software design matters to our analysis for two reasons. First, we devote only modest attention to the "engineering" aspects of OS design that often loom large in textbook discussions of computer programming techniques.[26] Principles matter in software development, as does the issue of meeting design objectives at reasonable cost. But the inherent flexibility of software code, coupled with the very large size of the market for OS products, implies that the engineering costs of software programming are unlikely to outweigh strong commercial incentives for achieving a particular design objective.

Second, design flexibility implies that the boundary between OS and applications software is fuzzy and mutable – and will in all likelihood remain so. Hence, we think that efforts to draw a bright line between operating systems and applications software on the basis of technical design criteria are misguided. We view OS software as a commercial product, not simply a technological object, and we recognize that the functionality of commercial OS products must evolve in response to technological and market forces.

Functional and Whole-Cloth Integration of New Features

To most PC users, "integration" means that the software features and hardware components work together smoothly and with modest effort. Computer buyers value the perception and experience of integrated performance – whether or not there is integration in a technical sense.[27] Hence, in marketing their software, firms refer to integration in the casual sense of integrated look and function, rather than in terms of internal design architecture.[28] PC users also value integration in the sense of easy, automated installation of distinct software products, even when the products are simply bundled together on the same CD-ROM.[29] In a parallel manner, much of our analysis flows from a functionality-based perspective on integration and product design. From this perspective, it is the result that matters, not the means to that end.

Nonetheless, the technical distinction between integration and bundling does bear on an economic analysis of OS design. Whole-cloth or "tight" integration, in the sense of multiple cross-dependencies among major components of the OS, involves costs and benefits. On the cost side, whole-cloth integration makes it harder for a PC user to economize on disk usage by deleting (or never installing) unneeded files or fragments of code. OS design can also affect memory usage on the PC, because an entire file must be loaded into memory even if only a portion of the code in the file is required for the execution of a particular task.[30] The bottom line: OS integration (in the sense of cross-dependencies) can place greater demands on the storage and memory resources needed to operate a PC. Hence, the huge size of a modern integrated operating system like Windows 98 or the MacOS imposes a cost – literal and figurative – on system resources.

But this cost is modest and falling rapidly. By 1999, disk storage costs per megabyte were less than one-half of 1 percent of 1990 levels.[31] And the capacity of the hard drive on a typical new PC system was 9,100 megabytes – up from 65 megabytes in 1990.[32] Thus, as of May 1999, even a 50 percent reduction in the size of Windows 98 would free only 1.2 percent of the disk space on a typical new PC system at an implied savings in hardware cost of just $2.25.[33]

As we noted earlier, random access memory installed on new computers has also increased dramatically in recent years, and the cost of RAM has declined more than proportionately. Over the course of the 1990s, the memory capacity of the typical new PC system rose from 2 megabytes to 64 megabytes, while the buyer's outlay per megabyte fell to less than 2 percent of 1990 levels.[34] What's more, effective memory usage is no longer severely constrained by the technical parameters of PC operating systems, as it was with PC-DOS.

In analyzing the efficiency of software integration, it's also worth noting that, although "small" files dedicated to narrowly defined tasks may economize on memory requirements, the organization of the OS into fewer, larger files also has technical advantages.[35] First, it takes longer to load many small files into random access memory than to load one large file composed of the same code. Second, the "calling file," which also resides in memory, must contain more code to load many small files than to load one large file. Third, breaking software programs into small files increases disk storage requirements, because each file, no matter how small, uses a minimum amount of disk space.[36]

That said, there is little doubt that, on balance, whole-cloth OS design increases the demands on disk storage and, in some circumstances, on the memory resources required to operate a PC. However, these resource demands are a minor factor in light of the development of larger, cheaper storage disks and memory chips. Thus our economic analysis of OS design places little weight on considerations related to storage and memory requirements, even though they loom large in some technically oriented discussions of OS design.[37]

More important, whole-cloth integration can serve both end users and applications developers by promulgating a common standard provided by an OS product. The shared files and other cross-dependencies make it less attractive to tinker with the OS, because such tinkering is likely to degrade overall performance. And by preserving a standardized environment, a highly integrated OS like Windows 98 assures hardware and software vendors that the full set of capabilities and APIs is available in every installation of the product. By reducing the number of configuration possibilities for the code modules, a standardized environment also lowers the cost and difficulty of testing OS performance and its interaction with complementary software and hardware products.

Thus whole-cloth integration protects a platform vendor and other software and hardware firms from poor performance caused by unpredictable differences across installations of the platform. The bottom line is lower testing and customer-support costs for the platform vendor, lower development and customer-support costs for the suppliers of complementary products – and greater customer satisfaction.[38]

COMPONENTIZED DESIGN ARCHITECTURES

Computer users value software for performance, ease of use, and compatibility with other elements of a computer system. The internal design of software – *how* it accomplishes tasks or achieves ease of use and compatibility – is typically of little intrinsic interest to them. If two software products offer comparable capability, ease of use, and compatibility, end users value them equally, even if they rely on radically different internal designs.

Nevertheless, internal design can greatly influence the market response to software products and their capacity to evolve successfully. Software platforms require useful applications programming interfaces (APIs) to encourage the development of complementary applications. Better APIs lead to more and better software applications, which benefit consumers, the platform vendor, and independent software developers. Indeed, good APIs are essential for the success of a software platform, even though few users of, say, Windows or the Mac OS could identify specific APIs or explain how they smooth the way for applications software.

Turn now to another aspect of internal software design, often referred to as "componentization." Like APIs, a componentized design provides indirect benefits that are not readily apparent to end users. Componentization can facilitate product development, design, and testing, and thereby reduce the cost of supplying software. It can also facilitate continual improvements in a large, complex system like one made up of a software platform and thousands of complementary applications. But there's a downside, too: Componentization can diminish performance or add to product development costs.[39]

What Is Componentization?

Componentization refers to a modular design architecture that structures and constrains the interactions among elements of a software system. This design architecture prescribes the pathways along which components communicate, and the precise manner in which one component "requests" information or processing services from another.

A few analogies can make this abstract concept more tangible and clarify some of the tradeoffs involved in a componentized design.

• Consider two alternative "design architectures" for an integrated TV-VCR system. One is a closed system housed in a one-piece construction. This architecture makes the machine compact, easy to use, and cheaper to manufacture. A second is a modular construction with separate units for the TV and the VCR. The units are only "integrated" in the sense that they easily connect and work together. This design makes it easy to upgrade individual pieces of the system. If the modular system is "open," it can also accommodate new components, like a DVD player, later on. Thus the modular design makes for a more flexible system, even though it may be less efficient or more costly in the short run.

• Consider the distinction between open-stack and closed-stack policies for book retrieval in a library. An open-stack policy permits patrons to take books directly from the stacks, and by whatever route seems desirable or convenient. In computer parlance, the user can "make calls" on the library services in an unconstrained manner. In contrast, a closed-stack policy processes all requests for book retrieval through a designated checkpoint. Here, there is a single pathway (or a limited number) by which users "make calls" upon library services. Like a closed-stack library, componentized software prescribes and limits the pathways by which a user (or other software) can call upon the processing services produced inside the component.

• Consider the provision of french fries as a metaphor for the provision of computing resources or processing services. Because patrons have different appetites, one size portion does not fit all, and a dispensary might be designed to distribute one fry at a time in order to meet every customer's wishes on the button. However, because most customers want many fries, this design solution involves a very large number of individual "calls" on the kitchen, slowing deliveries and reducing the dispensary's total capacity to deliver the goods. A more efficient design would dispense many fries at a time – but not too many, because a lot would be wasted if they came in orders of 500 when the typical customer wanted just 100. Thus, designing an efficient dispensary requires forethought about the optimal batch size.

• Consider the development of a new fighter jet that incorporates several distinct, but interacting, technological advances. A fighter is a complicated technological "system" with many subsystems and interacting components. Each must properly work and interact in order for the overall system to perform at maximum capacity. An intelligent design architecture will make it possible to organize development and testing around many small teams, each of which focuses on a subsystem or component. This approach allows development to proceed along many fronts, tackling many relatively small problems simultaneously. Of course, it is essential that the components work together when reassembled into an overall system. This reassembly may take place many times in the course of developing, testing, and refining a new fighter jet or other system product. So, clearly, the "componentization" of the fighter jet system cannot be carried out in a haphazard way. It requires forethought about how the components will interact once put back together.

Each of these analogies captures an important aspect of software componentization. The TV-VCR combination highlights the concept of modularity, which often involves a tradeoff between long-run "dynamic" benefits and short-run "static" costs. The library example illuminates the constraints on the pathways by which users retrieve information or make calls on system services. As explained below, this type of constraint also involves a tradeoff between dynamic benefits and static costs. The french-fry example, although contrived, shows the importance of forethought about the manner in which components are linked and the nature of requests for processing services. The fighter-jet example highlights the virtues of a componentized approach to the development and testing of a new system-like product.

The Costs and Benefits of Componentization

Designing intelligently componentized software is difficult and time consuming – and thus expensive. According to Microsoft's Paul Maritz, componentized design "requires a great deal of abstract thinking of a sort that human beings aren't naturally good at."[40] It is especially difficult to componentize an existing large-scale software product that was not originally designed that way.

An ill-conceived decomposition can generate tremendous demands on the microprocessor by increasing the number of calls between interfacing components. Even with the powerful processing capability of today's computers, it is very easy to slow execution dramatically. Thus it is not enough that software components work together; they must do so in a way that avoids excessive demands on the overall system.

Even a well-designed decomposition can degrade performance. Paul Maritz offers an example involving the HTML "renderer," which is essential technology for Web browsing.[41] The HTML renderer functions as a distinct component within Microsoft's Internet Explorer, but in Netscape Navigator the renderer is closely mingled with other functionality and code. This mingling of the HTML renderer with other functionality in Navigator allows for faster processing than a componentized design would. As a consequence, Microsoft had to put more effort into streamlining operations within the components of Internet Explorer in order to achieve processing speeds in Web-browsing activities comparable to Navigator's.

On the other side of the ledger, a componentized design delivers many benefits. Some of these are obvious; others are subtle.

First, componentization facilitates code sharing across same-generation programs and code reuse in new products. Code sharing has several benefits:

- It reduces the need to reinvent the same wheel for each program, thereby economizing on development costs.
- Since the code has a longer useful life, developers have greater incentives to invest in optimizing a component's technical performance.
- By simplifying the interactions among blocks of software code, componentization reduces product testing and debugging costs. This benefit comes in addition to cost savings afforded by the reuse of code that is already tested and debugged.
- Code sharing across products (e.g., Microsoft's Word, Excel, and PowerPoint) helps to harmonize the user interface and other aspects of the user experience.[42]

Second, componentization makes it easier to integrate new functionality into existing software by restricting and simplifying interactions within the program.[43] And when the introduction of new functionality does cause problems, a componentized design makes it easier to identify the source and to fix it. This advantage becomes more important as software products and systems become larger, because more complicated systems increase the potential for unforeseen interactions that create bugs. Hence, by simplifying and compartmentalizing design, componentization makes it easier to handle modern systems with hundreds of thousands or even millions of lines of code.

Third, componentization makes it easier to maintain the "backward compatibility" of platforms as they evolve.[44] Recall the closed-stack versus open-stack book retrieval analogy. The rearrangement of book stacks disrupts the pathways by which library users retrieve books under an open-stack policy. Hence, users must "reprogram" their "calls" on library services when the stacks are rearranged. Under a closed-stack policy, however, library patrons continue to present book-retrieval requests in the same manner as before. Likewise, computer users (or other software components) can continue to present their requests to a redesigned software component, so long as the component's interface remains unchanged.

This advantage is especially valuable in a product like Windows that serves as a platform for thousands of software applications. To attract users, after all, a new Windows release must continue to serve as a platform for the existing stock of Windows applications.[45] Componentization makes it easier to sustain the legacy even as the system expands its functionality.

Fourth, componentization facilitates a small-teams approach to software development by making it easier to break a project into discrete tasks. This benefit is obviously more valuable in the development of large-scale products like software platforms or integrated collections of software applications like the Microsoft Office Suite. In fact, Microsoft places great emphasis on a small-teams approach to the development of even the largest, most complicated software.[46]

The preceding discussion identifies some interesting tradeoffs in software design related to componentization. First, there is a tradeoff between static efficiency and dynamic efficiency – between short-run and long-run advantages.[47] Intelligently componentized software is more flexible in that it eases the integration of new functionality into an evolving software system. However, a one-piece design may be less costly to achieve and deliver faster processing.

Second, there is a tradeoff between scope and specialization. When the same basic functionality is used in many related (but not identical) products and circumstances, there is a greater payoff to the careful design of a single component that delivers the functionality widely. Alternatively, when the functionality is required in essentially the same product and circumstances repeatedly, it becomes more attractive to embed it within software dedicated to a narrower range of activities.

An Example

Consider the different internal designs of Microsoft's Internet Explorer and Netscape's Navigator and Communicator software. Early on, Microsoft decided to pursue a highly componentized design strategy for its Web-browsing technologies.[48] Netscape's browser software lacked the same degree of design modularity.[49]

As explained by the CEO of Intuit, the maker of Quicken financial software, a componentized browser provides the ability to show "an HTML frame within the context of the user interface of our products,"[50] permitting a seamless experience for the users of Quicken products.[51] Basically, the user remains within the Quicken environment, even when calling upon browser technology to retrieve information from the Web. Early browsing software did not have this capability.

Intuit faced this issue squarely in 1996 and early 1997.[52] Netscape Navigator was not componentized as of early 1997, which led to discussions between Intuit and Netscape about the development of a componentized version of the then-leading browser. The componentized nature of Microsoft's Internet Explorer technologies in Windows 95 became an important factor in

Intuit's decision to switch from Navigator to IE as its primary browser for Quicken products.[53] Intuit subsequently distributed some 5 million copies of IE with 1997 versions of Quicken, Turbotax, and Quickbooks.[54]

Also in this period, America Online (AOL) sought to provide a "seamless consumer interaction ... when [going] from one environment to another," such as from AOL's proprietary network to the Web.[55] Netscape's browser technology required a visible leap from one environment to another, whereas the componentized nature of IE (which AOL adopted) allowed for a seamless experience.[56]

It's clear, then, that the componentized design of IE made it more attractive to some providers of complementary software applications and Internet services – and, in the process, enhanced the value of Windows as a software platform. The examples also illustrate how design flexibility allowed for the same basic functionality – browsing technology – to be implemented in different ways that, in turn, had an important influence on market outcomes.

Componentized Software: Why, Especially, at Microsoft?

Microsoft platform products like Windows XP and business applications like the Office Suite are among the largest software systems offered by any mass-market software vendor. Because a componentized design architecture facilitates a small-team approach, it is especially valuable in the development and improvement of these large software systems. Componentization also helps maintain backward compatibility in the evolution of platform products.[57] Microsoft owns the most successful commercial software platforms. It also has a larger, more diverse set of independent software vendors writing to its platform than does any other software firm.

In addition, Microsoft has the broadest line of software and the largest revenues from software of any firm in the world. The company spends more on software development than does any other firm. Hence, it has the most to gain from code reuse, from optimizing the inner workings of a software component, and from harmonizing features and performance across software products. The emphasis on componentization at Microsoft has intensified over the past decade in line with the increase in its software development efforts, the expanding breadth of its software product line, and the increasing scale and complexity of products like Windows and Office.[58]

This interpretation of Microsoft's approach to software development and design also fits with the observation that Microsoft has become a leading developer of object-oriented software design tools. These tools facilitate the use of a componentized design strategy.

By the early 1990s, and perhaps earlier, Microsoft's approach to software development emphasized several of the virtues associated with componentized design architecture. In an August 1993 interview, Microsoft CEO Bill Gates stated that two key principles for managing software development are "a development process that allows large teams to work like small teams" and "product architectures that reduce interdependencies among teams."[59]

Since the late 1980s, Microsoft has made a conscious effort to harmonize user interfaces, feature sets, and performance characteristics across its major software products. Initially, this effort focused on external user-oriented aspects of software such as the user interface and the content of pull-down menus. With time, though, code sharing and functional integration received greater emphasis. This process is especially evident in the MS Office Suite. Originally, Word, Excel, and PowerPoint were independent products with little or no shared code and limited integration. As discussed at length in Cusumano and Selby (1995), much changed by the mid-1990s. The Office products are now closely integrated and share much of their code. What's more, their ongoing development is now closely coordinated. Seen in this light, the move toward componentized design at Microsoft is one step in a long-term effort toward greater harmonization of features and greater functional integration across software.

EFFICIENT MANAGEMENT OF INTERACTING FEATURES AND COMPONENTS

Simplifying the End-User Experience

To perform properly, technologically advanced products often require complex coordination of many interacting components. Achieving the necessary degree of coordination presents challenges in design, installation, and operation. Most consumers, however, place a high premium on ease of use, even for products that depend on arcane technology. They want no-fuss installation, push-button performance, and automated management of interacting components. When problems arise, they expect quick solutions.

It should be no surprise, then, that many product improvements are responses to customer demand for ease of use. Examples include cable-ready televisions, integrated home stereo systems, factory-installed automobile air conditioners, fax-copier machines, internal PC modems, and PC distributors who preinstall the OS and other software. As these examples suggest, greater ease of use often involves the integration of distinct components that could be sold separately.

Consider the example of automobile air conditioners. When they first became available, air conditioners were installed by the auto dealer or by a specialized firm hired by the dealer. Problems were common and often involved the interaction between the air conditioner and components of the automobile engine. For example, cooling systems designed for cars without air conditioning often boiled over when subjected to the added demands of an air conditioner.

Other potential interaction problems were more subtle or specific to certain engine designs. A/C compressors have very high peak power requirements, which can stall the engine. A slippable connection between the engine and the A/C compressor, such as a belt drive, can solve the problem. But with a rigid coupling – such as a gear system – serious problems arise if the A/C compressor clicks on when the engine is already under high load. By the same token, diesel engines have a different power curve from gasoline engines and different acceleration characteristics. So it may be necessary to shut the A/C compressor off in diesel-powered vehicles during warm-up and acceleration. Gasoline engines, by contrast, rarely require this type of regulation of the air conditioning system.

Because of such complications, the availability of "factory air" became a big selling point for automobile manufacturers. Although "factory air" was often still installed by the dealer, the system was designed to the automaker's specifications and carried the automaker's warranty. Automobile cooling systems were beefed up to account for the added load, and boil-over problems – common in the 1960s – became a thing of the past. Today, car buyers take all this for granted. They buy a car, push the "A/C ON" button, and it works.

The preceding remarks can be distilled into three assumptions that inform a theory of product integration:

(a) Customers and dealers have a limited capacity or desire to manage the complexities generated by interacting components.

(b) Greater ease of operating the product often involves the integration of distinct components that can be sold separately.

(c) Integration requires up-front design costs beyond initial product development costs.

Two other factors influence the timing of integration:

(d) When a new product or feature is introduced, performance, cost, and demand are initially uncertain. The uncertainty may involve the ultimate level of consumer acceptance, which version of the product will ultimately achieve the greatest commercial success and technological performance, and the size of up-front design costs required for seamless integration.

(e) The demand for a successful new product grows over time as information about its availability, characteristics, and performance diffuses among the base of potential users.

Assumption (a) implies a latent demand for integration, but not every new feature or product will eventually be integrated into a larger system. Other things being equal, integration is more attractive to the manufacturer of the system product – and likely to generate greater social gains – when more buyers use the stand-alone feature or product,[60] when the design and production costs of integration are lower, and when the stand-alone feature interacts with other features of the system in a complicated way.

Uncertainty about the technical performance of a new product and its interaction with system components creates an incentive to delay integration. As technical problems are identified and resolved, this concern diminishes, so that integration becomes more attractive. From the perspective of both economic efficiency and the system manufacturer's profitability, technological uncertainty adds value to the option of waiting to integrate. This "option value" arises because a manufacturer incurs irreversible costs when it commits to one approach to design and integration. The costs may involve direct expenditures, or they may take the form of harm to the system manufacturer's reputation for quality and reliability if the newly integrated feature performs poorly or interferes with other system components. By retaining the option to select its approach to integration, the manufacturer leaves room to act on information not yet available.

In short, the option value of waiting induced by technological uncertainty reflects two issues: whether integration involves acceptable performance gains relative to the cost of achieving integration, and, when more than one technical option is available, how best to integrate the new product. Of course, this option value is not the only consideration that governs the timing of integration. If the benefits of integration are large or the up-front costs of integration are small, early integration becomes more attractive.

Uncertainty about demand for the new product also induces an option value of waiting to integrate. This option value of waiting reflects two issues: whether demand is sufficiently high to justify the fixed integration costs, and which version of the new product or feature to integrate. As demand-side sources of uncertainty diminish, integration becomes more attractive.

Delay may be rational, even when eventual integration is assured. Both technical uncertainty about how to integrate and demand uncertainty about which version to integrate encourage delay. Even when there is no technical or demand uncertainty, a pure "discounting" effect – the time-value of money invested – encourages delay if the up-front costs are high relative to the initial rewards from integration.

Hence, there are strong economic incentives to postpone integration until kinks and performance problems in the new product are identified and resolved, and demand for the new product is revealed to be sufficiently high to justify the costs. Large benefits and small sunk costs encourage earlier integration.

This type of theory delivers the following stylized introduction–innovation path for new products:

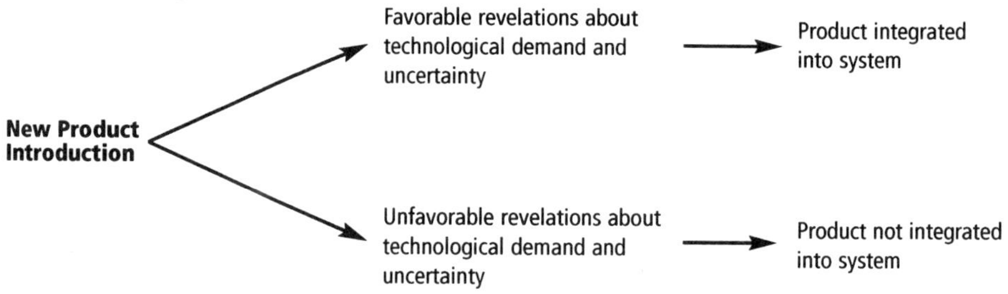

The theory also points to a potentially important complementarity between the integration of existing features and products into a system and the development of new stand-alone products that interact with the system. The integration of existing products into a computer OS, for example, economizes on the limited capacity of users and dealers to manage interacting components. Integration thereby opens the door to the development and introduction of additional non-integrated products. For example, the integration of better support for video display hardware and software into the OS simplifies the use of video-intensive applications and encourages the customer to make greater use of non-integrated products like scanners and digital cameras.[61]

In the extreme scenario in which customers and dealers have a fixed tolerance for managing interacting components, halting integration eventually stifles the development and introduction of new products. In this regard, it is striking that despite the automation of everything from the clutch to the choke to radio tuning, the modern automobile has about as many user-operated controls as the earliest autos. Drivers, it seems, will put up with just so much distraction when they are in motion. Moreover, even if there is no absolute upper bound on the capacity of consumers and dealers to manage interacting components, assumption (a) implies that integration of existing products into a system increases the demand for new non-integrated products that make use of the system.

Facilitating Applications Development

We can summarize the foregoing theory: Product integration simplifies end-user experience by helping to manage the interacting components in a system product. We now sketch a parallel and complementary theory that focuses on how integration facilitates the development of new applications for the system product. In the case of computers, the integration of software building blocks (APIs) into the PC operating system promotes innovation and product variety by reducing the cost of innovation.[62]

The key assumption in this theory of how OS integration facilitates applications development is analogous to assumption (a) above: Software applications developers have a limited capacity or desire to manage the complexities generated by interacting software and hardware components. Other assumptions in this theory parallel assumptions (b)-(e) above.

Most developers of software applications focus on "high-level" design and functionality while leaving critical but routine tasks such as file management, memory management, graphical displays, and video and audio management to the operating system. This division of labor relieves developers of the need to reinvent the wheel in each application and allows them to focus on their areas of expertise and commercial interest.

Specialization at this broad level is reflected in the often-drawn distinction between "systems programmers" and "applications programmers." The distinction is usefully applied to firms as well as individuals. Norton, for example, is a successful, well-respected software firm that mostly employs system programmers and specializes in operating system functions. Adobe, another respected software firm, mostly employs applications programmers and focuses almost entirely on applications-oriented software.

Many software developers are highly specialized in a particular application – e.g., financial analysis, architecture, electric power distribution, or laboratory automation – and they focus on specialized aspects of their field. Their knowledge, when embodied in software applications, is often the main source of added value and commercial viability for their products. For example, the local power company buys a computer-aided design package from AutoDesk primarily because of the expert knowledge embodied in the software, not because the CAD package offers better standard features (e.g., toolbars) than other software products.

Likewise, the incorporation of TCP/IP and other popular networking protocols into Windows provides independent software vendors a larger standard set of system services to leverage into specialized applications. Because the Hypertext Markup Language (HTML) has become a standard for Web applications, its use by the Windows Help facility in place of a proprietary language makes it easy for developers to code sound and video into Help files and to provide Help links to the developer's Web site.

This efficient division of labor among software developers implies that the integration of richer support tools into the OS leads to better, less costly software applications. Software developers know they can design applications with Internet Explorer functionality in mind because the IE technologies are integrated into the Windows OS. In addition, as explained in the previous section, the "componentized" nature of IE technologies affords greater flexibility in program design.

Thus, an applications program can call on the HTML display facility of the browser interface – one component of the IE technologies – whether or not the computer user is on the Internet. Alternatively, by calling on other components of the IE technologies, an applications program can execute Internet transactions without displaying Web pages or making any activity visible to the user. Intuit's Quicken is now designed so that a Windows user can access the latest interest rates and stock prices from the Web without leaving the Quicken application. This unobtrusive use of components of the IE technologies is more convenient than the need to retrieve the same information by initiating a browser shell program with a separate user interface.

For another indication of how the integration of software into the PC operating system facilitates specialization and product variety, consider some responses by software developers to improvements in IE technology that were integrated into Windows 98. According to *Business Week*, "at least four new browsers" that ride on top of IE were introduced shortly after the release of Windows 98.[63] Because Microsoft built the complex software into Windows needed to run Java applets, display graphics, play audio and video, and perform other tasks expected of browsers, even the simplest browser designed around IE technology can do these things.

In this way, OS integration gives product developers stronger incentives to create specialized browsers. IBM's Lotus Development, for example, has developed a browser built on IE technology that "works well and has a distinctive Notes look." Similarly, MediaLive has developed Surf Monkey, a "kid-safe" browser that uses IE technology.[64]

Note, too, that the integration of software building blocks into the PC operating system makes online distribution of new software faster. *Business Week* offers the example of the stand-alone Netscape Communications Navigator browser, whose 8 MB of code take at least 45 minutes to download on a 33.6 kilobit-per-second connection. By contrast, Bigfoot's NeoPlanet Browser, which makes use of IE components that are already part of Windows, occupies just 791 KB and can be downloaded in five minutes. Consequently, the wide dissemination of IE technology through OS integration increases competition and innovation in browser shell programs.

Basically, OS integration reduces the cost of innovation in the applications market. This positive effect on the supply side of innovation adds to the demand-side effects discussed above, whereby OS integration opens the door to new PC applications by simplifying the use of interacting components in a computer system.

OS integration is also a useful way to standardize the computing and software development environment. Furthermore, by facilitating online distribution, it reduces the cost of distributing applications products. Online distribution is especially important for specialized software products that are unlikely to be carried by traditional retail outlets.

Regarding which software building blocks become integrated into the OS and when, it should be clear that an analysis parallel to the one developed in the preceding section applies here as well. For example, once a platform supplier publishes a set of APIs that developers come to rely on, it becomes costly to remove the APIs or to alter them in ways that damage backward compatibility. Hence, a platform vendor has strong incentives to postpone the introduction of new APIs until the company is confident about both their usefulness and its ability to offer continued support for the APIs as the platform evolves.

Reducing Customer Support Costs

Another motive for integrating stand-alone elements into the OS is the desire to hold down customer support costs. For many software firms, customer support is a major cost of business and, in a world of dirt-cheap CD-ROMs, the main incremental cost of selling software.

This point comes through loud and clear in Microsoft's experience with customer support.[65] In the early 1990s, Microsoft was fielding about 60,000 customer support inquiries per day, including 20,000 phone calls that had to be handled by product support engineers. Microsoft personnel in the customer support division actually outnumbered the firm's software developers.[66]

Microsoft answered one customer support call for every three software units sold, at an average cost of $12 each. At that rate, just a few calls from a customer can wipe out the profit from selling most software products, even before factoring in development costs. As of 1993, in fact, customer support costs equaled 20 percent of the gross revenues from Windows and 25 percent from Windows NT. Most calls came from customers who had purchased the software within the previous 90 days, and about half of these "relate to setting up or installing the software...printing, usage of new or changed features, the operating environment, and interoperability with other products."[67]

This stark reality encouraged Microsoft to focus on design advances that would reduce customer support calls and costs. These innovations drew heavily on usability studies for new software products along with detailed statistical summaries of the problems that prompted support inquiries.[68]

The careful integration of software functionality into the OS can dramatically reduce the costs of customer support. Consider, for example, what it took for a PC user to get online in, say, 1993. The user had to acquire and install an operating system, a modem, a browser or other Internet software, an Internet provider, an Internet account, and a TCP/IP "stack." He or she also had to enter the appropriate parameters and data for each piece of software and hardware. Getting online required that all the information be entered correctly and that all the pieces worked together properly. As many who undertook this task can ruefully recall, getting online also required innumerable calls to customer support centers. By contrast, the integration of these elements into modern operating systems like Windows and MacOS 9 allows today's PC user to stroke just a few keys to get online the first time. At Microsoft, and no doubt other firms, this type of OS integration has dramatically reduced the resources devoted to helping customers connect to the Web and other networks.[69]

The integration of the HTML-based Help system into Windows 98 was also motivated, in part, by the desire to reduce customer support costs. Frequent Web references point users to documents that provide background, examples, technical information, and links to other Web-based information sources. This system can be used at all levels of the software development hierarchy – OS tools, applications, and company-based Intranet software.

Not all stand-alone elements will eventually be integrated into OS products. As discussed earlier in the chapter, integration becomes more attractive as the use of the stand-alone element increases, when integration leads to lower design and production costs, and when the stand-alone element interacts with the other elements of the OS in a complicated way. This section simply adds another potential benefit that must be weighed against the costs. In parallel with our earlier discussion, the timing of integration is influenced by uncertainty regarding the magnitude of customer support costs and how integration might most effectively reduce such costs.

The demand for OS integration can also arise from customer preferences for dealing with a single vendor – especially in cases where there are many interacting components in a complex system. Computer software systems can be extremely complicated, sometimes involving several subsystems with a million lines of code each.[70] When problems arise, customers want to know where to turn for solutions. And when a single seller supplies all the components, the answer is clear.

Early users of microcomputers had to assemble the systems, piece by piece. No one, except for an occasional "techie," attempted the task without assistance from customer support centers. If something went wrong with the computer after assembly, the user had to determine which parts vendor to contact for advice before the user could even hope to return the computer to working order. Altair was the first to build a microcomputer system that included a power supply, motherboard, CPU, memory, I/O and OS (BASIC interpreter). The present-day predominance of this form of integration suggests, among other things, that customers highly value the opportunity to buy all the pieces assembled and supported by a single vendor.

Or consider a more personal example. One of us (MacCrisken) worked as the database administrator for Intel in the early 1980s. During that period, Intel experienced a variety of network performance problems, which often involved the interaction of the mainframe OS, the communications software, and the network hardware. Fortunately for Intel, all of these products came from IBM. So when problems arose, Intel called on IBM – and the buck stopped there.

However, if a customer buys routers from Cisco, computers from Dell, and modems from 3Com, and the components don't interact properly, what options are open? Too often the choice is between bouncing from finger-pointing vendor to finger-pointing vendor, or hiring a third-party troubleshooter to solve the problem. [71]

Sometimes, the customer's demand for a single vendor can be met by the integration of additional features into a computer's operating system. This permits the seller to test the integration exhaustively before putting the components on the market, *and* it assigns clear responsibility for the failure of interacting components to work together. Less-informed and less-sophisticated computer users are especially likely to value the acquisition of software products from a single firm with a well-established reputation for quality and customer support.

DEMAND-BASED MOTIVES FOR SOFTWARE BUNDLING

Software is frequently bundled in the sense that multiple features or applications are packaged together or distributed jointly. Often, one or more items in the bundle are (or were) previously sold as separate products.

A few examples highlight the ubiquity of software bundling. PCs often come bundled with a large collection of software applications at no extra charge. Adobe, Corel, Lotus, Microsoft, Norton, and other software firms often bundle stand-alone applications in "suites" or multi-feature packages. PCTools, for example, offered a large collection of distinct software features on a single CD-ROM. And software vendors routinely bundle large collections of utilities and features with OS and platform products. In 1993, for example, Microsoft Windows for the first time included disk compression features similar to Stac's Stacker and fax functions similar to Delrina's WinFax product (Markoff, 1996).

As some of these examples suggest, the joint distribution of software features and applications often takes place even when there are no technical benefits or cost savings from code-level integration. In line with this observation, we show that demand-based effects alone can provide powerful motives for software bundling. We also explain why software bundling motivated by demand considerations leads to economic efficiency.

Before we develop the economic logic of bundling, some preliminary remarks help place this section's analysis in proper perspective.[72] First, demand-based motives for software bundling are distinct from, but fully consistent with, the motivations for OS integration discussed in earlier sections. Second, the benefits of bundling can be achieved by any method of joint distribution, including integration. As a practical matter, a mix of technological, timesaving, and demand-based factors may motivate the integration of particular software functionality. But for analytic clarity, we emphasize purely demand-based motives in this section. Third, demand considerations can lead a profit-maximizing firm to offer certain software applications at a zero or negative price. When this occurs, even a tiny technological benefit or cost saving makes integration the preferred strategy for achieving joint distribution.

Complementary Demand with the Operating System

The zero-price bundling and integration of certain software features with Microsoft's Windows OS has been criticized as predatory and anticompetitive.[73] It is important to recognize, however, that the most basic theory of pricing by a multi-product firm with downward sloping demand points to a very different explanation for this behavior – an explanation implying that zero-price bundling of software applications with OS products is a socially beneficial form of competition.

Start with the standard theory of pricing for a firm that sells multiple products with complementary demands. Two products are said to be complements when greater sales of one stimulate demand for the other. As an example familiar to many parents, sales of Barbie dolls stimulate the demand for Barbie clothes. After reviewing the pricing implications of complementary demand, we apply the logic to the bundling of OS and applications software. We then consider some implications of complementary demand for market structure and consumer welfare.

Consider a multi-product firm with downward sloping demand for each product. To focus on demand-based explanations for bundling, assume that production costs are unrelated across products. Also, set aside the motivations for product integration treated in earlier sections. To further simplify the exposition, assume that all of the firm's products are complements, so that greater sales of any one product increase demand for the others.

Under these conditions, complementary demand encourages the multi-product firm to set lower prices than would a collection of independent firms, each selling a single product. The logic is straightforward: A lower price on any one product generates additional sales of that product and all products with complementary demands. A multi-product firm internalizes this demand spillover onto the complementary products, whereas independent single-product firms do not.[74] In fact, complementary demand can lead the firm to price some products below marginal cost.

This point can be demonstrated with a simple model. Assume that the firm sells two complementary products with linear demand curves,

$$q_1 = a_1 - b_1p_1 - dp_2$$

$$q_2 = a_2 - b_2p_2 - dp_1$$

where q and p denote quantities and prices, and the a, b, and d parameters describe demand. Positive values for a and b imply positive, downward-sloping demand curves, and a positive value for d corresponds to the case of complementary demands. Assume that d is less than b_1 and b_2, so that own-price effects dominate. In addition, assume that the firm produces and sells each product at constant marginal costs denoted by c_1 and c_2.

Consider a numerical example in which the first product has bigger demand. The following parameter values fit this situation: $a_1 = 100$, $a2 = 50$,

$b_1 = b_2 = 1$, $c_1 = c_2 = 10$, and $d = .5$. With these values, profit maximization yields the prices, $p_1 = 55$ and $p_2 = 5$.[75] The firm prices good 2 below marginal cost in order to generate more profits by stimulating additional sales of good 1.

Now apply this logic to Microsoft's bundling of OS and applications software. The complementarity requirement certainly holds in this case, because Microsoft's PC software applications typically run on computer platforms that make use of its Windows OS products. So sales of PC applications software stimulate demand for Windows, and vice versa. To understand why complementary demand easily leads to zero-price bundling of applications software, it is important to recognize that the marginal cost of software sales may be quite low.[76] If we modify the previous example so that marginal cost is zero for each product, the profit-maximizing prices become $p_1 = 33.3$ and $p_2 = 0$.

Zero marginal costs are not necessary for a zero-price outcome, although low marginal costs make such an outcome more likely. If we modify the numerical example so that $a_2 = 20$ and retain the assumption that marginal cost equals 10 for each good, the firm's profit-maximizing prices become $p_1 = 65$ and $p_2 = -15$. The relatively low demand for good 2, coupled with complementary demand and low (but positive) marginal costs, leads the firm to set the price of good 2 below zero in order to stimulate sales of good 1.

In practice, a negative price may or may not exploit complementary demand more effectively than a zero price. If a negative price can be conditioned on actual use, then the firm can earn more profits in the preceding example by paying others to use product 2. Alternatively, if paying someone to take possession of a product provides no guarantee or incentive that he or she will actually use it, there is no point in offering the product at a negative price. Instead, by distributing the product at no charge, the firm maximizes product usage (and any effects of complementary demand) without incurring the additional expense of paying customers to take possession. Taking this observation into account and setting $p_2 = 0$ in the example with $a_2 = 20$ leads to a profit-maximizing price for the first good of $p_1 = 57.5$.

Adobe has pursued this pricing strategy for complementary software products with great success. As Shapiro and Varian (1999, p. 254) observe, Adobe allowed its portable document format (PDF) to "become an open standard but cleverly exploited the complementarities between creating and viewing a document. Adobe charged for the PDF creation software, while giving away the viewing software." Adobe successfully pursued a similar strategy with its Postscript page-description language and related software products.

Although extremely simple, the examples capture three salient aspects of the pricing and bundling of OS and applications software. First, OS and applications software are complementary in use. Second, marginal costs (of production, distribution, and customer support) are quite low for many types of software. Third, the demand for OS software is typically greater than the demand for a particular applications product. The third point, in particular, indicates that OS products play the role of good 1 in the numerical examples, and applications play the role of good 2.

We have now developed a simple explanation for the zero-price bundling of software features or applications with the OS that does not involve any dynamic or strategic considerations. Nor does it involve any direct technological or timesaving benefits of integration or reductions in customer support costs of the sort highlighted in earlier sections. Instead, the key elements in this explanation are low marginal costs for the bundled feature and complementary demand with the OS. Other things being equal, zero-price bundling is more likely for complementary goods that have relatively low demand.[77]

Two additional cost factors reinforce this complementarity motive for zero-cost bundling of software applications and features with the OS. First, this method of bundling is more convenient for the consumer than any other distribution method because it eliminates the time and effort associated with acquiring and installing the zero-price item.[78] Second, this form of bundling is also less costly for the software firm than other forms of distribution. There are no separate distribution costs and no customer support costs related to installation.

Other aspects of Microsoft's pricing behavior lend support to this interpretation of zero-price bundling with the OS. In particular, Microsoft has been a price-cutter in many software application categories such as CD encyclopedias, Web browsers, personal financial planning, and core business applications.[79] This behavior is a natural consequence of Microsoft's broad software product line, given that distinct categories of software applications are complements in use and, especially, the strong complementarity between Microsoft's OS products and its software applications that run on the OS. Complementary demand across product lines gives Microsoft a stronger incentive than its competitors have to set low prices, even when it has the same development and production costs and the same degree of market power for particular software products.[80]

Implications for Market Structure and Consumer Welfare

Whether it involves zero-price bundling of features with the OS or lower prices on stand-alone products, this type of behavior improves economic efficiency and helps consumers. The incentive for a multi-product firm to set lower prices in the face of complementary demand leads to higher output, more consumer benefits, and greater economic efficiency.[81]

Indeed, in the simple two-good model, consumers are unambiguously better off when a single, integrated firm sells both products than when a different firm sells each product. What's more, total profits are higher with a single, integrated firm. Since profits are higher and consumers are better off when a single firm sells both goods, economic efficiency must also be greater.[82]

Complementary demand (d>0) is the critical assumption that underlies the favorable effects of the single-firm market structure on consumer welfare and economic efficiency. Although our mathematical model is highly stylized, the economic logic of complementary demand is general, and the model carries important implications for thinking about market structure, efficiency, and consumer welfare in software markets.

To appreciate some of these implications, consider the evolution of the software market during the 1990s. Many commentators remark with concern – even alarm – that Microsoft became the leading vendor for many business and consumer software products during the 1990s.[83] One source of this concern is a perception that Microsoft enjoys an unfair competitive advantage over other software firms because of the tremendous success of the Windows platform.

Without pretending to address this issue in full, we can garner some important insights by applying our analysis to the question of market structure and consumer welfare. Suppose that two complementary products – let us call them OS and WB – have been developed by separate firms. The demand structure and marginal costs of production are the same as above. Initially, the two firms independently price and sell their products. Recognizing that the action of each affects the other, the two firms behave strategically in the manner of Bertrand (prices as strategies) or Cournot (quantities as strategies).[84]

We have already established that total profits are higher when a single, integrated firm sells both products. Hence, the two firms have a strong incentive to merge. Under the assumptions set forth here, a merger would be profitable for the firms *and* beneficial for consumers. Nonetheless, suppose that the two firms do not merge, because other aspects of their businesses do not mesh well, or perhaps because of opposition by the antitrust authorities.[85]

In the absence of a merger or acquisition, each firm might subsidize the price charged by the other. In this manner, the two firms could try to internalize the demand complementarity without actually merging. Firms sometimes do enter into mutual promotion agreements that contain cross-subsidies of this sort. Of course, if this option were a perfect substitute for merging, there would be no incentive to merge. In practice, though, inter-firm subsidies often run into serious practical problems. If the OS firm subsidizes the sale of WB, the WB firm may respond by expanding into market segments that are not especially helpful to the OS firm. Practical problems with this type of subsidy arrangement are apt to be especially severe when the net-of-subsidy price for WB is zero or negative, as in some of our numerical examples. An even more basic problem with the cross-subsidy solution is that it does not confer common ownership and control. The two firms may have imperfectly aligned incentives over how to market or design their respective products. Thus, even if a successful cross-subsidy arrangement is feasible, there will remain incentives to bring the two complementary products under common ownership and control.

This brings us squarely to the issue of market entry. We tailor our assumptions so that the analysis speaks to government claims in *U.S. v. Microsoft Corp.* Rule out cross-firm subsidies, and consider four specific assumptions. First, the two goods are initially owned and sold by separate firms. Second, it is costly for the OS firm to develop its own version of WB but much more costly for the WB firm to develop its own version of OS. Third, the demand structure and marginal production costs are such that it is profit-maximizing for an integrated firm to sell WB at a zero or negative price. Fourth, demand is great enough so that entry into the WB market is profitable for the OS firm. These four assumptions reflect key aspects of the market situation circa 1994 as it pertains to Microsoft and its Windows OS, on one hand, and Netscape and its Navigator Web browser, on the other hand.

Given these assumptions, the OS firm finds it profitable to develop its own version of WB, although the development costs are quite high. After incurring these large development costs, it then proceeds to offer its version of WB at no charge. It may even pay others to distribute WB or pay consumers to use it. This course of action obviously harms the firm that originally developed the WB product. Indeed, in our stylized model, the OS firm drives the original WB firm out of the market.

On first encounter, the decision by the OS firm to spend large sums to develop a "zero-revenue" product might appear anticompetitive or predatory. The government has drawn just such inferences in *U.S. v. Microsoft Corp.* from facts that parallel the assumptions in our stylized analysis. Indeed, the government's chief economic expert in the case draws the conclusion that "Microsoft had monopoly power, and its bundling and related actions 'made no business sense' save for the protection of that power." (Fisher [2000], p. 183.)

But it is clear from our analysis that even the most basic two-good model of complementary demand delivers a simple, pro-consumer interpretation of

Microsoft's behavior regarding the development and pricing of Internet Explorer. There is nothing esoteric about this explanation – no strategic or dynamic considerations are at play. Just basic economics.

If this complementary demand interpretation of Microsoft's pricing behavior is correct, Microsoft's large and broad presence in software markets has highly beneficial effects for consumers and overall economic efficiency. By the same token, breaking Microsoft into an OS company and a separate software applications company, as the trial judge ordered in *U.S. v. Microsoft Corp.*, would lead to lower output and higher consumer prices in both market segments.

Complementarities with Other Sources of Profit

Another simple demand-based explanation for zero-price bundling emphasizes complementarities with profit opportunities in other markets, rather than complementarity in use with the OS. To borrow Klein's (1999) terminology, product A has "negative marginal costs" when its adoption and use by customers generate additional profits for the firm in other markets, say B and C, that exceed the marginal costs of producing, distributing, and supporting product A. In principle, this form of complementarity can arise even when there is no direct complementarity in use between product A and products B or C. In practice, "negative marginal costs" may reinforce the bundling motive that stems from direct complementarity in use.

Web browsers like the IE browser shell and Netscape Navigator are examples of software with this potential. Greater use of Navigator, for instance, increased traffic flow on Netscape's Web site, which enabled Netscape to earn more from Web advertisements and from commissions on Internet commerce.[86] The commissions arise in connection with revenue-sharing agreements that Netscape made with firms that sell products and services over the Internet. Netscape earned a commission on the sales that resulted when Navigator directed Web traffic to another firm's Web site.

This type of revenue-sharing arrangement is an important aspect of Internet commerce and is by no means limited to Web browsers. For example, AOL and Yahoo generate revenue through such agreements. PC manufacturers Compaq and Gateway have also taken steps to generate revenues from Internet commerce in connection with their hardware sales. These PC makers redesigned their keyboards to give prominent placement to the Web sites and services of their online partners. When a customer uses a Compaq PC to access AOL, for example, Compaq gets a share of the customer's monthly AOL fees (Ramstad, 1998).

Klein (1999) stresses negative marginal costs of this sort in his explanation for Microsoft's vigorous efforts to distribute its browser software through zero-price bundling and integration with its OS products.[87] This negative marginal cost feature of browsers reinforces the complementarity motive for zero-price bundling that we developed above. In other words, negative marginal costs and complementarity in use with OS products are distinct forces that favor zero-price bundling. Either force alone can lead to zero-price bundling. When both forces are in play, the demand-based motive for zero-price bundling or integration with the OS becomes stronger.

We think Klein overstates the role of "negative marginal costs" in Microsoft's decision to distribute Internet Explorer at no charge. Microsoft, unlike Netscape, generated little revenue from advertisements and commissions earned in connection with customer flow through its Web portal. Furthermore, Microsoft's decision to componentize the design of Internet Explorer involved a sacrifice of potential portal-related revenues, because the componentized design made it easier for other companies to use IE technologies to build their own browsers and thereby direct customers to non-Microsoft Web portals.[88]

Nonetheless, we agree with Klein's basic point that Web browsers are highly complementary with other sources of profits. Prominent examples include Netscape itself, AOL and other online service providers, Internet aggregators like Yahoo, and Internet retailers like Amazon.com. For this reason, it seems likely that the price of Web browsers would have gravitated toward zero regardless of whether Microsoft had pursued a zero-price policy for Internet Explorer. Microsoft's actions simply accelerated the process.

Two additional points should help clarify the relationship between the negative marginal cost and complementarity-in-use explanations for zero-price bundling with OS products. First, browsers exhibit negative marginal costs because they are complementary to other activities with profit-making potential for the browser firm – namely, Internet sales and Web advertisements. In this respect, negative marginal costs involve a complementarity, but not a direct complementarity in use with the OS. Second, even the negative marginal cost explanation for the zero-price bundling of browsers requires some form of complementarity with the OS. Otherwise, the browser could just as well be freely distributed on street corners rather than bundled with the OS. In addition to the complementarity in use at the heart of our first demand-based explanation for bundling, three complementarities in distribution play a role in the zero-price bundling of browsers with the OS: (a) It is cheaper to distribute browser and OS software together; (b) it is more convenient for customers to acquire them together; and (c) customers who place a high value on the OS are more likely to also place a high value on a browser.

Reducing the Diversity of Buyer Valuations

A third demand-based explanation for product bundling begins with the observation that buyer valuations of a bundle are often much less dispersed than valuations of the individual items in the bundle. So, by combining many items into a single package, the high and low valuations a customer attaches to particular items tend to average out. Hence, a seller can more confidently predict what customers will pay for the bundle than what they will pay for any individual item in the bundle.

A newspaper is a good example of this type of bundled product. Customer valuations of the entire newspaper are much less dispersed than their valuations of individual sections devoted to sports, weather, international news, and so on. The same idea applies to individual articles. Customer valuations of particular articles about baseball's home run leaders, the likelihood that Michael Jordan will resume his NBA career, and predictions for the upcoming football season are much more dispersed than the valuations attached to the sports section as a whole.

Uncertainty regarding the value that consumers place on individual products undermines effective pricing from the firm's standpoint. If individual valuations for a product are highly dispersed, the firm must choose between higher prices that exclude many consumers with low valuations and lower prices that forgo substantial surplus to many consumers with high valuations. By bundling items, the firm can reduce the diversity in customer valuations for the bundled product relative to the individual items – or, at a minimum, reduce the diversity in customer valuations as a percentage of bundle value as its size grows.[89] The firm may then be able to set a price for the bundle that generates more revenue than it could obtain by separately pricing the individual items. Hence, provided that the costs of including multiple goods are not high, bundling can lead to higher profits.[90]

A simple numerical example shows how bundling can lead to higher profits and greater economic efficiency by reducing the diversity of buyer valuations. Consider a firm that owns the rights to 100 "information goods" such as software products. Assume the firm can replicate these items at zero cost. The firm sells the items in a market with anonymous buyers who differ in the value that they attach to individual items. In particular, suppose that there are also 100 consumer types, indexed by i = 1, 2,...100. The ith consumer places a value of 101 on the ith item and a value of 1 on the other 99 items.[91] Consumers purchase one or zero units of each item, and there are equal numbers of each consumer type.

Table 2 displays the firm's profit-maximizing outcomes for bundles of various sizes, given these assumptions. If the firm sells items individually, then it faces the following demand curve for each item: At a price less than or equal to 1, everyone buys; at a price greater than 1 but less than or equal to 101, only the high-valuation type buys; and at a price greater than 101, no one buys. Clearly, the firm will never find it advantageous to sell individual items for a price less than 1 or between 1 and 101. If the firm prices individual items at 1, it sells them to every type, and its profits on all items amount to 10,000 per hundred consumers. If it prices individual items at 101, it sells only to high types, and its profits amount to 10,100 per hundred consumers. So, given that the firm sells items individually, the profit-maximizing price is 101 and the total profit is 10,100 per hundred consumers. In this way, we determine the profit-maximizing outcomes for the first row in the table. The other rows are filled in using parallel logic.

As the table shows, the firm maximizes profits in this example by selecting the largest bundle. This result reflects the effect of bundling on the diversity of buyer valuations for the bundled product relative to the individual items in the bundle. Indeed, in this simple example, *every* consumer attaches a value of *exactly* 200 to the bundle that contains all 100 items. More generally, column (6) shows that the diversity among potential customers in the valuations attached to a bundle declines with bundle size. This diversity reduction aspect or "predictive value" of bundling leads a profit-maximizing firm to choose a lower price per item in a larger bundle. The firm more than makes up for the lower price per item by selling the bundled items to a larger number of customers. Total profits rise with bundle size, as indicated by column (5).[92]

The predictive value of bundling improves economic efficiency by promoting the widespread distribution and use of the firm's information goods. To understand why widespread distribution is efficient, recall that the firm can replicate its information goods at zero cost. Because replication is costless, and because every consumer type places a positive value on each information good in this example, economic efficiency calls for the widest possible distribution. Bundling leads to wider distribution and use, as shown in column (7) of the table. The largest bundle maximizes the distribution and use of the individual information goods.

A major barrier to this type of bundling in many cases is the cost of including additional items in the bundle. High marginal costs for individual

Table 2. **Profit-Maximizing Outcomes for Bundles of Various Sizes**

1 Bundle Size (# of types who buy each bundle)	2 Number of Product Bundles	3 Bundle Price	4 Price per Bundle (3/1)	5 Profits per 100 Consumers (1x2x3)	6 Coefficient of Variation of Bundle Variations*	7 Fraction of Items Used by Each Consumer
1	100	101	101	10,100	497.5	0.01
2	50	102	51	10,200	350.0	0.02
4	25	104	26	10,400	244.9	0.04
5	20	105	21	10,500	217.9	0.05
10	10	110	11	11,000	150.0	0.10
20	5	120	6	12,000	100.0	0.20
25	4	125	5	12,500	86.6	0.25
50	2	150	3	15,000	50.0	0.50
100	1	200	2	20,000	0.0	1.00

* Column (6) reports the coefficient of variation of buyer valuations for a bundle of the indicated size. The coefficient of variation is calculated as 100 times the standard deviation of buyer valuations divided by the mean of buyer valuations. The mean and standard deviations are calculated over all buyers, whether or not they actually purchase the bundle at the profit-maximizing price. The resulting coefficient of variation measures the diversity of buyer valuations placed on the bundle, expressed as a percentage of the mean valuation for the bundle. In this example, the coefficient of variation is the same for all bundles of a given size.

items greatly reduce the attractiveness of bundling when customers place little or no value on many individual items. Even modest marginal costs can undermine bundling. If we modify the example in Table 2 so that the marginal cost of each item is 2 rather than 0, the profit-maximizing bundle size is one item, instead of 100 items. For this reason, bundling to reduce buyer diversity is much more attractive for information goods than for physical goods, which typically involve non-negligible marginal costs. For information goods stored in electronic form, the marginal costs of replication and transmission are near zero.

These observations help explain important aspects of pricing behavior by firms that sell digital products. For example, many Internet aggregators provide access to enormous information libraries and a wide range of services for a single flat fee. For $23.95 a month (as of July 2001), AOL provides unlimited access to a wide range of services including Internet access, stock quotes, foreign exchange and commodity market information, e-mail, and instant messaging to other online users. All of these services are accessible from local phone numbers in most localities in the United States.

E-library (http://www.elibrary.com) is another example. Bakos and Brynjolfsson (1999) write: "As of 1997 and 1998, E-library provides access to a bundle of 150 newspapers, 800 magazines, 2,000 works of literature, 18,000 photos, and thousands of additional information goods for a fixed price of $59.95 per year for individual users."

The same economic rationale that explains the bundling approach adopted by AOL, E-library, and many other Internet firms also helps explain bundling by software firms. The key elements in this theory of software bundling are low marginal costs and a desire to reduce the diversity of buyer valuations. Hence, software features or applications that create large customer support burdens are unlikely to be bundled if the only motive is a reduction in the diversity of buyer valuations.

Unlike the complementarity-based explanation for bundling, the buyer diversity explanation requires no particular relationship among the bundled items. Thus, according to this theory, it is not surprising that a grab-bag collection of software utilities and applications is often bundled with OS products. For example, an OS upgrade might contain some Internet utilities, Plug-and-Play functions, Multimedia support, WebTV, and 1394/USB support.[93]

Product bundling motivated by a desire to reduce buyer diversity promotes economic efficiency for much the same reason that it allows firms to increase profits. The predictive value of bundling leads firms to price and market low-marginal-cost goods in such a way that they become more widely distributed. Consequently, consumers acquire and use many products that they would not purchase separately in the absence of bundling. For goods with a zero marginal cost of replication and transmission, the widespread distribution and use promoted by bundling is an efficiency-enhancing outcome.

The consumer welfare implications of bundling motivated by a desire to reduce buyer diversity are less clear. Salinger (1995) considers a case where bundling leads to higher consumer welfare. Bakos and Brynjolfsson (1999) make clear that this result is not general. However, both analyses approach the consumer welfare effects of bundling from a static perspective. In a dynamic setting, the higher profits generated by bundling provide incentives to develop the items or features in the bundle.[94] This point is especially pertinent in the context of software and other information goods, because their costs of development are often high, even if their costs of replication are low.

CONCLUDING COMMENTS

Improvements in the software that provides hardware management, user interface, and platform functions have played a central role in the growth and transformation of the personal computer (PC) industry. Several forces shape the design of these operating system products and propel their evolution, including:

• The need to efficiently manage the interacting components of PC systems so as to keep pace with rapid advances in computer technologies, simplify computer use and facilitate the development of applications software.

• The need to maintain compatibility with existing applications while preserving the flexibility to incorporate additional functions that support new applications.

• The desire to economize on customer support costs and assign clear responsibility for making the interacting components of the PC work together.

• The desire to bundle multiple software features into a single package so as to more effectively meet the demand for complementary applications or reduce the diversity in product valuations among consumers.

The integration and bundling of new features and functions into operating system products spurs growth in the PC industry and fosters innovation through several channels. By making PC systems easier to set up and use, integration opens the door to new, non-integrated hardware and software products. It also expands the number of PC users and the range of PC uses. In addition, the integration of APIs (software building blocks) into operating system products enables applications developers to concentrate on their areas of expertise. This specialization leads to an increase in the quality, number, and variety of software applications. As a related point, the integration of widely used features and software development tools into operating system products also promotes a standard computing environment. As a separate point, demand-based motives for bundling applications and utilities with operating system products lead to wider and cheaper distribution of software among PC users. Bundling also adds to consumer welfare by stimulating the development of software applications that would otherwise be unprofitable.

These beneficial effects of operating system integration (and bundling) enlarge the market for both software and hardware. Because scale economies are important in the computer industry, the market-enlarging effects of integration mean greater enjoyment of network benefits (as PC usage grows) and lower average costs (as up-front product development expenditures are spread more widely). Hence, the full benefits derived from adding features and functions to operating system products are greater, perhaps much greater, than the immediate benefits. In short, our analysis indicates that the integration and bundling of new features and functions into PC operating system products have been both highly beneficial for consumers and a major stimulus to growth and innovation in the computer industry.

We thus conclude that judicial or regulatory restrictions on software design would likely retard innovation in the computer industry and hurt consumers. To be sure, there are circumstances under which it is feasible and profitable for a firm with market power to design products for anticompetitive purposes, and to harm consumers in the process. Whinston (1990) shows that product design can be used to exclude a rival from the market for a tied good while raising the tying firm's profit and harming consumers.[95] Farrell and Katz (2000) identify conditions under which product integration by the monopoly supplier of one component in a system can reduce the incentives for innovation by other firms. And a firm might intentionally design a platform product to raise costs for rivals who compete in the sale of complementary applications.

A full assessment of the issues raised by anticompetitive product designs is beyond the scope of this study. However, a few points should help to place the matter in perspective.[96] First, theoretical demonstrations of profitable, but anticompetitive, product design are fragile in the sense that they do not survive natural modifications to the underlying assumptions. Second, the circumstances that lead to the possibility of anticompetitive product designs also give rise to the possibility of other harmful anticompetitive strategies. Hence, it is unclear whether product design restrictions can prevent or ameliorate anticompetitive conduct. Third, as a practical matter, it can be extremely difficult to distinguish anticompetitive product designs from pro-competitive designs, or to determine whether the harm caused by an allegedly anticompetitive design outweighs the beneficial effects.[97] Fourth, even if it were possible to discern, say, anticompetitive forms of integration and bundling and respond with legal restrictions on design that address the underlying problem, there would remain the danger that the design restrictions would impede beneficial forms of integration and bundling. As this study shows, highly beneficial forms of product integration and bundling are ubiquitous for software platforms and software products generally.[98] These points reinforce our view that legal restrictions on the design of software products are likely to slow innovation and harm consumers.

As we stressed at the outset, software is inherently malleable, and competition in many software product categories revolves around innovation. This reality partly motivated our focus on design issues rather than the pricing of software. Of course, pricing also matters because it directly affects consumer welfare, profits, and the incentives to innovate. Pricing and design also interact in many ways in addition to the connection between pricing and bundling that we discussed – see Shapiro and Varian (1999).

Davis, Murphy and Topel (2001) stress that product design changes can either intensify or soften price competition. Rival firms with secure positions in the same market have strong incentives to differentiate their products in ways that relax price competition.[99] To bring this about, a firm can focus on design improvements that appeal more strongly to its existing customers than to its rivals' customers. In contrast, when a firm seeks to displace a rival, it becomes attractive to intensify price competition by improving products in ways that appeal strongly to the rival's customers.

The durability of software raises dynamic pricing issues of the sort identified by Coase (1972). The seller of any durable product competes against its own past and future sales, a fact that can strongly affect the profitability of alternative design strategies. See the analyses by Fudenberg and Tirole (1998) and Ellison and Fudenberg (2000) and our discussion in Davis, MacCrisken, and Murphy (1999). Product design choices also play an important role in the evolution of standards for system products and affect compatibility with products supplied by other firms. Besen and Farrell (1994), Katz and Shapiro (1994), and Shapiro and Varian (1999) contain useful discussions on these topics and references to related work.

[1] Civil Action 98-1232 (D.D.C. 1998).

[2] The district court's Findings of Fact (11/5/1999), Conclusions of Law and Final Order (4/13/2000), and Final Judgment (6/7/2000) in *U.S. v. Microsoft* are available at http://www.usdoj.gov/atr/cases/ms_index.htm. The court of appeals opinion (6/28/2001) in the matter is available at http://www.ll.georgetown.edu/Fed-Ct/cadc.html. In the wake of the appellate court opinion, the government abandoned divestiture as a remedy on September 6, 2001. At this juncture (September 2001), there remains the possibility that a future remedy will include restrictions on the design of Microsoft software. Economic analyses of the case include Economides (2000), Evans, Nichols, and Schmalensee (2001), Fisher and Rubinfeld (2000), Gilbert and Katz (2001), Klein (2001) and Whinston (2001).

[3] *U.S. v. Microsoft Corp.* involved allegations of an illegal tie of Microsoft's Windows 9x software, which provides hardware management functions, a user interface, and an applications platform, to its Internet Explorer Web-browsing software. Another recent antitrust case, *Caldera, Inc. v. Microsoft Corp.* (72 F. Supp.2d 1295 [D. Utah 1999]) involves an allegedly illegal tie of the MS-DOS operating system to Microsoft Windows 3.1, which provides a user interface and applications platform. See Hylton and Salinger (2001) for a detailed assessment of tying law and theory that analyzes these cases.

[4] On dynamic competition in software markets, in particular, see Evans, Nichols, and Reddy (1999), Evans and Schmalensee (2001), and Liebowitz and Margolis (1999). Other studies of dynamic competition include Gans, Hsu, and Stern (2000), Reinganum (1985), and Vickers (1986).

[5] We interviewed James Allchin, Hillel Cooperman, Paul Maritz, and Tod Nielsen at the

Microsoft corporate campus in Redmond, Washington, on August 24, 1999. At the time of our interviews, Allchin was senior vice president for personal and business systems, Cooperman was a project manager for a version of Windows under development, Maritz was group vice president for platforms and applications, and Nielsen was vice president, developer marketing. Allchin and Maritz were also major witnesses in *U.S. v. Microsoft Corp*.

[6] An OS product can function as a software platform, but another platform can also be layered on top of an OS. For example, Microsoft Windows 3.x consisted of a graphical user interface and applications platform layered on top of the DOS operating system. Later, this graphical user interface was integrated with other operating system functions to become the Windows 9x and Windows NT line of products. A software application can also serve as a platform for other add-on software products, and the hardware in a computer system can be viewed as a platform for running software. See the second section in Evans, Nichols, and Schmalensee (2001; this volume) for a more detailed discussion of alternative types of software platforms.

[7] David Farber, professor of telecommunication systems at the University of Pennsylvania's Moore School of Engineering, remarks in his October 5, 1998, deposition (p. 91) that memory management systems were add-ons in early versions of DOS, but it became efficient over time to "include them integrally" in the OS. John Soyring, director of network computing software at IBM, discusses IBM's development of Internet browsing software and its inclusion in OS/2 on pages 35, 37, and 38 of his November 18, 1998, a.m. live testimony. Avadis Tevanian, senior vice president of software engineering at Apple Computer Corporation, discusses the integration or bundling of Internet functionality with the Mac OS on pages 37-38, 43, 47, and 65-66 of his November 5, 1998, p.m. live testimony. James Gosling, vice president and Sun fellow at Sun Microsystems and chief scientist of the Java Software Division, discusses "built-in Web support" for a Web-enhanced version of the Solaris OS on pp. 34 and 36 of his December 9 1998, p.m. live testimony. Steven McGeady, Intel vice president and participant in Intel's early Internet and Java development efforts, expresses the view in his October 8, 1998, deposition (pp. 59-61) that multimedia software should be built into standard PCs. Glenn Weadock, president of Independent Software, Inc., states in his January 8, 1998, deposition (pp. 103-104) that the definition of basic OS functionality has evolved over time. Edward Felten, assistant professor of computer science at Princeton University, notes with approval in his December 14, 1998, a.m. live testimony (p. 44) that new versions of software products often have more functionality and give users more choice. William Harris, president and CEO of Intuit, Inc., also remarks upon the expanding functionality of the OS over time in his January 4, 1999, a.m. live testimony (pp. 50-51). According to Harris, the benefits to Intuit of expanded OS functionality include additional code for modem support and the management of printer drivers. Harris also notes (pp. 51-52) that Intuit itself has expanded the functionality of its software products over time by integrating new Web functionality and by bundling different application products together. Here and below, all citations to live, deposition, and filed testimony refer to *U.S. v. Microsoft Corp.*, unless otherwise noted. Written testimony and transcripts of oral testimony by Microsoft witnesses, along with Microsoft's legal filings, are available at http://www.microsoft.com/trial/mswitness/default.asp. Court and government filings and the testimony of government witnesses are available at http://www.usdoj.gov/atr/cases/ms_index.htm. The court of appeals Web site at http://ecfp.cadc.uscourts.gov provides links to the filings in the appeals portion of the case.

[8] We compiled the data for Figures 1 through 5 and Table 1 in this section from advertisements in back issues of trade and advertising publications for the PC industry. To construct Figures 1, 2, and 3, we first identified the characteristics of new mid-range PCs at each date (Intel processor, memory amount, and hard disk capacity). We then priced each of these components as separate, stand-alone items. The data underlying Figures 1 through 5 and Table 1, and additional information about their construction and sources, are available from the authors upon request.

[9] In 1981, DOS Version 1.0 supported an 8-sector 160 KB floppy (single sided). Version 1.1, released in 1982, supported an 8-sector 320 KB floppy (double sided). Version 2.0 (1983) supported a 9-sector 360 KB floppy, and Version 3.0 (1984) supported a 1.2 MB floppy. See "DOS Versions" in Computer Language Company (1999).

[10] Berndt and Rappaport (2001, Table 1) estimate that the quality-adjusted price of desktop personal computers fell at an average rate of 27 percent per year from 1976 to 1999 and more than 35 percent per year in the 1990s.

[11] Based on offer from Gateway's Web site, http://www.gateway.com/home/prod/updatetotal.asp (accessed Sept. 9, 2001).

[12] Cusumano and Selby (1995, p. 148) provide a more detailed narrative of how the first several generations of DOS evolved in response to hardware advances.

[13] See Gookin (1992). As Evans and Schmalensee (2001) note, analysts also disagreed over whether OS/2 Warp 3.0 (introduced in November 1994) would prevail over Windows 95 (introduced in August 1995) to become the leading OS product for PCs.

[14] See Quarterman and Wilhelm (1993), chapter 2.

[15] According to a recent survey by Compaq, a major PC manufacturer and vendor, online services are now the number-one reason consumers buy PCs (Ramstad, 1998). Reid (1997) describes the explosive growth of the Internet.

[16] The quotation is drawn from a 1994 column explaining Mossberg's reason for initiating the column three years earlier.

[17] TCP/IP stands for transmission control protocol/Internet protocol. Because of its position in the software hierarchy between the Internet application and the communication I/O system (e.g., a modem or LAN), the configuration of a non-integrated TCP/IP package is extremely difficult for the non-technical user.

[18] In an interview, Todd Nielsen, Microsoft vice president of developer marketing, stressed that independent software vendors want a rich infrastructure, but they don't want to "do the plumbing." He also stressed that Microsoft undertakes extensive efforts to cultivate relationships with independent software vendors, to educate them about new and existing APIs in Microsoft platform products, to encourage their participation in beta testing, and to respond to their concerns.

[19] See Cusumano and Yoffie (1998), pp. 76-78, for a discussion of Netscape's use of APIs to promote its Navigator and Communicator products as applications platforms. Typically, platform vendors also devote considerable additional resources to stimulating the development of complementary applications by independent software firms. As of 1995, Microsoft spent about $65 million annually supporting independent software developers and had about 400 technical support engineers who exclusively served independent developers. See Microsoft (1995). According to the same document, Microsoft hosts about 200 developer conferences and seminars per year that are attended by more than 30,000 developers worldwide. Microsoft also engages in an extensive consultation and

testing program with developers prior to the release of new OS software. As an example, approximately 7,500 copies of an early version of Windows 95 were distributed to independent hardware and software vendors by December of 1993. About 12,000 beta-1 kits for Windows 95 were distributed by June of 1994. See p. 20 of Microsoft (1995).

[20] The integration of Internet Explorer into the Windows 98 OS is one of Microsoft's allegedly anticompetitive actions in *U.S. v. Microsoft Corp.*, but other leading suppliers of OS products have also made the integration of Web-support features and Internet functionality an important focus of OS development efforts. IBM has "Internet-enabled" OS/2 and other software products and perceives "tremendous value" in doing so. (Soyring, November 18, 1998, a.m. live testimony, pp. 36-37.) Some Internet protocols and functionality are "built into" the Mac OS, and other Internet functionality is bundled with the Mac OS. (Tevanian, November 5, 1998, p.m. live testimony, pp. 43, 63, 66, and 67.) Similarly, "built-in Web support for the Web-enhanced Solaris" OS includes TCP/IP, NFS protocols, and limited URL support. (Gosling, December 9, 1998, p.m. live testimony, pp. 34 and 36.)

[21] Soyring also remarks upon the great flexibility in software design on pp. 66-68 of his November 18, 1998, a.m. live trial testimony and on p. 11 of his filed testimony. The same theme is implicit in much of the live testimony of Felten and Tevanian, much of the live and deposition testimony of Weadock, and much of the deposition testimony of William Harris (president and CEO of Intuit, Inc.). Weadock explicitly discusses flexibility in software design on pp. 48-49 of his January 8, 1998, deposition testimony. Harris discusses the contrast between the componentized design of Internet Explorer and the design of Netscape Navigator on pp. 9-10, 45, and 73 of his January 4, 1999, p.m. live testimony and pp. 34-35 of his September 29, 1998, deposition testimony. Tevanian discusses how Apple weighed the choice between full technological integration and bundling of Internet protocols and functionality into the Macintosh OS on pp. 37-39, 43, 47, 63, 65, and 66 of his November 5, 1998, p.m. live testimony and p. 47 of his July 17, 1998, deposition testimony. A central theme of Felten's testimony is that Microsoft chose to design Windows 98 in a tightly integrated manner, even though technical efficiency does not require such a design.

[22] Weadock stresses that shared program libraries create indeterminacy in delineating a specific code set that defines a software product. See pp. 110, 115-116, and 119-120 of his January 8, 1998, deposition testimony. He also states (pp. 56-57) that "The delineation of what is system software versus what is OS software is a difficult and, except perhaps in legal proceedings, irrelevant distinction." Farber (October 5, 1998, deposition, pp. 103-104) argues that most people can agree about which file systems are sufficiently basic to be considered part of the OS.

[23] Weadock's deposition testimony quite effectively highlights the difficulties. He returns several times to the issue of what constitutes integration with the OS, what properly qualifies as part of the OS, and what functionality is properly deemed within the domain of the OS. However, it is difficult or impossible to distill any general principles regarding these matters from Weadock's testimony, because he advances often-conflicting criteria and many exceptions to particular rules. See pp. 13-14, 46, 48-58, 62, 65, 101-104, and 115-121 of his January 8, 1998, deposition testimony. Weadock is aware of these tensions and ambiguities. For example, he remarks that a disk defragmentation utility falls into a gray area as regards OS integration. This type of utility performs a basic housekeeping function, which tends to confer OS status in Weadock's view, but it can also be acquired from third-party vendors, which argues against OS status in his view.

[24] Some witnesses make this point explicitly. See, for example, p. 55 of Weadock's January 8, 1998, deposition testimony.

[25] A partial review of expert testimony in *U.S. v. Microsoft Corp.* turned up 10 distinct criteria for determining whether particular software components (files or groups of files) are properly deemed integrated, "built into," or part of the PC operating system:

1. Whether there exist multiple cross-dependencies among the components. (Soyring, November 18, 1998, a.m. live testimony, pp. 48 and 67, and October 15, 1998, deposition testimony, pp. 167 and 189.)
2. Whether the component in question exposes APIs to third-party users. (Soyring, November 18, 1998, a.m. live testimony, p. 48, and October 15, 1998, deposition testimony, p. 167.)
3. Whether the component in question is called upon by a wide variety of applications software. (Weadock, January 8, 1998, deposition, pp. 48-49.)
4. Whether the component performs services that are not directly available to end users. (Weadock, January 8, 1998, deposition, pp. 49-53.)
5. Whether the component performs "low-level" services; i.e., interacts in a fairly detailed and specific way with specific devices. (See pp. 49-53 of Weadock's January 8, 1998, deposition testimony, where he mentions network card drivers and Winsock as examples of software features that lie within the boundaries of the OS because, in part, they perform low-level services. Farber (October 5, 1998, deposition, pp. 91-92) defines a computer OS "as something that provides low level services, [but an] operating system platform or product or release, as commercially understood, is a lot more.")
6. Whether the component performs housekeeping functions. (Weadock, January 8, 1998, deposition, p. 53.)
7. Whether the component provides security and protection for other essential operating system functions. (Farber, filed testimony, page 10.)
8. Whether the component performs a function also performed by a separate software product available on the market from another vendor. (Soyring, October 15, 1998, deposition, pages 207-208; Weadock, January 8, 1998, deposition, pp. 46, 48, 56-58, 62, and 65.)
9. The extent to which the component is essential to basic OS functionality. (Weadock, January 8, 1998, deposition, pp. 101-102.)
10. The extent to which the component can be traced back to earlier versions of the OS. (Weadock, January 8, 1998, deposition, p. 46.)

[26] Farber discusses some principles of software engineering and design in his filed testimony.

[27] Several witnesses in *U.S. v. Microsoft Corp.* testify to this effect. See pp. 35-37, 52, and 54 of the November 18, 1998, a.m. and p. 86 of the November 19, 1998, p.m. live testimony and pp. 165-166 of the October 15, 1998, deposition testimony offered by John Soyring (IBM), pp. 59 and 62-63 of the November 5, 1998, p.m. live testimony by Tevanian (Apple), and p. 37 of the October 28, 1998, p.m. live testimony by David Colburn, senior vice president of business affairs for America Online, Inc.

[28] See, for example, pp. 37-38 of the December 9, 1998, p.m. live testimony by James Gosling. Gosling is shown a Sun marketing document that reads in part, "In addition to its HotJava Browser, the Web-enhanced Solaris operating environment also comes standard with Java Virtual Machine, JIT compiler and integrated Java API's. ... Through the Web-enhanced Solaris operating environment we offer Web-based client server computing." Gosling responds as follows: "But when it talks about the Java software being built

in as an integral part of the operating environment, it doesn't mean anything stronger than the Java Virtual Machine is another application that runs on top of the OS. ... The CD-ROM is nothing much different than sort of the digital equivalent of a paper bag into which you throw, you know, whatever you think is appropriate." See p. 35 of Soyring's November 18, 1998, a.m. live testimony for a very similar exchange regarding an IBM marketing document on the "integration" of Internet functionality into OS/2.

[29] As a case in point, IBM decided to install multiple different software products within its OS/2 offering in response to customer complaints about difficult, time-consuming installation procedures (Soyring, deposition testimony, pp. 165-166).

[30] See pp. 55-57 of the December 14, 1998, p.m. live testimony by Professor Edward Felten, a specialist in operating systems, Internet software, and Web-browsing programs.

[31] Based on advertisements in back issues of *PC Magazine*, disk storage costs per megabyte fell from $5.92 in May 1990 (Windows 3.0 release date) to $2.95 in April 1992 (Windows 3.1 release date) to 33 cents in August 1995 (Windows 95 release date) to 3 cents in June 1998 (Windows 98 release date) to 2 cents in May 1999.

[32] The 1990 figure is from *PC Magazine*'s annual review of best products, and the 1999 figure is based on advertisements in the May 5, 1999, issue of *PC Magazine*.

[33] Based on a PC system with a 9.1-gigabyte hard drive and a Windows 98 system requiring 225 megabytes of disk storage. At 2 cents per megabyte, the approximate cost of disk storage as of May 1999, the disk space freed up by a 50 percent reduction in the size of Windows 98 amounts to about $2.25.

[34] Based on advertisements in back issues of *PC Magazine*, memory costs per megabyte fell from $99 in May 1990 to $37.25 in April 1992 to $36.13 in August 1995 to $2.95 in June 1998 to $1.55 as of May 1999.

[35] Farber discusses several criteria that govern how software files are organized into files on pp. 7-8 of his filed testimony. He observes that "The most technically efficient size for a file is generally larger than a single routine and smaller than an entire application."

[36] Four kilobytes under Windows 98, 32 kilobytes under many earlier PC operating systems.

[37] See, for example, pp. 11-12 of Professor Farber's filed testimony and p. 44 of the December 14, 1998, a.m. live testimony and pp. 55-59 of the December 15, 1998, p.m. live testimony offered by Professor Felten.

[38] Of course, the standardized feature set promulgated by whole-cloth integration may not suit all users of OS software. Weadock, Farber, and other witnesses for the government in the Microsoft antitrust action stress this point in connection with the whole-cloth integration of Internet Explorer into Windows 98.

[39] Cusumano and Yoffie (1998), pp. 180-198 and 201-221, provide an insightful discussion of Netscape's struggle to achieve a componentized design architecture for its Navigator and Communicator products, the obstacles it encountered in pursuit of that goal, and the difficulties it faced because of its limited success in achieving a componentized architecture. Baldwin and Clark (2000) provide an extensive description and analysis of modular design strategies.

[40] Interview with the authors. See Chapter 4 in Cusumano and Yoffie (1998) for an account of the difficulties that Netscape faced in the pursuit of a componentized design architecture for its Navigator and Communicator software.

[41] Interview with the authors.

[42] Cusumano and Selby (1995) sound similar notes in their discussion of Microsoft's approach to software design architecture. For example, they write on p. 235 that "Sharing helps to harmonize the 'look and feel' of different products; it also facilitates user tasks that require more than one application, reduces redundant writing of code, and cuts down the size of individual applications."

[43] Drawing on their interview with Microsoft developer Jon De Vaan, Cusumano and Selby (1995, p. 245) provide a nice example of how software code that is not properly compartmentalized makes it difficult to add new features. In their discussion of the "revert to save" feature in Excel 5.0, they write that "The original procedure was very complicated, affecting as many as twenty different parts of the program. Since people did not commonly use the feature, developers would often forget it existed and 'break' the feature when making an unrelated change. As a result, it has been historically riddled with bugs. De Vaan replaced this with a much simpler design that centralizes the function in one place in the code, so that developers working on other parts of the system do not have to worry about it."

[44] The absence of a proper design strategy for maintaining backward compatibility can be disastrous for a software firm. Shapiro and Varian (1999, p. 194) make this point with a concrete example. "In some cases, the desire to maintain compatibility with previous generations has been the undoing of market leaders. The dBase programming language was hobbled because each new version of dBase had to be able to run programs written for all earlier versions. Over time, layers of dBase programming code accumulated on top of each other. Ashton-Tate, the maker of dBase, recognized that this resulted in awkward "bloatware," which degraded the performance of dBase. Unable to improve dBase in a timely fashion, and facing competition from Borland's more elegant, object-oriented relational database program, Paradox, dBase's fortunes fell sharply."

[45] Brad Silverberg, then senior vice president at Microsoft, emphasizes this point in an August 1993 interview with Cusumano and Selby (1995, pp. 167-168): "[Windows] 3.0 was pretty big and pretty slow; 3.1 made a lot of improvements ... [But] at some point you can't break compatibility, either. It's the interfaces. Some of them define the APIs through the applications. In some ways, if we could do them over again, we know how we could do it so we could write the system faster. But once you have those interfaces, you're pretty much locked. You can't just change them and break applications. A system like we have, we don't own it; the ISVs [independent software vendors] own it. We [the Windows/MS-DOS group] exist for one purpose, which is to run applications. And [if] you break an application, you don't have a reason for being any more."

[46] Cusumano and Selby (1995, especially chapter 2) develop this theme in rich detail.

[47] See Chapter 4 in Cusumano and Yoffie (1998), especially pp. 194-196, for a discussion of the dynamic tradeoffs that Netscape faced in the creation of modular design architectures for its software products.

[48] See the Declaration of David Cole (November 8, 1997) in *U.S. v. Microsoft Corp.* for an informative description of Internet Explorer's componentized design architecture.

[49] See pp. 183-185 in Cusumano and Yoffie (1998) on the contrast between the highly componentized design of Microsoft's Internet Explorer software and the design of Netscape's Navigator and Communicator software.

[50] Harris, September 29, 1998, deposition testimony, pp. 34-35.

[51] Harris, January 4, 1999, p.m. live testimony, p. 45.

[52] Harris, January 4, 1999, p.m. live testimony, pp. 9-12, and September 29, 1998, deposition

testimony, pp. 34-36.

[53] Harris, January 4, 1999, p.m. live testimony, pp. 9-10.

[54] Harris, January 4, 1999, p.m. live testimony, p. 75.

[55] Colburn, October 28, 1998, p.m. live testimony, p. 37, and October 29, 1998, a.m. live testimony, p. 34.

[56] Colburn, December 9, 1998, p.m. live testimony, pp. 37-40. Colburn speaks about an "integrated browser" as providing the seamless user experience that AOL sought, but the context of his remarks make clear that he is using this terminology to refer to the componentization of browser technology.

[57] The costs of maintaining backward compatibility come through loud and clear in some remarks by Lou Perazzoli, software engineering manager for Windows NT in 1993. In the course of discussing Microsoft efforts to incorporate Windows 3.1 features into Windows NT 3.0, Perazzoli states that in a typical week, about 1,000 new bugs get opened. "And the question is, how the hell can anybody developing software have so many bugs? It turns out that it is called "compatibility." If we didn't have to be compatible with Windows [3.1], we wouldn't have so many bugs." (As quoted on p. 319 of Cusumano and Selby [1995].)

[58] Microsoft's move toward greater emphasis on modularity and componentization over time is a clear theme in the discussions of Cusumano and Selby (1995), although they do not use the term "componentization." Paul Maritz and James Allchin confirmed this move in the course of our interviews with them.

[59] Cusumano and Selby (1995), pp. 25 and 237.

[60] In some cases, the stand-alone product may be unpopular because it is difficult to use (e.g., TCP/IP), but a smart developer can foresee that it would be popular if integrated.

[61] See Boyce (1998) for an evaluation of the integration of new features into Windows 98.

[62] This sort of integration also facilitates the online distribution of software products, a point we take up below.

[63] Wildstrom (1998).

[64] The creation of custom browsers is explicitly taught in the Microsoft documentation on IE4. Chapter 11, pp. 135-145, in Microsoft (1998) describes the WebBrowser Control, from which custom browsers can easily be built.

[65] This paragraph draws on pp. 224 and 362-370 of Cusumano and Selby (1995).

[66] According to remarks by Mike Maples, former Microsoft vice president, as quoted in Cusumano and Selby (1995) on p. 367.

[67] This quotation is from p. 365 in Cusumano and Selby (1995), who cite a document titled "Case Study: The New Microsoft Support Network."

[68] Cusumano and Selby (1995), pp. 375-384. Our interviews with Hillel Cooperman and other Microsoft personnel indicate that intensive usability studies have become an even more important factor in software design decisions at Microsoft in recent years.

[69] Personal communication with James Allchin.

[70] The complexity of microcomputer OS software has increased dramatically over time. MS-DOS 1.0 was designed for the original IBM PC in 1981 and had about 4,000 lines of code, MS-DOS 3.0 was designed for the IBM PC/AT in 1984 and had about 40,000 lines of code (Ichbiah and Knepper, 1991, pp. 252-253), and Windows 95 has about 11 mil-

lion lines of code (Reid 1997, p. 149).

71 See, e.g., McCartney (1986). In discussing the pros and cons of using more than one vendor for a computer system, the writer reports that "when a problem develops on a multi-vendor network, suppliers tend to pass the buck." And "no one takes responsibility."

72 See Shapiro and Varian (1999, pp. 73-79) for a broad, introductory perspective on bundling.

73 For example, see the complaint filed by the U.S. Department of Justice on May 18, 1998 in *U.S. v. Microsoft Corp.* and the Plaintiffs' Revised Proposed Findings of Facts filed on August 10, 1999.

74 Tirole (1988) treats the pricing behavior of multi-product firms with interdependent demands at length. He also provides extensive references to the relevant literature. Portions of his treatment in chapters 1 and 3 are especially pertinent to the discussion at hand.

75 The mathematical supplement to Davis and Murphy (2001) derives expressions for the profit-maximizing prices.

76 The marginal costs of software production (i.e., replication) and distribution are often quite low, but customer support costs are high for many software products. So the full marginal cost is low for some, but certainly not all, software products.

77 In fact, with zero marginal costs, $(a_1/a_2)>(b_1/d)$ is a necessary and sufficient condition for $P_2<0$ in the two-good model.

78 The relevance of this point is borne out in testimony by IBM's director of network computing in *U.S. v. Microsoft Corp.* See the deposition testimony of John Soyring, pp. 165-166.

79 See Liebowitz and Margolis (1999), especially pp. 154-157, for some systematic evidence. Khanna and Yoffie (1996) discuss how deep discounting on Microsoft's Office Suite helped bring about a steep decline in the price of business applications software during the 1990s.

80 We develop this point more fully in Section IX of Davis, MacCrisken, and Murphy (1999). Shapiro and Varian (1999) also emphasize this point. See their chapter 6, especially p. 162.

81 This point regarding complementary demand is closely related to standard arguments about the social benefits of vertical integration when both upstream and downstream firms exercise market power.

82 The mathematical supplement in Davis and Murphy (2001) contains a precise statement of these claims and a proof.

83 See, for example, the remarks on pp. 37-38 by Katz and Shapiro (1999), two prominent and highly respected economists with extensive backgrounds in industrial organization and antitrust matters. Their tone is one of concern, not alarm.

84 The mathematical supplement in Davis and Murphy (2001) spells this out explicitly and derives explicit solutions for prices and quantities in the Bertrand and Cournot cases.

85 Opposition by the antitrust authorities in the presence of important demand complementarities is quite plausible. In 1994, the U.S. Department of Justice denied a proposed acquisition of Intuit by Microsoft. Intuit sells the popular Quicken line of software, which was and is the leading personal finance software for PCs. Intuit's line of software products is highly complementary to Microsoft's operating system software. Nonetheless, the DOJ denied the proposed acquisition, because Microsoft Money was the leading competitor to

Quicken. See Katz and Shapiro (1999). To take another example, it is highly unlikely that the DOJ would have acquiesced to a Microsoft acquisition of Netscape in 1994 when Microsoft had no browser, or in 1995 when Microsoft's Internet Explorer was clearly inferior to Netscape's Navigator.

[86] See Cusumano and Yoffie (1998), pp. 36-38, 149-151, 200-201, and 325-328.

[87] Klein uses the term "packaging" to refer to bundling motivated by demand complementarities in use with the OS.

[88] We confirmed this point in our interview with Paul Maritz. According to Maritz, Microsoft recognized that its decision to componentize IE, and especially its decision to license the componentized IE technology to AOL, would detract from the growth and revenue potential of MSN, Microsoft's Web portal. However, the full integration of Web-support functionality into Windows, including the componentization of IE, was viewed as essential to preserve the viability of the Windows platform.

[89] To be more precise, suppose that customer valuations have the same mean and standard deviation for each item. With a negative correlation across customers, even a weak one, in the valuations attached to individual items, the variance in valuations for the bundled product can shrink with bundle size. The example we develop below has this property. Even with a zero or positive correlation (but less than one) across customers in the valuations on individual items, the average valuation per item in the bundle converges to a constant by the law of large numbers, while the standard deviation of the valuation attached to the entire bundle grows less than proportionately to bundle size. Hence, the ratio of the standard deviation of the bundle value to the total bundle value declines with bundle size.

[90] This idea dates to Stigler (1963), who showed how bundling can increase profits when consumer valuations for two goods are negatively correlated. Schmalensee (1984) showed that bundling can increase profits even when consumer valuations of the two goods are uncorrelated or positively correlated. Bakos and Brynjolfsson (1999) develop this type of bundling theory in a direction that is especially applicable to information goods. McAfee, McMillan, and Whinston (1989) and Bakos and Brynjolfsson consider motives for mixed bundling, in which the firm sells the same product separately and as part of a bundle. Adams and Yellen (1976) provide an insightful early treatment of how bundling affects consumer surplus and economic efficiency.

[91] To be more precise, we assume that the ith consumer places a value of 101+z on the ith good, where z is a very small positive number that we ignore in the calculations below.

[92] In this example, bundling raises profits by facilitating consumer acquisition of low-valuation items that they would not otherwise buy. Bundling can also raise profits by enabling the firm to more effectively extract consumer surplus on high-valuation items that consumers would buy in any event. To see this point, modify the example in the text by introducing 100 new consumer types as follows. Assume that the ith new type places a value of 200 on the ith item and a value of zero on the other 99 items, for i=1,2,...100. Provided that the number of new-type consumers is sufficiently small, the profit-maximizing price at each bundle size is the same as in Table 2. Furthermore, efficiency and profits still rise with bundle size. However, consumer surplus now declines with bundle size. For a more general treatment, see Bakos and Brynjolfsson (1999, 2000).

[93] 1394 and USB refer to standards for high-speed serial communication.

[94] Even in a static setting, bundling may enable a firm to earn enough revenues to cover fixed costs and continue serving customers, when it would otherwise exit the market. See

Bakos and Brynjolfsson (2000).

[95] See Carlton and Waldman (2000) for a related analysis that is motivated by allegations in *U.S. v. Microsoft Corp.*

[96] See Hylton and Salinger (2001) and Evans and Schmalensee (2001) for an extended treatment of these issues. Also, see Easterbrook (2000) and Posner (2000), who emphasize the limited capacity of the judicial process and antitrust enforcement machinery to effectively respond to allegedly anticompetitive conduct in information and technology-intensive sectors. Easterbrook and Posner are federal judges who sit on the U.S. Court of Appeals. Davis, MacCrisken, and Murphy (1999, Section IX) consider whether a platform supplier can profit by adopting a design that raises costs for rival suppliers of complementary applications.

[97] Harm to rivals and the exclusion of rivals from a significant share of sales are not good indicators of anticompetitive behavior or consumer harm. For example, Davis, Murphy, and Topel (2001) show that a product design that excludes rival sales can be highly beneficial for consumers.

[98] Tying can also have other benefits not emphasized in our study, such as lower production costs.

[99] See also Shaked and Sutton (1982), Economides (1986) and Chapter 7 in Tirole (1988).

References

Adams, William James, Yellen, Janet I. 1976. "Commodity Bundling and the Burden of Monopoly," *Quarterly Journal of Economics*, 90, no. 3, pp. 475-498.

Bakos, Yannis, Brynjolfsson, Erik. 1999. "Bundling Information Goods: Pricing, Profits and Efficiency," *Management Science*, 45, no. 12 (December).

Bakos, Yannis, Brynjolfsson, Erik. 2000. "Bundling and Competition on the Internet: Aggregation Strategies for Information Goods," *Marketing Science* (January).

Baldwin, Carliss Y., Clark, Kim B. 2000. *Design Rules: Volume 1, The Power of Modularity*. Cambridge, Massachusetts: The MIT Press.

Berndt, Ernst R., Rappaport, Neal J. 2001. "Price and Quality of Desktop and Mobile Personal Computers: A Quarter-Century Historical Overview," *American Economic Review*, 91, no. 2 (May), pp. 268-273.

Besen, Stanley, Farrell, Joseph. 1994. "Choosing How to Compete: Strategies and Tactics in Standardization," *Journal of Economic Perspectives*, 3, no. 2.

Boyce, Jim. 1998. *Inside Windows 98*. New Riders Publishing.

Carlton, Dennis W., Waldman, Michael. 2000. "The Strategic Use of Tying to Preserve and Create Market Power in Evolving Industries," George J. Stigler Center for the Study of the Economy and the State, Working Paper No. 145 (March). Available at http://gsb-www.uchicago.edu/research/cses/WorkingPapersPDF's/145.pdf.

Coase, R.H. 1972. "Durability and Monopoly," *Journal of Law and Economics*, 15, pp. 149-149.

Computer Language Company. 1999. *Computer Desktop Encyclopedia*. Point Pleasant, Pennsylvania. Searchable at http://www.computerlanguage.com/sitemain/content.html.

Cusumano, Michael A., Selby, Richard W. 1995. *Microsoft Secrets*. New York: Simon & Schuster.

Cusumano, Michael A., Yoffie, David B. 1998. *Competing on Internet Time: Lessons from Netscape and its Battle with Microsoft.* New York: The Free Press.

Davis, Steven J., MacCrisken, Jack, Murphy, Kevin M. 1999. "The Evolution of the PC Operating System: An Economic Analysis of Software Design," June 29. Available at http://gsbwww.uchicago.edu/fac/steven.davis/research.

Davis, Steven J., Murphy, Kevin M. 2000. "A Competitive Perspective on Internet Explorer," *American Economic Review*, 90, no. 2, pp. 184-187. Republished in expanded form with mathematical supplement at http://gsbwww.uchicago.edu/fac/steven.davis/research.

Davis, Steven J., Murphy, Kevin M., Topel, Robert H. 2001. "Entry, Pricing and Product Design in an Initially Monopolized Market." Available at http://gsbwww.uchicago.edu/fac/steven.davis/research.

Easterbrook, Frank H. 2000. "Information and Antitrust." Keynote address delivered at a symposium on "Antitrust in the Information Age" at the University of Chicago on October 29, 1999. Revised version is dated October 4, 2000.

Economides, Nicholas. 1986. "Minimal and Maximal Product Differentiation in Hotelling's Duopoly," *Economic Letters*, 21, pp.67-71.

Economides, Nicholas. 2000. "The Microsoft Antitrust Case," Working Paper 2000-09, Stern School of Business, New York University. Available at http://www.stern.nyu.edu/networks.

Ellison, Glenn, Fudenberg, Drew. 2000. "The Neo-Luddite's Lament: Excessive Upgrades in the Software Industry," *Rand Journal of Economics*, 31, no. 2 (Summer), pp. 253-272.

Evans, David S., Nichols, Albert, Reddy, Bernard. 1999. "The Rise and Fall of Leaders in Personal Computer Software," National Economic Research Associates. Available at http://www.neramicrosoft.com/NeraDocuments/Analyses.

Evans, David S., Nichols, Albert, Schmalensee, Richard. 2001. "An Analysis of the Government's Case in *U.S. v. Microsoft*," *Antitrust Bulletin*, 46, no. 2 (Summer).

Evans, David S., Schmalensee, Richard. 2001. "Some Economic Aspects of Antitrust Analysis in Dynamically Competitive Industries," NBER Working Paper 8268 (May).

Farrell, Joseph, Katz, Michael L. 2000. "Innovation, Rent Extraction, and Integration in Systems Markets," *Journal of Industrial Economics*, 48, no. 4 (December), pp. 413-432.

Fisher, Franklin M. 2000. "The IBM and Microsoft Cases: What's the Difference?" *American Economic Review*, 90, no. 2 (May), pp. 180-183.

Fisher, Franklin M., Rubinfeld, Daniel L. 2000. "United States v. Microsoft: An Economic Analysis," in *Did Microsoft Harm Consumers? Two Opposing Views*. Washington, DC: AEI–Brookings Joint Center for Regulatory Studies.

Fudenberg, Drew, Tirole, Jean. 1998. "Upgrades, Trade-Ins and Buybacks," *Rand Journal of Economics*, 29, no. 2 (Summer).

Gans, Joshua S., Hsu, David H., Stern, Scott. 2000. "When Does Start-Up Innovation Spur the Gale of Creative Destruction?" NBER Working Paper 7851.

Gilbert, Richard J., Katz, Michael L. 2001. "An Economist's Guide to *U.S. v. Microsoft*," *Journal of Economic Perspectives*, 15, no. 2 (Spring), pp. 25-44.

Gookin, Dan. 1992. "Windows 3.1 vs. OS/2 2.0," *InfoWorld*.

Hylton, Keith N., Salinger, Michael. 2001. "Tying Law and Policy: A Decision Theoretic Approach," Boston University School of Law Working Paper Series, Law and Economics Working Paper No. 01-04. Available at http://www.bu.edu/law/faculty/papers.

Ichbiah, Daniel, Knepper, Susan L. 1991. *The Making of Microsoft*. Prima Publishing.

Katz, Michael, Shapiro, Carl. 1994. "Systems Competition and Network Effects," *Journal of Economic Perspectives*, 3, no. 2.

Katz, Michael L., Shapiro, Carl. 1999. "Antitrust in Software Markets," in *Competition, Innovation and the Microsoft Monopoly: Antitrust in the Digital Marketplace*, Jeffrey A. Eisenach and Thomas M. Lenards, editors. Boston, Massachusetts: Kluwer Academic Publishers for the Progress & Freedom Foundation.

Khanna, Tarun, Yoffie, David. 1996. "Microsoft, 1995," Harvard Business School Case Study 9-795-147.

Klein, Benjamin. 1999. "Microsoft's Use of Zero Price Bundling to Fight the Browser Wars," in *Competition, Convergence and the Microsoft Monopoly*, Jeffrey A. Eisenach and Thomas M. Lenard, editors. Boston, Massachusetts: Kluwer Academic Publishers for the Progress & Freedom Foundation.

Klein, Benjamin. 2001. "The Microsoft Case: What Can a Dominant Firm Do to Defend Its Market Position?" *Journal of Economic Perspectives*, 15, no. 2 (Spring), pp. 45-62.

Liebowitz, Stanley J., Margolis, Stephen E. 1999. *Winners, Losers and Microsoft: Competition and Antitrust in High Technology*. Oakland, California: The Independent Institute.

Markoff, A. 1996. "Tomorrow, the World Wide Web," *The New York Times*, July 16, p. D1.

McAfee, R., Preston, J. McMillan, Whinston, Michael D. 1989. "Multiproduct Monopoly, Commodity Bundling, and Correlation of Values," *Quarterly Journal of Economics*, 104 (May), pp. 371-384.

McCartney, Laton. 1986. "The Pros and Cons of Going Multi-Vendor (Practicality of Companies Utilizing More Than One Vendor for Computer Systems)," *Dun's Business Month*, 128 (November), 93.

Microsoft. 1995. "Microsoft Developer Relations: Proving Microsoft's Commitment to Third Parties," Microsoft Corporation White Paper.

Microsoft. 1998. *Microsoft Internet Explorer Resource Kit*. Microsoft Press.

Posner, Richard. 2000. "Antitrust in the New Economy." Address delivered to a conference on antitrust sponsored by the American Law Institute–American Bar Association Committee on Continuing Professional Education, September 14, 2000, New York, and published in *Tech Law Journal*. Available at http://www.techlawjournal.com/atr/-20009l4posner.asp.

Quarterman, John S., Wilhelm, Susanne. 1993. *UNIX, POSIX, and Open Systems: The Open Standards Puzzle*. Addison–Wesley.

Ramstad, Evan. 1998. "PC Makers Hunt for Gold in Internet Hookups," *The Wall Street Journal*, August 12, Page B1.

Reid, Robert H. 1997. *Architects of the Web: 1,000 Days that Built the Future of Business*. New York: Wiley.

Reinganum, Jennifer F. 1985. "Innovation and Industry Evolution," *Quarterly Journal of Economics*, 99, no. 1, pp. 81-99.

Salinger, M.A. 1995. "A Graphical Analysis of Bundling," *Journal of Business*, 68, no. 1, pp. 85-98.

Schmalensee, Richard L. 1984. "Gaussian Demand and Commodity Bundling," *Journal of Business*, 57 (January), S211-S230.

Shaked, Avner, Sutton, John. 1982. "Relaxing Price Competition through Product Differentiation," *Review of Economic Studies*, 49, pp. 3-17.

Shapiro, Carl, Varian, Hal R. 1999. *Information Rules: A Strategic Guide to the Network Economy*. Boston, Massachusetts: Harvard Business School Press.

Stigler, George J. 1963. "United States v. Loew's, Inc.: A Note on Block Booking," *Supreme Court Review*, pp. 152-157.

Tirole, Jean. 1988. *The Theory of Industrial Organization*. Cambridge, Massachusetts: MIT Press.

Vickers, John. 1986. "The Evolution of Market Structure When There Is a Sequence of Innovations," *Journal of Industrial Economics*, 35, no. 1, pp. 1-12.

Whinston, Michael D., 1990, "Tying, Foreclosure, and Exclusion," *American Economic Review*, 80, no. 4 (September), pp. 837-859.

Whinston, Michael D. 2001. "Exclusivity and Tying in *U.S. v. Microsoft*: What We Know, and Don't Know," *Journal of Economic Perspectives*, 15, no. 2 (Spring), pp. 63-80.

Wildstrom, Stephen H. 1998. "Build Your Own Browser," *Business Week*, July 20, p. 17.

Section 2: Antitrust Policy and the New Economy

Essay 11

Preserving Competition: Economic Analysis, Legal Standards, and Microsoft

by Ronald A. Cass and Keith N. Hylton*

On its face, this essay by two Boston University School of Law professors is simply a critique of an article by Steven Salop and Craig Romaine that defends the government's position in the Microsoft case. But while Ronald Cass and Keith Hylton certainly engage the issues raised by the landmark antitrust suit, their reach is much broader.

Cass and Hylton use the Salop–Romaine piece to illustrate that antitrust policy is now caught between competing views. One is loosely known as the Chicago school, which "explains why conduct that courts might view as threatening competition either does not, or is so far from a rational business strategy as to be an improbable occurrence." The other, which the authors dub the "nip and tuck school," has taken many of its cues from game theory. It "postulates reasons why seemingly innocent – or at least ordinary – business activity could be designed to subvert competitors and, perhaps, competition."

Cass and Hylton argue that Salop and Romaine's focus on intent makes it possible to find anticompetitive behavior in a wide variety of ambiguous circumstances. For example, Salop and Romaine see insidious purpose in the fact that the expiration dates of Microsoft's software licensing contracts with various computer makers were staggered: "If all the contracts expired at the same time," they explain, "the entrant might be able to coordinate its entry and the start dates of its own contracts."

But does anyone doubt, Cass and Hylton ask, that Salop and Romaine would have been equally condemning if all of Microsoft's contracts had been written to expire simultaneously? After all, that would have limited the window in which potential rivals could have made comparable deals with any of Microsoft's contract partners.

By the same token, Cass and Hylton argue that Salop and Romaine rationalize market intervention by identifying the possibility – rather than the probability – of harm to consumers. Thus, Salop and Romaine see the need for activist antitrust policy in so-called network markets because there is a chance that the dominant firm will deter innovation along alternative paths. But they offer no evidence this possible outcome is inevitable or even likely.

All told, this deconstruction of the case against Microsoft is a cautionary tale with a clear moral: There may well be a high price to pay in abandoning antitrust policy built on a bedrock of demonstrable consumer harm.

— D.S.E.

Antitrust law is a hammer, not a scalpel. It is a blunt instrument that can have a powerful impact – but only against something very much like a nail. It cannot be used effectively against small imperfections, to nip and tuck so that the economy is shaped just so.

That reality is evident to all who have been on the receiving end of antitrust enforcement, and to all who seriously contemplate this prospect.[1] It is not, however, evident to many who write about this field.

A recent article by Professor Steven Salop and Dr. Craig Romaine illustrates both the attractions of and the problems associated with the nip-and-tuck school of antitrust analysis.[2] Professor Salop and Dr. Romaine (S&R, for short) use the Microsoft litigation as their focus for discussion of antitrust law, or perhaps it's the other way around.[3] Their article reports the allegations that plaintiffs say are antitrust violations by Microsoft.[4] S&R argue that each allegation could constitute evidence of Microsoft's design to reduce competition and to preserve or extend the monopoly they assume Microsoft already possesses.[5] They also argue that the right legal standard to apply is one that draws conclusions about intent from the effects of specific behavior, and they consciously frame this standard so that the benefit of the doubt goes to plaintiffs.[6] Tilting the standard against defendants such as Microsoft is justified, according to S&R, by the need to protect markets against the vices that Microsoft's alleged acts might generate.[7]

We believe the S&R approach is misguided. Though purporting to offer a middle ground, they would dramatically expand the reach of antitrust law and would give decision makers broad discretion to characterize ordinary business activity as antitrust violations. The standard that S&R suggest is the wrong standard under current law, and is at odds with better economic analysis. This article exposes problems with their approach, explains why it departs from current antitrust standards, and urges an approach consistent with current standards that respects the hammer-like quality of antitrust law.

THE ANTITRUST FRAMEWORK

Three Lessons from the Law

The basic charter of U.S. antitrust law is the Sherman Act of 1890 ("the Act").[8] While not a model of clarity, the Act does make three things plain.

First, its provisions are intended to reach extreme, not ordinary, conduct – which is why violations of the Act's major provisions constitute felonies.[9] Section 2, the provision primarily addressed by S&R, says, "Every person who shall monopolize, or attempt to monopolize ... any part of the trade or commerce among the several States, or with foreign nations, shall be deemed guilty of a felony ..."[10] Similarly, Section 1 declares, "Every person who shall make any contract or engage in any combination or conspiracy [in restraint of trade] shall be deemed guilty of a felony ..."[11]

Felonies are serious crimes, and these provisions expressly authorize substantial prison terms as well as hefty fines.[12] They target conduct that Congress thought fundamentally threatened the competitive structure of the economy.[13]

Second, the Sherman Act is entirely negative in character. The law does not say that the attorney general must ensure that every market is perfectly competitive, or even that every market is competitive in any measure. It does not guarantee competitors equal shares of markets, equal access to credit, to retailing space, to customers, or to anything else. Competitors are not granted any positive rights. As a byproduct of the law's prohibitions, however, consumers and producers alike share the benefits of markets that are free from the effects of practices that are utterly inimical to a competitive environment.[14]

Third, a great deal turns on interpretation of the text. Its spare language does not proscribe specific conduct, but targets a few generically described behaviors that undermine the operation of competitive markets. Just what those generic behaviors do and do not include – what specific activity will get a business hammered – is not obvious on the face of the statute.

Why, for example, does Section 2 punish someone who "monopolizes" a market, but not someone who *has* a monopoly? It has been up to courts (aided by administrative agencies and commentators) to put flesh on the law's bones, to determine which conduct falls within one of the law's prohibitions and which does not.[15]

Interpretation and Economics

Increasingly, judges have turned to economic analysis to distinguish conduct inimical to competition.[16] Economic analysis, however, does not always provide a single, accepted answer.

Broadly speaking, two schools of thought have emerged. One explains why conduct that courts might view as threatening competition either does not, or is so far from a rational business strategy as to be an improbable occurrence.[17] The approach of this school (often referred to as the Chicago School) is akin to the rationalist's reaction to reports of flying saucers – if *that* is what you think you saw, think again before spending too much time and effort deciding what to do with the little green men.

The other school postulates reasons why seemingly innocent – or at least ordinary – business activity could be designed to subvert competitors and, perhaps, competition.[18] Writings in this genre deploy sophisticated arguments to establish that conduct that looks ambiguous or even benign should be treated as contrary to the antitrust law's constraints. These writings frequently rely on subtle distinctions to separate the conduct they would stigmatize from the conduct they find pro-competitive. The writings further advocate antitrust remedies that assertedly do, if not perfect justice, its next of kin. These writings also typically rely on complex mathematical or game-theoretic models to demonstrate that important aspects of ordinary market competition can break down under certain assumptions that are difficult, if not impossible, to verify from observable data.[19]

We refer to writings in this vein as belonging to the "nip-and-tuck" school of antitrust analysis. Professor Salop is one of its leaders, and his article on "raising rivals' costs" was one of the first missiles launched in the counterrevolution to Chicago.[20]

We use the S&R article as our foil not because we have any special quarrel with the authors, but because their work illustrates the problems that nip-and-tuck analysis can generate, even in the hands of its ablest craftsmen. Its focus on the Microsoft case throws into sharp relief what is at stake in the analytical game economists are presently playing.

FINDING ANTICOMPETITIVE CONDUCT

Microsoft: Looking for Mr. Badbar

S&R run through a litany of allegations against Microsoft, touching on assertions in past investigations and those advanced in current litigation. They acknowledge that many of these allegations are contested, but they treat them as facts for their discussion of possible anticompetitive effects of business conduct. It is worth briefly reviewing the principal allegations.

Over the past decade, complaints by Microsoft competitors focused on Microsoft's contracting practices, product development, product distribution, and marketing – in other words, on practically every aspect of Microsoft's operation. In the early 1990s, the Federal Trade Commission (FTC) considered charges that Microsoft had violated the antitrust laws in agreeing to develop operating systems in cooperation with IBM.[21] The investigation quickly turned from that assertion to others, but after three years the commission declined to pursue these matters further.[22] The Department of Justice (DOJ) then instituted its own investigation.

Four of the practices investigated by the FTC or DOJ deserve note here. First, the agencies considered complaints that Microsoft allowed computer makers (commonly referred to as original equipment manufacturers or OEMs) to license software on a "per processor" basis. These licenses gave an OEM a small discount if it agreed to pay Microsoft royalties on all computers shipped with the particular microprocessors. They essentially relieved Microsoft of the need to monitor actual shipments of its software, allowing it instead to track only reported shipments of, for example, computers using Intel's 386 microprocessor.

A second focus of the investigation was allegations regarding Microsoft's treatment of OEMs that failed to ship the agreed number of computers with Microsoft software. Microsoft did not automatically permit such licensees to use "prepaid balances" from one license agreement to offset amounts due under successor license agreements.[23]

Third, firms complained that Microsoft announced products far in advance of their release – so-called vaporware – to stifle sales of competitors' products.

Fourth, the investigators examined complaints that Microsoft did not share information about the application programming interfaces (APIs) in its operating system soon enough with other software producers. The APIs allow applications software to use parts of the operating system to perform routine functions such as accessing files. The agencies considered the assertion that antitrust laws required Microsoft to make such copyrighted information available in a timely fashion.

Although nearly all of the issues the FTC–DOJ investigated are mentioned by S&R,[24] Microsoft settled the matter with a consent decree focusing almost entirely on terms for OEM contracts.[25] Additionally, despite S&R's casual assertion that the contract terms at issue "raised the costs of rival operating system entrants ... and created strong incentives for OEMs to deal exclusively with Microsoft,"[26] DOJ's own expert, Kenneth Arrow, thought the practices had relatively little impact on Microsoft's fortunes: "[Microsoft's OEM] licensing practices ... made only a minor contribution to the growth of Microsoft's installed base. Even this minor contribution overstates the impact of Microsoft's licensing practices on its installed base barrier to the entry and growth of competing operating systems."[27]

Professor Arrow's assumption that there is a barrier to entry – implicitly accepting the DOJ characterization of a narrow market for operating systems[28] – is far from self-evident. Even accepting the disputed assumption, however, he found the licensing practices of little moment. In his judgment, factors that were not significantly affected by the challenged licensing practices or even by the ability of competing operating systems to gain access to particular channels of distribution drove the success of Microsoft's operating system.[29]

Litigation against Microsoft by non-governmental entities echoed some of the assertions not pursued in the earlier case, and plaintiffs (including DOJ) added new allegations as well. Two sets of allegations are especially important to S&R's argument.[30] One is that Microsoft gave its Web browser away and integrated the browser into its operating system to undercut Netscape's competing Web browser.[31] The other is that Microsoft insisted on contract terms with OEMs, independent software vendors (ISVs), and Internet service providers (ISPs) that effectively foreclosed consumers' access to Netscape software, or that handicapped Netscape in its competition with Microsoft's Internet Explorer.

S&R state that Microsoft had a "policy of reducing the price of its browser or giving it away to some customers by bundling it with Windows."[32] The intimation of a change in pricing over time is wrong, but the assertion that Microsoft's Web browser has been available at low cost or no cost is correct. From the outset, Microsoft included its Internet Explorer browser at no separate charge with OEM versions of Windows 95. It also made the browser available free to those who downloaded it from Microsoft's Web site.[33]

The program's third generation and later versions were more tightly integrated with the operating system, making various functions – such as the ability to parse Web addresses and to decipher and display Web pages – available to other software vendors through documented APIs. Installing newer versions of Internet Explorer upgrades the relevant operating system files (deleting and replacing code) and provides an icon that makes the Internet Explorer features available directly to the end user. Thus, unlike stand-alone programs, Internet Explorer becomes part of the operating system when it is installed. In that sense, it is always, as S&R say, "bundled" with Windows.[34]

The second set of allegations, those related to Microsoft contracts, stand on less firm footing. S&R report that "Microsoft allegedly made exclusive deals requiring certain ISPs (e.g., AOL) and OEMs (e.g., Compaq, Apple) to carry Microsoft's Internet Explorer browser instead of Netscape's browser."35 These contracts can be sorted into two groups. Neither group involves a requirement that the other contractual party deal exclusively with Microsoft.

One group, primarily contracts with OEMs, consists of non-exclusive licensing arrangements.[36] These contracts require licensees to provide consumers with a copyrighted program in its entirety. They do not, however, limit OEMs' ability (a) to add other software that the user could substitute for some service of the operating system, (b) to place icons for other products on the computer desktop in positions as favorable as those occupied by Microsoft software, or (c) to provide prompts that make it easy to use the non-Microsoft program as a default.[37]

The other group – principally the contract with AOL – comes closer to fitting S&R's description. These contracts, however, do not provide for exclusivity in the sense of S&R's argument. The contracts also do not support the conclusion that whatever level of "exclusivity" they granted was imposed at Microsoft's behest to give Microsoft an advantage over a competitor.

AOL, for example, provides proprietary software to subscribers that allows users to perform several functions, including gaining access to the Internet.[38] AOL distributes this software to potential subscribers at no cost, in the hope of inducing them to join AOL. Initially, the software included AOL's own Web browser. Improvements in other browsers, however, prompted AOL to discuss the prospect of using Netscape or Internet Explorer. Whichever firm won that competition would have an "exclusive" contract with AOL.[39]

The question in this instance is not so much what the contract between AOL and Microsoft provides as what should be made of it. Microsoft argues that a winner-take-all competition in which one party wins necessarily results in exclusion of other competitors. Such a result, however, should not be deemed anticompetitive.[40] If it is consistent with competitive interests – either from a normative economic perspective or from the vantage of the antitrust laws – for AOL to award the contract to Netscape or to decide that neither Netscape nor Microsoft offered sufficient advantages to change from its own browser, why should it be inconsistent with those interests for AOL to choose Microsoft?

S&R have a more skeptical view of all of these activities, alleged and actual. That is where we disagree most strongly with their approach.

Thermos Problems in Antitrust Analysis

S&R's discussion of Microsoft is instructive in part because it illustrates the critical role of attitude in performing the analysis they suggest. The old canard about the thermos is that it must possess a marvelous intelligence; it keeps hot things hot and cold things cold – but how does it know which to do? By analogy, S&R's approach depends on thermos-like intelligence. Consider three of their allegations of anticompetitive conduct by Microsoft.

One is that Microsoft entered into contracts with OEMs that did not all expire at the same time. S&R explain: "[C]ontracts that do not all expire at the same time ... increase the coordination problem and entry costs facing the new entrant. If all the contracts expired at the same time, the entrant might be able to coordinate its entry and the start dates of its own contracts."[41] For S&R, a commitment to use Microsoft's product necessarily excludes competing products from access to those customers. This implies that other products can compete effectively only when such contracts expire. Viewed from the perspective of concern over any action that raises rivals' costs, the increase in coordination problems for competitors to Microsoft leads to the conclusion that use of contracts without uniform termination dates is anticompetitive.

Yet, imagine if Microsoft had insisted that all OEMs, ISPs, or others that contracted to use Microsoft's copyrighted product agree to the same termination date. Is there any doubt that S&R would see the coordination as inimical to competition? After all, during the period of the group contracts, a prospective entrant would be excluded from access to the business of *all* of the contract parties. Furthermore, because all contracts would be concurrent, it would be difficult for a new entrant to break into the market. The newcomer could not sign up a few customers as a signal to others that they should consider switching when their contracts with Microsoft expired. Accordingly, the newcomer would have to persuade a larger group to switch at once.[42]

The S&R approach would support arguments that staggered contracts are bad *and* that coordinated contracts are bad. Its protean quality makes every business action a potential basis for liability. Some judgment must be made to screen the actions that will be deemed anticompetitive from those that will not. It appears that, in S&R's world, liability depends, in the first instance, on whether the decision maker believes the defendant is wrongly keeping potential entrants out of a market in which the defendant has too much power or believes instead the defendant is rightly competing aggressively.[43]

Economic analysis should help resolve those issues. Its purported benefit is its capacity to replace subjective judgments with objective ones. The contribution of economic analysis should not be dependent on a decision maker's predisposition respecting the issues that are its critical inputs.

Yet that is precisely where S&R's economic analysis would leave us. It opens the specter of a world in which one court could find a defendant engaged in anticompetitive conduct for insisting on contracts with a uniform termination date, then another court could find that switching to contracts with staggered expiration dates is anticompetitive.

The result suggested above is not peculiar to that example. The same problem surfaces in considering how S&R would treat the "prepaid balances" issue. Recall that the FTC–DOJ investigation considered complaints about Microsoft's failure to credit a licensee with payments made in contemplation of shipments the licensee committed to, but did not make. Assertedly, Microsoft's failure to routinely credit OEMs for such payments was anticompetitive.[44] It seems likely that S&R would concur. The refusal to rebate funds for software not shipped would give OEMs an incentive to ship all the Microsoft software they could under the license agreement, up to the full quantity covered by the agreement. This term presumably would put a competing software vendor at a disadvantage. Payment to Microsoft for the full quantity covered by the license would be a sunk cost, so the marginal cost of shipping a Microsoft program already contracted for would be zero.[45] Other software, then, either would have to be offered at a similar price – which in all likelihood would not be profitable for the other firm – or would have to enjoy such a marked advantage over Microsoft's product as to be worth the added cost. S&R deploy essentially the same argument in discussing the competition between Microsoft and Netscape, addressed below.[46]

The conclusion that *refusing* to rebate "prepaid balances" is anticompetitive, however, does not exclude the prospect of finding that *granting* such rebates is *also* anticompetitive. After all, if prepaid balances were subject to rebate in future license agreements with Microsoft, then OEMs could be induced to enter successor agreements with Microsoft rather than with competitors.[47] If, as S&R urge, it is anticompetitive to have license agreements that expire at different times (which has only the mildest possible effect on licensee incentives to continue using Microsoft's product), then a rebate policy would surely fall within S&R's definition of anticompetitive conduct. Indeed, the plaintiffs advanced that exact argument in current litigation against Microsoft.[48] Ironically, the plaintiff making that claim is the successor firm to a Microsoft competitor that urged the FTC and DOJ to find Microsoft's actual contracting practice unlawful.[49]

If *both* refusing to grant rebates and granting them *could* be anticompetitive, how will the S&R analysis sort things out? As with the timing of contract expiration, the approach provides ample ammunition for arguing that particular business practices are anticompetitive. It does not, however, provide a ready way to distinguish competitive practices from anticompetitive ones.

Or consider S&R's report that Microsoft misbehaved by offering ISPs and OEMs "favors, such as ... low or zero prices" for its Web browser in exchange for ISPs' and OEMs' agreement to "favor Internet Explorer over Netscape,"[50] and that Microsoft gave "its browser to consumers for free."[51] They suggest that these activities are part of a predatory strategy by Microsoft against Netscape and other potential competitors.[52]

Again, however, the S&R analysis can be turned on its head. Discussing markets with network externalities, S&R assert that to compete effectively, entrants must engage in costly activities that attract consumers. Such activities include "selling ... initially at a very low price or giving [the product] away to gain market share."[53] In other words, selling at a very low or zero price is *either* a predatory strategy *or* a competitive necessity.[54]

S&R indicate that low-price browser distribution was an essential competitive strategy for Netscape but was an anticompetitive effort to extend or preserve a monopoly for Microsoft.[55] Neither conclusion is self-evident. When Microsoft began distributing Internet Explorer free, Netscape was the dominant provider of Web browsers. Indeed, Netscape enjoyed a 70 to 80 percent share of browser use in 1996 and certainly above half the browser market, however measured.[56] Although Microsoft had determined that it would add Web browser functionality to its operating system before Netscape began marketing its Web browser, Netscape was the clear leader in this arena when Microsoft's Web browser became available to consumers with the release of Windows 95.[57]

Why, then, is Microsoft cast as the firm that distributed at zero cost to preserve monopoly (which it is asserted to have done in what S&R treat as a product market different from browsers)[58] and Netscape cast as the firm competing to break into a market? Why not the other way around?

One answer might be that Microsoft's share of browser use (or of browser users or other measure of relative success) increased during the period considered by S&R.[59] That, of course, is the likely outcome when one introduces a new product. Whatever the nature of the competition, the odds are that the new product – which starts without any share of the market – will gain market share and that competing products will lose market share. There simply is nothing inherently suspect about an increase in market share.[60]

Perhaps S&R's position rests not on the simple fact of increasing market share but on the magnitude of the change. Certainly, there was a significant increase in the use of Microsoft's Internet Explorer.[61] Though the browser's early generations did not attract users in substantial numbers, that changed after Microsoft introduced the third and fourth generations of the software. The trade press extolled these versions as vast improvements, over Microsoft's earlier browsing technology, and consumers agreed, increasing Microsoft's market share rapidly.[62]

But significant market success cannot be the test. Beyond its implausibility as an interpretation of antitrust law, such a standard would conflict with the public interest – it would, for example, give no place to differences between competing products, to product improvements, or to other plausible sources of success in competitive markets.[63]

A second answer could be that S&R misconstrued the relevant market. In the ongoing litigation with DOJ, Microsoft argues that the relevant arena for understanding these activities is the competition among software *platforms*, whether those platforms are operating systems, Web browsers, or other software embodying a particular set of programming standards.[64] Applications software (word processors, spreadsheets, games, and so forth) is typically written for a specific software platform. An operating system typically can serve as a platform, but so can other products – for example, Sun Microsystems' Java programming language.

A focus on platforms plainly would encompass Microsoft's competition with Netscape and with Sun Microsystems.[65] If the arena for competition is the market for *platforms* rather than for a particular type of software, then Microsoft, not Netscape, was the heavyweight when they began competing for customers.

But S&R, along with DOJ's experts in its litigation with Microsoft, resist this market definition – doubtless because that definition would make it quite difficult to cast Microsoft as a monopolist rather than a competitor. After all, there are many actual or potential competitors in the platform market.

That, of course, is the argument's appeal to Microsoft. Whether the platform market is, in fact, the correct market definition is beside the present point. Our observation is simply that acceptance of the platform market definition offers one possible source of coherence to the choice S&R made in casting Microsoft as the predator and Netscape as the prey, and not the other way around.

A third possible solution to the problem presented by S&R's analysis is to look at intent. This approach is forcefully pressed by the government's chief economic expert in the case against Microsoft, who makes corporate purpose the touchstone of his argument.[66] Professor Frank Fisher asserts that one can look at what company officials say in context with the structure of their market and determine whether particular actions are motivated by a desire to compete or by an interest in undermining competition.[67]

Perhaps, as Professor Fisher suggests, it is easier to divine an anticompetitive purpose than to discern which *possibly* anticompetitive effects truly are inimical to competition. We should not, however, jump to that conclusion. Group purpose is notoriously difficult to construct under the best of circumstances, given the array of goals that motivate individuals.[68] Also, the materials from which a corporation's "intent" can be ascertained are particularly difficult to parse. Individual employees and officers routinely discuss matters of importance to their personal vision for the firm with an eye to a particular goal and a particular audience. Even statements from a firm's CEO often are unreliable indicia of overall corporate intent. That is why, prior to his involvement in the Microsoft case, Frank Fisher so adamantly opposed placing any weight on evidence of intent:

> The subjective intent of a company is difficult to determine and will usually reflect nothing more than a determination to win all possible business from rivals – a determination consistent with competition … .
>
> … To premise their legality on an inquiry into the specific motivations of subjective intent of the firms that engage in such conduct (when it is clear that all firms engaged in competition attempt and intend to win as much business as they can) or on retrospective evaluation of whether there were more "desirable" alternative actions that could have been chosen, would be to elevate competitors above competition and threaten the entire competitive process for the sake of those who are not intended to be its beneficiaries and at the expense of those who are.[69]

We believe that Professor Fisher was right the first time.

S&R do not make a similar error. They would allow some scope for corporate intent, saying that it "throws light on the likely effect of the conduct" being examined.[70] That observation, however, comes only as a footnote to their declaration that "a strong case can be made … that antitrust should dispense with the separate intent requirement and focus solely on the effects of the alleged anticompetitive conduct."[71]

As explained below, in practice there *is* no separate intent requirement for corporations. The law tends to take as a given that actions with a credible efficiency explanation are within the ordinary course of business activity, no matter what the firm's employees thought or said.[72] We think this a wise course, but it does not, then, provide an escape from the dilemma presented by the S&R approach.

The road that S&R lay out could be a perilous one for any number of businesses to travel. It places a premium on knowing how to tell the monopolists from the competitors, but it provides no ready mechanism for figuring out before the fact where the dividing line lies. After looking at the various alternatives, we can find no analytical structure in the S&R analysis that answers the question. Perhaps only the thermos knows.

Economic Analysis: Another View

Our quarrel is not with the substance of S&R's speculations about what effects *might* flow from particular conduct. They rightly observe that in markets with significant network effects, a variety of actions by firms with a large market share might create impediments to competition by smaller rivals. S&R also identify plausible effects of each type of action asserted in complaints against Microsoft. As observed earlier, much of the recent writing in economics provides insight into how activity that could be seen as ordinary competitive conduct also could plausibly impede rivals' competition with a dominant firm.[73]

The problem comes in trying to apply that insight. If the analysis stops at the academic exercise of observing the potential impact on rivals, it is interesting but essentially disconnected from important applications. If, however, the analysis becomes the predicate for imposing substantial penalties, it is problematic. To be useful to decision makers, economic analysis must do more than establish *possibilities*. It must establish the *probability* that the activity subverts market competition. This finding is the minimum goal for economic analysis of antitrust issues – issues that courts, requiring proof, not speculation, ultimately resolve. Typical of those in the nip-and-tuck school, S&R have not met this goal.

Consider, for example, their discussion of predatory threats. An impressive array of articles in academic journals over two decades discuss predation and predatory threats.[74] S&R draw on some of the more sophisticated entries in that literature, but their analysis gives the reader only *coulds* and *maybes* and *mights*:

> [P]redatory threats *might* be credible, even though following through on the threats would inflict a cost on the monopolist. ... [*I*]*f* carrying out the threatened conduct drives the rival to exit the market, the monopolist *could* recoup by preserving its monopoly profits. Second, it *may be* profitable for the monopolist to gain a reputation as a predator. That reputation *may* lead future victims to fear the monopolist's threats. Third, the monopolist sometimes *may be* able to make a binding commitment to carry out a threat that otherwise would not be credible.[75]

That all translates into speculation that, if a monopolist can drive all its rivals from the market and can keep them and others from the market over the long term, there is a possibility that the monopolist can make enough money to recover what was lost during a period of predatory pricing. If that is true, the monopolist may get its rivals' attention with a mere threat. But when are we apt to find a monopolist who can do that?

S&R come closer to completing the analysts' task when discussing Microsoft directly. They opine that, as Microsoft has "far 'deeper pockets' than [most of its potential competitors, it] can outlast [them] in a war of attrition and so a threat to continue to do so is credible."[76] Establishing a credible predatory threat is an essential step for their analysis, and they recognize one factor that enhances credibility.

But the *capacity* to outlast a rival is only one requisite of a credible story of predation or of a credible predatory threat. The essential question is why it is in a firm's interest to commit the predatory act. In a nuclear arms "game," my having more missiles than you bolsters your conviction that I could win if we go to war; but what evidence is there that war makes sense for me, even if I can win? The doctrine of mutually assured destruction, which dominated thinking about such matters for many years, rested on the theory that no one would care about "winning" a nuclear war if the devastation visited on both combatants was sufficiently high.[77] Predatory pricing encounters the same problem.

S&R nod in this general direction, but they do not explain their contrary conclusion that Microsoft is a plausible predator. They recognize that a firm with a large volume of business (which is apt to include any business with a large market share) has much to lose in a war of attrition, and the market leader typically stands to lose a great deal more than most rivals.[78] The utility of a predatory threat depends on the firm's ability to maintain a closed market long enough after ousting its rivals to recoup the losses incurred during the predatory activity.[79] S&R do not produce a good reason to believe that Microsoft could drive rivals away and then keep competitors out long enough and raise prices high enough to make up for the losses. S&R provide no calculations of the sort of losses that would be likely, of the elasticity of demand for Microsoft's products (indeed, they do not specify which Microsoft product they have in mind), or of other factors necessary to resolve this issue.

On the other hand, if the DOJ is to succeed in its litigation against Microsoft, it must provide just the sort of information missing from S&R's article. One might view the article and the DOJ evidence as theory and practice in this area. But it is not a practice that should make the theorists comfortable. Indeed, the practice looks just as theoretical and perhaps even more open-ended than the theory propounded by S&R.

The testimony, presented primarily by the government's chief economic expert witness, Frank Fisher, states that Microsoft engaged in predation by integrating its browser with Windows – a move Professor Fisher concludes cost Microsoft millions of dollars.[80] Fisher asserts that Microsoft could have sold the browser for a substantial profit, and its failure to do so can be explained only as a conscious decision to hurt itself in order to inflict greater harm on its potential competitors.[81] Having adopted the DOJ market definition – Intel-compatible PC operating systems – Professor Fisher identifies browsers as complements to the product that the DOJ's case concerns.[82] Microsoft's alleged predation in browsers is problematic in that view because the predation sustains a monopoly in operating systems.

Making Web browsers a product market separate from operating systems is critical to the predation claim; recognizing them as complements creates difficulties. The importance of separating the products should be obvious: It permits a simple focus on the price charged for browsers. Given that Microsoft makes Internet Explorer available at a zero price, the pricing-below-cost aspect of predation becomes far easier to establish.

But acknowledging that browsers are complements to operating systems complicates the government's argument. If the operating system and Web-browsing technology are complements, providing such technology at a very low or even at a zero price very well could be highly remunerative.[83]

This latter outcome is exactly what Microsoft's economic expert, Dean Richard Schmalensee, says occurred. Dean Schmalensee explains that Internet Explorer's contribution to the utility of Windows increases both the price that consumers will pay for Windows and the volume of sales. Slight increases in either – in the 1 to 3 percent range – more than pay for Microsoft's investment in Internet Explorer.[84] Integration of Internet Explorer into Windows to offer additional, attractive functions parallels Microsoft's integration of numerous other functions into Windows. This implies that Microsoft's strategy is remunerative and not predatory.[85] Simply put, the firm makes money not by selling every possible stand-alone product separately, but by integrating the most attractive complementary features into the operating system and encouraging consumers to become familiar with those features.

Professor Fisher agrees that Microsoft makes money on the sale of Windows and that the revenue from Windows more than pays for the costs of developing technologies incorporated in each new version. Given his recognition that Internet Explorer and Windows are at least complements, this recognition would seem to end the predation claim. But Professor Fisher offers a new twist to the predation argument. He declares that, even if it covers all of its Internet Explorer-related costs, Microsoft is making *less money than it might have made* had it priced and marketed Internet Explorer differently.[86]

Although Fisher casually conflates below-opportunity-cost pricing with the more conventional below-cost-pricing calculation,[87] this is a novel approach to predation. The standard approach asks whether pricing is below a firm's marginal costs.[88] That determination leaves open questions regarding the appropriate measures of cost and the apposite time frames for computing below-cost pricing. Both are matters of importance in lines of business with substantial economies of scale and immature products.[89] Professor Fisher's test asks instead what the *theoretical profit-maximizing price* is for a given product and commands that the firm *must* charge that price in order to avoid engaging in predation. This test requires a very different set of inquiries and implies far greater knowledge by the decision maker – regarding matters such as the nature of the demand curve faced by the individual firm – than the standard legal test.[90] It is a test that leaves virtually every business open to charges of predatory pricing, as no one will be able to anticipate with reasonable certainty precise calculations of the best price for each product.[91]

Far from providing the detailed calculations missing from S&R's analysis – factors necessary to decide whether Microsoft reasonably could engage in predation given the losses it would incur and its prospects for preventing competitive entry – Fisher's approach elides any precise calculation at all.[92] To circumscribe the set of candidates for predatory pricing claims, Fisher relies once again on his assessment of Microsoft's intent together with an assumption that defeating competition is especially valuable – and, hence, illicit efforts to that end are especially likely – in a market with strong network effects.[93]

The network effects argument brings us back to the initial question of DOJ's market definition, as the market with strong network effects must be the *platform* market.[94] Using that market definition makes the predatory pricing claim difficult, as explained earlier. Moreover, invocation of network effects does little to buttress the contention that a firm has engaged (or is likely to engage) in predatory behavior. As we explain later, we certainly find vigorous competition in the platform market plausible, but that in no way establishes that the competition is more or less vigorous, or more or less licit than competition in other markets.[95]

In the end, the DOJ and Professor Fisher have failed to reduce concern that the S&R approach is merely an open door to claims of anticompetitive conduct. They have not provided credible evidence that Microsoft engaged in predatory pricing, much less that market conditions are consistent with a reasonable expectation that Microsoft would recoup its current losses with future earnings.[96] Rather, the DOJ and Fisher see evidence of intent and the presence of network externalities as part of a pattern of illicit behavior. That approach replaces hard analysis of actual and probable effects with surmise based on fragmentary evidence and assumption. The problems created by this approach become more pronounced if such analysis is combined with the legal standard proposed by S&R. We turn next to consideration of their suggested legal standard.

LEGAL STANDARDS

S&R on the Legal Standard under Section 2

S&R tell readers that the legal standard used to judge violations of Section 1 of the Sherman Act is a well-settled balancing test. That test weighs the harm to consumer welfare of anticompetitive conduct against the benefits to consumer welfare (e.g., from efficiency gains).[97] Their crisp discussion of this standard contrasts sharply with their exploration of the monopolization standard under Section 2. They title the section on the monopolization test "Section 2's Unsettled Standard,"[98] and their discussion reinforces the sense that title conveys.

Actually, the problem is not strictly a matter of identifying the abstract standard. The recognized test for Section 2 cases is the *Grinnell* test, which requires possession of monopoly power and "willful acquisition or maintenance of that power as distinguished from growth or development as a consequence of a superior product, business acumen, or historic accident."[99] S&R accept that as the governing test, but they say the meaning of this test is uncertain. The reason, they suggest, is the ambiguity of the *willful acquisition* component of *Grinnell*.

S&R identify three "views" of the willful acquisition prong of *Grinnell*: the *avoidable exclusionary conduct* test, the *sole purpose and effect* test, and the *unnecessarily restrictive conduct* test.[100] They argue that the first two views – we will refer to them as alternative tests – are defective, while the third is not.

As S&R cast these tests, the *avoidable exclusionary conduct* test holds the monopolist liable whenever it creates barriers to competition (that the monopolist "has the ability to forego"), whether or not there are efficiencies associated with the monopolist's conduct.[101] The *sole purpose* test holds the monopolist liable only when the creation of competition barriers is the sole purpose of its conduct. One version of this is a "but for" test, which asks whether the monopolist's conduct would have been unprofitable in the absence of competition barriers imposed by the monopolist.[102] The *unnecessarily restrictive conduct* test holds the monopolist liable when the exclusionary effects of its conduct outweigh the associated consumer benefits.

S&R state that courts have applied each of these tests at various times. The *avoidable conduct* test was first articulated and applied by Judge Learned Hand in the celebrated Alcoa decision.[103] The Supreme Court applied the *unnecessarily restrictive conduct* test, according to S&R, in its *Aspen Ski* decision.[104] S&R note that the *sole purpose* test, rejected by Judge Hand in *Alcoa*, "has been used by some courts."[105] The one example they provide of an application of the *sole purpose* test is the recent *United States v. Microsoft Corp.* decision in the United States Court of Appeals for the D.C. Circuit,[106] a decision they plainly wish to distance from the test to be used in the current litigation.

Having found all three tests within the legal landscape, S&R concentrate on a normative discussion of the appropriate legal standard. After all, the "unsettled" state of the law fairly cries out for a normative answer; one can imagine judges pleading for someone to tell them which of the three tests is best.

S&R's normative position is based on a straightforward "error-cost" argument. The *avoidable exclusionary conduct* test of Judge Hand is inappropriate, they argue, because it generates a high rate of "false convictions," i.e., convictions in cases where the defendant's conduct led to a net increase in consumer welfare. The *sole purpose* test is inappropriate in their view because it generates a high rate of false acquittals – i.e., acquittals in cases where the defendant's conduct on balance reduced consumer welfare. The *unnecessarily restrictive conduct* test is best in their view because it can be applied in a manner that minimizes the total cost of error by trading off increases in one type of error for declines in the other type.

In other words, S&R's normative goal is to maximize consumer welfare.

In addition, they view the Goldilocks ("just right") solution to be a test that, like the Section 1 test, essentially balances expected consumer harm against expected consumer benefit.[107]

What's Wrong with the S&R View

We think S&R's positive claim regarding the standard under Section 2 is incorrect in most important respects, and their normative claim is simply misguided. S&R's positive analysis of the Section 2 legal standard presents the law as more ambiguous and up-for-grabs than it really is.

As Oliver Wendell Holmes noted long ago, the law for most purposes is a prediction of what a court is likely to do.[108] The lawyer's craft is making that prediction accurately. This notion applies to antitrust, as it does to other areas of the law: Antitrust lawyers and scholars sift through the legal authorities (which in antitrust overwhelmingly consist of case law) to predict how antitrust courts will treat a specific claim.

S&R's analysis, does not, however, predict how courts today – especially the courts that address the Microsoft litigation – will apply the current legal standard. S&R instead divide the authorities into three disparate tests, but they do not tell us which is most likely to be applied by a court in a monopolization case. For positive analysis, that is the question that counts.

Positive Analysis of the Legal Standard

It also is a question that most antitrust lawyers could answer, for the field is not so muddled as S&R suggest. Of the three tests defined by S&R, the *sole purpose* test (or the "but for" version of it) is the best description of the current legal standard under Section 2. The most important line of recent Supreme Court and appellate decisions articulating the standard under Section 2 is composed of predatory pricing cases. Among those cases are the Supreme Court's decisions in *Matsushita*[109] and *Brooke Group*,[110] the First Circuit's decision in *Barry Wright*,[111] and the Seventh Circuit's decision in *Rose-Acre Farms*.[112] These decisions share a clearly expressed view that the costs of false convictions are especially worrisome. The recoupment test set forth in *Matsushita*, and further developed in *Brooke Group*, is properly viewed as the version of the *sole purpose* test S&R were most at pains to dismiss. The recoupment test asks whether the defendant's price-cutting would have been unprofitable in the absence of barriers to competition. This is essentially the "but for" test that S&R identify as a special case of the *sole purpose* inquiry.[113]

Although S&R cite *Aspen Ski* as an application of their preferred *unnecessarily restrictive conduct* standard, this case is a poor example in two respects. First, as a predictor of the tests that will be used in the future, *Aspen Ski* is a poor choice because it does not enjoy widespread acceptance as a good decision. Indeed, it has been roundly criticized, and appellate courts have treated the *Aspen Ski* doctrine as limited to the facts of that case.[114]

Second, and more important, the Aspen Ski case is weak evidence even for the modest proposition that antitrust courts have applied the unnecessarily restrictive conduct test to any case. The defendant in Aspen Ski failed to provide a credible consumer-benefit or efficiency justification for its decision to withdraw from a joint marketing arrangement with its weaker competitor. The Supreme Court upheld the jury's determination in Aspen Ski largely because the defendant failed to introduce any evidence to counter the plaintiff's claim that the defendant's motivations were purely anticompetitive. That is, the Supreme Court upheld the finding of a Section 2 violation in Aspen Ski not because it thought that anticompetitive harms outweighed the defendant's efficiency justifications, as S&R would have us believe, but because the defendant failed to offer any efficiency justification.

Even if one passes that hurdle – if someone can find a case in which a court legitimately can be said to have adopted the *unnecessarily restrictive conduct* test – courts have not applied this test in Section 2 cases with sufficient frequency for it to be treated as an accepted legal doctrine. Antitrust courts holding defendants liable for anticompetitive exclusion generally have not reached this result through balancing pro-competitive benefits against anticompetitive harms. They reached this result when, and pretty much *only* when, the defendant failed to provide a credible efficiency justification.

The much-discussed *Lorain Journal Co. v. United States*[115] is exemplary. The *Lorain Journal* newspaper enjoyed a local monopoly in advertising and news dissemination. When a local radio station was licensed to begin broadcast operations and started signing up advertisers, the *Journal* refused to deal with firms that bought advertising time on the radio station. It presented advertisers a stark choice: them or us. The court found a violation of Section 2 for attempted monopolization. It rejected *Lorain Journal*'s argument that the newspaper had a right to deal with whomever it wished, and gave no credit to the defendant's justification that it acted according to a larger implicit agreement to protect local businesses from competing firms located outside Lorain.

In the absence of any credible consumer welfare justification, the court inferred that the *Lorain Journal* specifically intended to regain its monopoly in advertising. As in *Aspen Ski*, the Supreme Court upheld a lower court finding of monopolistic exclusion not because it thought that the anticompetitive harms outweighed the proffered consumer benefits, but because the defendant failed to provide any credible consumer-benefit justification.

Of the three tests identified by S&R – *avoidable exclusion*, *sole purpose* and *unnecessarily restrictive conduct* – antitrust courts have applied only the first two under Section 2. S&R correctly cite *Alcoa* as the key application of *avoidable exclusion*. Most modern antitrust courts, however, have rejected it. For example, in *United States v. Syufy Enterprises*,[116] Judge Kozinski had this to say about the Alcoa doctrine:

> [T]he government trots out a shopworn argument we had thought long abandoned: that efficient, aggressive competition is itself a structural barrier to entry. ... [T]he wisdom of this notion has been questioned by just about everyone who has taken a close look at it. ... [T]he antitrust laws protect competition, not competitors.[117]

Judge Kozinski's is a stronger and blunter statement of the point than is typical, but its substantive content is nonetheless within the mainstream of antitrust law.[118]

Admittedly, American law provides ample anecdotes of courts heading in unexpected directions, and an unusually lucky antitrust plaintiff might find a judge willing to apply S&R's *unnecessarily restrictive conduct* test. But you shouldn't bet your own money on that result – especially not when a defendant has substantial efficiency justifications on his side.

The present state of U.S. antitrust law is fairly clear: Only the *sole purpose* is generally applied under Section 2. S&R are simply wrong in suggesting that the legal standard is a lottery involving three potential tests, with a court equally likely to choose among them. They should receive high marks for creativity. But lawyers, law students, and bar applicants would be well advised to identify the *sole purpose* test as the standard actually applied in monopolization claims.

Normative Analysis of the Legal Standard

There are good reasons that courts have coalesced around *sole purpose*. These reasons take us directly into S&R's normative position regarding the proper legal standard under Section 2. S&R claim that applying the *unnecessarily restrictive conduct* test minimizes overall error costs. Antitrust courts generally have reached a different conclusion during their 100 years of applying the Sherman Act. It would be a wonderful advertisement for economics – and a bit amazing – if two economists discovered a superior approach to deciding cases that courts had failed to discover on their own. Of course, nothing so amazing has happened; the S&R analysis of error costs reaches the wrong conclusion. S&R's argument also relies on rather speculative claims about the relative costs of false convictions and false acquittals to get to this conclusion.

Start with the simple, basic principles case for preferring *sole purpose* to the *unnecessarily restrictive conduct* test on error-cost grounds. The *sole purpose* test certainly increases the likelihood of a false acquittal relative to the *unnecessarily restrictive conduct* test. The cost of a false acquittal, however, will be small whenever entry is easy. A firm that excludes a competitor in a market with easy entry will not enjoy the fruits of its exclusionary efforts; consequently, consumers will not be harmed.

S&R know that, so they emphasize instances in which entry is difficult. This fact, however, does not make their error-cost case. Of course, the difficulty of entry is a datum in the calculation, but it is not determinate in assessing the long-run consequences of false positives versus false negatives in antitrust. So long as entry is feasible, even if difficult, consumers will not suffer harm in the long run as a result of a dominant firm's exclusionary efforts. For in the long run, entry will occur and economic profits will be driven to zero. Whether consumers suffer harm at all and the extent of that harm will depend on whether and how long the dominant firm can exclude entry.

The point we want to stress here is that there is a market constraint on the cost of false acquittals. Monopoly profits attract entrants, and entry leads to an equilibrium in which consumer welfare is maximized. This proposition is true even where entry is difficult. In those instances, monopoly profits will attract entry to the point at which expected revenues will just compensate each firm for the opportunity costs of all types of capital employed as well as for the cost of entry.[119] An incumbent, dominant firm can prevent entry in this setting only by keeping its price sufficiently low that no potential competitor would find it profitable to invade its market. In that instance, consumer harm, if any, will be at a minimum.

There is no such self-limiting quality to the effects of false convictions. These are more likely if Section 2 cases are decided under the *unnecessarily restrictive conduct* test rather than under the *sole purpose* test. As many commentators and courts have noted,[120] false convictions can be costly. In particular, there are three types of cost associated with false convictions.

First, false convictions encourage firms to avoid aggressive competition and engage in collusive conduct. For example, false convictions for predatory pricing punish firms for cutting their prices. As the probability of a false conviction for predatory pricing increases, firms increasingly avoid price competition. Similarly, false convictions for competitive output decisions, such as the introduction of a new product (which, if successful, almost invariably raises rivals' costs), encourage firms to seek market- and information-sharing arrangements with their competitors. Such sharing can easily develop into implicit or explicit collusion.[121]

Second, false convictions encourage, and in effect teach, firms to seek compensation in the courts for actions by competitors that harm them. The higher the rate of false convictions, the more pronounced this lesson. A regime in which false convictions occur frequently generates a market in which no firm has an incentive to compete aggressively, for fear that any competitive act may give rise to a suit for treble damages. Further, each firm has an incentive to enforce this norm by taking competitors to court. The monopolization lawsuit becomes an especially important tool for firms that are disadvantaged by competition. These firms are apt to enjoy a relative advantage in litigation.[122]

Third, false convictions encourage firms to bring monopolization claims irrespective of their validity, which increases the frequency of frivolous or bad-faith litigation. Frivolous litigation is costly to society even if it has no other harmful side effects. Frivolous litigation, however, is likely to have harmful side effects. As the frequency of frivolous monopolization claims increases (holding fixed the rate of false convictions), firms will find it increasingly hard to tell whether damages have been awarded appropriately in any given case. But this situation only increases the incentive to bring frivolous claims and to avoid competition, as firms lose faith in the competence of courts to distinguish good claims from bad.

Thus, even if all firms comply with a non-competition norm – an undesirable byproduct of a false-convictions regime – as long as there is a substantial risk of a false conviction, each firm will have an incentive to seek damages from a competitor after any event that causes a shift of business from one firm to another. For example, if a reduction in the ozone layer causes a shift of business from one maker of sunglasses to another, the loser will have an incentive under a false-convictions regime to seek treble damages from the winner, on the theory that the winner's output and price decisions were predatory.

This may seem to be a ludicrous example. But the lure of treble damages has brought forth novel and ingenious legal arguments in the past, such as the claim by the plaintiffs in *Matsushita* that Japanese television manufacturers had engaged in a predatory conspiracy for roughly 20 years.[123]

False convictions for monopolization thus appear substantially more threatening to consumer welfare than do false acquittals. False acquittals leave the market in a condition in which competition is more likely over the long run. Although competition sometimes is brutal and can seem unfair to competitors, it serves to maximize consumer welfare. That is why promoting competition, not protecting competitors, is so widely recognized as antitrust's goal.[124] Notwithstanding temporary departures from the competitive equilibrium, the general trend of competitive forces toward greater output, variety, and lower prices remains intact in a market with false acquittals.

False convictions, on the other hand, generate a process that retards competitive markets. Firms learn to avoid competition and to share the benefits of high prices with rivals and input providers.[125] Output is lower, relative to the market with false acquittals, and prices are higher. This should not be surprising when the choice – as it is in monopolization cases, in contrast to cases involving collusive behavior such as price fixing – is between errors favoring too much competition and errors favoring too little.

This divergence in error costs is likely to be greater when the dynamic nature of competition is taken into account. Because monopoly profits attract entrants, there always will be competitors ready to take business away from a dominant firm that gouges consumers with high prices and poor products. The presence of these competitors, some already in the market and others waiting in the wings, continually puts pressure on the dominant firm to keep its prices low and to improve its products.[126] This process constrains the social cost of false acquittals and reduces it over time. In a regime of false convictions, however, no comparable market mechanism constrains false-conviction error costs over time. Entry cannot constrain false-conviction costs because each entrant would be subject to an attempted monopolization claim if it went at the market too aggressively. Entrants would learn to behave as incumbents do, avoiding competition.

Given the asymmetry in error costs, we think the *sole purpose* test used most consistently in monopolization cases is superior to the *unnecessarily restrictive conduct* test proposed by S&R. S&R are able to reach the opposite conclusion only because they severely discount the error costs associated with false convictions.

S&R seem to think that the cost of false convictions can be kept to a tolerable level under their proposed test. They ignore, however, the incentive for rent-seeking litigation in a regime that fails to minimize false monopolization convictions. There is an important fact of life that economists often fail to realize when they apply their tools to antitrust: Hypothetical legal rules that seem to work well in economic models may work quite poorly in real courts. The reason is that judges are fallible, information needed to apply complex rules is not readily gathered, and those who bring cases to court and present the relevant information to judges are motivated to exploit any legal rule to their personal advantage. Thus, a rule that would work well if always applied accurately, but would generate costly rent-seeking litigation if sometimes applied inaccurately, is unwise where rent-seeking costs are likely to dominate.[127] This general criticism applies to the legal standard proposed by S&R.

We noted that antitrust courts generally have been unwilling to apply the S&R *unnecessarily restrictive conduct* test. Some courts have openly defended this conservative approach on the basis of a comparison of relative error costs.[128] Generally, antitrust courts have been reluctant to conduct the sort of cost-benefit balancing that S&R recommend because it pushes judges beyond their area of competence and requires courts to take on some of the functions of public utility regulators.

To determine whether a dominant firm expanded its capacity to preempt a rival or to meet projected demand, a court would have to delve deeply into business records and market demand projections. The Supreme Court was reluctant to take on that kind of inquiry in the earliest cases interpreting the Sherman Act.[129] Since then, antitrust courts have avoided the duties of regulatory boards.[130]

Of course, the issue of institutional competence is closely related to that of error costs; they are, in a sense, two sides of the same coin. It is no accident that courts sometimes adopt bright-line rules instead of complicated balancing tests. Courts prefer bright-line rules when they believe that the alternative is likely to be applied so inaccurately that, even though a bright-line rule errs systematically in favor of one party, it still minimizes total error costs.[131]

For example, courts hearing tort disputes often adopt "custom" rules, shielding the defendant from liability as long as he or she has complied with the custom of his or her profession or industry.[132] These rules prevent courts from independently applying the negligence test (a general cost-benefit test) when the defendant complied with the custom. Physicians, for example, are not held liable for malpractice when they complied with the customs of the medical profession.[133] Courts have accepted this standard uniformly in the common – and intuitively compelling – belief that erroneous decisions would occur more frequently if judges or juries defined the appropriate standard of conduct in each malpractice case.[134] Antitrust courts have adopted the *sole purpose* test in Section 2 monopolization cases for the same reason.

As part of their normative argument regarding the proper standard under Section 2, S&R state that anticompetitive intent should not be a consideration unless it explains an otherwise ambiguous action. They believe courts should focus primarily – perhaps exclusively – on the anticompetitive effects of the defendant's conduct.[135] They suggest that courts might try to find actual evidence of intent to clarify the true purposes of corporate actions with potentially anticompetitive effects.[136] Our defense of the *sole purpose* test suggests why courts will continue to treat intent in applying the monopolization standard in a different way than S&R envision. Intent, as noted above, is a vague and typically useless concept in antitrust law.[137] Every competing firm wants to monopolize the market and drive its competitors out of business, and given this fact it would seem that every firm is guilty of possessing an anticompetitive intent.[138]

Typically, judges deciding Section 2 cases find anticompetitive intent when the defendant fails to offer any pro-consumer justification for its conduct. This was the case in *Aspen Skiing* and in *Lorain Journal*.[139] In both, the Supreme Court upheld lower-court findings of anticompetitive intent. These opinions indicate that the defendants were not punished merely because they sought to dominate their respective markets. They were punished because they could not offer a reasonable efficiency justification for challenged actions that were suspect on their face; given this failure, the proper inference is that their actions were purely anticompetitive rather than the mixed sort involving a combination of potential benefits to consumers and potential barriers to competition.[140]

The fact that courts often refer to anticompetitive intent is not, as S&R suggest, an odd feature that remains largely as a result of some useless precedent. Nor, on the other extreme, is it an indication that judges engage in the perilous activity of divining actual intent in these cases by looking at what corporate personnel said to each other, to customers, or to reporters.

As we said, unlike price-fixing cases or other settings where the statements of corporate personnel are important for their effect on other actors, monopolization cases are extremely unlikely to offer meaningful opportunity *or reason* to inquire into individuals' state of mind.[141] S&R are quite right in saying that "[w]hen there are multiple motives and effects, it is impossible to talk about *the* purpose of the conduct."[142] Courts could reach the right conclusions without referring to intent, and when they use the term in monopolization cases, they are referring more to an analytical construct in the nature of a burden of persuasion than to an inquiry into personal motives and beliefs.[143]

What S&R fail to note, however, is that the limited use now made of the "intent" concept in Section 2 cases takes the law in a very different direction than either they or DOJ would. Reference to "intent" serves the useful purpose of constraining courts to apply a *sole purpose* standard to monopolization cases. It reminds decision makers that only if no legitimate purpose is plausible will courts presume conduct to be sufficiently anticompetitive as to violate Section 2's commands.[144] This approach filters out monopolization claims against defendants where the conduct involves potential consumer benefits coupled with potential barriers to competition. Courts have decided, correctly in our view, that monopolization strictures are inappropriate for these types of cases.

The "Special Case" of "Network Markets"

To this point, we have considered the general case for choosing the *sole purpose* test over the *unnecessarily restrictive conduct* test. S&R's argument, however, includes the claim that the market for operating software is different, largely because of network effects. They claim that monopoly is more durable, and entry more difficult in markets with network externalities.

Even if these observations are true, they do not justify modifying a legal standard that has been applied reasonably well across the board to all sorts of industries with varying entry conditions. The key question is whether network effects prevent entry, or make entry so difficult that it would be appropriate to treat network industries under a unique legal standard. We know of no evidence proving entry infeasible in markets with network effects, or demonstrating that network industries should be judged under a different legal standard.

Moreover, in assessing the difficulty of entry, it is not enough simply to mention the existence of network effects or the chicken-and-egg problem, features asserted by S&R as reasons for treating Microsoft differently from dominant firms in other markets.[145] Network effects imply only that successful entry is difficult, not that it is impossible. Moreover, although network effects imply that the *probability* of successful entry is lower than it would be otherwise, they also imply that the *payoff* from successful entry is larger than it would be otherwise.

The incentive to enter is determined by the *expected payoff* from entry, which is the product of the probability of successful entry and the payoff from successful entry. Network effects theory tells us that the probability is lower and the payoff is higher. It should be clear that this model falls far short of offering a theoretical demonstration that entry conditions should be assumed to be radically different in network industries.

Before concluding that the incentive to enter is lower in a network market, a few questions must be answered. Is the probability of successful entry lower in a network market than in a comparable market without network effects? If the probability of successful entry is indeed lower, is the payoff from successful entry larger than in a comparable market without network effects?

It is a commonplace tenet of economic analysis that as expected return on an investment rises, so does the magnitude of the investment made to compete for the return.[146] This relationship tends to drive investment in such industries to the point at which the expected return from marginal investment in that arena equals the return expected elsewhere.[147] Why should that not hold for investment in industries with network effects just as much as for other investments?

While the equal-expected-payoff story is an analytically sound starting point, there is no guarantee that the equality will hold in all cases. It is possible, for instance, that risk aversion will skew investment decisions. If there is a systemic tendency toward underinvestment in riskier propositions, there could be a reduction in the risk-adjusted value of low probability–high payoff investments. So far as we know, however, there is no robust explanation for why thick capital markets would systematically tilt in this direction (which would overvalue low-risk, low-return investments). Indeed, for at least some sectors of the market, there is well-developed literature exposing widespread tendencies to *over*invest in risky propositions.[148]

These explanations primarily address situations involving exogenous constraints on capital markets – the U.S. savings-and-loan debacle is a prime example.[149] Agency-cost theory attempts to extend the analysis to corporate investment more broadly, but these extensions are questionable.[150] At present, the most that can be said with confidence is that the equal-expected-payoff story is plausible and has not been replaced by any strong alternative.

Let us, however, give S&R the benefit of the argument here. Assume there is a tendency to underinvest in low probability–high payoff events. If that is so, and if that describes investment in markets with large network effects, it still does not provide unambiguous support for intervention. Indeed, intervention in such markets is analogous to a tax on a successful entrant. If the reward of a high payoff is undervalued already, the threat of an additional penalty to investments that yield such payoffs would seem a peculiar way of encouraging additional investment.

S&R have a great deal to say about a related topic, the connection between network effects and innovation incentives. But most of what they say is inconclusive and openly speculative. Consider, for example, their observation that one "might argue that exclusion does not increase total innovation, but actually decreases innovation competition by reducing the incentives of new entrants to attempt to compete on the basis of better products."[151]

Such observations are weak analytical reeds on which to base important policy prescriptions. The probability-payoff framework discussed above applies to the innovation issue as much as to other investments needed to enter a network industry. If network markets are different in the sense that a favorable market position, once achieved, is more durable, this merely implies that the incentive to innovate is generally greater in network markets. The same arguments applicable to investment generally also apply to innovation investments.

Indeed, if there is greater durability to returns from investment because of greater insulation from the erosion of successes in network markets (which, we repeat, is not necessarily a correct assumption), that describes the basic structure thought to *encourage* innovation. Intellectual property rights enhance the payoff from successful innovation while raising other firms' costs of competing with the right holder.[152] In that sense, the S&R analysis is at odds with the basic theory behind intellectual property rights.

Such rights are granted to enhance both the quantity and the quality of new products.[153] Weakening them may have effects exactly opposite those suggested by S&R. Whether our intellectual property laws in fact have the incentive issue right – both the direction and magnitude of effects from issuance of those rights – is debated.[154] But S&R do not purport to be rewriting those laws. Instead, they cast their effort as one of analyzing other consumer welfare issues. Furthermore, antitrust litigation hardly seems the right venue for altering the basic underpinnings of copyright and related laws.

Ultimately, we do not know whether network markets have sufficiently distinctive characteristics from other markets to merit different treatment under the law. When S&R ask for a new antitrust standard for those markets, however, they have a burden of providing more than speculation that investment may be discouraged and innovation reduced. As with other aspects of their analysis, they have provided a set of possibilities. In each case these possibilities are no more likely than the obverse. Such weak speculation is an unlikely and unwise source of guidance for changing antitrust law. Such an approach is especially ill advised where the changes would also reduce the intellectual property protections generally thought to encourage innovation.

CONCLUSION

Mark Twain has a wonderful passage in *Life on the Mississippi* poking fun at pseudo-science of his time. Twain begins with the observation, gleaned from a news story, that soil was being carried down the Mississippi River and deposited at the delta near the mouth of the river; as the deposits built over time, the river was becoming shorter, according to the story. From that humble start, Twain spun a series of possible consequences, ending with Chicago and New Orleans joining and electing a single mayor. He asks where but in science can you find such wholesale returns in conjecture for such a trivial investment in facts.[155] Twain had not encountered modern economic analysis of antitrust issues.

* The authors gratefully acknowledge the financial and administrative support provided by Boston University, the International Centre for Economic Research, and Microsoft Corporation. We also thank Hilary Holbrook, Pete Rinato, and Russell Sweet for research assistance, and David S. Evans, Albert L. Nichols, and Bernard Reddy for helpful comments. This chapter was published initially in volume 8 of *George Mason Law Review* (1999) and is reprinted with permission.

1 See, e.g., Franklin M. Fisher et al., *Folded, Spindled and Mutilated: Economic Analysis and U.S. v. IBM* (MIT Press), 1983 (describing the government's economic analysis in the IBM litigation and the costs imposed by such litigation).

2 Steven C. Salop and R. Craig Romaine, "Preserving Monopoly: Economic Analysis, Legal Standards and Microsoft," 7 *George Mason Law Review* 617 (1999).

3 The authors of this paper are consultants to Microsoft, whereas Professor Salop and Dr. Romaine are consultants to clients involved in possible antitrust litigation against Microsoft. It would be a mistake, however, to view the debate between us and S&R as simply the product of different client interests. It is more accurate to say that the different affiliations we have reflect differences in perspective on antitrust and competition issues that are thrown into sharp relief in arguments over the Microsoft litigation. Nothing in this reply should be construed as an assertion that positions taken in the S&R paper are litigation-driven rather than principled.

4 See Salop and Romaine, *supra* note 2, pp. 619-624, 626-627, 629-630, 632-640, 642.

5 *Ibid.*, pp. 619-620, 622-642.

6 *Ibid.*, pp. 655-665.

7 *Ibid.*, pp. 661-665, 670-671.

8 15 U.S.C. sections 1-7 (1994) (as amended).

9 Originally, the Act specified that violations of its provisions were misdemeanors, though it specifically authorized prison sentences as punishment. The length of potential prison terms was later extended, resulting in the classification of violations as felonies. See Act of July 2, 1890, ch. 647, Section 1, 26 Stat. 209; Act of July 7, 1955, ch. 281, 69 Stat. 282.

10 15 U.S.C. section 2 (1994).

11 *Ibid.*, Section 1 (1994).

12 Initially, the law provided for one year in prison and a fine of $5,000, later increased to three years in prison and fines of $50,000, then $100,000 for individuals (now $350,000) and $1 million for corporations (now $10 million). See Act of July 2, 1890, ch. 647, Section 1, 26 Stat. 209 ($5,000 fine, 1 year imprisonment); Act of July 7, 1955, ch. 281, 69 Stat. 282 ($50,000 fine, 3 years imprisonment); Act of Dec. 21, 1974, Pub. L. 93-528, Section 3, 88 Stat. 1708 ($100,000 individual, $1 million corporate fine); Act of Nov. 16, 1990, Pub. L. 101-588, Section 4(a), 104 Stat. 2880 (amending Sherman Act section 1 to

increase fines from $1 million to $10 million against corporations, and from $100,000 to $350,000 against individuals). See S. Rep. No. 101-287, pp. 1-2 (1990) (summarizing changes). The initial $5,000 fine in 1890 would be roughly equivalent to $100,000 today, adjusting simply for changes in the consumer price index. If the fine were adjusted to remain the same size in relation to GNP, it would be roughly $3.2 million today.

[13] See *United States v. Socony Vacuum Oil Co.*, 310 U.S. 150, 221 (1940); *Appalachian Coals, Inc. v. United States*, 288 U.S. 344, 359 (1933); *Increasing Criminal Penalties Under the Sherman Antitrust Act: Report of House Comm. on Judiciary*, 84th Cong., 1st Sess., H.R. Rep. No. 84-70, p. 5 (1955); *Protection of Trade and Commerce Against Unlawful Restraints and Monopolies: Report of House Comm. on Judiciary*, 51st Cong., 1st Sess., H.R. Rep. No. 51-1707 (1890) (seeking to protect against "evils and oppression of trusts and monopolies" within the limits of federal power).

[14] For explication of this point in a series of antitrust contexts, see Robert H. Bork, *The Antitrust Paradox: A Policy at War with Itself* (1978); Richard A. Posner, *Antitrust Law: An Economic Perspective* (1976).

[15] See, e.g., *Business Elec. Corp. v. Sharp Elec. Corp.*, 485 U.S. 717, 732 (1988); Posner, supra note 14, p. 3; William F. Baxter, "Separation of Powers: Prosecutorial Discretion, and the "Common Law" Nature of Antitrust Law," 60 *Texas Law Review* 661 (1982).

[16] See, e.g., William E. Kovacic, "Reagan's Appointees and Antitrust in the 1990s," 60 *Fordham Law Review* 49 (1991); Andrew M. Rosenfield, "The Use of Economics in Antitrust Litigation and Counseling," 1986 *Columbia Business Law Review* 49.

[17] See, e.g., Phillip Areeda and Donald F. Turner, "Predatory Pricing and Related Practices Under Section 2 of the Sherman Act," 88 *Harvard Law Review* 697, 699 (1975); Frank H. Easterbrook, "Predatory Strategies and Counter-Strategies," 48 *University of Chicago Law Review* 263 (1981) (hereafter Easterbrook, "Predatory Strategies"); Benjamin Klein and Kevin Murphy, "Vertical Restraints as Contract Enforcement Mechanisms," 28 *Journal of Law & Economics* 265 (1988); John S. McGee, "Predatory Pricing Revisited," 23 *Journal of Law & Economics* 289, 296-300 (1980). For overviews of this approach, see William H. Page, "The Chicago School and the Evolution of Antitrust: Characterization, Antitrust Injury, and Evidentiary Sufficiency," 75 *Virginia Law Review* 1221 (1989); Richard A. Posner, "The Chicago School of Antitrust Analysis," 127 *University of Pennsylvania Law Review* 925, 932 (1979).

[18] See, e.g., Joseph Farrell and Garth Saloner, "Installed Base and Compatibility: Innovation, Product Preannouncements, and Predation," 76 *American Economic Review* 940 (1986); Michael H. Riordan and Steven C. Salop, "Evaluating Vertical Mergers: A Post-Chicago Approach," 63 *Antitrust Law Journal* 513 (1995); Steven C. Salop, "Strategic Entry Deterrence," 69 *American Economic Review* 335 (1979). See also Lawrence A. Sullivan, "Post-Chicago Economics: Economists, Lawyers, Judges, and Enforcement in a Less Determinate Theoretical World," 63 *Antitrust Law Journal* 669 (1995).

[19] See, e.g., Franklin M. Fisher, "Games Economists Play: A Noncooperative View," 20 *Rand Journal of Economics* 113, 117-119 (1989) (critiquing nip-and-tuck analysis as poor examples of "exemplifying theory" – theory that "does not tell us what must happen [but instead] what can happen.").

[20] See Steven C. Salop and David Sheffman, "Raising Rivals' Costs," 73 *American Economic Review* 267 (1983).

[21] Professor William Page concluded that the government initiated the investigation independent of complaints by Microsoft competitors, but that the competitors played an active

role in pressing for examination of certain issues. Indeed, he opines that "[T]he magnitude and frequency of the contacts between Microsoft's rivals and the enforcement agencies raise the question whether some form of regularity should be imposed on the lobbying process in major cases." William H. Page, "Microsoft and the Public Choice Critique of Antitrust," 44 *Antitrust Bulletin* 5, 11 (1999).

[22] *Ibid.*, p. 12 (citing James Wallace, *Overdrive: Bill Gates and the Race to Control Cyberspace* [1997]). Both the commissioners and the staff split on the question of whether there was any matter worthy of further action. The commission declined to move forward on a 2-2 vote with the remaining commission member not participating. The two bureaus that looked into these matters advanced conflicting recommendations, one suggesting further inquiry, one opposing it. Page, *supra* note 21, pp. 16-17 (citing Wallace).

[23] Some FTC staff thought that Microsoft should grant offsets against payments due under successor contracts, whereas others thought that Microsoft simply should rebate payments whenever an OEM did not ship the contracted numbers. Other commission staff thought that there was nothing problematic about Microsoft's treatment of OEM payments, just as staff divided on other issues in the FTC investigation. See *supra* note 22. This issue did not arise for OEMs whose shipments exceeded their committed volumes; they simply owed Microsoft the agreed-upon royalty rate for their extra shipments.

[24] See Salop and Romaine, *supra* note 2, p. 622, n.14 (contracting), 626, 634, n.49 (APIs), 637, n.57 (vaporware).

[25] *United States v. Microsoft Corp.*, 1995-2 Trade Cas. (CCH) paragraph 71,096 (D.D.C. 1995). In addition to regulating use of license provisions such as the per-processor license, the decree regulated the length of license contracts and nondisclosure terms in certain agreements with other software developers.

[26] Salop and Romaine, *supra* note 2, p. 622, n.14.

[27] Declaration of Kenneth J. Arrow, *United States v. Microsoft Corp.*, 1995-2 Trade Cas. (CCH) paragraph 71,096 (D.D.C. 1995), available at http://web.lawcrawler.com/microsoft/usdoj.cases/ 0049.htm (hereafter Arrow Declaration). The portion of the quote elided in the text states Arrow's view that the contested practices were a "significant impediment to the use of the OEM distribution channel by competing operating system suppliers." In Professor Arrow's view, the practices, hence, were "anticompetitive" even though they did not alter the demand for Microsoft's operating system.

[28] In the agency investigations, the 1994 DOJ complaint and the current DOJ litigation, the government has defined a narrower market than the text suggests, limited to operating systems for computers with Intel or Intel-compatible microprocessors. See Complaint, *United States v. Microsoft Corp.* (D.D.C. filed July 15, 1994) (No. 94-1564) Paragraph 13, available at http://www.usdoj.gov/atr/cases/f0000/0046.htm (1994 Complaint); Complaint, *United States v. Microsoft Corp.* (D.D.C. filed May 18, 1998) (No. 98-1232) Paragraph 54, available at http://www.usdoj.gov/atr/cases/f1700/f1736.htm (1998 Complaint).

[29] Professor Arrow agreed with the DOJ's characterization of the contested practices as "anticompetitive" and also agreed that the practices impeded use of the OEM distribution channel by competing operating systems' suppliers. However, he did not support DOJ's assertions respecting the degree to which those practices noted above affected demand for Microsoft operating systems. See Arrow Declaration, *supra* note 27. Nonetheless, Professor Arrow observed that the consent decree was forward-looking: "The complaint and proposed Final Judgment address the effects of Microsoft's licensing practices on

future sales of competing operating systems." The end of the challenged licensing practices five years ago, however, has not led to a surge in popularity of "competing operating systems" on Intel-compatible computers. *Ibid*. The continued success of Windows following the elimination of the disputed contract terms provides at least prima facie support for Arrow's conclusion that the contracting practices did not account for the demand for Microsoft's products.

30 S&R also spend some time on a third set of allegations involving Microsoft's version of the "Java Virtual Machine" (JVM). See Salop and Romaine, *supra* note 2, pp. 632-633. Similar allegations gave rise to litigation between Microsoft and Sun Microsystems (Sun). Sun is the principal pioneer and promoter of the Java programming language that, in some versions, assertedly allows programs to run on any computer that contains JVM software. The allegations at issue in the Sun–Microsoft litigation are fairly complex and not essential to understanding our criticism of S&R's arguments. The important claims in the litigation, referenced by S&R, concern Microsoft's implementation of its license agreement with Sun in two respects. The first involves Microsoft's decision to allow a Java program to gain access to specific Windows features if a program is written to take advantage of this aspect of Microsoft's JVM. The second addresses Microsoft's decision to restrict a Java program to access capabilities located outside the JVM (Sun claims the license agreement requires outside access and Microsoft asserts it does not). Apart from the interpretation of contract language, the Sun–Microsoft controversy is over a choice between two different methods for allowing Java programs to gain access to a program external to the JVM. The choice is *not* between a restricted technology and a cross-platform technology. S&R note that the Microsoft JVM does not necessarily degrade Java program operation. See Salop and Romaine, *supra* note 2 (discussing three possible effects of Microsoft's version). They treat the creation of Microsoft's Windows-oriented version of the JVM as potentially anticompetitive even though it appears to provide an additional alternative for software programs. At present, programmers can choose to use the Windows-specific features in Microsoft's JVM, can write a Java program that takes advantage of features associated with certain other JVMs, or can write a Java program that should be able to run on Sun's, IBM's, or Netscape's JVM as well as on Microsoft's JVM. (This is possible, for example, using the JVM being produced by Transvirtual Technologies, which implements both Sun's and Microsoft's enhancements to Java and should run programs designed for either approach. See *Transvirtual Technologies, Inc.* [accessed September 23, 1999], http://www.transvirtual.com [advertising "cross-platform Java solutions"].) In this context, it is hard to see the Sun–Microsoft contest over Java license terms as central to the arguments S&R advance. That, along with the complexity of the factual disputes, informs our decision not to treat this subject further here.

31 S&R assert that Microsoft provided benefits that made the price of its Internet Explorer "negative" in some instances. Salop and Romaine, *supra* note 2, p. 639.

32 *Ibid*., p. 636.

33 Microsoft's initial release of Windows 95 as an upgrade for consumers did not include Internet Explorer, though subsequent releases did. Also, downloads from Microsoft's Web site were available prior to the upgrade release in an integrated version.

34 Microsoft's view, however, is that the concept of "bundling" is inapposite, as all of the various versions of Internet Explorer were improvements to the Windows operating system, not unrelated programs. Hence, rather than combining two different products, Microsoft was adding new or improved features to its operating system to make the system more attractive to potential customers. The different conceptions of the software – and con-

comitant differences in terminology – often make the discussions of a single event by Microsoft supporters and opponents difficult to follow. Even where we find Microsoft's view compelling, we will try to describe events in ways that will be comprehensible to those who approach matters from a different vantage.

[35] Salop and Romaine, *supra* note 2, p. 636.

[36] See Ronald A. Cass, "Copyright, Licensing, and the 'First Screen,'" 5 *Michigan Telecommunications and Technology Law Review* 35 (Issue No. 2, 1999). See also *United States v. Microsoft Corp.*, No. 98-1232 (D.D.C. 1998) and New York ex rel. *Vacco v. Microsoft Corp.*, No. 98-1233 (D.D.C. 1998), direct testimony of Richard L. Schmalensee, January 3, 1999, Paragraph 357, available at http://www.microsoft.com/presspass/trial-mswitness/schmal/schmal.htm (hereafter Schmalensee Direct).

[37] See Cass, *supra* note 36, pp. 57-59.

[38] Although subscribers can rely strictly on AOL's software to access AOL features through the dial-in network or to access and browse the Internet, the AOL software allows flexibility in both access to and use of the Internet. The current version of AOL's software allows subscribers with other Internet connections to access AOL without using the AOL dial-in network. In addition, subscribers who access the Internet through AOL can use browsers other than that provided with the AOL software and can even use AOL keywords to download copies of Netscape's browser.

[39] The government argues that AOL decided to contract with Microsoft because Microsoft offered AOL "preferential treatment" in its visibility on the Windows desktop. Microsoft did offer to distribute AOL's software with Windows and to make the software accessible to the user through a folder on the Windows desktop. Evidence in the record, however, suggests that the basis for the choice of Microsoft over Netscape principally was the former's provision of a "componentized" browser that allowed greater flexibility to AOL. See Schmalensee Direct, *supra* note 36, Paragraphs 285, 405-407, 412.

[40] *Ibid.*, Paragraph 203. See also Harold Demsetz, "*Why Regulate Utilities?*," 11 *Journal of Law and Economics* 55 (1968) (under appropriate conditions – specifically, all production inputs available to bidders at prices determined in the market and no collusion among bidders – competitive bidding in natural monopoly setting results in competitive prices); Richard A. Posner, "*The Appropriate Scope of Regulation in the Cable Television Industry*," 3 *Bell Journal of Economics* 98, 115 (1972) (critiquing overregulation of bidding for cable franchises: "As long as there [is] more than one bidder and collusion among bidders [is] prevented – conditions that ought not to be insuperably difficult to secure – the process of bidding subscriber rates down and quality of service up would eliminate monopoly pricing and profits.").

[41] Salop and Romaine, *supra* note 2, p. 638, n.58.

[42] For similar arguments, see Thomas G. Krattenmaker and Steven C. Salop, "*Anticompetitive Exclusion: Raising Rivals' Costs to Achieve Power Over Price*," 96 *Yale Law Journal* 209, 223-230 (1986); Thomas G. Krattenmaker and Steven C. Salop, "*Analyzing Anticompetitive Exclusion*," 56 *Antitrust Law Journal* 71 (1987).

[43] S&R would not make this the sole determinant of liability, as a firm engaged in conduct with anticompetitive effects could avoid liability under their test if its conduct were shown to generate greater benefits for consumers than harm. See Salop and Romaine, *supra* note 2, pp. 659-665. We address their proposed legal standard later in this article, but we object at the outset to casting the net of possible anticompetitive effects as broadly as the S&R approach does.

[44] See discussion, *supra* note 23, and accompanying text.

[45] Of course, this is only true looking at the matter after the fact, after the contract is signed. It does not reflect the OEMs' calculation when considering the contract before the fact.

[46] See Salop and Romaine, *supra* note 2, pp. 627-629, 638-639.

[47] This concern apparently influenced some FTC staff participating in the investigation of Microsoft. See *supra* notes 22 and 23.

[48] See Complaint, *Caldera, Inc. v. Microsoft Corp.*, 181 F.R.D. 506 (D. Utah 1998) (No. 96-CV-645-B).

[49] Caldera purchased Novell's DR DOS assets in July 1996. Its litigation against Microsoft was filed on the day it completed the purchase. See Caldera, Inc., *Software Developer Caldera Sues Microsoft for Antitrust Practices*, Jul. 24, 1996 (press release).

[50] Salop and Romaine, *supra* note 2, p. 623.

[51] *Ibid.*, p. 623.

[52] *Ibid.*, pp. 624-645.

[53] *Ibid.*, pp. 621-622.

[54] See Michael Cusumano and David Yoffie, *Competing on Internet Time* (1998), p. 99; Schmalensee Direct, *supra* note 36, Paragraphs 248, 270-282.

[55] We believe this is an accurate characterization of S&R's argument. S&R do not, however, analyze Microsoft's position carefully. They do not find that PC operating systems is the relevant antitrust market; instead, they assume that it is, just as they assume that Microsoft has monopoly power, declaring that it "is not implausible that Microsoft has monopoly power in a market for operating systems." Salop and Romaine, *supra* note 2, p. 620.

[56] Estimates of past browser share vary, but all estimates give Netscape the lead for a considerable time, certainly including all of 1995-97. If the AOL browser (which is based on Internet Explorer) is included with Internet Explorer use, then Internet Explorer became the leading browser in 1998. If the AOL browser is classified as a separate browser, Netscape would still be the leading browser through 1998 and into 1999, with a share of overall use estimated at approximately 40 percent. Estimates of a browser share as high as 80 percent for Netscape in 1996, however, appear exaggerated and based on data that fail to count many users who accessed the Internet using a browser provided by AOL or other online services. See Schmalensee Direct, *supra* note 36, App. D (Estimates of Use of Browsing Software), Paragraphs 3, 44, 47-52.

[57] See Schmalensee Direct, *supra* note 36, Paragraphs 207-214.

[58] Although S&R treat browsers as a separate market from operating systems, they expressly abjure reliance on that, stating that "whether the browser is treated as part of the operating system or as a separate market is not crucial to our analysis." Salop and Romaine, *supra* note 2, p. 620.

[59] See Schmalensee Direct, *supra* note 36, Paragraphs 289-290.

[60] That is true regardless of the identity of the competitor(s) losing share to the new entrant, despite S&R's focus on the fortunes of Netscape's browser. See Salop and Romaine, *supra* note 2, pp. 636-642. In the case of Internet Explorer, moreover, survey data suggest that its gain in relative share of browser use primarily came through success against competitors other than Netscape, and especially from consumers using Internet Explorer in preference to AOL's Booklink Web browser. Indeed, Dean Schmalensee's review of the survey data concluded that roughly 85 to 90 percent of the relative increase in Internet

Explorer's use between the fall of 1996 and early 1998 resulted from consumers choosing Internet Explorer over those *other* browsers and less than 15 percent from a relative decline in use of Netscape. See Schmalensee Direct, *supra* note 36, Paragraphs 289-290.

[61] That much is not disputed, though the sides in the DOJ–Microsoft case debate how much of the increase for Internet Explorer came at Netscape's expense. See *supra* note 60.

[62] See Stanley J. Liebowitz and Stephen Margolis, *Winners, Losers and Microsoft: Competition and Antitrust in High Technology*, chapter 8 (Independent Institute), 1999.

[63] Many of these factors, however, also are targeted by S&R as possible antitrust violations. Product improvement, such as that attained through improved integration of desirable features, can be exclusionary conduct under the S&R analysis. Although they would offset consumer benefits from such conduct (at least some consumer benefits), they are unwilling to exempt from antitrust penalties conduct that enhances consumer enjoyment of a product, improves its operation, or creates other forms of efficiency. See Salop and Romaine, *supra* note 2, pp. 643-645.

[64] Dean Schmalensee has taken the position, earlier advanced by Professor Fisher, that market definition is as apt to be misleading as instructive in many cases. *See United States v. Microsoft Corp.*, No. 98-1232 (D.D.C. 1998) and New York ex rel. *Vacco v. Microsoft Corp.*, No. 98-1233 (D.D.C. 1998), cross-examination testimony of Richard L. Schmalensee, Jan. 13, 1999, p.m. Session, transcript, pp. 25-26, available at http://www.microsoft.com/presspass/trial/transcripts/jan99/01-13-pm.asp. For that reason, he has spoken of a "competitive arena" rather than a "market" for platforms. We do not believe that there is any important difference in this terminology and will use the terms interchangeably.

[65] See discussion, *supra* note 30.

[66] See *United States v. Microsoft Corp.*, No. 98-1232 (D.D.C. 1998) and New York ex rel. *Vacco v. Microsoft Corp.*, No. 98-1233 (D.D.C. 1998), cross-examination testimony of Franklin M. Fisher, Jun. 3, 1999, a.m. Session, transcript, pp. 33-34, available at http://www.microsoft.com/presspass/trial/transcripts/jun99/06-03-pm.asp (hereafter Fisher Cross).

[67] See *United States v. Microsoft Corp.*, No. 98-1232 (D.D.C. 1998) and New York ex rel. *Vacco v. Microsoft Corp.*, No. 98-1233 (D.D.C. 1998), testimony of Franklin M. Fisher, Jan. 5, 1999, Paragraphs 124-126, available at http://www.usdoj.gov/atr/cases/f2000/2057.htm (hereafter Fisher Direct).

[68] See, e.g., Kenneth J. Arrow, *Social Choice and Individual Value* (rev. ed., John Wiley), 1963, pp. 186-194; Allan Feldman, *Welfare Economics and Social Choice Theory* (Nijhoff), 1980, pp. 186-194; Frank H. Easterbrook, "Ways of Criticizing the Court," 95 *Harvard Law Review* 802 (1982); Eugene F. Fama and Michael C. Jensen, "Separation of Ownership and Control," 26 *Journal of Law and Economics* 301 (1983); Kenneth Shepsle, "Congress is a They, Not an It: Legislative Intent as Oxymoron," 12 *International Review of Law and Economics* 239 (1991).

[69] See Fisher et al., *supra* note 1, p. 272.

[70] Salop and Romaine, *supra* note 2, p. 660, n.121.

[71] *Ibid.*, p. 660.

[72] See discussion *infra* notes 135-144 and accompanying text.

[73] See authorities cited in note 18.

[74] See, e.g., Areeda and Turner, *supra* note 17; Joseph F. Brodley and George Hay, "Predatory Pricing: Competing Economic Theories and the Evolution of Legal Standards," 66 *Cornell Law Review* 738 (1981); Avinash Dixit, "Entry and Exit Decisions Under Uncertainty," 97 *Journal of Political Economy* pp. 620, 620-638 (1989); Easterbrook, "Predatory Strategies," *supra* note 17; Paul Joskow and Alvin Klevorick, "A Framework for Analyzing Predatory Pricing Policy," 89 *Yale Law Journa*l 213 (1979); McGee, *supra* note 17; Paul Milgrom and John Roberts, "Predation, Reputation, and Entry Deterrence," 27 *Journal of Economic Theory* 280 (1982); Paul Milgrom and John Roberts, "Limit Pricing and Entry Under Incomplete Information: An Equilibrium Analysis," 50 *Econometrica* 443 (1982); Janusz Ordover and Garth Saloner, "Predation, Monopolization, and Antitrust," in *The Handbook of Industrial Organization*, vol. 1, pp. 537-596 (Richard Schmalensee and Robert D. Willig, eds., North-Holland), 1989; Garth Saloner, "Predation, Mergers, and Incomplete Information," 18 *Rand Journal of Economics* 165 (1987).

[75] Salop and Romaine, *supra* note 2, p. 641 (emphasis added).

[76] *Ibid.*, p. 642.

[77] See, e.g., Thomas C. Schelling, *The Strategy of Conflict* (Harvard University Press), 1960, pp. 119-161, 230-254 . Our point here is not that mutually assured destruction was the best strategy, only that it raises a critical analytical issue.

[78] Salop and Romaine, *supra* note 2, p. 641. See also Easterbrook, "*Predatory Strategies*," *supra* note 17.

[79] In noting as a possible explanation for predatory pricing the predator's interest in gaining a reputation as a predator, S&R might intend to offer an explanation divorced from the predator's expectation of recoupment. Although the concept is controversial, Judge Posner has explained why a strategy of predation without recoupment is plausible in peculiar circumstances. See Posner, *supra* note 14, pp. 185-186. The Microsoft example, however, does not come close to the circumstances Judge Posner describes. Microsoft competes in markets that are not nearly so closed to competition as would be necessary to make a plausible case for predation for reputation's sake alone.

[80] Fisher Direct, *supra* note 67, Paragraph 122.

[81] *Ibid.*, Paragraphs 123-124.

[82] See *United States v. Microsoft Corp.*, No. 98-1232 (D.D.C. 1998) and New York ex rel. *Vacco v. Microsoft Corp.*, No. 98-1233 (D.D.C. 1998), redirect testimony of Franklin M. Fisher, Jan. 12, 1999, a.m. Session, transcript, p. 38, available at http://www.microsoft.com/presspass/trial/transcripts/jan99/01-12-am.asp (hereafter Fisher Redirect).

[83] This could be true even if the browser were distributed at a "negative" price. See *supra* note 31.

[84] Schmalensee Direct, *supra* note 36, Paragraphs 556, 563; *United States v. Microsoft Corp.*, No. 98-1232 (D.D.C. 1998) and New York *ex rel. Vacco v. Microsoft Corp.*, No. 98-1233 (D.D.C. 1998), direct examination testimony of Richard L. Schmalensee, Jun. 21, 1999, p.m. Session, transcript, pp. 56-60, available at http://www.microsoft.com/presspass/trial/transcripts/jun99/06-21-pm.asp; Defense Exhibit 2763, *United States v. Microsoft Corp.*, No. 98-1232 (D.D.C. 1998) and New York ex rel. *Vacco v. Microsoft Corp.*, No. 98-1233 (D.D.C. 1998), available at http://www.microsoft.com/presspass/trial/exhibits/jun99/2763/sld001.asp.

[85] Schmalensee Direct, *supra* note 36, Paragraphs 577-562. Microsoft's construction of

Internet Explorer as part of its operating system is consistent not only with past behavior by Microsoft but also with industry norms. Nearly all (perhaps all) commercially available desktop operating systems incorporate browsing functions, including Apple's MacOS, IBM's OS/2, Sun's Solaris, Be's BeOS, and the Caldera and Red Hat versions of the Linux operating system. At least one firm, IBM, integrated browsing functions with its operating system prior to Microsoft's release of Windows 95. And all of these firms integrated browsing functions without separate charges.

[86] *United States v. Microsoft Corp.*, No. 98-1232 (D.D.C. 1998) and New York *ex rel. Vacco v. Microsoft Corp.*, No. 98-1233 (D.D.C. 1998), direct examination testimony of Franklin M. Fisher, Jun. 1, 1999, a.m. Session, transcript, p. 70, available at http://www.microsoft.com/presspass/trial/transcripts/jun99/06-01-am.asp.

[87] *Ibid.*, pp. 38-39.

[88] See, e.g., Posner, *supra* note 14, p. 189 (pricing below short-run marginal cost is predatory; pricing below long-run marginal cost is predatory only if coupled with anticompetitive intent); Areeda and Turner, *supra* note 17.

[89] In the case of an industry in which there are substantial scale economies, short-run marginal cost is greater than long-run marginal cost for levels of output below the long-run minimum-cost scale. A firm that takes a long-term view has an incentive in this setting to set its price below short-run marginal cost. With respect to "immature" products or industries, predatory pricing doctrine has recognized the difficulties in this area by creating exceptions for firms that use promotional discounts in order to establish themselves in a competitive market. See, e.g., *A.A. Poultry Farms, Inc. v. Rose Acre Farms, Inc.*, 881 F.2d 1396, 1400 (7th Cir. 1989) (on promotional discounts, *citing Buffalo Courier-Express, Inc. v. Buffalo Evening News, Inc.*, 601 F.2d 48 [2d Cir. 1979]).

[90] Professor Fisher himself had difficulty answering questions that are critical to this inquiry, and he declined to offer an opinion on a key variable in making this calculation (price elasticity of demand). Notably, the colloquy on this issue occurred in a context that should make the calculation much more straightforward than typically would be the case, as Fisher was asked only to find the theoretical short-run profit-maximizing price for Windows on the assumption that Microsoft enjoyed a monopoly in the market defined by the government. See Fisher Cross, *supra* note 66, pp. 40-42. For this purpose, a monopolist can be assumed to face the industry demand curve, avoiding a need for firm-specific demand information.

[91] Indeed, several empirical studies of pricing find that managers typically use cost-based rules of thumb largely as a way of coping with uncertainties in the estimation of demand. See Frederick M. Scherer and David Ross, *Industrial Market Structure and Economic Performance* (Houghton-Mifflin Co.), 3d ed., 1990, p. 262 (reviewing empirical studies of price setting). Presumably firms use rules of thumb because it is too costly to obtain accurate estimates of the demand functions for their products before setting price.

[92] See Fisher Cross, *supra* note 66, p. 13 (answering that, due to the complexities involved, Fisher does not believe that an econometric model can be constructed to estimate the amount by which Microsoft's conduct has raised rivals' costs). See also Joseph Nocera, "*The Big Blue Diaries*," *Fortune*, July 5, 1999, pp. 132, 134 ("[Professor Fisher's] testimony is almost entirely lacking in hard figures.").

[93] Fisher Redirect, *supra* note 82, pp. 21-22.

[94] As distinct from the market for PC operating systems.

[95] See *infra* notes 145-154 and accompanying text.

[96] The argument in fact is not that Microsoft will recoup losses on Internet Explorer through higher future charges, but that losses on Internet Explorer allow Microsoft to continue to charge a monopoly price for Windows today. *See United States v. Microsoft Corp.*, No. 98-1232 (D.D.C. 1998) and New York *ex rel. Vacco v. Microsoft Corp.*, No. 98-1233 (D.D.C. 1998), cross-examination testimony of Franklin M. Fisher, Jan. 7, 1999, a.m. Session, transcript, pp. 13-15, available at http://www.microsoft.com/presspass/trial/transcripts/jan99/01-07-am.asp; direct examination testimony of Franklin M. Fisher, Jun. 2, 1999, a.m. Session, transcript, p. 27, available at http://www.microsoft.com/presspass/trial/transcripts/jun99/06-02-am.asp. We know of no case that adopts such a quasi-predation, quasi-tying approach to predatory pricing. Indeed, the concept of "recoupment" is an odd fit with other testimony of Professor Fisher about the price at which Microsoft sells its Windows operating system. See Fisher Cross, *supra* note 66, pp. 30-43, 53-54.

[97] Salop and Romaine, *supra* note 2, pp. 647-648.

[98] *Ibid.*, p. 649.

[99] *United States v. Grinnell Corp.*, 384 U.S. 563, 570-71 (1966).

[100] Salop and Romaine, *supra* note 2, p. 649.

[101] *Ibid.*, pp. 649-650.

[102] *Ibid.*, p. 650. S&R credit Professors Ordover and Willig for this test. See Janusz A. Ordover and Robert D. Willig, "*Access Bundling in High-Technology Markets*," in *Competition, Innovation and the Microsoft Monopoly: Antitrust in the Digital Marketplace* (Jeffrey A. Eisenach and Thomas M. Lenard, eds., 1999).

[103] See *United States v. Aluminum Co. of America*, 148 F.2d 416 (2d Cir. 1945).

[104] See Salop and Romaine, *supra* note 2, p. 650 (referring to *Aspen Skiing Co. v. Aspen Highlands Skiing Corp.*, 472 U.S. 585 [1985]).

[105] *Ibid.*, p. 650.

[106] See *United States v. Microsoft Corp.*, 147 F.3d 935 (D.C. Cir. 1998).

[107] As a concrete example of the type of case for which the *unnecessarily restrictive conduct* test is appropriate, S&R offer the following hypothetical:

> [S]uppose the efficiency benefit involves improved performance of the product. Suppose that it were known that the improved product performance has a value to users of $5. To make the example extreme in order to illustrate the differences among alternative antitrust approaches, suppose further that the higher barriers to competition [resulting from the product improvement] were known to allow the monopolist to charge an additional $50.
> (Salop and Romaine, *supra* note 2, p. 646.)

This example immediately raises questions that S&R never address. For example, if a firm improves its product in a way that adds $5 to consumer benefits, and then raises the product price by $50, why wouldn't consumers simply stay with the old version of the product, given that the old version gives them a greater consumer surplus (specifically, $45 more surplus)? Is it reasonable to assume that consumers are so closely tied to the dominant firm's product that they will switch to the new version under these conditions? If the dominant firm behaves in this manner, why wouldn't a competitor offer a substitute product that gives consumers more surplus?

[108] See Oliver Wendell Holmes, Jr., "*The Path of the Law*," 10 *Harvard Law Review* 457, 461 (1897).

[109] *Matsushita Elec. Indus. Co. v. Zenith Radio Corp.*, 475 U.S. 574 (1986).

[110] *Brooke Group Ltd. v. Brown & Williamson Tobacco Corp.*, 509 U.S. 209 (1993).

[111] *Barry Wright Corp. v. ITT Grinnell Corp.*, 724 F.2d 227 (1st Cir. 1983).

[112] *A.A. Poultry Farms, Inc. v. Rose Acre Farms, Inc.*, 881 F.2d 1396 (7th Cir. 1989).

[113] Salop and Romaine, *supra* note 2, p. 650.

[114] See, e.g., *Olympia Equip. Leasing Co. v. Western Union Tel. Co.*, 797 F.2d 370, 379 (7th Cir. 1986) ("If [*Aspen Ski*] stands for any principle that goes beyond its unusual facts, it is that a monopolist may be guilty of monopolization if it refuses to cooperate with a competitor in circumstances where some cooperation is indispensable to effective competition.").

[115] *Lorain Journal Co. v. United States*, 342 U.S. 143 (1951).

[116] *United States v. Syufy Enter.*, 903 F.2d 659 (9th Cir. 1990).

[117] *Ibid.*, pp. 667-668.

[118] See, e.g., *Olympia Equip. Leasing Co. v. Western Union Tel. Co.*, 797 F.2d 370, 375 (7th Cir. 1986) ("Opinion about the offense of monopolization has undergone an evolution. Forty years ago it was thought that even a firm with a lawful monopoly ... could not be allowed to defend its monopoly against would-be competitors by tactics otherwise legitimate; it had to exercise special restraint – perhaps, indeed, had to hold its prices high, to encourage new entry. So Alcoa was condemned as a monopolist because it had assiduously created enough productive capacity to supply all new increments of demand for aluminum. ... Later, as the emphasis of antitrust policy shifted from the protection of competition as a process of rivalry to the protection of competition as a means of promoting economic efficiency it became recognized that the lawful monopolist should be free to compete like everyone else; otherwise the antitrust laws would be holding an umbrella over inefficient competitors.") (citations omitted). See also Ernest L. Gellhorn and William E. Kovacic, *Antitrust Law and Economics* (West Pub. Co., 4th ed.), 1994, p. 130 ("In general, the path of Section 2 jurisprudence since *Alcoa* has led toward allowing dominant firms greater discretion to choose and implement competitive strategies, even if specific tactics vanquish individual rivals."); E. Thomas Sullivan and Jeffrey L. Harrison, *Understanding Antitrust and Its Economic Implications* (Matthew Bender, 3d ed.), 1998, p. 300 ("Whether Alcoa, at least as far as the excess capacity issue is concerned, would be decided the same way today is open to serious question.").

[119] See, e.g., William J. Baumol et al., *Contestable Markets and the Theory of Industry Structure* (Harcourt, Brace, Jovanovich, rev. ed.), 1988, p. 201.

[120] See, e.g., *Barry Wright Corp. v. ITT Grinnell Corp.*, 724 F.2d 227, 231-32 (1st Cir. 1983).

[121] See, e.g., George J. Stigler, "*A Theory of Oligopoly*," 72 *Journal of Political Economy* 44 (1964).

[122] See, e.g., *The Causes and Consequences of Antitrust: The Public Choice Perspective* (Fred S. McChesney and William F. Shugart II, eds., Univ. of Chicago Press) 1995, pp. 180-181 (discussing incentives of weak competitors to use antitrust laws). See also William J. Baumol and Janusz A. Ordover, "*Use of Antitrust to Subvert Competition*," 28 *Journal of Law and Economics* 247 (1985). These incentive effects exist even if lobbying alone is insufficient to secure government cooperation in the litigation. See Page, *supra* note 21.

[123] *Matsushita Elec. Indus. Co. v. Zenith Radio Corp.*, 475 U.S. 574, 591 (1986).

[124] See, e.g., Bork, *supra* note 14, pp. 56-61, 81-89 (demonstrating that the language of the antitrust statutes point to consumer welfare as the sole criterion and enumerating the

advantages of a single-goal antitrust law); Posner, *supra* note 14, pp. 101-113 (criticizing horizontal merger cases for deviating from accepted principles of protecting competition). But see Robert H. Lande, "*Wealth Transfers as the Original and Primary Concern of Antitrust: The Efficiency Interpretation Challenged*," 34 *Hastings Law Journal* 65 (1982) ("Congress intended to subordinate all other concerns to the basic purpose of preventing firms with market power from directly harming consumers.").

[125] See, e.g., Posner, *supra* note 14, pp. 214-216 (discussing perverse consequences of restraining competitive acts of dominant firm).

[126] See, e.g., Baumol et al., *supra* note 119, pp. 191-242 (discussing general theory of equilibrium with entry); Fisher et al., *supra* note 1, pp. 24-25 ("Firms in a competitive market cannot choose to use inefficient methods of production and survive.").

[127] See, e.g., Ronald A. Cass and Michael S. Knoll, "*The Economics of 'Injury' in Antidumping and Countervailing Duty Cases: A Reply to Professor Sykes*," in *Economic Dimensions in International Law: Comparative and Empirical Perspectives* (Jagdeep S. Bhandari and Alan O. Sykes, eds.), 1997, pp. 126-165; McChesney and Shugart, eds., *supra* note 122 (exploring the theory that antitrust could be protecting small, ineffective firms).

[128] See, e.g., *Barry Wright Corp. v. ITT Grinnell Corp.*, 724 F.2d 227, 235-36 (1st Cir. 1983).

[129] See, e.g., *United States v. Trans-Missouri Freight Assn.*, 166 U.S. 290, 331-32 (1897).

[130] See, e.g., Donald F. Turner, "*The Definition of Agreement Under the Sherman Act: Conscious Parallelism and Refusals to Deal*," 75 *Harvard Law Review* 655, 669 (1962) (rejecting public-utility interpretation of the Sherman Act).

[131] See, e.g., Richard A. Epstein, *Simple Rules for a Complex World* (1995) pp. 6-7; Antonin Scalia, "*The Rule of Law as a Law of Rules*," 56 *University of Chicago Law Review* 1175 (1989).

[132] See, e.g., W. Page Keeton et al., *Prosser & Keeton on the Law of Torts*, Section 33, pp. 193-196 (5th ed. 1984).

[133] *Ibid.*, pp. 186-187.

[134] *Ibid.*, pp. 187-188.

[135] Salop and Romaine, *supra* note 2, p. 660.

[136] *Ibid.*, p. 660, n.121.

[137] See discussion *supra* notes 66-72 and accompanying text.

[138] See, e.g., *A.A. Poultry Farms, Inc. v. Rose Acre Farms, Inc.*, 881 F.2d 1396, 1396 (7th Cir. 1989); Fisher et al., *supra* note 1, p. 17.

[139] *Aspen Skiing Co. v. Aspen Highlands Skiing Corp.*, 472 U.S. 585, 608-09 (1885); *Lorain Journal Co. v. United States*, 342 U.S. 143, 154-55 (1951).

[140] See *Aspen Skiing*, 472 U.S., pp. 608-610; *Lorain Journal*, 342 U.S., pp. 154-155.

[141] See discussion *supra* notes 66-72 and accompanying text.

[142] Salop and Romaine, *supra* note 2, p. 653.

[143] See, e.g., *Brooke Group Ltd. v. Brown & Williamson Tobacco Corp.*, 509 U.S. 209, 231-32 (1993); *Barry Wright Corp. v. ITT Grinnell Corp.*, 724 F.2d 227, 231-32 (1st Cir. 1983); *Rose-Acre Farms*, 881 F.2d at 1400-02.

[144] See, e.g., *Barry Wright*, 724 F.2d at 232; *Rose-Acre Farms*, 881 F.2d at 1400-02.

[145] Salop and Romaine, *supra* note 2, p. 663.

[146] This is an implication of basic investment theory; see, e.g., Richard Brealey and Stewart

Myers, *Principles of Corporate Finance* (McGraw-Hill, 2d ed.), 1984, pp. 180-181 (discussing investment on the basis of present value, with adjustment of risk).

[147] See, e.g., William J. Baumol, *Economic Theory and Operations Analysis* (4th ed.), 1977, pp. 648-649.

[148] James L. Pierce, *The Future of Banking* (1991), pp. 63-66 (discussing incentives of banks to lend in risky markets).

[149] *Ibid.*, pp. 73-74 (discussing record of bank lending in risky markets, and subsequent crises, including the savings-and-loan debacle).

[150] One setting in which a firm has an excessive tendency to invest in risky projects is the case in which the firm expects to go into bankruptcy if the project fails, or under other conditions in which the firm will be excused from having to pay for the failed project. For example, a borrower who does not intend to repay his or her loan will have an incentive to choose the riskiest project available, because he or she has to think only about the upside risk. This incentive explains the tendency of lenders to ration credit in settings where they cannot distinguish high- from low-risk borrowers. For an excellent discussion of this incentive problem, see Debraj Ray, *Development Economics* (1998), p. 554. Of course, in ordinary settings, one also could make the opposite argument, that managers, in order to protect their firm-specific human capital investments, have an incentive to choose the safest projects, perhaps unduly safe projects. The stories of both excessively risky investment and excessively safe investment draw on plausible agency-cost explanations.

[151] Salop and Romaine, *supra* note 2, p. 655.

[152] See, e.g., Kenneth W. Dam, "The Economic Underpinnings of Patent Law," 23 *Journal of Legal Studies* 247, 249-50 (1994); William M. Landes and Richard A. Posner, "An Economic Analysis of Copyright Law," 18 *Journal of Legal Studies* 325 (1989).

[153] See, e.g., *Sony Corp. of Am. v. Universal City Studios*, 464 U.S. 417, 429 (1984) (explaining that the grants of monopoly privileges by Congress are for public purposes, not individual gain); *Mazer v. Stein*, 347 U.S. 201, 219 (1954) (stating that the principle behind the copyright power is to encourage "individual effort by personal gain"); Edmund W. Kitch, "*The Nature and Function of the Patent System*," 20 *Journal of Law and Economics* 265 (1977) (presenting "prospect theory," which emphasizes incentive of patent holder to enhance the quality of an invention). See also Mark F. Grady and Jay I. Alexander, "*Patent Law and Rent Dissipation*," 78 *Virginia Law Review* 305 (1992); Jack Hirshleifer, "*The Private and Social Value of Information and the Reward to Inventive Activity*," 61 *American Economic Review* 561 (1971).

[154] See, e.g., Stephen J. Breyer, "The Uneasy Case for Copyright: A Study of Copyright in Books, Photocopies, and Computer Programs," 84 *Harvard Law Review* 281 (1970); Richard Gilbert and Carl Shapiro, "Optimal Patent Length and Breadth," 21 *Rand Journal of Economics* 106 (1990); Wendy J. Gordon, "An Inquiry into the Merits of Copyright: The Challenges of Consistency, Consent, and Encouragement Theory," 41 *Stanford Law Review* 1343 (1989); Grady and Alexander, *supra* note 153; Paul Klemperer, "How Broad Should the Scope of Patent Protection Be?," 21 *Rand Journal of Economics* 113 (1990); Robert P. Merges and Richard R. Nelson, "Market Structure and Technical Advance: The Role of Patent Scope Decisions," in *Antitrust, Innovation, and Competitiveness* (Thomas M. Jorde and David J. Teece, eds.), 1992, p. 185. See generally William D. Nordhaus, *Invention, Growth, and Welfare: a Theoretical Treatment of Technological Change* (1969).

[155] Mark Twain, *Life on the Mississippi* (Harper & Row 1917) (1883), p. 156. We owe Glen Robinson for reminding us of this story.

Section 2: Antitrust Policy and the New Economy

Essay 12

The Returns to Investments in Innovative Activities: An Overview and an Analysis of the Software Industry

by Josh Lerner

For antitrust enforcers, one of the classic signs of market power – and likely consumer harm – is high and sustained profits. "Supernormal" profits imply that barriers to entry have prevented competition from driving down the rate of return to just the opportunity cost of capital. Microsoft, arguably the most successful corporation of the last two decades, seems to fit this criterion well: Earnings per share have increased 24-fold between 1990 and 2000, and the return on stockholder equity in the latter year exceeded 20 percent. But two factors specific to so-called New Economy industries alter this calculus. First, much of the profit may be a return to intellectual capital, which may not show up on the corporate balance sheet. Second, and more relevant here, investments in firms before they were successful were enormously risky.

Here, Josh Lerner of the Harvard Business School examines the returns to high-risk New Economy startups. While the rates of return on large portfolios of such investments have been reasonably high, the distribution of returns has been heavily skewed: A small percentage of enterprises account for virtually all of the portfolios' gains in market value, revenues, and employment. Moreover, the risk in investing in startups apparently can't be substantially reduced by means of sophisticated analysis. Professional venture capitalists also experienced many disappointing investments.

Thus, from the policymaker's perspective, the potential consequences of regulating the returns of the winners (through price regulation or antitrust enforcement) can be quite dramatic.

Lerner illustrates this with two case studies: Comsat (the first successful communications satellite enterprise), and Genzyme (a maker of biotechnology-derived pharmaceuticals). In both cases, the government intervened, or threatened to intervene, after the fact to limit the company's profits. And in both cases, the market reacted by subsequently reducing the industry's access to risk capital.

"Because it is often impossible to predict which innovations will succeed," Lerner concludes, "investors need to be assured that they will receive substantial returns from successful investments to offset the unsatisfactory returns from the many failed or less successful projects." Lerner's bottom line: "If investors believe that they will be denied these returns by regulators, their willingness to fund the development of the next generation of innovative technologies will be greatly reduced." — *D.S.E.*

INTRODUCTION

This paper considers the structure of returns to investments in innovative activities, and its implications for public policy. The paper highlights, through both statistical and case-study analyses, the importance of allowing attractive returns to the financiers of successful innovations. The failure to do so can have a chilling effect on the willingness of private investors to fund the development of subsequent generations of innovative technologies.

This paper is divided into three parts. The first section considers the theoretical literature on the economics of technological change. It highlights two propositions. First, the returns to innovative projects are likely to be highly skewed. Second, a variety of factors make it difficult for investors to select firms that are likely to be successful in advance.

The second section considers the empirical evidence. It shows that, measured in a variety of ways, a small number of projects generate the bulk of the returns. This is true whether licensing revenues to universities, financial returns to venture capitalists, rewards to investors in initial public offerings, implicit patent valuations, or overall firm growth is used as a yardstick. The section reviews earlier studies examining a variety of industries, and then undertakes an original analysis demonstrating that these patterns hold for the software industry.

The third section considers the implications for public policy. The highly skewed distribution of returns and the great difficulty of determining in advance which projects will succeed have stark implications: Regulation limiting the return of even a few of the most successful projects is likely to deter further investments in risky projects. Without the assurance that they can realize a high return from their most successful investments, rational investors are unlikely to be willing to incur the losses associated with the many failures.

The fourth section illustrates these conclusions with two case studies, cases in which regulators limited the return of successful innovators. In both cases, the regulation had a chilling impact on subsequent investment. Although it is problematic to generalize from case studies, these episodes certainly raise concerns about the impact that regulatory intervention can have in high-technology industries such as software.

THE DISTRIBUTION OF RETURNS TO INVESTMENTS IN INNOVATIVE ACTIVITIES

Before considering the evidence on returns to investments in innovation, it is important to understand the *reasons* for these investment patterns. Why do investors in innovative activities – for example, corporations choosing among internal projects or venture capitalists screening business plans – select so many poor investments for every truly successful one funded?

I consider this question in two parts. This section first offers reasons why the returns to high-technology innovations are highly skewed. Second, it considers why selecting successful innovative projects in advance is difficult. I describe the factors that make it difficult for investors to identify the projects that will ultimately generate the bulk of the returns.

Why Are the Returns to High-Technology Projects Skewed?

Since the late 1970s, economists have developed a rich array of "racing" models to describe technological competition between firms.[1] These simple models depict technological competition between two or more firms. As originally specified by Gilbert and Newbery (1982), the literature considered a setting where innovations were not too large and were certain to be made by the party that spent the most on R&D. The model suggested that, although there might be a number of firms competing initially in an industry, as the industry evolved there would be a separation between successful and successful firms. The leaders would generate all the profits, and the rivals would drop out and receive nothing.

Reinganum challenged some of these assumptions. In her "cannibalization" models (1983, 1984), she considered a setting in which an incumbent monopolist's position is endangered by a potential innovation. The innovation is a radical one – i.e., the discoverer will enjoy a monopoly position. The time of the actual discovery is not known, with the probability of discovery increasing with the amount spent on research and development. The time until the next innovation – and hence the duration of the current leader's monopoly profits – declines with each firm's investment. In this setting, she demonstrates that the incumbent will have less incentive to invest in research than the entrant, who enjoys no profits in the current period. The leader is consequently likely to be surpassed by the follower.

This model, as generalized by Fudenberg et al., and Harris and Vickers, generates predictions of skewed outcomes similar to the Gilbert and Newbery model. Fudenberg et al. consider a race in which there is a lag between the time the follower and leader learn of each other's progress (1983). During each period, a firm may invest and advance one or two spaces. Thus, it is possible for the following firm to leapfrog the leader. As long as the follower has some chance of becoming the leader during the information lag, it will continue to invest in R&D. There will be vigorous competition until the follower trails the leader by more than one space, at which point the follower will drop out of the race. A similar result emerges from Harris and Vickers' more general treatments of R&D races (1985, 1987): Intense competition lasts only as long as the leader is not "too far" ahead. Again in these models, there is likely to be a skewed distribution of outcomes. Intense competition takes place between a few successful firms, while most firms that fall behind will drop out of the technological competition.

Why Can't Investors Identify Successful Innovations in Advance?

It is also important to realize that it is difficult for investors to discover in advance which firms are likely to be the successful ones. The reason lies in the formidable incentive and information problems associated with the financing of innovation. Innovative projects are typically associated early on with a great deal of uncertainty, where wide gaps in information between researchers and investors are commonplace. These projects typically generate substantial intangible assets, which are difficult to value and may be impossible to resell if the project fails. Similarly, market conditions in many of these industries are highly variable. The nature and magnitude of these problems create many opportunities for unsuccessful investment decisions.[2]

The first of these four problems, uncertainty, is a measure of the array of potential outcomes for a company or project. The wider the dispersion of potential outcomes, the greater the uncertainty. By their very nature, efforts to accomplish significant innovations are associated with high levels of uncertainty. In addition to questions about the technical feasibility of the proposed innovation, often the magnitude of the returns to successful projects remains uncertain. The extent of intellectual property protection that a new high-technology product will receive is also often very unclear. High uncertainty means that investors and researchers cannot confidently predict what the returns to the project will be.

Uncertainty affects the willingness of investors to contribute capital and the inclination of suppliers to extend credit, as well as the decisions of researchers and their managers. If the researchers and managers are averse to taking risks, it may be difficult to induce them to make the right decisions. Conversely, if they are overly optimistic, they may spend on projects that have little chance of success, and consequently generate negative returns.

The second factor, asymmetric information, is distinct from uncertainty. Because of his day-to-day involvement, the researcher knows more about a project's prospects than investors, suppliers, or strategic partners. Various problems arise in settings where such asymmetry prevails. For example, the researcher may take detrimental actions that investors cannot observe, undertaking a riskier strategy than initially suggested or not working as hard as the investor expects. The entrepreneur might also invest in projects that build his reputation at the investors' expense.

Asymmetric information can also lead to selection problems. The scientist who makes a potentially important discovery may exploit the fact that she knows more about the project – or her own abilities – than her investors do. Investors may find it difficult to distinguish between truly revolutionary technologies and impractical ones. Without the ability to screen out unacceptable projects, investors are unable to make efficient and appropriate decisions.

The third factor is the nature of the assets created by research and development. Firms that have tangible assets – e.g., machines, buildings, land, or physical inventory – may find financing easier to obtain or may be able to obtain more favorable terms. The ability to abscond with the firm's source of value is more difficult when it relies on physical assets. But when the most important assets are intangible, raising outside financing from traditional sources may be more challenging. For many innovative projects, the primary assets are patents, trade secrets, or informal "know-how." In this setting, it is often difficult to attract investors, because there can be little assurance that returns will accrue to the investors.

Market conditions also play a key role in determining the difficulty of financing innovation. Product markets may be subject to substantial fluctuations. By the same token, the supply of capital from public investors and its cost may vary dramatically. These variations may be a response to regulatory edicts or shifts in investors' perceptions of future profitability. As a result, investors may find that projects they have financed fail for reasons that are entirely unforeseen and have little to do with the behavior of the firm.

These problems may appear to be quite abstract. But as seen below, they have very real implications for the returns that investors in innovative technologies enjoy.

THE EMPIRICAL EVIDENCE

This section reviews the published empirical evidence on the pattern of returns to innovative activities, as well as presenting original evidence. It first summarizes the patterns from a variety of studies across high-technology industries, and then considers new evidence from the Corporate Technology Information Services database regarding returns in the software industry.

Review of Cross-Industry Studies

A wide variety of studies have examined the returns from investments in innovative activities. Despite the varying measures employed and the different industries under study, the conclusions are remarkably consistent: The returns are highly skewed, with a small subset of projects generating the bulk of the profit.

This section summarizes the evidence from a wide variety of studies that assess the returns to investments in innovative projects across high-technology industries. It does not consider the numerous studies of returns in particular industries. Those results, however, appear to be generally consistent with the cross-industry evidence.[3]

Perhaps the most detailed level at which the returns to investments in innovative projects can be studied is the patent level. (In many cases, firms will take out multiple patents on a single innovation.) Unfortunately, it is frequently difficult to determine the costs of developing a particular patent: Analysts are typically confined to examining the distribution of patent valuations instead.

An extensive literature has sought to infer the distribution of patent values from the propensity of patent holders to renew their awards. In many nations, patent holders must pay renewal fees at fixed intervals in order to continue to receive protection for their ideas. Since the pioneering work of Pakes and Schankerman (1984) and Pakes (1986), researchers have examined these issues using European data: European countries adopted renewal fees earlier than the United States, and these fees have typically been higher. By examining the percentage of patents renewed at each interval, we can infer the overall distribution of patent values.

The most recent and sophisticated treatment of these issues (Lanjouw, 1993) demonstrates that the distribution of patent values is highly skewed. She suggests that the top 10 percent of patents account for a disproportional share of the value of all patents across a variety of industries. In patents related to computer hardware, for example, the most valuable decile of patents accounts for 40.2 percent of their total value. In textile patents, the share of the top decile is 43.1 percent; in engines, 34.7 percent. Thus, if innovators were not allowed to receive the full returns from the most valuable patents, the average value of a patent would drop dramatically. For example, if innovators did not receive any value from the top 5 percent of computer hardware patents, the average value of a patent would fall by more than one-quarter.

An alternative measure of patent value is the royalty income generated from licensing. Unfortunately, only a subset of corporate patents are licensed. These licenses often involve large numbers of patents, making the observation of the returns from particular patents impossible. Furthermore, it might be thought that in many cases the patents that are licensed are not representative of all patents awarded to the corporation. For example, a corporation may be reluctant to license its most valuable patents because it believes that it will not be fairly compensated (because of the information problems discussed above).

Scherer, Harhoff, and Kukies (1998) address this problem by examining the distribution of licensing revenues generated by universities. Universities are likely to license all valuable patents, because they are unlikely to undertake commercial development themselves. Using data on 576 licensed patents (or "bundles" of several patents) from seven universities, the authors show that the top 10 percent of patents account for between 84 and 93 percent of the total revenues generated from patent licensing by these institutions.[4]

As discussed above, one of the inherent limitations with studies of patents is that it is very difficult to measure the timing or magnitude of the costs associated with their development. This concern can be addressed by examining the returns from investments in companies specializing in innovative projects.

Studies have focused on the financial returns from two subsets of firms where firm value is highly tied to the pursuit of innovative activities: privately held firms backed by venture capitalists, and initial public offerings (IPOs) of high-technology firms.

Venture capitalists typically specialize in investing in young, privately held firms pursuing innovative activities. More than 80 percent of venture capital investments have been in the information technology and life science fields, where firm value is inextricably linked to product and process innovations (Gompers and Lerner, 1998). A major focus of venture capitalists is screening out proposals that are unlikely to be successful: Field studies suggest that between 100 and 200 proposals are rejected by the typical venture organization for every one funded. Financings are often made conditional on extensive due diligence and the identification of another venture organization that is willing to co-invest.

Despite these efforts, the financial returns to venture capital investments are highly skewed. Huntsman and Hoban (1980) review 110 investments by three venture capital organizations made between 1960 and 1975. The aggregate gross rate of return (i.e., before any deductions for management fees or incentive compensation for the venture capitalists, but after some deduction for fees associated with the transactions) was 18.9 percent. As Figure 1 illustrates, however, the distribution of the returns across particular transactions was highly uneven. Investors suffered complete losses (100 percent) in 17 percent of the sample, and the median return was only 4 percent. Just one-quarter of the sample exceeded the average return of the portfolio. If the nine top performers (8 percent of the sample of 110 firms) are removed, the rate of return of the entire portfolio falls from 18.9 percent to 7.6 percent. If the top 17 performers (15 percent of the sample) are removed, the return of the portfolio is negative.[5]

These results appear to have changed little as the venture capital industry has matured. For example, Horsley (1997) examines a crude measure of the return from 1004 venture capital investments between 1985 and 1992. Rather than calculating an internal rate of return, he simply measures the difference between the cost of each investment and the value at the time that the venture capitalist liquidated the firm or sold or distributed its shares.[6] The total difference between cost and value was \$6.1 billion: The original investment was \$2.8 billion, and the value as calculated was \$8.9 billion. Of this \$6.1 billion, however, the best 76 investments (the top-performing 7.5 percent) accounted for \$3.5 billion, or more than one-half, of the total gains. Although this measure is a cruder one than that employed by Huntsman and Hoban (1980), it

Figure 1. **Annualized Rate of Return of 110 Venture Capital Investments, 1960-1975**

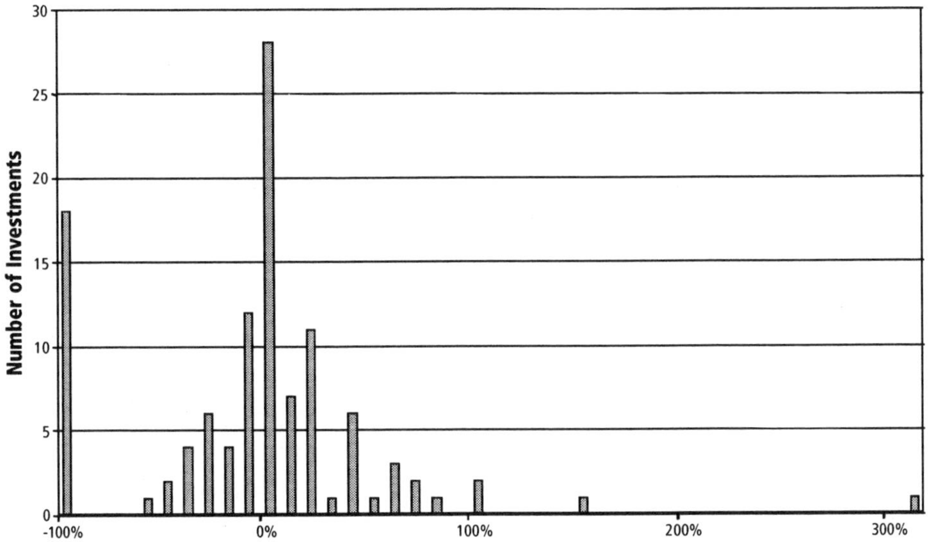

Source: Huntsman and Hoban (1980).

suggests that the extreme skewness of returns that they observed continues to characterize the industry.

An alternative measure is that of the performance of IPOs of high-technology firms. Because many of these firms go public while they are still pursuing significant innovations, the stock returns should reflect the evolution of their innovative efforts. Scherer, Harhoff, and Kukies (1998) examine the distribution of values at the end of 1995 of 110 venture-backed firms that went public between January 1983 and December 1986. Although the authors make no effort to market-adjust returns, and their treatment of acquired and delisted firms is somewhat ambiguous, skewed outcomes are again the rule. The top 10 percent of the IPOs account for 62 percent of the value at the end of 1995.

Analysis of the Software Industry

The analyses summarized above suggest that, using a variety of measures, the returns to innovative activities are very skewed across a variety of industries. This section examines whether these patterns hold as well in computer software. It might be thought that, because of the particular characteristics of the industry (e.g., low manufacturing costs), the distribution of returns to innovation would be different. But using a proxy for the change in value – the growth of software firms – I show that the same distribution seen in other industries holds here. A very modest number of firms account for the bulk of the industry's success.

Ideally, I would have examined the change in value of software companies. Unfortunately, only a small fraction of companies are publicly traded: Of the more than 12,000 software enterprises identified in the database described below, a little more than 5 percent were stand-alone publicly traded entities. I focused instead on two alternative measures: sales and employment growth. The valuations assigned to private firms by venture capitalists have been shown to be highly correlated with these two measures (Gompers and Lerner [1998a]).

I employ a panel data set of computer software companies between 1990 and 1998 compiled by the consulting firm Corporate Technology Information Services (CorpTech). This firm's *Corporate Technology Directory* is the most comprehensive directory of U.S. high-technology firms. It precisely identifies the industry in which each firm belongs, as well as estimating employment and sales for each firm based on survey responses and independent estimates. The *Corporate Technology Directory* is one of the few business directories that uses rigorous procedures to identify (and correct) problematic responses, and is very aggressive in tracking down and ascertaining the status of non-respondents. This data set includes all software firms active during this period that CorpTech could identify, including those that were acquired or liquidated in the interval.

I employ a special tabulation of the database undertaken by CorpTech that had not previously provided archived data to academic researchers. The resulting data set consisted of all software firms in its database that were active between January 1990 and July 1998.[7] The data set consists of 12,268 firms. Table 1 summarizes their characteristics. The firms are located disproportionately in California and Massachusetts. Most are quite young, with over two-thirds having been founded after 1980. A relative handful – a total of 896 – have received venture capital financing.[8] The low share of firms funded through venture investors is consistent with the general patterns discussed above.

The data set includes annual observations of sales and employment of firms between 1990 and 1998. In some cases, the firm reports only a range. In these cases, I employ the midpoint of the range. All sales figures are converted to constant 1997 dollars.[9] I then compute the difference between each pair of adjoining years where I have sales and employment data: in all, there are more than 37,000 such cases with adjoining observations of employment, and a little under 29,000 such observations of sales.[10]

Table 1. **Characteristics of the Sample**

The sample consists of 12,268 software firms in the Corporate Technology Information Services database active between 1990 and 1998. The first panel indicates the number of firms in the sample located in each of five states. The second panel indicates the year in which the firms were formed. The final panel indicates the number of firms that relied on venture capital, corporate investment, and public equity issues. (Some firms relied on several of these avenues; most firms relied on none of the three.)

State of Firm's Headquarters		Year of Firm's Formation		Source of Firm's Financing	
California	2554	1960 or before	232	Venture Capital	896
Massachusetts	1184	1961-1970	686	Corporate Investor	541
Texas	856	1971-1980	3,026	Public Equity Markets	733
Pennsylvania	650	1981-1990	6,207		
New York	649	1991 or after	2,117		
Other	6375				

I also compute the difference in employment and sales over the entire period in which a firm is in the database. These computations may consider as short a period as one year or as long as eight years. In total, these values can be computed for 10,300 firms (in the case of sales) and 10,491 firms (employment). In the remaining firms in the sample, there are less than two observations of sales and/or employment.[11]

Table 2 provides some summary statistics for these firms. The table presents the mean and median of each measure of firm growth, as well as other breakpoints of the distribution. It shows that the growth of employment and sales are both highly skewed: For example, in the case of long-run employment, fully 85 percent of the firms were below the mean. In each case, the top percentile of firms contributed the overwhelming amount of the growth. For example, in the case of employment, the aggregate growth between the first and last observation of the 10,491 firms in the sample was 413,000 jobs. The growth of the top percentile (the 105 firms with the greatest employment growth) was just over 373,000 jobs.

Another way to draw conclusions from the sample is to examine the percentage change in employment and sales, both on an annual basis and during the entire period that the firm is in the sample. I annualize the long-run growth figures in order to control for the different time periods over which the observations are made. The distributions of these growth rates are depicted in Figures 2 and 3, and tabulated in Table 3. Once again, the skewness of the returns, whether measured in the short or the long run, is apparent.

A natural concern about these results is that they may establish the first

***Table 2.* The Employment and Sales Growth of the Sample Firms**

The sample consists of 12,268 software firms in the Corporate Technology Information Services database active between 1990 and 1998. The table presents the number of observations, the mean and standard deviation of the firms' growth, and various percentiles of the distribution of firm growth. The first two columns present this information on an annual basis: Each pair of adjoining records of employment and sales is used as an observation. The third and fourth columns use the difference between the first and last levels of sales and employment for each firm. All sales figures are in millions of 1997 dollars.

	Short-Run Growth		Long-Run Growth	
	Employment	Sales	Employment	Sales
Number of Observations	37,253	28,673	10,491	10,300
Mean	9.32	1.78	39.33	4.65
Standard Deviation	403.55	286.38	653.44	296.33
1st Percentile	-100	-24.18	-220	-52.78
5th Percentile	-15	-3.47	-45	-8.92
10th Percentile	-5	-1.26	-20	-3.94
25th Percentile	0	-0.30	-5	-0.89
Median	0	-0.05	0	-0.21
75th Percentile	1	-0.02	8	1.04
90th Percentile	15	2.70	60	8.92
95th Percentile	40	10.18	155	22.21
99th Percentile	256	74.20	910	177.67

***Figure 2.* Annualized Long-Run Employment Growth of Software Enterprises**

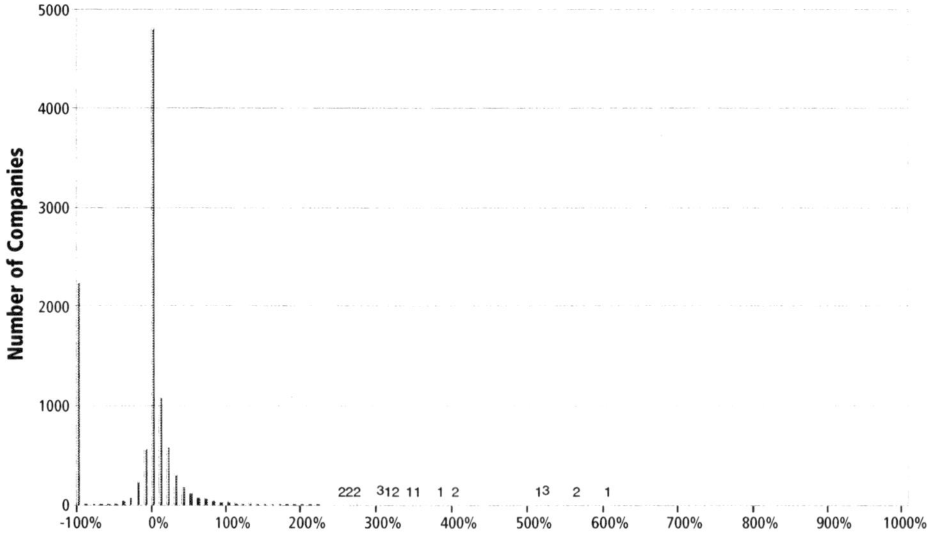

Note: The count of all entries in each 10% interval above 250% is noted. One positive outlier is not depicted.

Figure 3. **Annualized Long-Run Sales Growth of Software Enterprises, 1990-1997**

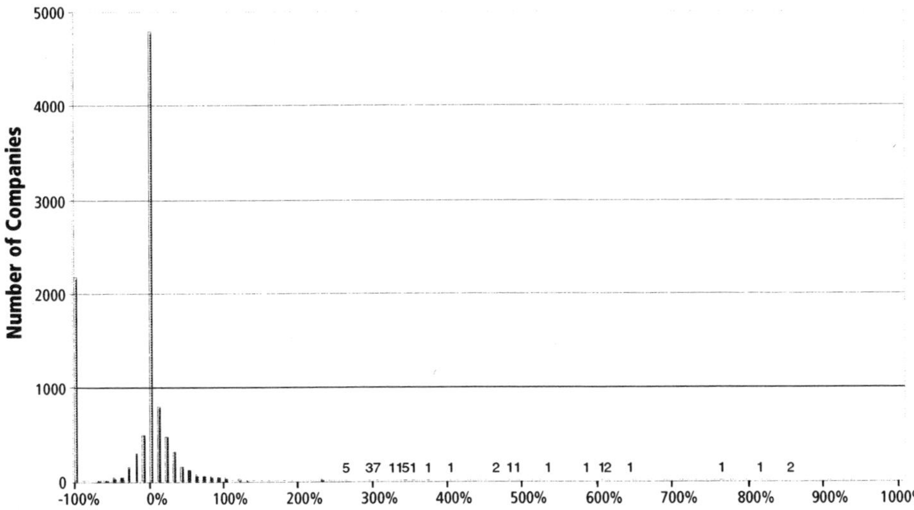

Note: The count of all entries in each 10% interval above 250% is noted. Five positive outliers are not depicted.

Table 3. **The Annualized Percentage Growth in Employment and Sales of the Sample Firms**

The sample consists of 12,268 software firms in the Corporate Technology Information Services database active between 1990 and 1998. The table presents the number of observations and various percentiles of the distribution of the annualized percentage growth rate of the firms. The first two columns present this information on an annual basis: Each pair of adjoining records of employment and sales is used as an observation. The third and fourth columns use the difference between the first and last levels of sales and employment for each firm. All sales growth calculations are made using 1997 dollars.

	Short-Run Growth		Long-Run Growth	
	Employment	Sales	Employment	Sales
Number of Observations	37,253	28,575	10,491	10,212
Minimum	-100.0%	-100.0%	-100.0%	-100.0%
1st Percentile	-100.0	-100.0	-100.0	-100.0
5th Percentile	-100.0	-52.2	-100.0	-100.0
10th Percentile	-40.0	-18.8	-100.0	-100.0
25th Percentile	0.0	-5.6	-18.8	-23.4
Median	0.0	-4.6	0.0	-4.8
75th Percentile	7.6	-2.9	9.2	7.0
90th Percentile	40.0	65.8	26.5	28.2
95th Percentile	66.7	107.1	43.5	47.5
99th Percentile	200.0	344.0	102.7	130.4
Maximum	44,344.5	482,899.8	1,650.0	4,171.4

***Table 4.* The Employment and Sales Growth of the Venture-Backed Sample Firms**

The sample consists of 896 software firms in the Corporate Technology Information Services database active between 1990 and 1998 that received professional venture capital financing. The table presents the number of observations, the mean and standard deviation of the firms' growth, and various percentiles of the distribution of firm growth. The first two columns present this information on an annual basis: Each pair of adjoining records of employment and sales is used as an observation. The third and fourth columns use the difference between the first and last levels of sales and employment for each firm. All sales figures are in millions of 1997 dollars.

	Short-Run Growth		Long-Run Growth	
	Employment	Sales	Employment	Sales
Number of Observations	2,382	1,842	682	666
Mean	23.41	6.04	100.88	22.42
Standard Deviation	224.25	66.17	701.79	246.49
1st Percentile	-220	-42.86	-350	-67.30
5th Percentile	-45	-8.73	-95	-21.51
10th Percentile	-15	-3.59	-45	-8.60
25th Percentile	0	-0.86	-5	-2.04
Median	0	-0.12	10	0.07
75th Percentile	16	2.92	63	9.80
90th Percentile	64	15.12	196	34.62
95th Percentile	125	32.98	375	76.12
99th Percentile	425	162.06	2,250	392.05

proposition outlined in the introduction to this paper – that the returns to innovative projects are highly skewed – but not the second – namely, that it is difficult to select successful firms in advance. It may be, after all, that many of these firms were begun and financed by unsophisticated individuals.

To address this concern, I proceed in two ways. First, I examine the subset of firms funded by professional venture capitalists. As discussed above, they engage in an extensive screening and due diligence process before investing in new firms. Tables 4 and 5 replicate Tables 2 and 3, but present the results only for the subset of 896 firms that were backed by venture capitalists. A similar skewness emerges from these tabulations, with the vast bulk of the growth accounted for by a few firms.

Another way to illustrate the difficulty of predicting before the fact which firm will be successful is to employ a regression analysis. I use as observations all firms that had employment data in at least two years in the CorpTech sample between 1990 and 1998. The dependent variable in the two regressions reported in Table 6 is the growth in employment and the annualized percent-

***Table 5.* The Annualized Percentage Growth in Employment and Sales of the Venture-Backed Sample Firms**

The sample consists of 896 software firms in the Corporate Technology Information Services database active between 1990 and 1998 that received professional venture capital financing. The table presents the number of observations and various percentiles of the distribution of the annualized percentage growth rate of the firms. The first two columns present this information on an annual basis: Each pair of adjoining records of employment and sales is used as an observation. The third and fourth columns use the difference between the first and last levels of sales and employment for each firm. All sales growth calculations are made using 1997 dollars.

	Short-Run Growth		Long-Run Growth	
	Employment	**Sales**	**Employment**	**Sales**
Number of Observations	2,382	1,821	673	637
Minimum	-100.0%	-100.0%	-100.0%	-100.0%
1st Percentile	-100.0	-100.0	-100.0	-100.0
5th Percentile	-54.5	-44.0	-100.0	-100.0
10th Percentile	-28.6	-20.7	-100.0	-100.0
25th Percentile	0.0	-5.3	-3.5	-5.6
Median	0.0	-4.4	7.7	-0.6
75th Percentile	28.6	27.5	25.2	23.4
90th Percentile	71.4	102.3	55.7	59.4
95th Percentile	113.3	137.9	77.6	91.2
99th Percentile	253.0	443.7	200.0	269.4
Maximum	733.3	8,850.7	512.5	1,090.2

age growth in employment between the first and last observations multiplied by 100 (e.g., a 25 percent annualized growth rate is recorded as 25.0). As independent variables I employ the age of the firm at the time of the first observation (in years), the employment in the year of the first observation, the count of other software firms in the firm's state and zip code in the year of the first employment observation (to control for any regional agglomeration effects that may influence firm success), a dummy variable that takes on the value of one if the firm attracted venture capital financing (and zero otherwise), and dummy variables for the year of the first observation and the sub-segment of the software industry into which the firm was classified by CorpTech.[12] Because the time spans over which I observed the firms' growth differed, I feared that the precision of the various estimates of annualized growth might vary. I consequently employed heteroscedastistic-consistent standard errors, with the data grouped by the number of years between the first and last observation.[13]

***Table 6.* Ordinary Least Squares Regression Analysis of Employment Growth and the Annualized Percentage Growth in Employment**

The sample consists of 12,268 software firms in the Corporate Technology Information Services database active between 1990 and 1998. The dependent variable in the first regression is the growth in employment between the first and last observations of each firm; in the second regression, the annualized percentage growth in employment multiplied by 100. Independent variables are the age of the firm at the time of the first observation (in years), the employment in the year of the first observation, the count of other software firms in the firm's state and zip code in the year of the first employment observation, a dummy variable that take on the value of one if the firm attracted venture capital financing, and dummy variables for the year of the first observation and the sub-segment of the software industry into which the firm was classified by CorpTech (not reported). Absolute heteroscedastic-consistent standard errors are in brackets.

	Dependent Variable	
	Change in Employment	**Annualized Growth**
Age of firm	5.99 [1.51]	-0.03 [0.51]
Employment of firm	-0.001 [0.44]	0.0001 [2.61]
Software firms in state	-0.01 [1.76]	-0.001 [2.25]
Software firms in zip code	2.83 [2.01]	0.77 [4.08]
Venture capital backed?	14.88 [0.77]	13.72 [5.55]
R^2	0.014	0.109
F-statistic	58.01	25.22
Number of observations	8,232	8,232

As Table 6 reports, the regressions explain only 1 to 10 percent of the total variance in outcomes. Investors, of course, would employ many other considerations in assessing a potential software investment, but the low goodness-of-fit of this regression does suggest how difficult it is to predict the success of firms.

Venture capitalists appear to be better at selecting firms than other investors or at ensuring success by adding value after the investment: The employment in a typical venture-backed firm grows at a 14 percent greater rate than the others. At the same time, it is clear that they also face many challenges in identifying successful firms. I illustrate this point by repeating the regression where the venture capital dummy variable was significant (the second regression in Table 5), while now restricting the sample to venture-backed firms. The increase in variance explained by the independent variables – from 0.11 to 0.13 – is only marginal. Venture capital investors also face a great deal of uncertainty in their investments in software firms.[14]

IMPLICATIONS FOR PUBLIC POLICY

The distribution of returns from investment in innovative activities, and the inability of even the most sophisticated investors to determine in advance which projects will be successful, have profound implications for public policy. In particular, private investors will undertake investments in firms only if they believe they will earn an attractive return. Regulatory actions that affect the returns of investors in a few successful companies can have a dramatic impact on the overall return. If even a small number of successful high-technology companies are not allowed to earn an attractive return because of after-the-fact regulatory activity, it may lead to a dramatic reduction in the willingness of investors to fund similar companies in the future.

In this section, I illustrate these claims with two cases in which federal regulation called into question the ability of successful high-technology firms to earn the returns that their investors expected. In each case, regulators argued that the firms had earned an excessive rate of return, without taking into consideration the very modest probability that the firm would succeed in the first place. In each case, the regulatory action had a chilling effect on the willingness of private investors to make subsequent investments in high-risk projects in that industry.

The Case of Communications Satellite Corporation[15]

The Communications Satellite Corporation (Comsat) was established in 1963. The Communications Satellite Act of 1962 created a new private corporation to establish a communications satellite network. Due to the riskiness of the firm's business plan and the intangible nature of its assets, the firm could not finance its activities with debt. Instead, it undertook an IPO in June 1964, raising $200 million in equity.

Comsat's initial operations were far more successful than originally anticipated. It began commercial satellite service in April 1965, two years ahead of schedule. The incidence of satellite failures during and after launch was considerably less frequent than expected, and the technological progress with each generation of satellite more substantial. One indication of its extraordinary success was that in only one month during its first decade of operation did a satellite failure cause a revenue loss for Comsat. This technological success was reflected in the rapid growth in its revenues and profitability.

Comsat's financial success, however, attracted the attention of the Federal Communications Commission. Under the provision of the Communications

Satellite Act, Comsat was subject to the regulation of the FCC, the governmental body responsible for the oversight of communications carriers. In March 1972, the FCC initiated hearings, which lasted for over two years, to determine a fair rate of return for Comsat.

During the hearings, the commission's staff argued that the firm had been charging excessive rates. It recommended that Comsat be forced to reduce its rates, and refund excessive profits the company had earned in previous years. In particular, it urged the FCC to allow the firm a return on equity of approximately 8 percent over the previous decade. The recommended rate was slightly below that allowed the telecommunications giant AT&T during the same period.[16]

Comsat responded that the technological and business risks it had faced over the previous decade were far greater than those of AT&T, which had an installed network and stable customer base. As compensation for these risks, it demanded a higher rate of return (between 12 percent and 15 percent). In response, the FCC staff pointed to the many technological and business successes that Comsat had enjoyed. It argued that this success was evidence that the risks were actually quite modest.

This rebuttal apparently persuaded the FCC commissioners. In December 1975, they ruled that Comsat had overstated and exaggerated its risks. It allowed the firm a rate of return on capital of 9.5 percent, a slight premium over that of AT&T. The decision stated that Comsat's investors "knew or should have known" that this would be the allowed rate of return when they invested in the firm. The commissioners also sharply reduced the base on which Comsat could calculate its profits. Comsat appealed the decision, but was ultimately forced to cut its rates by nearly one-half.

The decision had substantial implications for Comsat's investors. During the year of the FCC's decision, 1975 (a year of generally rising equity prices), Comsat's stock price fell by nearly one-half. In the 10-day window around the FCC's decision, its share price fell by 30 percent. The impact on Comsat was long lasting. Between 1964 and 1990, a period during which the Ibbotson large-capitalization stock market index appreciated by over 1,300 percent, investors in Comsat experienced a negative return.

These negative consequences apparently extended beyond Comsat's investors. Searches of the press accounts and analyst reports suggest that there was little new private investment in space-related industries until the launch of Orbital Sciences Corporation in 1983 (shortly after the dramatic rollback in regulation associated with the Reagan administration). It was not until the 1990s that investors felt sufficiently comfortable to undertake large-scale investments in satellite communications (Graham, 1996). Although this shift undoubtedly reflected in part shifts in demand and technological opportunity, concerns about the after-the-fact regulation of the firm that proved so successful were clearly also a major consideration.

The Case of the Biotechnology Industry[17]

Between 1992 and 1994, the price of the relatively few successful biotechnology-derived drugs was greatly scrutinized. The biotechnology industry had begun in the mid-1970s with the promise of rapidly exploiting the new discoveries in genetic engineering. A major focus of the approximately 1,500 firms that entered the industry – including at least 350 that received venture capital backing – was the development of new pharmaceuticals.

This proved to be much more difficult than originally foreseen. Only 22 biotechnology-based therapeutics and vaccines were approved between 1975 and 1993. Losses across the period were enormous: In 1993 alone, the industry as a whole lost $3.6 billion. The development of new drugs via biotechnology proved to be extraordinarily expensive: Amgen, for example, had raised $405 million in equity before its first drug reached the market.

During the efforts to reform the health-care system between 1992 and 1994, the prices of the biotechnology drugs became a focus of public interest. In the ensuing debate, the prospect was raised that the federal government would enforce provisions that would allow it to limit the prices on drugs that were derived from federally funded research. Because virtually all biotechnology-derived drugs were based on federally funded research, this posed a substantial concern to the industry and its investors.

The focus of much of this controversy was the Genzyme Corporation, one of the relatively few companies to have an approved bioengineered drug. Genzyme had been founded in 1981, and had received venture capital backing in 1983. After several false starts, it had obtained approval from the FDA for the enzyme Ceredase for the treatment of Gaucher disease in 1991. Prior to this point, the firm had raised $328 million in equity. The company estimated that it had invested $70 million in researching and obtaining approval for the drug, for which it believed there were 5,000 to 6,000 sufferers worldwide whose symptoms were serious enough to need the Ceredase treatment.

Genzyme's pricing of Ceredase (estimates for the annual cost of the treatment for the typical patient ranged from $20,000 to $350,000) was intensely criticized. One patient activist characterized it as "one of the worst illustrations of corporate greed I've ever seen" (Flanagan, 1993). In an October 1992 report, the U.S. Office of Technology Assessment criticized the drug's pricing, noting that much of the original research had been funded by the U.S. National Institutes of Health. In response to this pressure, Genzyme cut the price of Ceredase several times. Like other biotechnology firms, it experienced negative returns during this period of scrutiny, with its market capitalization falling by more than one-half between the beginning of 1992 and the end of 1993.

The impact on young biotechnology firms more generally was also severe. For example, the amount raised by publicly traded biotechnology firms in initial and follow-on offerings (measured in 1995 dollars) went from $4.2 billion in 1991 to $2.2 billion in 1992, and reached a nadir of $1.1 billion in 1994. The number of biotechnology firms attracting venture financing for the first time fell from 46 in 1992 to 20 in 1995. Equity valuations for publicly traded biotechnology stocks fell by 32.6 percent in 1993, a year in which the market as a whole rose.[18] Wall Street analysts attributed the rapid falloff in investment and valuations to concerns about the ability of biotechnology investors to earn sufficiently attractive returns from firms with approved drugs to compensate them for the many unsuccessful projects and companies.

CONCLUSIONS

The distribution of the returns to innovative activities, whether in the software industry or more generally across high-technology industries, is highly uneven. A small number of firms account for the bulk of the returns. An extensive theoretical literature on technological competition suggests that this empirical regularity is not surprising. This is true not only in high-technology firms in general, but also in the software industry specifically.

Moreover, predicting the success of high-technology firms is exceedingly difficult. Information problems and the intangible nature of the companies' assets make it difficult for investors to avoid making numerous unsuccessful investments for each successful one. If investors are denied profits from even a handful of their most successful investments in innovative activities, their overall return is likely to fall dramatically.

Finally, this highly skewed distribution of rewards has substantial implications for the designers of regulatory policy. Because it is often impossible to predict which innovations will succeed, investors need to be assured that they will receive substantial returns from successful investments to offset the unsatisfactory returns from the many failed or less successful projects. If investors believe that they will be denied these returns by regulators, their willingness to fund the development of the next generation of innovative technologies will be greatly reduced.

[1] Reviewed in Reinganum (1989).

[2] For a more detailed discussion of these problems, see Lerner (1998).

[3] For example, Grabowski and Vernon (1990, 1994) show that the top 10 percent of new drugs approved in the 1970s and 1980s generated 55 percent and 48 percent, respectively, of the net present value of earnings from all new drugs approved in this period.

[4] One concern with this analysis is the treatment of equity. In many cases, universities receive equity in spinout firms in exchange for reduced licensing or royalty payments. The equity can thus be regarded as the capitalized value of payments that in a traditional arrangement would be spread out over many years. The authors assume that the entire value of equity received in a licensing agreement is realized in the year the equity is sold. This may make the distribution of university revenues from patents appear more skewed than it actually is.

[5] The study by Huntsman and Hoban, like the other ones below, examines only the distribution of the raw returns, not adjusted by the returns of comparable companies in the public market during the same interval. Properly adjusting the returns of venture-backed firms is a challenging process (Gompers and Lerner, 1998b). The variance in the returns in these samples, however, is so great that the results would be little changed.

[6] Companies that had not been "exited" by the venture capitalists as of September 1996 were assigned the valuation that the venture capitalist used in its report to its investors at the close of that quarter.

[7] I eliminate approximately 200 firms whose industry was apparently misclassified. I also eliminate observations in which firms that were acquired or subsidiaries of other firms reported the employment and sales of the parent firm, and not that of the entity itself.

[8] The remaining firms have been financed through cash flow from operations and by corporate and individual investors.

[9] An additional complication is introduced by firms that disappear from the database and that CorpTech identifies as having gone bankrupt or having been liquidated. Typically, these firms are dropped from the database when they cease to respond: There is no final observation reflecting the firm's termination. An analysis of the differences in the reported data would be upwardly biased, since I would not observe the consequences of these firms' bankruptcies or liquidations. In these cases, I add a final observation for these firms, consisting of zero employees and/or sales.

[10] There are multiple observations of many firms.

[11] In Table 2, I present the simple change in employment and sales: I make no effort to correct for the fact that the observations are made over durations of varying length. In Table 3, all percentage changes are annualized to correct for these differences.

[12] The final two sets of dummy variables are not reported in Table 6.

[13] The sample sizes are somewhat smaller because CorpTech was not able to ascertain the financing history of all firms. The results are robust to the deletion of the venture capital dummy variable and the use of a larger sample.

[14] A related question, not answered by the above analysis, is how the *level* of returns in the

computer software industry compares to those in other industries. It might be thought that the best way to approach this problem would be to analyze accounting returns, such as return on equity. The essential problem here is that both the numerator (net income) and the denominator (shareholders' equity) in the calculation of the return on equity of a software firm are problematic. Software firms have different approaches to treating software product development expenses: unlike R&D, firms can capitalize these expenditures, which may inflate earnings. As in many knowledge-intensive industries, important assets are not included on the balance sheet (e.g., intellectual property, installed user base, etc.), and hence are not reflected in the shareholders' equity. An alternative approach is to examine the stock-market returns of publicly traded firms in the industry. In their analysis of returns between 1964 and 1994, Fama and French (1997) show that the computer industry's "excess returns" – i.e., the returns adjusted for the various factors that are correlated with riskinesss on a market-wide basis – are not statistically different from zero.

[15] This section is based primarily on Mullins (1976), Fruhan and Mullins (1992), and Stevenson, Sahlman, and Turner (1986).

[16] In addition, the commission staff argued that the calculation be made assuming the firm had a capital structure similar to that of AT&T: i.e., that the allowed rate of return employ the (counterfactual) assumption that almost half of firm's capital was lower-yielding debt.

[17] This section is based on, among other sources, U.S. Office of Technology Assessment (1992, 1993), Genzyme Corporation (1992), Teisberg and Rossi (1993), and Barrett (1994).

[18] These patterns are documented in Lerner and Merges (1998).

[19] The inability of small biotechnology firms to raise capital had substantial and long-lasting effects. For instance, these problems diminished their ability to negotiate favorable agreements with pharmaceutical companies, who were aware of these firms' weak financial positions [Lerner and Merges, 1998]. The relatively unfavorable alliances that were negotiated further reduced the willingness of investors to finance new biotechnology firms.

References

Barrett, M. James. 1994. "Testimony of M. James Barrett, Ph.D., Chairman and Chief Executive Officer, Genetic Therapy, Inc.," Joint Economic Committee, U.S. Congress.

Fama, Eugene F., French, Kenneth R. 1997. "Industry Costs of Equity," *Journal of Financial Economics*, 43, pp. 153-193.

Flanagan, Patrick. 1993. "Drug Prices: What's the Rationale?," *Management Review*, 82 (July), pp. 10-15.

Fruhan, William E., Jr., Mullins, David W., Jr. 1992. "Communications Satellite Corporation: Teaching Note," Harvard Business School Teaching Note No. 5-292-046.

Fudenberg, Drew, Gilbert, Richard J., Stiglitz, Joseph E., Tirole, Jean. 1983. "Preemption, Leapfrogging and Competition in Patent Races," *European Economic Review*, 22, pp. 3-31.

Genzyme Corporation. 1992. "OTA Report on Ceredase Alglucerase Injection Released," *Business Wire*, October 5.

Gilbert, Richard J., Newbery, David M.G. 1982. "Preemptive Patenting and the Persistence of Monopoly," *American Economic Review*, 72, pp. 514-526.

Gompers, Paul A., Lerner, Josh. 1998a. "Money Chasing Deals? The Impact of Fund Inflows on Private Equity Valuations," Unpublished Working Paper, Harvard University.

Gompers, Paul A., Lerner, Josh. 1998b. "Risk and Return in Private Equity Investments: The Challenge of Performance Assessment," *Journal of Private Equity*, 1 (Winter), pp. 5-12.

Gompers, Paul A., Lerner, Josh. 1998. *The Venture Cycle*. Cambridge: MIT Press.

Grabowski, Henry, Vernon, John. 1990. "A New Look at the Returns to Pharmaceutical R&D," *Management Science*, 36, pp. 804-821.

Grabowski, Henry, Vernon, John. 1994. "Returns on New Drug Introductions in the 1980s," *Journal of Health Economics*, 13, pp. 386-406.

Graham, John. 1996. "The Surge in Satellite Finance," *Institutional Investor*, 30 (November), pp. 117-124.

Harris, Christopher, Vickers, John. 1985. "Perfect Equilibrium in a Model of a Race," *Review of Economic Studies*, 52, pp. 193-209.

Harris, Christopher, Vickers, John. 1987. "Racing with Uncertainty," *Review of Economic Studies*, 54, pp. 1-22.

Horsley, Phillip. 1997. *Trends in Private Equity*. San Francisco: Horsley | Bridge.

Huntsman, Blaine, Hoban, James P. 1980. "Investment in New Enterprise: Some Observations about Risk, Return, and Market Structure," *Financial Management*, 9 (Summer), pp. 44-51.

Lanjouw, Jean O. 1993. "Patent Protection: Of What Value and for How Long?," National Bureau of Economic Research Working Paper No. 4475.

Lerner, Josh. 1998. "'Angel' Financing and Public Policy: An Overview," *Journal of Banking and Finance*, 22, pp. 773-783.

Lerner, Josh, Merges, Robert P. 1998. "The Control of Technology Alliances: An Empirical Analysis of the Biotechnology Industry," *Journal of Industrial Economics*, 46, pp. 125-156.

Mullins, David W., Jr. 1976. "Communications Satellite Corporation," Harvard Business School Case No. 276-195.

Pakes, Ariel. 1986. "Patents as Options: Some Estimates of the Value of Holding European Patent Stocks," *Econometrica*, 54, pp. 755-784.

Pakes, Ariel, Schankerman, Mark. 1984. "The Rate of Obsolescence of Knowledge, Research Gestation Lags, and the Private Rate of Return to Research Resources," in *Patents, R&D and Productivity*, Zvi Griliches, editor. Chicago: University of Chicago Press for the National Bureau of Economic Research.

Reinganum, Jennifer R. 1983. "Uncertain Innovation and the Persistence of Monopoly," *American Economic Review*, 73, pp. 741-748.

Reinganum, Jennifer R. 1984. "Practical Implications of Game Theoretic Models of R&D," *American Economic Review Papers and Proceedings*, 74, pp. 61-66.

Reinganum, Jennifer R. 1989. "The Timing of Innovation: Research, Development and Diffusion," in *The Handbook of Industrial Organization*, Richard Schmalensee and Robert D. Willig, editors. New York: North-Holland.

Scherer, F.M., Harhoff, Dietmar, Kukies, Joerg. 1998. "Uncertainty and the Size Distribution of Rewards from Technological Innovation," Unpublished Working Paper, Harvard University.

Stevenson, Howard H., Sahlman, William A., Turner, James Z. 1986. "Orbital Sciences Corporation (A)," Harvard Business School Case No. 9-386-175.

Teisberg, Elizabeth O., Rossi, Sharon. 1993. "Genzyme Corp.: Strategic Challenges with Ceredase," Harvard Business School Case No. 9-793-120.

U.S. Congress, Office of Technology Assessment. 1992. *Federal and Private Roles in the Development and Provision of Alglucerase Therapy*. Washington: U.S. Government Printing Office.

U.S. Congress, Office of Technology Assessment. 1993. *Pharmaceutical R&D: Costs, Risks and Rewards*. Washington: U.S. Government Printing Office.